Lecture Notes in Computer Science 10295

Commenced Publication in 1973
Founding and Former Series Editors:
Gerhard Goos, Juris Hartmanis, and Jan van Leeuwen

More information about this series at http://www.springer.com/series/7409

Panayiotis Zaphiris · Andri Ioannou (Eds.)

Learning and Collaboration Technologies

Novel Learning Ecosystems

4th International Conference, LCT 2017
Held as Part of HCI International 2017
Vancouver, BC, Canada, July 9–14, 2017
Proceedings, Part I

 Springer

Editors
Panayiotis Zaphiris
Cyprus University of Technology
Limassol
Cyprus

Andri Ioannou
Cyprus University of Technology
Limassol
Cyprus

ISSN 0302-9743   ISSN 1611-3349 (electronic)
Lecture Notes in Computer Science
ISBN 978-3-319-58508-6   ISBN 978-3-319-58509-3 (eBook)
DOI 10.1007/978-3-319-58509-3

Library of Congress Control Number: 2017939726

LNCS Sublibrary: SL3 – Information Systems and Applications, incl. Internet/Web, and HCI

Printed on acid-free paper

This Springer imprint is published by Springer Nature
The registered company is Springer International Publishing AG
The registered company address is: Gewerbestrasse 11, 6330 Cham, Switzerland

Foreword

The 19th International Conference on Human–Computer Interaction, HCI International 2017, was held in Vancouver, Canada, during July 9–14, 2017. The event incorporated the 15 conferences/thematic areas listed on the following page.

A total of 4,340 individuals from academia, research institutes, industry, and governmental agencies from 70 countries submitted contributions, and 1,228 papers have been included in the proceedings. These papers address the latest research and development efforts and highlight the human aspects of design and use of computing systems. The papers thoroughly cover the entire field of human–computer interaction, addressing major advances in knowledge and effective use of computers in a variety of application areas. The volumes constituting the full set of the conference proceedings are listed on the following pages.

I would like to thank the program board chairs and the members of the program boards of all thematic areas and affiliated conferences for their contribution to the highest scientific quality and the overall success of the HCI International 2017 conference.

This conference would not have been possible without the continuous and unwavering support and advice of the founder, Conference General Chair Emeritus and Conference Scientific Advisor Prof. Gavriel Salvendy. For his outstanding efforts, I would like to express my appreciation to the communications chair and editor of *HCI International News*, Dr. Abbas Moallem.

April 2017   Constantine Stephanidis

HCI International 2017 Thematic Areas and Affiliated Conferences

Thematic areas:

- Human–Computer Interaction (HCI 2017)
- Human Interface and the Management of Information (HIMI 2017)

Affiliated conferences:

- 17th International Conference on Engineering Psychology and Cognitive Ergonomics (EPCE 2017)
- 11th International Conference on Universal Access in Human–Computer Interaction (UAHCI 2017)
- 9th International Conference on Virtual, Augmented and Mixed Reality (VAMR 2017)
- 9th International Conference on Cross-Cultural Design (CCD 2017)
- 9th International Conference on Social Computing and Social Media (SCSM 2017)
- 11th International Conference on Augmented Cognition (AC 2017)
- 8th International Conference on Digital Human Modeling and Applications in Health, Safety, Ergonomics and Risk Management (DHM 2017)
- 6th International Conference on Design, User Experience and Usability (DUXU 2017)
- 5th International Conference on Distributed, Ambient and Pervasive Interactions (DAPI 2017)
- 5th International Conference on Human Aspects of Information Security, Privacy and Trust (HAS 2017)
- 4th International Conference on HCI in Business, Government and Organizations (HCIBGO 2017)
- 4th International Conference on Learning and Collaboration Technologies (LCT 2017)
- Third International Conference on Human Aspects of IT for the Aged Population (ITAP 2017)

Conference Proceedings Volumes Full List

1. LNCS 10271, Human–Computer Interaction: User Interface Design, Development and Multimodality (Part I), edited by Masaaki Kurosu
2. LNCS 10272 Human–Computer Interaction: Interaction Contexts (Part II), edited by Masaaki Kurosu
3. LNCS 10273, Human Interface and the Management of Information: Information, Knowledge and Interaction Design (Part I), edited by Sakae Yamamoto
4. LNCS 10274, Human Interface and the Management of Information: Supporting Learning, Decision-Making and Collaboration (Part II), edited by Sakae Yamamoto
5. LNAI 10275, Engineering Psychology and Cognitive Ergonomics: Performance, Emotion and Situation Awareness (Part I), edited by Don Harris
6. LNAI 10276, Engineering Psychology and Cognitive Ergonomics: Cognition and Design (Part II), edited by Don Harris
7. LNCS 10277, Universal Access in Human–Computer Interaction: Design and Development Approaches and Methods (Part I), edited by Margherita Antona and Constantine Stephanidis
8. LNCS 10278, Universal Access in Human–Computer Interaction: Designing Novel Interactions (Part II), edited by Margherita Antona and Constantine Stephanidis
9. LNCS 10279, Universal Access in Human–Computer Interaction: Human and Technological Environments (Part III), edited by Margherita Antona and Constantine Stephanidis
10. LNCS 10280, Virtual, Augmented and Mixed Reality, edited by Stephanie Lackey and Jessie Y.C. Chen
11. LNCS 10281, Cross-Cultural Design, edited by Pei-Luen Patrick Rau
12. LNCS 10282, Social Computing and Social Media: Human Behavior (Part I), edited by Gabriele Meiselwitz
13. LNCS 10283, Social Computing and Social Media: Applications and Analytics (Part II), edited by Gabriele Meiselwitz
14. LNAI 10284, Augmented Cognition: Neurocognition and Machine Learning (Part I), edited by Dylan D. Schmorrow and Cali M. Fidopiastis
15. LNAI 10285, Augmented Cognition: Enhancing Cognition and Behavior in Complex Human Environments (Part II), edited by Dylan D. Schmorrow and Cali M. Fidopiastis
16. LNCS 10286, Digital Human Modeling and Applications in Health, Safety, Ergonomics and Risk Management: Ergonomics and Design (Part I), edited by Vincent G. Duffy
17. LNCS 10287, Digital Human Modeling and Applications in Health, Safety, Ergonomics and Risk Management: Health and Safety (Part II), edited by Vincent G. Duffy
18. LNCS 10288, Design, User Experience, and Usability: Theory, Methodology and Management (Part I), edited by Aaron Marcus and Wentao Wang

Learning and Collaboration Technologies

Program Board Chair(s): **Panayiotis Zaphiris and Andri Ioannou, Cyprus**

- Ruthi Aladjem, Israel
- Mike Brayshaw, UK
- Jitender Kumar Chhabra, India
- Anastasios A. Economides, Greece
- Maka Eradze, Estonia
- Mikhail Fominykh, Norway
- David Fonseca, Spain
- Francisco J. García Peñalvo, Spain
- Evangelos Kapros, Ireland
- Tomaž Klobučar, Slovenia
- Efi Nisiforou, Cyprus
- Antigoni Parmaxi, Cyprus
- Marcos Roman Gonzalez, Spain
- Telmo Zarraonandia, Spain
- Maria Zenios, Cyprus

The full list with the Program Board Chairs and the members of the Program Boards of all thematic areas and affiliated conferences is available online at:

http://www.hci.international/board-members-2017.php

HCI International 2018

The 20th International Conference on Human–Computer Interaction, HCI International 2018, will be held jointly with the affiliated conferences in Las Vegas, NV, USA, at Caesars Palace, July 15–20, 2018. It will cover a broad spectrum of themes related to human–computer interaction, including theoretical issues, methods, tools, processes, and case studies in HCI design, as well as novel interaction techniques, interfaces, and applications. The proceedings will be published by Springer. More information is available on the conference website: http://2018.hci.international/.

General Chair
Prof. Constantine Stephanidis
University of Crete and ICS-FORTH
Heraklion, Crete, Greece
E-mail: general_chair@hcii2018.org

http://2018.hci.international/

Contents – Part I

Beyond the Classroom

Games and Gamification for Learning

Contents – Part II

Diversity in Learning

Learning Analytics

Improving the Learning and Collaboration Experience

Multimodal and Natural Interaction for Learning

Immersive Visualization Technologies to Facilitate Multidisciplinary Design Education

Jorge D. Camba[1(✉)], José Luis Soler[2], and Manuel Contero[2]

[1] Gerald D. Hines College of Architecture and Design, University of Houston,
4200 Elgin Street, Houston, TX 77204-4000, USA
jdorribo@uh.edu
[2] Instituto de Investigación e Innovación en Bioingeniería (I3B), Universitat Politècnica de Valéncia, Camino de Vera s/n, 46022 Valencia, Spain
{josodo,mcontero}@upv.es

Abstract. This paper reports on an integrated project-based course for undergraduate students in industrial design, architecture, and interior architecture, where emerging technologies are used to develop 3D visualization experiences for projects that effectively combine elements from the three design disciplines. The course emphasizes design as a multidisciplinary activity that can benefit from skills that span traditional departmental boundaries. The curriculum moves through the different types of mixed reality technologies such as virtual and augmented reality, and explores how these tools can be combined to harness the design potential across disciplines and create compelling and engaging outcomes. The course follows a student-centered collaborative approach where projects are completed as a team with members from different majors. Student to student collaboration is actively encouraged in an effort to promote dialogue and community and foster creative thinking. The proposed initiative provides an integrative and unifying experience for students and their design concepts and project outcomes, as well as an opportunity for expanding their creative portfolios.

Keywords: Multidisciplinary education · Design disciplines · Mixed reality · 3D visualization

1 Introduction

Modern approaches to design pedagogy are largely influenced by constructivist theories, which emphasize the importance of interpreting and contextualizing educational contents to provide effective learning experiences [1, 2]. In constructivism, it is essential that the educational material is not only lectured but learners have the opportunity to experience it in their own context and reflect on those experiences [1].

To facilitate phases of individual construction and contextualization, design pedagogy generally takes the form of collaborative project-oriented learning where a studio-centered environment encourages teamwork, cooperation, hands-on activities, and the creative exploration of ideas [3, 4]. Design studio instruction is based on the premise that creative design is learned through the act of doing and making, or "leaning-by-doing" [5]. A design studio

P. Zaphiris and A. Ioannou (Eds.): LCT 2017, Part I, LNCS 10295, pp. 3–11, 2017.
DOI: 10.1007/978-3-319-58509-3_1

is expected to promote a culture where students work side by side to share and benefit from exposure to a variety of ideas from peers and instructors [6, 7].

However, the unique characteristics and requirements of each individual design discipline often make it difficult to deliver an integrated curriculum that promotes truly multidisciplinary work. For example, a project that involves the design of a new line of urban bicycles may be exciting to industrial design students but would likely be of little to no interest to students majoring in architecture. Similarly, designing the interior space of an office building or a hotel lobby would likely be exciting to interior architecture students, but unstimulating to most industrial designers.

In this paper, we describe a new multidisciplinary course that is currently being offered to students of industrial design, architecture, and interior architecture at the University of Houston. The curriculum uses emerging visualization technologies as a catalyst for the creation of collaborative projects and the development of integrated outcomes. In this regard, this paper was written as a way of distributing the results of our initiative to the design education community.

2   Educational Needs and Multidisciplinary Programs

Researchers across various disciplines have stressed the importance of cross-disciplinary education. This kind of education aims to supplement traditional domain-specific knowledge skills with the development of "boundary-crossing" skills such as the ability to synthesize knowledge from different disciplines and being able to change perspectives based on specific aspects of a problem [8].

According to Berezin [9], the proper balance between specialized technical training and a general social human knowledge is essential to avoid fragmented knowledge in poorly interacting specialties [9]. Similarly, authors Borrego and Newswander [10] state that "researchers from other disciplines 'see' things differently, but by understanding the underlying differences and how these can expand possibilities for research, would-be collaborators can learn lessons invaluable to cooperation, communication, and ultimate understanding [10]." Evidence suggests that cross-disciplinarity facilitates comprehensive understanding [8, 11]

Cross-disciplinary collaborations can take the form of either multidisciplinary or interdisciplinary approaches. In a multidisciplinary approach, collaborators work together on a problem and each collaborator brings his or her own expertise to the team [12, 13] and split apart after the common work is completed. In contrast, in interdisciplinary collaborations, researchers from different disciplines work in a more integrated manner by combining their knowledge from their own disciplines to work toward a common goal [10, 12, 13]. As stated by Borrego [10], "at the end of a truly interdisciplinary collaboration, each collaborator is changed by the experience."

The differences between multidisciplinary and interdisciplinary approaches are illustrated in Fig. 1.

We are familiar with efforts at a number of universities (from faculty to departmental to college to university levels) to promote cross-disciplinary education. For example, successful collaborations between engineering, humanities, and applied sciences have

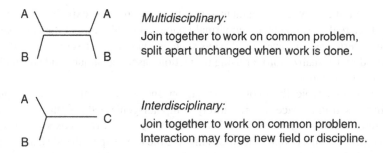

Fig. 1. Difference between multidisciplinary and interdisciplinary collaborations (adapted from [13]).

been reported [14] as well as initiatives that combine design and communication [15], or engineering, business, and art [16]. A pilot interdisciplinary course on climate solutions was also reported which involved faculty from seven different disciplines including engineering, political science, philosophy, meteorology and foreign languages [17]. Researchers agree that support from the academic institution is a key factor to the successful implementation of interdisciplinary courses [10].

The integration of various disciplines into a cross-disciplinary curriculum is generally implemented as project-based team courses (particularly if the disciplines are closely related), which emphasize teamwork as the focus for learning. Some examples include partnerships among architecture, engineering, and construction [18] as well as civil, mechanical and electrical engineering [19]. Cross-disciplinary project-based education is also common among first-year engineering programs as a strategy to improve retention and attract new students into engineering [20, 21]. In some cases, students work closely with sponsors and external companies that support the course.

Some major obstacles to successfully implementing cross-disciplinary education were identified by Ackerson [22]. These obstacles include (1) fragmentation of disciplinary information, (2) inability to digest the extensive volume of existing information, and (3) a lack of access to relevant information [22].

The multidisciplinary course presented in this paper was designed to address the first obstacle (i.e., fragmentation of disciplinary information) by facilitating an environment where students can work in teams toward a common goal while naturally dividing tasks based on students'individual interests, backgrounds, and majors.

3   Emerging Visualization Technologies

For the purposes of this paper, the concept of "emerging visualization technologies" refers to advanced 3D visualization tools that can be used to present and experience design information, concepts, and outcomes in an immersive manner. These technologies include the various types of augmented reality technology (e.g., direct, indirect, marker-based, projection-based, etc.), virtual reality, and holographic visualization.

Augmented Reality (AR) is a visualization technology that combines real-time three-dimensional computer-generated imagery and real-life footage to create an enhanced representation of reality [23]. Augmented reality allows users to experience a modified version of the real world by blending virtual images and real views of the environment. It can be experienced in a variety of ways such as via computer screens and portable devices (indirect visualization), or using projection based techniques and special headsets (direct visualization).

Virtual Reality typically involves immersion. In a virtual reality environment, the user is immersed in a space that is entirely computer-generated (i.e. the real world is entirely replaced by a virtual world) [24]. There are many ways to experience virtual reality worlds. The most popular methods involve the use of specialized Head Mounted Displays (HMD) such as the Oculus Rift® [25] or the HTC Vive® [26].

Holographic visualization is a type of direct mixed (augmented) reality experience popularized by Microsoft and their recent Head Mounted Display, the Hololens® [27]. This technology offers a more integrated view of reality, as real spaces can be mapped in 3D, making virtual content "aware" of the real environment. According to Microsoft, holographic visualization allows users to "visualize and work with digital content as part of the real world" and "feel present in the environment by enabling them to move naturally, interact, and explore in three dimensions [27]."

Visualization technologies have always been at the heart of the design disciplines. In addition to CAD software, immersive technologies have been used to develop and visualize design concepts [28–30]; visualize construction processes and scheduling [31]; or analyze engineering and construction equipment [32, 33]. Research has shown that immersive technologies in design studios can increase the awareness of the designer and facilitate the selective reinterpretation and immediate evaluation of a particular design instance [34].

From an educational standpoint, however, immersive visualization technologies have generally been used merely as tools to complement or facilitate other tasks, but not necessarily as the focus of the course. In fact, these types of courses are often very technical and offered only to computer science students as a complement to a computer graphics course [35, 36]. Burdea identified some of the problems regarding the teaching of these technologies, particularly virtual reality [37].

Nevertheless, a number of educational initiatives on virtual reality courses have been reported, including some multidisciplinary ones. For example, an educational framework for developing VR applications was described by Miyata et al. [38]. Using this framework, graduate students worked in teams to develop a number of visualization experiences, mostly games. Authors Zimmerman and Eber [39] described an interdisciplinary course with students from computer science and art. Similarly, a practical course on virtual reality designed for engineering students from different fields (e.g., mechanical engineering, electrical, etc.) was also reported [40].

In this paper, we describe a pilot course for design majors where immersive visualization technologies are studied from a non-technical standpoint. The course examines how these technologies can benefit designers, particularly in terms of the presentation and delivery of visual content.

4 Approach

As part of an initiative supported by the College of Architecture and Design at the University of Houston to offer courses that are interdisciplinary among the degree programs within the College (Interior Architecture, Industrial Design, and Architecture), a pilot course on emerging visualization technologies was offered in the Spring 2017 semester. The goal of this initiative is aimed at providing new cross-disiplinary areas of inquiry to students in the context of the following four approaches: (1) Human Factors, (2) Materials/Systems, (3) History/Theory, and (4) Entrepreneurial Processes.

Although the new course is organized around a student-centered project-based collaborative curriculum, it is not offered as a traditional design studio but as a regular lecture/lab course. Upperclass undergraduates and graduate students from all three majors were eligible to enroll. The course is divided into four major learning blocks, each of which covering a relevant emerging topic on visualization technology:

- Fundamentals of 3D and stereoscopy
- Augmented Reality (Direct and Indirect)
- Virtual Reality
- Holographic Visualization

The course emphasizes (1) 3D visualization, presentation, and visual communication as fundamental skills that are common across different specialties; (2) the integrative and versatile nature of visualization technologies; and (3) their inherent applicability to different design fields. Through a combination of lectures and project-based exercises, students investigate emerging topics in 3D visualization, including the limitations, areas of application, and contexts of use. Students investigate how immersive 3D visualizations can enrich the delivery of design information; enhance presentations and simulations in their respective fields, and impact user perception, cognition, and engagement. The general schedule of topics of the course is described in Table 1.

Table 1. Schedule of topics

Week	Learning block	Topic	Project
1	3D fundamentals	Introduction	Project 1
2		Stereoscopic 3D	
3		360 Video	
4	Augmented reality (AR)	Augmented reality	Project 2
5		AR indirect view	
6		AR direct view	
7		Projection mapping	
8	Virtual reality (VR)	Virtual reality	Project 3
9		Designing immersive environments	
10		User experience in VR environments	
11	Holographic visualization	Introduction to holograms	Project 4
12		Interactivity	
13		Interactivity	
14		Spatial mapping	

Given the design background of the students enrolled in the course, topics and specific technolgies were discussed almost entirely from an "authoring" or content-creation point of view, emphasizing user experience. Emphasis was also put on the visual quality of the deliverables. No programming, software development, or computer graphics concepts were discussed beyond basic interactions and interface design.

A team project was assigned for each major topic. Teams were comprised of no less than three students. Attempts were made to diversify all teams so at least one member of each team would be from a different design discipline. Projects involved the creation of an interactive visualization experience that combined elements of all three majors. The experience would be designed for the specific technology being discussed in class at the time the project was assigned. As an example, for the virtual reality learning block, an architecture student may create an immersive visualization of a building where all the details can be experienced at true scale. Similarly, an interior architecture student may build on the previous work by modeling a particular interior space within the previous building, whereas an industrial design student could do the same for a particular piece of furniture for that interior space. All three concepts are integrated in a seamless manner to provide a comprehensive visualization of a particular design space.

In addition, for each major learning block (described above), students were required to reflect back on their respective fields, describe how the technology can be applied and used effectively, and be encouraged to use their 3D models and designs (including those completed in previous courses and studios) to create additional experiences that are relevant to their specific area or interest.

The final deliverables for each project required a poster session, an oral presentation, a final report, and a demonstration of the experience. Project topics were discussed between the faculty and each individual team and reflected the interests of the students: immersive visualization of living spaces, public spaces and community development, furniture design and applications, customization of interior spaces and its impact on user perception, examination of immersive technologies as a tool to evaluate user preferences, urban farming, and visualization of large urban areas.

Student to student collaboration was actively encouraged in an effort to promote dialogue and community, foster creativity and unconventional thinking, and expand students' perspectives. The proposed initiative provides not only a multidisciplinary course for students, but also an integrative and unifying experience for their design concepts and project outcomes as well as an opportunity for expanding their creative portfolios.

5   Discussion

The development and affordability of innovative immersive 3D visualization technologies are opening new doors to design exploration, documentation, and presentation. Furthermore, visualization technology is increasingly influencing the design process itself, particularly during initial concept phases. As designers, being able to show the audience a virtual version of a future product or environment can foster reliability and consensus, reduce uncertainty, and help make decisions throughout refinement and planning processes.

Using visualization technologies, layers of digital information can be combined with traditional media and physical spaces to create truly unique and immersive experiences that go far beyond classic presentation boards and computer screens. As a practical hands-on exploration of emerging technologies for design visualization and presentation, we developed a new course where students learn to deliver three-dimensional experiences that merge the physical with the virtual and allow audiences to interact with the content.

The multidisciplinary experience of the course is founded on (1) 3D visualization as a fundamental component of design that is common to all disciplines; (2) the integrative and versatile nature of visualization technologies; and (3) their immediate applicability to different design fields. In this regard, new visualization technologies have the potential to drastically change the way design is experienced, shared, and presented.

A dedicated course that explores state of the art tools and visualization technologies was designed to prepare students with the means to provide richer and more engaging experiences to diverse audiences. The proposed course is intended to have a significant impact on the nature of the presentation deliverables that students submit to their studio courses and theses. In addition, the integrated curriculum offers students from Industrial Design, Architecture, and Interior Architecture (both at the undergraduate and graduate levels) a path toward experiencing state of the art visualization technology and applying it to their respective fields.

The difficulties encountered with the multidisciplinary format of this pilot course involve mostly administrative challenges. In some cases, however, the challenge is not a result of the multidisciplinary aspect of the course, but one involving teamwork. For example, working and managing small groups can often be difficult for both faculty and students, especially when one or more students are not fully engaged in the project.

In addition, faculty and students agreed that the lack of particular resources dedicated to the teams was unfortunate, as all specialized equipment had to be shared among multiple teams. The fact that the Head Mounted Displays such as the Oculus Rift and the Microsoft Hololens are costly and require powerful computers to run was a major obstacle for students. There were consistent complaints from the students that they could not test their experiences adequately because they did not have easy and exclusive access to the technology outside class meetings. They suggested that even a small budget to purchase more equipment could have been helpful. An alternative option was proposed where each team would complete each project at a different time during the semester to reduce scheduling conflicts for a specific device. This option would naturally add complexity in terms of course management, as more content would have to be delivered at the beginning of the semester in order to accommodate all projects.

There are several implications of our pilot experience. First, students benefit from exposure to a diversity of design backgrounds from their colleagues and opportunities to share their areas of expertise within their groups. Second, student also benefit from explicit instruction on cross-disciplinary teamwork, dynamics, and problem solving. Third, student get different perspectives on design by interacting with other students and being exposed to how other disciplines approach the design process itself. Finally, students benefit from the resulting project outcomes, which provide an integrated piece for their creative design portfolios. In the near future, we would like to examine how this course influences the quality and delivery of design information in other courses. We plan to collaborate with other faculty to track these students and determine whether the use of immersive technologies has a significant impact on their future presentations.

References

1. Piaget, J.: The Child's Conception of the World, vol. 213. Rowman & Littlefield, Lanham (1951)
2. Dewey, J.: Experience & Education. Kappa Delta Pi, New York (1938)
3. Maitland, B.M.: Problem-based learning for an architecture degree. In: Boud, D., Feletti, G. (eds.) The Challenge of Problem-based Learning. Kogan Page, London (1991)
4. Green, L.N., Bonollo, E.: Studio-based teaching: history and advantages in the teaching of design. World Trans. Eng. Tech. Educ. 2(2), 269–272 (2003)
5. Schön, D.: The Reflective Practitioner. Basic books, New York (1983)
6. Waks, L.J.: Donald Schon's philosophy of design and design education. Int. J. Technol. Des. Educ. 11, 37–51 (2001)
7. Chiu, M.L.: An organizational view of design communication in design collaboration. Des. Stud. 23(2), 197–210 (2002)
8. Spelt, E.J., Biemans, H.J., Tobi, H., Luning, P.A., Mulder, M.: Teaching and learning in interdisciplinary higher education: a systematic review. Educ. Psychol. Rev. 21(4), 365 (2009)
9. Berezin, A.: Interdisciplinary integration in engineering education. In: Proceedings, IECON 2001. 27th Annual Conference of the IEEE Industrial Electronics Society (Cat. No.37243), vol. 3, pp. 1740–1745 (2001)
10. Borrego, M., Newswander, L.K.: Characteristics of successful cross-disciplinary engineering education collaborations. J. Eng. Educ. 97(2), 123–134 (2008)
11. Newell, W.H.: Decision making in interdisciplinary studies. In: Morçöl, G. (ed.) Handbook of Decision Making. CRC, New York (2007)
12. Klein, J.T.: Interdisciplinarity: History, Theory, and Practice. Wayne State University Press, Detroit (1990)
13. Committee on Facilitating Interdisciplinary Research: Facilitating Interdisciplinary Research. National Academies Press, Washington (2005)
14. Shields M., O'Connell, J.P. Collaborative teaching: reflections on a cross-disciplinary experience in engineering education. In: Proceedings of the 1998 Annual ASEE Conference, Seattle, WA, 28 June–1 July 1998
15. Hirsch, P.L., Shwom, B.L., Yarnoff, C., Anderson, J.C., Kelso, D.M., Olson, G.B., Colgate, J.E.: Engineering design and communication: the case for interdisciplinary collaboration. Int. J. Eng. Educ. 17(4,5), 342–348 (2001)
16. Wesner, J.W., Amon, C.H., Bigrigg, M.W., Subrahmanian, E., Westerberg, A.W., Filipski, K.: Student team formation and assignment in a multi-disciplinary engineering design projects course: a pair of suggested best practices. Int. J. Eng. Educ. 23(3), 517–526 (2007)
17. Rhee, J., Cordero, E.C., Quill, L.R.: Pilot implementation of an interdisciplinary course on climate solutions. Int. J. Eng. Educ. 26(2), 391 (2010)
18. Fruchter, R.: Dimensions of teamwork education. Int. J. Eng. Educ. 17(4,5), 426–430 (2001)
19. Skates, G.W.: Interdisciplinary project working in engineering education. Eur. J. Eng. Educ. 28(2), 187–201 (2003)
20. Frolik, J., Keller, T.: Wireless sensor networks: an interdisciplinary topic for freshman design. In: American Society for Engineering Education Annual Conference & Exposition, ASEE, pp. 1–7 (2005)

21. Knight, D.W., Carlson, L.E., Sullivan, J.F.: Improving engineering student retention through hands-on, team based, first-year design projects. In: Proceedings of the International Conference on Research in Engineering Education, Honolulu, HI (2007)
22. Ackerson, L.G.: Challenges for engineering libraries: supporting research and teaching in a cross-disciplinary environment. Sci. Technol. Libr. **21**(1,2), 43–52 (2001)
23. Azuma, R.T.: A survey of augmented reality. Presence-Teleoperators Virtual Environ. **6**(4), 355–385 (1997)
24. Jerald, J.: The VR Book: Human-Centered Design for Virtual Reality. Morgan & Claypool, San Rafael (2015)
25. Oculus Rift. https://www.oculus.com/rift/. Accessed 20 Feb 2017
26. HTC Vice. https://www.vive.com/. Accessed 20 Feb 2017
27. Microsoft Hololens. https://www.microsoft.com/microsoft-hololens. Accessed 20 Feb 2017
28. Shibano, N., Hareesh, P.V., Kashiwagi, M., Sawada, K., Takemura, H.: Development of VR experiencing system with hemi-spherical immersive projection display for urban environment design. In: Proceedings of the Seventh International Conference on Virtual Systems and Multimedia, VSMM 2001 (2001)
29. Schmitt, G.: Virtual Reality in Architecture. In: Thalmann, N.M., Thalmann, D. (eds.) Virtual Worlds and Multimedia. Wiley, Chichester (1993)
30. Messner, J.I., Yerrapathruni, S.C., Baratta, A.J., Riley, D.R.: Cost and schedule reduction of nuclear power plant construction using 4D CAD and immersive display technologies. In: Computing in Civil Engineering: Proceedings of the International Workshop of Information Technology in Civil Engineering, pp. 136–144 (2002)
31. Whisker, V.E., Baratta, A.J., Yerrapathruni, S., Messner, J.I., Shaw, T.S., Warren, M.E., Rotthoff, E.S., Winters, J.W., Clelland, J.A., Johnson, F.T.: Using immersive virtual environments to develop and visualize construction schedules for advanced nuclear power plants. Proc. ICAPP **3**, 4–7 (2003)
32. Lipman, R., Reed, K.: Using VRML in construction industry applications. In: Web3D – VRML 2000 Symposium, Monterey, CA, pp. 1–7 (2000)
33. Opdenbosch, A., Hastak, M.: Virtual reality environment for design and analysis of automated construction equipment. In: 2nd Congress for Computing in Civil Engineering, Atlanta, GA, 566–573 (1994)
34. Abdelhameed, W.A.: Virtual reality use in architectural design studios: a case of studying structure and construction. Procedia Comput. Sci. **25**, 220–230 (2013)
35. Zara, J.: VR course - a natural enrichment of computer graphics classes. Comput. Graph. Forum **25**, 105–112 (2005)
36. Cliburn, D.: Incorporating virtual reality concepts into the introductory computer graphics course. In: Proceedings of the SIGCSE. ACM, Houston, Texas, USA, pp. 77–81 (2006)
37. Burdea, G.: Teaching virtual reality: why and how? Presence: Teleoperators virtual Environ. **13**, 463–483 (2004)
38. Miyata, K., Umemoto, K., Higuchi, T.: An educational framework for creating VR application through groupwork. Comput. Graph. **34**(6), 811–819 (2010)
39. Zimmerman, G.W., Eber, D.E.: When worlds collide!: an interdisciplinary course in virtual-reality art. In: Proceedings of SIGCSE. ACM, New York, pp. 75–79 (2001)
40. Häfner, P., Häfner, V., Ovtcharova, J.: Teaching methodology for virtual reality practical course in engineering education. Procedia Comput. Sci. **25**, 251–260 (2013)

Peacemaking Affordances of Shareable Interfaces: A Provocative Essay on Using Technology for Social Change

Andri Ioannou[✉] and Chrystalla Antoniou

Cyprus Interaction Lab, Department of Multimedia and Graphic Arts,
Cyprus University of Technology, Limassol, Cyprus
andri.i.ioannou@cut.ac.cy, chg.antoniou@edu.cut.ac.cy
http://cyprusinteractionlab.com/

Abstract. This article is a provocative essay on the topic of educational applications of shareable interfaces, with a focus on the use of multitouch interactive tabletops in peacemaking school initiatives. Based on the already researched affordances of tabletops in education, as well as promising empirical results from the limited application of this technology in peacemaking contexts, the authors of this manuscript would argue for the integration and further investigation of interactive tabletops in peacemaking school initiatives, pushing the boundaries of the technology to positively influence our societies.

Keywords: Peacemaking · Peacebuilding · Peace education · Technology enhanced learning · Peace and technology · Multitouch tabletops · Shareable interfaces

1 Introduction

The potential of using technology for peace has received considerable attention in the recent days. The role of technology in peacemaking, peacebuilding, and peace education, in terms of initiatives and ideas as well as technology infrastructures for peace, is recently being discussed in prestigious academic conferences and journals [11, 14, 24, 25]. Overall however, promoting peace or educating for peace through the means of technology is a topic we rarely see addressed in school contexts. There are a few established models for conflict management in schools, which mainly involve conflict resolution education (i.e., conflict management skills training) infused into the daily school curriculum; yet, very little work is done in this area that takes advantage of current technologies and innovations. This provocative essay aims to start the dialog and encourage research that unpacks the largely unexplored potential of shareable interfaces – that is, technologies designed to support collocated collaboration – in technology-enhanced peacemaking, peacebuilding and peace education initiatives. The essay focuses on multitouch interactive tabletops, as a form of shareable interfaces, pointing to relevant literature and calling for research that expands their potential application in this area.

© Springer International Publishing AG 2017
P. Zaphiris and A. Ioannou (Eds.): LCT 2017, Part I, LNCS 10295, pp. 12–21, 2017.
DOI: 10.1007/978-3-319-58509-3_2

2 Background Work

2.1 Peace and Technology

As Hourcade and Bullock-Rest [12] explained, there are many opportunities for research in the area of human-computer interaction and peace including "the design of technologies to enable connections between opposing camps, tools to present news stories from several points of view, and technologies to support international monitoring missions to prevent the escalation of conflicts", yet the same authors acknowledge that empirical work is very limited and sporadic (p. 443). In educational contexts and initiatives, some technologies have been used to promote peace and peace-related outcomes, although the focus of these efforts mainly revolve around the use of Internet technologies mediating long-distance collaboration in particular, (i) *virtual learning environments* to host learning activities related to peace, (ii) *Web 2.0 and communication technologies* including blogs, wikis, social networking sites, video sharing sites, email and video conferencing to promote communication and collaboration among people of diverse backgrounds, and (iii) *serious games or MMORPGs* to promote exposure to diverse populations and social interaction, such as the PeaceMaker game which simulates the Israeli-Palestinian conflict and engages dyads in negotiating peace [4], or *simulations* used to teach about conflict management [2]. A review of these previous efforts is found in Veletsianos and Eliadou [25].

The benefits emerging from the use of communication and collaboration technologies are numerous, especially when those are employed in cases where participants' physical co-presence is obstructed by insurmountable barriers, such as physical distance, high costs in time and money, fear and suspicion, or external events like war, conflicts and attacks. Without overlooking the advantages of using technologies to support remote interaction in peace-related initiatives, the authors of this work would argue that sharing an experience in a common physical space, e.g., via shareable interfaces, affords yet more powerful peace-making opportunities.

It is acknowledged that peace education takes different shapes in practice, as for instance, human rights education, development education, conflict resolution education, international education and environmental education [8]. According to Harris [8], this results out of the controversy surrounding the concept of 'peace' in combination to educators' attempts to address different forms of violence in different cultures and in different social contexts. Despite the different approaches, practices that aim to promote peace-related outcomes have several features in common, as they are mainly oriented towards fostering collaboration, communication and understanding of the 'other' – parameters which function as prerequisites for peace [25]. We support that these factors can be enhanced by the means of shareable interfaces, when the technology is used by learners to carry out meaningful tasks and to share structured experiences that involve or even require their physical co-existence and collaboration in collocated settings.

Sharing mutually meaningful experiences in a common physical space is a way of enhancing social connections [19], which in turn can enable the aforementioned prerequisites for peace. We, therefore, argue that technology-infused practices which require collocation, e.g., learning tasks mediated by shareable interfaces, have the potential to provide shared experiences that can activate social bonding and the other above-mentioned peace factors. Moreover, physicality and collocation can be essential in peacemaking efforts in the rather typical case in which language barriers exist between those in conflict (e.g., Israeli-Palestinian conflict, Greek-Turkish Cypriots conflict). Overall, however, technology-enhanced peacemaking research in collocated settings is almost non-existent to date. Even opportunities for such research were lacking until a few years ago, when tabletops became commercially available, affordable and compelling for small-group, collocated work [6, 9]. The rest of this essay focuses on multitouch interactive tabletops, as a form of shareable interfaces which presents an opportunity to nourish peacemaking efforts in collocated educational settings.

2.2 Interactive Tabletops

Tabletops are large horizontal displays that enable interaction by multiple concurrent users. They have been commercially available since 2009 with the introduction of MS Surface [6]. In terms of hardware, commercial tabletops can typically respond to more than 40 simultaneous inputs, therefore can easily support groups of four to six students. In terms of software, today commercial operating systems, such as Windows 8 (or above) and Android, support native touch input and offer a repository of thousands of touch applications that can be easily downloaded from the Web and used on a commercial tabletop. Also, if funds, time and expertise permit, custom-built tabletop applications can be designed and developed.

There is already substantial work on their use to support various types of communication collaboration and learning. A summary of work on the pedagogical considerations of tabletops is found in Higgins et al. [9]. Also, a summary of work on the technological considerations of tabletops is found in Dillenbourg and Evans [5]. Briefly, studies on tabletops have shown that "being able to see another's physical actions on the shared display can enhance awareness, which in turn can support fluid interaction and coordination" (p. 167) [10]. Also, the horizontal orientation of a tabletop display allows users to hover their hands easily over the surface, and as a result, gesture-based communication can supplement or even replace verbal communication around tabletops [22]. This might be particularly useful in cases where language barriers may inhibit participation and interaction among the collaborators.

Moreover tabletops have been found to enhance the sense of teamwork [18], 'invite' interaction and willingness to participate in groups tasks [23], increase equity in physical interaction compared to other devices [7, 15, 17], promote joint attention on the task [5, 7], encourage playfulness in interaction [16, 20], improve the (learning) experience and motivation to engage in the task [3], enable collaborators to negotiate conflict [7, 14, 21], and help engage users in 'creative conflict', that is, arguing and disagreeing directed at ideas rather than people [1]. One might consider all of the above as 'peacemaking affordances' of the technology, although none of these studies have perceived it as such, setting tabletops pertinent to work on peacemaking, peacebuilding and peace education.

2.3 Tabletops for Peace

A couple of previous studies have endorsed the idea of collocated, technology enhanced peacemaking exploring the potential of tabletops in this context. In particular, Stock et al. [24]

designed a collocated tabletop interface, the NNR-Table, as a tool for reconciliation. NNR-Table allowed multimedia narrations to be contributed from two opposing sides; participants worked together to achieve a narration acceptable to both viewpoints (i.e., by revising and completing the narration together). NNR-Table interventions were found successful in helping Jewish-Arab pairs of youth reach a compromise and learn more about each-other's viewpoints [24, 26]. Moreover, Ioannou et al. [14] designed a collocated brainstorming tabletop activity to facilitate dialog and consensus decision-making in groups of college-students discussing sensitive and controversial topics, including peace-building in a country in long-term ethnic conflict. The authors found that discussion around the tabletop was fluent with no evidence of tension, anxiety or strong disagreement among the participant.

Furthermore, Ioannou and Antoniou [13] used tabletops to promote playful collaboration and learning among students in conflict (verbal and physical bullying) in an elementary school, leading to positive changes in their attitudes and behaviours from pre to post intervention testing. In particular, a SUR40 tabletop was used with freely available applications and designed game-like learning activities which required students, in conflict-laden groups, to collaborate around the tabletop (see Fig. 1.). Once such activity for instance, required students to learn about animals (top image of Fig. 1) or to categorize the various types of musical instruments (bottom image of Fig. 1) by sorting images on the tabletop [13]. In a follow-up study in the spirit of technology-enhanced peacemaking, the same authors conducted an intervention study with 44 young children (aged 9–10 years old) of multiple ethnicities in an elementary school with a large number of migrants. In this work (see Fig. 2), tabletop technology and associated learning activities aimed at promoting communication and collaboration, perspective taking and feeling of acceptance (authors' reference under review).

The aforementioned studies showed that tabletop technology can function as mediator for peace, through two different approaches. On the one hand, Ioannou et al. [14], Stock et al. [24] and Zancanaro et al. [26] provided evidence supporting that peacemaking can be fostered when students are given opportunities to deal explicitly with sensitive issues directly linked to the existing conflicts of the students' micro or macro environment. In these cases, tabletops appear to facilitate perspective-taking processes, in a tensed-free way. On the other hand, findings provided by Ioannou and Antoniou [13] indicated that it is not always necessary to talk about peace issues in order to achieve peace-related outcomes. In fact, the particular study was diversified from the previous and was innovative in that technology was used by students in conflict-laden groups for game-like tasks which were not directly or explicitly related to the experienced conflict per se. In this way, students' attention was intentionally shifted from the existing conflict amongst them and was placed to the gamified learning tasks that students had to jointly carry out. The tabletop activity, as an attractive and challenging force, shaded the stated ongoing conflict between the group members, who simply aimed to successfully complete the game-task. Despite the fact that the students had barely discussed about their conflict as such, or about peace-related issues, the emerged findings revealed students' positive behavioral and attitudinal shifts, highlighting tabletops' potential as 'peace-enforcing' technology. This was achieved by providing a shared common physical space of equal access and of distributed power, where students could collaborate over structured, game-like activities through which they could engage in a mutual goal.

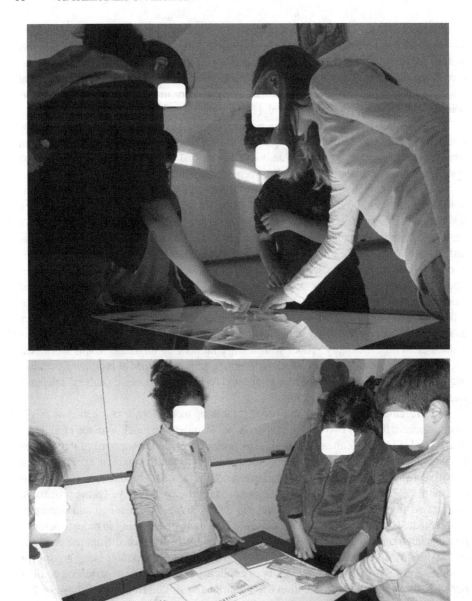

Fig. 1. Tabletop collaboration in conflict-laden groups (Ioannou and Antoniou 2016)

Fig. 2. Tabletop collaboration promoting feeling of acceptance (under review)

In other words, the focus of the particular study was not solely on what students communicated about, but on creating an attractive technology-infused social environment in which they could communicate and work together [13].

In accordance to Nardi and Whittaker [19], given that "social bonding is affected through two linked processes, namely engagement of the human body in social interaction and informal conversation" (p. 86), current research findings document that tabletops can respond to both of these processes, thereby promoting communication, collaboration and interaction, the so-called, by Veletsianos and Eliadou [25], 'antecedents to peace'. Either by directly targeting peace topics or by deliberately going around them, the use of multitouch interactive tabletops appear to have the potential to mediate peace-related outcomes, regardless the adopted approach.

Overall, considering the encouraging but limited research work on tabletop-enhanced peacemaking, as well as their already researched affordances for communication and collocated collaboration, one could argue that tabletops are well suited technologies for integration in peace education initiatives and interventions. We would argue that tabletops and other shareable interfaces, such as for example integrative walls and floors [6], can be 'peace-enforcing' technologies which can enable a shared workspace for collaboration and interaction among people in conflict, allowing 'power' to be shared and distributed and, in this way, 'forcing' the participants to take into account the interests of the 'other'.

3   Discussion

The potential of shareable interfaces, including multitouch interactive tabletops, in peacemaking and peace education is largely unexplored. This provocative essay calls for research that expands the potential application of such technology in peacemaking school initiatives. Based on the already researched affordances of tabletops in educational settings, as well as promising empirical results from its limited application in peacemaking contexts, the authors argue that tabletops, but also other forms of shareable interfaces, can have a stimulating effect in education if their peacemaking affordances are perceived more widely.

Shareable interfaces, such as interactive tabletops and interactive walls and floors [6], are now commercially available whilst becoming more robust and affordable every year. In terms of software, interactive tabletops have an advantage compared to other shareable interfaces: commercial operating systems, such as Windows 8 (or above) and Android, support native touch input and offer a repository of thousands of touch applications that can be easily downloaded from the Web and used on. For example, a beginner's attempt to integrate the technology, might involve the use of off-the-shelf applications from the Windows Store in the categories of Education and Entertainment. There is a number of freely-available applications in the Windows Store, such as iMath, English Club, Puzzletouch, and Kids Play & Learning (see application descriptions in the Windows Store) around which school teachers can design learning activities linked to aspects of the everyday curriculum. These apps come with levels of difficulty and other various settings which can be customized and personalized according to the grade-level and knowledge of the participating groups, as in Ioannou and Antoniou [13]. Also, the technology can either be integrated in the curriculum or can be used for extracurricular activities, with similar peacemaking goals in mind.

All in all, the authors present a position that tabletops, and other shareable interfaces, can be 'peace-enforcing' technologies allowing 'power' to be shared and distributed and giving the chance for people in conflict to share a common space. Future research should benefit from further empirical investigations in this area, potentially leading to the formation of some theoretical or methodological account of:

(i) how shareable interfaces might promote peacemaking by eliciting and supporting various types of interactions amongst collocated learners, and
(ii) how learning design, mediated by such technology, can be tailored to changing perceptions, improving relationships and breaking down social barriers.

Closing, tabletops in particular, and shareable interfaces in general, are a new generation of educational technologies that offer new possibilities for engaging students in communication and collaboration. In the future, new forms of collaborative practice will be supported by this technology, especially as it gets more advanced and equipped with relevant software. What is also important, this kind of technology is attractive for young people who can stay engaged and enjoy the experience [3, 14]. Tailoring this technology to enhance peace education efforts is a great area for research and development while serving an important purpose.

The authors of this work believe that tabletops, and other shareable interfaces such as interactive walls and floors, can provide a revolutionary approach to peacemaking school initiatives, pushing the boundaries of the technology to positively influence our societies and giving educators the opportunity to deal with social issues perhaps in ways they have not had the chance to do before. This provocative essay aims to start the dialog and encourage research that unpacks the largely unexplored potential of shareable interfaces in the unique areas of peacemaking, peace-building, and peace education.

Acknowledgements. Authors acknowledge funding from the European Union's Horizon 2020 Framework Programme through NOTRE project (H2020-TWINN-2015, Grant Agreement Number: 692058).

References

1. Basheri, M., Munro, M., Burd, L., Baghaei, N.: Collaborative learning skills in multi-touch tables for UML software design. Int. J. Adv. Comput. Sci. Appl. **4**(3), 60–66 (2013)
2. Brynen, R., Milante, G.: Peacebuilding with games and simulations. Simul. Gaming **44**(1), 27–35 (2013)
3. Buisine, S., Besacier, G., Aoussat, A., Vernier, F.: How do interactive tabletop systems influence collaboration? Comput. Hum. Behav. **28**(1), 49–59 (2012)
4. Burak, A., Keylor, E., Sweeney, T.: PeaceMaker: a video game to teach peace. In: Maybury, M., Stock, O., Wahlster, W. (eds.) INTETAIN 2005. LNCS, vol. 3814, pp. 307–310. Springer, Heidelberg (2005). doi:10.1007/11590323_40
5. Dillenbourg, P., Evans, M.: Interactive tabletops in education. Int. J. Comput. Support. Collab. Learn. **6**(4), 491–514 (2011)
6. Evans, M.A., Rick, J.: Supporting learning with interactive surfaces and spaces. In: Spector, J.M., Merrill, M.D., Elen, J., Bishop, M.J. (eds.) Handbook of Research on Educational Communications and Technology, pp. 689–701. Springer, New York (2014). doi: 10.1007/978-1-4614-3185-5_55

7. Fleck, R., Rogers, Y., Yuill, N., Marshall, P., Carr, A., Rick, J., Bonnett, V.: Actions speak loudly with words: unpacking collaboration around the table. In: Proceedings of the ACM International Conference on Interactive Tabletops and Surfaces, pp. 189–196. ACM, November 2009

8. Harris, I.M.: Peace education theory. J. Peace Educ. 1(1), 5–20 (2004)

9. Higgins, S.E., Mercier, E., Burd, E., Hatch, A.: Multi-touch tables and the relationship with collaborative classroom pedagogies: a synthetic review. Int. J. Comput. Support. Collab. Learn. 6(4), 515–538 (2011)

10. Hornecker, E., Marshall, P., Dalton, N.S., Rogers, Y.: Collaboration and interference: awareness with mice or touch input. In: Proceedings of the 2008 ACM Conference on Computer Supported Cooperative Work, pp. 167–176. ACM, November 2008

11. Hourcade, J.P., Bullock-Rest, N., Davis, J., Jayatilaka, L., Moraveji, N., Nathan, L., Zaphiris, P.: HCI for peace: preventing, de-escalating and recovering from conflict. In: CHI 2012 Extended Abstracts on Human Factors in Computing Systems, pp. 2703–2706. ACM, May 2012

12. Hourcade, J.P., Bullock-Rest, N.E.: HCI for peace: a call for constructive action. In: Proceedings of the SIGCHI Conference on Human Factors in Computing Systems, pp. 443–452. ACM, May 2011

13. Ioannou, A., Antoniou, C.: Tabletops for peace: technology enhanced peacemaking in school contexts. Educ. Technol. Soc. 19(2), 164–176 (2016)

14. Ioannou, A., Zaphiris, P., Loizides, F., Vasiliou, C.: Let's talk about technology for peace: a systematic assessment of problem-based group collaboration around an interactive tabletop. In: Interacting with Computers, iwt061 (2013)

15. Ioannou, A., Zenios, M., Stylianou, A.: Dialogue, knowledge work and tabletops: lessons from preservice teacher education. In: Zaphiris, P., Ioannou, A. (eds.) LCT 2014. LNCS, vol. 8523, pp. 410–418. Springer, Cham (2014). doi:10.1007/978-3-319-07482-5_39

16. Jamil, I., O'Hara, K., Perry, M., Karnik, A., Subramanian, S.: The effects of interaction techniques on talk patterns in collaborative peer learning around interactive tables. In: Proceedings of the SIGCHI Conference on Human Factors in Computing Systems, pp. 3043–3052. ACM, May 2011

17. Marshall, P., Hornecker, E., Morris, R., Dalton, N.S., Rogers, Y.: When the fingers do the talking: a study of group participation with varying constraints to a tabletop interface. In: 3rd IEEE International Workshop on Horizontal Interactive Human Computer Systems, TABLETOP 2008, pp. 33–40. IEEE, October 2008

18. Morris, M.R., Huang, A., Paepcke, A., Winograd, T.: Cooperative gestures: multi-user gestural interactions for co-located groupware. In: Proceedings of the SIGCHI Conference on Human Factors in Computing Systems, pp. 1201–1210. ACM, April 2006

19. Nardi, B.A., Whittaker, S.: The place of face-to-face communication in distributed work. In: Hinds, J.P., Kiesler, S. (eds.) Distributed Work, pp. 83–110. MIT Press, Cambridge, London (2002)

20. Piper, A.M., Hollan, J.D.: Tabletop displays for small group study: affordances of paper and digital materials. In: Proceedings of the SIGCHI Conference on Human Factors in Computing Systems, pp. 1227–1236. ACM, April 2009

21. Pontual Falcão, T., Price, S.: Interfering and resolving: how tabletop interaction facilitates co-construction of argumentative knowledge. Int. J. Comput. Support. Collab. Learn. 6(4), 539–559 (2011)

22. Rick, J., Marshall, P., Yuill, N.: Beyond one-size-fits-all: how interactive tabletops support collaborative learning. In: Proceedings of the 10th International Conference on Interaction Design and Children, pp. 109–117. ACM, June 2011

23. Rogers, Y., Lindley, S.: Collaborating around vertical and horizontal displays: which way is best? Interact. Comput. **16**(6), 1133–1152 (2004)
24. Stock, O., Zancanaro, M., Koren, C., Rocchi, C., Eisikovits, Z., Goren-Bar, D., Tomasini, D., Weiss, P.T.: A co-located interface for narration to support reconciliation in a conflict: initial results from Jewish and Palestinian youth. In: Proceedings of the SIGCHI Conference on Human Factors in Computing Systems, pp. 1583–1592. ACM, April 2008
25. Veletsianos, G., Eliadou, A.: Conceptualizing the use of technology to foster peace via adventure learning. Internet High. Educ. **12**(2), 63–70 (2009)
26. Zancanaro, M., Stock, O., Eisikovits, Z., Koren, C., Weiss, P.: Co-narrating a conflict: an interactive tabletop to facilitate attitudinal shifts. ACM Trans. Comput. Hum. Interact. **19**(3), 1–30 (2012)

Acoustic Filter

New Virtual Reality Audio Format Pretends to Enhance Immersive Experience

Josep Llorca[1(✉)], Ernesto Redondo[1], Francesc Valls[1], David Fonseca[2], and Sergi Villagrasa[2]

[1] AR&M, Barcelona School of Architecture, BarcelonaTech, Catalonia Polithecnic University, Av/Diagonal 649, 08028 Barcelona, Spain
{josep.llorca,ernesto.redondo,francesc.valls}@upc.edu
[2] GRETEL – Grup de Recerca en Technology Enhanced Learning, La Salle – Ramon Llull University, C/Sant Joan de la Salle 42, 08022 Barcelona, Spain
{fonsi,sergiv}@salle.url.edu

Abstract. The implementation of sound in a virtual environment enhances immersive experience, and some audio formats have been developed for virtual reality. These formats are very powerful but they have also some limitations. Here we build upon this previous work by examining the properties of these formats. The aim of this study is to present the possibility of a new audio format based on the characteristics of the soundscape. Following the principles of audio correlation, an acoustic filter with the properties of the space is defined. The filter contains the acoustic information of the space and is able to be used whether in virtual reality and in acoustic analysis applications. This indicates that there is a possibility of obtaining a new audio format that contains the properties of the place.

Keywords: Architecture · Urban design · Acoustics · Virtual reality · Audio filter

1 Introduction

Virtual Reality (VR) has received much attention in the last decades due to its multiple applications in a broad range of fields: conductor training (look for references), military strategies, entertainment, blind rehabilitation, neurological testing, surgery training, etc. VR is an environment generated in the computer, which the user can operate and interact with in real time [1]. It has also many applications in the architectural field such as designer training [2, 3] or citizen participation in urban design process [4, 5]. But a remarkable feature is that the majority of architectural applications of VR rely only on the visual aspects and doesn't pay much attention to the acoustic ones, although other architectural-related fields use images combined with sound, such as computer games. The lack of attention to the acoustic aspects in VR architectural representations presents big interest to those who search for an immersive architecture experience.

There are several ways to include audio in VR and there has been extensive research regarding the development of these formats. The three most common and successful

© Springer International Publishing AG 2017
P. Zaphiris and A. Ioannou (Eds.): LCT 2017, Part I, LNCS 10295, pp. 22–33, 2017.
DOI: 10.1007/978-3-319-58509-3_3

ones are named Multi-Channel audio, Object-Based audio [6] and Ambisonics [7]. Although each of these technologies present their own advantages over the others, none of them is capable of containing the soundscape of the place and allowing the free movement of the listener without a big array of speakers, a huge use of CPU power, or a multiple path recording, respectively. Firstly, not everybody has the chance for a big array of speakers. Secondly, the average of personal computer's power cannot be big enough for the support of a game as that presented, Finally, a multiple path recording would be too expensive and tedious for an architectural VR study.

This paper presents a set of criteria for the generation of a new VR audio format that can fulfil the lacks that the other formats have. This new format is based on the creation of a filter which contains the place information. On the basis of these criteria it then describes the preparation of a set of study cases where the filter can be tested.

The last step in the experimental process will consist of the evaluation of this acoustic filter by architecture students and by generic users. This evaluation will show us the satisfaction grade of both students and users in a similar way that some studies made before [8]. The intention of these studies was to understand the city as a digital educational environment and use it as an experimental frame for the implementation of the new technologies both in academic curriculum and in informal education.

2   Background

Architecture necessarily deals with use, place and technique [9]. The three basic components contain the questions that architecture must answer: how do you live in this architecture, where is this architecture located, and how is this architecture made. The study of these three components leads to the architectural discipline. It seems to be logical that if a representation of an architectural ambience pretends to be immersive, it must represent the three basic components with success. This means that the representation (and more exactly VR) must explain how do you live there, where is this located and how is that made.

The first component (how do you live in this architecture) has always been represented by a wide range of methods commonly known as geometry. These methods consist on showing the facilities of the space to the user: the comfortable measures of the rooms, the suitable position of furniture or the convenient disposition of the walls between rooms. VR representations have developed ways for the visualization of these features by representing the geometry of a place in a perspective in a convincing way. It was also shown that viewing a graph in a virtual reality display is three times as good as 2D diagram [10].

The second component (where is this architecture located) can be firstly found in the science of place called geography. This science is able to define the physical characters of place and represent them through cartographic drawings. VR representations have developed ways for the visualization and navigation through these spaces not only by a desktop but also by a head-mounted display [11]. What is more, architectural models need to include landscape elements such as trees, mountains and other buildings in order to locate the represented architecture in an exact environment.

The third component (how is this architecture made) representation counts with a long tradition of drawing techniques that are able to explain the nature of the construction: materials, textures, colours, brightness, transparency or blurriness are some of the large number of the characteristics of the built environment. VR representations have also developed ways for the visualization of these features by representing the qualities of an object under the effect of natural or artificial light.

As we can see, the three components need to be convincing in order to achieve an immersive environment. Nevertheless, we have presented architecture as a discipline only dealing with visual data. While use, place and technique embrace also haptic, tactile or acoustic factors [1]. In fact, some critiques from within the discipline of architecture itself argue the importance of the other senses, apart from sight, for the discipline of architecture. Juhani Pallasmaa [12], Ted Sheriden and Karen Van Lengen [13], Björn Hellstrom [14], Stephen Holl and Rafael Pizarro [15] are some of the architects who have noted what the discipline of architecture may profit from considering the hidden realm of the auditory and the multisensory [16].

These reasons conduce our attention to the acoustic representation in VR. As Vorländer says, if the behaviour of an acoustic object or system is shown in a more complex way than numerically, including the creation of acoustic signals in time or frequency domain, we talk about "simulation" and "auralization" [1].

The implementation of audio information from the surroundings is what is needed for an enhanced immersive experience of the represented architecture. For this purpose, several VR audio formats for auralization have been developed during the last decades: Multi-channel audio, Object-Based audio and Ambisonics. In this part of the article we are going to explain the main features of these audio formats and to point out the main strengths and weaknesses of each of them.

2.1 Multi-channel Audio

In the Multi-channel audio representation, the listener is located in the centre of the scene and an array of speakers surround them. The unit of information is the loudspeaker, where each channel is associated to a loudspeaker. Here, the sound reproduction is made by mixing the various channels on several speakers. In Multi-channel audio, the more channels, the more spatial sound capabilities. This method has been the traditional sound representation used for the past 50 years or more. The Stereo, 5.1, 7.1 formats are multi-channel horizontal representations. 3D is obtained by adding elevated speakers, like in the 11.1 format, where 4 ceiling speakers are added to a 7.1 horizontal speaker layout. One of the main drawback of the Multi-channel audio representation is that it is loudspeaker set up dependent and that one needs one mix tor type of each set-up, whereas Object-Based and Ambisonics contents are independent of the loudspeaker set-up [17]. Another disadvantage is that a Multi-channel audio system needs an array of speakers and relies on the number of speakers. When the number of speakers is limited the system becomes poor and without possibilities.

2.2 Object-Based Audio

In the Object-Based representation, the listener is located on the centre of the scene with headphones and some virtual sound sources surrounds them. The unit of information is the virtual sound source. The scene is made of several virtual sound sources and information about their locations, their directivity patterns and the rendering environment (room size, reverberation parameters...). The 3D audio rendering is made by calculating the combination of all the sources, including the reverberation, at the listener position. This is a great paradigm to interactively create content, but it also uses a lot of CPU resources. The more complex (number of sound sources) and realistic (precision of the reverberation) the scene, the more CPU is needed [17]. Moreover, Object-Based audio has to render the environment according to the virtual model, what is not always the most exact approximation to the reality. This last drawback is pretended to be solved with our filter proposal, as we explain afterwards.

2.3 Ambisonics

Unlike the two other representations, the Ambisonics format does not rely on the description of individual sound sources (speakers or objects) but instead represents the resulting sound field at the listener's position. The mathematical formalism used to describe the sound field is called spherical harmonics and the unit of information is the number of component (or the Order) of this spherical representation. The more components or the higher order you have, the more precision in the spatial representation of the scene you get. This paradigm is not new and has been used by a small sound professional community for several decades with a concept called the B-Format which is in fact a Higher Order Ambisonics representation at the 1st order. The representation of the resulting sound field at the listener's position is one of its main advantages when computing the information, but can be also one of its main drawbacks when considering the listener's position as a fixed point. If one wants to record a whole place, one must make as Ambisonics recordings as possible positions of the listener, and this can be a tedious task.

Ambisonics can be understood as a three-dimensional extension of M/S (mid/side) stereo, adding channels for height and depth. The resulting signal set is called B-format. Its component channels are labelled:

- W: for the sound pressure (the M in M/S).
- X: for the front-minus-back sound pressure gradient.
- Y: for the left-minus-right (the S in M/S).
- Z: for up-minus-down.

The W signal corresponds to an omnidirectional microphone, whereas XYZ are the components that would be picked up by figure-of-eight microphones oriented along the three spatial axes.

The simplest Ambisonic panner (or encoder) takes a source signal S and two parameters, the horizontal angle θ and the elevation angle ϕ. The different gains of the Ambisonic components are the following:

$$W = S \cdot \frac{1}{\sqrt{2}} \tag{1}$$

$$X = S \cdot \cos\theta \cos\phi \tag{2}$$

$$Y = S \cdot \sin\theta \cos\phi \tag{3}$$

$$Z = S \cdot \sin\theta \tag{4}$$

3 Methodology

In this part of the article we are going to expose the features of our new VR audio format. We must remain that the purpose of our work consists of the definition of a way of representing the soundscape of an architectural environment able to be implemented in a VR environment or to make an acoustic analysis of a place. For the definition of the Acoustic Filter, we need to make an experiment. The materials required for the experiment are an anechoic chamber for the sound recording in a pure state, a recording equipment consisting on a Zoom H6 recorder with two incorporated microphones and two KM 183 Newmann omnidirectional microphones, and a dodecaedrical ball for the reproduction of the sound into the anechoic chamber and into the analyzed places. Additionally, we need a software sound editor as Adobe Audition and the knowledge of correlation of acoustic wave principles. Our experiment consists of some steps derived from the audio correlation technique.

First of all, a known and *basic sound* is reproduced in the anechoic chamber with a dodecaedrical ball. This *basic sound* is recorded in the anechoic chamber with the KM 183 Newmann matched pair omnidirectional microphones connected to the Zoom H6. As the environment in the anechoic chamber is free of interferences from the ambience and additional noise, the basic sound recorded contains the acoustic information of the pure basic sound.

Secondly, the pure *basic sound* is analyzed and its frequency range is tested to be complete.

Thirdly, the pure *basic sound* is reproduced in the case study place. This sound is reproduced with the same dodecaedrical ball which was recorded in the anechoic chamber, in order to reproduce the basic sound under the same conditions as the first recording. This *resulting sound* is recorded in the case study place by the KM 183 Newmann matched pair omnidirectional microphones connected to the Zoom H6. The recording of the sound can be made from several points in the case study place, simulating the different positions of the listener.

Fourthly, the *resulting sound* is analyzed. The presence of an urban and architectural environment, city sound and position from the sound, modifies the *basic sound* in a way that the *resulting sound* registers. Usually, the *resulting sound* is attenuated, colorized, enriched or delayed by the presence of the environmental agents.

Finally, by a cross-correlation process [18] we can compare the *basic sound* with the *resulting sound*. In order to search the environment features, which are recorded in the *resulting sound*, it is easy to make the difference between the *resulting sound* and the *basic sound*. The sonic difference contains only the features of the place, which we denominate as the *place sound*.

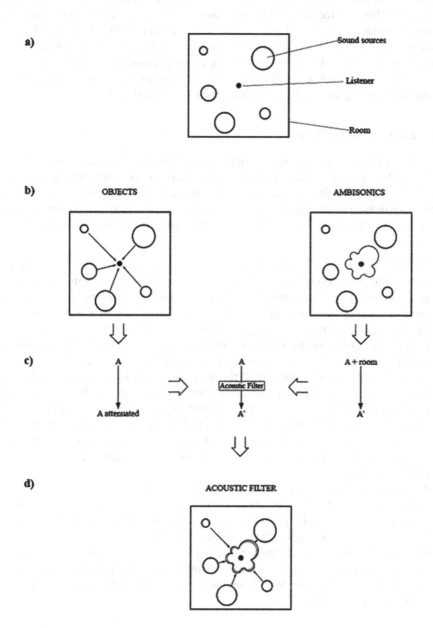

Fig. 1. Graphic comparison between the two audio formats (Objects and Ambisonics) with the new Acoustic Filter: (a) above all, the generic scenario is presented; (b) then the working process of Objects and Ambisonics; (c) the basic properties of Objects and Ambisonics and the main feature of the Acoustic Filter; (d) the resulting scenario for the Acoustic Filter.

This *place sound* can be treated as a function [19] and constitutes the basis of our Acoustic Filter. The Acoustic Filter is able to reproduce the acoustic features of the place with any *basic sound*. This is the reason why the Acoustic Filter is very useful in architectural VR, because the different *basic sounds* that take place in an environment can be treated under the Acoustic Filter in order to get the impression of the sound in that place without a complete virtualization of the acoustics in the model, as Object-Based audio does, and without a prerecorded image of the environment acoustics, as Ambisonics does. The design of this Acoustic Filter is required and in the next part of the article we are going to introduce the basics of filter design (Fig. 1).

3.1 The Case Study Places

Five urban places are selected for the study cases. All of them are located in the ancient center of Barcelona, near the cathedral. Each of them has got a principal actor that is usually located there. Our intention is to relate the acoustic study to the type of music they make in each place. For this reason, we are going to record the particular music played in this place to be compared between them. Here we describe the places and their principal actors:

- The crossroad between *Carrer del Bisbe* and *Carrer de Santa Llúcia*. Its principal actor usually sings every weekend night. He is an opera tenor singer that, sometimes, is accompanied by other opera singers. His actuation consists of the interpretation of some opera arias and fragments over an orchestra basis sang by a portable speaker. The orchestra accompaniment has got no voice recorded in a way that our actor sings in front of some spectators. The actor is placed in *Carrer de Santa Llúcia* and singing towards the *Carrer del Bisbe*, where people circulation is not blocked.
- The crossroad between *Carrer del Bisbe* and *Carrer de la Pietat*. Its principal actors vary from a guitar soloist, an arpist, or a clarinetist accompanied by a guitar. Their position in front of a door in *Carrer de la Pietat* does not block the people circulation.
- *Plaça de Sant Iu*, in front of the East door of the Barcelona Cathedral. Its principal actors vary forma a guitar soloist, an arpist, or a clarinetist accompanied by a guitar. Their position in the *Palau del Lloctinent* façade does not block the people circulation.
- *Plaça del Rei*. Their principal actors are usually guitar soloists, or violin soloists. But because of its spatial configuration, there have been made some choir or band concerts. They are usually placed on the stairs on the north corner, those that allow the access to the *Santa Àgata* chapel and the *Tinell Room*.
- *Plaça de Sant Jaume*. The presence of the bells of the *Generalitat* and its musical interpretations every week, give a unique soundscape to this square and its surroundings. Moreover, *Plaça de Sant Jaume* is a usual scenery for some concerts and projections with music.

4   Audio Filter Design and Analysis: Basic Parameters

A filter, generally, is a system that avoids some parts of the processed object, following one or more attributes. For example, a gravel filter, or sieve, allows the sand passing but stops the stone passing. In a similar way, a processing signal filter is a very wide concept, because it can be any system treating signal. The filtering concept is very important for our experiment. For this reason, it is necessary a correct definition of the filter concept and types (Fig. 2).

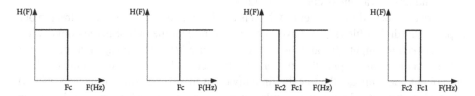

Fig. 2. Frequency representation of the following ideal filters, from left to right: (a) low-pass; (b) high-pass; (c) band-stop; (d) bandpass. The filters are symmetric from the horizontal axis.

We can define the classical types of filters, in a similar way that Ruiz and Duxans [20] do:

- A low-pass filter that allows low frequencies pass and attenuates high frequencies.
- A high-pass filter that allows high frequencies pass and attenuates low frequencies.
- A band-stop filter, that is complementary to bandpass filter because it eliminates a band of frequencies, allowing the rest of the frequencies.
- A bandpass filter, that allows a band of frequencies, eliminating the high and low frequencies.

A digital classic filter can be defined as a system that modifies a digital signal in a way that allows the pass of an interval of frequencies and attenuates the others. It has a main objective: an output with some features [20]. For our experiment, we need to study the feasible digital filters. These feasible digital filters must verify some properties: linearity, time invariance, causality, and stability:

- If it verifies the linearity, we know that the filter does not modify the signal form. It can postpone it, but it maintains the signal form. A lineal filter, in discrete time or non-discrete time, is that one which verifies the superposition property: if an input consists of the pondered sum of some signals, the output is simply the superposition (the pondered sum) of the answers of the filter to each one of those signals [21].
- If it verifies the time invariance, we know that the behavior and features of the filter are fixed in time. A filter is time invariant if a time sliding in the input signal causes a time sliding in the output signal. The property of time invariance tells us that the answers of a time invariant system to time slid unitary impulses, are simply scrolled versions one from each other [21].
- If it verifies the causality, we know that the filter output, in any moment, depends only from the input value in the present moment and in the past. Sometimes, this

filter is called a non-anticipative filter, because the filter output doesn't anticipate future values of the input [21].

- If it verifies the stability, we know that the little inputs of the filter lead to non-divergent answers. If the stable filter input is limited (that is, if its magnitude doesn't increase in a non-limited way), the output is also limited and it cannot diverge [21].

In the next part of this section, we describe the characterization of a filter regarding its impulse response and transfer function.

In the temporal domain, the impulse response relates the input and the output of a lineal and time invariant system (SLIT) [20].

If we talk about digital systems, which is the domain that we are going to treat in our experiment (digital filters), we have to bear in mind that the output is the convolution sum between the input $x[n]$ and the impulse response $h[n]$. This means that the output is the sum of the input, plus the answer, plus the echoes [21]. From now and ahead we are going to denominate the lineal a time invariant filter (linear time invariant system) as SLTI. In the filters' case, the impulse response and the transfer function determine the next concepts:

- The gain (G(f)) is defined as the amplification of the output signal regarding the input signal. If it is negative, it is called attenuation.
- The amplitude response of a filter is defined as the modulus of the filter frequency response.
- The phase response of a filter is defined as the phase of the impulse response.
- The order of a filter is the rate that a filter has got and it matches up with the maximum delay (in terms of samples) used or with the input signal or previous outputs in order to calculate y[n].
- The bandpass of a filter is the frequency range that a filter allows the pass from the input to the output with an attenuation.
- The group delay evaluates the output signal compared to the input signal in samples for each frequency. Hence, the global delay experimented by a signal is evaluated. If the group delay is constant, the phase is lineal.

The definition of a filter in finite differences equation allows us to make a clear distinction between two types of filters:

- Non-recurrent filters: the impulse response of the filter has got a finite number of samples different from zero and, for this reason, they are called under the name of FIR filters (finite impulse response).
- Recurrent filters: those in which the impulse response has got a non-finite number of samples different from zero, and they are named as IIR filters (infinite impulse response).

The basis of the filter design technique assumes that measurements can be made in the reproduced sound field in order to compare the reproduced signals with the signals that are wanted to be reproduced [22].

5   Filter Design

Having seen the basic parameters of the filters, based on the system features, we are going to consider the design of our filter.

We have already seen that a feasible, lineal, invariant, causal and stable FIR filter has got an impulse response of a finite length L, and an output that depends only on input values, never on output values. If we want to have lineal phase (without distortion of the wave form of the original signal), the impulse response must be symmetric or asymmetric.

The filter design should be flexible enough for its implementation in a Virtual Reality environment. In particular, a Gamification of the study cases that were previously exposed is been developed. The final intention is to implement the Acoustic Filter to the VR environment in order to listen the current soundscape in its actual version, and afterwards to listen the different urban proposals of the same place only by changing the sound sources.

The filter design implies a complete comprehension and application of the cross-correlation tools applied to audio filter production. The definitive Acoustic Filter design will be explored in future research.

6   Conclusion

The present study confirms that a new audio format for virtual reality can be possible. Based on the initial hypothesis, it is now possible to state that the up-to-date audio formats for virtual reality are not suitable for the characterization of the acoustic features of the urban environment because they do not interact with the environment (Objects) or they do not split the environment from the sound sources (Ambisonics).

The current findings add substantial information to our understanding of the acoustic properties of a place. In particular, the proposed Acoustic Filter can be considered a sound filter containing spatial information of the place. This finding suggest that architect's conception of space can be approached not only by visual parameters, but also acoustic ones.

Finally, an important limitation needs to be considered. If the proposed Acoustic Filter is required for the complete acoustic comprehension of a public space, several measurements must be done in order to interpolate the results and predict a possible acoustic plan. This means that the more measurements are made, the better is the resolution of the acoustic plan.

Further research is required in order to establish a complete design and put into practice of the Acoustic Filter. In particular, next steps will be done in audio filtering design by means of cross-correlation methods and the field measurements in the places above mentioned will be carried out. With these future objectives, it is logical that the experiment will show the results that are searched.

Acknowledgments. This research was supported by the National Program of Research, Development and Innovation aimed to the Society Challenges with the references

BIA2016-77464-C2-1-R & BIA2016-77464-C2-2-R, both of the National Plan for Scientific Research, Development and Technological Innovation 2013-2016, Government of Spain, titled "*Gamificación para la enseñanza del diseño urbano y la integración en ella de la participación ciudadana* (ArchGAME4CITY)", & "*Diseño Gamificado de visualización 3D con sistemas de realidad virtual para el estudio de la mejora de competencias motivacionales, sociales y espaciales del usuario* (EduGAME4CITY)". (AEI/FEDER, UE).

References

1. Vorländer, M.: Auralization: Fundamentals of Acoustics, Modelling, Simulation. Algorithms and Acoustic Virtual Reality. Springer, Heidelberg (2008). ISBN 9783540488293
2. Henry, D., Furness, T.: Spatial perception in virtual environments: evaluating an architectural application. In: Proceedings of IEEE Virtual Reality Annual International Symposium, pp. 33–40. IEEE (1993). doi:10.1109/VRAIS.1993.380801
3. Vicent Safont, L., Villagrasa, S., Fonseca Escudero, D., Redondo Domínguez, E.: Virtual learning scenarios for qualitative assessment in higher education 3D arts. J. Univ. Comput. Sci. **21**, 1086–1105 (2015). doi:10.3217/jucs-021-08-1086
4. Wu, H., He, Z., Gong, J.: A virtual globe-based 3D visualization and interactive framework for public participation in urban planning processes. Comput. Environ. Urban Syst. **34**, 291–298 (2010). doi:10.1016/j.compenvurbsys.2009.12.001
5. Fonseca, D., Valls, F., Redondo, E., Villagrasa, S.: Informal interactions in 3D education: citizenship participation and assessment of virtual urban proposals. Comput. Human Behav. **55**, 504–518 (2016). doi:10.1016/j.chb.2015.05.032
6. Bleidt, R., Borsum, A., Fuchs, H., Weiss, S.M.: Object-based audio: opportunities for improved listening experience and increased listener involvement. SMPTE Motion Imaging J. (2014). doi:10.5594/M001546
7. Ma, G.: Multidirectional sound reproduction systems, UK-patent no. 3 997 725 (1976)
8. Domínguez, E.R., Riera, A.S., Sala, J.M.: La ciudad como aula digital: enseñando urbanismo y arquitectura mediante Mobile Learning y la realidad aumentada: un estudio de viabilidad y de caso. ACE Archit. city Environ. 0 (2012)
9. Armesto, A.: Arquitectura y naturaleza: tres sospechas sobre el próximo milenio. DPA Doc. Proj. d'arquitectura (2000). ISBN 2339-6237
10. Ware, C., Franck, G.: Viewing a graph in a virtual reality display is three times as good as a 2D diagram. In: Proceedings of 1994 IEEE Symposium on Visual Languages, pp. 182–183. IEEE Computer Society Press (1994). doi:10.1109/VL.1994.363621
11. Sousa Santos, B., Dias, P., Pimentel, A., Baggerman, J.-W., Ferreira, C., Silva, S., Madeira, J.: Head-mounted display versus desktop for 3D navigation in virtual reality: a user study. Multimed. Tools Appl. **41**, 161–181 (2009). doi:10.1007/s11042-008-0223-2
12. Pallasmaa, J.: The Eyes of the Skin: Architecture and the Senses. Wiley, New York (2012). ISBN 9781119941286
13. Sheridan, T., Van Lengen, K.: Hearing architecture: exploring and designing the aural environment. J. Archit. Educ. **57**, 37–44 (2003). doi:10.1162/104648803770558978
14. Hellström, B.: Noise design: architectural modelling and the aesthetics of urban acoustic space. Bo Ejeby Förlag, Göteborg, Sweden (2003). ISBN 9188316386
15. Pizarro, R.E.: Teaching to understand the urban sensorium in the digital age: lessons from the studio. Des. Stud. **30**, 272–286 (2009). doi:10.1016/j.destud.2008.09.002
16. Fowler, M.: Sound, aurality and critical listening: disruptions at the boundaries of architecture. Archit. Cult. **1**, 162–180 (2013). doi:10.2752/175145213X13756908698766

17. Developers - 3D Sound Labs. http://www.3dsoundlabs.com/category/developers/
18. Bracewell, R.N.: The Fourier Transform and its Applications. McGraw-Hill, Boston (1978). ISBN 007007013X
19. Kester, W.: Data Conversion Handbook. Elsevier, Analog Devices, Inc. (2005). ISBN: 9780750678414
20. Barrobés, H.D., Costa-Jussà, M.R.: Procesamiento de Audio, Barcelona (2012)
21. Oppenheim, A.V., Willsky, A.S., Nawab, S.H.: Signals and Systems. Prentice Hall, Upper Saddle River (1997). ISBN: 0138147574
22. Nelosn, P.A., Orduña-Bustamante, F.: Multichannel signal processing techniques in the reproduction of sound. J. Audio Eng. Soc. **44**(11), November 1996

Gesture Deviation in Interactive Communication – A Cross Cultural Study of Indian Case Examples

Ravi Mokashi Punekar[✉] and Sarath Paliyath

Indian Institute of Technology Guwahati, Guwahati, Assam, India
{mokashi,p.sarath}@iitg.ernet.in

Abstract. This paper presents a study following a user-centered method in examining cross-cultural variations in the use of body gestures among Indian user groups in the age group of 21–30. Twenty-six participants belonging to a cross section of eight states located across different geographical regions of India, were subject to group discussions deliberating on a short film clipping presented to them during the test. The analysis based on study of video recording examined the different hand gestures involuntarily used by the participants to communicate during their discussions. These were identified, grouped and classified based on taxonomy of gestures outlined by McNeill. The communicative aspects of the gestures involved were analyzed to gain insights of regional similarities and differences specific to each region. Based on the findings the paper discusses the scope of these findings in the development of an inventory of gestures and their relevance in the design and development of gesture based interactive products. Considering the increasing move towards gesture based interaction modes for man–product interactions the paper outlines the scope for culture based variations in the design of gestures that meet the needs of culturally diverse communities in the rapidly growing domain of ICE based communication technologies.

Keywords: Cultural diversity · Gesture based communication · Man-machine interaction design · User centered design method

1 Introduction

The Government of India in December 2016 took a decision of de-monetization of the Indian currency. With the withdrawal of highly used currency denominations for every day financial transactions, this was a highly disruptive intervention with far reaching implications. The government introduced a new financial service platform – BHIM to be used on a mobile phone. This was to be used by the public at large to shift financial exchange from a cash rich to a less-cash economic mode of transaction. This dramatic and unexpected disruption brought to surface the immediacy and challenge of socio-economic and cultural factors that need to be urgently addressed if such an alternative solution is to find acceptance as an alternate service.

With the rapid growth and penetration of mobile telephony, companies in Information, Communication and Entertainment (ICE) sector, are faced with the design and development of interactive products and new services that concurrently address the challenges,

© Springer International Publishing AG 2017
P. Zaphiris and A. Ioannou (Eds.): LCT 2017, Part I, LNCS 10295, pp. 34–45, 2017.
DOI: 10.1007/978-3-319-58509-3_4

aspirations and expectations of cultural diversity for their acceptance and success. With the increasing shift towards gesture based modes of product–user interaction, there is an urgent need for design research in the study of socio-cultural considerations that can affect gesture based interaction in such mass based product mediated services.

2 Related Work on Gesture Based Studies

The diversity of cultural variations in non-verbal modes of communication through body language is presented in two excellent anthropological publication titled 'Man watching' [1]) and 'Body watching' [2]. Since the early 2000, there is a distinct move towards developing gesture based interaction in the design and development of ICT based information, communication and entertainment (ICE) based products. Early attempts in the development of gesture based interaction in products were algorithm based [3]. More recent studies have explored the use of gestures for the control of mobile phones [4]. Their study was essentially non-technical in nature and focused on the study of natural human gestures that the subjects may use in devices such as a mobile phone. Some studies have explored the use of gestures in the navigation of the different functional tasks to be performed on a smart phone [5]. Their paper outlines a gesture taxonomy involving 19 different tasks to be performed on the device. Study in the use of gestures on iPad was undertaken to help identify gestures that can be used to transfer data from an iPad to a PC [6].

In India, a recent study amongst semi-literate rural users in the state of Assam, examined the potential of its use for the domain of neonatal healthcare for a television based product user interaction for the Indian context [7]. The study resulted in the development of gesture based interaction using a Kinect based platform that was developed for maternal healthcare [8] for semi-literate rural women users. This doctoral research followed a user-centered approach and identified gestures that were commonly understood amongst low literacy and low-income rural communities in northeast India. Unfortunately such gesture based user-product interactions studies are in their infancy in the Indian context.

These research studies however, show that communication through gestures is definitely not universal. They vary from one community to another, one region to another and also can be different for different religious groups - signifying different meanings in their use. The study of gestures and their communicative meanings in multi-cultural, multi-linguistic and multi-religious dimensions is an interesting subject for design research. Its implications in the designs of man/machine interaction system will necessary have to factor this cultural dimension.

This paper examines cultural variations in communication through body gestures amongst Indian user groups following the taxonomy outlined by McNeill [9]. The findings help to reflect upon their implication in design of gesture based man-machine interaction. The experiments are planned to examine the following specific questions: Are there cross-cultural variations in the use of hand gestures among a pan Indian user groups? Are there gestures that are common to the different groups? Do similar gestures mean differently to the different cultural groups? Can individuals articulate and explain the gestures common in their culture?

3   Methodology

Researchers have developed different methods for development of gesture based interactive systems [10]. Gestures have been derived from subjects identified by semantic representation of their associated function [11]. Participatory design method has been used for generation of gestures for surface computing [12]. Studies have been undertaken to examine what gestures signify to people [13].

In most of these methods user participation in the process of generation and reading of gestures is followed. Participatory approach that involved participants from the different regions of India was adopted for this study.

In the experiment planned, attempt is made to study hand gestures involved in communication by participants coming from different states in India and the findings are summarized to answer the above queries for their implication in design of gesture based man-machine interaction.

4   Planning the Experiment and Methodology Used for the Cross-Cultural Study of Gestures Amongst Indian Users

4.1   Selection of Content for the Study

The objectives of the experiment essentially focused on identifying cultural variations in the involuntary use of non-verbal communication using hand gestures. It was planned that hand gestures involved during a conversation be captured in a natural and unobtrusive manner without making the subject conscious. Engaging the participating group to discuss a cinema clip screening offered suitable scope to capture the different hand gestures involved during conversation. An Iranian film titled 'Two and Two' directed by Babak Anvari was selected for the screening. Duration of screening was for 7 min. Although in Persian language, the clip being rich in human emotions participants were encouraged to discuss aspects of the visual language after the screening. The Persian language used in the film not being familiar, enabled the participants to focus on the visual content in their discussion. This helped to overcome any individual bias of the region that the participant belonged to or that of his regional language and cultural background.

4.2   Selection of Subjects

Drawing strength of a multi-cultural and multi regional mix of students selected for admission to its programs, the participants selected for this study were 26 senior students of Design who were coming from seven different states in India viz. Kerala (kl), Tamil Nadu (t) and Andhra Pradesh (ap) the southern states (10 participants); Delhi (d) and Kashmir (ks) the northern states (5 participants); Maharashtra (m) from the western state

(4 participants) and Jharkhand (j) and Assam (a) from the eastern states (7 participants) - a pan India cross section of 26 participants in all, covering a mix of multi-cultural diversity, religious background and regional languages (Fig. 1). They were formed into small groups comprising of two to three member belonging to each region. The film clip was screened separately for these different groups and the members of each group were asked to discuss the film after the screening.

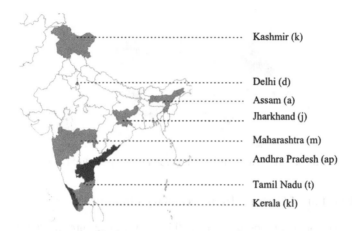

Fig. 1. States in India to which participants belong.

4.3 Selection of the Medium for Documentation

Video recording being a powerful enabler was the chosen medium for documenting the conversation of the participants. This was subsequently reviewed for the study of hand gestures they involuntarily used during their discussions. The video helped to record movement, capture gestural speed in real time, faithfully show how many repetitions were used, and even present the hand gestures along with other involuntary body nonverbal behavior (facial grimaces, postural changes, etc.) as they occur. Video could even record for the viewer the participant's (or "encoder's") own contextual account about how the gesture is used, circumstances that illustrate a use of this gesture, the probable consequences of using the gesture etc.

4.4 Design and Studio Setup

The video documentation was done using Canon 650D DSLR cameras. A schematic position of the subjects, the camera positions and ceiling light settings is as shown (Fig. 2). It may be noted that people generally are found to use gestures effectively while standing. The participants from each state were allowed to discuss the cinema clipping while standing. They were positioned to stand in manner so that they come face to face as in a casual talk. Three cameras have been used to capture the discussion so as to get the front view of each person clearly.

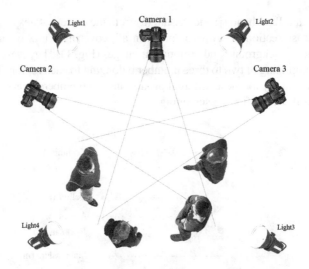

Fig. 2. Studio and camera setup for 4-participant discussion.

4.5   Identification of Gestures from Secondary Literature

Based on the taxonomy proposed by McNeill in a study of gestures in HCI [9] the video recording was reviewed to identify, categorize and analyze the following hand gesture categories (Fig. 3).

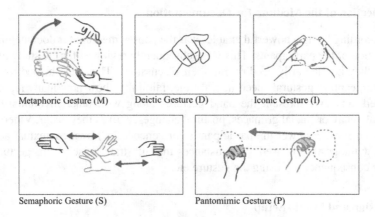

Fig. 3. Category of gestures

4.6   Method for Analysis of Video Recordings

Video recording were transferred to a Macbook pro computer and reviewed on a video editing Final cut Pro application software. The video editing software helped to run over individual visual frames across a time line. The video recordings of each participating group were viewed on an average for 30 times. Around 149 video clips were sorted from the video footage, to collect and identify more than 250 non-verbal hand gestures and categorize using the following legend:

'X_{YZ}': X = Taxonomy of the of gesture category, y = State the subject belongs, z = Serial number.

Non-verbal hand gestures involuntarily engaged during the conversations by each participant were analyzed for each group from the video recordings. Both duration of the gestures and the visual image frames were noted for each subject and the gesture classified under the seven categories. A sample of data logging is shown in Table 1.

Table 1. Sample of data logging

	Participant	Time	Gesture for	Comment
1	Shyam	01:32:17	Following	
2	Shyam	01:52:03	To mimic a gun	Only single hand used
3	Faris	02:11:00	That's wrong	
...	....	....	....	....

4.7 Data on Total Gesture Types Taken for Observation and Study

The Table 2 below summarizes the list of gestures shortlisted for the study:

Table 2. State-wise distribution of gesture type

Taxonomy of gesture type (X)	State to which subject belongs (y)					
	Delhi (d)	Jharkhand (j)	Kashmir (k)	Kerala (kl)	Maharashtra (m)	Tamilnadu (t)
Deictic (D)	1	5		3	10	3
Iconic (I)		1	3			
Metaphoric (M)	5	4	2	8	16	13
Pantomimic (P)	5	1	1	4	4	7
Semaphoric (S)	5	5	2	7	7	4
	Number of gestures (z)					

5   Results and Observations

5.1   Deictic Gestures (D)

Deictic gestures are used to indicate objects and directions.

The study did not show significant differences in the use of this hand gesture among the 26 participants across the states. Most subjects while they were talking used the pointing gestures in similar ways with variations of use of single hand or both hands (Fig. 4).

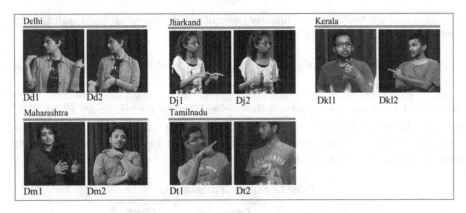

Fig. 4. Deictic gestures made by participants grouped state-wise

5.2 Iconic Gestures

Metaphoric Gesture (M). Metaphoric gestures are also representational, but the concept they represent has no physical form; instead the form of the gesture comes from a common metaphor.

E.g. "the meeting went on and on" accompanied by a hand indicating rolling motion.

The uses of metaphoric gestures by participants across the different regions were high but also significantly varying in their meaning. The most diverse range of gestures came in this category. The participants were found to use the same kind of gesture to convey different meaning. It was also found that participants used different gestures to convey same meaning. For e.g. The metaphoric gesture (M1) used by participants - waving the hand forward keeping the palm downward (Fig. 5) - signified different meaning.

Delhi (Md3) - Suppressed
Kerala(Mkl1,2) - Forcing
Maharashtra(Mm2) - This has to be done
Tamilnadu (Mt4,8) - Forcing

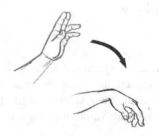

Fig. 5. Metaphoric gesture (M1)

Other Metaphoric gestures (Fig. 6) used often by the participants are given below.

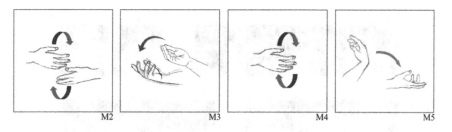

Fig. 6. Metaphoric gestures used by the participants

These five gestures (M1 to M5) were used by the participants in distinct context. Table 3 shows this.

Table 3. Similar metaphoric gesture with different meaning used by the participants

State	M1	M2	M3	M4	M5
Delhi	Suppressed (Md3)	Someone else (Md2)			After that (Md4)
Jharkhand	–		Said (Mj1)		Someone else (Mj2)
Kashmir		After that (Mk2)		That happened (Mk1)	
Kerala	Forced to do (Mkl1, Mkl2)				Forward (Mkl3)
Maharashtra	It has to do (Mm2)	Part of that (Mm5)		Trying to (Mm1)	Some one (Mm11)
Tamilnadu	Forced to do (Mt4)		New one (Mt3)	After that (Mt2)	Going (Mt8)

Another important thing that can be observed from the table is that some participants used distinct gestures for the same context.

This diversity was there among the people from the same state itself. For e.g. from the observation of participants from Kerala, almost similar gesture is used to represent "focused" (Mkl1), "Forced" (Mkl2) and "forward" (Mkl3) by waving hand forward (Fig. 7).

5.3   Semaphoric Gestures (S)

Semaphoric gestures are hand postures and movements, which are used to convey specific meanings. Mostly gesture and meaning are completely unrelated and strictly learned. Therefore, semaphoric gestures are most dependent on the participant's background and experience.

Semaphoric gestures in this experiment show complete variations in their use among the participants. A wide variety of gestures are observed to be used. Few gestures that are used frequently are shown (Fig. 8).

All these gestures were used in entirely different context by the participants.

Fig. 7. Metaphoric gestures made by participants grouped state-wise.

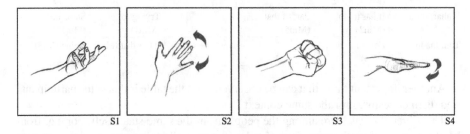

Fig. 8. Semaphoric gestures used by the participants

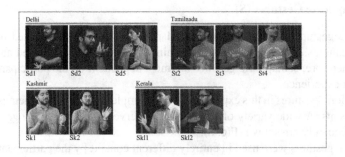

Fig. 9. Semaphoric gestures made by participants grouped state-wise.

Here 'S1' is a gesture performed by showing hand palm upward like a flower. This has been used in entirely three distinct context to mean "Anything", "but", "I didn't understand" etc. (Sd1, Sd2, St1) (Fig. 9).

Other three semaphoric gestures and the contexts in which they were used is shown in the Table 4:

Table 4. Semaphoric gesture with different meaning used in different states

Gesture	Kashmir	Kerala	Delhi	Tamilnadu
S2	Sometimes (SK2)	Wrong (Skl1)		No one (St3)
S3	Power (Sk1)			Truth (St4)
S4		Death, Wrong (Skl, Skl2)	Kill (Sd5)	

5.4 Pantomimic Gestures

As pantomimic gestures are used to show the movement or action performed by a tool or object. These are the gestures often used in showing the use of movement of some invisible tool or object in the speaker's hand. The important feature of mimic gestures is that they strive for reality.

The gestures performed by the participants to indicate the object, in this instance a gun, were similar (Fig. 10). Variations if any were seen in the gesture performed using a single hand or two hands.

Fig. 10. Pantomimic gestures made by participants grouped state-wise.

6 Conclusion

Insights drawn from this study have implications in the design and development of gesture based interface for product interactions. Gestures to be developed for man/machine interaction system do not follow a universal language. There are cultural differences in the meaning and use of gestures used by people belonging to different regions across India. The gestures analyzed from different part of India were categorized into Deictic, Iconic, Metaphoric, Semaphoric and Pantomimic gestures. From the study it is seen that there are only minor difference in the gestures that belong to Deictic, Iconic, Pantomimic categories. Identification of a family of Deictic, Iconic, Pantomimic gestures may prove to be useful in the design of man-machine interactive systems. Iconic gestures that specify a manner in which action is carried out; Deictic gestures that help pointing or directing the users attention to specific events in the machine environment and Pantomimic gestures showing the use of movement of some invisible tool or object in the speaker's hand can be identified in the design of gesture based interfaces for man –machine systems.

In comparison, there are noticeable differences in Metaphoric and Semaphoric gestures used by the participants across different regions in India. Since metaphoric gestures are also representational but the concepts they represent show variations from one region to anther. It may be suggested that an inventory of region specific gestures be identified and be offered as optional choice for users to personalize them as per their own preferences. Similarly Semaphoric gestures offer a similar challenge as there are variations in the hand postures and movements used to convey specific meanings and are specific to each region and culture of use. These again need to be offered as a basket of choice to accommodate individual users preference and choice.

7 Implication for Interaction Design

The above factors have implications for the interaction designers. A detailed study with a larger sample size needs to be undertaken by the design research team to identify these commonalities and differences of use of gestures, their signification and meaning across by undertaking a pan Indian survey. It will go a long way towards understanding cultural factors that will impact the acceptance in intelligent and interactive products for their usability and market success.

As a growing economy, for a multicultural country like India, the market potential for usable and intelligent products is very large. The modes of interaction vary. The importance of making gesture based interfaces for region specific diversity will be imperative.

References

1. Desmond, M.: Man Watching - A Field Guide to Human Behavior. Grafton Books, London (1977)
2. Desmond, M.: Body Watching – A Field Guide to the Human Species. Grafton Books, London (1987). ISBN 0-586-20274-9
3. Schlomer, T., Poppinga, B., Henze, N., Ball, S.: Gesture recognition with a Wii controller. In: Proceedings of the 2nd International Conference on Tangible and Embedded Interaction, pp. 11–14. ACM, New York (2008)
4. Kray, C., Nesbitt, D., Dawson, J., Rohs, M.: User defined gestures for connecting mobile phones, public displays, and tabletops. In: Proceeding of the 12th Human computer Interactions With Mobile Devises and Services, pp. 239–248. ACM, New York (2010)
5. Ruiz, J., Li, Y., Lank, E.: User defined motion gestures for mobile interaction. In: Proceeding of the SCGHI Conference on Human Factors in Computing Systems 2011, pp. 11–14. ACM, New York (2011)
6. Kurdyukova, E., Redlin, M., Andre, E.: Studying user-defined iPad gestures for interaction in multi-display environment. In: Proceedings of 12th ACM International Conference on Intelligent User Interfaces 2012, pp. 93–96. ACM, New York (2012)

7. Keyur, S.: Gestural Interfaces for maternal healthcare: a case study of rural Assam, North – East India. Doctoral Dissertation. IIT Guwahati (2015)
8. Keyur, S., Minal, J., Mannu, A., Punekar, R.M., Saurabh, S., Nitendra, R.: Gesture selection study for a maternal healthcare information system in Rural Assam, India. J. Usability Stud. **11**(1), 7–20 (2015)
9. McNeill, D.: Hand and Mind: What Gestures Reveal About Thought. University of Chicago Press, Chicago (1992)
10. Nanceta, M., Kamber, Y., Qiang, Y., Kristensson, P.O.: Memorability of predesigned and user defined gesture sets. In: Proceedings of the SIGCHI Conference on Human Factors in Computing Systems 2013, pp. 1099–1108. ACM, New York (2013)
11. Nielsen, M., Störring, M., Moeslund, Thomas B., Granum, E.: A procedure for developing intuitive and ergonomic gesture interfaces for HCI. In: Camurri, A., Volpe, G. (eds.) GW 2003. LNCS, vol. 2915, pp. 409–420. Springer, Heidelberg (2004). doi: 10.1007/978-3-540-24598-8_38
12. Morris, M., Wobbrock, J., Wilson, A.: Understanding user's preferences for surface gestures. In: Proceedings of Graphics Interface 2010, pp. 261–268. Canadian Information Processing Society, Toronto (2010)
13. Wobbrock, J.O., Aung, H.H., Rothrock, B.A., Myers, B.A.: Maximizing the guessability of symbolic input. In: CHI 2005 Extended Abstracts on Human Factors in Computing Systems, pp. 1869–1872. ACM, New York (2005)

Brain Tagging: A BCI and HCI Tagging System to Evaluate the Learning Contents

Yang Ting Shen[1(✉)], Pei Wen Lu[2], and Xin Mao Chen[1]

[1] School of Architecture, Feng Chia University, Taichung, Taiwan
yatishen@fcu.edu.tw, a543385100@hotmail.com
[2] Department of Geography, National Changhua University of Education,
Changhua, Taiwan
peiwenlu@cc.ncue.edu.tw

Abstract. In this paper, we propose a novel interactive video-based learning system, Brain Tagging. Through collecting both the passive BCI and the active HCI tagging information, the learns' objective and subjective metadata to the video contents are generated. The system gives a way to visualize the learning pattern by timeline chart consisted of BCI metadata (attention and meditation) and HCI metadata (good, question, and disagree). This can help to understand the learning process and performance, and thereby to provide proper improvement in e-learning.

Keywords: e-learning · BCI · HCI · Tagging · Metadata · EEG

1 Introduction

Video-based e-learning, due to its effectiveness and boundless, has become a promising alternative approach that helps the learning process to be more lifelong and on-demand [32]. It offers considerable knowledge in an attractive and consistent way beyond the time-space constraint. Learning platforms, such as YouTube, TED, and MOOCs, are keen to provide video-based contents for seamless learning. Video-based e-learning approach can also be contributive to the tradition of teaching. It allows teachers to uploading well-prepared videos according to their learning plans. By excluding the uncertainties, the quality of teaching can therefore to be more sustained. This forms a new environment for teaching and learning.

From the research perspectives, we consider the video-based e-learning approach with a great potential to support quantitative evaluations – not only addressed in the afterward assessment but also representing the real-time performances. This drives to the needs of more effective methods for the learning content evaluation and learner performance analysis [12]. Engaging learners to create metadata when accessing the video contents helps to make the real-time assessment applicable.

Learners contribute to the metadata through both the subjective and the objective ways [25]. Learners' subjective expression, such as tagging or annotation, generates the

© Springer International Publishing AG 2017
P. Zaphiris and A. Ioannou (Eds.): LCT 2017, Part I, LNCS 10295, pp. 46–54, 2017.
DOI: 10.1007/978-3-319-58509-3_5

subjective metadata. Gibeo[1] [8] presents an example of web-based annotation system which generate metadata from learners' explicit cognition. Through adding "gibeo.net" to the target webpage URL, a set of options is displayed to allow the learner to specify the quality of the highlighted text with labels, e.g., important, wrong, good, or cool, if a part of the text on the page is selected. This offers the learners to remark their perceptions as feedbacks. The objective metadata are generated from learner's physiological signals such as tiredness, emotion, and attention. Koelstra and Patras [11] present a multi-modal approach that collects both facial expressions and electroencephalography (EEG) of the learners and convert the information into affective tagging implicitly.

In regard to the assessment techniques, however, there is a lack of assessment tools that can collect both the subjective and the objective information. This causes a difficulty to examine the performance between the two approaches. We in this paper introduce an interactive video-based tagging system, Brain Tagging, that integrates subjective and objective metadata of the learning experiences. We firstly review the existing works of active tagging and passive tagging. The description of Brain Tagging is addressed in follow and leads to the conclusion.

2   A Review of Affective Metadata

Studies of affective metadata are mainly derived from the affective computing [19]. Affective computing is a broad area that deals with the detection, recognize and interpretation of human emotions – with a high integration among the professions of computer science, psychology, and cognitive science [24]. The existing approach of affective metadata collection can be divided in two categories: active tagging records subjective reactions of the expressed emotion, while passive tagging collects the objective reaction, i.e., brain information, spontaneously when the user experiencing the content.

2.1   Active Tagging: Knowledge Exchange and Experience Sharing

What we tag for? In regard to teaching and learning, the collected tagging information can be useful to assess learner's performances, so thereby to improve their learning experiences. The active tagging often set up a focus of knowledge exchange and experience sharing. It stands on its functions to describe the feedbacks that record the tagger's experiences and beliefs [7]. Active tagging can contribute in two ways. One is meant for exchanging and sharing the information among a group of learners. Through co-tagging a shared material, e.g., selected videos, it can offer a great benefit on collaborative learning. The most famous system is Annotea [8], which improves the collaborative development of the Semantic Web via shared web tags and annotations.

Another contributive way of active tagging is specifically for single learners to organize and to define the information. The "web discussion" feature of Microsoft Office 2000 provides an useful example. It allows collaborative tagging of any web page, so

---

[1] htttp://gibeo.net.

thereby to generate learner-centric tagging information. Gibeo is another example. It allows the user to specify the quality of the highlighted text on the webpage, with labels such as important, wrong or cool. The JavaScript web tagging system, Marginalia [19], presents a similar case that allows users to highlight any part of the text and write associated comments in the margin of the pages.

In regard to video-based e-learning, tagging techniques to contribute to create the metadata for annotating, classifying, retrieving, or analyzing the content. This helps the videos to be more beneficial. Several examples illustrate the situation. The video analysis application, EVA [14], allows users to tag events in real-time for behavioral video analysis. Marquee [28], developed for video annotation and tagging, segments the video according to the time zones, to help the users 'paint' their selections. Both examples present an interesting way for users to 'tag' in the text-based or video-based learning contents – whilst the tagging results can be collected to improve the selection. This makes the systems be more meaningful and powerful for sustainable use.

2.2 Passive Tagging: The EEG Signal Analysis

Different from active tagging that requires direct efforts in records, passive tagging, i.e., human-centered implicit tagging, gathers tags and annotations without any effort from the users [3]. The main idea behind is to collect users' spontaneous reactions as a given signal to identify tags. Passive tagging mostly relies on the information collected by the electroencephalography (EEG) signals when processing in brain. The EEG headset is one of the collecting techniques. It is a non-invasive monitoring technique for measuring a user's brainwave patterns. A cap or headset is worn on the user's head to measure the voltage fluctuations resulting from ionic current within the neurons of the brain. An international standard known as the 10–20 system determines the location of the electrodes on the scalp [11]. The combinations of different electrodes represent human's emotions such as angry, attention, meditation etc.

Brain-computer interfacing (BCI), advances in cognitive neuroscience and brainwave technologies, has found its way in representing the activities in the brain [17]. The term "Brain-Computer Communication," from Vidal in 1973, indicates any computer-based system that produced detailed information on brain function [27]. Vidal developed a system which recorded the scalp over visual cortex to determine the direction of eye gaze, and thus to determine the direction of the cursor movement. In 2002, Wolpaw proposed a framework of BCI to individuals with severe motor deficits. The system controlled process included both signal acquisition and signal processing to translate brainwave features into devices control commands [29].

Most of BCI applications allow the user to send voluntary and directed commands that control the connected computer system to communicate through it. Some studies [4, 31] propose an extended approach to integrate BCI technology with cognitive monitoring. This provides valuable information about the users' intentions, situational interpretations and emotional states to the computer system. The passive brain-computer interface (passive BCI), called also the implicit BCI, provided information from the user's mental activities to without the need of direct brain activity controlling. This helps to interpret human emotions derived from brain activities.

According to Fowler [5] and Shen [20], the relationship between learning perform-ance and the arousal is a type of inverted-U curve. People learn best when their emotions are at a moderate optimal arousal level. These results are recognized as references in developing the assessment tool.

3 Brain Tagging: The System Design

Brain Tagging is a system that collects both the learners' active expressions and the received passive physiology signals for evaluation. The active expression is about learners' subjec-tive opinions to the learning contents, such as good, question, or disagree. Those opinions are generated from learners' cognition levels, which are hard to be measured by BCI tech-niques. Passive signals, such as attention and meditation, are more direct. This causes the information to be more applicable for machine measurements.

Benefit from the BCI and the HCI, Brain Tagging allows learners to instantly eval-uate video-based learning contents at the same time. This externalizes the invisible cognitive and physiological data, which are called affective metadata, and apply them to assist the learning process evaluation.

3.1 Active HCI Tagging

Active tagging allows the learners to record their opinions during the learning process. As we know, in some video-based or lecture-based learning situations, the learning process would be difficult to interrupt. For the sake of annotating and retrieving needs, the appropriate method is to tag their opinions in parallel with the process. OATS (Open Annotation and Tagging System) project [1, 2] presented an example. It integrates a content-tagging and a note-taking tool that allow students to motivate the learning contents, at the meanwhile gathers learner-centric metadata.IBM In Sight project [26], another example, presents a way for collaborative editing with micro-tags. In the micro-tagging mode, learners are allowed to attach a tag to a subset of large media, such as a segment in a video. The whole video can be segmented into selected fragments according to the sort of collaborative tagging.

Our previous studies [6, 21–23], focusing on the active tagging, have been acknowl-edged to decrease the complicated and laboring works in assessing the contents. We also learn that the preliminary opinion buttons would perform more sufficient than the free texts in generating learners' opinions. According to this, we remove the textual tag input in Brain Tagging. Three kinds of tagging buttons are addressed: the positive tagging button "GOOD", the neutral tagging button "QUESTION", and the negative tagging button "DISAGREE". The tagging outcomes will be marked along with the timeline chart synchronously to visualize the feedbacks of interaction process.

3.2 Passive BCI Tagging

The passive BCI tagging collects physiology signals of the learners. It aims to dig the implicit but objective information – mostly emotional. Fowler [5] and Shen [20] both acknowledge the relationship between learning performance and emotions. The EEG techniques have been recognized to be a useful tool to monitor the emotions. Many studies devote to explore the possibility of using EEG as a means for detecting or differentiating between human basic emotions such as happiness, joy, distress, surprise, anger, fear, disgust and sadness [16, 18], or between learning related emotions such as engagement, boredom and frustration [15, 20]. The EEG techniques have also been used for automatic implicit emotional tagging of multimedia content, as an alternative to explicit approaches that require learners to tag the clips themselves [30].

Brain Tagging uses the NeuroSky commercial EEG headset to measure and to convert learners' brainwaves into evaluable information [13]. The non-invades EEG headset detects and translates the EEG power spectrums (alpha waves, beta waves, etc.) into two kinds of outcomes: ATTENTION and MEDITATION according to Keller's ARCS model that scales the degree of learners' mental status from 1 to 100 [9, 10]. The outcomes are visualized as line charts along with the video timeline. The interface and the layout are presented in follow.

3.3   The Integrated Interface

We expect the interface to be applicable, friendly and encouraging for use. As shown in Fig. 1, the field of project information allows the learner to create a new video-based learning project or to retrieve an old one. When the learner creates a new project, the video source can be input from the computer webcam or videos saved in the computer. The video can therefore be displayed on the video canvas. The HCI mode provides alternative way that the learner can tag his opinions within the accurate video periods by clicking buttons. As mentioned above, we provide three tagging buttons: GOOD, QUESTION and DISAGREE. The outcomes are marked on the timeline chart according to individual tagging times.

The learner are encouraged to wear the EEG headset and to activate the BCI mode. Once the connection between EEG headset and computer is built, the learner's attention and meditation data will be automatically documented in the timeline chart along with the video (Fig. 2).

3.4   The Timeline Chart

Both the HCI and BCI tagging outcomes are integrated to become visualization data shown in the timeline chart. The BCI tagging information (ATTENTION and MEDITATION) is presented as individual continuous line charts. Attention is displayed in red and meditation is displayed in green. The HCI tagging (GOOD-circle symbol, QUESTION-triangle symbol, and DISAGREE-cross symbol) are marked on the line charts according the clicking time.

The timeline chart is designed in this way for the learner performance analysis and for learning content evaluation. In regard to the learner performance analysis, the timeline chart documents and illustrates the learner's interactive learning process including the BCI and HCI tagging results. It provides the opportunity to analyze the learner's learning performance by observing the waviness of BCI tagging chart. We can see how many and how long the attention and meditation higher levels present in the timeline to evaluate the learning performance. In addition, we also can compare the relationship between the BCI tagging waves and HCI tagging markers to understand the learner's learning preference or tendency.

In regard to the purpose of learning content evaluation, the tagging results provide a novel way to assess and extract the valuable video contents. For example, by mass learners' tagging collection to the same video, we can analyse the video contents and locate the specific video segments with higher and denser tagging outcomes. In other words, we not only evaluate the whole video but also detail to the special video intervals.

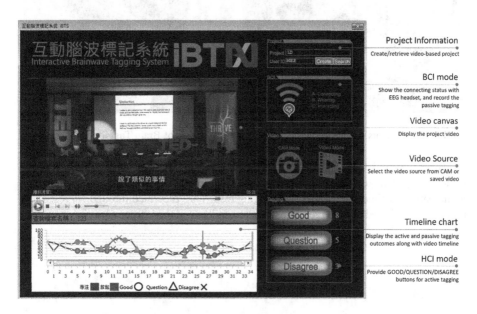

Fig. 1. The interface design of Brain Tagging system

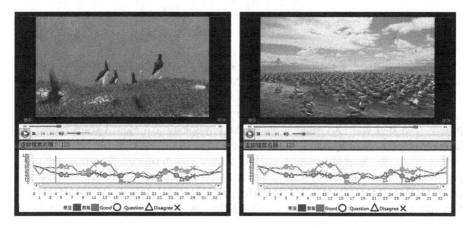

Fig. 2. No texts

4   Conclusion

In this paper we describe the intention, the theoretical backgrounds and the design of the BCI and HCI tagging system, Brain Tagging. Students who voluntarily participate in our experiment are asked to watch the same video for pilot study experiments (see Fig. 3).

Fig. 3. Students participating the pilot study experiments of Brain Tagging voluntarily

The results of the experiment are shown as Fig. 4. The HCI tagging results are remarked in circles: good in green, question in purple and disagree in blue. These results are addressed in the particular time points. The BCI tagging results are presented through curves: attention in blue and meditation in red. This helps to understand the learner's learning patterns.

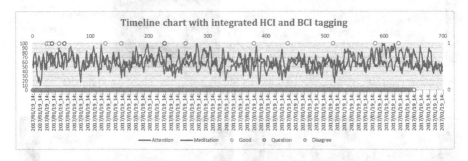

Fig. 4. The visualized metadata included tagging buttons (GOOD/QUESTION/DISAGREE) outcomes and brainwave values (ATTENTION/MEDITATION) outcomes (Color figure online)

In conclusion, Brain Tagging provides an innovative method to visualize the learning pattern. The BCI and HCI tagging record the physiology and mental states during the learning process. As a system of collecting the metadata, it provides the opportunity to further assess the learning content and the learner's performance. The periodic study presents only the result of a small group. It is still a long way before we can conduct concreted remarks in regard to learner performance analysis and learning content evaluation. We expect to conduct more experiments in following semester to collect data for learning pattern finding. This will help us to design more proper learning contents and processes based on learners' physiological and cognitive performance.

Acknowledgements. The financial support from Ministry of Science and Technology (MOST) including project "Brain Tagging System" (MOST 105-2221-E-035-070-) and project "Resilient Livable Smart City:" (MOST 105-2627-M-035-008-), is greatly acknowledged.

References

1. Bateman, S., Brooks, C., Mccalla, G., Brusilovsky, P.: Applying collaborative tagging to e-learning. In: Proceedings of the 16th International World Wide Web Conference (WWW 2007), May 2007
2. Bateman, S., Farzan, R., Brusilovsky, P., McCalla, G.: OATS: the Open Annotation and Tagging System. In: Proceedings of I2LOR (2006)
3. Cadiz, J.J., Gupta, A., Grudin, J.: Using web annotations for asynchronous collaboration around documents. In: Proceedings of the 2000 ACM Conference on Computer Supported Cooperative Work, pp. 309–318. ACM, December 2000
4. Cutrell, E., Tan, D.: BCI for passive input in HCI. In: Proceedings of CHI, vol. 8, pp. 1–3. ACM Press, New York, April 2008
5. Fowler, C.J.H.: The role of arousal in memory and attention, Doctoral dissertation, Royal Holloway, University of London (1977)
6. Hsu, Y.C., Jeng, T.S., Shen, Y.T., Chen, P.C.: SynTag: a web-based platform for labeling real-time video. In: Proceedings of the ACM 2012 Conference on Computer Supported Cooperative Work, pp. 715–718. ACM, February 2012
7. John, A., Seligmann, D.: Collaborative tagging and expertise in the enterprise. In: Collaborative Web Tagging Workshop in Conjunction with WWW 2006, May 2006
8. Kahan, J., Koivunen, M.R., Prud'Hommeaux, E., Swick, R.R.: Annotea: an open RDF infrastructure for shared Web annotations. Comput. Netw. **39**(5), 589–608 (2002)
9. Keller, J.M.: Motivational design of instruction. In: Instructional Design Theories and Models: An Overview of Their Current Status, vol. 1, pp. 383–434 (1983)
10. Keller, J.M.: Strategies for stimulating the motivation to learn. Perform. Improv. **26**(8), 1–7 (1987)
11. Koelstra, S., Patras, I.: Fusion of facial expressions and EEG for implicit affective tagging. Image Vis. Comput. **31**(2), 164–174 (2013)
12. Lin, C.Y., Tseng, B.L., Smith, J.R.: VideoAnnEx: IBM MPEG-7 annotation tool for multimedia indexing and concept learning. In: IEEE International Conference on Multimedia and Expo, pp. 1–2, July 2003
13. Luo, A., Sullivan, T.J.: A user-friendly SSVEP-based brain–computer interface using a time-domain classifier. J. Neural Eng. **7**(2), 026010 (2010)
14. Mackay, W.E.: EVA: an experimental video annotator for symbolic analysis of video data. ACM SIGCHI Bull. **21**(2), 68–71 (1989)
15. Mampusti, E.T., Ng, J.S., Quinto, J.J.I., Teng, G.L., Suarez, M.T.C., Trogo, R.S.: Measuring academic affective states of students via brainwave signals. In: 2011 Third International Conference on Knowledge and Systems Engineering (KSE), pp. 226–231. IEEE, October 2011
16. Nie, D., Wang, X.W., Shi, L.C., Lu, B.L.: EEG-based emotion recognition during watching movies. In: 2011 5th International IEEE/EMBS Conference on Neural Engineering (NER), pp. 667–670. IEEE, April 2011

17. Nijholt, A., Tan, D., Allison, B., del R Milan, J., Graimann, B.: Brain-computer interfaces for HCI and games. In: Extended Abstracts on Human Factors in Computing Systems, pp. 3925–3928. ACM, April 2008

18. Petrantonakis, P.C., Hadjileontiadis, L.J.: Emotion recognition from EEG using higher order crossings. IEEE Trans. Inf. Technol. Biomed. **14**(2), 186–197 (2010)

19. Picard, R.W., Picard, R.: Affective Computing, vol. 252. MIT Press, Cambridge (1997)

20. Shen, L.P., Leon, E., Callaghan, V., Shen, R.M.: Exploratory research on an affective e-learning model. In: Proceedings of Workshop on Blended Learning, pp. 267–278, August 2007

21. Shen, Y.T., Lu, P.W.: Learning by annotating: a system development study of real-time synchronous supports for distributed learning in multiple locations. In: 2012 6th International Conference on New Trends in Information Science and Service Science and Data Mining (ISSDM), pp. 701–706. IEEE, October 2012

22. Shen, Y.T., Lu, P.W.: Engage the power of social community in the lecture-based learning by using the collaborative tagging system. J. Convergence Inf. Technol. **8**(11), 485 (2013)

23. Shen, Y.T., Jeng, T.S., Hsu, Y.C.: A "live" interactive tagging interface for collaborative learning. In: Luo, Y. (ed.) CDVE 2011. LNCS, vol. 6874, pp. 102–109. Springer, Heidelberg (2010). doi:10.1007/978-3-642-23734-8_16

24. Tao, J., Tan, T.: Affective computing: a review. In: Tao, J., Tan, T., Picard, R.W. (eds.) ACII 2005. LNCS, vol. 3784, pp. 981–995. Springer, Heidelberg (2005). doi: 10.1007/11573548_125

25. Tkalčič, M., Burnik, U., Košir, A.: Using affective parameters in a content-based recommender system for images. User Model. User-Adap. Inter. **20**(4), 279–311 (2010)

26. Topkara, M., Rogowitz, B., Wood, S., Boston, J.: Collaborative editing of micro-tags. In: Extended Abstracts on Human Factors in Computing Systems, CHI 2009, pp. 4297–4302. ACM, April 2009

27. Vidal, J.J.: Toward direct brain-computer communication. Ann. Rev. Biophys. Bioeng. **2**(1), 157–180 (1973)

28. Weher, K., Poon, A.: Marquee: a tool for real-time video logging. In: Proceedings of the SIGCHI Conference on Human Factors in Computing Systems, pp. 58–64. ACM, April 1994

29. Wolpaw, J.R., Birbaumer, N., McFarland, D.J., Pfurtscheller, G., Vaughan, T.M.: Brain-computer interfaces for communication and control. Clin. Neurophysiol. Off. J. Int. Fed. Clin. Neurophysiol. **113**(6), 767–791 (2002)

30. Yazdani, A., Lee, J.S., Ebrahimi, T.: Implicit emotional tagging of multimedia using EEG signals and brain computer interface. In: Proceedings of the First SIGMM Workshop on Social Media, pp. 81–88. ACM, October 2009

31. Zander, T.O., Kothe, C.: Towards passive brain–computer interfaces: applying brain–computer interface technology to human–machine systems in general. J. Neural Eng. **8**(2), 025005 (2011)

32. Zhang, D., Zhao, J.L., Zhou, L., Nunamaker, J.F.: Can e-learning replace traditional classroom learning? Evidence and implication of the evolving e-learning technology. Commun. ACM, **47**(5) 75–79 (2004)

Analytical Steps for the Validation
of a Natural User Interface

Madlen Wuttke[✉], Sabine Völkel, Peter Ohler, and Nicholas H. Müller

Media-Psychology, Faculty of Humanities, Chemnitz University of Technology,
Thüringer Weg 11, 09126 Chemnitz, Germany
{madlen.wuttke,sabine.voelkel,peter.ohler,
nicholas.mueller}@phil.tu-chemnitz.de

Abstract. Pedagogical Agents are primarily researched regarding their depiction or appearance on screen, rather than their capabilities to react to a learner in front of it. As it has been previously reported, we developed an agent system, which is based on an electronic educational instance for a learning module to incorporate information from the environment as well as non-verbal reactions of a user. The system is then capable of proactively reacting to this additional information, establishing a natural user interface as it might be expected by any user. In order to validate our approach, the steps for our experimental setup are presented and discussed.

Keywords: Pedagogical · Agent · Proactive · Validation

1 Introduction

Within this paper, the authors refer to their validation efforts of the previously described concept [5]. A user study with 160 participants was conducted with four different variations of learner support aspects. To check for the persona effect, as stated by Lester et al. [9], the electronic educational instance (Fig. 1. EEI [6] and Enhanced capabilities [5].) is used in conjunction with a depicted pedagogical agent or without. The persona effect formulates that there is a per se beneficial effect of including a depicted agent onscreen. This might be true due to the expectancy of social adequate behavior [8], which is why the experimental setup displayed the agent onscreen and had variations where the agent's voice was audible but there was no depiction visible on the screen.

The development of our agent has been deeply influenced by the research activities of Reeves and Nass [8] who postulated a user's expectancies of a social adequate behavior when interacting with a machine. Our process of creating the electronic educational instance has been previously published [5–7, 12, 13]. Therefore, we will only present a limited overview of our previous development and focus on the validation aspects.

Ever since Lester et al. established the persona effect [9] research regarding pedagogical agents is heavily focused on the outward appearance of an agent. For example, the various depictions of an agent as well as their embodiment [2] have been a focus of research as has been their outward appearance, including their manners and behavior [3, 14–16]. Research regarding their appearance also includes their vocalization of learning material and

© Springer International Publishing AG 2017
P. Zaphiris and A. Ioannou (Eds.): LCT 2017, Part I, LNCS 10295, pp. 55–63, 2017.
DOI: 10.1007/978-3-319-58509-3_6

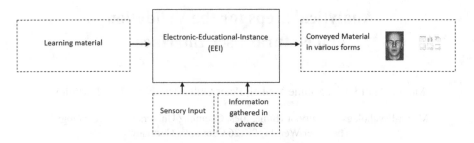

Fig. 1. EEI [6] and Enhanced capabilities [5]

their conversational behavior in general [4, 17, 18]. Heidig and Clarebout [1] published an overview of various aspects of pedagogical agents and their possible benefits for electronic learning.

These aspects of exploration all focus on one dimension of the user-agent relation-ship, namely having an agent appear more lifelike or to behave and communicate most helpfully. Within our approach, we argue for a shift to include additional input channels for the agent to get a more thorough grasp of the learning situation and about the context in which a learner is situated.

Based on our research, the possibilities for a user to interact with a learning system are still limited to traditional input channels like keyboard and mouse interfaces. Although, as Krämer [19] pointed out, the raw processing power of computer systems is already on a level, which would allow the implementation of much more natural ways of communication. Even though recent advances in the form of speech and gesture recognition has opened up new ways of interaction, this still has not advanced to the implementation of system-based reactions to a user's behavior in front of the screen or to environmental cues related to the learner. As it has been previously established by conceptual research [5] the integration of advanced input channels for computer and web based trainings should provide a measurable benefit during the conveyance of information, simply by being able to pause a training program if a student is looking away from the screen or there is too much noise in the environment. By implementing an electronic educational instance [6, 7] it is possible to enhance a wide array of possible variations of learning software. The idea behind the electronic educational software is to enable the computer system to behave in accordance with the media equation theory as postulated by Reeves and Nass [8]. As they stated, humans tend to subconsciously expect technical devices to behave as another human being would. Including the expect-ance of transporting non-verbal cues. An agent-system capable of identifying such cues would be immensely more useful when conveying learning material due to its capability to factor real time information into the presentation. Within our system, this explicitly means environmental cues like the noise level of the learning environment as well as the focused gaze of the learner in front of the computer. For the presented experimental validation, the attention onto the screen is key in having a thorough understanding of the learning material and the capability of actively utilizing learned knowledge.

2   Real-World Applications

Implementing a proactive functionality to any technology promises broad new forms of human computer interactions in general. Due to the EEI and its enhanced capabilities as being a standalone component, it is possible to implement our sensory concept into pretty much any form of technology. For example, Smart TV systems, which would pause and resume a movie or a sports game until the attention is reverted back onto the screen or the audience remains within the visible reach of the television screen. Another form would be the implementation into the modern aspects of mobile learning scenarios, in which a system would react to the users surrounding and would be able to proactively offer another form of material conveyance, e.g. an audio transcript while waiting at a bus stop and a combined audio-video demonstration once seated and commuting [20].

Given a real-world learning scenario, a human teacher would be able to react to a student. Would there be a noise disturbance in the environment of the classroom, a teacher would wait for the disturbance to go away or reaches a low enough level to be sure that audible information would be understandable. In addition, if one or more students divert their gaze away from what is shown by the teacher, the presentation would be paused until attention has been reverted to the topic at hand. Additionally, if a teacher would detect confusion amongst students, a different approach would be used to look at a specific topic from another perspective and thus possibly have the learning material conveyed more easily.

3   Experimental Validation

Therefore, we enhanced the electronic educational instance [8] to be able to detect a users' gaze. A commonly used webcam is able to detect the eyes of a user and therefore infers that the learning material is actively consumed (Fig. 2. The experimental setup with webcam and eye-tracking-camera.). Once the user is looking away from the screen and the software notices a deviation of the gaze away from the monitor, the presentation is paused and only resumed, once the gaze and therefore the attention is reverted back to the learning material.

Test subjects were asked to study an already established web-based training in use at the institute of media research from 2006 to 2012. Within the WBT, the basic functions of the Adobe Dreamweaver Suite are explained. Three basic ideas were to be tested during the experimental run.

- Does the proactive function lead to a better understanding of the learning material once the learner's attention is diverted?
- Does the depiction of the agent (persona effect) have a measurable impact on the understanding of the learning material?
- Is it necessary to include an intervention of the proactive functionality in order to allow a learner to repeat a session or to continue from the point of diverted attention?

To ensure that our experiment is capable of testing for various empirical aspects (e.g. the persona effect [9]) six groups of participants were tested (Table 1).

Fig. 2. The experimental setup with webcam and eye-tracking-camera

Table 1. Experimental groups

Group 1	Depicted agent, with proactivity
Group 2	Depicted agent, without proactivity
Group 3	Audio-only agent, with proactivity
Group 4	Audio-only agent, without proactivity
Group 5	Audio-only agent, with proactivity, no intervention message
Group 6	Depicted agent, with proactivity, no intervention message

In order to create a lifelike agent onscreen, we used the FaceShift software, which, using a Microsoft Kinect camera, allows the immediate capture of mimic and voiced mouth movements onto a 3D head model (Fig. 3. Faceshift capture of speaker).

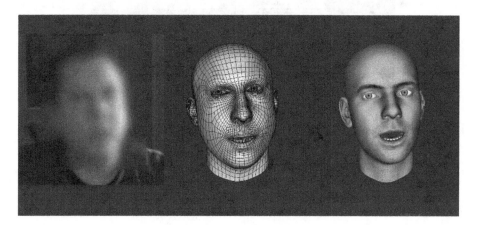

Fig. 3. Faceshift capture of speaker

The recorded re-readings of the information material were recorded and afterwards synchronized with the original web based training by using Adobe Premiere (Fig. 4. Synchronization of WBT and character animation).

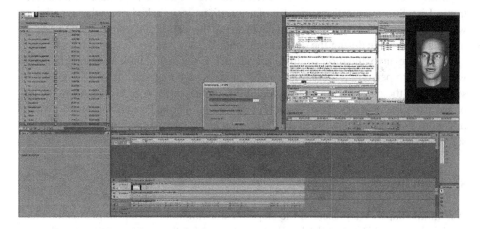

Fig. 4. Synchronization of WBT and character animation

The displayed Agent interaction onscreen differs only marginally from group to group in order to test for aspects of the persona effect, the benefits of proactivity and the intervention of the agent system (Fig. 5. Displayed variations onscreen). Main differences are the depiction of the agent itself and the display of interaction buttons once the presentation stopped during the experiment due to an averted gaze.

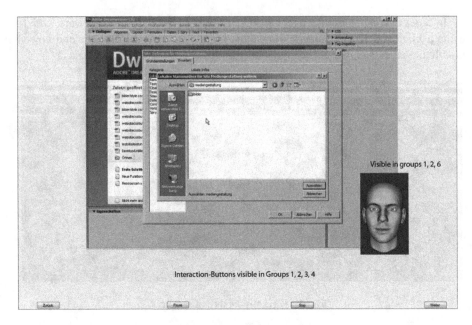

Fig. 5. Displayed variations onscreen

Before the experimental variations started, the general knowledge of participants regarding websites, html code and the Dreamweaver software is gathered via an electronic LimeSurvey questionnaire. Similar questions were asked once the experiment was over to check for increased knowledge due to the web-based training and to expose missing knowledge during the diverted attention.

To ensure any validation could be traced back to the manipulations, the participants were asked to perform a second task while studying the material. At two standardized segments of the presentation, at a critical information conveyance, a monitor to the left of the participants flashed and a speaker played an alarm. Participants were given a password before the experiment and told to enter it, once something happens on the screen to their left.

4   Conclusion

Within this paper, we presented the steps for the validation of our implemented electronic educational instance (EEI). We argue to broaden the scope of pedagogical agent research to include various other aspects when deciding how to better enable an information conveyance using electronic learning media. Especially, not to focus any longer on instructional design methods and new forms of information segmentation, but to include new and readily available input channels into electronic learning systems.

Even nowadays, most modern e-learning software is limited to mouse and keyboard inputs and learning success is mostly defined by having a learning success test implemented at the end of a chapter. However, the information whether or not a learner is able and capable to understand certain information is available long before this end point of the conveyance – it is visible due to non-verbal cues of averted attention. Due to the proposed EEI module, any existing learning software could be rapidly upgraded to notice any diversion from the screen and due to ubiquitous webcam-in-screen-frame designs of modern notebooks, tablets and 2-in-1 computers; there are not even monetary investments necessary.

Preliminary analysis of our validation shows a clear proof of the obvious: it is beneficial to the information conveyance, if a user is actually looking at the screen and attentive when said information is delivered.

Furthermore, our next steps for implementation will include a cognitive workload assessment based on recorded pupil dilations [10]. Due to this, we will be able to know in real-time whenever any given material is too hard to understand for any given user in front of the learning system. Therefore, the agent system is capable to proactively change the conveyance of the material, to repeat certain aspects until cognitive load levels [21, 22] normalize or to change the mode of presentation. This would allow for a unique learner calibration of learning material, which right now is, if at all, performed by questions about preliminary knowledge beforehand.

In addition, we are about to implement and auditory sensor array which checks for environmental noise levels and decides whether or not the speaker output-level is suitable for the current situation or if it would be beneficial to raise the amplitude. If noise levels were too disruptive, the presentation would be stopped proactively entirely while the system waits for the surrounding circumstances to normalize.

Moreover, beyond these readily available modes, we are currently working on implementing a facial action coding reconnaissance module. This FACS [11] would present another non-verbal cue about the learner's inner state as the cognitive workload module. Due to certain facial muscle activations, it is possible to detect basic emotions on a user's face and therefore compute an emotional valence level. As long as this would be in a neutral or positive domain, the information conveyance might be all right or even entertaining. However, once the emotional valence level threshold is crossed into a negative sphere, the system should be able to incorporate this information. Further closed eyelids might indicate boredom or at least sleepiness and is therefore not beneficial for a learning success. Therefore, the system would be able to know when a unique learner is not able to follow the conveyance of information and suggest either a break or to choose another variation of conveyance by, for example, switching to an easier but more time-consuming variant.

Due to these non-verbal detection modules, it would be possible to detect specific instances where additional learner support would be beneficial instead of the standard time for the detection of faulty conveyance – during the learner success test at the end of a computer or web-based training program.

Although we discuss all of these non-verbal cue detection modules inside a learning setting, there are numerous possible applications, which would benefit from a proactive sensory phalanx. Smart home systems and self-driving cars would benefit from knowing a user's valence state, as would streaming-services when recommending movies or tv-shows. The cognitive load level could be used to detect a pilot's overextension in aviation and deviations from established gaze patterns in air-traffic-controllers might indicate a problem.

Therefore, although this paper is merely outlining the implementation aspects of our validation, we showed what steps are necessary to implement a proactive agent system and we will continue to include said non-verbal detection modules into every-day-life human-computer-interactions.

References

1. Heidig, S., Clarebout, G.: Do pedagogical agents make a difference to student motivation and learning? Educ. Res. Rev. **6**, 27–54 (2011)
2. Lusk, M.M., Atkinson, R.K.: Animated pedagogical agents: does their degree of embodiment impact learning from static or animated worked examples? Appl. Cogn. Psychol. **21**, 747–764 (2007)
3. Wang, N., Johnson, W.L., Mayer, R.E., Risso, P., Shaw, E., Collins, H.: The politeness effect: pedagogical agents and learning outcomes. Int. J. Hum.-Comput. Stud. **66**, 98–112 (2008)
4. Veletsianos, G.: How do learners respond to pedagogical agents that deliver social-oriented non-task messages? Impact on student learning, perceptions, and experiences. Comput. Hum. Behav. **28**, 275–283 (2012)
5. Wuttke, M., Heidt, M., Rosenthal, P., Ohler, P., Müller, N.H.: Proactive functions of a pedagogical agent – steps for implementing a social catalyst function. In: Zaphiris, P., Ioannou, A. (eds.) Learning and Collaboration Technologies, LCT 2016. LNCS, vol. 9753, pp. 573–580. Springer, Cham (2016). doi:10.1007/978-3-319-39483-1_52
6. Wuttke, M.: Pro-active pedagogical agents. In: Fakultät für Informatik (ed.) Proceedings of International Summer Workshop Computer Science, pp. 59–62, July 2013
7. Wuttke, M., Heidt, M.: Beyond presentation - employing proactive intelligent agents as social catalysts. In: Kurosu, M. (ed.) HCI 2014. LNCS, vol. 8511, pp. 182–190. Springer, Cham (2014). doi:10.1007/978-3-319-07230-2_18
8. Reeves, B., Nass, C.: The Media Equation. How People Treat Computers, Televisions, and New Media Like Real People and Places. Cambridge University Press, New York (1996)
9. Lester, J.C., Converse, S.A., Kahler, S.E., Barlow, S.T., Stone, B.A., Bhogal, R.S.: The persona effect: affective impact of animated pedagogical agents. In: Pemberton, S. (ed.) Human Factors in Computing Systems: CHI 1997 Conference Proceedings, pp. 359–366. ACM Press, New York (1997)
10. Rosch, J.L., Vogel-Walcutt, J.J.: A review of eye-tracking applications as tools for training. Cogn. Technol. Work **15**(3), 313–327 (2013)
11. Ekman, P., Friesen, W.V., Hager, J.C.: Facial Action Coding System - The Manual. Research Nexus Division of Network Information Research Corporation, Salt Lake City (2002)
12. Wuttke, M., Martin, K.-U.: Natural forms of communication and adaptive behaviour in human-computer-interaction. In: Kurosu, M. (ed.) HCI 2014. LNCS, vol. 8511, pp. 641–647. Springer, Cham (2014). doi:10.1007/978-3-319-07230-2_61
13. Wuttke, M., Belentschikow, V., Müller, N.H.: Storytelling as a means to transfer knowledge via narration – a scenario for a narrating pedagogical agent. i-com **14**(2), 155–160 (2015). doi: 10.1515/icom-2015-0034
14. Graesser, A.C., Person, N.K., Harter, D., Group, T.R.: Teaching tactics and dialog in AutoTutor. Int. J. Artif. Intell. Educ. **12**, 257–279 (2001)
15. Kim, Y., Baylor, A.L., Shen, E.: Pedagogical agents as learning companions: the impact of agent emotion and gender. J. Comput. Assist. Learn. **23**, 220–234 (2007)
16. Chan, T.W., Chou, C.Y.: Exploring the design of computer supports for reciprocal tutoring systems. Int. J. Artif. Intell. Educ. **8**, 1–29 (1997)

17. Domagk, S.: Do pedagogical agents facilitate learner motivation and learning outcomes? The role of the appeal of agent's appearance and voice. J. Media Psychol. **22**(2), 82–95 (2010)
18. Nass, C., Isbister, K., Lee, E.J.: Truth is Beauty, Researching Embodied Conversational Agents: Embodied Conversational Agents, pp. 374–402. The MIT Press, Cambridge (2000)
19. Krämer, N.C.: Soziale Wirkungen virtueller Helfer. Gestaltung und Evaluation von Mensch-Computer-Interaktion. Kohlhammer, Stuttgart (2008)
20. Martin, K.-U., Wuttke, M., Hardt, W.: Sensor based interaction mechanisms in mobile learning. In: Zaphiris, P., Ioannou, A. (eds.) Learning and Collaboration Technologies. Technology-Rich Environments for Learning and Collaboration, LCT 2014. LNCS, vol. 8524, pp. 165–172. Springer, Cham (2014). doi:10.1007/978-3-319-07485-6_17
21. Chandler, P., Sweller, J.: Cognitive load theory and the format of instruction. Cogn. Instr. **8**(4), 293–332 (1991)
22. Sweller, J., Chandler, P.: Evidence for cognitive load theory. Cogn. Instr. **8**(4), 351–362 (1991)

Monitoring Cognitive Workload in Online Videos Learning Through an EEG-Based Brain-Computer Interface

Yun Zhou[1]([✉]), Tao Xu[2], Yanping Cai[3], Xiaojun Wu[4], and Bei Dong[4,5]

[1] School of Education, Shaanxi Normal University, 199, South Chang'an Road,
Xi'an 710062, Shaanxi, People's Republic of China
zhouyun@snnu.edu.cn

[2] School of Software and Microelectronics, Northwestern Polytechnical University,
Xi'an, People's Republic of China
xutao@nwpu.edu.cn

[3] School of Mechanical Engineering, Xi'an Jiaotong University, No.28, Xianning West Road,
Xi'an 710049, Shaanxi, People's Republic of China
caiyanping502@163.com

[4] Key Laboratory of Modern Teaching Technology, Ministry of Education,
Shaanxi Normal University, Xi'an, People's Republic of China
{xjwu,dongbei}@snnu.edu.cn

[5] School of Computer Science, Shaanxi Normal University, Xi'an, People's Republic of China

Abstract. Student cognitive state is one of the crucial factors determing successful learning [1]. The research community related to education and computer science has developed various approches for describing and monitoring learning cognitive states. Assessing cognitive states in digital environment makes it possible to supply adaptive instruction and personalized learning for student. This assessment has the same function as the instructor in a real-world classroom observing and adjusting the speed and contents of the lecture in line with students' cognitive states. The goal is to refocus students' interest and engagement, making the instruction efficiently. In recent years, increased researches have focused on various measures of cognitive states, among which physiological measures are able to monitor in a real-time, especially electroencephalography (EEG) based brain activity measures. The cognitive workload that students experience while learning instructional materials determines success in learning. In this work, we design and propose a real-time passive Brain-Computer Interaction (BCI) system to monitor the cognitive workload using EEG-based headset Emotiv Epoc+, which is feasible for working in the online digital environment like Massive Open Online Courses (MOOCs). We choose two electrodes to pick up original EEG signals, which are highly relevant to the workload. The current prototype is able to record EEG signals and classify levels of cognitive load when students watching online course videos. This prototype is based on two layers, using machine learning approaches for classification.

Keywords: Electroencephalography (EEG) · Passive brain-computer interface (BCI) · Cognitive workload · Learning

© Springer International Publishing AG 2017
P. Zaphiris and A. Ioannou (Eds.): LCT 2017, Part I, LNCS 10295, pp. 64–73, 2017.
DOI: 10.1007/978-3-319-58509-3_7

1   Introduction

Nowadays, the Web and its technologies have revolutionized our vision to deliver courses and learning models to students. As one of the contributions of the Web in education, the Massive Open Online Courses (MOOCs) generate a new digital learning environment, which provide open learning for large scale and support learners to study at their own pace with instructional video clips. Although these online courses and the digital environment show their popular, they are still far away from delivering effective education strategies. One of the issues is on detecting student's cognitive states (One step further, the affective states) and supplying adaptive instruction in such digital environments. In a real-world classroom, an instructor easily observes the cognitive state of students and adjusts the speed and contents of the lecture. This strategy regains students' interest and engagement in learning. Current MOOCs platforms do not support cognitive states recognition and miss the adaptive presentation of videos and other learning materials.

Recently, increased researches have focused on physiological measures on cognitive states, among which electroencephalography (EEG) based brain activity measures are able to monitor in a real-time, compared with self-reported assessment and learning performance measures. One current focus on cognitive states is to enhance student engagement, including measuring features, classifying attention levels, and modelling. In the work [2], the passive brain-computer interfaces are leveraged to enhance user engagement and learn how to better deliver the best reading experience. Szafir and Mutlu [3] design and build a system in which a robotic agent informs of real-time measurements of student attention obtained from EEG data employed cues that human instructors use to recapture student attention when it declines. However, in the learning context, the engagement drops possibly due to student's lack of interest, possibly due to the inappropriate workload levels. The cognitive workload that students experience while learning instructional materials determines success in learning. With the workload real-time assessment tool, the instructor could observe whether the adjustment of strategies is successful when decreasing or increasing the workload levels of student by optimizing the instructions, using more cases to explain, etc. In digital unsupervised environment, the system embedded with detection modules could provide automatic adaption and personalized learning paths for students. Therefore, in the learning context, it is crucial to monitor and analyze the cognitive workload.

In this work, we design and propose a real-time passive Brain-Computer Interaction (BCI) system to continuously monitor the cognitive workload using EEG-based wireless headset Emotiv Epoc+, which is feasible for working in the online digital environment like Massive Open Online Courses (MOOCs). We choose two electrodes to pick up original EEG signals, which are highly relevant to the workload. The current prototype is able to record EEG signals and classify levels of cognitive load when students watching online course videos. This prototype is based on two layers, using machine learning approaches for classification.

2   Related Work

2.1   Cognitive Workload

The cognitive load theory (CLT) built by Sweller [4] indicates that learning happens best under conditions that are in line with learner's cognitive structure. In this theory, cognitive load refers to the total amount of metal effort being used in the individual cognitive system in a specific working period. The intensity and type of cognitive load that students experience while learning instructional materials determines success in learning. Sweller classified the workload into three types [5], including intrinsic cognitive load (ICL), extraneous cognitive load (ECL) and germane cognitive load (GCL), based the sources of the workload. Even though the nature of cognitive load is unclear and the workload type cannot be observed directly, through assessing workload we could adjust the load to an expected level by the materials difficulty (related to ICL), the representation and forms (related to ECL) and the cases (related to GCL). Brunken et al. [6] classified various methods of assessing cognitive load along two dimensions: objectivity (subjective and objective) and causal relation (indirect and direct). Along to the time when to detect the workload, these measures could be regarded roughly as real-time and non-real-time. Physiological measures often provide a real-time detection, like EEG-based BCI, heart rate, eye movements, etc. Self-reported assessment and learning performance (learning outcome measures, dual-task performance) are usually conducted before or after tasks.

2.2   Brain-Computer Interface on Workload Recognition

Due to its high temporal resolution, EEG is an appropriate tool to record brain activities and recognize patterns in complex cognitive tasks in learning. EEG headsets can be classified casually as medical caps and portable caps. Usually, the medical cap have 128 channels and expensive. It requires a specific environment or lab to conduct the experiment, and well-trained technicians to operate the device. Each procedure takes at least half an hour to prepare the device. Even though the medical cap performs with more accuracy and has more channels, the system using this cap is impractical for a wide use. On the contrary, the portable cap is cheaper and simpler to use.

As shown in Table 1, we survey and list several existing EEG-based cognitive workload recognition systems. The workload is measured by using the improved method in study [7], which has investigated memory workload in the n-back task using wireless EEG signals. This work was based on the Proximal Support Vector Machine (PSVM) algorithm, using signal power features, statistical features, morphological features, and time-frequency features, to distinguish high, medium and low levels. Honal and Schultz [8] employed SVM and Artificial Neural Networks (ANNs) for classification of EEG signals on workload in lecture and meeting scenarios (Table 1).

Table 1. Existing EEG-based cognitive workload recognition systems

References	Workload levels	Stimulus/ context	Device	Features measured	Classifier
[7] Wang et al. (2016)	Three: 1-back, 2-back, 3-back.	n-back Task	Emotiv Epoc	• Signal power • Statistical features • Morphological features • Time-frequency features	Proximal Support Vector Machine (SVM) algorithm (PSVM)
[8] Honal and Schultz (2008)	Two: Low, high.	The lecture and meeting scenarios	Electro-Cap and a self-made EEG-headband	Feature vector consisted of spectral features	SVM and Artificial Neural Networks (ANNs)
[9] Grimes et al. (2008)	Three: 1-back, 2-back, 3-back.	n-back Task	Biosemi Active Two 32 channel system	Signal power Ratio theta/alpha Ratio theta/ (alpha + beta)	Naïve Bayes density model
[10] Antonenko and Niederhauser (2010)	Two high level (without lead), low level (with lead)	Hypertext learning environment	Biopac MP30	Event-Related Desynchronizati on percentage (ERD%) for alpha, beta, and theta rhythms	/
[11] Heger et al. (2010)	Load index in the range between 0 and 1	The flanker and the switching paradigms	Brain Products actiCAP	Feature vector consisted of spectral features	SVM

From these studies [9, 12–14], results indicated that increased memory load was associated with increased theta band power in the frontal midline area by Gevins et al. and other researchers. Besides, alpha band activity changes have been observed in the studies of detecting memory load.

3   EEG-Based Brain-Computer Interface to Assess Cognitive Workload

3.1   System Structure

This passive BCI system is designed for using in a ubiquitous environment, which supports monitoring when student learning online at any place. It consists of two layers: the offline layer for training the classifier and the online layer for real-time recognition of workload levels. As shown in Fig. 1, with regards to both layers, the process is based on the machine learning approaches and includes raw EEG signals recording from headset, artifacts removal, feature extraction, and classification. The implementation of machine learning approaches typically requires training. Then the learning model is used for test or prediction. The parameters are trained and accomplished in the offline layer. We will discuss the components in the subsections.

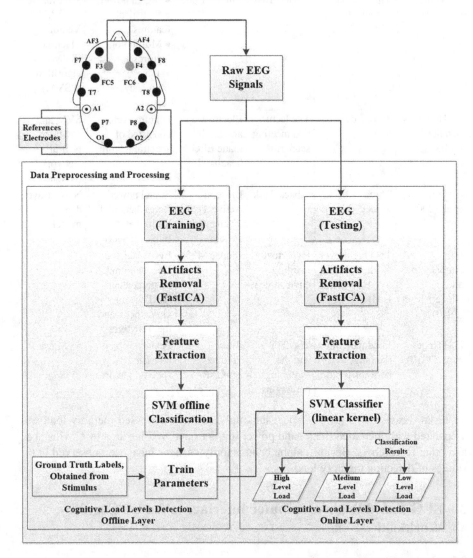

Fig. 1. The passive BCI system architecture for recognizing cognitive load levels in the context of online courses learning

3.2 Apparatus

In this work, we leverage the Emotiv Epoc+ to record EEG signals and its SDK to develop related processing models (see Fig. 2). The Epoc+ is low-cost and ubiquitous, which has been proved to be accuracy and feasibility to access cognitive activities. This wireless acquisition device connects to a computer via a USB and records the raw EEG data via a headset. The headset features 14 channels plus 2 references based on the 10–20 format, with a resolution of 128 samples/s. Its low cost, lightness and channels makes it appropriate and competent to work in online learning environment. The Emotiv SDK allows to program to log EEG signals and train for cognitive states recognition. It supports C++ and other common languages like Python, Matlab. In this work, we use Matlab to build and test the offline system. Then we develop the online system in C++.

Fig. 2. The Emotiv Epoc + headset

3.3 EEG Data Recording and Denoising

We adapted two electrodes to gather raw signals for gaining a fast processing, including F3 and F4 (see Fig. 1), with two reference channels A1 and A2. F3 and F4 are frontal channels. These two channels are highly related to the cognitive workload. As aforementioned, the theta and alpha waves reflect the variation of workload. Therefore, F3 and F4 are selected for recording EEG.

The raw EEG data are mixed with noises that impact the signal analysis and classification. These noises, namely the artifacts, are generated from the outside of the brain, including eye and body movements, and electronic inference. To remove artifacts, independent component analysis (ICA) has been proved as a feasible method, which attempts to decompose the brain signal into independent non-Gaussian signals, determine the noisy signals and reconstruct the brain signals by excluding those artifacts. However, ICA is highly user dependent and requires operating manually by experts to some extent. Therefore, FastICA and other extended ICA algorithms are used more often in many studies. In our context, we leveraged an automatic ICA-based ADJUST algorithm [15]. ADJUST identifies and removes artifact-related components based on the combined use of spatial and temporal features. In this way, we eliminate the confounding elements introduced by the motor activities.

3.4   Transformation and Feature Extraction

To monitor the workload, it requires obtain features related to theta and alpha. Epoc + headset samples at a rate of 128 Hz and has a bandwidth in the range of 0.2–43 Hz, which could be resolved to delta (0.5–4 Hz), theta (4–8 Hz), alpha (8–13 Hz), and beta (13–30 Hz) waves. The Fast Fourier Transforms (FFT) are used to process the cleaned EEG data and transformed it to theta and alpha bands.

Since the linear feature extraction requires less time to calculate, we employ 6 linear features, that is, mean absolute amplitude, mean square, variance, activity, mobility and complexity. The mean absolute amplitude, mean square and variance are statistical features, which are calculated as below:

$$\text{Mean absolute amplitude} = E(x) = \frac{1}{N} \sum_{i=1}^{N} |x_i| \tag{1}$$

$$\text{Mean square} = E(x^2) = \frac{1}{N} \sum_{i=1}^{N} x_i^2, \tag{2}$$

$$\text{Variance} = E\{(x - E(x))^2\}. \tag{3}$$

The latter three features are based on Hjorth parameters. Hjorth parameters [16] was proposed by Bo Hjorth in 1970, indicating the statistical properties used in signal processing. Activity parameter represents the signal power in frequency domain. It is calculated by the Eq. (3) as below:

$$\text{Activity} = var(y(t)). \tag{4}$$

Where $y(t)$ refers to the signal. Mobility is defined as the mean frequency or the proportion of standard deviation of the power spectrum:

$$\text{Mobility} = \sqrt{\frac{var(y'(t))}{var(y(t))}}. \tag{5}$$

Complexity parameter indicates the similarity of the signal to a pure sine wave:

$$\text{Complexity} = \frac{mobility(y'(t))}{mobility(y(t))}. \tag{6}$$

Hjorth parameters require less time and resources to calculate. To sum up, we have 24 features, counting from 6 features for 2 frequency bands and 2 channels.

3.5   Classification

In our study, the sample size is smaller than the feature numbers. Therefore, we employ the Support Vector Machine (SVM) [17] to classify EEG data, based on the statistical learning theory. SVM algorithm has a fast processing ability. As one of the machine learning approaches, it has shown promising empirical results in many practical applications, including text categorization, classification of images, handwritten digit recognition, biological science, etc. The basic idea behind SVM is to find out a maximal margin hyperplane to make the classification. In addition to performing linear classification, SVM could efficiently perform a non-linear classification using the kernel trick. Concerning the kernel function, we employ the linear kernel, since from previous researches, it performs better with EEG data than the polynomial and the Gaussian radial basis function kernel (RBF).

With regards to the classifier in our current prototype, we have two cognitive load level: high level and low level. The high level is related to the video contents requiring more effort to understand. The low level is related to the contents that are easy to understand and master. Therefore, the ground truth labels are gained from the difficulty levels of instruction materials.

4 Experiment and Discussion

We develop our passive BCI system and train it in a lab environment. This system is built based on a laptop, with Windows 10 and 8.00G RAM, a headset of Emotiv Epoc+, and two monitor screens. As shown in Fig. 3, in our experiment, the tasks that subjects perform are watching the clips of online courses videos. Each of the clip are made at about 3 to 4 min. The meta process includes preparing, watching and doing the questionnaire. After the training, the performance and self-report questionnaire is asked to fill to verify the difficulty levels of the video materials. In this training experiment, we build the learning model and training parameters for the prototype.

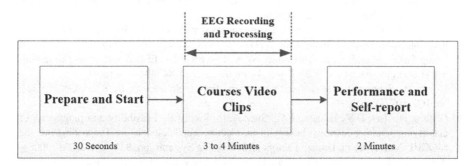

Fig. 3. The process of training.

5 Conclusion and Future Work

This study is motivated due to missing studies on passive BCI system in online courses learning context. In this preliminary work, we design and propose a real-time passive Brain-Computer Interaction (BCI) system to continuously monitor the cognitive workload using EEG-based wireless headset Emotiv Epoc+, which is feasible for working in the online digital environment like Massive Open Online Courses (MOOCs). We choose two electrodes to pick up original EEG signals and decompose the signal to theta and alpha bands. The current prototype is able to record EEG signals and classify levels of cognitive load when students watching online course videos. This prototype is based on two layers, using machine learning approaches for classification.

In our future work, we are going to verify the classifier at first. Then we will seek for more features to increase the accuracy of this BCI system. Finally, it is interesting to know how to distinguish the adjustment of intrinsic cognitive load, extraneous cognitive load and germane cognitive load based on our BCI approach.

Acknowledgements. Authors gratefully acknowledge the National Natural Science Foundation of China (Grant No. 11372167), the Key Science and Technology Innovation Team in Shaanxi Province, China (Grant No. 2014KTC-18), and the 111 Project (Grant No. B16031).

References

1. D'Mello, S., Olney, A., Williams, C., Hays, P.: Gaze tutor: a gaze-reactive intelligent tutoring system. Int. J. Hum Comput Stud. **70**, 377–398 (2012)
2. Andujar, M., Gilbert, J.E.: Let's learn!: enhancing user's engagement levels through passive brain-computer interfaces. In: CHI 2013 Extended Abstracts on Human Factors in Computing Systems, pp. 703–708. ACM (2013)
3. Szafir, D., Mutlu, B.: Pay attention!: designing adaptive agents that monitor and improve user engagement. In: Proceedings of the SIGCHI Conference on Human Factors in Computing Systems, pp. 11–20. ACM (2012)
4. Sweller, J.: Cognitive load during problem solving: effects on learning. Cogn. Sci. **12**, 257–285 (1988)
5. Sweller, J., Van Merrienboer, J.J., Paas, F.G.: Cognitive architecture and instructional design. Educ. Psychol. Rev. **10**, 251–296 (1998)
6. Brunken, R., Plass, J.L., Leutner, D.: Direct measurement of cognitive load in multimedia learning. Educ. Psychol. **38**, 53–61 (2003)
7. Wang, S., Gwizdka, J., Chaovalitwongse, W.A.: Using wireless EEG signals to assess memory workload in the-back task. IEEE Trans. Hum. Mach. Syst. **46**, 424–435 (2016)
8. Honal, M., Schultz, T.: Determine task demand from brain activity. In: BIOSIGNALS (1), pp. 100–107 (2008)
9. Grimes, D., Tan, D.S., Hudson, S.E., Shenoy, P., Rao, R.P.: Feasibility and pragmatics of classifying working memory load with an electroencephalograph. In: Proceedings of the SIGCHI Conference on Human Factors in Computing Systems, pp. 835–844. ACM (2008)
10. Antonenko, P.D., Niederhauser, D.S.: The influence of leads on cognitive load and learning in a hypertext environment. Comput. Hum. Behav. **26**, 140–150 (2010)
11. Heger, D., Putze, F., Schultz, T.: Online workload recognition from EEG data during cognitive tests and human-machine interaction. In: Annual Conference on Artificial Intelligence. pp. 410–417. Springer (2010)
12. Gevins, A., Smith, M.E., Leong, H., McEvoy, L., Whitfield, S., Du, R., Rush, G.: Monitoring working memory load during computer-based tasks with EEG pattern recognition methods. Hum. Factors J. Hum. Factors Ergon. Soc. **40**, 79–91 (1998)
13. Gevins, A., Smith, M.E.: Neurophysiological measures of working memory and individual differences in cognitive ability and cognitive style. Cereb. Cortex **10**, 829–839 (2000)
14. Lei, S., Roetting, M.: Influence of task combination on EEG spectrum modulation for driver workload estimation. Hum. Factors J. Hum. Factors Ergon. Soc. **53**, 168–179 (2011)

15. Mognon, A., Jovicich, J., Bruzzone, L., Buiatti, M.: ADJUST: an automatic EEG artifact detector based on the joint use of spatial and temporal features. Psychophysiology **48**, 229–240 (2011)
16. Hjorth, B.: EEG analysis based on time domain properties. Electroencephalogr. Clin. Neurophysiol. **29**, 306–310 (1970)
17. Vapnik, V.: The Nature of Statistical Learning Theory. Springer, New York (2013)

Learning and Teaching Ecosystems

Lessons Learned from Evaluating an Authoring Tool for Learning Objects

André Luiz de Brandão Damasceno[1]([⊠]), Carlos de Salles Soares Neto[2],
and Simone Diniz Junqueira Barbosa[1]

[1] Pontifical Catholic University of Rio de Janeiro, Rio de Janeiro, RJ, Brazil
{adamasceno,simone}@inf.puc-rio.br
[2] Federal University of Maranhão, São Luís, MA, Brazil
csalles@deinf.ufma.br

Abstract. Teachers and students often adopt technologies that allow new ways of teaching and learning, and multimedia resources such as slideshows, videos and games have been increasingly used in both distance and face-to-face instruction. These multimedia learning environments handle several media resources (e.g., video, image, text). One such environment is the multimedia authoring tool Cacuriá. Cacuriá allows teachers to create multimedia educational content for interactive TV and Web without requiring programming skills. In this paper we present a case study which was conducted to show how learning objects could be created using Cacuriá without requiring the user to previously know programming concepts. Finally, usability tests results show that Cacuriá can be used by teachers with effectiveness and consistency.

Keywords: Usability test · Mental-model · Navigation/search design · Participatory design · Interaction design · Learning objects

1 Introduction

Learning Objects (LOs) are defined as any content used to support the learning process by computer(s) [1,2]. In the last years there was an increase in authoring tools providing teachers with different ways to create content (e.g., slideshows, videos, and games). They can be used in both forms of education: classroom and distance [3–6].

Cacuriá is a multimedia authoring tool that serves that purpose [7]. Cacuriá allows teachers to create multimedia educational content for interactive TV and the Web without requiring programming skills. The tool also enables the teacher to create applications which adapt to students' interactions. Cacuriá is integrated with the iVoD (Interactive Video on Demand) service from RNP, a National Research and Educational Network responsible for promoting the development of networks in Brazil, including the development of innovative applications and services. iVoD was specified to allow the storage and distribution of LOs integrated into the authoring tool. Figure 1 describes the architecture of the iVoD service.

© Springer International Publishing AG 2017
P. Zaphiris and A. Ioannou (Eds.): LCT 2017, Part I, LNCS 10295, pp. 77–89, 2017.
DOI: 10.1007/978-3-319-58509-3_8

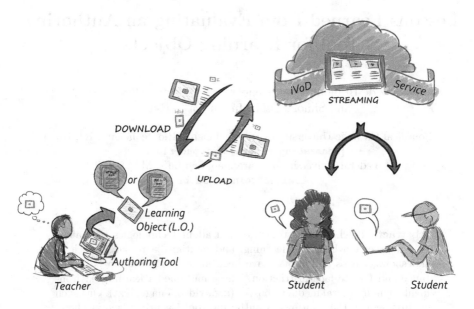

Fig. 1. Service architecture.

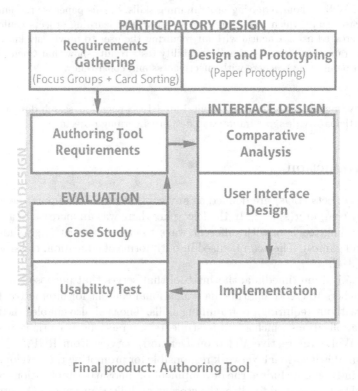

Fig. 2. Research methodology.

First, a teacher creates a LO using Cacuriá and then submits it to the iVoD cloud storage. Then, students can watch and interact with the content created by the teacher with various devices with Internet access, such as tablets, computers, and smartphones. The service is used by 15 universities in different regions of Brazil and nearly 30 LOs have been created between 2015 and 2016.

The methodology used in the development of Cacuriá is presented in Fig. 2. As described elsewhere [7], the Cacuriá's design process integrates Participatory Design [8] and Interaction Design [9] methods. In order to present the Cacuriá's evaluation process, this paper considers that usability is an important factor which influences the quality of a software design. The lack of usability in a software system can lead users to dissatisfaction, low productivity and wasted time. In this paper, we present the results of usability tests performed with users of the tool and the main lessons learned from them. Moreover, we also show a case study which was conducted to demonstrate how learning objects can be created using Cacuriá.

This paper is structured as follows. Section 2 presents some related works. Section 3 describes the evaluation process of a multimedia authoring tool for learning objects, and Sect. 4 presents its results. Finally, Sect. 5 provides some final considerations.

2   Related Works

Usability can be defined as the "effectiveness, efficiency and satisfaction with which specified users achieve specified goals in particular environments" [10]. To ensure a system has high usability, several usability evaluation methods have been proposed by experts and researchers [11], and many works in the literature present usability evaluations of softwares for distinct domains [12–15].

Feizi and Wong performed an empirical study with 32 user interfaces designers and software developers to investigate the usability attributes of effectiveness, efficiency and satisfaction scores for learning Adobe Flash CS4 and Microsoft Expression Blend 4 [12]. Their goal was to compare the impacts of adopting different user interface styles: graphical user interface (GUI) and command-line interface (CLI). The results showed that participants perceived CLI as more difficult to learn and use and, although participants perceived GUI as simpler to learn, the results highlighted the need to provide menu labels and icons that are familiar and easy to find.

Cabada et al. [13] describe a collaborative learning environment called Educa. Educa is composed of five modules: an authoring tool, two repositories (resources and courses), a delivery engine, and a recommendation engine. The authoring tool was implemented to create adaptive learning material. The authors evaluated the authoring tool with 30 participants through a 5-point Likert scale questionnaire. The results showed that most participants "agreed" or "strongly agreed" with respect to the software interfaces' ease to generate an intelligent tutor, learning time for using the tool, time to produce a content and the course organization.

In turn, Marchiori et al. present a system named WEEV (Writing Environment for Educational Video games), whose main goal is to facilitate educational video game development by educators [14]. This authoring tool was tested with 20 software engineering students and 9 educators. The goal of evaluation was to discover problems in the user interaction with the system and to assess the perception of the system by educators. Some users detected problems in the software such as, some saved files were unreadable, some constructs needed to be deleted in order to be modified and help panels provided lots of information of limited relevance. All the students implemented an application using the WEEV around 50 min. On the one hand, the students did not seem to value the usefulness of the software. On the other hand, the educators showed interest in using technologies that would allow them to create their own games. Nevertheless, although the evaluation took around 90 min, the educators did not have time to fully develop the test application. They found usability problems (e.g. the system was complex to use, especially in the creation of new elements). The results point to the need to help the educators to understand the metaphor used in tool and to provide sample games in order for them to understand the purpose of the system.

3 Evaluation Process

This section describes the evaluation process, which consisted of two steps: a case study and a usability test. The first step aimed to evaluate whether it is possible for experts to build interactive applications with Cacuriá. The second one aimed to evaluate the usability of Cacuriá and to investigate whether end users can successfully create an interactive application.

3.1 Case Study

The goal of the case study was to identify a range of applications that can be created using Cacuriá. We therefore analyzed the tool and identified the models of learning objects that could be created with it.

To illustrate the development process of the interactive application, we describe here the process of authoring an application about tourist spots in Rio de Janeiro. This application is called "Roteiro do dia" (Tour of the day) and, as Fig. 3 shows, it is composed of four images and five videos. It starts with an introduction video describing some places in Rio. Then, the video offers the possibility of getting to know more about two locations (Central do Brasil and Copacabana). At the end of whichever video the user may choose, two additional locations are offered (Gafieira Estudantina and Jardim Botânico) for users to obtain more information.

The temporal synchronism with the video happens in the exhibition of the images "Central do Brasil.png", "Copacabana.png", "Gafieira Estudantina.png" and "Jardim Botânico.png", which are shown just in the final seconds of each video. The nonlinear authoring is characterized by offering a choice of place about which the student may want to obtain further information. This choice may appear to users as a kind of customized experience.

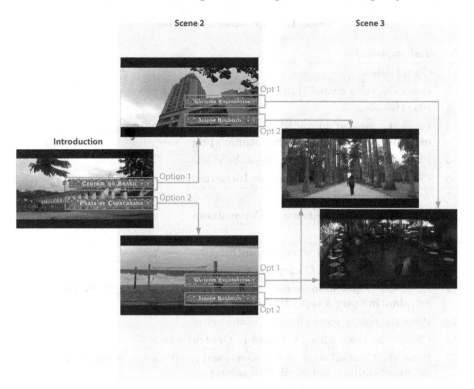

Fig. 3. The "Roteiro do dia" application.

3.2   Usability Test

The evaluation was performed with 44 teachers distributed in sessions of 6 to 10 participants (Fig. 4). They had little or no experience in using authoring tools. The overall goal of the usability test was to evaluate user satisfaction, effectiveness and efficiency of the tool and to investigate whether the prototype supports teachers in the creation of interactive content.

The tests were carried out using computers containing a software for capturing the actions of the participant and the authoring tool for learning objects. A folder in each computer contained a shortcut to access the tool and the media to be used when building the application. Moreover, a 30-step task script for the construction of the application was distributed among the participants (Table 1).

Each session started with a brief introduction about the authoring tool. Then the "Roteiro do dia" application was run. Finally we asked participants to build the application using Cacuriá. After developing the application, each teacher answered an online multiple choice questionnaire, based on version 7.0 of the

Table 1. Script tasks user testing.

No.	Task explanation
1	Open Cacuriá
2	Insert the video named **B2.mp4**
3	Play the scene
4	Pause the scene at 40 seconds and insert images: **menu.png**, **estudantina.png** and **jardimbotanico.png**
5	Place the images on the left side of the video
6	Change the current scene name to **Introduction**
7	Add a new scene
8	Change the new scene name to **Copacabana**
9	Add a new scene
10	Change the new scene name to **Central**
11	Add the video named **C3.mp4** in **Copacabana** scene
12	Pause the **Copacabana** scene at 40 seconds and insert images: **menu.png**, **estudantina.png** and **jardimbotanico.png**
13	Place the images on the left side of the video
14	Change the video named **C2.mp4** in **Central** scene
15	Pause the **Central** scene at 40 seconds and insert images: **menu.png**, **estudantina.png** and **jardimbotanico.png**
16	Place the images on the left side of the video
17	Add a new scene
18	Change the new scene name to **Jardim**
19	Add a new scene
20	Change the new scene name to **Estudantina**
21	Add the video named **E2.mp4** in **Jardim** scene
22	Add the video named **E1.mp4** in **Estudantina** scene
23	Make a link from **Introduction** to the **Central** and **Copacabana** scenes through **central.png** and **copa.png** images
24	Make an automatic link from **Introduction** so that the **Copacabana** scene will play at the end of the source scene
25	Make a link from **Copacabana** to the **Estudantina** and **Jardim** scenes through the **estudantina.png** and **jardimbotanico.png** images
26	Make an automatic link from **Copacabana** so that the **Estudantina** scene will play at the end of the source scene
27	Make a link from **Central** to the **Estudantina** and **Jardim** scenes through the **estudantina.png** and **jardimbotanico.png** images
28	Make an automatic link from **Central** so that the **Estudantina** scene will play in the end of the source scene
29	Export the current project to "HTML"
30	Run the project in a browser

Fig. 4. Tests performed with the tool.

Questionnaire for User-Interaction Satisfaction (QUIS)[1], whose objective is to measure user satisfaction [16]. The questionnaire was adapted so as not to be long and to assess just what was relevant for the tool. It therefore included only 44 of the 126 QUIS questions. Moreover, the original scales were reduced from 9 to 5 points, ranging from 1, representing the user's dislike, to 5, representing the user's satisfaction with the corresponding aspect.

The questionnaire used in the evaluation was divided into 6 sections. The first section was related to the user identification and contains fields to enter the name, occupation, experience as a teacher or tutor, as well as programming skills. Next, the participants should answer questions to assess their overall perception of the tool. The third section aimed to evaluate the tool interface. The fourth section contained questions related to terminology and system information. The fifth section consisted of questions focused on the evaluation of learning to use the tool. The sixth and final section was associated with system capabilities such as speed, response time, correcting typos, etc. At the end of sections 3 to 6, participants could make free-form textual comments about the aspects of the tool addressed in the corresponding section.

---

[1] Available in: http://lap.umd.edu/quis/.

4   Results and Findings

In this section we present the results of case study and the usability test, which show the effectiveness and efficiency of the authoring tool Cacuriá. The participants' feedback raised new requirements and recommendations for refining the tool.

4.1   Case Study

Based on the results obtained during the Participatory, Interface Design and Implementation phases [7], we defined and developed Cacuriá as a tool to support users in generating nonlinear learning objects composed of synchronized media (e.g., video, image and text). The "Roteiro do dia" application was used to illustrate the content model generated by the tool and some other features the tool offered, such as the synchronism between media objects and the insertion of links on the scenes to demonstrate the nonlinearity of content. As the study involved skilled users, there was no need to follow the step-by-step task script provided to users in the usability testing activity.

When Cacuriá is run, the first action to be taken is to click on the video icon to choose the first video for the scene. Then, the video is added in the Library View and its first frame is shown in the Layout View. In addition, the timeline of the Temporal View receives the total duration of the video and the options in the Properties View are enabled.

Next, four scenes are added through the option "add scene" located in the Scene View. Then, the second scene is selected in the same view, in order to add the

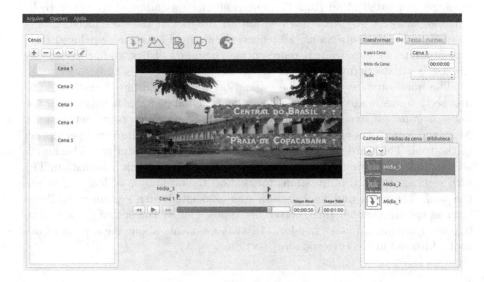

Fig. 5. Cacuriá's interface.

"Central do Brasil.mp4" video. Similarly, the "Copacabana.mp4", "Gafieira Estudantina.mp4" and "Jardim Botânico.mp4" videos are inserted in the third, fourth and fifth scenes, respectively.

Then, back to the first scene to add and position the "Central do Brasil.png" and "Copacabana.png" images on the video. Next, the links from the first scene are created. The images recently added are selected and links to the second and third scene are set in the Properties View, as Fig. 5 illustrates. Similarly, the "Gafieira Estudantina.png" and "Jardim Botânico.png" images are inserted and positioned in both the second and third scenes. Lastly, a link is also configured for each image to trigger the fourth and fifth scenes, respectively.

4.2   Usability Test

The usability test was performed in seven days. Only 6 of the 44 participants failed to perform all the tasks. We noticed a certain degree of difficulty to start the application development: the average learning time was around 10 min. Most participants built the application in less than 40 min, which was the expected time. Although the tool still requires improvements in its efficiency, the results demonstrate that an adequate degree of effectiveness was achieved.

The results are presented through graphs with percentages of agreeing and disagreeing responses to each question. The use of color in the graphs aims to make it easy to identify where there are agreements on the proposed model and what problems were found in the tool. The evaluation analysis also includes the comments provided by the participants at the end of each stage. The results considered satisfactory are those for which the participant choses option 4 or 5 (green color) on the scale. But when the option 1, 2 or 3 (red and gray color) was selected, the result is classified as a problem and considered a feature to be improved.

Figure 6 shows the results of the general impressions that the participants had after using Cacuriá. It can be observed that most users believed Cacuriá to be a useful tool (Q1). Furthermore, it was though as motivating for the construction of learning objects through the tool (Q2). More than half of participants assessed the tool features as sufficient (Q4) and both its use (Q3) and the options offered to make the activities (Q5) were deemed satisfactory. Based on these data, we notice overall positive general impressions about the tool.

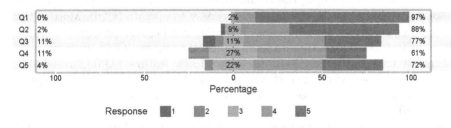

Fig. 6. General impressions about the tool. (Color figure online)

According to Fig. 7, over half of the users rated the letters used in the tool interface as easy to identify (Q6), with adequate font sharpness (Q7) and good readability (Q8). In addition, most of them thought it was easy (Q10) to find the media properties and (Q9) to identify the corresponding icons to add video, image, text, shapes, as well as to publish a learning object. Regarding system colors (Q11), although they were considered appropriate in general, some users found them a little confusing. Meanwhile, most participants reported as adequate the arrangement of information (Q12) and the progression of work-related tasks (Q13).

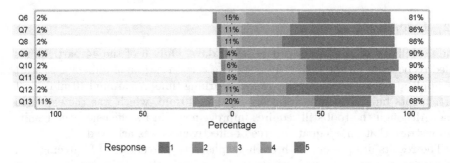

Fig. 7. Overall results about the user interface. (Color figure online)

The results regarding the terminology and system information are shown in Fig. 8. Most of the participants perceived as consistent the system terminology (Q14), the messages displayed on the user interface (Q19), and the terms related to the task (Q15) and the computer (Q16). They also agreed that performing an operation in Cacuriá leads to a predictable results (Q22). Moreover, the computer terms used in the tool (Q17) and displayed on the system interface (Q18) were evaluated as appropriately and precise. However, the feedback messages issued by the tool can be improved. The scores about the instructions for correcting errors (Q20) and about whether the system keeps the user informed about what it is doing (Q21) were satisfactory. Moreover, issues regarding the error messages (Q23), the phrasing of error messages (Q25) and if error messages clarify the problem (Q24) were assessed as unsatisfactory.

As can be seen in Fig. 9, the results obtained in the evaluation of learning demonstrate that Cacuriá was perceived as easy to operate (Q26). Most of the participants positively assessed issues regarding getting started (Q27), learning advanced features (Q28), time to learn to use the system (Q29) exploration of features by trial and error (Q30), discovery of new features (Q31), straightforwardness of tasks performance (Q32), number of steps per task (Q33), logical sequence of steps to complete a task (Q34), and feedback on the completion of steps (Q35).

Some participants made comments regarding the ease, simplicity, and speed in learning to use the tool. A participant reported that: "for people like me who

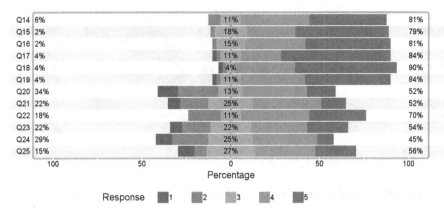

Fig. 8. Overall results about the terminology and system information. (Color figure online)

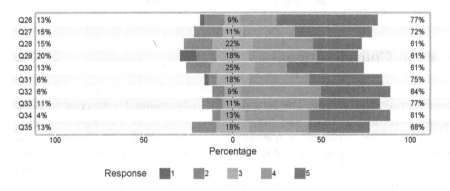

Fig. 9. Overall results about the learning. (Color figure online)

have worked with some video editor or even Microsoft PowerPoint, learning is not time-consuming because the symbols follow the same standard and were well applied in Cacuriá". Despite the satisfactory results, participants also gave interesting suggestions for the user to learn to operate Cacuriá more efficiently. The main suggestions were related to the use of a manual and videos embedded in the tool to demonstrate system features.

Figure 10 shows the evaluation results of system capabilities. Satisfactory results were obtained on issues related to system speed (Q36), response time for most operations (Q37), rate at which information is displayed (Q38), correcting typos (Q40), whether the ease of operation depends on the user's level of experience (Q42), and whether the user could accomplish tasks knowing only a few commands (Q43). Most users considered it easy to correct their mistakes (Q39) and to use shortcuts to perform actions (Q44). Nevertheless, the support to undo operations (Q41) was classified as inadequate. Despite satisfactory results in Q39 and Q44, they were also considered as features to be improved due to the

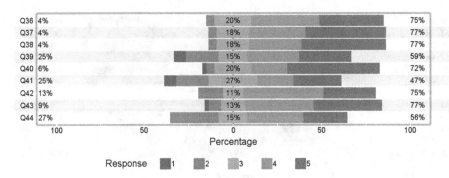

Fig. 10. Overall results about system capabilities. (Color figure online)

number of participants' suggestions. In addition, many participants remarked that the tool needs to offer users an option to undo, triggered by the "Ctrl + Z" key combination, as well as more shortcuts to perform functions.

5   Final Considerations

The evaluation of the current version of Cacuriá achieved satisfactory results regarding its effectiveness. The tool proved to be useful for teacher to build classes for distance learning and supplementary content for classroom teaching. The main positive results of the usability tests were related to the learnability of the tool user interface in terms of its "intuitiveness" and reduced learning time. However, some improvements would be welcome, related both to the colors used in the user interface and the feedback messages issued by the tool.

We also evaluated the use of Cacuriá in a rural region in a poor state of Brazil. The challenge was to allow teachers in those areas to create their own educational contents based on their local reality. This experience had interesting preliminary results. Teachers used the tool to create different classes. In a geometry class, teachers showed how to measure the area of polygons using the city's main square. In a geography class, teachers talked about the pollution of the local river. Despite the regional limitations and the lack of experience by the teachers, the students described that they feel more engaged with interactive and multimedia contents than with conventional classes.

Based on the development experience of Cacuriá, it seems that the effectiveness was achieved in the first cycle, due to the inclusion of the stakeholders in the tool design process. However, more cycles are necessary to improve the tool's efficiency. It seems that the proposed methodology can help the general usability of multimedia tools.

Acknowledgments. The work presented in this paper was funded by RNP, a National Research and Educational Network from Brazil, and was developed in context of RNP Working Groups programme, in projects was run during the cycles 2012/2013, 2013/2014 and 2015. The authors would like to thank the LAWS laboratory team who contributed to this work, in special Antonio Busson, Mauricio Pessoa, Rosendy Galabo and Thacyla Sousa. The authors also thank CAPES, FAPEMA, and CNPq for their support.

References

1. IEEE Learning Technology Standards Committee (LTSC): Draft standard for learning object metadata. IEEE Standard 1484.12.1 (2012)
2. Wiley, D.A.: Connecting learning objects to instructional design theory: a definition, a metaphor, and a taxonomy. In: Wiley, D.A. (ed.) The Instructional Use of Learning Objects (2000). http://reusability.org/read/chapters/wiley.doc
3. CourseLab. http://www.courselab.com
4. Sousa Neto, F., Bezerra, E., Dias, D.: ITV-Learning: a prototype for construction of learning objects for interactive digital television. In: Proceedings of International Conference of the future of Education, pp. 486–490 (2012)
5. eXe Learning. http://www.exelearning.org
6. HotPotatoes. http://hotpot.uvic.ca
7. Damasceno, A.L.B., Soares Neto, C.S., Barbosa, S.D.J.: Integrating participatory and interaction design of an authoring tool for learning objects involving a multidisciplinary team. In: Proceedings of the International Conference on Human-Computer Interaction HCII 2017 (2017)
8. Simonsen, J., Robertson, T.: Routledge International Handbook of Participatory Design. Routledge, Abingdon (2012)
9. IXDA. http://www.ixda.org/
10. ISO 9241:1992, Ergonomic requirements for office work with visual display terminals (VDTs)
11. Madan, A., Dubey, S.K.: Usability evaluation methods: a literature review. Int. J. Eng. Sci. Technol. 4(2), 590–599 (2012)
12. Feizi, A., Wong, C.Y.: Usability of user interface styles for learning a graphical software application. In: 2012 International Conference on Computer & Information Sciences, pp. 1089–1094. IEEE Press, New York (2012)
13. Cabada, R.Z., Estrada, M., Garcia, C.A.R.: EDUCA: a web 2.0 authoring tool for developing adaptive and intelligent tutoring systems using a Kohonen network. In: Expert Systems with Applications, vol. 38, pp. 9522–9529 (2011)
14. Marchiori, E.J., Torrente, J., Blanco, A., Moreno-Ger, P., Sancho, P., Fernández-Manjón, B.: A narrative metaphor to facilitate educational game authoring. Comput. Educ. 58, 590–599 (2012)
15. Urquiza-Fuentes, J., Velázquez-Iturbide, J.A.: A survey of successful evaluations of program visualization and algorithm animation systems. ACM Trans. Comput. Educ. 9(2), 1–21 (2009)
16. Harper, B., Slaughter, L., Norman, K.: Questionnaire administration via the WWW: a validation and reliability study for a user satisfaction questionnaire. In: Proceedings of World Conference on the WWW, Internet and Intranet. Association for the Advancement of Computing in Education, Charlottesville (1997)

ECoLab: A Cooperative System to Improve Training Processes

Ángel Fidalgo-Blanco[1(✉)], María Luisa Sein-Echaluce[2],
and Francisco J. García-Peñalvo[3]

[1] LITI Laboratory, Technical University of Madrid, Madrid, Spain
angel.fidalgo@upm.es
[2] GIDTIC Research Group, University of Zaragoza, Zaragoza, Spain
mlsein@unizar.es
[3] GRIAL Research Group, University of Salamanca, Salamanca, Spain
fgarcia@usal.es

Abstract. The goal of the qualitative research is to achieve information regarding the attitudes and opinions of a group of individuals with similar habits, needs and interests. The selection of the participants is a key element in the qualitative research. This paper presents a new model, ECoLab (Experiencial Cooperative Laboratory), of qualitative research that integrates the following methods: Focus Group, Delphi, After Action Review, LivingLab and MediaLab. This new model is designed to improve educational processes and works with the information from the tacit knowledge of the persons, specifically with their experience. For this reason, any person who participates must have participated (or be participating) in the process on which it is desired to investigate and improve. Thus, the group of people participating in ECoLab should be heterogeneous in terms of their role, experience and commitment to the subject matter of the study. ECoLab consists of different groups of people working cooperatively. The criterion of configuration of each group is based on the homogeneity of the role that they play or have played in the action to investigate. Therefore, the heterogeneity of the participants is integrated with the homogeneity in their grouping. This paper presents the ECoLab model (with two variants, iterative ECoLab and ECoLab lego) and a case study where the most urgent improvements of the Spanish University Education System are investigated in a qualitative way.

Keywords: Qualitative research · Cooperative learning · Experiential learning · ECoLab

1 Introduction

The goal of the quality research is to achieve information regarding the attitudes and opinions of a group of individuals with similar habits, needs and interests [1]. The most commonly used methods are Focus Group and Delphi. In both cases, we work with a small group of people. The Focus Group method seeks a set of homogeneous and representative users about the product or aspect to investigate [2], while the Delphi method assembles previously identified experts, since the random selection of participants is not

© Springer International Publishing AG 2017
P. Zaphiris and A. Ioannou (Eds.): LCT 2017, Part I, LNCS 10295, pp. 90–99, 2017.
DOI: 10.1007/978-3-319-58509-3_9

valid in this case [3]. The selection of the participants is a key element in the qualitative research, thus the criteria they should meet must be specified and they will be different according to the topic to be investigated.

Also, there exist other more recent qualitative research methods that maintain a common selection criterion of participants, regardless of the subject of the investigation. The After Action Review (AAR) method, from US Army, is devoted to investigate how to improve military actions. This method imposes a common condition on the components of the group, having participated in the action. In this way information is obtained from the tacit knowledge of the people about the subject to investigate. The AAR method is usually located in the discipline of knowledge management and is widely used in the industrial sector.

The LivingLab is other method that joins the qualitative research with the development of a project [4, 5]. It integrates the lab idea, as an innovative and creative space with resources enough to develop a project and it is open for people to participate independently of the knowledge they have about the topic of the project to develop. In this case, even citizens with no knowledge of the project could participate, but who may be affected by it. The most commonly used method is the spaces called MediaLab used by municipal administrations as an element for citizens to participate in municipal projects.

In this paper, we present a new original model of qualitative research that integrates traditional methods such as the FocusGroup or Delphi, methods based on knowledge management (such as AAR method) and the LivingLab model. The result is a new structure of group organization, which allows to refine the degree of abstraction of the research as well as its application, both in general and specific contexts.

The rest of the paper is organized as follows: Sect. 2 is devoted to present the ECoLab model with a double perspective, the methodological one and the process one. Section 3 describes a case study to understand better the application of the proposed model. Finally, Sect. 4 concludes the paper.

2   ECoLab Model

The proposed qualitative research model is called ECoLab (Experiential Cooperative Laboratory) and has been designed to improve educational processes. ECoLab works with the information from the tacit knowledge of the persons, specifically with their experience, based on the criteria of the AAR method, where the only condition is to have participated in the action, and therefore having experience in it. For this reason, any person who participates must have participated (or be participating) in the process in which it is desired to investigate and improve. The selection criterion is common and no matter the degree of experience (beginners can participate along with experts). Thus, the group of people participating in ECoLab should be heterogeneous in terms of their role, experience and commitment to the subject matter of the study.

Also, ECoLab is organized in a physical space where the different groups are located. There exist a series of multimedia devices for each group and for the people who direct the activity. In this sense, it is based on the structure of the Medialab, where a suitable context is created to produce knowledge. All the media are interconnected. In the research process, the work done by each group in a private way is alternated with common debates among all the groups and the people who direct the activity.

The description of the model is made on the basis of two visions: the *methodological model* and the *continuous refinement model*.

2.1 Methodological Model

One of the most important differences with respect to other qualitative research methods is that ECoLab consists of different groups of people working cooperatively. The configuration criterion for each group is based on the homogeneity of role that they are playing or have played in the action to investigate. Therefore, ECoLab integrates the heterogeneity of the participants with the homogeneity in their grouping.

Figure 1 shows a distribution of participants, which as a whole is heterogeneous, but the clusters per work table correspond to homogeneous profiles, similar of a Focus Group organization.

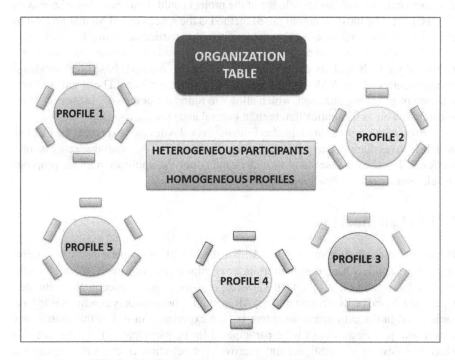

Fig. 1. Distribution of participants in an ECoLab session

The ECoLab process is based on the formulation of a set of common questions to all participants. Each table debates to obtain an agreed response by the components of the table. After a time, each table presents its conclusions, which are commented by all the session participants in an open debate. Parallel to the exhibition and discussion, people assigned to the coordination identify convergences and divergences with respect to each contribution.

Now, we are going to describe the mission and structure of each of the main components: the organizational table and the homogeneous profile tables.

The organizational table has the mission of managing the ECoLab knowledge creation process, those expressed in Fig. 2 (points 1 to 4). There must be two people at least, due to the tasks corresponding to item 3 is done parallel to point 4.

1. Formulating the common questions, including the decision about the available time to debate and reach the consensual conclusions in the tables.
2. Moderating the presentation of conclusions of each table and the debate associated with each topic.
3. Identifying convergences and divergences for each answer to the different questions.
4. Producing a map of knowledge that reflects the main points of what happened or using a repository to classify the knowledge generated by participants and provide a personalized search [6].

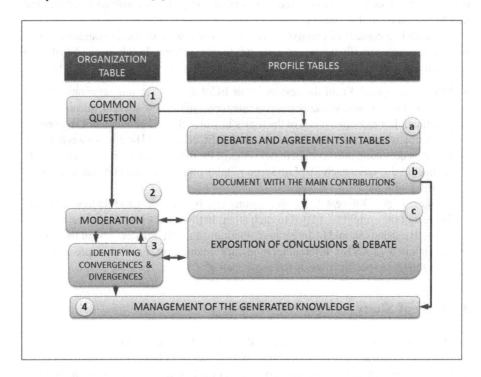

Fig. 2. Cooperative tables model

The homogeneous profile tables should be composed by a limited number of people, between 4 and 6. All people participate in the internal debate and agree together the information to be displayed in the room (Fig. 2-a). But in addition to the participant role, there must be three more roles: moderator, secretary and spokesperson. The same person can assume several roles. The moderator's mission is to agree on a common vision in the time available for discussion; the secretary must write the common vision into a minutes document (Fig. 2-b); and the spokesperson is the person who exposes the conclusions (Fig. 2-c) and participates in the debate in response to any clarification requested by any member of the rest of the profile tables or the organization table itself.

2.2 Continuous Refinement Model

ECoLab is designed to work with both generic aspects, for example, how to improve Education; and with very specific concepts, for example, how to increase students' participation in a specific subject.

The affinity degree among the participants who share the same profile is the key element for a successful instance of the model; for example, if the objective is to study how to improve Education, in the faculty profile table, it will be enough the participants belong to this professional body, regardless of their academic level or the subject matter. However, if the objective is oriented to a specific subject, the involved teaching staff should be related to that subject.

ECoLab is a context of creative force; this means, we can obtain conclusions that may be not-foreseen, divergent and even imply new actions. In this sense, ECoLab is designed to integrate with other ECoLab sessions. There are two types of integration:

- *ECoLab in spiral.* From the results of an ECoLab session, new sessions may be organized to continue working on the same topic. In the new session, questions may be refined. For example, if one of the topics in which there is convergence to improve Education is about student motivation, another ECoLab could be done to work deeper in that issue, taking into account that profiles of the different tables could significantly change. In this case, each ECoLab spiral obtains more precision and concreteness in the results [7, 8].
- *ECoLab Lego.* Different ECoLab sessions can be considered to address different issues, but they might be related to each other. In this case, the results of the different ECoLab sessions should be integrated, obtaining a much broader view of the subject to be studied, as well as different relationships. In this case, an ECoLab process starts from the most specific towards the most abstract.

3   Case of Study

ECoLab has been defined in the scope of the ideas lab of the International Conference on Learning, Innovation and Competitiveness [9, 10]. This laboratory tries to innovate in the improvement and innovation processes in the learning scope and to apply them in the biennial call of the International Conference.

The objective of ECoLab session we are going to use as case study is to obtain an overview of the impact that an educational innovation [11] should have on the university context and the most immediate actions to improve education. In order to achieve this, we wanted to give social value to the action by reconciling interests and committed people to improve Education.

The experience was made at the Technical University of Madrid during the month of June 2016 and for the session, all the tables (profiles and the organization ones) used a computer with wi-fi connection.

3.1 Description

As shown in Fig. 3, four tables were created with the following profiles:

- *University student.* The composition had different student profiles (masters, first courses, belonging to associations, etc.).
- *University Teachers.* The common thread is that all the participants had experience in educational innovation.
- *Retired University Faculty.* Belonging to retired associations of the Technical University of Madrid (2 people) and people who were pioneers in educational innovation in Spain.
- *Academic managers.* With political and managerial responsibilities in the government of universities.

Fig. 3. Tables with different profiles

Figure 4 shows the different roles of the coordination table. One member of the organization moderates the interventions of each table ("general moderator") during the sharing and another member realizes, in real time, a common vision of what happens in the room.

Fig. 4. Coordination table

A total of four questions were given to the profile tables' members, which were delivered a few days in advance:

- Q1 - In what aspects of teaching should the educational innovation impact?
- Q2 - What changes should be most urgently made to improve learning?
- Q3 - What barriers and drivers have the application of educational innovation?
- Q4 - Do you know any examples of educational innovation that improve the learning process? Identify some indicators that define this good practice.

The mission of the organizing table, in terms of the sharing, was to elaborate:

- Common aspects.
- Differences.
- Contradictions.
- Reconciliation of interests.

The duration of the session was 4 h, one hour per question (40 min for the internal debate and 20 min for the presentation of the conclusions).

3.2 Case of Study Results

Each table provided a report with the name and profile of its members, and the main conclusions associated with each of the questions. This information was made public to all the participants of the different tables.

Also, a concept map was generated where the contributions of the different tables were organized. There was a coincidence in the type of contribution in each table. Thus, all the tables gave information about *general aspects of education* and about *specific aspects of the students*. For this reason, all interventions were classified under these two categories.

Figure 5 shows the concept map for question Q1, obtained from the contributions of the faculty table.

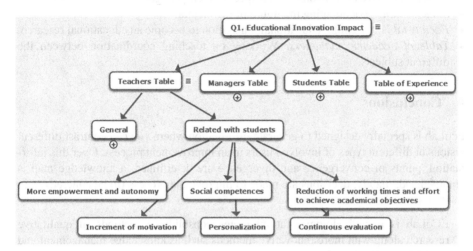

Fig. 5. Faculty table Q1 answers. Conceptual map after an ECoLab

The **common aspects** are obtained from the analysis of the nodes. For example, one of the aspects, with greater convergence among the tables, was the *motivation of the students*. Despite this convergence, each table made contributions that are complementary, for this same indicator "motivation" each table approached the following way:

- *Table of the experience:* Types of motivation and reasons why students are not motivated.
- *Students table:* Direct relationship between the lack of motivation and the active participation of the students.
- *Faculty table:* The need to increase motivation is related to students' willingness to learn.
- *Table of academic managers:* Motivation should be focused on how students can acquire various competences such as self-learning and decision making.

As it can be observed, although there is a coincidence in one of the aspects where educational innovation should impact, each table brings a joint vision. In this case, the students relate it to specific aspects of their learning; the table of experience based its opinion on the causes and methodological aspects; the faculty table thinks emotional issues are the main cause; and the table of academic managers relates the conclusions with the achievement of certain competencies. All the contributed aspects are complementary and with the them is possible elaborating concrete actions taking into account the different approaches.

Also, there are **different aspects** for each table and, as a result of the same question Q1, each table had different perspectives:

- *Table of the experience:* Identifying in what the students have improved and in which the teachers have been wrong with respect to their pedagogy.
- *Students table:* Encouraging the figure of the mentor.
- *Faculty table:* Orienting educational innovation to become an educational research.
- *Table of academic managers:* Working on teaching coordination between the different subjects.

4   Conclusions

EcoLab is specially designed to generate information where you can contrast different visions of different types of involved users in an improvement process. Over this information, points of convergence and divergence are determined, a knowledge map is obtained and, mainly, decisions are made to improve the process (to be concretized in a set of actions).

- ECoLab is a methodology that integrates consolidated methods in qualitative research along with more innovative methods such as knowledge management and open laboratories to citizens.
- It allows grading the accuracy of the information according to the characteristics of the analysed problem. It permits iterations and associations with other EcoLab sessions, to give this way a greater scope to the solution.
- It is able to integrate different visions. This increases the scope of the solution, also it allows establishing relational networks among the different concepts.

One of the main conclusions is that this method generates a great amount of information for each question; that information is both convergent and divergent. Therefore, a process of management and organization of the same is required due to it is difficult to deal with large volumes of organizational data.

The people who make up the tables are highly motivated to present their points of view, even though these are done internally at each table, they have to bring their personal vision during the debate too. This causes the debates lengthen considerably and the information provided in a personal way does not coincide with the consensus opinion of the bureau. To manage this circumstance, moderators with experience are needed in order to respect the stablished timing.

It has been observed that an hour for each question is a short time to leave, since the expositions and debate require more than 20 min.

The obtained information is very valuable, it allows the decision-making to propose concrete actions and also this information includes different visions, often complementary.

As future work, ECoLab will be exported to other fields different than Education, because of the model can be adapted to any area of knowledge. Also, it will be important to improve issues related to the organizational table, such as new tasks (for example, agreeing on a pooling of the three most convergent and divergent aspects).

The experience will be applied in the International Congress CINAIC, establishing this way a new form of interaction between the participants of the conference and generating information with different visions for all attendees. We will work with a virtual model of ECoLab, using social networks where the conditions of participation and organization can be changed.

References

1. Barrios, E., Costell, E.: Review: use of methods of research into consumers opinions and attitudes in food research. Food Sci. Technol. Int. **10**(6), 359–371 (2004)
2. Langford, J., McDonagh, D.: Focus Group: Supporting Effective Product Development. CRC Press, New York (2003)
3. Ludwig, B.: Predicting the future: have you considered using the Delphi methodology? J. Ext. **35**(5), 1–4 (1997)
4. Yañez-Figueroa, J.A., Ramírez-Montoya, M.S., García-Peñalvo, F.J.: Systematic mapping of the literature: social innovation laboratories for the collaborative construction of knowledge from the perspective of open innovation. In: García-Peñalvo, F.J. (ed.) Proceedings of the Fourth International Conference on Technological Ecosystems for Enhancing Multiculturality (TEEM 2016), Salamanca, Spain, pp. 795–803. ACM, New York, 2–4 November 2016
5. Yañez-Figueroa, J.A., Ramírez-Montoya, M.S., García-Peñalvo, F.J.: Open innovation laboratories for social modeling sustainable society sensitive to social needs. In: García-Peñalvo, F.J. (ed.) Proceedings of the Fourth International Conference on Technological Ecosystems for Enhancing Multiculturality (TEEM 2016), Salamanca, Spain, pp. 1133–1138. ACM, New York, 2–4 November 2016
6. Sein-Echaluce, M.L., Fidalgo-Blanco, A., García-Peñalvo, F.J.: Students' knowledge sharing to improve learning in academic engineering courses. Int J. Eng. Educ. **32**(2B), 1024–1035 (2016)
7. Fidalgo-Blanco, Á., Sein-Echaluce, M.L., García-Peñalvo, F.J.: Knowledge spirals in higher education teaching innovation. Int. J. Knowl. Manag. **10**, 16–37 (2014)
8. Fidalgo-Blanco, Á., Sein-Echaluce, M.L., García-Peñalvo, F.J.: Epistemological and ontological spirals: from individual experience in educational innovation to the organisational knowledge in the university sector. Prog. Electron. Libr. Inf. Syst **49**, 266–288 (2015)
9. Fidalgo Blanco, Á., Sein-Echaluce Lacleta, M.L., García-Peñalvo, F.J.: La Sociedad del Aprendizaje. Actas del III Congreso Internacional sobre Aprendizaje, Innovación y Competitividad, CINAIC 2015, Madrid, España. Fundación General de la Universidad Politécnica de Madrid, Madrid, 14–16 de Octubre de 2015
10. CINAIC: Congreso Internacional de Aprendizaje, Innovación y Competitividad (2017). http://cinaic.com. Accessed 20 Feb 2017
11. García-Peñalvo, F.J.: Mapa de tendencias en Innovación Educativa. Educ. Knowl. Soc. (EKS) **16**, 6–23 (2015)

A Metamodel Proposal for Developing Learning Ecosystems

Alicia García-Holgado[✉] and Francisco José García-Peñalvo

GRIAL Research Group, Computer Sciences Department,
Research Institute for Educational Sciences, University of Salamanca, Salamanca, Spain
{aliciagh,fgarcia}@usal.es

Abstract. The definition and development of learning ecosystems is a complex process with a wide range of requirements. Although two different institutions or companies share the same problems and goals regarding their learning and training processes, the learning ecosystems to support them are different. The components of the ecosystem, including the human factor as a key element, and the relationships between them, change over time. In other words, learning ecosystems evolve as natural ecosystems; there are many factors, both internal and external, that influence an entity. The authors have defined and developed different learning ecosystems. Moreover, they have transferred the same learning ecosystem, specifically a learning ecosystem for knowledge management in a PhD Program, to different domains. These experiences have provided the required information to define the ecosystems metamodel following the Model Driven Architecture proposed by the Object Management Group. The aim of this metamodel is define a Domain Specification Language to develop learning ecosystems.

Keywords: Learning ecosystems · Metamodel · MOF · Model-Driven Architecture · Information systems

1 Introduction

The technological ecosystems are the evolution of the traditional information systems. They provide support to information and knowledge management in heterogeneous environments [1, 2]. The learning ecosystems are a type of technological ecosystems focus on learning management processes.

The metaphor of technological ecosystem transfers the main properties of biological or natural ecosystems to the technological area. The organisms of the natural ecosystems are the users and the software components from a technological point of view; the relationships among the organisms are the information flows between the components; and the physical environment are the mechanism to stablish and support such flows [3]. This relationship between technology and nature appears in many authors that provide their own definitions of technological ecosystems, also called Software ECOsystems (SECO) [4–9].

Technological ecosystems should connect and relate the different tools and services that arise and serve for the knowledge management, building technological ecosystems,

© Springer International Publishing AG 2017
P. Zaphiris and A. Ioannou (Eds.): LCT 2017, Part I, LNCS 10295, pp. 100–109, 2017.
DOI: 10.1007/978-3-319-58509-3_10

increasingly complex internally, from the semantic interoperability of its components to transparently provide more functionality and simplicity to its users [10].

One of the main problems to define and develop technological ecosystems, particularly learning ecosystems, is the need to adapt them to the natural evolution of the companies and institutions. A technological ecosystem should adapt to different contexts or domains, i.e. it should be transferable between different domains.

Currently, the development of a learning ecosystem is influenced by many factors, both internal and external. Although the main goals are the same, the software components and information flows can change even in the same entity. Each new ecosystem or the transfer of an existing one involves carrying out a large number of ad-hoc developments.

Within the Research Group in InterAction and eLearning (GRIAL) of the University of Salamanca, the authors have participated in the development of several learning ecosystems in different contexts to solve real problems [11–14]. Moreover, they have transferred the same learning ecosystem, specifically a learning ecosystem for knowledge management in a PhD Program [15], to different domains.

To improve the definition and development of learning ecosystems, it is needed to provide a platform-independent solution. The main objective of this paper is to define a metamodel for developing learning ecosystems following the Model-Driven Architecture (MDA) proposed by the Object Management Group (OMG).

The paper has the following structure: Sect. 2 describes the methodology used to formalize the metamodel proposal. Section 3 sets the high-level requirements for the learning ecosystems development. Section 4 describes the metamodel as a M2-level model in OMG four-layer metamodel architecture. In Sect. 5 a real learning ecosystem is modelled using the Ecosystems Metamodel. Finally, Sect. 6 summarizes the main conclusions from this study.

2   Methodology

Model-Driven Architecture provides a framework for software development that uses models to describe the system to be built [16]. It allows to separate the data and operations specification of the system from the details of the platform or platforms on which it will be built. MDA is the proposal of the Object Management Group to apply Model Driven Development (MDD) using the OMG standards for visualizing, storing, and exchanging software designs and models [17]: Meta Object Facility (MOF), Unified Modeling Language (UML), XML Metadata Interchange (XMI) and Query/View/Transformation (QVT).

In this work, the MDA is used as guidelines to define learning ecosystems using high-level conceptual models, platform-independent models (PIM). These models can later be translated to concrete executable specifications or code using standard-mappings. This is performed according the OMG four-layer metamodel architecture. In this architecture, a model at one layer is used to specify models in the layer below [18]. The four layers are the meta-metamodel layer (M3), the metamodel layer (M2), the user model layer (M1) and the user object layer (M0).

The Ecosystems Metamodel is an instantiation of the meta-metamodel layer using MOF language, the abstract language used to describe MOF metamodel.

3   High-Level Requirements

The main problems associated with the definition and development of learning ecosystems have been identified in a previous work through a comparative analysis of the Strengths, Weaknesses, Opportunities and Threats (SWOT) of several real case studies developed in different contexts [19]. Based on this analysis, the identified problems were modelled with Business Process Model and Notation (BPMN) to provide a high abstraction level of the main problems in learning ecosystems and define an architectural pattern to resolve them during the definition phase [20].

Learning ecosystems modeling involves the proposed architectural pattern, a pattern based on the Layers pattern defined by Buschmann [21] with a top-down scheme composed of four layers. Modelling of learning ecosystems must be supported by a formal Ecosystems Metamodel. This metamodel is not focus on capturing the requirements related to the software or human components of the ecosystem. The components are black boxes; the Ecosystems Metamodel does not enable capture of the description of a specific component because of learning ecosystems are based on connect or adapt existing components. The metamodel should enable capture of a small set of modeling elements to define the relationships among components.

The high-level requirements for ecosystems metamodel are the following:

- The metamodel shall enable capture of the high-level description of the learning ecosystem components.
- The metamodel shall enable capture of the human factor as part of the learning ecosystem.
- The metamodel shall enable capture of the information flows between the learning ecosystem components.
- The metamodel shall enable capture of the configurations of the software components.

4   Ecosystems Metamodel

In this section, the formal semantics of the Ecosystems Metamodel is described. The metamodel is a M2-level model in the four-layer metamodel architecture. The Ecosystems Metamodel is an instance of the MOF meta-metamodel (M3-level model) (Fig. 1).

The Ecosystems Metamodel defines an ecosystem following the architectural pattern proposed in a previous work [20]. The pattern is composed by four layers – presentation, services, static data management and infrastructure – and two input streams which introduce the human factor as a key element. Also, the pattern provides a set of software components that should be part of a learning ecosystem to resolve some problems of this kind of technological solutions. The layers and the components proposed are reflected in the metamodel.

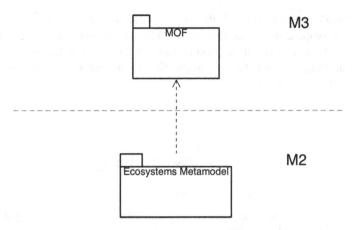

Fig. 1. Model layers. The meta-metamodel layer, M3, and the metamodel layer, M2.

An ecosystem is made up of a collection of two type of components, software tools and people. Both components are abstract classes that inherit from a root class named *Component*. The software tools are organized in a hierarchical structure that provides three layers of the pattern: the service layer through *Tool* class; the static data management layer with the *DataRepository* class; and the infrastructure layer through a class with the same name. The authors have decided that the presentation layer is not part of the metamodel due to the interfaces of the software components are closely related to the technology used in each component.

Moreover, the ecosystem can be composed by software tools that contains others ones, this is modeled with a recursive association in *SoftwareTool* class.

The set of software components are part of the hierarchy describe above. *MailServer*, *Monitorization* and *UserManagement* inherit from *Infrastructure* class. Moreover, other child classes can be defined from *Infrastructure*.

Regarding the tools in the service layer, these are modeled as child classes of the *Tool* class, *InternalTool* and *ExternalTool*.

The human factor is modeled through *Management*, *Methodology* and *User* classes. *User* performs management and establishes one or more methodologies. Moreover, the *Management* is composed by zero or more objectives modeled by the *Objective* class.

These objectives are the key element to define the information flows. An *InformationFlow* is an abstract root class that establishes a relationship between two *SoftwareTool* instances. The information flows are based on services. This requirement is modeled through a leaf class, *Service*. The four classes related to the services are a very simplified version of the service capability view of the services metamodel proposed by Jegadeesan and Balasubramaniam [22]. *ServiceDescription* has a semantic description of the service and also includes the endpoint of the service. *ServiceInterface* represents the underlying capabilities brought to bear by a service. *ServiceOperation* represents an underlying capability and allows modeling event-driven scenarios using the *isNotification* and *isListener* attributes.

Finally, the *Property* class provide the semantic to model the configuration provided by some software components and used by another. This part of the metamodel complements the information flows to establish different relationship levels among the components.

The metamodel proposed in the Fig. 2 is completed with a set of constraints defined with Object Constraint Language (OCL).

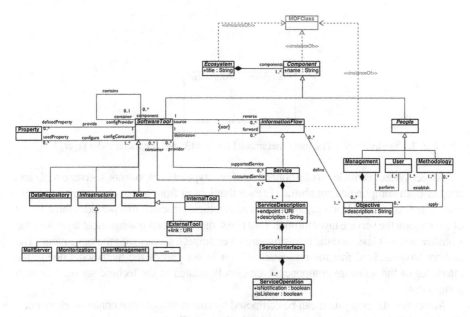

Fig. 2. Ecosystems metamodel

An ecosystem must have one mail server, one monitorization system, one user management system, and at least one internal tool, one management input stream, one methodology input stream and one user:

```
context Ecosystem inv:
self.components -> select(c |
  c.oclIsTypeOf(MailServer)) -> size() = 1 and
self.components -> select(c |
  c.oclIsTypeOf(Monitorization)) -> size() = 1 and
self.components -> select(c |
  c.oclIsTypeOf(UserManagement)) -> size() = 1 and
self.components -> select(c |
  c.oclIsTypeOf(InternalTool)) -> notEmpty and
self.components -> select(c |
  c.oclIsTypeOf(Management)) -> notEmpty and
self.components -> select(c |
  c.oclIsTypeOf(Methodology)) -> notEmpty and
self.components -> select(c |
  c.oclIsTypeOf(User)) -> notEmpty
```

The value of the endpoint attribute defined in the service descriptions should be unique in the whole ecosystem:

```
context ServiceDescription inv:
ServiceDescription.allInstances -> forAll (p1,p2 |
   p1 < > p2 implies p1.endpoint < > p2.endpoint)
```

A software tool cannot consume a service provided by itself, that is to say, the information flows always involve two different software tools:

```
context SoftwareTool inv:
self < > self.consumedService.provider
```

The mail server must provide at least one property:

```
context MailServer inv:
self.definedProperty -> notEmpty
```

5   Modeling the Ecosystem for Scientific Knowledge Management in a PhD Program

The learning ecosystem modeled from the Ecosystems Metamodel is oriented to manage the scientific knowledge generated in the scope of the PhD Program on Education in the Knowledge Society at the University of Salamanca (https://knowledgesociety.usal.es). This ecosystem is described by García-Holgado, García-Peñalvo and Rodríguez Conde [15].

This learning ecosystem is composed by three elements in the infrastructure layer: (1) a mail server provided by the University of Salamanca; (2) a user management tool that is part of a component located in the service layer, the portal; (3) and a monitorization tool that is also part of the portal.

The static data management layer is provided by the institutional repository of the University of Salamanca.

Finally, the service layer has a main component, a user-centered portal which provides most features required by the business logic; and a set of external tools focused on the dissemination of the scientific knowledge in different social networks (Twitter, YouTube, SlideShare and Facebook) and sending bulk emails (Mailchimp).

The model (M1-level) has been divided in three packages: the ecosystem tools model; the ecosystem users model; and the ecosystem services model. Furthermore, the classes from the metamodel (M2-level) are represented to indicate which classes are used to model the example.

In Fig. 3, the main software components of the learning ecosystem are modeled. The *PhDEcosystem* is composed by: a *GmailSmtpServer*, modeled using the MailServer class; the *InstitutionalRepository* that instances the *DataRepository* class; the *PhDPortal* which contains the *PortalUserManagement* and the *PortalMonitorization*, instances of *InternalTool*, *UserManagement* and *Monitorization*, respectively; and a set of modeled elements using the *ExternalTool* class.

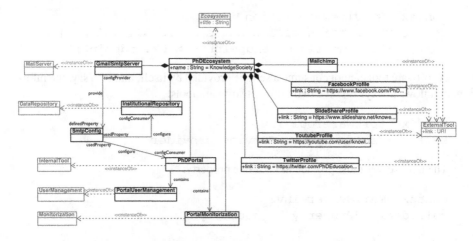

Fig. 3. Ecosystem tools model

The human factor is represented by the Academic Committee that is in charge of the management of the PhD Program, including the learning ecosystem. And a Quality Committee that provide the methodology to ensure the quality of the Program and the learning ecosystem.

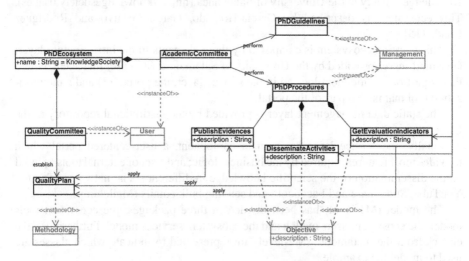

Fig. 4. Ecosystem users model

In Fig. 4, the human factor is modeled. The *AcademicCommittee* performs the *PhDGuidelines* and the *PhDProcedures*, both modeled using the *Management* class. The *QualityCommittee* establishes the *QualityPlan* modeled using the *Methodology* class. The

PhDProcedures provides a set of objectives, that are involved in the modeling of the information flows.

Finally, the information flows of the learning ecosystem are modeled in the Fig. 5. The relationships among the components are supported by several services to achieve the objectives (*PublishEvidences, DiseminateActivities* and *GetEvaluationIndicators*) that are part of the *PhDProcedures* in Fig. 4. Each service is modeled using *Service* class and involves two instances of *SoftwareTool*.

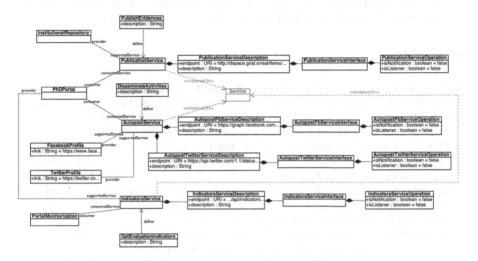

Fig. 5. Ecosystem services model

The *PublicationService* is provided by *InstitutionalRepository* and it is consumed by *PhDPortal* to support the *PublishEvidences* objective. The *AutopostService* is provided by two instances of *ExternalTool*, *FacebookProfile* and *TwitterProfile* to support the DiseminateActivities objective. And the *IndicatorsService* is defined by the *GetEvaluationIndicators* objective and involves *PhDPortal* and *PortalMonitorization*.

It should be noted that the *PhDPortal* consumes two services and provides another. Also, there is a service, *AutopostService*, composed by two instances of *ServiceDescription*, *AutopostFbServiceDescription* and *AutopostTwitterServiceDescription*.

6   Conclusions

This paper presents an ecosystems metamodel based on MOF to model different perspectives of learning ecosystems development. The metamodel have been used to model a real learning ecosystem for a PhD Program, which have been transferred to other domains. The modelling example demonstrate how a real ecosystem could be modeled using the Ecosystems Metamodel.

This work provides a base to define a UML profile for the Ecosystems Metamodel in order to leverage existing tool support. Furthermore, a set of transformation rules using QVT could be defined to transform the models into executable specifications to provide an ecosystem prototype.

Acknowledgement. This research was performed within the University of Salamanca PhD Program on Education in the Knowledge Society scope (http://knowledgesociety.usal.es) and was supported by the Spanish Ministerio de Educación, Cultura y Deporte under a FPU fellowship (FPU014/04783).

This work has been partially funded by the Spanish Government Ministry of Economy and Competitiveness throughout the DEFINES project (Ref. TIN2016-80172-R).

References

1. García-Peñalvo, F.J., Hernández-García, Á., Conde, M.Á., Fidalgo-Blanco, Á., Sein-Echaluce, M.L., Alier, M., Llorens-Largo, F., Iglesias-Pradas, S.: Learning services-based technological ecosystems. In: Proceedings of the 3rd International Conference on Technological Ecosystems for Enhancing Multiculturality, pp. 467–472. ACM (2015)
2. Ochoa, A., Yañez, S., Martinez-Arevalo, C., Alvarez, F., Caja, J., Maresca, P., Adrada, T., Merino, M., Zanón, A.: Competencias en el contexto del Proyecto Mentor de una Escuela de Ingeniería. In: Fidalgo Blanco, Á., Sein-Echaluce Lacleta, M.L., García-Peñalvo, F.J. (eds.) La Sociedad del Aprendizaje. Actas del III Congreso Internacional sobre Aprendizaje, Innovación y Competitividad, CINAIC 2015, Madrid, España, 14–16 de Octubre de 2015, pp. 670–675. Fundación General de la Universidad Politécnica de Madrid, Madrid (2015)
3. García-Holgado, A., García-Peñalvo, F.J.: The evolution of the technological ecosystems: an architectural proposal to enhancing learning processes. In: Proceedings of the First International Conference on Technological Ecosystem for Enhancing Multiculturality, TEEM 2013, Salamanca, Spain, 14–15 November 2013, pp. 565–571. ACM, New York (2013)
4. Chang, E., West, M.: Digital ecosystems a next generation of the collaborative environment. In: Eighth International Conference on Information Integration and Web-Based Application and Services, pp. 3–23 (2006)
5. Chen, W., Chang, E.: Exploring a digital ecosystem conceptual model and its simulation prototype. In: IEEE International Symposium on Industrial Electronics, ISIE 2007, pp. 2933–2938 (2007)
6. Dhungana, D., Groher, I., Schludermann, E., Biffl, S.: Software ecosystems vs. natural ecosystems: learning from the ingenious mind of nature. In: Proceedings of the Fourth European Conference on Software Architecture: Companion Volume, pp. 96–102. ACM (2010)
7. Laanpere, M.: Digital learning ecosystems: rethinking virtual learning environments in the age of social media. In: Open and Social Technologies for Networked Learning, IFIP-OST 2012, Taillin (2012)
8. Messerschmitt, D.G., Szyperski, C.: Software Ecosystem: Understanding an Indispensable Technology and Industry, vol. 1. MIT Press Books, Cambridge (2005)
9. Pata, K.: Meta-design framework for open learning ecosystems. In: Mash-UP Personal Learning Environments (MUP/PLE 2011). Open University of London (2011)
10. Pardo, A., Delgado Kloos, C.: Stepping out of the box: towards analytics outside the learning management system. In: Proceedings of the 1st International Conference on Learning Analytics and Knowledge, LAK 2011, pp. 163–167. ACM, New York (2011)

11. García-Holgado, A., García-Peñalvo, F.J.: Knowledge management ecosystem based on drupal platform for promoting the collaboration between public administrations. In: García-Peñalvo, F.J. (ed.) Proceedings of the Second International Conference on Technological Ecosystems for Enhancing Multiculturality, TEEM 2014, Salamanca, Spain, 1–3 October 2014, pp. 619–624. ACM, New York (2014)

12. García-Peñalvo, F.J., Conde-González, M.Á., Zangrando, V., García-Holgado, A., Seoane Pardo, A.M., Alier, M., Galanis, N., Brouns, F., Vogten, H., Griffiths, D., Mykowska, A., Alves, G.R., Minović, M.: TRAILER project (Tagging, Recognition, Acknowledgment of Informal Learning ExpeRiences). A methodology to make visible learners' informal learning activities to the institutions. J. Univ. Comput. Sci. **19**, 1661–1683 (2013)

13. García-Peñalvo, F.J., Johnson, M., Alves, G.R., Minović, M., Conde-González, M.Á.: Informal learning recognition through a cloud ecosystem. Future Gener. Comput. Syst. **32**, 282–294 (2014)

14. Orueta, J.L., Pavón, L.M. (eds.): Libro Blanco de la Universidad Digital 2010. Ariel. Colección Fundación Telefónica. Cuaderno 11 (2008)

15. García-Holgado, A., García-Peñalvo, F.J., Rodríguez Conde, M.J.: Definition of a technological ecosystem for scientific knowledge management in a PhD programme. In: Proceedings of the Third International Conference on Technological Ecosystems for Enhancing Multiculturality, TEEM 2015, Porto, Portugal, 7–9 October 2015, pp. 695–700. ACM, New York (2015)

16. Mellor, S.J., Scott, K., Uhl, A., Weise, D.: Model-driven architecture. In: Bruel, J.-M., Bellahsene, Z. (eds.) Workshops on Advances in Object-Oriented Information Systems, OOIS 2002 Montpellier, France, 2 September 2002, pp. 290–297. Springer, Heidelberg (2002)

17. Frankel, D.: Model Driven Architecture: Applying MDA to Enterprise Computing. Wiley, New York (2002)

18. Álvarez, José M., Evans, A., Sammut, P.: Mapping between levels in the metamodel architecture. In: Gogolla, M., Kobryn, C. (eds.) UML 2001. LNCS, vol. 2185, pp. 34–46. Springer, Heidelberg (2001). doi:10.1007/3-540-45441-1_4

19. García-Holgado, A., García-Peñalvo, F.J.: Architectural pattern for the definition of eLearning ecosystems based on open source developments. In: Sierra-Rodríguez, J.L., Dodero-Beardo, J.M., Burgos, D. (eds.) Proceedings of 2014 International Symposium on Computers in Education (SIIE), Logroño, La Rioja, Spain, 12–14 November 2014, pp. 93–98. Institute of Electrical and Electronics Engineers (2014). IEEE Catalog Number CFP1486T-ART

20. García-Holgado, A., García-Peñalvo, F.J.: Architectural pattern to improve the definition and implementation of eLearning ecosystems. Sci. Comput. Program. **129**, 20–34 (2016)

21. Buschmann, F., Meunier, R., Rohnert, H., Sommerlad, P., Stal, M.: Pattern-Oriented Software Architecture: A System of Patterns (1996)

22. Jegadeesan, H., Balasubramaniam, S.: An MOF2-based services metamodel. J. Object Technol. **7**, 71–96 (2008)

Needs Analysis as a Cornerstone in Formation of ICT Competence in Language Teachers Through Specially Tailored In-service Training Course

Nadezhda Kabanova[1(✉)] and Marina Kogan[2]

[1] Foreign Language Teaching and Translation,
Peter the Great St. Petersburg Polytechnic University, St. Petersburg, Russia
kabanova@bk.ru
[2] Department of Linguistics and Cross-Cultural Communication,
Peter the Great St. Petersburg Polytechnic University, St. Petersburg, Russia
m_kogan@inbox.ru

Abstract. ICT competence is becoming an integral part of foreign language teachers' professional competence. However, syllabus design of efficient in-service courses aiming at improving ICT competence in specialists outside the IT domain is still quite a challenge. This paper looks specifically at needs analysis as a key to efficient professional development course design. This paper addresses practical concerns about ambiguity of the concept of *needs*, and focuses on learners' *wants* rather than *necessities* as the basis of needs analysis. Findings allowed the authors to develop a framework for a specially tailored in-service training course aiming at improving foreign language teachers' professional ICT competence. The study also focuses on identifying University teachers' needs related to sustainable development of their ICT skills and challenges that may be encountered in this field.

Keywords: Component · In-service language teachers training · ICT competence · Needs-based analysis · In-service training course syllabus

1 Introduction

Technological advances of the digital era require that teachers in institutions of HE be able to make use of them in their every day work for improving quality of teaching their disciplines. While debates about necessary changes in curricula of training pre-service teachers (e.g., language teachers) are very fruitful, most today's teachers have to find formal (through in-service training courses) or informal (through occasional workshops, webinars, conferences, self-directed learning, learning from colleagues and students, etc.) ways of improving their professional competence in using Information and Communications Technology (ICT competence) [11].

Educators in different disciplines in different countries stress that this competence "is not simply about the technology, but also requires an understanding of the pedagogical considerations, and the skills that are needed, to effectively facilitate them" [21].

© Springer International Publishing AG 2017
P. Zaphiris and A. Ioannou (Eds.): LCT 2017, Part I, LNCS 10295, pp. 110–123, 2017.
DOI: 10.1007/978-3-319-58509-3_11

So, as G. Karlsson put it in-service training should cover such issues as Student centered learning, Curriculum design, Quality of teaching, ICT enhanced learning, Technologies of e-learning [13]. Besides the issues common for most professionals in today's HE there are discipline specific ones that should be taken into account while considering in-service courses syllabus.

In the language teaching domain, which we represent, it was discovered that the online context of language learning needs new teaching approaches and teaching skills that are different from those used in teaching face-to-face language courses [9]. These new skills are crucial for teaching online language courses whose subject matter is communication. This discovery resulted in a good deal of fruitful research aiming at detailed analysis of the skills, approaches and responsibilities a language teacher should have to teach on-line (see for example, [4, 18, 19]), development of self-assessment questionnaires similar to ICT "can do" lists composed by Prof. G. Davies [5], helping language teachers to evaluate what they know about technology, what exactly they can do or apply into practice, and what they would like to learn to improve their ICT competence.

Based on these studies we refer to ICT competence of a language teacher as a combination of four groups of skills: *cognitive level skills* (the ability to learn and to master new technology, understanding its place in the teaching process and instructional design), *technical level skills* (the ability to use computer programs, internet resources, CMS, LMS, etc. for teaching purposes), *motivation level skills* (the ability to feel the need in professional development in online teaching, to enjoy using technology, etc.), and *experience level skills* (sustainability in using technology, ability to use new skills, time management, etc.)

The burning issue, however, is how to realize a formal in-service training of language teachers in the most efficient way. Ph. Hubbard considers 13 possible approaches focusing on either the amount of content covered (breadth vs depth dilemma); or ways of delivery such as online, hybrid, in the classroom 'mentor-based', self-directed learning which is now a feasible possibility with manuals like [7, 10, 16] being available; or desirable outcomes (portfolio-based, project based, situated learning), and some others [11].

According to Titova, in order to be efficient, an ICT professional development course has to be based on the standards of ICT competence structure, as well as on a number of existing frameworks both on the international and national level, like the Russian Federal State Standard for Higher Education Institutions introduced in the Russian Federation recently; and, in addition to this, be in the hands of subject specialists rather than ICT specialists to avoid being too general or too technical; be practically oriented; help teachers create professional networks or virtual teaching environment [19]. However, literature review, as well as our own experience and observation, allow us to suppose that relatively short, in-service training courses for language teachers will be the most efficient if they are built around one or a very limited number of applications or meet the criteria for a situated learning environment where teachers can immediately connect their work in CALL (Computer Assisted Language Learning) to the classrooms in which they are currently teaching.

Examples of 'depth-first courses' allowing teachers to acquire both technical and pedagogical skills and knowledge through firsthand experience described in literature are built around

- development of a WebQuest [3];
- computer mediated communication (tele-collaboration project for in-service teachers from different countries) [6];
- considering/mastering features of virtual learning environments (VLE) or learning management systems (LMS) Moodle [17];
- Interactive White Board (IWB), for example, at Peter the Great Polytechnic University (St. Petersburg, Russia) such a course providing in-service training for faculty members proves to be very popular. This goes in good agreement with Dudeney & Hockley's opinion stating that only training for teachers in the use of a complex tool such as an IWB can ensure 'effective uptake' [7, p. 124];
- a specific skill area, such as development of learner autonomy through VLE (Coalea project described by Bailly [1]) or learner motivation to use a powerful potential of modern ICT technologies for development of communicative skills in a target language within University curriculum [2].
- effective use of corpora in language education [8, 14].

Few studies which focus on follow-up on impact of the in-service training on teachers' practice show that applying the acquired skills is a problematic area: only 10% of all teachers participating in in-service courses produced their own materials for publication (websites, blogs, wikis, etc.) and 7% were actually involved in some sort of telecollaborative event a year after completing an international telecollaboration in-service training course [6].

All these considerations made us assume that it proves practically impossible to develop an in-service training course aiming at increasing language teachers' ICT competence which meets all the above requirements. We postulate that the course syllabus should be based on the results of would-be learners needs analysis.

Saying this, it's important to focus on the concept of *needs*. In his comprehensive paper R. West suggests that there still exists certain ambiguity in understanding the very concept of *needs analysis*, depending on the meaning of *needs* considered. He states that there is a contradiction between various concepts of need: *necessities* or *demands* (also called *objective, or product-oriented, or perceived* needs) and learners' *wants (subjective, or felt* needs) [20]. The latter refer to what the learners want or feel they need. These needs are considered to be personal and can be referred to as *subjective needs*. They could be hidden from an external observer and therefore not easily definable.

The aim of this study is to identify university language teachers' subjective needs concerning their professional ICT competence with subsequent use of these findings to design a specially tailored in-service training course and test its efficiency.

2   Methods

To analyse the ICT skills and professional development needs of Russian HE foreign language teachers, an online questionnaire was designed, aiming at checking cognitive, technical, experience level skills, as well as teachers' motivation to use technology in their practice in and outside the classroom. To provide better access to the on-line questionnaire, the link to it was given in social networks (Russian network "vkontakte" vk.com, facebook), sent directly to the researcher's e-mail contact list, and referred to in the skype account of the author (kabanovanadezhda) and on the Moodle site of the researcher's affiliated institution (moodle.lingua.spbstu.ru). All the addressees mentioned had a choice whether to participate or not, to insure anonymous and willing contribution. The questionnaire was open for three months for distant participants.

To compare the ICT skills of language teachers with the skills and educational needs of university lecturers from different fields, another questionnaire was designed and distributed via Google forms service among the participants of a general ICT course developed by the SPbPU electronic resource department.

Regarding the first questionnaire, after 3 months of data collecting the feedback came from 56 foreign language teachers from 18 universities (the Russian Federation) located in 7 cities and regions of the Russian Federation from Kaliningrad on the west to Khabarovsk on the east.

The online questionnaire consisted of five blocks of multiple choice questions (though the possibility to leave comments was provided for each question), each of which refers to different components of ICT competence of a language teacher:

- Basic Skills of using ICT (cognitive and operational level skills), e.g. the ability to use text-processing software, create and edit presentations;
- Use e-mail, social networks, blogs, forums, wikis, websites, search tools, etc. for personal needs;
- Using ICT for foreign language teaching (FLT) (cognitive, operational, experience level skills), e.g. ability to use text-processing software, create and edit presentations, use e-mail, social networks, blogs, forums, wikis, websites, search tools, multimedia etc. for creating teaching resources and enhancing communication with students; experience in using VLE, LMS, CMS available in their institutions to organize students' individual and collaborative learning and project work; ability to use authoring tools (test-makers, like *hot potatoes*) to create and use interactive tasks;
- Professional Development in the field of ICT (experience and motivation level skills), e.g. previous experience of pre-service and in-service courses in ICT and CALL; fields of special interest in ICT (online or hybrid learning, evaluation and assessment tools, instructional design and ICT, using LMS or social networks in FLT, etc.);
- Attitude towards using ICT for FLT (motivation level skills), e.g. the desire to develop professional competence in ICT and CALL, obstacles teachers encounter when using ICT in their institutions, etc.
- BIO data (experience level), e.g. age, position, institution, experience in FLT, ICT, CALL.

In addition to the questionnaire, off-line observation was used for deeper understanding of the needs of three focus groups (totally of 54) of would-be participants of the in-service face-to-face course for FL teachers at Peter the Great Polytechnic University (St. Petersburg, Russia). To identify the key skills that teachers already have we carried out practical skills analysis based on the study of real teaching resources they use (computer-based and internet-based), and observation of teaching practice (use of ICT during face-to-face lessons and for independent learning support for students) of six teachers chosen randomly among those who expressed the intention to participate in the course.

Needs analysis allowed us to set out the objectives of the skills-based, practically-oriented in-service course of professional development in the field of ICT, its content, instructional technology, and teaching facilities. Three groups of foreign language teachers working at Peter the Great Polytechnic University did in-service courses covering 72 h of active learning. The training lasted for 3 to 6 months in different groups to support maximum flexibility. The formal in-service course was followed by one year informal and non-formal individual professional development controlled by the tutor.

After the course we analysed the outcomes, doing qualitative and quantitative analysis of teaching skills, resources and practice observation. We also used Wilcoxon signed-rank test to check the validity of measuring ICT competence improvement. Based on the analysis, we suggested a course syllabus update, that is, a set of recommendations for instructional designers to improve further teacher training process.

3 Findings

When the on-line questionnaire for distant participants was closed, we analysed the answers and comments, which enabled us to summarize the data as follows.

3.1 BIO Data

Participating teachers fairly equally represented five different age groups (approximately 20% each): under 35 (young professionals, born after 1980, attending high school and HE institutions during the period of active reforms in Russia and Russian education system), from 35 to 45 (experienced instructors, mostly taught in more traditional Russian academic universities), from 46 to 54 (experienced teachers, less than 10 years before retirement age for women in Russia), and over 55 (age of retirement for women). 61% had more than 15 years of professional experience in foreign language teaching. More than 50% stated their position as "Senior Lecturer" (faculty members at Russian Universities who usually do not have PhD degree and thus less intend to share their experience and reflect on it in scientific papers) working in different universities, mostly/mainly teaching a general English course to students majoring in Applied Linguistics, Information Science, Physics, Economics, Design and other subjects.

3.2   Basic Skills of Using ICT and Using ICT for Foreign Language Teaching

All participants demonstrated fairly confident use of basic ICT skills for personal needs that can be explained by the used means of disseminating the information about this survey. We assume that most participants found hyperlinks to the questionnaire either in their e-mail inboxes or in the news feed of social networks. However, it is clear that very limited ICT skills were necessary and sufficient for filling in the Google forms.

Most participants (more than 60%) identified their ability to use ICT for personal needs as "experienced user", which involved the ability to use different text processing tools; manage files and folders; set up software, drivers for hardware, programs and applications; learn how to use new programs and even help friends and colleagues solve some simple problems with software and hardware use. All participants have regular access to either desk-top or laptop computer with good internet connection, both at home and in their institution, but when asked about the purposes of using computer and internet access, they mentioned checking e-mail and searching information for personal needs. About 75% of participants who use internet regularly mentioned information search for professional purposes, and even fewer (50%) use the internet to organize and manage teaching practice.

37% of participants answered that they were registered and regularly used their accounts in social networks (mostly facebook, twitter, and vkontakte) not only to access information, but also to create their own messages, pages, groups, blogs and discussions. This fact means that teachers are ready to create and share content on the internet. However, only 16% have their own content in LMS or CMS in their institutions. This tendency might mean that teachers' technical level skills are developed enough to create their own content, but their motivation level of professional ICT competence is relatively low, as they do not apply their knowledge in professional context.

41% of participants regularly use computers and the internet to prepare activities for face-to-face lessons and to deliver their content at the lessons, but only discouragingly few (8%) claimed that they use their own teaching resources or the content they created and uploaded to LMS. Most teachers prefer to use media and technical equipment they are well familiar with (CD players, DVD players, overhead projectors for audio and video content delivery – 19%; internet-based resources and e-textbooks – 14%). To support students' independent work most teachers (about 70%) prefer to send files with tasks and hyperlinks via e-mail, while only about 10% mentioned communicating with students in forums and blogs, and organizing project work in LMS as part of their support.

3.3   Professional Development in the Field of ICT

45% of participants have taken in-service professional development courses in the field of ICT at least once in their career, and 32% have done a course of ICT for FLT. Although most teachers admit that they have improved their professional ICT competence, only 16% are completely satisfied with their progress and skills development. On the one hand, these data may question the level of the courses the participants have completed, but, on the other, confirms the need to further develop teachers' ICT for

FLT skills. 63% of participating teachers stated that they would like to develop their ICT competence in FLT, and some of them mentioned that in-service courses format alone was not always appropriate, that is, a short course is not enough to master ICT skills and to learn how to apply them in practice.

When it comes to the content of the course, we offered a wide range of options in a multi-select question, so that all participants could choose as many topics and fields of interest as they liked. The following topics were chosen most often (18 to 21%): planning and designing activities and working in LMS/VLE; creating computer-based teaching resources for FLT; teacher-student communication in digital environment (using different means, such as social networks, blogs, and forums). Basic general ICT skills like text processing, working in Power Point, searching for information in the internet received lowest percentage of answers (approximately 4%). These data confirmed our assumption that practically oriented and subject-specific courses would be more popular among language teaching professionals than general, technology-centered ones.

3.4   Attitude Towards Using ICT for FLT

Most participating teachers stated that they support ICT use for FLT (80%), but only 36% were prepared to take active part in implementation of technology into their everyday working routine. They added that they might agree to be more active provided their institutions supported them both technically (providing equipment, training, hardware and software) and financially (higher salary or bonus on a regular basis). These data show a lack of teachers' internal motivation (motivation level skills) and demonstrate a tendency to expect some extra benefits from institutions if they use ICT in teaching, although professional ICT competence is nowadays considered by most employers in education as a must (see [11], for example). Nevertheless, most participants admitted that using ICT is an innovative trend in foreign language teaching and instructional design, which allows us to express hope that, in case of improving teachers' motivation during in-service courses, it might be possible to increase the number of language teachers who actually use ICT skills in practice.

When asked about preferences concerning creating and sharing digital course materials, ways of communicating with students, and managing activities, teachers agreed that they are ready to provide students with general information about the language course (explain the agenda and requirements in LMS or via e-mail), share course content in the form of files, presentations, hyperlinks to audio and video resources; answer students' questions via e-mail, forums and instant messaging tools in VLE; less often - manage and assess students' individual project in the internet. Most teachers said, however, that they were not yet prepared to manage their personal website, professional blog or professional digital network (for students or for colleagues).

3.5   Analysis

Six full-time female teachers aged 35–47 from St. Petersburg Polytechnic University who intended to join the in-service course were selected for further research, namely for analysis of teaching resources and technology enhanced methods of teaching English they use.

All participating teachers demonstrated clear understanding of the necessity to use computer-based and internet-based teaching resources already available. 4 out of 6 have used LMS (Moodle site available on the institutional level) to organize students' independent work, but admitted that they were displeased with its design and content. Most participants (5 out of 6) have not had any experience in developing their own materials for LMS, though they would like to improve their technical skills as well as instructional design skills. All the teachers often created and used .pdf documents and Power Point presentations (for face-to-face lessons), and only 2 used interactive tools and special programs (test-makers, quiz-makers like Hot Potatoes), though this process lacks systematic planning and reflexive attitude.

As for motivation level skills, 4 of 6 claimed that there were different bureaucratic and financial obstacles as well as technical limitations (lack of the Internet access in Universities' classrooms, impossibility to hold language classes in the computer labs) preventing them from using technology in their practice on a regular basis or as M. Dooly put it "...teachers are often working in less than ideal environment" [6, p. 366].

3.6   Second Questionnaire Analysis

In order to find out if the ICT competence for languages teachers differ from the ICT competence for University teachers from other fields, the second questionnaire was designed. The questionnaire was focused on the issues presented in Table 1. Totally, 21 participants from a group of 28 teachers who just completed the above mentioned SPbPU ICT course responded to the on-line questionnaire.

Table 1. Results of analysis of Questionnaire 2

	Question	Analysis of answers	Comments
1	The subject area of lecturers	8 language teachers; 8 specialists from economics and management domain; 1 applied psychologist; 2 teachers from engineering domain (metallurgy); 1 IT specialist;	The majority come from Humanities and Economics Departments showing that teachers from these domains feel the need to improve their ICT competence
2	Self-evaluation of ICT skills using three-point scale: beginner - experienced user - professional level	beginner - 0, experienced user - 71%, professional level - 29%	
3	Aims and objectives of using ICT for professional needs	Most participants use e-mail and forums for communication, and web search to look for teaching resources	

(continued)

Table 1. (*continued*)

	Question	Analysis of answers	Comments
4	Services and programs used	76% of all the participants stated that they use only e-mail, 23% have experience in using distant courses in LMS. Practically nobody does blogging or has accounts in social networks	This is in a good agreement with the answers of the Survey 1 respondents (see Sect. 3.4 above)
5	Professional development in the field of ICT	Most teachers mentioned the in-service course in ICT provided by SPbPU	
6	Attitude towards using ICT in teaching, e.g. the desire to develop professional competence, obstacles teachers encounter when using ICT, etc.	All the participants stated that they are ready to use ICT in teaching. As for the obstacles, about 30% mentioned financial problems (hardware and software upgrade, research funding, etc.). More than a half sees a lack of instructional and technical support as the main obstacle	
7	BIO data (experience level), e.g. age, position, and teaching experience	90% are aged 35–55, 71% have been teaching for more than 15 years (others slightly less)	
8	Lecturers were asked to express their ideas of what an ideal professional development course should be like, and what areas need to be highlighted during the course	Answers varied including LMS Moodle administration, Financial Analysis software, MatLab, DBMS, Mathematical Modeling applications, Visual Design software, etc. However, 30% of the participants were unable to identify the particular services and software they would like to familiarise with. Only one participant demonstrated the readiness to master any software that could be of any interest in his field	We suggest that this very ability to specify professional needs in the field of ICT could serve as a sensitive indicator in identifying the real level of professional ICT competence
9	Awareness of any national or international standards concerning ICT competence of a university teacher (e.g. UNESCO ICT Competency Framework for Teachers, Russian Federal State Standard for Higher Education Institutions)	71% of the participants stated that they are unaware of ICT competence frameworks, either local or international	This result shows that self-evaluation of ICT competence is unlikely to include formalised requirements for professional ICT competence of university teachers

4   Outcomes

Based on the above data we defined the objectives of the in-service professional development course for foreign language teachers and identified core blocks of its content. The agenda included technical skills development (searching for information on the internet, use of specific computer programs, e.g. test-makers; working in LMS/VLE), instructional technology (activities aimed at cognitive and motivation level skills development: evaluation of teaching resources, use of computer-based and internet-based activities and tests, using social networks for teaching purposes, assessment, e.g. peer assessment in LMS, etc.), practice (aimed at developing experience level skills, e.g. designing and moderating Moodle courses and computer-based activities). All these blocks are *not* taught separately in a lecture form, but rather studied by course participants under the supervision of the teacher instructor, in an integrated form. The detailed description of the content is given in Table 2.

Based on our research and the results of needs analysis we published a coursebook (in Russian) [12] E-learning and CALL, accompanied with a Moodle course. The aim of this was to allow the participants to have access to all the course, no matter which format of delivery (electronic or printed) they preferred. We also assumed that not all teachers had an opportunity to attend 100% of face-to-face sessions, so they would need additional practice and support.

The Moodle course we designed contained resources and activities that help teachers practice real ICT skills by creating their own teaching materials and uploading them to the Moodle site. Another feature was that the resources were presented so that, for example, a wiki activity was explained through a wiki page; the study of hot potatoes quiz was presented by a series of hot potatoes quizzes, etc. This way of course delivery was aimed at increasing motivation and making the course more practical and task-oriented.

As mentioned above, the 72 h course lasted for 3 to 6 months, depending on how many hours a week teachers were able to attend. A specially designed Moodle course was used to accompany the learning process, which allowed teachers to get 24/7 support. At the end of the course all participants were required to develop their own set of activities in the form of a Moodle course.

The professional development course was based on the constructivist approach, which meant active participation in the formation of the course agenda, collaborative work, group work and peer-assessment. This approach also helps built professional networks, develop creativity and improve motivation.

On the completion of the course we again analysed teachers' ICT skills (cognitive, technical, motivation and experience level skills), paying more attention to the teaching resources and practical application of the skills. Each category of skills was assessed using scores from 0 (no skills in this area) to 3 (professional level). The criteria of the assessment were based on ICT4LT Questionnaire and Can do List (http://www.ict4lt.org/en/ICT_Can_Do_Lists.doc), developed by the author and described in a PhD thesis by Kabanova (2014).

To check the assumption about significant (as opposed to negligible) increase of teachers' professional ICT competence on completion of the course, Wilcoxon

Table 2. In-service training course syllabus

Topic	Modules and topics	Content
1.1	**Module 1 Introduction to e-learning and CALL** Introduction to E-learning	Basic theoretical concepts of e-learning. Philosophy of digital age. Terminology, legal issues, government acts and laws concerning use of ICT in formal education (mostly HE institutions). Success stories in implementing e-learning, best practice and case studies
1.2	Constructivist and connectivist approaches to e-learning. Networked learning	Social constructivism and connectivism in e-learning: fundamentals, instruction strategies, learner autonomy. Active learning, interaction, project work. Networked learning, social media and open education. The phenomenon of MOOC, its advantages and limitations
1.3	Introduction to CALL	Definitions of CALL. The development of CALL. CALL programs and activities. Roles of the computer, tutor and student in FL learning and teaching. Teaching in the computer network environment, self-access learning, distance learning
2.1	**Module 2 Instructional design for Foreign language teaching using ICT** Introduction to Instructional Design	Teachers as designers in digital age. Instructional design principles. Visualization, interaction (human-machine and human-human). Designing presentations. Goal setting and outcome planning in language teaching
2.2	Information search and hypertext	Using hypertext in instructional design. Searching for specific information. Information relevance and authenticity in language teaching. Copyright and licensing
2.3	On-line resources, encyclopedia and libraries in FLT	Web resources for FLT. Sites, podcasts, video. E-libraries, dictionaries, databases. Translation software. Delivering and receiving multimedia
3.1	**Module 3 Computer programs and internet services for FLT** Test-makers. Hot Potatoes	Test-makers, quiz-makers (software and internet-based templates). Hot Potatoes Quizes: matching exercise, crossword, multiple choice exercise, open cloze. Creating and using hot potatoes web pages
3.2	Web services in FLT	Web 2.0. Social networks (practical use in FL teaching and learning). Professional networks (for FLT and CALL professionals). Wikis, blogs, chatrooms, forums in ELT

(continued)

Table 2. (*continued*)

Topic	Modules and topics	Content
3.3	Webinars in FLT	Web-conferences and webinars in language teaching. Synchronous activities in CALL. Software and web services for webinars (Adobe Connect Pro, Big Blue Button, Open Meetings, Sclipo). Methodology of preparing for and holding an on-line seminar
4.1	**Module 4 LMS MOODLE** Starting with Moodle	Moodle terminology (course, course section, resource, activity, editing mode, etc.). Course menu. Creating the course. Course settings, main page. Files and folders
4.2	Course administration and settings	Editing mode. Moodle roles, Moodle labels (icons). Text processing in Moodle. Uploading files (text, audio, video, presentations). Hyperlinks in Moodle
4.3	Moodle Resources	Creating, managing and using Moodle resources (files, web-pages, text pages, labels, directories). Teaching strategies for using Moodle resources (multimedia, links, web-pages) in FLT
4.4	Moodle Activities	Creating, managing and using Moodle activities for FLT (hot potatoes quiz, assignment, forum, glossary, wiki, workshop, and test). Project work, collaborative work and peer assessment in Moodle
4.5	Assessment in Moodle. Choosing Moodle features for your course	Communication and assessment in Moodle. Messages, Scores in Forum, scales, statistics, reports in Moodle. Groups and roles for assessment. Choosing activities to reach the goals of the course

Signed-rank Test (in this case, repeated measurements on a single sample) was used. The calculations were made automatically on-line, using the template provided on the site for psychological research and statistics (http://www.psychol-ok.ru/statistics/wilcoxon/).

The values were calculated for n = 50 (50 participants of the face-to-face course, which was maximum for the template mentioned). The critical values for this number are T = 466 at $p < 0.05$. Our obtained value was T = 28, which is less than critical values, so we rejected the null hypothesis and accepted the alternative hypothesis: growth of the participants' ICT competence owes the in-service training course.

5   Conclusions

Stanley suggests that the availability of technology today makes it impossible to follow it all, as well as incorporate all its forms into curriculums [17]. Our findings show that the issue of teachers' ICT skills development may be tackled with careful needs analysis, followed by skills-based course design. However, this approach does not guarantee success if technical, organizational, and motivational problems are not taken into account.

According to Liu and Kleinsasser, there are lots of questions yet to be answered by researchers in this field, concerning, for example, teachers' reflection on students' feedback after implementing CALL, institution administration support, and teachers' willingness to apply CALL in classroom instruction [15].

The content and agenda of the in-service hybrid course, based on the needs analysis, allowed the participants to increase significantly the level of professional ICT competence with the help of the instructor. However, the content alone cannot guarantee successful implementation of the professional development program. To reach sustainable development of teachers' ICT skills, it is vital to choose appropriate topics, methods and teaching techniques applicable for particular institutions and relevant for their current instructional settings.

Acknowledgements. The authors would like to acknowledge and express their gratitude to Prof. Maria Akopova, who died unexpectedly and well before her time. The authors are grateful for her inspiration and devotion, which set a perfect example for them and their colleagues, and enabled them to continue their research into the field of CALL and professional development.

References

1. Bailly, S., Ciekanski, M., Guély-Costa, E.: Training language teachers to sustain self-directed language learning: an exploration of advisers' experiences on a web-based open virtual learning environment. EUROCALL Rev. **21**(1), 35–53 (2013)
2. Boulton, A., Azzam-Hannachi, R., Pereiro, M., Chateau, A.: Learning to learn languages with ICT – but how? CALL-EJ Online **9**(2) (2008) https://hal.archives-ouvertes.fr/hal-00273307/document
3. Chao, C.: How WebQuests send technology to the background: scaffolding EFL teacher professional development in CALL. In: Hubbard, P., Levy, M. (eds.) Teacher Education in CALL, pp. 221–223. John Benjamins, Amsterdam (2006)
4. Compton, L.K.L.: Preparing language teachers to teach language online: a look at skills, roles, and responsibilities. Comput. Assist. Lang. Learn. **22**(1), 73–99 (2009). doi:10.1080/09588220802613831
5. Davies, G.: ICT "Can Do" lists for teachers of foreign languages (2009). http://www.ict4lt.org/en/ICT_Can_Do_Lists.doc
6. Dooly, M.: New competencies in a new era? Examining the impact of a teacher training project. ReCALL **21**(3), 352–369 (2009). doi:10.1017/S0958344009990085
7. Dudeney, G., Hockly, N.: How to Teach English with Technology. Pearson-Longman, Harlow (2008)

8. Ebrahimi, A., Faghih, E.: Integrating corpus linguistics into online language teacher education programs. ReCALL **29**(1), 120–135 (2017). doi:10.1017/S0958344016000070
9. Hampel, R., Stickler, U.: New skills for new classrooms: training tutors to teach languages online. Comput. Assist. Lang. Learn. **18**(4), 311–326 (2005). doi:10.1080/09588220500335455
10. Hockly, N., Clandfield, L.: Teaching Online: Tools and Techniques, Options and Opportunities. Delta Publishing, England (2010)
11. Hubbard, P.: CALL and the future of language teacher education. CALICO J. **25**(2), 175–188 (2008)
12. Kabanova, N.A., Kolonitskaja, O.L.: Metodika prepodavanija anglijskogo jazyka. Jelektronnoe obuchenie inostrannym jazykam s ispol'zovaniem LMS MOODLE. [Methodology of Teaching English. Electronic Teaching Foreign Languages using LMS MOODLE] SPb: Izd-vo Politehn. un-ta, 2013 (in Russian)
13. Karlsson, G., Hellstrom, M., Holotescu, C., Grosseck, G., Dumbraveanu, R.: Are we ready to move towards a new type of teacher training? Case study: The WETEN Project. In: Göran Karlsson, G., Dan Burdescu, D., Krämer, D. (eds.) The Third International Conference on Mobile, Hybrid, and On-line Learning (eL&mL 2011), Guadeloupe, France, pp. 36–39. IARIA (2011)
14. Leńko-Szymańska, A.: Is this enough? A qualitative evaluation of the effectiveness of a teacher-training course on the use of corpora in language education. ReCALL **26**(2), 260–278 (2014). doi:10.1017/S095834401400010X
15. Liu, M.H., Kleinsasser, R.C.: Exploring EFL teachers' CALL knowledge and competencies: in-service program perspectives. Lang. Learn. Technol. **19**(1), 119–138 (2015)
16. Stanford, J.: Moodle 1.9 for Second Language Teaching. Packt Publishing, Birmingham (2009)
17. Stanley, I.: Teacher education in CALL: using workshops to train a faculty in the use of Moodle. J. Kanda Univ. Int. Stud. **21**, 369–384 (2009)
18. Sysoyev, P., Evstigneev, M.N.: Foreign language teacher's competence in using information and communication technologies. Lang. Cult. **1**, 142–147 (2014)
19. Titova, S.: Developing of ICT competence of language teachers through an online professional development course in Moodle: strategies and challenges. In: Gómez Chova, L., López Martínez, A., Candel Torres, I. (eds.) Proceedings of 6th International Technology, Education and Development Conference, INTED 2012, Valencia, Spain, pp. 4378–4385, March 2012
20. West, R.: Needs analysis in language teaching. Lang. Teach. **27**(1), 1–19 (1994)
21. White, S., Folley, S., Williams, S., Allen, J.: Preparing higher education tutors for delivering online courses. In: White, S., Marquand, M. (eds.) The Seventh International Conference on Mobile, Hybrid, and On-line Learning (eLmL 2015), Lisbon, Portugal, pp. 20–26. IARIA (2015)

Design Considerations for Competency Functionality Within a Learning Ecosystem

Irina Kondratova[✉], Heather Molyneaux, and Helene Fournier

Human-Computer Interaction Team, Information and Communications Technologies,
National Research Council of Canada, Ottawa, Canada
{Irina.Kondratova,Heather.Molyneaux,
Helene.Fournier}@nrc-cnrc.gc.ca

Abstract. This paper provides a review of the current trends within competency based training and management and the challenges with competency management frameworks in Canada. The paper builds on earlier work by the authors related to digital systems for competency management, a market analysis report for competency management systems and a literature review on competency management systems in Canada. The authors also elaborate on current and proposed design solutions for competency functionality in the context of the Learning and Performance Support (LPSS) program at the National Research Council of Canada (NRC) and on the results of user surveys and usability studies of the LPSS system related to competency and skills development.

Keywords: Competency management · Learning and performance support · Personal learning environment · Collaborative learning

1 Introduction – Competency Management

In this paper we explore the literature on competency management frameworks in Canada and elaborate on how competency functionality is being approached for the Learning and Performance Support (LPSS) program at the National Research Council of Canada (NRC). The paper is based on the results of literature and market reviews as well as user feedback through surveys and usability studies.

A competency is defined as a set of characteristics of an individual that are observable, measurable and predictive of superior performance in a given role. They define how people get their job done [1]. Others have suggested that competencies include a combination of observable and measurable knowledge, skills, abilities and personal attributes that contribute to enhanced employee performance and ultimately result in organizational success [2].

Competencies act like a bridge to connect job requirements with the desired skill set (of an individual) through appropriate training and development [3]. Competencies balance both the theoretical and practical experiences and can be developed through knowledge management within organizations by human resource development activities such as: competence recognition (through interviews or other means); acquiring competence (through e-learning or other training/learning methods); assessing competence

© Her Majesty the Queen in Right of Canada 2017
P. Zaphiris and A. Ioannou (Eds.): LCT 2017, Part I, LNCS 10295, pp. 124–136, 2017.
DOI: 10.1007/978-3-319-58509-3_12

(through monitoring within e-learning or other training/learning methods); and optional utilization of competence (through coaching/mentoring) [3]. Competencies are developed into competency frameworks within organizations or are based on existing national competency frameworks. The difficulty with this approach is that competency frameworks tend to be specific to particular organizations and countries.

Competency-based education is a topic frequently mentioned in relation to competency management, prior learning experience assessment and the informal learning paradigm: "Competency-based education" (CBE) refers to a method of organizing learning based on the achievement of competency, rather than on a defined set time. The two basic methods and forms of CBE are: (1) course-based where students work on their own time through a set of competencies organized into a course; and (2) direct assessment where students demonstrate the achievement of predefined competencies based on prior learning or experience" [4]. The 2016 Gartner report on business trends impacting higher education claims that CBE is currently at the peak of inflated expectations on the digital learning technologies hype curve. The other findings by Gartner related to the status of CBE in North America include the following observations [4]:

- CBE is becoming increasingly popular among institutions that are interested in increasing student outcomes, such as mastery of the subject matter, graduation rates and preparation for the world of work.
- Interest in competency-based education is very strong in the U.S. and is growing globally, as it delivers scalable, any-pace education and connects with competence and mastery initiatives in other countries.
- Currently, most of the activity around CBE is at the planning level since only a relatively small number of institutions have actually implemented it.
- There is a close logical relationship between CBE and outcomes - or performance-based funding, a funding formula to reward a defined policy outcome. Performance-based funding should not be confused with the concept of competency-based education (an education model built on mastery). Most of the experience with CBE has been at institutions with a nontraditional student body. As CBE is implemented at institutions with a more conventional 18- to 24-year-old student population or with a less-disciplined student body, new challenges are likely to emerge.

In addition to the United States, the area of competency management, frameworks, competency-based education and competency matching is a very active and extensively funded research area in the EU. There are several EU funded projects that develop technologies for competency management and competency based education such as TENCompetence (Building the European Network for Lifelong Competence Development), PROLIX (Process-oriented Learning and Information eXchange), TRACE (TRAnsparent Competence in Europe) and WATCHME (Workplace-based e-assessment technology for competency-based higher multi-professional education). EU projects on competency management and competency based education develop technologies focused on lifelong competence development, personal competency management, authoring tools to help users organize and coordinate learning environments, activities, competencies and learning paths, as well as ePortfolios to help lifelong learners to reflect on the competences and competence profiles they have acquired [5–10].

Regrettably, the area of competency management and competency-based education does not get similar attention and research funding from the Canadian government and industry, with the exception of healthcare industry. The next section of our paper provides an overview of competency frameworks, competency management and competency-based education in Canada.

2   Canadian Competency Frameworks

Competency frameworks are most commonly used within the medical profession including medical education, professional training and accreditation –and in the public service. Details of the medical and professional competency frameworks in Canada are addressed in the sections below.

2.1   Medical Competency Frameworks

In 1986 a physician's strike in Ontario raised concerns about the public perception of doctors and their competence, and the importance in ensuring that medical education fits societal needs [11]. This resulted in the 1996 introduction of the Canadian Medical Education Directives (CanMEDS) Framework by the Royal College of Physicians and Surgeons of Canada (the Royal College) that implemented a competency framework for Canada's postgraduate training programs. The CanMEDS framework has since been modified for use in other countries [12]. CanMEDS currently outlines seven roles: medical expert, communicator, collaborator, manager, health advocate, scholar and professional. Some of these roles are easy to teach and assess while others are more challenging. There is also a "tension between the need to meet accreditation standards and the development of meaningful assessment tools" [11].

Competency-based medical education (CBME) has its share of issues. Competencies are intrinsically contextual and culturally specific – that "individual views of competence communication, collaboration, professionalism and advocacy will be historically contingent, situational, changeable, and inevitably different from those from other backgrounds and cultures." There is also a need for medical training to align with community wants and needs [11].

CBME includes measuring competencies within medical simulations. For simulations involving interpersonal and communication skills, psychometric tools are used – the encounter is recorded and rated on a 7 point scale. Checklists are used for procedural skills, pre and post tests are used to assess knowledge and observational and non-observational tools are used to measure competencies. Observational tools include global rating scales, checklists (checking "respect for tissue, efficiency of time and motion, instrument handling, knowledge of instruments, use of assistants, flow of operation, forward planning and knowledge of specific procedural steps"). Non-observational tools include computer based measurements such as scores "generated based on errors, economy of movement, and time to complete the task" [13].

Issues with simulations and competencies "include the challenges and costs of obtaining and using appropriate simulation software and hardware, concerns about validation of simulations as an educational tool, and difficulty in creating normative standards for grading performance." To summarize, potential barriers to simulation and competencies include: access, cost, instructor availability, educational validity, assessment and outcome measurements [13].

Another implementation issue is that when competencies are considered in medical simulations sometimes important competencies are neglected and there is a need to include a greater degree of competency assessment. For example, when competencies are assessed during medical simulations of orotracheal intubation, force is usually not considered. In addition, traditional measures of observation and checklists are not always the best way to assess intubation competencies. In these cases, Garcia and colleagues reviewed additional assessment measures of force applied, number of attempts, time to intubation and hand position using checklists, and additional measures such as "sensors, transducers, and special pressure sensitive films secured to the laryngoscope" [14].

2.2 Professional Competency Frameworks

The bulk of the Canadian literature on competencies deals with medical education; few other professions and sectors in Canada employ competency based education and competency frameworks. For example, the competency framework has been developed for public service sectors in Canada based on the existing job classification system in place within the Canadian public service.

Bonder [15] outlines the implementation of a competency framework in the Canadian Federal Public Service. The framework was based on the existing job classification system in place within the Canadian public service. While the article indicates numerous core competencies for all public sector employees (making up more than 140 competency profiles), only "client focus" competency is listed and detailed within the article. The competency framework is available through the CBM (Competency Based Management) Web Suite 2 which is accessible to all employees and provides information on CBM and on various tools such as the national competency dictionary, competency profiles, competency self-assessment questionnaires for employees, assistance on developing learning plans and the "National Learning Inventory" which links all departmental learning and development activities to competencies. The site also provides online tools and information for managers to assist them in applying competencies to staffing and other HR processes.

In addition to public service workers, competency models are currently in place for professional training programs for new lawyers. Paquette [16] writes on the design of competency software for a professional law training program. The final system presents the users with a list of competencies from which the users then select their own competencies and performance level. Next the system provides the users with a global summary of their competency levels in order to show gaps and identify strengths and weaknesses. Finally the system presents the users with a plan of action by providing them with resources.

2.3   Competency-Based Education and Prior Learning Assessment

Competency-based education (CBE) and prior learning assessment (PLA) are both important strategies and companion tools for post-secondary education programs. CBE focuses
on what students should learn rather that where or when the learning occurs, while PLA
presents strategies for evaluating informal learning [17]. The Canadian Forces (CF) is one
of the few large Canadian organizations with a Prior Learning Assessment and Recognition
(PLAR) program. Other countries with PLAR in the military include Australia, New Zealand
and South Africa. The UK has a national qualification framework but PLAR is underutil-
ized. PLAR is not used in the United States military.

PLAR implementation in other Canadian workplaces, besides the Canadian military,
is limited. Not recognizing prior and informal learning does have significant consequences for the Canadian economy. Simpson and Vollick's report [18] on a 2001 study
from the Conference Board of Canada concluded that if the experiential learning of
Canadians was fully recognized, between \$4.1 and \$5.9 billion in income could be
generated. This same study found that Canadian post-secondary education has established barriers that prevent the recognition of credentials other than those gained through
formal education.

2.4   Implementation Challenges

Our literature review showed that there are significant challenges with the implementation
of competency-based education and management in Canada, including lack of a national
competency classification system, non-uniform implementation of accepted medical competency frameworks, such as CanMEDS, and the fact that competency assessment methods
vary widely and could be unreliable. Another challenge in broad implementation of competency frameworks is that they are not universal and generally not applicable outside of
specific countries, provinces and/or professions and need constant revisions. In addition,
researchers observed some significant user resistance to implementation of competency
frameworks in industry and in medical training [11, 12, 19, 20].

Competency management practices are closely intertwined with learning management. The functionality of both competency and learning management systems are
frequently included in a single software application, or two software systems might be
integrated. The tools can be used to schedule training sessions, keep track of attendees,
and create reports on who completed each session [21]. New learning management
systems (LMS) incorporate social media, training, certification and mentoring systems.
Similarly, highly evolved learning and performance ecosystems are made up of a
combination of talent management, performance management and knowledge management; they also provide access to experts, social networking and collaboration, and
structured learning [22, 23].

3   Competency Implementation Within LPSS

The National Research Council of Canada (NRC)'s Learning and Performance Support
(LPSS) program implements adaptive and personalization strategies and develops software

components for learning, training, performance support and enterprise workforce optimization. These technologies are designed to benefit NRC clients and their users by: facilitating lifelong learning, reducing learning and training costs, reducing demands on physical infrastructure, enabling streamlined and rapid skill development, reducing time to competency, supporting informal, personal and personalized learning, increasing learner engagement, optimizing sustainable workforces, and increasing operational performance and productivity [24].

The LPSS program is developing a learning and performance support suite of tools that will maximize a users' potential, by enabling them to manage and achieve competencies by matching their skills and expertise to stated customer or employer needs. The tools will help to understand training needs by automatically collecting and analyzing learning and performance reports to show gaps between existing competencies and learner or employer needs. The goal is to improve efficiency of training by using learning records and performance analytics to recommend the most useful learning services and resources specific to workplace environments and competency profiles. LPSS technologies will aid in lowering the cost of learning by enabling access to a wide range of learning services and resources from multiple providers from within the context of relevant multiple workplace

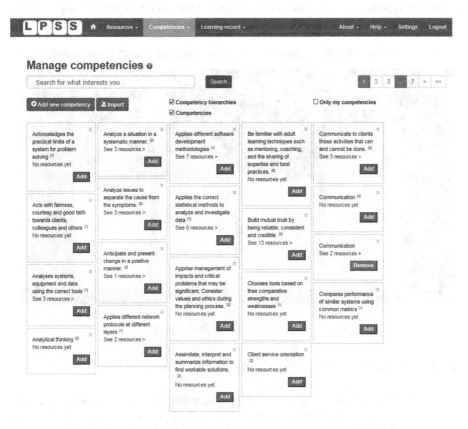

Fig. 1. User interface for personal competency management in LPSS

environments and productivity tools. LPSS tools originated as a web-based prototype open to the public at lpss.me that offers personal rather than personalized learning [24]. The prototype lpss.me was active from Fall 2014 to Fall 2016. Currently it is being redesigned as a set of tools to address the needs of NRC clients.

While the competency management functionality developed within the lpss.me platform is based on a set of preloaded competencies and competency profiles, the user can also define their own competencies and what they want to achieve such as "carpentry" or "creative writing". The user can choose a competency from the preloaded set or add user-defined competencies and receive recommendations for a set of learning resources for a chosen competency (or a set of competencies). The user also has the option to self-assess the level of skills acquired. A screenshot of the LPSS user interface for the competency management functionality is presented in Fig. 1.

Feedback from the users on the lpss.me prototype is being incorporated in the NRC's suite of learning and performance technologies and its showcase platform Techquity (see Fig. 2). The Techquity showcase platform provides the medium by which the benefits of individual LPSS research tools can be demonstrated to clients and allows for tool integration to create broader service offerings. The showcase site itself, named "Techquity" combines "technology" and "equity" and serves as a landing page where all LPSS tools (showcases) can be accessed. Some showcases may demonstrate single technologies, while others demonstrate how these technologies could work together.

Fig. 2. The NRC Techquity showcase platform

4   User Feedback on LPSS Competency Functionality

User feedback on functionalities within LPSS, including competency management and competency and learning resource matching, was elicited via an online survey of lpss.me users and through users' responses to questions regarding LPSS functionality in the course of the remote usability testing of lpss.me conducted in February of 2016.

4.1 Online Survey

An invitation to participate in the online survey was sent to 299 users who were registered with the lpss.me personal learning platform. Between November 2014 and October 2016, 57 users responded to the survey, a response rate of 19%. The majority of respondents were male, from 40 to 69 years old, involved in online learning and highly educated. As a result, the findings from the survey cannot be seen as representative of the general population, but are sample viewpoints from power users within the online learning community.

A total of 24 questions were asked, ranging from demographics questions (e.g. age, gender, education, and familiarity with online learning, etc.) to more specific questions about the LPSS system, including "Which of the LPSS pages or features have you looked at so far?" [24, 25]. LPSS questions that elicited responses concerning user competencies within the system included the open ended text questions: "What would you like a learning and performance management system (like LPSS) to do for you? How would you like to use it?"

4.2 User Feedback on Competency Functionality

The competency management functionality within LPSS attracted significant interest, with roughly 80% of the respondents indicating familiarity with the "My competency profile" functionality and 96% indicating familiarity with the "Browse competency" functionality.

When asked to give feedback on LPSS platform features, the participants provided feedback and suggestions for improving competency features, including:

- Making competency profiles less general and more specific, tied to a particular task.
- Making a better connection between competencies and resource recommendations.
- Adding social connections for people with similar competencies providing a way to network around competencies and learn from what others interested in similar competencies are studying.
- Providing the ability to browse competencies with the users profile associated, to optimize the social network effect.

Examples of user responses related to the LPSS competency functionality are listed below:

"...If I am correct, LPSS is about lifelong learning through the perspective of your competences. The idea and its features are interesting, but you can see the realization is too much inspired by research and less through how people actually want to experience stuff online. For example, I would suggest that at the start of the LPSS, LPSS already would know what kind of competences I might be looking for based on LinkedIn or something. It should give suggestions. Also, learning - for me at least - should be much more visual. Probably this is on the roadmap, but I would like to stress the importance of visual stuff, also to make competences more readable…"

"…Being linked into a group of other users who share common interests/competencies would help…"

"I like the idea of having competencies listed that I want to achieve as part of a personal learning and development plan. Then to point to resources that will help to achieve competencies. I would like more detail in the competencies section. I could see naming a competency area like Professionalism… and then have several more detailed competency statements… and then have some way to measure progress toward achieving each competency statement".

4.3 Feedback on the LPSS System and the User Interface

The survey respondents came up with some ideas on what they would like a learning and performance management system (like LPSS) to do for them, how they would like to use the system, and how the system should be designed to help them learn better:

"As a learner I like it to make suggestions for relevant resources within the competencies, I would like to develop. Based on my already achieved competencies it would also be interesting to see, what other people with a similar profile would recommend to study. Basically it has to (be) intuitive in use".

"I would like to find a way to connect these competencies with an online digital identity tool for employers/conference organizers to scrape so I don't need a dedicated website".

"Network me with other learners interested in similar competencies".

Users' feedback on the user interface design and suggestions on modifications that might help the usability of the system included comments such as:

"I was confused when trying to create my own competencies. It would be useful to have a support tool that guides you as you create competencies. Also, the format of competencies that I have doesn't seem to fit into the input boxes".

"Navigation is clear, clean look. Features that are functioning work well. Perhaps instead of a tick mark to indicate that a competency had been chosen it could change colour".

"Needs a better personal dashboard, with multiple competencies it will become a long page. When getting started the concept of resources is not clear. Love the concept".

"…Create an online sharing and learning environment that is transparent, accessible, personal, friendly, inviting…"

4.4 Usability Evaluation

In addition to the LPSS user survey, usability evaluation of the LPSS platform was conducted in February 2016 using remote usability software (Loop11). The users that signed on lpss.me within the period from December 2014 to December 2015 were invited via email to participate in the usability testing. LPSS users are all volunteers who were invited to sign up to use lpss.me as a website in development. An invitation email to participate in the study was sent to a total of 150 users, with the reminder email sent a week later. The remote usability study for lpss.me has involved users performing mandatory tasks within lpss.me and answering task-related and general questions on lpss.me use, as well as several demographic questions. The study contained some regular lpss.me tasks that users were asked to complete, for example: to add a topic to the competency profile. The questions that users were asked to respond to were either within a text box or Likert scale questions with radio buttons.

During the study period a total of 16 participants clicked on the study link in the invitation email; out of these 16 people, three users completed the study (known here as P1, P2 and P3). Two users (P4 and P5) provided some responses to questions but did not complete the study. The task analysis was done for the completed studies only, and responses to questions analysis included both completed and partial user responses.

At the end of the usability study participants were asked a series of general questions about the system, including would they use it, which features they liked the most, and which features are useful for learning or for doing their job. Two of the users who were able to do all the tasks gave some useful responses that point to the potential of LPSS as well as the need to push the system further and add greater functionality.

For example, in response to a question about the most liked features of the system user P3 commented: "Competencies. Easy to add" and added that "… I would like to have the opportunity to be able to showcase my competencies and abilities"; that the tool is useful for learning and job and that "…The tool is great to force you to reflect on your career".

Users were also asked which aspects of LPSS they found less useful, if they had any suggestions for new features, which additional features they would like to see, and if they had any issues with the lpss.me website. Participant 1's response was that it would be useful to have: "Link to my publications or similar demonstrations of competencies".

While providing important insights on the user's experience with lpss.me, the usability study was limited in that only a small percentage of LPSS users looked at the study, and an even smaller percentage finished the entire study which was comprised of tasks and survey questions. This is not surprising considering that this type of study is more time consuming than a straightforward survey (about 40 min for the study vs less than 10 min for the survey) and users were not compensated for their efforts.

5   Design Considerations for Future LPSS Development

Based on the results of the literature review and the user feedback on desirable LPSS functionality, future LPSS development will focus on greater functionality within LPSS, greater personalization for the user and a better user interface created through the use of multimedia. The development of competency functionality will focus on providing the ability to showcase the competencies, social networking for people with similar competencies and including the assessment of both formal and informal learning.

Competency assessment in most cases is a complex process that involves many actors and software; sometimes it might be too complex to automate. LPSS can provide functionality to access the learning records and activities related to a particular competency for actors such as experts, instructors, and for learning and performance analytics.

In addition, the LPSS research team plans to explore ways to connect competency assessment with NOC 2016 (Canadian National Occupational Classification) and with user resumes, similar to what is currently done with ESCO classification in EU [26]. LPSS technology components currently in development for competency management and competency-based training include competency key phrase extraction, matching courses to competencies, characterizing informal learning and recommender technologies to recommend learning resources based on existing and desired competencies.

6 Conclusions

This paper reports on the findings of the literature review on the current trends within competency-based education, training and management, as well as the challenges with competency management frameworks in Canada. Results from user surveys and usability study for the lpss.me learning and performance management platform related to the competency management functionality were presented. We found that in Canada competencies are most commonly used within the medical profession, including medical education, professional training and accreditation and in public service. One major concern is that frequently competencies are applied in a varied and un-uniform manner, and they can be assessed in sometimes unreliable ways. In addition, competencies might be too rigid or inflexible for some organizations, too focused on the cultural contexts of a specific country and have limited international transferability. Contextual factors also limit competencies transferability – for example, in the area referred to as public health human resources, the needs of each community are dependent upon the context, the place, location and its particular needs.

LPSS users want better resource recommendations, social connectivity with others with similar competencies and the ability to showcase the competencies. Future LPSS development of competency functionality will focus on providing capability to capture both formal and informal competencies and will target competency functionalities that address LPSS users' concerns such as the lack of ability to showcase their competencies, and the connection between their competencies, job opportunities, and social networking opportunities.

References

1. Gartner G00266384: Magic quadrant for talent management suites. Gartner Report (2015)
2. ADL CASS project (2016). http://www.cassproject.org/
3. Dave, M., Dave, M., Shishaodia, Y.S.: Knowledge management and organizational competencies: a harmonic collaboration. Int. J. Adv. Res. Comput. Sci. Soft. Eng. 2(12), 45–50 (2012)
4. Gartner G00294735: Top 10 business trends impacting higher education in 2016. Gartner Report (2016)
5. Lundqvist, K.Ø., Baker, K., Williams, S.: An ontological approach to competency management. Proc. iLearn 2007, 1–4 (2007)
6. Leyking, K., Chikova, P., Loos, P.: Competency and process-driven e-Learning: a model-based approach. Electron. J. e-Learning 5(3), 183–194 (2007)

7. Vogten, H., Koper, R., Martens, H., Van Bruggen, J.: Using the personal competence manager as a complementary approach to IMS learning design authoring. Interact. Learn. Environ. **16**(1), 83–100 (2008)

8. Koper, R., Specht, M.: TenCompetence: lifelong competence development and learning. In: Sicilia, M.-A. (ed.) Competencies in Organizational E-Learning: Concepts and Tools. Education Technology and Society, vol. 9, no. 2, pp. 8–14 (2006)

9. WATCHME project (2017). https://www.project-watchme.eu/

10. Kew, C.: The TenCompetence Personal Competence Manager (2007). http://ceur-ws.org/Vol-280/p08.pdf

11. Whitehead, C., Kuper, A., Hodghes, B., Ellaway, R.: Conceptual and practical challenges in the assessment of physician competencies. Med. Teach. **37**(3), 245–251 (2015)

12. Takahashi, S.G., Hodges, B., Waddell, A., Kennedy, M.: Innovations, Integration and Implementation Issues in Competency-Based Education in Postgraduate Medical Education. Members of the FMEC PG Consortium: 33 pages (2011)

13. Chetlen, A.L., Mendiratta-Lala, M., Probyn, L., Auffermann, W.F., DeBenedectis, C.M., Marko, J., Pua, B.B.: Conventional medical education and the history of simulation in radiology. Acad. Radiol. **22**(10), 1252–1267 (2015)

14. Garcia, J., Coste, A., Tavares, W., Nuno, N., Lachapelle, K.: Assessment of competency during orotracheal intubation in medical simulation. Br. J. Anaesth. **115**(2), 302–307 (2015)

15. Bonder, A., Bouchard, C., Bellemare, G.: Competency-based management – an integrated approach to human resource management in the Canadian Public Sector. Public Personnel Manage. **40**(1), 1–10 (2011)

16. Paquette, G.: An ontology and a software framework for competency modeling and management. Educ. Technol. Soc. **10**(3), 1–21 (2007)

17. Tate, P., Klein-Collins, R.: PLA and CBE on the Competency Continuum: The Relationship between Prior Learning Assessment and Competency-based Education. The Council for Adult and Experiential Learning, October 2015

18. Simpson, S., Vollick, S.: Rewarding learning: a review of prior learning assessment and recognition processes in allied militaries and large organizations. Canadian Forces, Department of National Defence, and Defence R&D Canada Report. DGMPRA CR 2013-001, January 2013

19. Molyneaux, H., Fournier, H., Kondratova, I., O'Donnell, S.: Literature review of competency management systems in Canada. Internal LPSS Report (2016)

20. Stokes, P., Orily, E.: An Evaluation of the user of competencies in human resource development – a historical and contemporary recontextualisation. EuroMed J. Bus. **7**(1), 4–23 (2012)

21. Frost & Sullivan: Enabling Productive Human Capital: New Methods and Tools Help Companies Cope with Changing Workforces, Work Environments, and Regulations, Market Insights (2014)

22. Kondratova, I., Molyneaux, H., Fournier, H., O'Donnell, S.: Market analysis report: TM, HCM and competency management systems. Internal LPSS Report (2016)

23. Rosenberg, M.J., Foreman, S.: Learning and performance ecosystems. Strategy, Technology, Impact, and Challenges. The ELearning Guild, White paper (2014). http://www.elearningguild.com/publications/?id=53

24. Lapointe, J.-F., Molyneaux, H., Kondratova, I., Viejo, A.F.: Learning and performance support - personalization through personal assistant technology. In: Zaphiris, P., Ioannou, A. (eds.) LCT 2016. LNCS, vol. 9753, pp. 223–232. Springer, Cham (2016). doi:10.1007/978-3-319-39483-1_21

25. Fournier, H., Molyneaux, H.: Learning and performance support systems: personal learning record: user studies white paper. NPARC #: 21275411, 19 pages (2015). http://doi.org/10.4224/21275411
26. Zotou, M., Papantoniou, A., Kremer, K., Peristeras, V., Tambouris, E.: Implementing "Rethinking Education": matching skills profiles with open nurses through linked open data technologies. Bull. IEEE Tech. Committee Learn. Technol. 16(4), 18–21 (2014)

Integrated Learning Environment for Blended Oriented Course

3-Year Feedback on a Skill-Oriented Hybrid Strategy

Walter Nuninger[✉]

Polytech'Lille, Université de Lille 1, Av. Paul Langevin, 59655 Villeneuve d'Ascq, France
Walter.nuninger@polytech-lille.fr

Abstract. A fully integrated pedagogical solution has been designed since 2013 to counter the diversity of previous training paths and work experience of the audience enrolled in studies leading to chartered engineer (master degree). The proposed innovative use of a diversity of pedagogical means, including multimedia, is a worthwhile reply to the time reduction of face-to-face lessons, the lack of commitment of learners in their training and the intrusion of digital in Higher Education courses. Such an evolution of the way to conduct the course scenario was motivated by the constraint of sandwich courses for Continuous Vocational Training (CVT) and the wish of the learners for upstream autonomous tools for prerequisites before starting the teaching unit. Based on an improvement development process that takes into account the learners' satisfaction and positive criticism, the solution is validated as a mix of known devices, improved ones and new digital tools integrated in a reasoned manner for the blended oriented course. In this way, it creates an Integrated Learning Environment (ILE) initiated by the trainer, then duplicated, enriched and transferred to other audiences. The results are a change in teaching practices, richness of the interactions with the audience and the completion of the HE issues: quality and efficiency, high level of learning outcomes and involvement of the parties. Such a process will question organization and functioning of HE providers, the culture in the pedagogical team, the aim of a Community of practice (CoP) and the personal objectives of the parties in the environment with levers and blocks.

Keywords: ILE · Blended-course · Digital pedagogical tools · Welfare at work · PBL · Reflexive learning · Collective intelligence · LMS · PLE

1 Introduction

1.1 The Issues of Higher Education

In Higher Education (HE), professors and associate professors further referred to as trainers are facing new constraints while in the classroom [1]. First, the audience (the students, apprentices and learners) has evolved with new personal needs, leading to a lack of involvement in the training. Second, they face bigger groups with a large diversity of previous learning routes and professional experiences, resulting in heterogeneity or

© Springer International Publishing AG 2017
P. Zaphiris and A. Ioannou (Eds.): LCT 2017, Part I, LNCS 10295, pp. 137–157, 2017.
DOI: 10.1007/978-3-319-58509-3_13

low prerequisites while the training becomes more accessible to all. Third, internet ubiquity [2] and generation ages [3] question the students' behaviors in work situations. But, the trainers are also under the pressure of changes in the HE organization to ensure the operational performance triangle (objectives, results and resources) with respect to quality issues by ENQA [4] (see Table 1). Time reduction affects the skill workforce with less face-to-face lessons but also limited asynchronous time due to personal life management, professional ambition and economic situation of learners. Then, the trainers whose responsibility is to achieve a minimal set of learning outcomes for recognized diplomas should adapt locally their practices and find optimal course scenario [5] based on a mix of pedagogical solutions (hybrid course) for their welfare at work.

Table 1. New issues of higher education adapted from Parmentier [13]

Motivation	Challenge
To face the democratization of the university	To develop student-centered learning and partnerships [6]
To make intelligible the hidden curriculum [7] in addition to the learning outcomes	To integrate the generic, cross-disciplinary (communicate, analyze, transfer) as basics
To enhance the students' learning ability and competences to help them enter labor world	To motivate Work Integrated Learning (WIL) for employability [8–10]
To prepare learners and HE providers to globalization and world competition	To develop learning organizations to support internationalization and CoP [11] for excellence
To face the uncertain evolution of society and complex challenges for anyone, including creativity and innovation	To develop modular Training all lifelong [12], i.e. made accessible at any age and from anywhere for personal route

1.2 Background on Pedagogical Approaches for Efficient Learning

Most of the effective pedagogical solutions are learner-centered and based upon the following non-exhaustive list of learning and teaching models:

- The **cone of learning experience** by Dale (1969) with a three-set of learning outcomes: "surface" for knowing; "intermediate" for reproducing ability and "deep-learning" for acting in new situations (skills);
- The **reflexive learning close-loop** (control, adaptation, reconfiguration) by McGills (1993) [14, 15] with focus on student development paradigm;
- The **learning recursive process cycle** by Kolb [16] to dynamically improve learning through experience, stressing on the continuous and voluntary act to grasp and transform experience: feel, think and watch-do, then assimilate, converge and accommodate to contexts;
- The **8-learning events model** by Leclercq and Poumay [17] connects the parties (learner/trainer) involved in the learning system, motivating interaction with action/reaction to improve the learning based on questioning behaviors.

Whatever the model, the active pedagogy should be progressive, adaptable to individual's personal route with targeted competences put into practice, based on previous knowledge ownership for further recognition. Then, the course is a set of learning activities articulated in time, continuous or not, in face-to-face or asynchronous time. The activities are problem-situations that can only be solved with an expected learning and leveraging solutions based on personal strategies as a response to a question that gives meaning. For the learning momentum, the trainer should **initiate, observe, guide, regulate, support and evaluate**. The formative assessment [18] allows remedial actions in the remaining time of the TU. Such considerations stress on the three processes in the pedagogical triangle [19] while the behaviors of the parties (teacher/trainer and learner/trainee) change to achieve the learning outcomes (knowledge-skill): *teaching* when learner is mostly *passive*; *training* when *practising*; and *learning* with a *passive teacher*. The underlying attitudes of teacher and learners will denote the ability to train and learn.

1.3 Proposal for a Digital Support for Guided Self-learning, Called ONAAG

The bias to create the pedagogical device ONAAG (acronym of the "Outil Numérique d'Appui d'Auto-formation guidée"; i.e. Digital Support for Guided Self-Learning [20]) is first, the integration of digital in the training, respecting the European Accessibility Act (2011) and the Equality Challenge for HE as a reply to the issues promoted by the United Nations (art. 24, since 2006). Second, the chosen Ldl approach introduced by Martin J.-P. [21]: "*learn by doing*" to develop the expertise in the topic based on validated knowledge; the learners will prepare the work, propose and apply concept in known and unknown situations, interact for problem-solving and present their results, going further than just "studying" but, identifying good practices, developing cross-disciplinary skills and expertise transfer. The aim is meta-learning and self-reflection with a set of gradual learning activities.

The new opportunities of IT developments allow a new use of time and place, in the classroom and outside, with real or virtual face-to-face thanks to new access to contents and new ways to interact within new media. In this context, ONAAG is a support for a flexible course that encourages the questioning of the learners and their commitment. The trainer motivates, follows and guides toward self-evaluation and peers recognition for individual and collective evolution. To that purpose, the device is based on two different technologies (see Fig. 1): first, a scenario-based Learning Management System (LMS) respecting the trainer's concern to transfer knowledge (ONAAG-1) and second, a dedicated workspace for case studies implemented on the net with a learner focus to develop the skills and achieved the learning outcomes (ONAAG-2). The two technical components motivate learners to solve problem-situations that stand as a set of learning activities with online individual feedback and collective debriefings in the classroom in order to develop reflexive learning [14, 15]. The process initiated by the trainer with blended-course target will boost the 3-loop regulation of the learner's behavior: act and modify action taking into account the results obtained, self-assessment to regulate the action to ensure the result and meta-reflect to adapt action to context and address the issue. This implies formative assessment. The flipped classroom is then the key to benefit from ONAAG during sandwich courses. First, the students autonomously study topics.

Second, they apply the knowledge by solving problems, doing and interacting with others and also with the trainer.

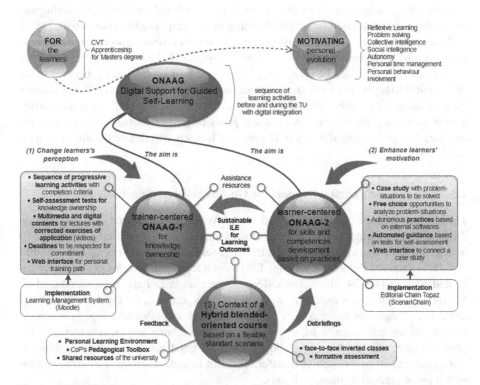

Fig. 1. ONAAG bull chart as the spine of the blended-course, enhancing the motivational dynamics process [22] thanks to basics (1) and abilities (2) developed in the context (3).

The purpose of this paper is to present the integrated hybrid pedagogical device developed since 2014 whose aim is to facilitate learning outcomes thanks to a better involvement in the training. The reminder of this paper is organized as follows. Section 2 presents the groups that motivated the change and experimented ONAAG. The validated scenario of the blended-oriented course is presented in Sect. 3 based on the use of ONAAG enriched by the actors' Personal Learning Environment (PLE) [23]. It integrates a mix of selected pedagogical solutions: conceptual map, serious pedagogical mini-games [24], multimedia and LMS. ONAAG appears as the spine of the ILE while learner-centered pedagogy is the core of the system to support a blended-oriented course [25]. Then, Sect. 4 gives the 3-year feedback based on the main points of evolution, satisfaction surveys and results of the teaching unit evaluation. A brief Sect. 5 puts the focus on the project development that respects the values of agile approaches and the steps of the U-theory of innovation: it affects the trainers' practices. After the future prospects, Sect. 6 provides a conclusion.

2 Training Context

2.1 Motivation and Description of the Audience

ONAAG was created in 2014 for the learners (group n° 1) enrolled in the last year of the CVT, leading to the Chartered Engineer diploma of Polytech'Lille in the field of "production" (master's degree) [26]. The overall objectives for the considered TUs of the WIL curriculum are more efficiency (doing the things right) and more effectiveness (doing the right things) with respect to the audience and learning outcomes, taking advantage of the opportunities offered by digital technologies to support active and learner-centered pedagogy. The device was then adapted to the group of apprentices (n° 2, same field) and finally spread to other groups of students (n° 3, Biological and Food engineering field) and Teaching Units (TUs). The evolution of the learners' flow (-25%, $+44\%$ and $+2\%$ in four years respectively for the groups in the above order) and various recruitment pools (previous higher diploma for 33%, 27% and 31%; average gender rates are 12%, 24% and 79%) requires further efforts for the parties (audience and trainer) to reach the learning outcomes, facing failures during final examinations. Even if formative training was already implemented for CVT and IVT with continuous follow-up, the younger (apprentices) seemed less involved with true difficulties to organize their learning and to work collectively during asynchronous and distance activities. The trainer's observations of group n° 1 encourage to teach part of the prerequisite in mathematics (only 14% are able to calculate on their own) and provide resources before starting the course especially for computer programming basics (16% are not autonomous) so that they could use simulation software as Scilab and be able to follow the automatic control TU. Before 2013, the solution was to provide supplementary documents and use part of the allocated hours (almost one third of the 40 h over two semesters). In 2013, a satisfaction survey confirmed these needs for prerequisite and the learner's demand for additional trainings before starting the TU. The group project guidance has also shown that they lacked skills in project management and collective intelligence (over 3 years, the number of project managers dropped by 20%): cross-disciplinary competences enhanced during their formative work situation. As a mean value over four years, 88% of the apprentices attending the computer programming TU do not consider having needs for coding skills (a stable reading) but at the same time, 27% do not feel autonomous with ITC. A rate that doubles in two years to reach 43% in 2016, in line with the reality observed during the practical sessions that year: only 35% have the ICDL basic level, showing the recruitment changes. This variability is measured with the other groups but is not easily predictable. Over the same period, a rising number of learners (n° 1) attending the automatic control TU feels independent in mathematics, from 8% in 2014 up to 22% in 2016. The trend is in contrast with the others groups, but the reverse is true with respect to coding competences (from 33% towards 11% in 2016). In 2013, 67% of the learners felt no need for this topic however enrolled in the production field! ONAAG, proposed since 2014 to the groups before the beginning of the course with a focus on prerequisite, had turned such a feeling inside out (11% in 2016), reflecting the impact of the tool for a higher commitment afterwards.

2.2   Opportunities to Create ONAAG Project

In 2014, such observations motivated the trainer to make best use of the possibilities offered by Moodle to set a sequence of autonomous learning activities realized before and during the course. Because alternation offers distance possibilities for work and asynchronous online feedback, the digital solution will replace the previous hard copy document and corrected homework. Now, final tests with multiple attempts allowed for self-assessment will follow web-based lessons with videos of corrected exercises. Face-to-face lessons will deal with debriefings and complementary explanations, targeting the flipped classroom. Based on Ldl [21], the group project will now be implemented digitally with automated guidance to develop collective skill. For the vocational trainings, the formative assessment with remedial actions were already an asset that favor the new way to drive the course with ONAAG. Meanwhile, the final assessment will not change. The ONAAG project took advantage of the CNL project by the Université de Lille 1 that supports digital online content, providing time recognition for the trainer's production (https://goo.gl/4eN9GB) and technical support.

2.3   Impacts of ONAAG Project

ONAAG goes further than Virtual Learning Environment and PLE while learner-centered pedagogy is the core of the system that drives the use of a mix of pedagogical solutions [23, 27]: serious pedagogical mini-games, problem-based learning (PBL) and formative assessments with comings and goings in and outside the classroom with a distance feedback and

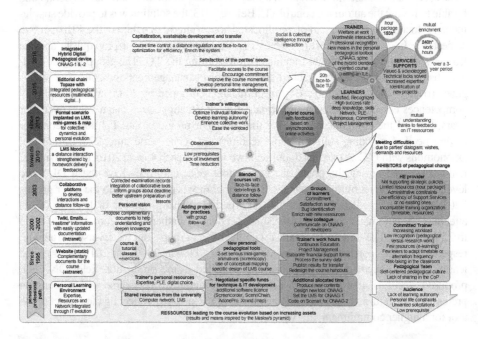

Fig. 2. Evolution of the course scenario (left) towards a blended-oriented hybrid course for sustainable results (up right) that complies with the satisfaction of the parties; inhibitors (right)

face-to-face debriefings. The agile project development motivated the innovation in the sense of the U-theory [28], driving the change towards a hybrid blended-oriented course (see Fig. 2): based on a validated standard scenario (see Sect. 3) it is flexible, helps course momentum, allows additional contents for evolving outcomes and could be transferred to new topics. The aim is to cope with the satisfaction of the parties through the ILE [20]: learners, trainers and members of technical support, motivating some kind of CoP for network and transfer.

3   Standard Scenario of the Blended-Oriented Hybrid Course

3.1   Scenario with ONAAG Spine

Taking into account PBL, the pedagogical device is a multi-level training solution [29] that better takes into account the context and group progression to adapt synchronous lessons (local momentum regulation, feedback and debriefing). Based on the identified competences and the use of digital technologies, the global objective is more efficiency, then quality. Figure 3 shows the proposed scenario for the blended-oriented course after a 3-year period of experiments with three essential lines of approach, now validated:

- An **upstream initialization** for prerequisite and identification of the TU outcomes that will resonate with the learners' personal needs thanks to feedback [30] (part 1);
- The **"learn by doing" approach** [21] for capacity building based on the two parts of the ONAAG device [20]: first one, for knowledge and learning ability and second one, for skills development, putting knowledge in practice autonomously (part 2);
- The **challenge of the alternating face-to-face sessions** to create the group dynamic with serious pedagogical mini-games [25], encourages reflexive learning [15] with activities like conceptual mapping project and debriefings [31] to sustain involvement in the training, and strengthen knowledge ownership (part 3);

This proposal is a way to handle the pedagogical approach rejection due to the discomfort felt by the learners put into problem-situations [32], demanding new skills for the parties involved. They expected the training to be easy but they face personal and external constraints (prerequisite, learning autonomy and personal life with economic and/or professional stress). One has to "learn to learn": a recursive learning process that involves errors, uncertainties and drives the change (socio-constructivist approach). The course timeline is adapted with respect to the observed progression of the group thanks to the modular concept of ONAAG that creates an area of freedom to conduct the course. The underlying requirement is to train the trainers [33] to make the best of the Information and Communications Technology for Education (ICTE) and transfer the approach: the richness of ONAAG comes from its use by the trainer who designed it as pointed out in Sect. 5. The peer review and self-assessment provide meaning, initiates collective intelligence and develops cross-curricular competencies [34].

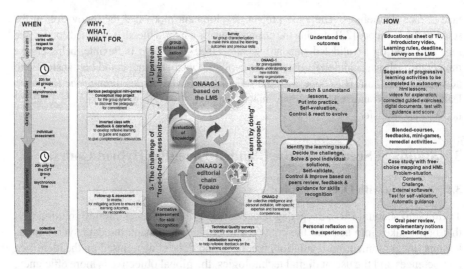

Fig. 3. Validated hybrid course scenario based on the ONAAG digital device in 2016 for CVT. Note that for IVT only ONAAG-1 is used followed by a collective project in class for abilities.

3.2 ONAAG-1, to Prepare Lessons, Consolidate the Prerequisites and Evolve

This first part of ONAAG targets the knowledge through a sequence of synchronized digital learning activities: prerequisite, then new notions dealing with the TU outcomes. This explains why learners begin studying with ONAAG-1 in autonomy (surface learning level: knowing) before the first lesson, then carry it out afterwards all along the course for the momentum, helped by feedback in class (intermediate level: reproducing). However, ONAAG-1 is a trainer-centered device that explains the technical solution adopted on the LMS Moodle, using the already integrated resources, it participates in developing the behavioral and learning competence. It proposes an alternative way to access information and build knowledge, giving the parties some clues to invent their PLE, mixing different origins and means for data access.

Figure 4 shows the standard functional solution for two activities of increasing "difficulty" (A1 and A2). The A1 activity is a digital lesson (A11) with web-based documents for lecture, multimedia for explanation and corrected guided exercises of application to understand, followed by a self-evaluation test (A12) with various attempts allowed based on a production to upload. The following A2 activity is of similar design but activated after completion of the previous one by the learner. Automatic feedback after the test encourages the learner to go backwards and forwards to overcome the blocks. ONAAG-1 is a way to tailor the training to the learners' personal learning rhythm. Created in 2014, the modular structure is copied to add new streams of specific activities required by other TU, then spread out in 2015 for different training audience, leading to the revision of the entire trainer's course handout material. The trainer has to set the tool in accordance with the blended-course organization, deciding the completion criteria of the activities to connect and giving deadline that strengthens personal time management ability. As an additional workload, he should adapt in real time the timeline to the evolution of the group taking benefit from debriefings during the face-to-face sessions to give complementary explanations, helping reflexivity and autonomy.

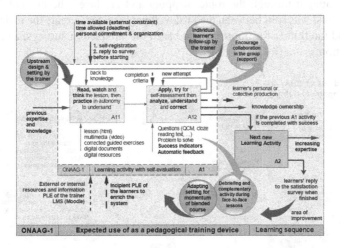

Fig. 4. Functional description of a learning sequence with triggering criteria for completion

3.3   ONAAG-2, to Implement Knowledge in New Contexts and Develop Expertise

This second part of ONAAG focuses the required competences within a dedicated workspace for case studies that provides free-decision making for problem solving. The autonomous learners (group n° 1) will meet a problem-situation to solve in a given context (in-depth learning), putting into practice their knowledge acquired with ONAAG-1. The allocated time is 12 h of the TU hours for synchronous group guidance and momentum in class based on a personal work (30% of the TU hours, i.e. 6 h/learners). The rest of the time serves complementary training based on the group demands.

ONAAG-2 is a learner-centered device for ramp-up skills based on a free-choice mapping of learning route by experience (see path excerpt in Fig. 5). The technical solution is built from the editorial chain Topaz (ScenariChain, scenari-platform.org) as a set of intertwined paths to guide the problem analysis within orientation nodes for decision-making. It is a discovery of the unknown, but considering one problem solving, the learners are expected to formalize the issue (see number 1 in Fig. 5), propose their solution synthesis to the challenge (2) and innovate with a step back and forward to develop higher skills (3). Reflexive learning is encouraged, implementing external tools and methods to overcome the issue thanks to information, calculus, simulation and brainstorming with the group. To avoid dead-ends, support resources are automatically proposed, depending on the score of self-assessment. The learners upload their self-validated group production on the LMS Moodle for follow-up, additional guidance based on formative assessment. They will present their work in class for final recognition and peers review. ONAAG-2 strengthens questioning and informal learning. It is a key for competence differentiation for individuals committed in the learning group, including the hidden curriculum [7]: problem-solving, project management, communication, social and collective intelligence. In 2015, the CVT group tested the prototype already integrated to the LMS [27] using a web link to the case-study HMI. The trainer thought through the route mapping and produced the content. Then, the coding workload was split between the IT developer service to create the main mapping structure and the trainer for improvement based on satisfaction surveys, and for small bugs correction.

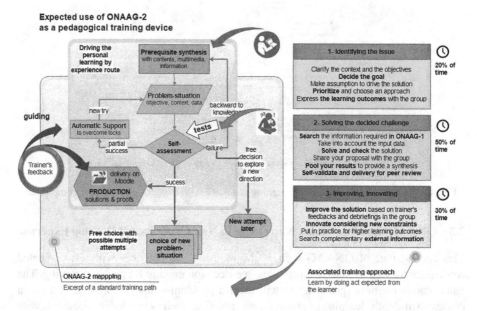

Fig. 5. Free-choice route example implemented with ONAAG-2 and associated PBL approach

4   Results After 3-Years of Experimentation with ONAAG

4.1   Some Figures About ONAAG

ONAAG is a 2-technology digital device integrated through the LMS. Various versions of ONAAG-1 were experimented during 3 years by more than 277 learners: four TUs dealing with computer programming (20 h) and automatic control (40 h) of three training paths leading to chartered engineer (two in WIL). The previous training paths and work experiences are heterogeneous. ONAAG project was supported over a 3-year period based on results by the university within a 153 h package for the trainer (44 h as an average value each year) plus 266 work hours for multimedia support service (64%: 76 h and 160 h for ONAAG-1 and -2 respectively). Many satisfaction surveys were proposed to identify areas of improvement and quality surveys for technical aspects. Data processing motivates new contents, modularity and additional videos of higher quality. Today, the prospect is to simplify the interconnection of resources in Moodle for ILE.

4.2   Better Learning Outcomes

Overall results to the TUs are better if we compare the final individual assessment for each group taken independently. For group n° 1 (CVT), as early as 2014 compared to 2013 when ONAAG was not proposed. 77% validated at the first examination and 100% after remedial activities in contrast with the 50% remediation the previous year. Full completion of ONAAG is a requirement. Indeed, the average grade for group n° 3 increases by 1.5 points with a standard deviation narrowing and higher extreme score; a group that completed ONAAG at a rate of 97%. The same good results apply for the apprentices (group n° 2) when completing ONAAG at 98% in 2014 and 2015 with a score distribution moving up by 5.4 points and a reduced standard deviation by 3 points. In 2016, the group is observed to be less autonomous during practical lessons with lower ownership, but ONAAG is only completed at 64%. This is the risk of digital native browsing through accessible multimedia resources without deep analysis, or practices for ownership. Allocating time, deadline and guiding are part of ONAAG requirements. The comparison of the behaviors of the groups during final examinations questions the assessment choices; how to recognize in the collective production the autonomous and committed individual, giving confidence? In 2016, one student stated *"the ONAAG test results should be taken into account and not only checking that the work was done: use ONAAG as an assessment tool!"*. An attractive proposition, but incompatible with the constraints of "diplomas" and non-face-to-face realization. This is a difficulty met for the MOOCs, what ONAAG is not: although, it can be stand-alone used as an e-learning means, the richness comes from blended-learning based on the designed online tool. It is therefore closer to a SPOC that motivates learning and collective work to raise the blocks, but taking support from integrated face-to-face sessions: this changes everything. A learner commented in 2016: *"ONAAG-2 is better than a MOOC because the learning steps are not prescribed: we can stop, change challenge then, come back later. The work with the colleagues, all together with debriefings, is valuable and lifts us up"*.

4.3   Learners' Satisfaction and Learning Attitudes

The final learning satisfaction is higher due to peer recognition as comments a learner in 2016: *"I really liked the pedagogical approach that take us out of our comfort zone, with a professional and engineering judgement instead of a schoolish assessing academic way"*. All along the TU duration, personal time management and organization evolve towards a greater evenness of decided learning periods during asynchronous time, showing a new behavior and commitment in their learning. In 2014, depending on external constraints for CVT the average data access peaks occur early in the morning, midday or late at night, with higher frequency in response to the trainer's inputs. Although, we do not have information about the use of data, the video time access varies from 30 s to 30 min for 2–5 min videos. This denotes quick data backup for later personal use or online reading with replay and pause, depending on generation age. The comments or observation in the classroom show that the oldest print documents whereas the youngest simply copy digital information and read on mobile phone. Surprisingly, low IT basics limit their quick adaptability to new digital technical choices and therefore, their efficiency. *"Read, write, count and code"* are the new prerequisites of learning digital solutions compliance and upgrade, explaining the use of Moodle for mobility a low cost. Students told us in 2016: *"It is clear with videos than with the course handout"*; *"It is easy to use from anywhere at school, at the library or at home"*. At the end of the first semester, this year a learner wrote, *"ONAAG-1 allowed me to understand the course basics, to hang on and also to exchange with the teacher or the group to get feedback and develop knowledge ownership. It allows me to identify the blocking points I need the teacher to explain while back in class"*.

4.4 Some Specificities Between the Two Parts of ONAAG

Collective assessment of the learning production of the group through ONAAG-2 is ethical thanks to individual examinations processed after ONAAG-1 completion that validate a shared basic level of learning outcomes for the further competence target. ONAAG-2 is learner-centered in contrast with the trainer-center ONAAG-1 that motivates evolution as noted by a learner, *"we expected a guided path framework as with ONAAG-1, but this is not the case: free-choice is disruptive. I thought tests were the finality, but our results shared with the group showed it us a different way"*. The learners were trained to follow a pre-decided path; they now have to decide freely, discovering the unknown. The main improvements from the prototype are first, to make clear such a difference thanks to instructional videos of learners working with the two devices. Second, add a route map with short videos to explain issues and allow shortcuts. Third, optimize the automated guidance and resources access for support based on supplemented test with indicators of success. Finally, better link ONAAG-2 to the LMS with structured digital returns of results, in form and time, to facilitate the trainer's assessment. This requires new technical developments for full autonomy of the group that will decide of the depth of his learning outcomes; pulled up by the device and the deadline for formalized work synthesis, limiting blocks with reactive feedback.

4.5 Impacts of Previous Training and Professional Routes

The initialization step, the gradual difficulty scope of learning sequences and the synchronous group activities under the trainer guidance in class are, with feedback for support and debriefings to motivate and reassure, the keys of success that limit rejection. Note in 2014, the apprentices: *"too much personal homework"*, *"I want the corrections and more face-to-face lessons"*, *"I don't like collective feedback with forums"* but also, *"this approach of autonomous education is interesting but for the complex notions, we need more guidance"*; even in 2016, a student wishes more lectures. Confidence should be given about the individual ability to perform, encouraging involvement in the training in order to overcome resistance to change. The reasons are the previous training and professional personal route, but also behaviors and dialogism between wishes, required efforts and unknown external brakes. It is clear that this approach questions previous knowledge and expertise, but also autonomy, personal organization and learning abilities. In 2015, a learner already wrote, *"my perception has evolved notably on tools for the TU objectives. I understood that everything is done to help learning and I am satisfied with my results"*. Even younger students comments in 2016: *"I appreciated the autonomous way to learn"*, *"I find rather good the grasp of digital but we are not always ready for it"*; *"I expected to learn the computer programming I did not need, but in the end, I am satisfied with my new skills"*. A committed audience in the learning momentum requires much less efforts by the trainer: *"I didn't see the time flew past, I did things at my own pace and saw them in a different way"* (student in 2016). Other keywords in replies to open question for group n° 3 are, more playful and interesting, easier access to notions, adaptable to personal learning rhythm, original and motiving. The digital allows **learning in a different way**, at any time and from anywhere, with educational videos for better explanation than in class due to the rhythm control. Nevertheless, all groups still expect direct access to bringing solutions online. In 2016, a CVT learner wrote, *"I feel more confident to follow the TU. ONAAG-1 allows us to go backwards and forwards through the learning to find levers, benefiting from forums and exchange with colleagues. It is a good tool to learn and prepare final examination"*. Finally, the shared assets is that all parties finished the training with a higher self-awareness: knowledge ownership, skills, behavior and personal needs. Indeed, after failure at the final examination, one apprentice said in 2016, *"You provided us all of it! It is our fault, we must evolve in behaviors"*, stressing learning ability and involvement. This is undoubtedly one of the limitations of digital technology: sharing contents but avoiding learners to skim through, ensuring availability after the training completion and retaining authorship in the context: PLE is the key.

4.6 Trainer's Satisfaction

Today, quality concern implies simplifying the interconnection of the parts of ONAAG with the LMS. The video quality has already been improved thank to multimedia services. The course is better received, enriched by the peers' interactions in the group that motivates. The workload is greater upstream to develop and set the device and during realization for follow-up, but for higher welfare at work. The good return on investment comes from the tools developed and the training expertise from the practice. Nevertheless, some external constraints cannot be easily taken into account without the support of the HE provider strategy (alternation frequency, assessment rules, global organization and planning) to provide sufficient autonomous learning time to limit backlash effect and make possible active pedagogy. This is a limitation to innovation. The success mostly depends on the trainer's willingness and efforts to get funds, technological solutions for a final adapted and operational device put into the training action to comply the pedagogical objectives. It is flexible, easy to access, attractive and based on existing facilities by the university for maintenance and possible transfer. It helps the awareness of one's own responsibility in the act of learning, developing a proactive attitude. The hybrid course benefits from contextualized and experiential activities but the trainer is put at risk and the personal workload of the parties should be estimated.

4.7 Technical Requirements and Final Results in 2016

Today, the trainer entirely manages the two parts of ONAAG with LMS setting and re-coded with JavaScript functions to develop specific indicators. The blocks for ONAAG-2 are the secured individual follow-up, automatic generation of the work synthesis and development of more standard tests to facilitate duplication with new cases studies, limiting new coding to only few settings. Further improvements, depending on funds, will consider the full integration of the digital resources to the LMS [25]. The standard scenario of the blended-oriented course is the achievement of a 4-year commit-ment of the trainer for the learners' satisfaction, giving them some complementary abil-ities. **It is summarized as follows**: 1- Initialize the activities for membership, grasping tools and identifying expectations. 2- Allow an upstream time before the introduction of new concepts to avoid rejection, providing the prerequisites with ONAAG-1. 3- Give milestones for autonomous, but obligatory, fulfillment of learning activities to prepare the flipped classroom. 4- Regulate in time and extend the duration of the TU over the semester to benefit from alternation and asynchronous learning time, inserting debrief-ings for complementary support for better ownership. 5- Assess and value the work carried out with ONAAG-2. ONAAG also integrates the other pedagogical means from the toolbox within two frameworks. First, **for mini-games**: a short upstream video with quiz on the LMS followed by synchronous collective work, then knowledge strength-ening with ONAAG-1. Second, **for collective projects** like mapping or case studies with ONAAG-2: 1- Start the group dynamic in face-to-face session for challenge discovery. 2- Ensure self-education for specific topics using ONAAG-1 (for instance conceptual maps). 3- Provide staged completion including debriefings and self-assess-ment (with ONAAG-2 for instance). 4- Motivate peer review for final recognition. The year 2017 will be the one of simplification with additional learner videos testimonials to encourage interest and explain, and a unique LMS to access all parts of ONAAG for readability, integrating the requirements of other pedagogical means.

5   ONAAG's Project Development

5.1 A Project that Respects the Agile Approach

The trainer's willingness to respond to the needs of the audience with a quick functional response and a constant adjustment of the technical solution in real-time with respect to the groups' satisfaction, made agile the ONAAG project [35]. The major thread to develop the device deals with the additional values it provides to the parties involved, based on an emerging idea developed with and for the audience. The satisfaction surveys were guarantees for sustainable results: an existing, used and validated pedagogical device that integrates existing means and new technical evolutions (LMS, ScenariChain, multimedia…). One of the key conditions of success is that the trainer is at the same time the Product Owner and the Leader of the project (Scrum Master in the sense of Scrum approach [36]) that energizes but leaves the IT development team free to organize (he is part of it), limiting the deviation to the specifications. It also proves the technical feasibility and interest of the pedagogical approach to motivate the colleagues to join the process.

5.2 A Project Leading to Innovation and CoP

ONAAG is an interesting lever for the CoP [37] that broadens the inner competences to include a wider culture as a learning organization. The device affects the behaviors of all the parties involved thanks to the interaction between teaching practices, learning abilities and technical developments. By seeking local solutions, an evolutionary process has begun in accordance with the U-theory of innovation [28] (see Fig. 6):

1. **Initiate** thanks to the triggers pushing away from the comfort zone of the pedagogical habits: the groups' needs, training constraint or organization demands.
2. **Experiment** in opposition to the culture of origin of the pedagogical team as a system: or felt opposed to;
3. **Act** voluntary and thoughtfully by integrating new approaches and tools for its own use and objectives;
4. **Co-evolve** thanks to a new dialogue and skill transfer (generative conversation) that broaden and develop the practices and the CoP: in our context, active pedagogy and digital to support reflexive learning and autonomy.

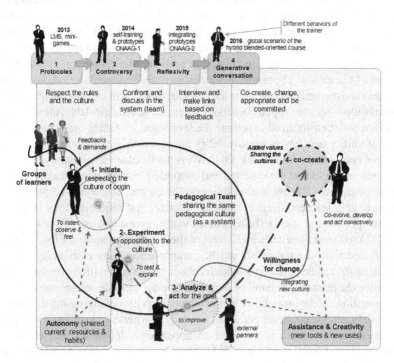

Fig. 6. ONAAG, the founding element of change in coherence with the U-Theory

In 2013, the learning activities were proposed on Moodle with pedagogical serious mini-games in class to encourage involvement. Then, some self-training opportunities with ONAAG are experimented as of 2014. Since 2015, all validated digital parts have been integrated into the improved ONAAG with a global course scenario formalized in 2016. Future prospects with the pedagogical team will ensure sustainability: a necessary path for the recognition and viability of the economic model in the medium term.

5.3   Projects Impact on the Parties: The Trainer's Responsibility

The course realization had changed with some benefits for the trainer with respect to the teaching interest and the adhesion of the audience. In the same way, learners face a new way of learning that might be better adapted to their needs and generation specificities (digital but not only). The consequence for the parties is to change behavior: first, the students looking for easier ways to learn through more attractive and iterative activities with less reading at first glance but they should be more able to learn autonomously with analysis abilities to select information; second, the trainer should develop new generic and operational skills and change practices. The training requirement specifications motivate the necessary behavior change to become an engineer with respect to the competency framework. It demands to enforce complex learning processes with new relationships between trainees and trainers. The context is neither predictable, nor reproducible but the learning approach can be framed. The trainer must initiate and boost the act of learning in a permanent interaction with the group because of various personal needs, unifying a shared consistent objective for all (see Fig. 6). In the scope of compe-tences, the means are problem-situations that motivate the change progressively with the support of the trainer. The reference situations make it possible to validate what has been learned and recognize the skills in the context; blocks will emerge, identified within continuous follow-up and flipped classroom. Then, in the time available, the remediation activities are better customized to actuate the levers and guarantee the gains: a personal mapping of ability that favors employability based on differentiation upon a common professional competency framework. ONAAG is the flexible and modular digital means to push questioning so that the solicited and supported learners will develop ownership and peer recognition. The innovation relies on the controlled use and responsibility of the trainer to help learners discover what is effective, first refraining their own experi-ences in an open state of mind to be able to act in the context and learn from the process. Indeed, ONAAG raises learner's awareness of their learning responsibility. To mitigate the risk of rejection, the trainer should be comprehensive and convincing. First, the trainer initiate the reflexive dialogue with feedback on the action (discover and involve). Second, once the learners are familiar with questioning (confidence and autonomy), the reflexive learning can be brought with effect using activities of increasing difficulty and collective debriefings, going deeper into knowledge ownership, leading to recognition. Sharing a common concern is therefore an appealing solution for efficient training, taking advantage of work-experience and situations for change, ability and knowledge ownership that lead to satisfaction, recognition and diploma. Behind the digital device, what makes the difference is the trainer's skill: an expert mentor that can supervise, guide and support [38]. As a trainer-tutor, he will take on three roles facing three behaviors of the leaner who evolves:

- **The master role** (course leader) in front of the *disciple* to help the step back on learning outcomes and pedagogical approach;
- **The informed advisor** (coach), the one "to-go" for the *dissenting learner* who discovers autonomy but still has to conceptualize it for ownership;
- **The expert** for the leaner acting as a *committed peer* with collective intelligence, free speech, creativity, reflect ability and autonomy.

The aim is to give comfort to facilitate testing actions and recognition through feedback and personal development [39]. The pedagogy is a learner-centered active one used in a course scenario that must adapt to the difficulties met by the learners. The skills required for the trainer-tutor are active listening to overcome locks manifested by the audience anxiety reaction (based on real or perceived skills) and the questioning of the trainer (based on justified and achievable expected learning outcomes). Consequently, the design of ONAAG and the associated learning standard scenario change the paradigms: the trainer is no longer the knowledge holder but the means, whereas the learner is imperatively a voluntary actor for personal evolution. The process reinforces the cross-disciplinary skills such as inter-personal abilities, problem solving, organization, positive criticism, self-nomination and intercultural to be able to act in new situations.

5.4 Future Prospects

Today, the solution appears as useful for the quality of course thanks to the ability of the trainer to guide the groups through the knowledge they autonomously discover and put into practice. The future prospects will meet the following issues. First, a pre-recruitment training process could encourage the applicants towards upstream and customized self-training based on ONAAG-1 framework to ensure knowledge and prerequisite. Second, specific distance training could enrich the training offer of the HE provider, targeting a set of competences in a limited amount of individualized time based on the use ONAAG-2 model within virtual face-to-face inverted lessons. The key benefit results from the possible interactions between modular and shorter trainings to allow the differentiation of the training route of the individual in time and space: life-long learning [41]. To this end, questions arise like the assessment mode and scoring, including online individual and collective evaluation. Finally, the experimentation and transfer in the pedagogical team will enrich the CoP, making links between topics.

6 Conclusion

In the beginning, the challenge was to find, in the given framework of the training organization, a way to give more flexibility to the course with respect to the audience specificity and the learning progression of the groups, while ensuring the diploma Ethics. The designed pedagogical device ONAAG, and the standard blended-course scenario for its use, require a new learning style of the parties who will strengthen their social and collective intelligence, motivating interaction and reflection over the training experience. They will evolve by acting voluntarily to overcome issues in a context they identify: an ability of the engineer as a recognized expert. The use of digital and multimedia means are only ways to support the pedagogical approach, favored by the tremendous development of ICTE, avoiding the viral effect of being fashionable with well-known multimedia platforms and permanent access to information: keeping focus on the learning target (skills) allows the validation of information. This evolution demands effective HE support services for the trainer and trainees: IT maintenance services and multimedia producing services for quality, safe and secured access to digital resources; but also a necessary training plan. Indeed, the trainers should be proficiency-users as expressed in DIGCOMP [40] with respect to digital competence: "*confident, critical and creative use of ICT to achieve goals related to work, employability, learning, leisure, inclusion and/or participation in society*". This also applies to the end-users learners that should enter the training as already independent-users; they are citizens in a digital word [41]. ONAAG encourages the trainer evolution to overcome the new challenges of digital natives and the new generation of learners. Developed as a prototype in a local context, this hybrid solution is an appealing way to solve dialogism: skills/diploma, personal path/standard for the group, freedom of the teacher in the classroom/training framework and autonomy/guidance. Such a process of proven effectiveness (adhesion and higher commitment of the audience) questions the organization and functioning of HE providers, team pedagogical culture, CoP goal and the personal objectives of the committed parties in their environment with levers and blocks.

The Return On Investment (ROI) comes from the satisfaction of the learners and their collective feedback that enrich the course, practices and device. In addition, the transfer of the hybrid solution to different training paths and TUs is a reality with quick adaptation of the contents by the trainer thanks to a duplicated modular structure for generic skills and prerequisites. ONAAG is not a MOOC, nor a full distance learning solution, but a support for autonomy with focus on knowledge first, then abilities in the framework of a blended-oriented course. Note that the same scope is shared with the WissBase and WissFit solutions proposed at DHBW Mosbach (www.wissbase.de) with scenarios on Moodle to help learners' learning and working skills; a program that benefits from more funding to cover all the training offer. This is not the case for the ONAAG project, limited to some TUs, which develops collective intelligence and skills through case studies, going further than just an optimized use of the LMS.

The main inhibitors to pedagogical innovation in contrast with the levers (see in Fig. 2) are strategic policies not supporting the change with too high administrative constraints, the lacks of efficient support services for technique, then local organization (timetable) incompatible with the TU requirements in addition to higher workload and low recognition that reduce the trainer's willingness. Finally, the self-centered pedagogical culture that limits the sharing in the pedagogical team in addition to the risk-taking with the audience. The innovation relies on the personal use of this hybrid solution that creates an ILE, initiated by the trainer that evolves with the richness of the audience met. The last asset is the contribution to the welfare at work in the classroom that relies on the trainer inner skills and behavior: the system is designed for his needs in order to achieve the learners' expectations for the training. To go further, the project development process takes into account the learner's satisfaction (as "clients") with rapid adaptation for improvement and can easily be copied and conducted but, for capitalization, the involvement of the pedagogical team and the inclusion in the HE strategy are a necessity for new developments. Today, technical improvements will focus on monitoring for a simpler follow-up of learners. Then, the assessment should be thought through for autonomous individuals involved in a collective work to ensure Ethics and equity. Today, we are at the edge of a culture break following the U-theory model of development for innovation. A change that expects a better internal communication on the pedagogical choices for a training offer strategy dealing with e-distance learning and life-long learning.

Acknowledgement. This research was supported by the University de Lille from 2014–2017 through the CNL bidding process (Digital Online Content) to support the creation of digital educational resources by the trainers. Our special thanks go to our demanding learners who experimented and gave us their worthwhile feedback to help us identify the areas of improvements. Thanks to Jean-Marie Châtelet, my colleague, for his support and positive critical view upon teaching practices.

References

1. Alava, S., Romainville, M.: Les pratiques d'étude, entre socialisation et cognition. In: Revue Française de pédagogie, vol. 136, pp. 159–180 (2001)
2. Tapscott, D.: Grown up Digital: How the Net Generation is Changing Your World. McGraw-Hill Education, New York (2009)
3. Tugan, B.: Not Everyone Gets a Trophy: How to Manage Generation Y. J-Bass (2009)
4. European Association for Quality Assurance in Higher Education – ENQA: Standards and Guidelines for Quality Assurance in the European Higher Education Area (ESG) (2015). http://www.enqa.eu/index.php/home/esg/. Accessed 10 Oct
5. Saroyan, A., Frenay, M. (dir.): Building Teaching Capacities in Higher Education: A Comprehensive International Model. Stylus Publishing (2010)
6. Fillol, C., Barbier, J.-Y.: Bridging Individual and Organizational Learning Through a Systemic Approach: Toward a Double Helix Knowledge Creation Model. University Paris, Paris (2007). Economics Papers
7. Konieczka, J.: The hidden curriculum as a socialization of schooling is in process at all times, and serves to transmit messages to students about values, attitudes and principles. In: Advanced Research in Scientific Areas, pp. 250–252, 2–6 December 2013
8. Ferns, S., Russel, L., Smith, C.: Designing work integrated learning to optimise student employment. In: Learning for Life and Work in a Complex World, vol. 38, pp. 161–175. ERDSA, Australia (2015)
9. Yang, J., Schneller, C., Roche, S.: The Role of Higher Education in Promoting Lifelong Learning. UNESCO Institute for Lifelong Learning (2015)
10. Davies, A., Fidler, D., Gorbis, M.: Future Work Skills 2020. Institute for the Future for University of Phoenix Research Institute (2011). http://www.iftf.org/uploads/media/SR-1382A_UPRI_future_work_skills_sm.pdf. Accessed 2015
11. Gibbs, G., Coffey, M.: The impact of training of university teachers on their teaching skills, their approach to teaching and the approach to learning of their students. Active Learn. Higher Educ. 5(1), 87–100 (2004)

12. European Commission: Europe 2020 (2010). http://ec.europa.eu/europe2020/index_en.htm. Accessed 2015
13. Parmentier, P.: Cinq leviers institutionnels pour la qualité de l'enseignement universitaire. In: Rege Colet, N., Romainville, M. (eds.) La pratique enseignante à l'université, pp. 199–215. De Boeck, Bruxelles (2006)
14. Borckbanc, A., McGill, I.: Facilitating Reflective Learning in Higher Education. Open University, Maidenhead, McGraw-Hill, New York (2007). ISBN 978-033522091-5368
15. Cendon, E.: Bridging theory and practice: reflective learning in higher education. In: Nuninger, W., Châtelet, J. (eds.) Handbook of Research on Quality Assurance and Value Management in Higher Education, pp. 304–324. IGI Global, Hershey (2016). doi: 10.4018/978-1-5225-0024-7.ch012
16. Kolb, D.A.: Experiential Learning - Experience as the Source of Learning and Development. Prentice-Hall, Englewoods Cliffs (1984)
17. Leclercq, D., Poumay, M.: The 8 learning events model and its principles (2008). http://www.labset.net/media/prod/8LEM.pdf. Accessed 1 Oct 2014
18. Brown, S.: Assessment for learning. Learn. Teach. HE 1, 81–89 (2005). 2004–2005
19. Houssaye, J.: The relevance of the pedagogical triangle: understanding operating principles of the pedagogical situation. In: Annual Meeting of the American Educational Research Association (AERA), New Orleans, USA (1994)
20. Nuninger, W., Châtelet, J.: Hybridization-based courses consolidated through LMS and PLE leading to a new co-creation of learning: changing all actors' behavior for efficiency. In: Fonseca, D., Redondo, E. (eds.) Handbook of Research on Applied e-Learning in Engineering and Architecture Education, pp. 55–87. IGI Global, Hershey (2016)
21. Grzega, J.: Learning by teaching. the didactic model LdL in university classes (2005). http://www.joachim-grzega.de/ldl-engl.pdf. Accessed Dec 2015
22. Viau, R.: La motivation en contexte scolaire. De Boeck (2003). ISBN-10: 2804143295
23. Conde-González, M.Á., García-Peñalvo, F.J., Alier, M.: Interoperability scenarios to measure informal learning carried out in PLEs. In: Xhafa, F., Barolli, L., Köppen, M. (eds.) Proceedings of the Third IEEE International Conference on Intelligent Networking and Collaborative Systems, IEEE INCoS 2011, pp. 801–806. IEEE CS Press, Los Alamitos (2011)
24. Nuninger, W., Châtelet, J.: Pedagogical mini-games integrated into hybrid course to improve understanding of computer programming. In: Gamification-Based e-Learning Strategies for Computer Programming Education, pp. 152–194. IGI Global, Hershey (2017)
25. Nuninger, W.: Common scenario for an efficient use of online learning: some guidelines for pedagogical digital device development. In: Vu, P., Fredrickson, S., Moore, C. (eds.) Handbook of Research on Innovative Pedagogies and Technologies for Online Learning in Higher Education, pp. 331–366. IGI Global, Hershey (2017)
26. Nuninger, W., Chatelet, J.: Engineers' abilities improved thanks to a quality WIL model in coordination with the industry for two decades. Int. J. Qual. Assur. Eng. Technol. Educ. (IJQAETE) 3(1), 15–51 (2014)
27. Conde-González, M.Á., García-Peñalvo, F.J., Rodríguez-Conde, M.J., Alier, M., García-Holgado, A.: Perceived openness of learning management systems by students and teachers in education and technology courses. Comput. Hum. Behav. 31, 517–526 (2014)
28. Scharmer C.O.: Theory U: Leading from the Future as it Emerges. Berrett-Koeheler Publishers, San Francisco (2009)
29. Kanuka, H.: Characteristics of effective and sustainable teaching development programmes for quality teaching in higher education. HE Manag. Policy 22(2), 69–81 (2010)
30. Stone, D., Heen, S.: Thanks for the Feedback: The Science and Art of Receiving Feedback. Viking, New York (2014)

31. Schein, E.H.: Humble Inquiry: The Gentle Art of Asking Instead of Telling. Berrett-Koehler Publishers, San Francisco (2013)
32. White, A.: From Comfort Zone to Performance Management: Understanding Development and Performance. White & MacLean Publishing, Belgium (2009)
33. Postareff, L., Lindblom-Ylänne, S.: Variation in teachers' descriptions of teaching: broadening the understanding of teaching in EH. Learn. Instr. **18**(2), 109–120 (2008)
34. Goleman, D.: Social intelligence: the new science of human relationships, Bantam (2007)
35. Agile Alliance-AA: The Agile Manifesto (2001). https://www.agilealliance.org/agile101/the-agile-manifesto/. Accessed Jan 2016
36. Radenkovic, D.: Conduire un projet avec la méthode Scrum, Tech. Ingénieur, FP0777 (2012)
37. Wenger, E.: Communities of practice and social learning systems. Organization **7**(2), 225–246 (2000). SAGE, London
38. Aguilar, M.: L'art de motiver. Dunod, Paris (2009)
39. Senge, P., et al.: The Fifth Discipline Fieldbook. Nicolas Brealey Publishing, London (1994)
40. European Commission-EC: A common European Digital Competence Framework for Citizens (DIGCOMP), Eramus+ (2014). http://openeducationeuropa.eu/sites/default/files/DIGCOMP%20brochure%202014%20.pdf. Accessed 2016
41. European Commission-EC: The key competences for lifelong learning – a European reference framework, EU 2006/L394, Edu. & Cult. DG. EC Official Publications (2007)

The Development of a Mediation Artifact for Representing Teaching Practices: A Study Connecting the Areas of Design and Learning Design

Patrícia B. Scherer Bassani[✉], Igor Escalante Casenote, Eduardo Guilherme Albrecht, and Diego Mergener

Feevale University, Novo Hamburgo, RS, Brazil
{patriciab,igor,eduardoalbrecht,diegom}@feevale.br

Abstract. Learning activities can be codified through different forms of representation. These are known as mediation artifacts. The design of a sequence of activities using a mediation artifact generates a document which can be shared with other teachers in order to exchange ideas for using digital technologies in the classroom. This research aims to contribute to the studies on mediation artifacts by introducing the design process of the development of a mediation artifact which articulates studies between Design and Learning Design. The research, based on a qualitative approach, was organized into three phases: (a) learning design study meetings; (b) the design process of the mediation artifact; (c) validation with pre-service teachers. The main characteristic of the produced mediation artifact is that it is based on a conceptual map model and it has been organized into colors and icons. An amount of 76 icons were organized into four groups: yellow for learning tasks, including learning outputs; purple for learning tools and resources; red for representing the involvement and/or support of the actors in a learning task; and a social media special group. The mediation artifact was tested within two groups of undergraduate teacher formation students using the conceptual map tool available on GoConqr.com. Results pointed out that the use of a visual pattern can facilitate the comprehension by teachers from different countries and languages; the proposed model does not require much time for appropriation; the online tool GoConqr is an interesting space for sharing learning practices using the mediation artifact.

Keywords: Educational technology · Learning design · Mediation artifact

1 Introduction

The activities or tasks which can be a lecture, a debate, a research, an exercise, and others, are the basic unit of the teaching and learning process. A sequence of activities is a set of ordered, structured, and articulated tasks meant to achieve certain educational goals [1].

Learning activities can be codified through different forms of representation such as text, visual/graphical representation, taxonomy, etc. These are known as mediation artifacts due to their role of mediating the design of sequences of activities [2].

© Springer International Publishing AG 2017
P. Zaphiris and A. Ioannou (Eds.): LCT 2017, Part I, LNCS 10295, pp. 158–172, 2017.
DOI: 10.1007/978-3-319-58509-3_14

The sharing of learning activities with the use of technologies is in the center of the studies of the Learning Design area [3]. The core concepts of Learning Design are guidance (ways for helping teachers to learn new methods and technologies), representation (tools and models for representing practices), and sharing (a way of enhancing the use of digital technologies in education) [3].

This study focuses on the representation and it aims to contribute to the studies on mediation artifacts for representing practices [2–10].

There are many tools that can be used to design a learning activity. Some of them were developed based on Learning Design concepts like CompendiumLD [11] or Web Instant Collage [12]. These tools are available only in English and require from the teachers considerable time for appropriation [2, 5, 6]. Tools for the development of conceptual maps, such as Mindomo [13], Popplet [14] and GoConqr [15] can also be used for representing learning activities [2, 5–7].

The design of a sequence of activities using a mediation artifact generates a document which can be shared with other teachers in order to exchange new ideas for using digital technologies in the classroom. This final document needs to follow a standard model in order to be understood and reused by others. However, studies on learning design show that there isn't currently a consistent model for learning design [2, 4]. Furthermore, workshops with teachers showed that existing representations are complex [2–4].

This study is complementary to an ongoing research project called *Pedagogical practices on cyberspace* and aims to promote the development and the documentation of learning activities with technologies in elementary schools based on Learning Design studies [5–7]. How can we, thus, develop a model for representing practices that can be easily understood and used by teachers to promote the sharing and reuse of learning activities with technologies?

This paper presents the design process of the development of a mediation artifact which articulates studies between Design and Learning Design.

In the following section we present a reflection about mediation artifacts for representing practices, followed by the research path presenting the design process of a mediation artifact. Subsequently, we discuss the proposed model and finish the paper by presenting the findings and making recommendations for future research.

2   Mediation Artifacts for Representing Practices

There are different mediation artifacts that can be used for representing practices such as models, narratives or case studies, vocabularies, diagrammatic or iconic presentations [2]. Each mediation artifact has its own characteristics and allows different degrees of abstraction and detailing. This way, different mediation artifacts highlight different aspects of a learning activity.

An individual example of a sequence of teaching and learning activities is called a *learning design*, and the implementation of a learning design with a particular group of students is called a *running learning design* or a *running sequence* [3].

The recording of a learning activity using a mediation artifact based on text is very used by teachers/professors especially in a lesson plan format. However, the diversity of presentation formats and non-standardized detailing reveals two possible problems [6, 7]:

(a) a very superficial detailing of the learning activity which makes it difficult to be understood and reused;
(b) an excessive detailing of the learning activity which makes it difficult to be applied in other contexts.

There are many interesting proposals for using visual representation as a mediation artifact [2–7].

Oliver and Herrington [8] proposed a framework for representing learning designs which comprises three interconnecting elements: learning tasks, learning resources, and learning support. They proposed a representation based on a temporal sequence.

This framework [8] was used in the context of the Learning Design project developed by the Australian Universities Teaching Committee (AUTC) [9, 10]. In this project the team created a graphical representation mechanism to describe and document a generic learning design which is known as a Learning Design Sequence.

The representation of a Learning Design Sequence uses the following graphical notation [9, 10]:

(a) Squares: represent tasks;
(b) Triangles: represent resources;
(c) Circles: represent supports.

Figure 1 shows an example of a representation using temporal sequence of an activity. There are three tasks that students undertake in a sequence and each task has an appropriate teacher's support. There is a resource available for the development of Task 1.

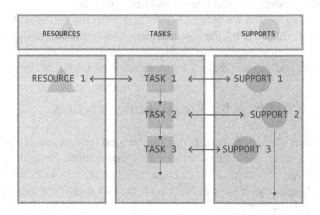

Fig. 1. Example of a learning design sequence (Source: created by authors based on [9, 10]) (Color figure online)

The Compendium LD [11] is a tool for representing learning designs. It provides a set of icons to represent the components of learning activities, as shown in Table 1.

Table 1. Learning design icons and their functions defined in the CompendiumLD tool

Icon	Function
	Role
	Task
	Tool
	Resource
	Learning output
	Stop

A learning activity in CompendiumLD comprises actors (students and teachers/professors/tutors), who perform actions (learning tasks such as discussing, etc.), making use of tools (e.g. online forums, text editor) and resources (e.g. course texts and videos) [11]. Figure 2 presents an example of a learning design produced using CompendiumLD tool.

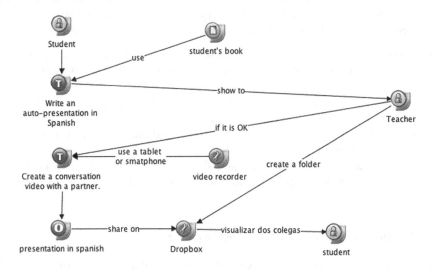

Fig. 2. Example of a learning design using CompendiumLD (Source: created by authors)

Tools for the development of conceptual maps, such as Mindomo [13], Popplet [14], and GoConqr [15] can be used for representing learning activities as well [2, 5–7]. Studies point out that these tools are relevant spaces to enhance the recording and sharing of learning activities. Another important point to highlight is that there are many free online conceptual map tools available, and they are easy to use. However, the learning design produced by teachers/professors in these tools needs to follow a standard model in order to be understood and reused by others [6].

The next section presents the research path for the development of a mediation artifact which articulates studies between Design and Learning Design.

3 The Research Path

The research, based on a qualitative and exploratory approach, was organized into three phases:

(a) learning design study meetings;
(b) the design process of the mediation artifact;
(c) validation with pre-service teachers.

Each phase is detailed below.

3.1 Study Meetings

Study meetings between educational technology researchers and designers were the first research phase. These meetings aimed to discuss the Learning Design area, the ongoing project, and the first research results about mediation artifacts using conceptual maps [5–7]. It was also a space to discuss the problem: the lack of a common visual representation and the necessity to develop a non complex representation of a mediation artifact.

Based on these studies we defined the guidelines to the design process:

(a) the concept of sequence of activities proposed by [1] is the basis of the design, and the organization of these sequences in a learning design will follow the representation proposed by [10];
(b) the proposed model for the development of a learning design must be easy to apply using an online conceptual map tool [6];
(c) the model must be constructed based on colors and images so that teachers of all languages can use it;
(d) the graphical representation can follow the model used by CompendiumLD tool [11], using icons to represent learning tasks, actors, tools, resources, and learning outcomes.

3.2 The Design Process of the Mediation Artifact

The second phase, involving the design process, was conduct by the Design Center of Feevale University. The design team conducted a design process that comprehended three stages (Table 2):

(a) informational, where the problem was analyzed;
(b) creative;
(c) technical.

The briefing was the first activity. The discussions carried out within the study meetings were important for the problem comprehension. Besides, the design team explored tools for representing teaching and learning activities including learning design tools and conceptual maps tools. The data organized during this *informational phase* was the basis of the *creative phase*.

The *creative phase* started with the definition of the concept which guided the mediation artifact development: the use of a visual language based on icons.

Table 2. Methodology used by the design team

Informational	Creative	Technical
Briefing	Definition of the concept	Application
Former research	Brainstorming	User manual
Theme Search	Icon classification	Simulation
Analysis	Visual language	Presentation
	Color's study	

The mediation artifact has been organized into colors and icons. Each color represents a component of the leaning design: the actors in red, the tasks in yellow, the resources in purple, the tools in pink, and the learning outputs in green.

Some icons were developed using AIGA's (American Institute of Graphic Arts) pictograms which are design standards for visual communication and are based on professional ethics issues in the design area. However, there are icons developed from scratch especially for this project (Fig. 3).

Fig. 3. The creative process for the development of the icons (Source: created by authors)

The development of the icons involved a study of flat colors with shadows for contrast and differentiation between groups of icons for the purpose of better aesthetics and logic. After color studies and layout tests the icons were digitalized in vector images (Fig. 4).

Additionally, there is another group of icons to represent social media tools (Fig. 5). Social media can be used as a resource or as a tool.

Fig. 4. Icons and colors to represent a learning design (Source: created by authors) (Color figure online)

Fig. 5. Icons for social media representation (Source: created by authors)

The main characteristic of the produced mediation artifact is that it is based on a conceptual map model. Conceptual maps are usually employed in educational contexts and teachers and students are familiar with this kind of tool. Thus, in the visual pattern created, a learning design is composed by a group of coloured text boxes with an icon, as shown on Fig. 6.

The visual pattern (Fig. 6) was tested on the online conceptual map GoConqr [15]. This tool was selected based on previous studies which indicated that it enables both the sharing and the remix of the documents produced [6].

At the end of the *technical phase* an amount of 76 icons were organized into six groups: the actors in red, the tasks in yellow, the resources in purple, the tools in pink, and the learning outputs in green, and the social media special group. These icons are available online combined with the user manual[1].

---

[1] https://drive.google.com/open?id=0B1lDz2CC6oyoSTdTcW5oVWttUEE.

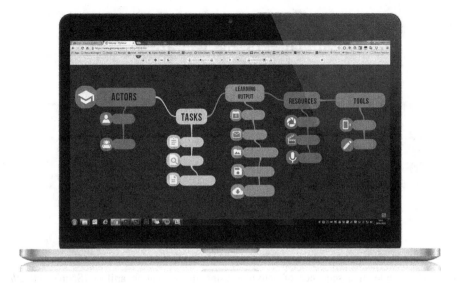

Fig. 6. Preliminary viewing of the visual pattern created (Source: created by authors) (Color figure online)

3.3   Testing the Mediation Artifact

Finally, in the third phase of the research the design solution was tested with two groups of undergraduate teacher formation students. The data were collected from observation in locus, digital photography, and from the learning designs produced by students using the proposed graphic pattern in the online tool GoConqr.

The first testing was realized in the first semester of 2016 and involved a group of undergraduate teacher formation students majoring in English/Portuguese. This group used the model to represent sequences of activities designed for a Portuguese Course for Foreign People. They produced five sequences of activities in GoConqr platform using the proposed mediation artifact[2]. The Figs. 7, 8, and 9 show three of these sequences of activities.

On Fig. 7 we can see that the colors of the icons don't match the colors of the text box as proposed. On this (Fig. 7) there is a list of tasks (in yellow) in vertical order, indicating a sequence to follow, but there are tasks represented side by side. Thus, according to Fig. 7, the comprehension of the sequence of activities could be complicated.

---

[2] The documents are available online: https://padlet.com/patriciab/yhisuily538b.

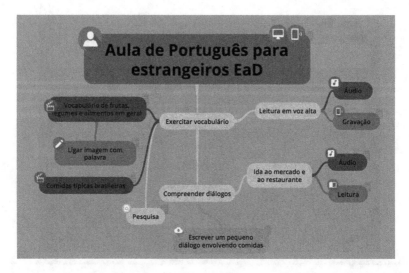

Fig. 7. Example of a sequence of activities using the mediation artifact (Source: https://www.goconqr.com/pt-BR/p/5787738-Aula-de-Portugu-s-para-estrangeiros-EaD-mind_maps) (Color figure online)

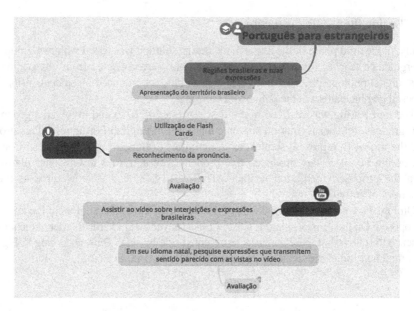

Fig. 8. Example of a sequence of activities using the mediation artifact (Source: https://www.goconqr.com/pt-BR/p/5558697-Portugu-s-para-estrangeiros-mind_maps) (Color figure online)

On Figs. 8 and 9 we find the same problem with the colors of the icons. On Fig. 8 the students represented the sequence of activities in a comprehensive way. However, on Fig. 9 there is a list of learning outputs (represented by a green text box) isolated from the tasks.

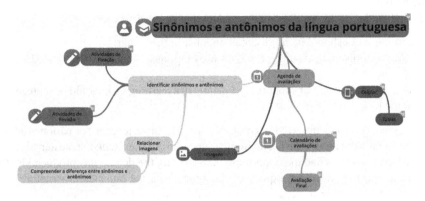

Fig. 9. Example of a sequence of activities using the mediation artifact (Source: https://www.goconqr.com/pt-BR/p/5820445-Sin-nimos-e-ant-nimos-da-l-ngua-portuguesa-mind_maps) (Color figure online)

This first testing revealed two issues:

(a)   the students had difficulty in differentiating tools and resources and this generated a confusion of colors between the text box and the icons, breaking the proposed visual pattern;

(b)   the lack of information of how to organize the learning design elements generated some non- comprehensible sequence of activities (Fig. 10).

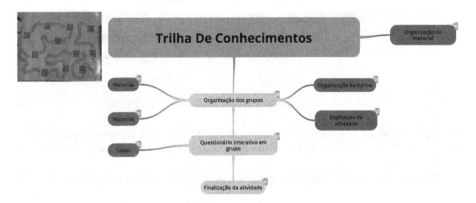

Fig. 10. Example of a sequence of activities using the mediation artifact (Source: http://www.goconqr.com/pt-BR/p/7161286-Trilha-De-Conhecimentos-mind_maps)   (Color   figure online)

Based on these first results we realized the importance of defining, in a formal way, the structure of the mediation artifact meant to guide the representation of the sequence of the activities.

Based on the [9, 10] studies we defined a transparent structure:

(a) learning tasks should be represented on a list in the center;
(b) learning tools and resources for each learning task should be represented on the left;
(c) the involvement and/or support of the actors in a learning task should be represented on the right.

The second testing involved a group of undergraduate teacher formation students enrolled in an Education and Technology course during the second semester of 2016. This group of students had the opportunity of verifying the documents produced by the first group and they received a quick explanation about the transparent structure they should follow in order to organize the learning design elements. They produced 15 sequences of activities[3] in GoConqr platform using the proposed mediation artifact. The Figs. 10 and 11 show some of these sequences of activities.

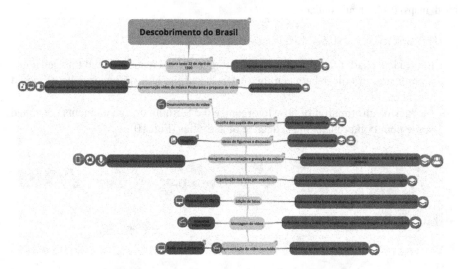

Fig. 11. Example of a sequence of activities using the mediation artifact (Source: https://www.goconqr.com/pt/p/7017545-Descobrimento-do-Brasil-mind_maps) (Color figure online)

The second testing revealed important issues about the mediation artifact:

(a) the students, as well as the first group, had difficulty to differentiate tools and resources, and it generated a confusion of colors between the text box and the icons;
(b) some students didn't apply the icons in the learning design;

---

[3] The documents are available online: https://padlet.com/patriciab/4bhif3qn4ofx.

(c) the proposed transparent structure based on [9, 10] was efficient and the learning designs developed by students showed an organized sequence of activities related to the appropriate resources, tools, and supports.

The next section presents an analysis of the mediation artifact based on these two testing experiences.

4 Discussion

The mediation artifact was tested within two groups of undergraduate teacher formation students. The documents were produced in the GoConqr platform [15] using the conceptual map tool. This tool was chosen because [6]:

(a) it is possible to attach a note to a text box: this feature enables the production of a learning design with two layers, the main layer presenting the general idea of the activities, and a second layer detailing in depth each activity;
(b) it is possible to insert a link to an external resource: this feature enables the creation of links to resources and tools as web pages or another online conceptual map (in this case it's possible to create integrated learning designs);
(c) the conceptual maps are available online through a public link;
(d) it is possible to use a remix feature (one person can reuse and adapt an existing conceptual map).

The students within both groups had to produce a sequence of activities with technologies using the proposed mediation artifact. The documents produced by students are available online[4] and were analyzed based on document analysis [16, 17]. The document analysis makes use of static documents available online which do not involve interaction between individuals [16].

Bowen [17] suggests that documents can serve to a variety of purposes as a part of a research. In the context of this research, the documents provided means for tracking change and development of the mediation artifact.

The first testing revealed a very relevant issue: the lack of information of how to organize the learning design elements. This problem affected seriously the results and some students produced a non-comprehensible sequence of activities. Based on this information, a transparent layer was proposed in order to guide the organization of these elements.

The first testing also revealed a problem with the visual pattern. The students had difficulty in differentiating tools and resources and this generated a confusion of colors between the text box and the icons, breaking the proposed visual pattern. We decided to proceed to the next testing before making some changes in the visual pattern.

The second testing showed that the proposed transparent structure was efficient and the learning designs developed by students showed an organized sequence of activities.

This second test, however, confirmed the need to redesign the visual pattern once the same problem appeared: the observation of the students *in locus* during both testings

---

[4] https://padlet.com/patriciab/yhisuily538b - https://padlet.com/patriciab/4bhif3qn4ofx.

revealed that they had difficulty in seeing the difference between tools and resources. Although a resource can be understood as a content-based artifact, and a tool as an artifact designed to support a specific task, the distinction between a resource and a tool is becoming blurred because the same tool can be used by the teacher/designer to create content and also by the students to create their own representation of subject matter [18].

Furthermore, the observation *in locus* and the analysis of the documents showed that students had also difficulty to understand a learning output as something different from an evaluation task.

Based on these findings, we developed a new design pattern for the mediation artifact (Fig. 12) based only in three groups of colors:

(a) learning tasks, including learning outputs, should be represented on a list in the center using the yellow color;
(b) learning tools and resources for each learning task should be represented on the left using the purple color;
(c) the involvement and/or support of the actors in a learning task should be represented on the right and using the red color.

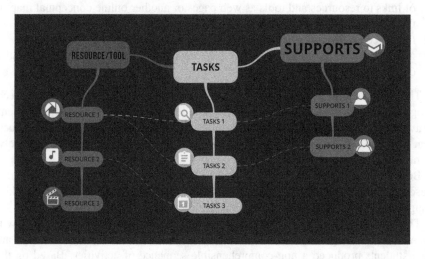

Fig. 12. Final visual pattern of the mediation artifact (Source: created by authors) (Color figure online)

At the end of the research process an amount of 76 icons were organized into four groups: the actors/support in red, the tasks/learning outputs in yellow, and the resources/tools in purple, and the social media special group. These icons are available online combined with the user manual[5].

---

[5] https://drive.google.com/open?id=0B1lDz2CC6oyoSTdTcW5oVWttUEE.

5   Final Comments

This study is complementary to an ongoing research project called *Pedagogical practices on cyberspace* which aims to promote the development and the documentation of learning activities with technologies in elementary schools based on Learning Design studies.

In this paper we described the research path meant to produce a mediation artifact for representing learning activities. This research had as starting point the following question: How can we develop a model for representing practices that can be easily understood and used by teachers to promote the sharing and reuse of learning activities with technologies?

The development of the mediation artifact articulated studies between Design and Learning Design. The mediation artifact was tested within two groups of undergraduate teacher formation students. The conceptual map tool available on online platform GoConqr.com [15] was used to produce the learning designs using the mediation artifact.

The analysis of the learning designs produced using the proposed mediation artifacts revealed:

(a)   the use of a visual pattern with different colors and icons to represent the learning design elements can facilitate the comprehension and the use by teachers from different countries and languages;
(b)   the proposed model does not require much time for appropriation;
(c)   the online tool GoConqr is an interesting space for sharing learning practices using the mediation artifact.

Although the research showed that online conceptual maps are a relevant and feasible space for producing and sharing learning designs using the proposed mediation artifact, we understand it would be interesting to develop a mobile application using our graphical pattern.

Future works should involve tests using the mediation artifact in a broader context, focusing on teachers and/or professors, and workshops to disseminate the study.

Acknowledgments.   We thank the National Council for Scientific and Technological Development - CNPq/Brazil (http://www.cnpq.br) for providing financial support for this study. We would also like to thank Feevale University (http://www.feevale.br) for making possible this research.

References

1. Zabala, A.: A Prática Educativa. Artmed, Porto Alegre (1998)
2. Conole, G.: Designing for Learning in an Open World. Springer, New York (2013)
3. The Larnaca Declaration on Learning Design. https://larnacadeclaration.wordpress.com
4. Falconer, I., Finlay, J., Fincher, S.: Representing practice: practice models, patterns, bundles. Learn. Media Technol. **36**(02), 101–127 (2011)
5. Bassani, P.S.: Documentação de atividades de aprendizagem com uso de tecnologias. In: III Jornada de Atualização em Informática na Educação, pp. 106–143. SBC, Brazil (2014)

6. Bassani, P.S., Lima, C., Dalanhol, D.: Documentação e compartilhamento de atividades de aprendizagem: um estudo sobre repositórios de prática e artefatos de mediação. Revista e-Curriculum, vol. 14, pp. 1423–1453. PUCSP, São Paulo (2016)
7. Bassani, P.S., Bassani, R.: Production and sharing of learning activities with technologies: designing for fearning in teacher formation courses. In: ATINER'S Conference Paper Series, No:EDU2016-1901. Atiner, Atenas (2016)
8. Oliver, R., Herrington, J.: Teaching and learning online: a beginner's guide to e-learning and e-teaching in higher education. Edith Cowan University. Centre for Research in Information Technology and Communications (2001)
9. Oliver, R., Harper, B., Hedberg, J., Wills, S., Agostinho, S.: Formalising the description of learning designs, in quality conversations. In: Proceedings of the 25th HERDSA Annual Conference, Perth, Western Australia, 7–10 July 2002
10. Learning Design. http://www.learningdesigns.uow.edu.au/project/learn_design.htm
11. Compendium LD. http://compendiumld.open.ac.uk
12. Web Instance Collage. http://pandora.tel.uva.es/WIC2
13. Mindomo. http://www.mindomo.com
14. Popplet. http://www.popplet.com
15. Goconqr. http://goconqr.com
16. Hewson, C., Laurent, D.: Research design and tools for internet research. In: Hughes, J. (ed.) Sage Internet Research Methods, pp. 165–193. Sage, London (2012)
17. Bowen, G.: Document analysis as a qualitative research method. Qual. Res. J. 9(2), 27–40 (2009)
18. Beetham, H.: An approach to learning activity design. In: Beetham, H., Sharpe, R. (eds.) Rethinking Pedagogy for a Digital Age, pp. 26–40. Routledge, New York (2007)

On the Potential of Using Virtual Reality for Teacher Education

Kalliopi-Evangelia Stavroulia[✉] and Andreas Lanitis

Visual Computing Media Lab, Department of Multimedia and Graphic Arts,
Cyprus University of Technology, Limassol, Cyprus
pstavroulia@gmail.com, andreas.lanitis@cut.ac.cy

Abstract. Virtual reality technology has the potential to be used in teacher training as it can provide innovative virtual teaching environments, offering teachers the ability to gain in-training feedback and knowledge that can be transferred and applied to real-life situations. As part of an initial investigation into the applicability of using VR for teacher training, two experiments were conducted. The first experiment had to do with teachers' understanding and detection of students' possible disorders such as vision disorders. The second experiment had to do the ability of teachers to identify and deal with bullying-related activities among students. The results indicated that through a VR-based role-changing mechanism teachers could enter students' position and understand their problems, while they experienced incidents that were like real-life incidents making the application a valuable training tool. The overall results of the preliminary investigations in combination with the findings of a related survey, highlight the potential of using VR for implementing real-life tools for teacher professional training. Building on the results of the preliminary experiments, a new application is currently under development aiming to address the lack of practice in teacher training and provide to young but also experienced teachers a VR-based school environment that represents real-life situations and will allow them to be trained, experiment, test their skills, make mistakes and learn from them but without the risk of harming real students.

Keywords: Virtual reality · Virtual classroom · Teacher preparation · Teacher training · Head Mounted Display (HMD)

1   Introduction

The integration of technology in the educational process gave new perspectives on teaching and learning aiming to equip students with the appropriate skills that will enable them to meet the demands and challenges of the modern world. In such a dynamically evolving environment, there is a necessity for educational systems to adjust to radical changes to meet the ever-increasing challenges of the 21st century. The transformation and modernization of the educational systems has become one of the strategic objectives of the European Union-EU [1], as the adjustment to the challenges will ensure that all European citizens will be equipped with the necessary competencies and skills required for sustainability and success in the labour market. Moreover, investment in education

© Springer International Publishing AG 2017
P. Zaphiris and A. Ioannou (Eds.): LCT 2017, Part I, LNCS 10295, pp. 173–186, 2017.
DOI: 10.1007/978-3-319-58509-3_15

is considered to be the solution to the current financial economic crisis, as it will promote economic growth, competitiveness, job-creation, productivity and prosperity.

However, the current educational systems were not designed to teach today's generation of students, the so-called 'Digital Natives', who have access to technology since their birth [2]. Thus, education must confront the problem of teachers, the so-called 'Digital Immigrants', who were not born into the digital world and are struggling to keep up with technology and adapt to the new circumstances and teach a generation that speaks the language of the digital world [2]. Unfortunately, teachers still believe that learners are the same as in the past and thus the traditional teaching methods can be effective. But todays' learners speak a different language and the traditional teaching and learning methods can no longer provoke their interest.

It is an undeniable fact that the transformation and modernization of the educational systems cannot be achieved without the contribution and active participation of teachers. Regardless the implementation of technology in education and the use of new and innovative teaching tools and practices, teachers remain the key wheel of education. Teachers are the strategic agents of educational change and with an enormous responsibility in the preparation of the future generations of active European citizens. In this new and challenging environment, teachers not only have to survive but they also have to respond with success to ever-changing class environments. As the classroom changed, the traditional role of teachers inevitably changed and they became students' partners, co-researchers, co-travelers and mentors between students and a rapidly changing world [3].

From this standpoint, teachers must renew their skills and competencies in order to confront the challenges and specificities of the framework within which they must act. It is essential that teacher education programs prepare candidate teachers with the necessary skills in order to respond with adequacy and effectiveness to the increased requirements of their profession. Teachers must have a deep understanding of their domain, use teaching strategies that will engage their students and build on their prior knowledge fostering their understanding. Additionally, teachers must find a new way to communicate with their students and new teaching methods to attract their interest and guide them in the acquisition of knowledge. Investing in teachers is essential to enhance their professionalism and provide education of good quality.

Nevertheless, research indicates that teacher education programs do not adequately prepare candidate teachers with the necessary knowledge, skills and competencies and as a result when teacher graduates enter the profession, they lack the knowledge for effective teaching [4]. Another concern is that little emphasis has been placed on 'learning to do' deriving learners from the opportunity to acquire through work experience the skills that will allow them to deal with difficult and unforeseen situations that might arise and learn to work with others [5]. Unfortunately, teacher training within the university is theoretical and there is a lack of practice and collaboration between schools and teacher preparation programs deriving candidate teachers from important resources and mentoring [4, 6, 7]. Without doubt, the lack of practice and connection between school and universities derive candidate teachers from the ability to acquire knowledge through experience and mentoring from experienced teachers [6, 7].

Beyond a shadow of doubt, the role of the teacher had to be redefined towards a new direction in this new multicultural and global arena. Virtual environments can address the need for practice in teacher preparation and can provide teachers (beginning and experienced) the feedback, the mentoring and the realistic view that they need [4].

The last few years, the use of virtual reality in the landscape of education has attracted the interest of the scientific community due to its potential educational effectiveness because of the high-fidelity simulation and representation of space they offer. Virtual reality (VR) learning is an ideal way to provide users a safe, controllable and flexible environment, allowing experimentation in real-life situations that in many cases cannot be accessed physically.

In the remainder of this paper the term Virtual Reality along with the use of VR in education is introduced followed by an analysis related the uses of virtual reality in education. In section four two experiments that were conducted are presented along with preliminary results followed by regarding description of the development of a novel application under development. Finally, some considerations, conclusions and plans for future work are presented.

2   Virtual Reality: Defining the Terms

The concept of virtual reality has been around for decades, although it became popular and drew much attention in the early 1990s. There is no consensus on the definition of virtual reality as it is a multidimensional concept with a variety of characteristics. Virtual Reality (VR) is defined as a 'computer-generated simulation of a three-dimensional image or environment that can be interacted with in a seemingly real or physical way by a person using special electronic equipment, such as a helmet with a screen inside or gloves fitted with sensors' [8]. For Lawson et al. [9], VR 'is a system which permits users to interact, move, look at, and be immersed in a 3D environment'. Moreover, VR is 'an absorbing, interactive, computer-mediated experience in which person perceives a synthetic (simulated) environment by means of special human-computer interface equipment. It interacts with simulated objects in that environment as if they were real' [10]. VR aims at making 'the user located in the three-dimensional data environment expressed by the computer, and travel in this environment by eyes, hands, ears or special three-dimensional device, to create a sense of being on the scene' [11].

The above definitions of VR point to several important characteristics related to the concept. First and foremost, VR aims to immerse or absorb the user in a more learner-centered and learner-controlled computer generated environment, leading to higher levels of engagement when compared to a traditional classroom setting [12]. The significance of virtual reality also lies in its ability to produce high levels of sense of presence allowing the users to feel like 'being there' [12, 13].

There are three key elements of VR known as the '3I' - Immersion, Interaction and Imagination [11, 14]. Immersion is one of the key elements of a virtual environment, as it refers to the sensation of being physically present in a non-physical world [8]. For Cheng [11], immersion or else called 'the sense on the scene, 'refers to the degree of reality that the user feels when he exists as hero in the virtual environment'. Deep engagement in the virtual environment causes lack of awareness of time and of the real world, convincing players that the virtual environment is real and making them feel that they are there.

In order for virtual reality to provide an authentic real-life experience to the user it is necessary to respond to the users' actions [15]. Thus, another important element of VR environments for user's successful experience is interactivity. Interactivity takes place when the computer responds to users' input. Finally, the element of imagination stresses 'that the virtual reality technology possesses a wide imaginable space, which can widen the knowing scope of human beings, not only represent a truly existing environment, but also mentally construct a non-existing environment, even an impossible environment' [11].

Technology allowed the development of immersive virtual reality applications that can be applied in many fields. VR has been used as a tool for the treatment of agoraphobia with and without panic disorder, public speaking anxiety, social anxiety disorder, fear of flying, spider phobia, eating disorders, psychological stress, schizophrenia and autism [13]. Moreover, VR offers the users the opportunity to live the life of someone else getting an idea of what someone else's life might be like [16] or even how one's life at a different age might be like [17]. For example, researchers from BeAnotherLab developed an interactive virtual environment called 'The Machine to be Another' in order to address the relationship between identity and empathy [18]. 'The Machine to be Another' aimed to help the users understand the Self though understanding the Other's point of view [18].

VR can also be used in domains as automotive industry. Car design is an expensive and time-consuming process that requires several modifications and reviews before the product goes to production. Thus, VR environments can be used in the design and development phase in order to reduce the time and cost required while maximizing the quality of the product [9]. Furthermore, VR environments have been used for pedestrian safety training. Many pedestrians are killed or injured annually with most of them being children, as children have not yet developed the cognitive and perceptual processing skills in order to cross the streets with safety. VR can offer children a safe, fun but also realistic training environment for repeated practice minimizing the risk of potential injury [19].

3   Using Virtual Reality in Education: State-of-the Art

As Ke et al. [20] state 'teaching is a complex problem-solving task that requires weighing many variables and adaptively implementing principles of instruction, communication, and content representation in a highly situated context'. Lately, teaching practice in schools with real students is becoming more difficult to accomplish. Nonetheless, beginning teachers are expected to be of highly professional quality and practice. Technology might give the answer to the request for a strong training in teacher preparation, enabling pre-service but also in-service teachers to improve the quality of their learning and performance. Additionally, one of the most significant problems of the teaching profession is that many teachers are leaving the profession during the first years. Thus, virtual training environments may result in reducing the percentage of teachers that leave the profession, as after virtual training teachers may feel more confident and well equipped.

Virtual learning environments can be used for the development of effective future teachers that will be successful in the classroom. Virtual reality provides the users with realistic environments that allow real time active learning and the transfer of knowledge and skills from the virtual to the real context [20]. Moreover, constant training within the virtual environment will better prepare teachers and will ensure their survival in todays' digital and multicultural classrooms. However, despite the extensive use of virtual technology in fields such as medicine and military, in the field of teacher education its use is extremely limited.

The significance of using immersive environments in teacher training lies in the fact that the diversity in the classroom is growing and teachers must attend multicultural classrooms and bilingual students with different cultural and ethnic backgrounds but without intercultural experiences [21]. Dieker et al. [21], also suggest that the purpose of using a virtual training environment is to 'positively impact teacher recruitment, preparation, and retention in education', and provide teachers a safe environment where they can be trained with virtual students that is a 'more ethical approach to learning the art of teaching'. Another key point is that within the virtual environment teachers can make mistakes but without influencing learning of real students and they can repeat the experience to work on their mistakes and no matter how many times teachers may was to experiment, the virtual students have no memory of the process.

Virtual classroom environments aim to provide an innovative training tool that can be used for constant professional development and update of teachers' skills so that teachers can remain productive [22]. Furthermore, the use of virtual environments will allow teachers to take control of their own learning, monitor their progress and thus learn more. Equally important is that the virtual environment will provide immediate feedback and data that in an actual classroom would be difficulty to identify [21].

The last few years some attempts have been made in the preparation of teachers via virtual training environments. Dieker et al. [21], propose the use of virtual environments in teacher training. A prototype virtual environment was developed called STAR simulator and aimed to identify and recruit the best teachers, and train them. The goal of the realistic virtual environment was to provide physical, emotional and social interaction like this that teachers face in reality. The objective of the virtual environment was to create a realistic urban middle school to provide rich experiences to the participating teachers through interactions with the virtual students and collect the data for analysis.

Overall, the results of the research related to the STAR classroom revealed that it is possible to develop a virtual environment that can provide teachers with realistic and compelling experiences as if they were in a real classroom with real students. Nevertheless, further research and evaluation is required for safer results. Based on the results, teachers found the virtual classroom environment realistic. However, teachers proposed several modifications for the future including the presence of more students in the classroom, ability to see students' work during the tasks, movement from the students (sitting up from the desk or movements around the room or even possibility to leave the room). Additionally, beginning teachers reported that such a simulator can be used to help them in behavior management. Finally, the participants found the STAR simulator a friendly and fun environment and expressed the desire to get trained again, experimenting with their approach.

TeachMe is another virtual environment that was developed for teacher training. The prototype focused on behavior and classroom management aspects and the goal was to train beginning teachers in mathematics, science and special education before entering in the classroom for the first time [23]. The results of the experiment with TeachMe virtual environment indicate the potential in training teachers in behavior management issues. Andreasen and Haciomeroglu [23], state that such a simulated environment can help teachers gain in depth knowledge of their domain and assist the development of behavior management strategies.

Ke et al. [20], also investigated the potential use of virtual reality in the training of teaching assistants. A virtual classroom environment was developed via an open-source platform called OpenSimulator, and the virtual students was a mixture of students controlled by scripts and students controlled by peer trainees. Kinect was also used enabling the participants to project and embody their real-time body movements and gestures onto their avatars in the virtual world. The results of the experiments indicated the potential use of virtual environment in teacher training. The use of Kinect that allowed the users to project and embody their real-time body movements and gestures, not only reinforced their sense of presence but there are also indications that it affected positively the pedagogical knowledge of the trainees. However, further research is a necessity for safer results.

The above studies suggest a potential for using virtual reality environments for active teacher training. Research so far has indicated that virtual environments can engage the users while reinforcing the sense of presence resulting in the acquisition of deeper knowledge and skills. Nevertheless, research is still at its infancy and further research is required in order to examine how virtual environment can be implemented effectively in teacher training maximizing teachers' competencies.

4 Preliminary Experimental Evaluation

The last few years the technological advancements changed dramatically the traditional classroom and the role of the teacher. From unique source of knowledge, teachers became guides to help the students conquer and construct their own knowledge. Moreover, the implementation of technology in education changed dramatically the traditional classroom that became digitalized and dynamic. Despite the changes in education teachers remain the main actors of every educational system and thus, the professional development of teachers became a priority for the European Union.

Unfortunately, initial teacher education does not adequately prepare pre-service teachers and thus beginning teachers entering the profession encounter several problems and feel unprepared to deal with the complexity of today's classroom. Moreover, most beginning teachers lack practical skills, as there is a lack of connection between Universities and schools deriving them from the mentoring and support that they need from experienced teachers.

As part of an initial investigation into the applicability of using VR for teacher training, two experiments were conducted [24, 25]. The first experiment had to do with teachers' understanding and detection of students' possible disorders such as vision disorders. More specifically, myopia disorder had been chosen as the students' disorder within the scenario. Students with myopia often feel embarrassed to wear glasses in the classroom as they are being targeted, bullied and teased by other classmates. As a result, teachers might be unaware of student's situation and believe that students' limited participation during the lesson is due to lack of interest rather than due to health reasons. During the VR application teacher-users could see through the eyes of a visually impaired avatar in order to raise their awareness towards students' eye conditions and help them identify students with myopia symptoms (see Figs. 1 and 2).

Fig. 1. The virtual environment showing clear and blur vision

Fig. 2. The virtual environment showing vision problems of the student as seen through an Oculus Rift

Both applications were developed as a first-person 3D virtual environment using the 'Unity3D' game engine. The avatars used in the virtual environments were created with the Maya Autodesk Character Generator student version and were imported in the Unity3D game engine. One aspect that had to be considered for the design of the virtual classroom was that it had to be realistic and like a real classroom to maximize the sense of presence. Therefore, photographs were taken from a real classroom and then the models for the classroom were designed in Maya. To create a realistic immersive experience for the teachers, Head Mounted Displays (HMD) and specifically Oculus Rift and headphones were used (see Fig. 3). Furthermore, to achieve higher level of realism in avatar movements, motion capture techniques that involved the use of a motion tracking suit in conjunction with multiple infrared cameras, were used to record human movements that were used to animate the avatars.

Fig. 3. Participants during the use of the virtual environment

In both experiments for the evaluation of the virtual environments two questionnaires consisted of closed-ended five-point Likert scale questions were developed. The first questionnaire aimed to collect demographic data and general information and was completed before the experiment. The second questionnaire was completed after the use of the virtual environment and aimed to collect data relative to participants' experience in the VR environment and the usefulness of the VR application as a training tool for teachers. Before taking part in the experiments all volunteers had to read and sign the consent document that provided general information about the research. Then participants had to test the virtual environment and at the end of the experiment they had to complete the second questionnaire.

The quantitative results indicated that participants found the virtual environment of the classroom a realistic representation of the real classroom setting. Thus, there were high levels of immersion and the participants felt like being in a real classroom setting and the use of an HMD and headphones also helped in participants' immersion. Moreover, all the participants experienced a sense of presence, like being in a real classroom. Teachers participated in the experiment reported that they could enter students' position and understand their disorder something that will be beneficial for their future teaching practice. Furthermore, participants reported that virtual environments like the one they experienced could be a useful tool for teachers in order to understand students' problems. Equally important is that all participants stated that they were problematized because they had never had the chance to enter the students' position before and through the current application they experienced their students' viewpoint. Moreover, many of the participants admitted that it was highly possible that in some cases they had misjudged real-life students due to their inability to consider the possibility that such students had a vision disorder.

The second experiment had to do the ability of teachers to identify and deal with bullying-related activities among students. As the aim of our application is to address the lack of practice in teacher training in school bullying, there was an effort to record real life incidents that could be incorporated in the scenario of the application. For this reason, a focus group interview took place with experienced teachers and school counselors in order to obtain information about real life bullying incidents. The participants provided multiple examples of school bullying incidents and they suggested that the most important aspect for new teachers is to be able to differentiate bullying incidents from simple teasing incidents among the students. As bullying is a repetitive action, teachers must observe carefully the behaviors and those students involved to identify bullying activities. Based on the feedback received by experienced teachers and school counselors the following scenario was drafted to fulfill the needs of required application.

Within the VR application the teacher-user experienced different types of in-class and outdoors student behavior incidents related to bullying. For each of the incidents the user can select one of a series of choices related to the appropriate actions that need to be enforced for each incident. The first incident was teasing and the second and third incidents constitute bullying as it is a repetitive action from the victimizer to the same target person. Thus, user-teachers must observe carefully the behaviors and the students involved in order to recognize bullying.

The quantitative results revealed that the behavior problems that pre-service teachers experienced were like their real-life incidents making the application a valuable training tool for identifying bulling, and taking the correct actions depending on the nature of the incident. It was also evident that most the participants consider bullying a serious problem within the school environment. What is interesting to be noted is the fact that in service and experienced teachers argued that training via a virtual environment cannot contribute significantly in the development of their skills as they already possess the skills to confront bullying due to their everyday experience. They proposed the use of the application for the training of pre-service teachers who lack the experience to identify bullying. However, most of the teachers failed to recognize and distinguish the teasing incident from the bullying incidents.

The overall results of our preliminary investigation proved that the use of virtual reality in teacher preparation has considerable potential. Moreover, the development of such a tool could be also an innovative and valuable life-long learning tool.

5 Developing an Integrated VR-Based Teacher Training Tool

Building on the results of the preliminary experiments, a new application is currently under development aiming to addresses the lack of practice in teacher education and the need for the professional development of teachers. In addition, a survey that aims to register teacher needs and opinions regarding the use of VR in their professional development was carried out. Preliminary results of the research indicate that there is a lack of practice in teacher training and a lack of experience among teachers related to the use of virtual reality. Teachers reported the need of further training in teaching students with special learning needs, in confronting students with disorders such as vision, hearing and speech disorders, in behavior management and in body language. Additionally, according to the results it is difficult for teachers to deal with students who show behavioral disorders (including violence, aggression), health disorders, learning disabilities and Attention Deficit Hyperactivity Disorder (ADHD). Furthermore, a significant number of participants report that teachers need additional training for all the above-mentioned issues but not in theory, but in practice within a virtual classroom environment.

The proposed application aims to address the lack of practice in teacher training and provide new but also experienced teachers a mentoring, support and life-long learning tool that they need for their professional development. A virtual reality school environment representing real-life situations will allow teachers to be trained, experiment on their skills, make mistakes and learn from them but without the risk of harming a real student. The logic for the proposed application is outlined in Fig. 4:

Fig. 4. The logic of the application

Based on the survey and the results concerning teachers' real needs, different scenarios for the application will be developed. The logic for the development of the scenario is presented in Fig. 5.

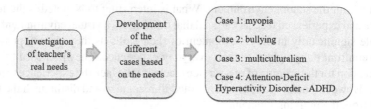

Fig. 5. The logic for the development of different scenarios

The new application is being developed using Unity software. From a hardware point of view, the set-up makes use of an Oculus Rift VR headset for a more immersive experience. Moreover, Maya is used for the development of the school and classroom models, while the models of the virtual students are designed with Maya Autodesk Character Generator student.

One important aspect that had to be considered for the design of the virtual school and classroom was that it had to be realistic and similar to real classrooms, in order to create the users a strong sense of presence that is the illusion of being an active part of the computer-generated virtual environment. For this reason, the model of the virtual classroom was designed based on photographs that were taken from real classrooms and on the specifications of the company 'Buildings Infrastructures' (http://www.ktyp.gr/en/) that is responsible for constructing Greek public buildings including schools (see Fig. 6 below). The virtual classroom models and the virtual students can be seen in Fig. 7 below.

Fig. 6. An image of the real classroom environment (left) and an image of a students' desk according to Buildings Infrastructures Company (right)

Fig. 7. The simulated classroom environment created with Maya without (left) and with students (right)

6   Conclusions

The introduction of educational technology in the classroom has a profound impact upon the role of the teacher and of the student. Teachers are no longer the source of information but they aim to facilitate students to conquer knowledge and develop their skills. Nevertheless, teachers' role remains significant since his/her educational techniques will provide students the experiences they need in order to gain new knowledge affecting their learning outcomes.

Teachers need to improve their skills through constant practice. However, there is limited training and lack of motivation. The recent technological developments have made it feasible to develop 3D VR environments for teaching, learning, and training. Integrating virtual reality environments supplementary to traditional university education will enhance teacher's motivation and professional development on classroom and behavior management aspects.

There are strong indications in preliminary research results [24, 25] that the use of VR environments in teacher training can improve teachers' skills and knowledge. Moreover, the results from the investigation of teachers' needs revealed a great interest from teachers for practical training within a safe virtual classroom environment. As virtual environments represent real-life situations, they create a strong sense of presence to the participants making them feel as if they are in an actual classroom. The sense of presence absorbs the participants to the virtual environments allowing them to focus on the scenarios reinforcing their skills. VR holds a promise in the domain of teacher training, nevertheless further research is needed in order to investigate and evaluate the impact of those environments in the development of teachers.

In the future, we plan to build on our early promising results and further develop the VR application tool and enrich it with scenarios that correspond to teachers' real needs. The results of the survey regarding the investigation of teachers' needs are still under analysis. Based on the results, interviews and focus groups with experienced teachers and counselors will take place in order to gain a deep understanding of teachers' problems, so as to develop scenarios that best fit their needs. Then, we will perform an extended evaluation of the application, that will provide feedback for changes in the VR environment and provide information relating to the impact of the VR environment in the development of teachers' knowledge and skills. Such actions will contribute towards the development of an innovative and useful tool for teacher training that will allow teachers to gain practical experience within a safe but also challenging environment.

Acknowledgements. Authors acknowledge funding from the European Union's Horizon 2020 Framework Programme through NOTRE project. This project has received funding from the European Union's Horizon 2020 research and innovation programme under grant agreement No 692058. Moreover, we would like to thank the teaching staff of the Secondary School of Agiou Spiridona, in Limassol, Cyprus for allowing us to run the initial experiments in their premises. We would also like thank the teachers and school counselors for their feedback and participation in the pilot test of the application and in the survey for the investigation of teachers' needs. Also, we would like to thank A. Ruiz-Harisiou, E. Manouchou, K. Georgiou and F. Sella for their contribution for the development of the prototype applications that formed the basis for the development of the new application.

References

1. European Commission/EACEA/Eurydice: The teaching profession in Europe: practices, perceptions, and policies. Eurydice Report. Publications Office of the European Union, Luxembourg (2015)
2. Prensky, M.: Digital native, digital immigrants (2001). http://www.marcprensky.com/writing/prensky%20-%20digital%20natives,%20digital%20immigrants%20-%20part1.pdf
3. Christodoulou-Gkliarou, N.: Methodological approaches that contribute to the development of communication and social skills for effective participation of children in the learning process. In: Makri-Botsari, E. (ed.) Issues of Introductory Training for Newly Appointed Teachers, pp. 7–14. PI-Pedagogical Institute of Greece, Athens (2007). (in Greek). http://www.pi-schools.gr/download/news/t_eisag_epimorfosis.pdf
4. Kirby, S., McCombs, J., Barney, H., Naftel, S.: Reforming Teacher Education: Something Old, Something New. RAND Corporation, Santa Monica (2006)
5. Delors, J., Al Mufti, I., Amagi, I., Carneiro, R., Chung, F., Geremek, B., Gorham, W., Kornhauser, A., Manley, M., Padrón Quero, M., Savane, M., Singh, K., Stavenhagen, R., Won Suhr, M., Nanzhao, Z.: Learning: the treasure within. Report to UNESCO of the International Commission on Education for the Twenty-first Century. UNESCO publishing, France (1996). http://www.unesco.org/education/pdf/15_62.pdf

6. Darling-Hammond, L., Hammerness, K., Grossman, P., Rust, F., Shulman, L.: The design of teacher education programs. In: Darling-Hammond, L., Bransford, J. (eds.) Preparing Teachers for a Changing World, pp. 390–441. Jossey-Bass, San Francisco (2005)
7. Woolfolk, A.: Educational Psychology, 9th edn. Pearson Education, Boston (2005)
8. Freina, L., Ott, M.: A literature review on immersive virtual reality in education: state of the art and perspectives. In: eLSE Conference, Bucharest, April 2015 (2015). http://www.itd.cnr.it/download/eLSE%202015%20Freina%20Ott%20Paper.pdf
9. Lawson, G., Salanitri, D., Waterfield, B.: Future directions for the development of virtual reality within an automotive manufacturer. Appl. Ergon. **53**, 323–330 (2016). http://dx.doi.org/10.1016/j.apergo.2015.06.024
10. Mandal, S.: Brief introduction of virtual reality and its challenges. Int. J. Sci. Eng. Res. **4**(4), 304–309 (2013)
11. Cheng, T.: Application and research of using the virtual reality technology to realize the remote control. Int. J. Control Autom. **7**(8), 427–434 (2014)
12. Schwienhorst, K.: Why virtual, why environments? Implementing virtual reality concepts in computer-assisted language learning. Simul. Gaming **33**(2), 196–209 (2002). doi:10.1177/1046878102332008
13. Valmaggia, L.R., Latif, L., Kempton, M.J., Rus-Calafell, M.: Virtual reality in the psychological treatment for mental health problems: a systematic review of recent evidence. Psychiatry Res. **236**, 189–195 (2016). doi:10.1016/j.psychres.2016.01.015
14. Li, Z., Yue, J., Jáuregui, D.A.G.: A new virtual reality environment used for e-Learning. In: IEEE International Symposium on IT in Medicine and Education, 2009-ITIME 2009, Jinan, 14–16 August 2009, vol. 1, pp. 445–449 (2009). doi:10.1109/ITIME.2009.5236382
15. Sherman, W.R., Craig, A.B.: Understanding Virtual Reality. Interface, Application and Design. Morgan Kaufmann Publishers, San Francisco (2003)
16. Axelrod, J.: A virtual reality means you don't have to be yourself (2014). http://www.pastemagazine.com/articles/2014/12/virtual-reality-means-you-dont-have-to-be-yourself.html
17. Zavlanou, C., Lanitis, A.: An age simulated virtual environment for improving elderly wellbeing. In: XIV Mediterranean Conference on Medical and Biological Engineering and Computing 2016, pp. 885–890. Springer, Cham (2016)
18. Bertrand, P., Gonzalez-Franco, D., Cherene, C., Pointeau, A.: The machine to be another: embodiment performance to promote empathy among individuals (2014). http://www.themachinetobeanother.org/wp-content/uploads/2013/09/THE_MACHINE_TO_BE_ANOTHER_PAPER_2014.pdf
19. Schwebel, D.C., Combs, T., Rodriguez, D., Severson, J., Sisiopiku, V.: Community-based pedestrian safety training in virtual reality: a pragmatic trial. Accid. Anal. Prev. **86**, 9–15 (2016). doi:10.1016/j.aap.2015.10.002
20. Ke, F., Lee, S., Xu, X.: Teaching training in a mixed-reality integrated learning environment. Comput. Hum. Behav. **62**, 212–220 (2016). doi:10.1016/j.chb.2016.03.094
21. Dieker, L., Hynes, M., Hughes, C., Smith, E.: Implications of mixed reality and simulation technologies on special education and teacher preparation. Focus Except. Child. **40**(6), 1–20 (2008)
22. Dieker, L., Hynes, M., Stapleton, C., Hughes, C.: Virtual classrooms: STAR simulator. Building virtual environments for teacher training in effective classroom management. New Learn. Technol. SALT **4**, 1–22 (2007)
23. Andreasen, J.B., Haciomeroglu, E.S.: Teacher training in virtual environments. In: Paper Presented at the Annual Meeting of the North American Chapter of the International Group for the Psychology of Mathematics Education, Atlanta, GA. Teacher Training in Virtual Environments (2009)

24. Manouchou, E., Stavroulia, K.E., Ruiz-Harisiou, A., Georgiou, K., Sella, F., Lanitis, A.: A feasibility study on using virtual reality for understanding deficiencies of high school students. In: The Proceedings of the 18th IEEE Mediterranean Electrotechnical Conference (MELECON 2016), Limassol, Cyprus, 18–20 April 2016. IEEE (2016). 978-1-5090-0058-6/16/$31.00 ©2016
25. Stavroulia, K.E., Ruiz-Harisiou, A., Manouchou, E., Georgiou, K., Sella, F., Lanitis, A.: A 3D virtual environment for training teachers to identify bullying. In: The Proceedings of the 18th IEEE Mediterranean Electrotecnical Conference (MELECON 2016), Limassol, Cyprus, 18–20 April 2016. IEEE (2016). 978-1-5090-0058-6/16/$31.00 ©2016

e-Learning, Social Media and MOOCs

Exploring the Impact of Social Learning Networks in M-Learning: A Case Study in a University Environment

Fisnik Dalipi[1,2(✉)], Florim Idrizi[2], and Arianit Kurti[1,3]

[1] Department of Computer Science, Linnaeus University, Växjö, Sweden
{fisnik.dalipi,arianit.kurti}@lnu.se
[2] Department of Informatics, Tetovo University, Tetovo, Macedonia
florim.idrizi@unite.edu.mk
[3] RISE Interactive, Norrköping, Sweden
arianit.kurti@tii.se

Abstract. The high penetration of Internet, advances in mobile computing and the rise of smartphone usage has largely enhanced the use of social media in education. Moreover, nowadays social learning network (SLN) platforms have become an important educational technology component in higher education. Despite the fact that SLN are becoming ubiquitous in the higher education, there is relatively not much empirical work done investigating their purposefulness when integrated into the learning activities. This paper aims at exploring the impact of SLN in mobile assisted learning and to provide empirical evidence as to what extent SLN and mobile learning (M-learning) can improve the learning experiences. For this purpose, a quantitative experimental approach is used, and two survey questionnaires were conducted. The data is collected from 120 participants. In this study, we focus our intention on Edmodo and Kahoot platforms, which represent social media based tools that aid and support collaboration, knowledge sharing and group activities among students. Computer science students of the Tetovo University (TU) used these tools throughout one semester. From this study, there is significant evidence that students are very interested to use this SLN in a M-learning setting, indicating that SLN can be one of the promising pedagogical technologies that could contribute effectively to learning process.

Keywords: M-learning · Social learning networks · Higher education · Edmodo · Kahoot

1 Introduction

It is well-established fact that higher education nature has been changed radically due to the rapid development of mobile computing devices and internet capabilities. Mobile technology has become an indispensable part of the educational landscape at higher education setting, as it brings many opportunities and challenges to both students and academics [1]. Therefore, pedagogy should be remodeled to match with the current digital era [2].

© Springer International Publishing AG 2017
P. Zaphiris and A. Ioannou (Eds.): LCT 2017, Part I, LNCS 10295, pp. 189–198, 2017.
DOI: 10.1007/978-3-319-58509-3_16

Rapid development of internet technologies also brought many innovations in terms of social media services, which has penetrated different application domain, including those applicable to learning domain. In this aspect, SLN encapsulates a range of scenarios in which a number of people learn from one another through structured interaction. Current research indicates that teachers and instructors are reaching out to the use of different SLN applications in order to mediate and enhance their teaching and instructions as well as promote active learning of the students [3]. The proliferation of online communication has given rise to a number of SLN applications, ranging from Question and Answer (Q&A) sites (e.g., Quora), to enterprise social networks (e.g., Jive), to platforms for online education (e.g. Edmodo) [4].

The portability of smart devices has increased the use of social media in everyday life, giving users the opportunity not only to access the educational content from anywhere and anytime but also to interact and collaborate on the educational tasks via social interaction tools through different eLearning systems [5]. Nowadays, students are increasingly using social media for educational purposes; they also prefer to use social media to communicate with peers and instructors, and when used effectively, social media promotes learning by facilitating communication and information sharing [6–8].

Our study investigated the impact of Edmodo and Kahoot platforms in mobile assisted learning environment by providing empirical evidences on how these platforms facilitate the learning process. Moreover, the article aims at investigating whether these platforms enhance the students' engagement, motivation and learning.

We use Edmodo as an eLearning platform and implement gamification via Kahoot to evaluate student assessment. Edmodo is a closed social learning platform based on Web 2.0 and mobile assisted learning, while Kahoot represents a new generation game-based learning tool and platform based on a quiz concept, focusing more on engaging and motivating the students through attractive graphical interface.

The rest of the paper is structured as follows. In Sect. 2, we present literature review. Section 3 gives an overview of the methodological approach followed by analysis and results discussion in Sect. 4. The last section presents conclusion and some insight into future directions.

2   Related Work

The Oxford English Dictionary defines learning as "the cognitive process of acquiring skill or knowledge". Within the research community, learning is defined as a social, intellectual activity that is primarily based on collaboration [9]. Wenger (2003) defines social learning in terms of social competence and personal experiences [10].

Technology has had a strong impact on the way people learn by providing new ways of collaboration, interaction and experiences. The technology nowadays has created new opportunities for interaction with learners and between learners. In this aspect, SLN emerges when learners exchange information on the educational topics in a structured way [4]. Edmodo and Kahoot represent instances of social media tools used to promote interaction and collaboration among learners. Despite being available for a while in the educational space, Edmodo (2008) and Kahoot (2013), there are few studies conducted on their use and application to learning activities. Some of the studies identified are conducted towards the application of Edmodo [11–14] and Kahoot in learning process [15–17]. In [11], Edmodo is discussed and implemented as the network-learning environment, where the teaching process is demonstrated under the concept of flipped classroom. This study proves that this platform can stimulate student's learning interest and improve their ability of comprehension.

The use of social learning platforms in conjunction with the flipped classroom concept has been further studied by [12], where again Edmodo is selected as the online learning environment. This work indicated that the flipped classroom and the use of Edmodo exposes some ontological changes with respect to the use of digital technologies within education; as the study suggests, the duality of the real and online worlds is no longer relevant as this two notions seamlessly integrate.

Wallace [13] conducts another interesting experiment, where authors try to investigate the student preference towards the incorporation of Edmodo on student's engagement and responsible learning. The study revealed that Edmodo encourages engagement and responsible learning, and the students' preference of the platform is mainly emphasized towards resources, communication, such as forums, and also for other online activities. The experiences of using Edmodo to support problem-based learning are addressed in [14]. Although the literature argues that cultural differences can play an important role in the acceptance of this platform [18], the results of the [14] indicate that Edmodo has positive acceptance in blended learning and supports problem based learning.

Recently, the innovative use of social media tools in higher education institutions for educational purposes is giving rise to the game-based pedagogy. Most of the works in this field is directed towards the use of game-based learning apps and their effect on the students. Hence, [15] study the specific elements in game-based learning, where authors investigate how to use points and audio effects by using the Kahoot platform. Their study reveal that there exist some differences whether audio and points are used in game-based learning for concentration, engagement, enjoyment and motivation. Authors in [16] perform another experiment where Kahoot is compared to traditional non-gamified assessment platforms, as well as the usage of traditional paper forms for formative assessment. The results show improvements with regard to motivation, engagement, enjoyment and concentration, but there is no evidence that there is a significant learning improvement. Another study [17] uses Kahoot in classroom activities to observe student's interaction, attention and motivation. The authors pointed out that this platform motivates interaction among students and allows students to concentrate more in order to achieve learning activities in the classroom.

Despite the substantial body of knowledge on the use of Edmodo and Kahoot tools in learning activities, there is still a need for further empirical addresses the impact of these two platforms (Edmodo and Kahoot) used together in a mobile assisted learning environment. Therefore, in this paper we have constructed one such study trying to contribute to the understanding of these two SNL tools and their contributions to the learning process.

3 Settings of the Study

In order to achieve the purpose of this study, which is to investigate the role and impact of Edmodo and Kahoot on the student's engagement, motivation and learning, we seek answers to the following research questions:

- **RQ1:** What are the learning experiences with the two observed SLN in an m-learning environment and to what extent they can contribute to learning process?
- **RQ2:** Can different SLN affect learner's experience in terms of engagement and motivation in the context of their course?
- **RQ3:** What are the learner's perceptions on the limitations, advantages and structural differences between the observed SLNs?

We use quantitative approach to perform the analysis of the questionnaire data. The main motivation to conduct this study is based on the scarcity of research works, where social-media based learning environments like Edmodo and Kahoot are incorporated together to perform m-learning and assessment in classroom context on higher education settings in a developing country context.

3.1 Sample and Study Instrument

This study is focused on the higher education students and it was conducted with the participation of students from Tetovo University, which is a public university in Macedonia. The participants include 120 bachelor students from Computer science department in the following courses: Data structures, Programming 1, Computer architecture, Digital circuits 1, IT ethics and System software. This study took place around 12 weeks during the 2016 fall semester. Data from the study has been collected with two online surveys.

The methodological framework is given in Fig. 1, and consists of three stages. We initially use a questionnaire to evaluate student's learning experiences and familiarity with social media and SLN in m-learning environment. This represent the first stage of our study. The questionnaire is conducted at the beginning of each of the courses. At the second stage, the learners are asked to attend lessons, have access to the course materials, upload assignments/homework and perform other educational tasks using Edmodo with their mobile devices. In this stage, in which the m-learning and assessment takes place, we observe and measure, among others, the user interaction with the SLN and by using Kahoot we perform an assessment for each of the courses. Moreover, learners were encouraged to use these platforms for doing teamwork assignments and project development. On the other hand, Kahoot is used to perform assessment activities, in a form of quizzes. Before commencement of this stage, students received a short introduction to Edmodo and Kahoot in their classroom class. The third stage involves another questionnaire (post-study), which was administered at the end of the courses, and is used to gather learners' experiences with Edmodo and Kahoot as well as their impact on learning.

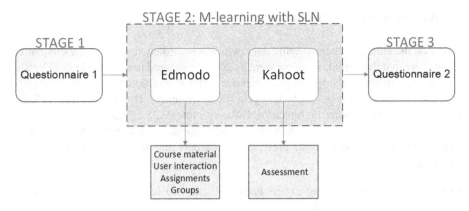

Fig. 1. Schematic representation of the methodological framework

3.2 Sampling Technique and Survey Structure

For this study we use the *Purposive homogeneous sampling* method where the participants are all members belonging to one similar subgroup (computer science students), and are carefully selected with the expectation that each participant will provide unique and rich information of value to the study [19].

Before starting to administer the questionnaires, an ethical approval from the Faculty and the students is obtained. All the participants were kindly informed that their participation in this study is on voluntary basis and the responses they provide will remain completely confidential.

The first questionnaire consists of 16 items (questions), and is made of three parts. The first part contained questions about participant's demography, including: name, e-mail address, study level, age, whereas the second part includes questions related to the student's familiarity and awareness about m-learning and also for social media tools as learning aid separately. The third part includes questions related to the student's experiences with the usage of SLN in a mobile assisted environment, with special focus to Edmodo and Kahoot apps.

The second questionnaire consisted of 30 five point Likert scale items whose values ranged from 1 = Strongly Disagree to 5 = Strongly Agree. The main idea behind these questionnaire relies on understanding as to what extent students are satisfied with these platforms as learning aid, and to examine the suitability of the platforms towards strengthening engagement, motivation and communication among students when used for M-learning in higher education. Sample items included "Do you think that social media learning networks encourage the student-student and student-teacher collaboration in M-learning", "The Edmodo app keeps me more focused with the subject", "Kahoot can help me get better grades", etc. Some items have been adopted from relevant studies, such as [14, 16].

4   Analysis and Discussion

Based on the student's demographic data, which were asked at the first questionnaire, results revealed that female students were 24.5% as compared to male students (75.5%). All the students are studying computer science at the undergraduate level, more specifically, 40.9% of students belong to first year (Programming 1, Digital circuits 1), 17.4% to second year (Computer architecture, Data structures), 25.5% to the third year (IT Ethics), while only 16.4% (System Software) are students attending their fourth year of studies. The rest of the sections presents the findings that answer our three research questions.

RQ1. What are the learning experiences with the two tested observed SLN in m-learning environment?

By analyzing the students' experiences and awareness towards social media and m-learning, results have indicated that before conducting this study, 67.3% of the students have already used social media (Facebook, Youtube, Twitter) for learning, as opposed to wikis, blogs, and audio/video podcast. On the other hand, it is interesting to note that only 47.3% have used mobile devices in their education, while the majority of them have used laptop and desktop computers (52.7%). As can be seen from Table 1, which presents the pre-study calculated results, the learners are uncertain about m-learning usage and advantages (Mode = 3), while the majority of them didn't have any experience of using SLNs, having also a poor perception for the suitability of SLN for m-learning (Mode = 2). They recognize the positive impact that in general SLN could contribute to learning (Mode = 4), but they lack information for the functionalities of Edmodo and Kahoot and have no previous experience with this tools for learning.

RQ2. Can different SLN (Edmodo and Kahoot) affect the learner experience in terms of engagement and motivation in the context of their course in a m-learning setting?

Table 1. Student's experiences and awareness towards m-learning and SLN tools

Question	Mean	Mode	Standard deviation
I have enough knowledge about the m-learning advantages	3.08	3	0.88
I use my smartphone for learning	2.78	3	0.82
Social media tools are suitable for m-learning	2.89	2	0.95
I frequently use social media tools for learning	1.96	2	0.86
I frequently use social media with my smartphone for learning	1.99	2	0.86
In general, social media tools can have positive impact on learning	3.55	4	0.86
I have information about the functionalities of Edmodo and Kahoot	1.78	2	0.78
We have already used Edmodo and Kahoot in the classroom	1.40	1	0.51

To determine the answer of this question, we asked students to reflect upon the impact of these tools on their engagement and motivation in learning. As indicated in the Table 2, approximately 44% of students agree that Edmodo helped them to engage more and discuss learning concepts with colleagues (M = 3.96, SD = 0.96), while only 28% of them agree when using Kahoot (M = 3.75, SD = 3). This result could be attributed to the fact that both these tools help learners' to increase the interaction since they have system functions to engage them in discussions, albeit having differences in the user interface.

Table 2. The impact of SLNs to engagement and motivation

Question	Mean	Mode	Standard deviation
Edmodo helps me to engage and discuss learning concepts with colleagues	3.96	4	0.96
Do you think Kahoot empowers dialog and discussions in the class	3.75	3	1.06
Learning with Edmodo in a smartphone increases my motivation	4.35	5	0.91
I enjoyed the assessment with Kahoot app and feel more motivated to learn	4.33	5	0.84

Concerning motivation, the study reveals that the majority of students strongly agree that both platforms have had high motivational impact on them.

The result could refer to the reason that no courses at all were previously introduced through SLN platforms in a m-learning setting at Tetovo University, but rather by using the conventional methods of teaching. Hence, the aspirations of learners towards m-learning with SLN are very high, as they found these tools very motivational and interesting.

RQ3. What are the students' perceptions on the limitations, advantages and structural differences between the observed SLNs?

The findings related to limitations, advantages and structural differences between Edmodo and Kahoot are presented in Table 3. Basic observations from the set of questions seems to be that student overall have had a positive experience on using Edmodo, but they are more toward neutral when it comes to the benefits of Edmodo for increasing the knowledge on the subject. One thing to be investigated is the fact if the course content affects the usefulness of SLN tools?

At the curiosity level students seems to find the use of the tool very interesting, especially through mobile device. They were very positive on the usefulness of the tool to support interaction and communication with the teacher. They seems to have good experiences with using of Edmodo app for submission of homework as well as they highly recommend the app to other users.

As far as Kahoot is concerned, it seems that we have a more converging situation. The majority of students agreed that the purpose of it is for assessment. In addition, as such it can provide the necessary support for personalized learning experience. The have

Table 3. Student's perceptions towards limitations, advantages and differences of the observed SLNs

Question	Mean	Mode	Standard deviation
Edmodo is suitable and satisfies my needs for m-learning	4.18	4	0.74
Edmodo makes easy to be updated with learning	3.94	4	0.99
Do you think Edmodo helped you to increase your knowledge for the subject	3.76	3	0.97
Learning with Edmodo in a smartphone increases my motivation	4.35	5	0.91
Edmodo helped me to get more information or assistance from the teacher	4.05	5	1.00
I always submit on time my homework with Edmodo	4.25	5	1.03
Would you recommend to others to use the Edmodo app	4.39	5	0.84
Kahoot platform is suitable for assessment	4.60	5	0.74
The Kahoot mobile app helps me to manage better my studies	3.84	4	0.98
Do you think that Kahoot can be used to follow the success for every student	3.92	5	1.05
Do you think that Kahoot based assessment is more effective and accurate than the traditional one	3.88	5	1.03
Do you believe Kahoot help you identify your weaknesses	4.09	4	0.96
Kahoot would enable me to get higher grades	3.85	5	1.02
Kahoot adds more value to m-learning	4.23	4	0.79

slightly lower score when it come to the use of Kahoot for managing of their studies. As well as supporting them identifying the weaknesses.

Students see a more usefulness on the Kahoot when it comes to ability to support them getting higher grades. Despite having the mode 5, still the mean value is lower while and standard deviation relatively higher. This indicates that the majority of students had an overall good experience with Kahoot when it comes to their course performance. In comparison to Edmodo, Kahoot seems to have been liked more by the students. Especially they were able to see a more tangible added value on the use of Kahoot compared to Edmodo. The most interesting result is that students suggest that they will continue using Kahoot in the future as well. Interesting observation seems to be that Kahoot sees to have influenced students perceptions that m-learning is more assessment oriented compared to traditional learning. The ability for faster feedback seems to have supported this understanding.

Another interesting observation that comes from this study is the fact that the use of technology seems to support the perception for increased creativity as well as motivation among students. In the context of higher education, the technology, in particular social media tools are instrumental to support the interactions between peers as well as with the teacher. Furthermore, they represent an effective tool for teachers to engage students and to encourage them to broaden their knowledge and skills aimed at making learning more meaningful, fun and effective [20].

5   Conclusions

Social media tools provide services and various new ways of communication, using computers and mobile devices. In this paper we presented an approach of application of SLN in m-learning and provide an insight on their impact for the learning activities. For this study, students in various computer sciences courses were participating in our study to share their perceptions and experience of working with social media based tools, attend lessons and conduct different learning activities with Edmodo and Kahoot, and finally provide their feedback related to the use of the observed SLN.

Findings from this work indicated that, overall, SLN tools support better engagement in the classroom and increase the potential for interactions among peers and teachers as they also help students to be part of the m-learning community without any restrictions of time and place. It seem that from the two tools investigated here, the students have better received Kahoot.

Further, results point to the need to conduct future research on the correlation between course content, pedagogical approaches and supporting tools used.

References

1. Gikas, J., Grant, M.M.: Mobile computing devices in higher education: student perspectives on learning with cellphones, smartphones, and social media. Internet High. Educ. **19**, 18–26 (2013)
2. Beetham, H., Sharpe, R.: Rethinking Pedagogy for a Digital Age: Designing for 21st Century Learning. Routledge, New York (2013)
3. Tess, P.A.: The role of social media in higher education classes (real and virtual) – a literature review. Comput. Hum. Behav. **29**(5), 60–68 (2013)
4. Brinton, C., Buccapatnam, S., Wong, F.M.F., Chiang, M., Poor, H.V.: Social learning networks: efficiency optimization for MOOC forums. In: The 35th Annual IEEE International Conference on Computer Communications, IEEE INFOCOM 2016, San Francisco, USA, 10–15 April 2016
5. Imran, A.S., Pireva, K., Dalipi, F., Kastrati, Z.: An analysis of social collaboration and networking tools in eLearning. In: Proceedings of Third International Conference, LCT 2016, Held as Part of HCI International 2016, Toronto, ON, Canada, 17–22 July 2016
6. Junco, R.: Too much face and not enough books: the relationship between multiple indices of Facebook use and academic performance. Comput. Hum. Behav. **28**(1), 187–198 (2012)
7. Lee, M.J.W., McLoughlin, C.: Social software as tools for pedagogical transformation: enabling personalization, creative production, and participatory learning. In: Lambropoulos, N., Romero, M. (eds.) Educational Social Software for Context-Aware Learning: Collaborative Methods and Human Interaction, pp. 1–22. Information Science Reference, Hershey (2010)
8. Selwyn, N.: Looking beyond learning: notes towards the critical study of educational technology. J. Comput. Assist. Learn. **26**(1), 65–73 (2010). Wiley
9. Brown, J.S., Duguid, P.: The Social Life of Information. Harvard Business School Press, Boston (2002)
10. Wenger, E.: Communities of practice and social learning systems: the career of a concept. In: Blackmore, C. (ed.) Social Learning Systems and Communities of Practice. Springer, London (2010)

11. Quingqing, H.: Research on flipped classroom design and implication based on Edmodo platform. In: 8th IEEE International Conference on Measuring Technology and Mechatronics Automation, Macau, China, 11–12 March 2016

12. Wallace, A.: Social learning platforms and the flipped classroom. Int. J. Inf. Educ. Technol. **4**(4), 293–296 (2014)

13. Balasubramanian, K., Jaykumar, V., Fukey, L.N.: A study on student preference towards the use of Edmodo as a learning platform to create learning environment. Procedia Soc. Behav. Sci. **144**, 416–422 (2014)

14. Paliktzoglou, V., Suhonen, J.: Microblogging as an assisted learning tool in problem-based learning in Bahrain: the Edmodo case. In: Handbook of Research on Interactive Information Quality in Expanding Social Network Communications, Advances in Social Networking and Online Communities. IGI Global, Hershey (2015)

15. Wang, A.I., Lieberoth, A.: The effect of points and audio on concentration, engagement, enjoyment, learning, motivation, and classroom dynamics using Kahoot! In: Proceedings of the European Conference on Games-Based Learning, January 2016

16. Wang, A.I., Lieberoth, A.: The effect of digitizing and gamifying quizzing in classrooms. In: Proceedings of the European Conference on Games-Based Learning, January 2016

17. Cutri, R., Marim, L.R., Cordeiro, J.R., Gil, H., Guerald, C.C.T.: Kahoot, a new and cheap way to get classroom-response instead of using clickers. In: Proceedings of American Society for Engineering Education conference, New Orleans, USA, 26–29 June 2016

18. Cheung, C.M., Chiu, P.-Y., Lee, M.K.: Online social networks: why do students use Facebook. Comput. Hum. Behav. **27**(4), 1337–1343 (2011)

19. Onwuegbuzie, A.J., Collins, K.M.: A typology of mixed methods sampling designs in social science research. Qual. Rep. **12**(2), 281–316 (2007)

20. Wankel, C.: Management education using social media. Org. Manag. J. **6**(4), 251–262 (2009)

Improving Concepts of E-Learning by Using ERP Systems for an Interactive Knowledge Diffusion

David Heim[(✉)], Marcus Fischer, and Axel Winkelmann

University of Wuerzburg, Wuerzburg, Germany
{david.heim, marcus.fischer,
axel.winkelmann}@uni-wuerzburg.de

Abstract. As digitalization reshapes consumer needs sustainably, enterprises must cope with an increasing complexity of products, processes, and job designs. On the one hand, business operations depend on specialists and their expert knowledge to provide high-quality products and services. On the other hand, customers get more connected and establish new, flexible ways of interacting with organizations throughout the entire product lifecycle. Therefore, interdisciplinary knowledge is the central source of competitiveness and employability. However, as higher education is influenced by technology, digitalization, and decentralization, the teaching paradigm becomes more teacher-centered. Consequently, most online courses focus on the distribution of facts, instead of mediating competencies in a problem-oriented environment. The purpose of this paper is to evaluate the use of enterprise simulations for traditional e-learning concepts. Enabled by cloud-based ERP systems, students participate in a decentralized course design, while cross-departmental interdependencies require communication, coordination, and knowledge diffusion. Thus, we propose that enterprise simulations can positively influence learning success in e-learning scenarios. To test our hypothesis, we conduct a survey from a university course using the cloud-based ERP system SAP Business ByDesign. Results of 32 participants reveal that the proposed course design positively influences process-orientation, communication and teamwork.

Keywords: Knowledge transfer · Computer-supported collaborative learning · Enterprise simulations · Cloud-based enterprise research systems

1 Motivation

In a continuously changing environment, knowledge is the central source of competitiveness for many organizations. As market pressure increases, products and services are continuously innovated and enterprises are forced to further specialize in their core competencies. Simultaneously, technological advancements allow customers to connect with their environment, establishing new ways of interacting with enterprises throughout the entire product lifecycle [1]. Thus, enterprises must provide an integrated customer experience to address new requirements on quality, flexibility, connectivity, and ubiquity. As organizations rely on an enterprise-wide coordination of processes

© Springer International Publishing AG 2017
P. Zaphiris and A. Ioannou (Eds.): LCT 2017, Part I, LNCS 10295, pp. 199–215, 2017.
DOI: 10.1007/978-3-319-58509-3_17

and activities, effective mechanisms of knowledge diffusion among organizational members must be established to enable process-orientation, communication, and coordination [2].

While organizations increasingly focus on cross-functional education efforts for their employees, initial competencies are limited by a teacher-centered paradigm course design in higher education [3]. Thus, courses rather focus on the distribution of facts, instead of mediating competencies in a problem-oriented environment [4, 5]. Consequently, potential employees frequently lack necessary communication and reasoning skills when entering the labor market and require additional educational effort. However, as higher education is increasingly influenced by technology, digitalization, and decentralization, a shift from traditional teaching approaches to e-learning scenarios can be observed. As most online courses only provide little opportunity to interact and collaborate, the prevailing lack of competency mediation tends to intensify [X].

To address those challenges, the present paper suggests integrating enterprise simulations based on cloud enterprise resource planning (ERP) systems into traditional e-learning concepts. Based on a common database, ERP systems are generally implemented to provide organization-wide support for business operations. Consequently, problem solving depends on the interaction and collaboration of organizational members. This research is summarized by the following research questions:

(**RQ1**)   Do traditional teaching concepts facilitate the perceived competiveness of students when entering the labor market?

(**RQ2**)   Do cloud-based enterprise simulations increase the likelihood of learning success in the context of online course designs?

This contribution is organized as follows: Sect. 2 provides background on ERP systems. In Sect. 3, a theoretical framework is introduced, describing the process of knowledge diffusion within an enterprise simulation. The methodology underlying this research endeavor is presented in Sect. 4. Subsequently, a comprehensive survey is conducted to draw implications on the effect of the proposed course design on the participants' learning success. Concluding this contribution, Sect. 6 summarizes the main findings and gives an overview of limitations and future research potentials.

2   Enterprise Resource Planning Systems

ERP systems can be defined as a special type of information system that enterprises use to collect, store, manage and interpret data gathered from executing their business operations [6]. In general, systems support the entire process organization and track business resources such as cash, raw materials, and production capacity as well as the status of transactional objects, such as customer orders, purchase orders, and payroll [7]. Based on an integrated, and centrally managed database, ERP systems share and provide data across functions and departments. Thus, employees access relevant data in real time, without the need for switching systems. Implementing ERP systems, enterprises aim to optimize business processes, support management decision making, increase data security, and to improve overall customer satisfaction [8].

The functions covered range from financial accounting to human resources and supply chain management [9]. However, as systems consist of multiple modules, functions can be parametrized and customized to align with enterprise-specific needs. A recently conducted survey revealed that more than 90% of small and medium enterprises (SME) in Germany use ERP systems to support their business operations [10].

As the market for enterprise software has been continuously growing during the last decades, a large variety of vendors and systems emerged [11]. Due to varying requirements across different industries, the market can be further distinguished into software solutions for large companies and SMEs. Though in the past, implementing and ERP system was linked to significant IT investments, today cloud-based technologies provide access without on-site hosting or maintaining IT infrastructures [12].

The paper at hand uses the cloud-based ERP system SAP Business ByDesign, which was especially developed for SMEs. The system was parametrized to cover the functions specified in Table 1. Activated modules were simultaneously used as departments to organize the enterprise simulation.

Table 1. Covered functions within the enterprise simulation [9]

SAP business by design		
Department	Abbreviation	Function
Customer relationship management	CRM	To manage the enterprise's current and future customer interactions
Material management	MM	To manage movement of materials, logistics, and the supply chain
Production planning	PP	To plan futureproductionbydeterminingandarrangingwhichfacilitiesareneeded
After sales	AS	To perform activities and services that tie customers to the enterprise
Finance and controlling	FICO	To manage financial flows and monitor the enterprise's performance
Human resource management	HRM	To maximize employee performance in the service of an employer's strategic objectives

3 Knowledge Transfer in Enterprise Simulations

Using ERP systems to support interactive course designs has become increasingly popular in recent years [5, 13, 14]. ERP-related teaching concepts have proven to enable process-oriented competency mediation with positive impacts on teaching quality and experience [15]. However, the suitability of traditional on-premise software is limited when transferred to an e-learning environment. Nevertheless, emerging technologies, such as Cloud Computing, allow ubiquitous accessibility and location independency [16].

Due to the definition of learning as an active process of constructing knowledge in the receiver's mind, knowledge cannot be exchanged like tangible goods [17–19]. In fact, aspects like social interaction, personal understanding, and sense making influence knowledge creation significantly [20, 21]. Following Wilkesmann et al., knowledge transfer can be described as a multi-level phenomenon that is realized on the individual, intra-organizational, and inter-organizational levels [22]. Inkpen and Tsang further define the process of organizational knowledge transfer as a change in knowledge or performance of the receiving unit [23]. While at the individual level, units are defined as organizational members, they represent departments on the intra-organizational level and entire organizations at the inter-organizational level. However, as the course design is naturally limited to the simulation of a single enterprise, aspects of inter-organizational knowledge transfer are not accounted for in this research.

In alignment with Wilkesmann and Wilkesmann, knowledge creation always includes the individual level, although mutual learning effects can be generated on the intra-organizational and inter-organizational level [24]. Thus, this study defines knowledge transfer as a process of knowledge exchange between experts and novices that are connected through an ERP system. A conceptual overview of the knowledge exchange process is illustrated in Fig. 1.

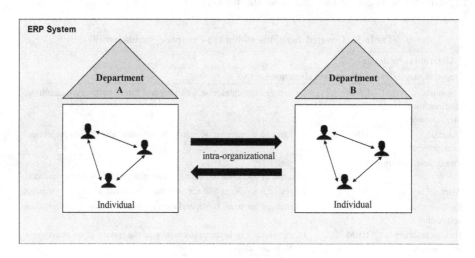

Fig. 1. Knowledge transfer in enterprise simulations [24]

To describe knowledge transfer on the individual level, we utilize the model of skill levels by Dreyfus and Dreyfus, who distinguish stages of knowledge acquisition as follows: novice, advanced beginner, competent, proficient, and expert [25]. The first three stages can be summarized as a person's knowledge that solution guidelines for a certain problem exist. The stages 'proficient' and 'expert' are characterized by knowing how to act in certain situations and how to use the acquired theoretical knowledge [24]. In fact, novices conform to rules, with no or little linkage of theory and its practical application. In contrast, experts use intuitive reasoning based on vast experiences in their field of expertise [25].

These differences mostly result from information asymmetries between both cohorts [24]. However, as individuals only absorb information that is relevant in certain situations, it facilitates knowledge diffusion. Table 2 illustrates the five stages of skill acquisition as well as their main characteristics.

Table 2. Stages of skill acquisition [25]

Skill level	Characteristics
1. Novice	Conformance to rules
	No discretionary judgment
2. Advanced beginner	Attribute-based action guidelines
3. Competent	Action planning based on long-term goals
4. Proficient	Holistic perspective on problems
5. Expert	No rule-based actions
	Intuitive, reflexive, and evaluative acting

Due to the variety of requirements, tasks, and activities, each person can be novice and expert in different fields simultaneously. According to Argyris and Schön, organizational learning works best in a problem-oriented environment in which actions lead to a mismatch of expected and accomplished results [26]. Thus, individuals aim to identify a problem's solution by performing a process of thought and further action. In general, the learning process starts with individuals perceiving a problem and acting on behalf of the organization. In line with that, Wilkesmann et al. suggest that a linkage of individual and organizational learning can be facilitated by performing routine and innovation games [27]. While routine games focus on recurring tasks, such as producing goods or services, innovation games aim to modify and optimize the current status quo of activities and processes. Participating in routine games, a novice's learning process is initiated by the acquisition of basic knowledge about social and functional interdependencies and requirements of an adequate problem solution. However, as routine games are repetitive, a steep learning curve is provided and the novice eventually becomes an expert. Thus, a former novice can advise and teach another novice solving unknown problems. Knowledge transfer is facilitated by the occurrence of complex problems, which are generally characterized by their innovativeness. Thus, the problem cannot be solved with the information of a single individual, since no established procedure to approach the problem exists [28]. In dealing with those situations, an individual must transfer his or her knowledge within a collaborative learning process, in which all participating members exchange opinions and integrate their perspectives into a single solution [24].

Organizational knowledge transfer can be facilitated by technologies providing direct channels for an immediate exchange of information [29]. Following Wilkesmann and Wilkesmann, direct interactions can be adequately supported by e-learning or knowledge management systems [24]. While e-learning aims to qualify persons in a certain direction, knowledge management supports the process of knowledge creation. As ERP systems provide a central source of information, the present paper defines them as a special type of knowledge management system. Following Wilkesmann and Wilkesmann, an ideal type of knowledge transfer from experts to novices can be modeled as illustrated in Fig. 2.

According to Wilkesmann and Wilkesmann, novices are less experienced and require broad and more elaborative presented information [24]. Thus, they can start their individual learning and qualification process by using e-learning tools, such as

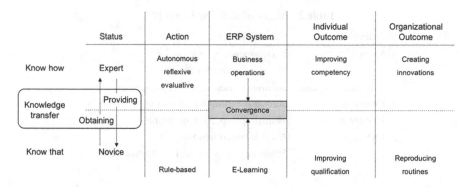

Fig. 2. Knowledge transfer as an interaction between experts and novices [24]

videos or online documentations. However, as experts know how to accomplish their predefined goals, they can search for specific pieces of information or data within an ERP system. Consequently, knowledge transfer is enabled by the integrated environment in which experts and novices collaborate. Compared to traditional knowledge management systems ERP systems further exhibit the advantage, that supported business processes connect every individual within an organization. Thus, information diffusion is facilitated and more complex problems can be solved.

4 Research Design

To evaluate our hypothesis and to answer the predefined research questions, we apply a quantitative research methodology. Thus, results can be analyzed using statistical methods, and the survey can be conducted anonymously.

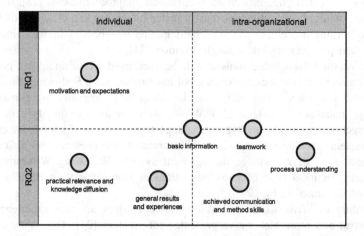

Fig. 3. Survey design based on research questions and theoretical framework

Constructing the survey, we aimed to cover multiple aspects of knowledge exchange, including previous knowledge, perceived skills, competencies, and expectations. Figure 3 summarizes the survey's scope and links the proposed research questions to the predefined theoretical framework. As the survey was conducted twice, impacts of the simulation can be analyzed from a longitudinal perspective. Table 3 gives an overview of sections covered at the courses beginning and end.

Table 3. Sections of the survey

Sections at the course's beginning (t = 0)	Sections at the course's end (t = 1)
1. Basic information	1. Basic information
2. Motivation and expectations	2. Achieved method skills
3. Teamwork	3. Teamwork
4. Cooperation and communication	4. Cooperation and communication
5. Practical relevance and knowledge diffusion	5. Practical relevance and knowledge diffusion
	6. General results and experiences
	7. Process understanding
	8. Achieved communication skills

Basic Information (t = 0, 1). Basic information includes the participants' age and gender. We further prompt for students' majors and alma maters, as this provides valuable insights into existing knowledge and fields of expertise. In fact, participants with a bachelor's degree from a university of applied sciences can exhibit a stronger linkage of theoretical knowledge and its practical application.

Table 4. Questions regarding motivation and expectations

Abbr.	Question
Mot&Exp.1	I am satisfied with the amount of practical references in existing course designs
Mot&Exp.2	I feel well prepared for entering the labor market
Mot&Exp.3	Existing teaching concepts enable interdisciplinary knowledge exchange
Mot&Exp.4	Existing curricula enable interdisciplinary knowledge transfer
Mot&Exp.5	I am willing to try new teaching concepts
Mot&Exp.6	I would appreciate more innovative teaching concepts at the university
Mot&Exp.7	I prefer innovative teaching concepts over traditional course designs
Mot&Exp.8	I am interested in applying theoretical knowledge in real-world scenarios
Mot&Exp.9	It is exciting to be a member of an organization
Mot&Exp.10	I look forward to be working in an interdisciplinary team during the course
Mot&Exp.11	Working in a team can be fun
Mot&Exp.12	I can yield knowledge from previous courses for this class
Mot&Exp.13	Working as a group has a positive influence on the quality of results
Mot&Exp.14	I can learn from working with students from other fields of expertise

Motivation and Expectations (t = 0). This section aims to shed light on the motivations and expectations of the participating students. Questions aim to reveal the students' motivation for signing up for the course and their general satisfaction with previously experienced teaching concepts at the university. The section further requests perceived labor market competitiveness within the participant's fields of specialization (Table 4).

Teamwork (t = 0, 1). The teamwork section aims to reveal participants' general willingness to share existing knowledge in a social group, their openness to actively assist other participants and their past teamwork experiences (Table 5).

Table 5. Questions regarding teamwork

Abbr.	Question
TW.1	I am interested in sharing my expertise with other participants
TW.2	I am excited to get in touch with other members of the team
TW.3	I can use my knowledge to facilitate accomplishing team objectives
TW.4	Teamwork helps to analyze theoretical concepts from various perspectives
TW.5	I feel uncomfortable working in team
TW.6	I do not like explaining something to others
TW.7	I do not know how to solve complex problems in a team
TW.8	Results from teamwork exhibit a higher quality
TW.9	When working in a team, it feels like a waste of time
TW.10	Working on your own is better when solving complex problems

Cooperation and Communication (t = 0, 1). This section aims to provide insights into the willingness of participants to cooperate with other students to accomplish overall objectives (Table 6).

Table 6. Questions Regarding Cooperation and Communication

Abbr.	Question
C&C.1	Our team can integrate different perspectives into a single solution
C&C.2	We draw innovative conclusions from discussing different ideas
C&C.3	We constantly develop new ideas and try to integrate them into a satisfactory solution
C&C.4	We ask questions if something is not clear
C&C.5	If a team member expresses his opinion, he is also interested in other opinions
C&C.6	When mistakes happen, the team is willing to find the causes together
C&C.7	If things go wrong, the team takes time to find a solution
C&C.8	If things go wrong, the team takes time to analyze and learn why
C&C.9	Our team shares mistakes to prevent other team members from experiencing similar one
C&C.10	We discuss mistakes as a team because they provide valuable information
C&C.11	Within our team, mistakes are analyzed in a productive way

Practical Relevance and Knowledge Diffusion (t = 0, 1). In this section, students are asked to estimate their ability to transfer knowledge from theory to practical applications. Furthermore, participants are requested to assess the importance of this knowledge for future job applications (Table 7).

Table 7. Questions regarding practical relevance and knowledge diffusion

Abbr.	Question
PrRe&KnDi.1	I can transfer knowledge to practical applications
PrRe&KnDi.2	During my previous school experiences I acquired adequate social skills
PrRe&KnDi.3	I can link interdisciplinary knowledge from different fields
PrRe&KnDi.4	I can analyze logical dependencies in a business context easily
PrRe&KnDi.5	I can structure and solve unknown problems
PrRe&KnDi.6	Linking knowledge is crucial for earning my degree
PrRe&KnDi.7	I can solve practical problems easily
PrRe&KnDi.8	I can evaluate knowledge for its practical relevance
PrRe&KnDi.9	I can estimate the impact of my actions on members of other departments

Results and Course Experiences (t = 1). In this section, participants are asked to provide information about their experiences and overall satisfaction with the course. Answers can be compared to Sect. 2 (Mot&Exp). Furthermore, we evaluate the course's effectiveness in improving the practical relevance of university teaching concepts, and reassess the perception of future job opportunities. Consequently, this section includes questions regarding the applicability of existing knowledge and the quality of cooperation with other team members (Table 8).

Table 8. Questions regarding results and course experiences

Abbr.	Question
Re&Exp.1	I feel well prepared for entering the labor market
Re&Exp.2	This course helped improved my competiveness when applying for a job
Re&Exp.3	This course is characterized by an extensive interdisciplinary component
Re&Exp.4	I would appreciate being offered similar courses
Re&Exp.5	This course improved my ability to transfer knowledge from theory to practical applications
Re&Exp.6	We connected the expertise of each team member to find the best solution
Re&Exp.7	Knowledge from other classes helped me in this course
Re&Exp.8	I think I learned a lot during this course

Process Understanding (t = 1). This section aims to evaluate the participants' perception of individual process knowledge. Thus, corresponding questions focus on improvements in understanding business operations and business processes. Additionally, participants are asked to provide information about intra-organizational communication issues between different departments (Table 9).

Table 9. Questions regarding process understanding

Abbr.	Question
Pk.1	This course helped me understand business operations
Pk.2	I improved my ability to analyze and optimize business processes
Pk.3	I achieved a better understanding of interfaces and how to manage them
Pk.4	This course helped me understand complex business processes more easily
Pk.5	This course helped me understand and implement complex business processes

Achieved Communication and Method Skills (t = 1). This sections aims to evaluate improvements in terms of communication, cooperation and complementary social skills. Furthermore, it prompts perceived changes in methodical skills, e.g., regarding capabilities for complex problem solving. Results can be compared to the section on cooperation and communication (Table 10).

Table 10. Questions regarding achieved communication and method skills

Abbr.	Question
Cs&Ms.1	I feel more confident expressing my opinion in a group
Cs&Ms.2	I feel more confident questioning things in a group
Cs&Ms.3	I am able to communicate my thoughts more clearly
Cs&Ms.4	I can participate in discussions more effectively
Cs&Ms.5	I appreciated working together with students from different backgrounds
Cs&Ms.6	This course improved my ability to understand and structure problems in a business context
Cs&Ms.7	I can structure my work better than before
Cs&Ms.8	This course helped to improve my overall skills

5 Results

5.1 Experimental Setup

At the start of the course, an application phase offered participants the opportunity to apply for a department within the simulated enterprise. It is assumed that the decision was based on individual skills and preferences. Screening the applications, the research team carefully assembled teams in consideration of individual job experience, grades in relevant courses and other characteristics. As the course was open to students from different majors, a wide range of capabilities and skills was available. In fact, it was our goal to achieve a good composition of novices and experts in each department. Randomly conducted interviews provided evidence that each member felt like an expert in one or two fields within the range of departmental activities, while exhibiting only little knowledge in many other areas. Eventually, participants were assigned to functions as illustrated in Table 11. As departments vary in workload and functionality range, the number of participants was accordingly adjusted to meet the department-specific requirements.

Table 11. Distribution of participants to departments

CRM	HRM	PP	MM	AS	FICO
7	3	7	4	4	7

The simulation was based on the ERP system SAP Business ByDesign. As a cloud-based system, students could participate in the simulation independent of locality and time. Although the corresponding lectures were held twice a week, personal attendance was not mandatory. However, as the research team served as the enterprise´ s executive board, lectures provided a platform to discuss problems, track progresses, and define future goals. The course was further supported by a Massive Open Online Course (MOOC), which facilitated communication and cross-departmental problem solving. At the start of the productive phase of the course, participants were initially requested to identify and implement relevant business processes in their department. Due to the cross-functional character of business processes, interdependencies between departments required communication and interaction with other organizational members. At the beginning of the course, participants had to learn how to use the ERP system productively. Thus, qualifying e-learning materials, such as videos or documentations were offered on the MOOC platform. Driven by routine games, representing repetitive tasks, such as providing master data or creating new customers or invoices, participants achieved an understanding of basic tasks, processes and intra-organizational dependencies. They further experienced the advantages and other consequences of an ERP system´s integrated working environment. At times, the research team purposely initiated special incidents, such as the acquisition of another enterprise, unexpected large-scale orders, or a warehouse fire damage. Thus, the organization had to manage innovation games, which required further communication, coordination, and intra-organizational knowledge exchange.

5.2   Meta-analysis

First, a comprehensive meta-analysis provides information about each participant's socio-demographic background and summarizes existing skills, specializations, and interests.

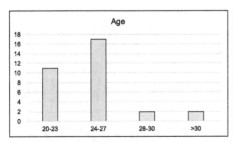
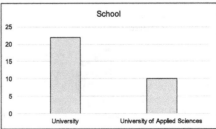

Fig. 4. Socio-demographic information

Figure 4 provides an overview of relevant background information. Since the course is offered in a master´s program, most participants were aged between 20 and 27. However, because of previous job experiences, a small number of students were 28 and above. Due to the German system of higher education, the student´s alma mater can influence their ability to transfer theoretical knowledge to practical applications. Results from our survey reveal that 69% of participants completed their bachelor 's degree at a university, while 31% graduated from a university of applied sciences.

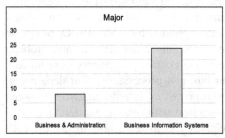 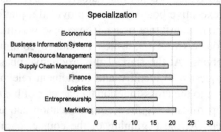

Fig. 5. Skills and interests

Furthermore, Fig. 5 provides information on majors and specializations of the participating students. While the course is open to students of different majors, most participants were enrolled in a degree in Business & Administration (B&A) or Business Information Systems (BIS). However, students with a BIS major were most numerous, since the course description is rather technical. In our investigation of students' fields of expertise, their skills and interests exhibit a roughly equal distribution on the available specializations. Thus, experts and novices were available in each department of the enterprise simulation and enabled a dynamic process of knowledge exchange.

5.3   Motivations and Expectation

To shed light on expectations and motivations, items of this section aim to reveal the participants' general satisfaction with existing teaching formats and their perceived labor market competiveness.

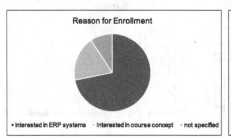 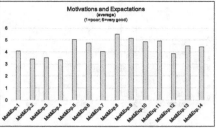

Fig. 6. Motivations and expectations

Results from this section are summarized in Fig. 6. Most students specified, that their main reason for signing up for the course is their interest in working with an ERP system. In addition, a smaller number of students were interested in the interactive course design and based their decision on positive reviews of students, who had previously completed the course. However, most students feel poorly prepared for their labor market entry and estimated their competitiveness as limited. In line with that, linking theoretical knowledge to practical applications is a major motivation for students attending this course (Mot.Exp.8). Most of the students further approve of being part of a simulated enterprise to learn in a problem-oriented environment (Mot.Exp.9). Consequently, they felt comfortable with learning in a group and assume, that they could learn from exchanging knowledge with students with other fields of expertise (Mot.Exp.14).

5.4 Effects on Teamwork, Cooperation and Communication

The sections 'Teamwork' and 'Cooperation and Communication' aim to analyze the willingness of participants to share their existing knowledge in a social group. Additionally, items in these sections address their openness towards interactive and learner-centered course designs. As ERP systems have proven to facilitate teamwork and skills of cooperation and communication, we aim to investigate, if these known advantages can be transferred to e-learning concepts [5].

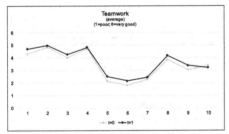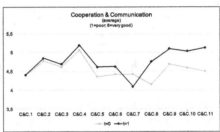

Fig. 7. Motivations and expectations

Figure 7 illustrates the effects on teamwork as well as communication and cooperation. While the course exhibits a positive impact on most teamwork-related items of the survey, most significant effects can be observed in the participants' willingness to share information from their fields of expertise with other group members (TW.1). Positive impacts are mainly due to the intra-organizational compositions of novices and experts. In line with that, participants noticed that linking complementary knowledge within the group resulted in an increased quality of problem solutions. However, most students experienced the necessary efforts on coordination and communication as cumbersome and time-consuming (TW.9). As suggested by the results, the course positively influenced the student's ability in problem solving (TW.10).

To analyze the effect on cooperation and communication, the results from corresponding survey items suggest a positive impact from our course design. While communicating opinions and problems within the group is enabled (C&C.4; C&C.5), it can further be observed that groups often did not take enough time to analyze problems and find an adequate solution (C&C.7). However, participants benefited from communicating mistakes straightforwardly, as the group gained new experiences from individual failures (C&C.9; C&C.10).

5.5   Effects on Practical Relevance, Knowledge Diffusion and Experiences

The following section investigates if the course design positively influences the perceived practical relevance of university teaching. Additionally, effects on students' ability to transfer knowledge and their overall satisfaction with the course are evaluated. Finally, we control for improvements in perceived competitiveness when entering the labor market (Fig. 8).

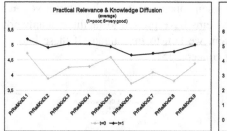 

Fig. 8. Practical relevance, knowledge diffusion and results

In our analysis of the perceived practical relevance of teaching concepts, the course exhibits a positive influence on every item of the survey. Results reveal that participants experience improved social competencies, which are crucial for working in a team (PrRe&KnDi.2). It can further be observed that the course supports the linkage of interdisciplinary knowledge and thus, enables participants to work in a more process-oriented manner (PrRe&KnDi.6). Finally, working with the ERP system improves students' ability to transfer theoretical knowledge to practical applications (PrRe&KnDi.7).

Results also show improved perceived competitiveness when entering the labor market (Re&Exp.1). This perception was caused by the process-oriented course structure, and participants acknowledge that solving cross-departmental tasks within the simulation require a high degree of cooperation and communication (Re&Exp.3). In their evaluation of the overall satisfaction, participants gained valuable knowledge and experience (Re&Exp.8).

5.6 Effects on Process Understanding and Skills Improvement

The concluding sections aim to evaluate individual process knowledge and improvements in communication and cooperation skills as well as other social competencies. The results are summarized in Fig. 9.

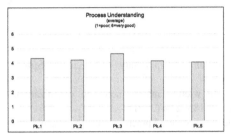 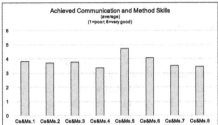

Fig. 9. Process understanding and skill improvements

In our investigation of participants' perceived process knowledge, they exhibit an adequate comprehension of organizational interdependencies. Thus, students achieved competencies in managing cross-departmental interfaces (Pk.3) and felt more confident understanding requirements and implementing them in business operations (Pk.4; Pk.5).

In line with results from previous sections, the course helped students develop and improve social competencies in terms of communication and cooperation. Students especially appreciated the exchange of interdisciplinary knowledge with participants from other fields of expertise (Cs&Ms.5). Results further suggest that the course supports participants in understanding and structuring business problems (Cs&Ms.6).

6 Conclusion and Future Research

The present paper aimed to integrate and evaluate cloud-based ERP systems into e-learning. As most e-learning scenarios focus on the distribution of facts rather than on the mediation of competencies, courses frequently lack appropriate mechanisms for knowledge diffusion. ERP systems proved to have a positive impact on the learning success of students in a higher education environment. This is mostly due to its underlying process structure and the cross-departmental integration of data and activities. However, previous studies have exclusively focused on the use of on-premise software, which is not suitable for e-learning scenarios. As higher education is increasingly influenced by digitalization and decentralization, using cloud-based ERP systems facilitates e-learning success and offers ubiquitous accessibility and location-independency. This research investigated a German course on information systems, using the ERP system SAP Business ByDesign. Our design of the course was built on well-known theories that define knowledge diffusion as an interaction of novices and experts supported by technology. To evaluate our hypotheses, a survey of 32 participants was conducted. It confirmed that ERP systems can be successfully used in e-learning and positively influence participants' skills regarding teamwork, communication, coordination, and process orientation. However, approaches of this kind are subject to well-known limitations. As data analyses were exclusively based on descriptive methods, large randomised controlled experiments and the application of inferential statistics are essential before drawing generalizable implications.

References

1. Aula, P.: Social media, reputation risk and ambient publicity management. Strateg. Leadersh. **38**, 43–49 (2010)
2. Gold, A.H., Malhotra, A., Segars, A.H.: Knowledge management: an organizational capabilities perspective. J. Manag. Inf. Syst. **18**, 185–214 (2001)
3. Schuh, K.L.: Learner-centered principles in teacher-centered practices? Teach. Teach. Educ. **20**, 833–846 (2004)
4. Saulnier, B.M., Landry, J.P., Longenecker, H.E., Wagner, T.A.: From teaching to learning: learner-centered teaching and assessment in information systems education. J. Inf. Syst. **19**, 169–175 (2008)
5. Leyh, C., Strahringer, S., Winkelmann, A.: Towards diversity in ERP education – the example of an ERP curriculum. In: Møller, C., Chaudhry, S. (eds.) CONFENIS 2011. LNBIP, vol. 105, pp. 182–200. Springer, Heidelberg (2012). doi:10.1007/978-3-642-28827-2_13
6. Shehab, E.M., Sharp, M.W., Supramaniam, L., Spedding, T.A.: Enterprise resource planning: an integrative review. Bus. Process Manag. J. **10**, 359–386 (2004)
7. O'Leary, D.E.: Enterprise Resource Planning Systems: Systems, Life Cycle, Electronic Commerce, and Risk. Cambridge University Press, Cambridge (2000)
8. Becker, J., Kugeler, M., Rosemann, M.: Process Management: A Guide for the Design of Business Processes. Springer, Heidelberg (2011)
9. Hufgard, A., Legner, C., Winkelmann, PA..: B2B-Geschäftsszenarien mit der Cloud-Lösung SAP Business ByDesign. In: Proceedings of the Multi-Konferenz Wirtschaftsinformatik (2012)
10. Konradin, M.: Konradin ERP-Studie 2011: Einsatz von ERP-Lösungen in der Industrie. Anwenderstudie, Leinfelden-Echterdingen (2011)
11. Jacobson, S., Shepard, J., D'Auila, M., Carter, K.: The ERP market sizing report, 2006–2011. AMR Research Inc., Boston, USA (2007)
12. Hufgard, A.: Business Integration mit SAP-Lösungen. In: Hufgard, A., Hecht, H., Walz, W., Hennermann, F., Brosch, G., Mehlich, S., Bätz, C. (eds.) Business Integration mit SAP-Lösungen, pp. 15–34. Springer, Heidelberg (2005)
13. Klima, C., Pfarr, F., Winkelmann, A.: ERP system environments in IS education: design and evaluation of a new course concept. Interact. Technol. Smart Educ. **11**, 112–122 (2014)
14. Seethamraju, R.: Enterprise systems (ES) software in business school curriculum - evaluation of design and delivery. J. Inf. Syst. Educ. **18**, 69–83 (2007)
15. Boyle, T.A., Strong, S.E.: Skill requirements of ERP graduates. J. Inf. Syst. Educ. **17**, 403–413 (2006)
16. Elragal, A., El Kommos, M.: In-house versus in-cloud ERP systems: a comparative study. J. Enterp. Resour. Plan. Stud. 1–13 (2013)
17. Savery, J.R., Duffy, T.M.: Problem based learning: an instructional model and its constructivist framework. Educ. Technol. **35**, 31–38 (1995)

18. Duffy, T.M., Cunningham, D.J.: Constructivism: Implications for the Design and Delivery of Instruction (1996)
19. Oliver, R.: Developing e-learning environments that support knowledge construction in higher education. In: Working for Excellence in the Economy, pp. 407–416 (2001)
20. Aamodt, A., Nygård, M.: Different roles and mutual dependencies of data, information, and knowledge — an AI perspective on their integration. Data Knowl. Eng. **16**, 191–222 (1995)
21. Willke: Systemisches Wissensmanagement. Lucius & Lucius, Stuttgart (1998)
22. Wilkesmann, U., Fischer, H., Wilkesmann, M.: Cultural characteristics of knowledge transfer. J. Knowl. Manag. **13**, 464–477 (2009)
23. Inkpen, A.C., Tsang, E.W.K.: Social capital, networks, and knowledge transfer. Acad. Manag. Rev. **30**, 146–165 (2005)
24. Wilkesmann, M., Wilkesmann, U.: Knowledge transfer as interaction between experts and novices supported by technology. Vine **41**, 96–112 (2011)
25. Dreyfuss, S.E., Dreyfus, H.L.: A five-stage model of the mental activities involved in directed skill acquisition. Oper. Res. Cent. 1–18 (1980)
26. Argyris, C., Schön, D.A.: Organizational Learning. Addison-Wesley Pub. Co., Reading (1996)
27. Wilkesmann, U.: Lernen in Organisationen: die Inszenierung von kollektiven Lernprozessen. Campus-Verl, Frankfurt (1999)
28. Hirokawa, R.Y.: The role of communication in group decision-making efficacy: a task-contingency perspective. Small Gr. Res. **21**, 190–204 (1990)
29. Szulanski, G., Bowman, N., Winter, S., Grant, R., Spender, J.C., Kogut, B., Miner, A., Ghoshal, S., Levinthal, D., Stuart, T., Lane, P., Argote, L.: The process of knowledge transfer: a diachronic analysis of stickiness. Organ. Behav. Hum. Decis. Process. **82**, 9–27 (2000)

Using Phenomenography to Understand Cultural Values in Facebook

Leantros Kyriakoullis[✉] and Panayiotis Zaphiris

Cyprus Interaction Lab, Department of Multimedia and Graphic Arts,
Cyprus University of Technology, 30 Archbishop Kyprianou Street, 3036 Lemesos, Cyprus
leantros@cyprusinteractionlab.com

Abstract. The purpose of this phenomenographic study is to investigate the role of cultural values in perceptions of privacy, friendships, trust and motivations for using Facebook among Greek Cypriots. The study used a mixed method of semi-structured interviews and an exploratory online survey. The results of our study show that Greek Cypriot students use Facebook primarily as a way of communication with friends and for maintaining existing relationships. This study contributes to existing literature on culture in HCI and social networks with data from an eastern Mediterranean country. We discuss the findings and their implications.

Keywords: Culture · Privacy · Trust · Information disclosure · Facebook · Social networks

1 Background

The emergence of Social Network Sites (SNS) has changed the way people interact with computers. One of the most important SNS today is Facebook which reached 1.01 billion daily active users on average in September 2015 [17]. Facebook is a platform which people maintain their own personal profile and engage with various activities. Some of these activities are posting photos, communicating with friends or family, playing games or simply like posts of others. Facebook users may follow pages or join groups that match their interests. In recent years, a number of research studies on Facebook examined factors such as privacy settings [26], support seeking [5], emotional outcomes [29], addiction, satisfaction, self-esteem [4] while some others examined human well-being [40], need to belong, need for self-presentation [35], need for popularity [8] teaching and learning [6]. Even though Facebook was developed from a western culture, it is now widely used across different regions worldwide. Despite its great success worldwide, several studies reveal behavioral differences between people living in disparate regions. One of the reasons why people behave differently is believed to be associated with the role of culture in society.

Culture is a complex term. According to Triandis [47] "culture is to society what memory is to the person". Similarly, Hofstede, Hofstede and Minkov [23] define culture as a "collective programming of the mind which distinguishes the members of one

P. Zaphiris and A. Ioannou (Eds.): LCT 2017, Part I, LNCS 10295, pp. 216–236, 2017.
DOI: 10.1007/978-3-319-58509-3_18

human group from another". In his research, Hofstede identified six dimensions, which can be used to differentiate nations according to their cultures:

- Power distance (PDI): The level to which people accept inequalities among other members of the society.
- Individualism versus collectivism (IDV): The level to which people take care only of their own selves or feel as though they belong to a strong group and always try to protect it.
- Masculinity versus Femininity (MAS): Masculinity refers to societies with clear distinction between the two genders. Femininity refers to societies in which there is less differentiation between the two genders.
- Uncertainty Avoidance (UAI): The level to which people in different cultures feel vulnerable in risky situations.
- Long-term versus short-term orientation (LTO): In long-term orientation cultures, tradition is an impediment to change. In short-term orientation cultures, change occurs faster as these beliefs do not constitute an obstacle towards change.
- Indulgence versus restraint (IVR): Indulgence refers to the tendency of the society to freely satisfy basic desires such as enjoying life and having fun. Restraint refers to a society in which enjoyment is restrained by social norms.

Hofstede argues that dimension scores remain stable for decades [22]. According to Hofstede, cultural values are acquired early in our life and these are the core of culture. Cultural values are those positive or negative feelings about a situation such as evil versus good, ugly versus beautiful, unnatural versus natural, forbidden versus permitted, dangerous versus safe. Hofstede claims that unlearning is even more difficult than learning. As a consequence, cultural values resist change and may require generations to change [23]. His research is widely used across the research community as a reference to explain differences in group behavior. It is applied in many domains such as education, healthcare, business or computer mediated communication. Baskerville [3] challenges Hofstede's work for the use of nations as the units of analysis in his cross-cultural research. As Baskerville highlights, cultures do not equate with nations. Minkov and Hofstede [34], however, support Hofstede's work by reporting that intermixture of nations is rather rare.

Hall [18] highlights culture as a crucial dimension in communication. In his research Hall distinguishes communication between high-context (HC) communication and low-context communication (LC). In HC cultures communication is fast, economical and effective but time is invested for the programming. In other words, in HC cultures the minimum information is transmitted in the message because most of the information is in the context. In LC cultures most of the information is in the transmitted message. Another major difference between the two contexts is the need for stability in HC and the need to adapt and change in LC. The Greek culture belongs to the high-context cultures. Hall also distinguishes cultures into polychronic and monochronic. In monochronic time (M-time) systems emphasis is given in schedules, segmentation, and readiness. In polychronic time (P-time) systems several things are happening at the same time. The focus in P-time systems is in the completion of transactions rather than strictly following predefined schedules. Greece belongs to the polychronic cultures [18].

Culture becomes more complex and dynamic over time. However, when a culture reaches at a very high point of complexity it then moves towards simplification. Extreme collectivism, for instance, results in a shift towards individualism and extreme individualism results in a shift towards collectivism [47]. Noteworthy is also the point that when a nation's wealth increases it becomes more individualistic. Personal goals in individualistic societies prevail in-group goals [21, 47].

2   Short History and Culture in Cyprus

Cyprus is an eastern Mediterranean island at the crossroads of Europe, Africa and Asia. Near the end of the Bronze Age Mycenaean Greeks reached Cyprus transmitting Greek language as the main language of the island. Mycenaean Greeks have also brought a number of other cultural traits with them such as their political system. At that time, this political system was belligerent monarchies operated from guarded fortress. The king was playing both religious and political role [41]. A number of scripts, from the 8th to 3rd century BC, have been found in Cyprus in most of the cases written in Greek language (Linear B) [44]. Cyprus came under domination of the Assyrian rule (8th century BC), Egyptian rule (6th century BC) and Persian rule (6th–4th century BC). The Hellenistic period followed Persian rule from 4th to 1st century BC. Cyprus became a Roman province in the 1st century BC and in the 4th century AC it became part of the Byzantine Empire until the 12th century AC. The Frankish (12th–15th century AC), Venetian (15th–16th century AC), Turkish (16th–19th century AC) and English (19th–20th century AC) rules then followed.

Cyprus became politically independent from British rule in 1960. "The Republic of Cyprus is de facto partitioned into two main parts; the area under the effective control of the Republic, comprising about 59% of the island's area, and the north, administered by the self-declared Turkish Republic of Northern Cyprus, which is recognized only by Turkey, covering about 36% of the island's area" [9]. On 1 May 2004 the Republic of Cyprus became a full member of the EU and in January 2008 Cyprus joined the Eurozone. Greek Cypriots are predominantly Christian and adhere to the Autocephalous Greek Orthodox Church of Cyprus. Turkish Cypriots are predominantly Sunni Muslims, while Maronite belong to the Maronite Catholic Church, Armenians predominantly to the Armenian Apostolic Orthodox Church and Latins to the Latin Catholic. Although Cyprus became under foreign domination for many years it never lost its Greek identity and culture. According to the demographic report of 2014 published by the Statistical Service of Cyprus, the population of the Greek Cypriot community was 694.700 (74, 0%) while the population of the Turkish Cypriot community was 91.400 (9, 8%). The population of foreign residents was 152.300 (16, 2%) [12].

3   Facebook and ICT Usage in Cyprus

The country's Internet penetration rate in 2014 was 95%. Greek Cypriots have a relatively high Facebook adoption rate. In 2015 the percentage of Facebook users was 69.7% of the total population [24]. In 2015, 23% of the total population aged 16 to 74 purchased online. The share of e-buyers was much lower compared to the EU average (53%). In 2014, about 22% of enterprises in Cyprus were purchasing electronically, while about 11% of them were selling electronically. This percentage of electronic purchases and sales was much lower compared to the EU average (40% and 19% respectively) [14].

4   Cultural Differences in Social Networks

Studies examining cultural differences in Facebook continues to grow. Abbas and Mesch (2015) claim that cultural values motivate young Palestinians to use Facebook for maintaining friendships. They associate this behavior with Hofstede's three cultural dimensions (collectivism, power distance, uncertainty avoidance) and Hall's theory of low vs. high-context culture. In more detail, the study found a positive association between high level of uncertainty avoidance and the use of SNS's for maintaining existing relationships and positive association between collectivistic values and the desire to maintain existing relationships [1]. The need of belonging, social connectedness and entertainment seem to motivate young Brazilians engage with Facebook [11]. Peters, Winschiers-Theophilus and Mennecke [38] report that Namibians tend to accept all friend requests on Facebook as they consider that by rejecting them is impolite. As a result, almost all Namibians befriended with unknown people who do not have an offline connection.

Cho and Park [7] report culture differences in SNS usage between Korean and US users. In general, Korean users unlike US users were unwilling to disclose personal information to introduce themselves. On the other hand, Korean SNS users provided details of their lives to their existing connections while US users did not want to reveal their daily life and feelings. For Koreans, SNS friends were considered close friends offline. On the contrary, the diversity of friends in U.S. users' friend lists inhibited them to have conversations at a more personal level. Korean participants with homogeneous in-group members in their circle of friends were more likely to self-disclose. This behaviour was due to their desire to maintain existing relationships. Cho and Park [7] highlight the existence of a generation gap between younger and older Hungarians. They demonstrate that younger Hungarians do not pay much attention to privacy settings on Facebook in contrast to elderly. As the study reports, the behaviour of older generation is a consequence of the presence of the Hungarian secret police during the Soviet occupation, between years 1945 and 1956. The secret police violently enforced policies of the Soviet and Hungarian governments. The study also found that the younger generation also expressed fear in discussing politics. This fear was transmitted by their parents' generation and a number of political episodes [48].

According to Karl, Peluchette and Schlaegel [25] the ratio of US students posting problematic content (i.e. substance abuse) on Facebook is much higher than German students. They indicate that this behaviour is partially affected by the countries cultures. According to Hofstede [45] USA is much more individualistic and lower uncertainty avoidance country than Germany. Vasalou, Joinson and Courvoisier [49] show that Facebook users from Greece do not consider status updates as important as users from U.S. In addition to this, Facebook groups are considered more important for UK users compared to US users. For Italians, groups and games in Facebook are considered more important compared to US users and for French status updates and photographs are less important compared to US users [49]. Recently, Kyriakoullis and Zaphiris [28] have reviewed several cultural studies in HCI and social networks highlighting the future directions of this field of research.

5   The Current Study

According to Hofstede, the Greek is a high uncertainty avoidance and low individualism culture. In high uncertainty avoidance cultures people tend to avoid taking risks. What is unknown or different to them is at the same time dangerous. In collectivistic cultures individuals avoid expressing their own opinion. Opinions are fixed in advance by the group [45]. In high uncertainty avoidance and collectivistic cultures people use social network sites to maintain existing relationships [1]. Previous research suggests that both anxiety and uncertainty are factors that anticipate avoidance during encounters with strangers of the same or foreign culture [13]. The Greek culture is also relatively homogeneous and tight. People in homogeneous cultures share similar norms and values. Homogeneous cultures are tight, meaning that all members assume to behave according to the norms of their society and "inappropriate" behavior is criticized [47]. "Inappropriate" behavior may be considered an individual's opinion that contradicts group beliefs [45]. Thus the following research questions are posed:

Research Question 1:   How do the characteristics of Greek culture influence the way that Facebook users form and use SNS relationships?

Research Question 2a: How do the characteristics of Greek culture influence the way that Facebook users form and use self-disclosing behaviors?

Research Question 2b: How do the characteristics of Greek culture influence the way that Facebook users form and use self-expression behaviors?

Research Question 3:   What is the relation of the collectivistic and high-context characteristics of Greek culture and online communication?

This study used semi-structured interviews to identify how Greek Cypriot students experience Facebook, from a phenomenographic perspective. "Phenomenography aims to reveal the qualitatively different ways of experiencing various phenomena" [32]. Phenomenographic research was initially used to understand the qualitative differences in the process and outcome of learning [33]. Some recent studies used phenomenography to investigate the educational potential of Facebook [42]. An important characteristic of phenomenographic research is that researchers aim to describe, analyze and understand experiences of various aspects of the world from the second-order perspective. In the second perspective, researchers are interested to investigate how people experience an aspect of the world. Their intention is not to describe a phenomenon on the basis of their own previous experiences, understanding, or viewpoint - first-order perspective [31]. Thus, in our study we sought to understand the different ways interviewees experience their interaction with Facebook and associate the findings with their cultural characteristics.

The most common data source used in phenomenographic research are interviews. The interview transcripts, however, cannot be understood independent of the context of the group of transcripts. The interpretation of each transcript must be on the basis of the transcripts as a whole. A typical phenomenographic interview is usually audio recorded and then transcribed. The categories of perceptions are revealed after the data analysis and not determined beforehand [2]. In this study, in order to avoid the risk of misinterpretation we have not relied solely on transcripts during the data analysis. That is why we listened to the recordings several times before and after transcription.

As far as ethical issues are concerned, the students were informed that the interviews were not mandatory and that all of the information they provided would be used for research purposes only. For this reason, the researchers provided a consent form signed by all interviewees before the interview. It was made clear to all participants that the information from the interviews would remain anonymous.

6   Method

6.1   Interview Process

For our primary study we conducted 25 semi-structured exploratory interviews. All the interviews were conducted in Greek. The interviews were voice recorded and then transcribed and translated in English language by the researchers. Subsequently, the interview data were imported into NVivo software for qualitative data analysis and then analyzed and coded according to themes and categories identified by the researchers. The transcriptions included pauses and laughs. The interview questions focused on the following topics: (a) what is the perception of Greek Cypriot students about Facebook (b) how they use it (their main activities), (c) whether they trust it (d) how they would respond to a friend request (e) whether their friends on Facebook are people they maintain offline connection and (f) demographic information.

6.2   Interview Participants

The study's interviewees were undergraduate students at the Cyprus University of Technology. In the fall semester of 2015, 25 students were recruited from the department of multimedia and graphics arts. All 25 volunteered to participate in the interviews, in which they were inquired to discuss some of their Facebook activities. They were also asked questions related to privacy, trust, self-disclosure and friendship requests. The students were composed of 12 male and 13 female. All of the participants were Facebook users. The average age of the participants was 19 years old. We verified that all participants were born and raised in Cyprus and that the language they spoke fluently before the age of 10 was Greek, to make sure the cultural identity of each respondent in this study was strictly Greek.

6.3 Online Survey

For our secondary study we conducted an exploratory online survey to understand the role of mutual friends in terms of accepting a friend request. The qualitative analysis of the interviews revealed that mutual friends seemed to play a decisive role among participants to accept a friend request. The majority of the participants mentioned mutual friends before accepting an invitation to connect. This survey provided a good basis for understanding the influence of mutual friends in terms of accepting a friend request. The online survey was available in English and Greek language. The raw data was collected from Google forms and analyzed with SPSS.

6.4 Online Survey Participants

In the sample, the respondents' ages ranged from 16 to 56 years old (N = 181), with a mean age of 28.44 (SD = 7.99). As to gender, 58.8% were female and 41.2% were men. Regarding the cultural background, we ensured that all participants were born and raised in Cyprus and the language they spoke fluently before the age of 10 was Greek. The participants who specified other language and/or country of residence before the age of 10 have been removed from the analysis.

7   Categories of Description

7.1 Facebook Usage and Activities

With regards time spent on Facebook, the majority of the participants 16 out of 25 (64%) use Facebook every day, while 5 out of 25 (20%) are always connected. Only 1 out of 25 (4%) use Facebook 4 days a week. The remaining participants, 2 out of 25 (8%) did not mention time spent on Facebook. This study found that the majority of students 23 out of 25 (92%) use Facebook mainly as a way to communicate with their friends. Almost half of them, 12 out of 25 (48%) use Facebook for posting pictures such as photos. Other activities Greek Cypriot students engage with Facebook are watching newsfeeds and posts of others (10 out of 25, 40%), joining groups of their interest (8 out of 25, 32%), reading news or other information (6 out of 25, 24%), spending/killing their time (5 out of 25, 20%), playing games (3 out of 25, 12%), for self-promotion (3 out of 25, 12%), meeting new people (2 out of 25, 8%), posting work-related material (1 out of 25, 4%) or for maintaining a page (1 out of 25, 4%).

Facebook seems to be a popular tool for online communication between Greek Cypriot students. Given that the Greek culture belongs to the high-context cultures, it is reasonable to assume that computer mediated communication, such as online chat, does not create a barrier to communication. It may also be easier for users from HC cultures to use online communication compared to LC cultures. The results are consistent with other studies in collectivistic countries which show that Facebook is a good communication channel for online chat [7, 16, 38].

7.2 Self-disclosure, Trust and Privacy

Self-disclosure has been an important concept for researchers. Previous research shows that the need for popularity on Facebook seems to be the driving force for information disclosure [8]. The willingness of people to share, however, relies on who they are sharing the information with [36]. People tend to disclose most with close family members or close friends and least with strangers [51]. The cultural background has also been identified as affecting the willingness of people to disclose personal information that could identify them easily [7].

Two distinct themes were identified on how the interviewees consider trust on Facebook. In the first group belong those who trust Facebook (11 out of 25 interviewees). In the second group, are interviewees who state that trusting Facebook depends on a number of factors (13 out of 25 interviewees). Only one participant (4%) does not trust Facebook. Those who do not completely trust Facebook protect themselves by being cautious of what personal information share online. In addition to this, their circle of friends are not strangers. As a result, this information is available only to friends they trust. Furthermore, those students who maintain few strangers in their friend lists seem to have no concerns about their posts. The reason for this is that if they did not want to show them their posts, they would not accept the friendship request in the first place.

"...and if I didn't want to show them [my posts] I wouldn't accept them in my friend list..." (P. 10, female student 19).

The results show that in general the interviewees trust Facebook. These findings are consistent to previous studies [1] which show a positive relation between collectivistic values and trust in Facebook. In 2011, Pingdom [37] found that Cyprus ranked at the first place in Facebook adoption as percentage of population.

With regards information sharing, students avoid posts that will reveal their personality characteristics. They are careful with what information they share online. That is why most of the times they share information such as music, videos, photos or work-related material. This behavior may be the result of a homogeneous and tight Greek culture. In tight cultures, people are aware of the requests of others. As a result, they avoid disclosing much information as by disclosing they may reveal certain aspects of the self that others might criticize [47].

"...usually I post something funny that I saw and liked or music. If somebody believes that these are valuable data then go get them..." (P. 1, male student 21).

"...My posts are more artistic ones, there is not something that is saying much about myself..." (P. 2, male student 20).

"To be honest I don't post a lot, if I post it will be just photos...I don't post frequently, every day or something...I don't have it for the public..." (P. 9, female student 19).

It worth to state though that one of the participants (P. 5) states that he avoids posting not because of any privacy concerns. He mentions that he will not post something if there is no reason for doing so.

Previous studies demonstrate the importance of perceived control in addressing users' privacy concerns in Facebook [20]. Overall, the findings of this study reveal that participants feel like they have control over their data. Their feeling of control derives either by avoiding the disclosure of personal information or restricting the public view of their posts. By changing privacy settings on Facebook participants allow only trusted members to view their posts.

"No [I don't have any issue with my personal data] because I can edit them [my posts]…I can edit who I would like to show them [my posts]…" (P. 10, female student 19).

Our research provides evidence that in general Greek Cypriot students avoid self-exposure on Facebook as they avoid disclosing personal information. The participants of this study are also not willing to disclose personal information that someone might identify them easily. Consistent with other studies [8], they avoid disclosing personal information such as home address, phone numbers or credit card numbers. These findings are consistent with a study by Abbas and Mesch [1] who associated higher scores of collectivism with privacy concerns. The following interview excerpts reveal that the participants are not willing to share information they consider as private on Facebook.

"I choose what I want to disclose. My e-mail…ok…others may get it from you…but it is you who decides whether to disclose your telephone number…it is not mandatory. I don't disclose any credit card numbers or anything else or my home address that they can create problems to me. These are not mandatory" (P. 1, male student 21).

"Debatable. Depends. I mean I will not disclose many things about me…I don't know…It's creepy to be on the internet. Maybe everybody can have your details. So I will not disclose telephones etc. something that you can actually find me" (P. 2, male student 20).

"Ok, I don't believe that someone will steal my data because…I don't know…why steal them? Anyway, credit card numbers are not required to provide them and if so I have never disclosed them or my home address…so these are OK. The telephone number is the most…but I don't think that I will lose something from Facebook…that someone will steal my data…" (P. 5, male student 21).

Previous studies show that the high uncertainty avoidance levels may be one of the reasons for the slow adoption of electronic commerce in Cyprus [10]. In e-commerce sites, purchasing online requires the disclosure of a bank account card number and home address for the purchase of goods or services online. The findings of this study reveal that any privacy concerns of the participants are repressed first by the strong influence of social interaction and second by the perceived control over their data. For instance, information considered as private, such as credit card numbers, telephone numbers or home address is not required for maintaining a profile at Facebook. As a consequence, it is easier to trust a social networking website such as Facebook (the operator), as users do not risk their bank account numbers. Unlike e-commerce sites in social network sites this information is not required.

7.3   Friendship Ties

Previous research shows that older SNS users have fewer friends compared to younger. They also prefer to connect with people they know very well as a result they are more careful and selective compared to younger [39]. Consistent with other studies [1, 7, 15] Greek Cypriot students use Facebook for maintaining existing relationships rather than forming new connections. Greek Cypriot participants agreed that they did not generally want strangers to be on their friend lists even though they still included strangers on their friends' lists. The majority of students' friend lists are people who have a kind of an offline connection or are known to them. Interestingly, 10 out of 25 students indicate that the majority of their circle of friends are people they know with few unknown, while for 6 out of 25 indicate that their friend lists consist only of friends they know or maintain an offline connection. Additionally, 7 out of 25 students indicate the inclusion of unknown friends in their circle of friends but did not specify which precedes the other. The remaining participants, 2 out of 25, did not mention about friendship ties.

7.4   Friend Request Invitation

Previous research suggest that people from collectivistic countries tend to accept friend requests from strangers on Facebook [38]. One of the interview questions of this study inquired participants to describe how they would respond to a friend request. Greek Cypriots tend to accept people they know or have met face-to-face before. The majority of participants, 20 out of 25 (80%), accept a friend request only if they know the person sending the friend request. The remaining participants either accept all friend requests or did not mention whether they accept strangers. Fake profiles seem to bother 2 out of 25 (8%) participants while 1 participant (4%) mentions that age is important to accept a friend requests. For example P. 10 [Greek Cypriot female student #10] would not accept a friend request from someone much younger or much older than her. The participants of this study consider mutual friends important before accepting a friend request. The findings show that the majority of the participants, 15 out of 25 (60%), mentioned the existence of "mutual friends" when inquired how they would respond to a friend request. In addition, 16 out of 25 (64%) participants visit the profile of the person who sends the request to look at their photos or their overall profile. Location such as the city of the person who sends the friend request is also mentioned in 3 out of 25 (12%) of the participants. Interestingly, one female participant (4%) would consult a close friend to advise her about the person sending the friend request, as she may not remember his face (P. 7, female student, 21). The weight given to the opinion of a close friend reveals a characteristic of the collectivistic culture.

The reason why Greek Cypriot students need to know the person who sends the friend request may be associated with the high uncertainty avoidance levels of the Greek culture. They would not risk to accept friend requests from people without any offline connection. The high level of uncertainty impulse Greek Cypriot students to avoid connecting with strangers. For Greek Cypriots, no prior offline contact and interaction prevents them from accepting strangers. An unknown person sending the friend request is considered as outgroup and therefore is being rejected. The following interview excerpts reveal the importance of mutual friends before accepting a friend request.

"I view the profile of that person…I see if that person is the one he claims to be and is not fake… and also age matters…I will not add someone much younger than me or much older than me… that we don't even have mutual friends…" (P. 10, female student 19).

"Depends…if there are mutual friends I will see [decide] if I will accept otherwise if there are no mutual friends I will reject" (P. 15, female student, 18).

Interestingly 3 out of 25 students mentioned that a minimum number of mutual friends is required before accepting the friend request. This indicates that a large number of mutual friends will positively influence their decision to accept a friend request.

"...but on the basis of mutual friends...I will not accept someone that I have 10–12 mutual friends...more than 100 usually" (P. 22, female student, 19).

"...If I indeed have more than 5 mutual friends..." (P. 25, male student, 20).

Few participants (3 out of 25) not only mentioned mutual friends as important but also the degree of friendship closeness as important too. In other words, they would most probably accept a friend request if mutual friends are close friends too or maintain frequent communication with them.

"I visit his profile...I see if I know that person...our mutual friends and from which town he comes from...mainly if we have mutual friends...for example my brothers...If my brothers have that person it means it might be someone known...that I may also know him too..." (P. 19, female student, 19).

"...or if they [existing friends] have him as a mutual friend and if [existing friend] is a close friend..." (P. 7, male student, 21).

"Yes I will accept [a friend request]...depending on who these [mutual] friends are...If mutual friends are friends we talk I will accept otherwise if these are mutual friends that we don't talk a lot it depends..." (P. 15, female student, 18).

The participants of this study seem to form a kind of "social network in-group", which is their circle of friends in Facebook. The majority of the members of this in-group have prior been accepted and probably trusted. We argue that the appearance of mutual friends seem to be an important interface feature, especially for users coming from collectivistic and high uncertainty avoidance cultures. When receiving a friend request, apart from knowing that person, mutual friends determine whether the person sending the request deserves a place in their in-group. The members of this in-group are considered as "trusted members". According to Triandis [47], the in-group-outgroup differentiation defines social behavior more strongly in collectivist than in individualistic cultures. The distinction between in-group and outgroup has already been identified in the domains of online gaming [27] and social networks [7].

The avoidance of accepting strangers on Facebook is a behavior similar between Greek Cypriot and U.S. students [38]. According to Hofstede the two cultures are characterized by large differences in both dimensions of uncertainty avoidance and individualism. Compared to Cyprus (or Greece) a collectivistic and high uncertainty avoidance country, USA is an individualistic and low uncertainty avoidance country. Nevertheless the results of this study reveal similar behavior with other collectivistic countries such as Indonesia [16] and Namibia [38], in terms of using Facebook as a way to communicate with friends (online chat). In addition, both the distinction between in-group and outgroup and the avoidance of revealing self-identifying information are consistent with the findings of a study by Cho and Park [7]. We cannot conclude, however, that maintaining existing relationships is a characteristic exclusively of a single dimension that of collectivistic culture. A study by Ellison et al. [15] for example, reports that Michigan State University (MSU) undergraduate students use Facebook to primarily maintain existing offline connections too. The cultural background of the participants in this study [15], however, was not investigated in detail.

Greek Cypriots tend to accept friendship requests from people they met offline, preferably from their existing circle of friends. The findings of this study contradict other studies [30, 38] in terms of associating a collectivistic culture with accepting all friendship requests, known or unknown. In more detail, one study [38] found that although the participants come from a collectivistic culture, the majority of them tend to accept friend invitations mainly from people they know or maintain an offline connection. In Namibia, a collectivistic country too, people tend to accept all friend requests, as they believe it is not appropriate to reject them [38]. Another country with similar behavior is India, a society with both collectivistic and individualistic traits. India, with a score of 48 is according to Hofstede [45], an intermediate collectivistic country. In India the majority of the SNS users tend to maintain online friends who have not met face-to-face [30]. It is not clear though, from the findings of this study [30] which percentage precedes the other: "online" or "real" friends. What is it then about the Greek culture that results in avoidance of accepting strangers? Perhaps it is insufficient to interpret the results by applying just one cultural dimension. For instance, a major difference between the three countries (Greece, Namibia and India) is in the uncertainty avoidance dimension level. For example, the Greek culture is a high uncertainty avoidance culture while Namibia and India are low uncertainty avoidance cultures. We believe that a high uncertainty avoidance culture results in more anxiety and uncertainty when it comes to accepting friend requests from unknown people. As a result, people from high uncertainty avoidance countries avoid connecting with strangers. Another possible reason for this may be that the Greek culture shifts towards a more individualistic society [10]. The collectivistic characteristics, however, remain noticeable such as the importance of mutual friends.

Previous research suggests that the acceptance rate of unknown friend requests is higher in low-income areas [19]. According to the Word Bank statistics [46] India belongs to the lower-middle-income economies, Namibia to the upper-middle-income economies while Cyprus to high-income economies. It may be the case that Cyprus, as a high income economy, shifts towards individualism (De Angeli and Kyriakoullis 2006). Hence, it is reasonable to assume that by applying just one of Hofstede's dimensions we cannot accurately explain cultural differences. This agrees with Hofstede's statement, who also claims that one cannot directly explain a certain behavior by only applying the cultural dimensions. Other factors such as national wealth, history, personalities and coincidences are factors that must also be taken into consideration [21]. Baskerville [3] too highlights other aspects beyond culture such as socio-political differences between nations, political and religious influence or education statistics. It is reasonable to examine in the future though, why people in some collectivistic countries behave different than other collectivistic countries and associate them with factors that extend beyond culture. One factor that may influence users seems to be associated with the income level.

7.5 Self-promotion

Previous studies show that Romanian users use Facebook more for the purpose of socialization and less for promotion of self-image [43]. Romania, similar to Greece, is a high uncertainty avoidance and low individualistic country. Consistent with the findings of Romanian Facebook users [43], our study found that only few participants use Facebook for self-promotion. Although self-promotion is a common characteristic between individualistic cultures, we identified this behavior in the answers of 3 out of 25 participants in this study too. These individualistic characteristics of students, however, are narrowed to the promotion of their work rather than self-image:

"…and what is happening recently is that you promote yourself…and I am also doing some paintings and I mostly add and accept friends for the potential of a job opportunity…maybe someone can see something [from my paintings] that would be interested in…" (P. 1, male student, 21).

"… then i thought of like a way to show my work from it…create a page…to show…drawings I create…things I want to show…" (P. 12, male student, 20).

"…because everybody is on Facebook now, it is a way to show yourself over the internet…" (P2, male student, 20).

7.6 Online Survey and Discussion

The majority of the participants (40%) of the online survey agree that mutual friends play an important role in their decision to accept a friend request, followed by 55 participants (30.5%) stated disagree and 53 (29.5%) stated that neither agree nor disagree (Fig. 1).

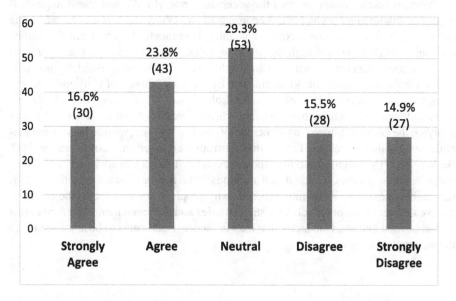

Fig. 1. Mutual friends play an important role in my decision to accept a friend request

The next two scenario-based questions aimed to find the effect of two different trust attributes. The first was the appearance of mutual friends and the second the appearance of profile photos. The scenarios asked participants how they would respond to a friend request. The first scenario question was: "I have received a friend request from a Facebook user. There are no uploaded photos in this user's profile and I cannot identify this person by his name. I have noticed that we have 10 mutual friends." Answers were given on a five-point Likert scale with the anchors 1 = strongly agree, and 5 = strongly disagree. Thus, higher scores indicate more negative attitudes towards accepting a friend request in Facebook.

As expected, the majority of the participants, 78%, would not accept a friend request if they cannot identify the person from a profile photo, even if they maintain 10 mutual friends. Only 10% of the participants would accept a friend request by only maintaining 10 mutual friends. The remaining participants (12%) neither agreed nor disagreed with the statement (Fig. 2).

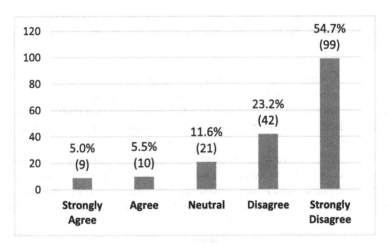

Fig. 2. I have received a friend request from a Facebook user. There are no uploaded photos in this user's profile and I cannot identify this person by his name. I have noticed that we have 10 mutual friends. I accept the friend request.

The second scenario question was: "I have received a friend request from a Facebook user. I can see that there is a photo in this profile and I can identify the person. I have noticed that we have no mutual friends". The majority of respondents (42%) of the second scenario would again not accept the friend request. This shows the importance of mutual friends as a trust attribute which determines the participant's decision to accept a friend request. It seems that even by identifying a person with a profile photo, it is not adequate for approving him or her to their circle of friends. This percentage, however, is considerably lower compared to the first scenario (78%) which is an indication that a profile photo is the most important trust attribute. About 31% would accept the friend request while 27% remain neutral (Fig. 3).

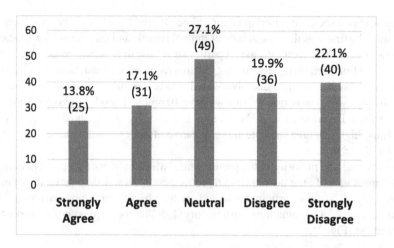

Fig. 3. I have received a friend request from a Facebook user. I can see that there is a photo in this profile and I can identify the person. I noticed that we have no mutual friends. I accept the friend request.

Participant answers of the two scenarios were analyzed by a paired samples t-test. Results indicate a significance difference between the two scenarios (t (180) = 8.108, p < 0.001). As a result we can conclude that the appearance of a profile photo is more important than the existence of mutual friends. Nevertheless, it can be argued that both the presence of a profile photo and mutual friends are important characteristics that determine the decision of participants to accept a friend request. It is reasonable to assume that Greek Cypriot students need to know the person, therefore a profile photo is essential for them to accept a friend request. Additionally, friendship ties with the existing members of their circle of friends form a peer pressure that pushes them to accept a friend request (Fig. 4).

Paired Samples Test								
	Paired Differences							
			Std. Error Mean	95% Confidence Interval of the Difference				
	Mean	Std. Deviation		Lower	Upper	t	df	Sig. (2-tailed)
Pair 1 Scenario1 - Scenario2	.97790	1.62260	.12061	.73991	1.21589	8.108	180	.000

Fig. 4. Paired samples t-test (profile photo vs. mutual friends)

The findings of the scenario questions are also confirmed by two follow up questions. These questions were tested on a five-point Likert scale too (1 = Strongly agree to 5 = Strongly disagree). The first question was: "I accept a friend request only when we have mutual friends, even if I am sure that I know this person". Interestingly, 23% of the participants would accept a friend request only if mutual friends exist, even if they are sure they know the person sending the friend request. The majority of the participants though (51%), would accept a friend request without the presence of mutual friends if they are sure that they know the person while about 26% of the participants neither agreed nor disagreed to this question (Fig. 5).

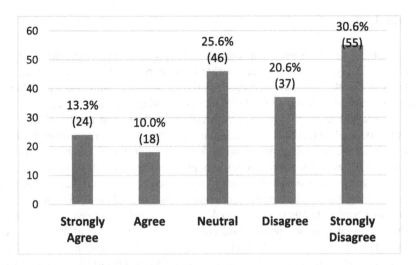

Fig. 5. I accept a friend request only when we have mutual friends even if I am sure that I know this person.

The second question "I accept a friend request when we have mutual friends even if I do not know the person who sends me the friend request" also revealed interesting results. In more detail, 20% of the participants accept a friend request only by maintaining mutual friends even if the person is unknown to them. The majority of the participants (64%), however, accept a friend request when they are confident that they know that person, without maintaining any mutual friends. About 16% remained neutral to this question (Fig. 6).

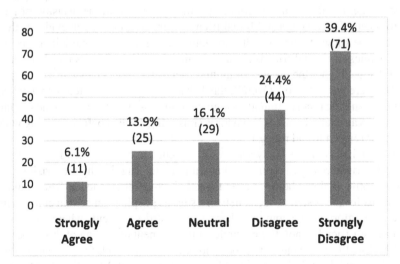

Fig. 6. I accept a friend request when we have mutual friends even if I do not know the person who sends me the friend request.

8 Conclusion

The main objective of this phenomenographic study was to explore the different ways in which Greek Cypriots experience Facebook. In more detail, the interview analysis revealed how Greek Cypriots conceptualize privacy, self-disclosure and friendship ties in Facebook. In addition, our attempt was to identify what motivates Greek Cypriots to use Facebook and relate the findings with cultural values. The results of this study suggest that depending on the cultural orientation, participants' perception of friendship ties, self-disclosure and self-expression in Facebook differ. Our findings are consistent with our predictions and previous studies in populations with high level of UAI and low IDV [1]. In more detail, the answer to research question one "how do the characteristics of Greek culture influence the way that Facebook users form and use SNS relationships?" is that Greek Cypriot students use Facebook mainly for maintaining existing friendship ties. These findings may be a result of the collectivistic, homogeneous and high uncertainty avoidance Greek culture. The high uncertainty avoidance level may inhibit Greek Cypriots to connect with someone unknown, especially if this person is unknown to their friends too - a collectivistic characteristic. These findings are consistent with previous studies [1, 7] that associate collectivism and the desire to maintain intimate relationships. Contrary, users in individualistic cultures use social networks for building social connections [7]. It is reasonable to assume therefore that cultural characteristics may influence Greek Cypriots to avoid connecting with strangers in Facebook. It appears that maintaining an offline connection positively influences Greek Cypriot students to accept a friend request.

The participants of this study exhibited a desire to form a Facebook in-group (circle of friends) of people they know and trust which is also a characteristic of a collectivistic culture. Our results show the importance of mutual friends in terms of accepting a friend request. The existence of mutual friends positively influenced the decision of participants to accept a friend request. Mutual friends, is at some degree, an evidence that the person may be known to them too. It also seems that it is easier for participants to accept a friend request if mutual friends are at the same time close friends too. Noticeable is the fact that the higher the number of mutual friends the more chance is for that person to be considered as "trusted". Overall, this behavior can be associated with a collectivistic culture and the relative importance given to groups such as close friends or family members. As an example of this behavior is consulting a friend before deciding whether to accept or reject a friend request.

The participants of this study search for evidence in order to identify if the person sending the friend request is someone known to them. That is why they visit the other person's profile to view photos or even tagged photos of their friends. This could have implications for the design of social network sites as people from certain cultures might require more information about the other person in order to decide whether to have this person as their friend or not. For example, at the moment of writing of this paper, there is no functionality available in Facebook to allow users search for content in a user's profile. Content search in a user's profile may be very useful functionality for people requiring more evidence about the other person. Users may search for evidence or more information by using keywords. A possible keyword search might be the name of a friend that the user observes is related with the other person. The results of this search could provide all posts, comments or even tagged photos of the searched keyword, in this case a name.

We found that Greek Cypriot students exhibited concerns about their privacy in Facebook. They seem to worry that by disclosing too much personal information someone might identify them easily. Thus, to answer research question 2a, "how do the characteristics of Greek culture influence the way that Facebook users form and use self-disclosing behaviors?" this behavior may be the result of a high UAI culture. Our explanation for this is that Greek Cypriot students feel vulnerable when disclosing personal information. They seem to worry of unauthorized people gaining access to their personal information without permission. That is why they avoid disclosing their mobile phone numbers or home address. Similarly, to answer research question 2b, "how do the characteristics of Greek culture influence the way that Facebook users form and use self-expression behaviors?" Greek Cypriot students avoid self-expression in Facebook. This behaviour may also be the result of a homogeneous and collectivistic culture where people avoid self-expression to reduce the risk of getting criticized. The freedom of expression, for example, may be repressed by the strong influence of their Facebook in-group. In order to avoid disagreements or conflicts with their in-group friends, they prefer to limit their activities by sharing content such as photos instead of sharing personal thoughts with others. Consistent with other studies in collectivistic countries [7, 16, 38] and to answer research question 3 "what is the relation of the collectivistic and high-context characteristics of Greek culture and online communication?" we also found that Greek Cypriot students use Facebook mainly as a way of communication, for instance online chat. We believe that apart from the collectivistic characteristics, the high-context culture favors online communication. This assumption is on the basis that in high-context cultures the context is predefined, therefore less information is required in communication [18]. Thus, this assumption makes online communication effective.

Overall this study revealed that by associating a single dimension of Hofstede's work to describe group behavior in social network sites may not be adequate. To fully understand cultural differences in the use of social network sites, further research that explores recent historical, political, economic, cultural and technological changes is essential. Developing trusting relationships in computer-mediated communication is a much more difficult task especially in certain cultures [10, 50]. Is the worldwide success of Facebook a result of a "global culture"? Information and communication technologies allow existing groups to coordinate more effectively instead of eliminating group boundaries [23]. Clearly, research studies show that culture is a major factor which determines group behaviour.

Facebook or other similar social network sites, satisfy basic human needs such as the need to belong, the need for social connectedness or the need for popularity. Inevitably, common behavioral characteristics will be identified in the use of social networks between users from diverse cultural backgrounds. We argue that this behaviour is not the result of a "global culture". It is due to the platform-specific functionality provided by the operator (i.e. Facebook). At a higher level it seems that Facebook usage is similar between people with different cultural backgrounds. At a deeper level the studies examining users' behaviour with different cultural backgrounds reveal those hidden cultural characteristics. These characteristics differentiate Facebook usage between users from diverse cultural backgrounds at a mental level. One example of this is the influence of mutual friends. Some cultures consider it as an important indication for accepting friend requests while others not. Finally, more research studies in the future, need to address the role of cultural values in Facebook from users with different cultural backgrounds.

References

1. Abbas, R., Mesch, G.S.: Cultural values and Facebook use among Palestinian youth in Israel. Comput. Hum. Behav. Sci. **48**(C), 644–653 (2015). doi:10.1016/j.chb.2015.02.031. Elsevier
2. Åkerlind, G.S.: Variation and commonality in phenomenographic research methods. High. Educ. Res. Dev. **24**(4), 321–334 (2005). doi:10.1080/07294360500284672
3. Baskerville, R.F.: Hofstede never studied culture. Acc. Organ. Soc. **28**(1), 1–14 (2003)
4. Błachnio, A., Przepiorka, A., Pantic, I.: Association between Facebook addiction, self-esteem and life satisfaction: a cross-sectional study. Comput. Hum. Behav. **55**, 701–705 (2016). doi:10.1016/j.chb.2015.10.026
5. Blight, M.G., Jagiello, K., Ruppel, E.K.: "Same stuff different day:" a mixed-method study of support seeking on Facebook. Comput. Hum. Behav. **53**, 366–373 (2015). doi:10.1016/j.chb.2015.07.029
6. Bosch, T.E.: Using online social networking for teaching and learning: Facebook use at the university of Cape Town. Commun. South Afr. J. Commun. Theor. Res. **35**(2), 185–200 (2009). doi:10.1080/02500160903250648
7. Cho, S.E., Park, H.W.: A qualitative analysis of cross-cultural new media research: SNS use in Asia and the West. Qual. Quant. **47**(4), 2319–2330 (2013). doi:10.1007/s11135-011-9658-z
8. Christofides, E., Muise, A., Desmarais, S.: Information disclosure and control on Facebook: are they two sides of the same coin or two different processes? Cyberpsychol. Behav. Impact Internet Multimedia Virtual Real. Behav. Soc. **12**(3), 341–345 (2009). doi:10.1089/cpb.2008.0226
9. Cyprus: Wikipedia (n.d.). https://en.wikipedia.org/wiki/Cyprus. Accessed Feb 2016
10. De Angeli, A., Kyriakoullis, L.: Globalisation vs. localisation in e-Commerce: cultural-aware interaction design. In: Proceedings of the Working Conference on Advanced Visual Interfaces, pp. 250–253 (2006). doi:10.1145/1133265.1133314
11. De Oliveira, M.J., Huertas, M.K.Z., Lin, Z.: Factors driving young users' engagement with Facebook: evidence from Brazil Mauro. Comput. Hum. Behav. **54**, 54–61 (2016). doi:10.1016/j.chb.2015.07.038
12. Demographic Report 2014, 27 November 2015. http://www.cystat.gov.cy/mof/cystat/statistics.nsf/populationcondition_21main_gr/populationcondition_21main_gr?OpenForm&sub=1&sel=4
13. Duronto, P.M., Nishida, T., Nakayama, S.: Uncertainty, anxiety, and avoidance in communication with strangers. Int. J. Intercult. Relat. **29**(5), 549–560 (2005). doi:10.1016/j.ijintrel.2005.08.003
14. E-commerce in EU Enterprises, 9 December 2015. http://ec.europa.eu/eurostat/web/information-society/publications
15. Ellison, N.B., Steinfield, C., Lampe, C.: The benefits of Facebook "Friends:" social capital and college students' use of online social network sites. J. Comput. Mediat. Commun. **12**(4), 1143–1168 (2007). doi:10.1111/j.1083-6101.2007.00367.x

16. Erlin, Fitri, T.A., Susandri: Using social networks: Facebook usage at the Riau College students. In: International Conference on Computer Science and Computational Intelligence (ICCSCI 2015), vol. 59, pp. 559–566 (2015). doi:10.1016/j.procs.2015.07.543
17. Facebook newsroom (n.d.). http://newsroom.fb.com/company-info/
18. Hall, E.T.: Beyond Culture. Anchor Books, New York (1977)
19. Hattingh, F., Buttendag, A., Thompson, W.: User willingness to accept friend requests on SNS: a Facebook experiment. In: Proceedings of the IST-Africa Conference, pp. 1–8 (2014). doi:10.1109/ISTAFRICA.2014.6880610
20. Hoadley, C.M., Xu, H., Lee, J.J., Rosson, M.B.: Privacy as information access and illusory control: the case of the Facebook news feed privacy outcry. Soc. Netw. Web 2.0, Special Issue 9(1), 50–60 (2010). doi:10.1016/j.elerap.2009.05.001
21. Hofstede, G.: Research and VSM (n.d.). http://www.geerthofstede.nl/research–vsm
22. Hofstede, G., Hofstede, G.J.: Dimensions of national cultures (n.d.). http://www.geerthofstede.nl/dimensions-of-national-cultures
23. Hofstede, G., Hofstede, G.J., Minkov, M.: Cultures and Organizations: Software of the Mind. Revised and Expanded, 3rd edn. McGraw-Hill, New York (2010)
24. Internet World Stats (n.d.). http://www.internetworldstats.com/europa.htm#cy
25. Karl, K., Peluchette, J., Schlaegel, C.: Who's posting Facebook faux pas? A cross-cultural examination of personality differences. Int. J. Sel. Assess. 18, 174–186 (2010). doi: 10.1111/j.1468-2389.2010.00499.x
26. Kowalewskia, S., Zieflea, M., Ziegeldorfb, H., Wehrleb, K.: Like us on Facebook! – analyzing user preferences regarding privacy settings in Germany. In: 6th International Conference on Applied Human Factors and Ergonomics (AHFE 2015) and the Affiliated Conferences, vol. 3, pp. 815–822 (2015). doi:10.1016/j.promfg.2015.07.336
27. Kwak, H., Blackburn, J., Han, S.: Exploring cyberbullying and other toxic behavior in team competition online games. In: 33rd Annual CHI Conference on Human Factors in Computing Systems, CHI 2015, pp. 3739–3748 (2015). http://dx.doi.org/10.1145/2702123.2702529
28. Kyriakoullis, L., Zaphiris, P.: Culture and HCI: a review of recent cultural studies in HCI and social networks. Univ. Access Inf. Soc. 15, 1–14 (2015). doi:10.1007/s10209-015-0445-9
29. Lin, R., Utz, S.: The emotional responses of browsing Facebook: happiness, envy, and the role of tie strength. Comput. Hum. Behav. 52, 29–38 (2015). doi:10.1016/j.chb.2015.04.064
30. Marshall, B., Cardon, P., Norris, D.T., Goreva, N., D'Souza, R.: Social networking websites in India and the United States: a cross-national comparison of online privacy and communication. Issues Inf. Syst. 9(2), 87–94 (2008)
31. Marton, F.: Phenomenography — describing conceptions of the world around us. Instr. Sci. 10(2), 177–200 (1981). doi:10.1007/BF00132516
32. Marton, F., Booth, S.: Learning and Awareness, p. 136. Lawrence Erlbaum Associates, Mahwah (1997). ISBN 0-8058-2455-3
33. Marton, F., Saljo, R.: On qualitative differences in learning: I. Outcome and process. Br. J. Educ. Psychol. 46(1), 4–11 (1976). doi:10.1111/j.2044-8279.1976.tb02980.x
34. Minkov, M., Hofstede, G.: Is national culture a meaningful concept? Cultural values delineate homogeneous national clusters of in-country regions. Cross Cult. Res. 46(2), 133–159 (2012). doi:10.1177/1069397111427262. Sage Publications
35. Nadkarni, A., Hofmannb, S.G.: Why do people use Facebook? Pers. Individ. Differ. 52(3), 243–249 (2012). doi:10.1016/j.paid.2011.11.007. Elsevier
36. Olson, J. S., Grudin, J., Horvitz, E.: A study of preferences for sharing and privacy. In: CHI 2005 Extended Abstracts on Human Factors in Computing Systems, pp. 1985–1988 (2005). doi:10.1145/1056808.1057073

37. Perez, S.: When ranking Facebook adoption as percentage of population, Cyprus is #1 (2011). http://techcrunch.com/2011/12/28/when-ranking-facebook-adoption-as-percentage-of-population-cyprus-is-1/
38. Peters, A.N., Winschiers-Theophilus, H., Mennecke, B.E.: Cultural influences on Facebook practices: a comparative study of college students in Namibia and the United States. Comput. Hum. Behav. **49**, 259–271 (2015). doi:10.1016/j.chb.2015.02.065
39. Pfeil, U., Arjan, R., Zaphiris, P.: Age differences in online social networking - a study of user profiles and the social capital divide among teenagers and older users in MySpace. Comput. Hum. Behav. **25**(3), 643–654 (2009). doi:10.1016/j.chb.2008.08.015
40. Satici, S.A., Uysal, R.: Well-being and problematic Facebook use. Comput. Hum. Behav. **49**, 185–190 (2015). doi:10.1016/j.chb.2015.03.005
41. Snodgrass, A.: Cyprus and early Greek history In: Cyprus: From Prehistory to Modern Times, pp. 108–109. Bank of Cyprus Cultural Foundation (1995). ISBN 9963-42-048-6
42. Souleles, N.: Perceptions of undergraduate graphic design students on the educational potential of Facebook. Res. Learn. Technol. **20**(3), 241–252 (2012)
43. Tasente, T., Ciacu, N., Sandu, M.: Facebook, between socialization and personal image promotion. Commun. Mark. J. **3**(5), 13–24 (2012)
44. Taylour, W.: The Mycenaeans. Thames and Hudson, London (1983). ISBN 0-500-27586-6 1983
45. The Hofstede Center (n.d.). http://www.geert-hofstede.com/
46. The World Bank (n.d.). http://data.worldbank.org/about/country-and-lending-groups
47. Triandis, H.C.: The self and social behavior in differing cultural contexts. Psychol. Rev. **96**(3), 506–520 (1989)
48. Ur, B., Wang, Y.: Online social networks in a post how hungarians protect and share on Facebook. In: Proceedings of the 2012 iConference, pp. 398–406 (2012). doi:10.1145/2132176.2132228
49. Vasalou, A., Joinson, A.N., Courvoisier, D.: Cultural differences, experience with social networks and the nature of "true commitment" in Facebook. Int. J. Hum. Comput. Stud. **68**(10), 719–728 (2010). doi:10.1016/j.ijhcs.2010.06.002
50. Zakaria, N., Stanton, J.M., Sarkar-Barney, S.T.M.: Designing and implementing culturally-sensitive IT applications: the interaction of culture values and privacy issues in the Middle East. Inf. Technol. People **16**(1), 49–75 (2003). doi:10.1108/09593840310463023
51. Zhao, C., Hinds, P., Gao, G.: How and to whom people share: the role of culture in self-disclosure in online communities. In: Proceedings of the ACM 2012 Conference on Computer Supported Cooperative Work, pp. 67–76 (2012). doi:10.1145/2145204.2145219

Exploring the Determinants Affecting the Adoption of Social Web Applications Used in Massive Online Open Courses

Tihomir Orehovački[1(✉)] and Snježana Babić[2]

[1] Department of Information and Communication Technologies,
Juraj Dobrila University of Pula, Zagrebačka 30, 52100 Pula, Croatia
tihomir.orehovacki@unipu.hr
[2] Polytechnic of Rijeka, Trpimirova 2/V, 51000 Rijeka, Croatia
snjezana.babic@veleri.hr

Abstract. High dropout rates are one of the major issues of Massive Online Open Courses (MOOCs). Benefits of social Web applications such as active participation in creating, sharing and managing content, simultaneous work on the same artefact, synchronous and asynchronous interaction, and variety of functionalities that stimulate productivity in performing assignments have the potential to boost students' motivation and thus address the aforementioned issue. Successful implementation of social Web applications in educational settings is largely influenced by their acceptance by students. With an objective to examine the forerunners of adoption in the context of social Web applications commonly used in MOOCs, an empirical study was conducted. Participants in the study were students of one Croatian higher education institution. Data was collected by means of the post-use questionnaire. Results of data analysis uncovered the extent to which evaluated social Web applications differ with respect to determinants of their adoption.

Keywords: Adoption · Collaboration · Education · Social Web application · Empirical study · Post-use questionnaire · Wiki · Google Docs · Massive Online Open Courses

1 Introduction

Fast development of information-communication technology and its applicability in all human endeavour have led to the emergence of information society, which strives increasingly to become a knowledge society on a global scale. Supporting e-inclusion is considered as very important as its aim is to eliminate the digital divide, i.e. an inequality between groups of individuals or communities regarding their efficient use of ICT in economy and other aspects of a knowledge-based society [16]. Education plays an important role in engaging every individual in the process of building a knowledge society and it is thus crucial to find models of learning and teaching that will promote social inclusion [16]. E-education has been recognized as one of the key components in the process of building a knowledge society. In recent years, different forms of online

© Springer International Publishing AG 2017
P. Zaphiris and A. Ioannou (Eds.): LCT 2017, Part I, LNCS 10295, pp. 237–248, 2017.
DOI: 10.1007/978-3-319-58509-3_19

learning have appeared, from closed ones to open learning. They have led to a new form called Massive Online Open Courses (MOOC's) [2].

1.1 Massive Online Open Courses

The main characteristics of Massive Online Open Courses (MOOCs) are mass and free access available to any individual, regardless of the nature of the participation, which can differ with respect to an individual's educational needs [17]. According to Rajabi and Virkus [34], one of the goals of MOOCs is to ensure online courses of high quality where all individuals have equal educational opportunities. MOOCs represent an innovation in education and their successfulness is derived from the fact that they "reflect the personal, networked, and openly collaborative practices and principles of Web 2.0" [17]. The power of the MOOCs is based on the engagement of a large number of self-organized students and their connections within a certain course platform or their interaction with particular social Web application [7]. Co-creation with learners, low marginal costs for the scaling, lack of location- and time-dependency, individualization of teaching services, and enhanced reputation on the educational market are just some of many advantages MOOCs offer to educational institutions [45].

Regarding the structural differences observed from pedagogical and technical standpoints, MOOCs can be divided into two basic categories [7, 34–36, 45]: cMOOCs and xMOOCs. These two categories represent completely different models of learning and teaching. While cMOOCs are drawing on connectivism and networking, xMOOCs rely on cognitive-behaviourist approach. In that respect, xMOOCs are more tutor-centric, whereas cMOOCs are student-centric models in which learners' autonomy, peer-to-peer learning and social networking are more prominent [35].

Saadatmand and Kumpulainen [36] have highlighted the importance of understanding networked learning that represents a form of learning in which social media and Web technologies intermediate in connecting human resources, content and digital artefacts. The results of their research have shown that involvement in MOOCs encourages participants to develop self-organization, self-motivation and a satisfactory level of technological knowledge to be able to manage a large amount of resources. It is important to note that in MOOCs there are participants with different personal characteristics, including socio-demographic factors, learning styles, competences, personal goals, etc. In that respect, understanding factors that influence acceptance and continued use of MOOCs by a heterogeneous group of participants is of great importance for the successful integration of MOOCs in different forms of education.

The number of MOOCs in higher education is growing exponentially [36]. However, practice and research have shown certain shortcomings of MOOCs pointed out by students. According to Rajabi and Virkus [34], some of them are: low rate of finishing MOOCs, lack of motivation for active participation and insufficient knowledge and skills to use ICT. The authors stated that students believe designing a more interactive platform could boost participants' motivation. Being social Web applications, wikis and collaborative editors are a representative sample of interactive educational platforms.

1.2 Social Web Applications as a Backbone of Massive Open Online Courses

Wiki is a set of structured pages and as such represents a universal mean for information exchange and knowledge management. In the educational environment, wiki refers to a collection of information which arises from active participation of students and teachers thus evolving with each new entry. According to Parker and Chao [33], wikis provide support for various approaches to learning including collaborative and constructivist paradigm as well as narrative analysis and cognitive apprenticeship. Drawing on their work, Orehovački et al. [23] determined following uses of this social Web application: (1) wiki as a tool for documenting group work where each wiki page represent a separate report; (2) wiki as a knowledge repository composed of artefacts created by means of other desktop, Web, or mobile applications and integrated with or connected to wiki page; and (3) wiki as a platform for asynchronous communication and collaboration among stakeholders of the educational ecosystem.

Owing to their features, wikis started to be actively employed in educational settings even before the emergence of other social Web applications. In the last decade, they have become an essential part of diverse educational processes including teaching a foreign language [13], mathematics [14], statistics [19], information systems [12], etc. However, results of prior studies on utilizing wiki as a collaboration tool for educational purposes are quite mixed. For instance, Elgort et al. [10] found that from students' perspective wiki encourages their participation in a group work and facilitates collecting and organizing information, while from teachers' viewpoint it simplifies managing students' work and monitoring of their progress. On the other hand, issues related to learning the wiki syntax, management of history logs, aesthetics of supported templates, consumption of server resources, and lack of commitment to regular use are considered to be the major obstacles that prevent students from embracing wiki as an educational tool [43]. In that respect, Ebner et al. [9] emphasized that research effort related to the use of wikis in educational context should be focused on revealing facets of usability and motivational aspects that contribute to their success.

Social Web applications for collaborative writing are designed to support concurrent work of multiple users on the same document. The main advantages of collaborative editors are simultaneous work on the same artefact, variety of functionalities that enable efficient formatting and editing of the content, and number of add-ons such as live chat, live markup and annotation etc., which significantly enhances and simplifies interaction among users [31]. Moreover, they enable monitoring who designed particular artefact and when facilitates artefacts management. Therefore, collaborative editors are commonly used for educational purposes. Serving as an effective replacement for the pen and paper, students can employ them for the purpose of taking notes during each lecture and lab-based exercise. Considering that social Web applications for collaborative writing have sharing functionality, students can supplement each other's notes, extend them with the content from literature in the field, and in that manner create educational materials which they will employ when preparing for the mid-terms and the final exam. Being a costless alternative to commercial office suites, students also use this type of social Web applications for the joint work on project documentation, preparing essays, participating in brainwriting sessions, creating various artefacts, etc. [4].

The aim of this paper is to explore facets of adoption in the context of social Web applications widely used in educational settings. The remainder of the paper is structured as follows. Brief overview of current advances in the field is offered in the next section. Employed research methodology is described in the third section. Study findings are presented and discussed in the fourth section. Concluding remarks are offered in the last section.

2   Background to the Research

White et al. [44] argue that the students' adoption of an application meant for conducting collaborative activities represents a strong determinant of successful completion of the group work in the virtual environment. Motivational factors that significantly contribute to the adoption of novel technologies in terms of users' continuance intentions are well-established in latest versions of Technology Acceptance Model (TAM) [40], Unified Theory of Acceptance and Use of Technology (UTAUT) [42], and Expectation-Confirmation Theory (ECT) [3]. However, only some of the forerunners of the aforementioned models have been enhanced and adapted to the context of collaborative Web applications and MOOCs. For instance, Liu [15] extended the original technology acceptance model with three new constructs (wiki self-efficacy, online posting anxiety, and perceived behavioural control) and discovered that wiki self-efficacy, perceived ease of use, perceived usefulness, and wiki use intention significantly affect wiki usage in the classroom. Drawing on the ECT, Alraimi et al. [1] explored factors that influence an individual's intention to continue to use MOOC. They found that perceived reputation, perceived openness, perceived usefulness and user satisfaction significantly affect continuance intentions related to the use of MOOCs.

In current studies on predicting adoption of social Web applications by students, TAM model has been enhanced with constructs from other relevant theories and models. For instance, Shiau and Chau [37] discovered that integrated model of ECT and TAM have greater power in explaining continuance intention related to the use of blogs than TAM alone. By using the Theory of Planned Behaviour (TPB) [39] as a foundation of their study, Taylor and Hunsinger [38] revealed significant positive interplay among attitude, subjective norms, control of behaviour and affect. As a follow up, Cheung and Vogel [5] combined constructs of TAM and TPB thus confirming significant impact of compatibility with existing tools and practices, perception of resources, self-efficiency and subjective norms on behavioural intentions to employ Google applications. White et al. [44] explored the ECT in the context of collaborative editors and confirmed that both perceived usefulness and satisfaction affect continuance intentions related to the use of Google Docs. By combining dimensions of TAM and ECT, Orehovački and Babić [22] found that confirmation of expectations, perceived usefulness, and perceived ease of use are strong predictors of satisfaction whereas satisfaction and perceived usefulness significantly contribute to continuance intentions when use of Google Docs is taken into account.

Apart from being solely focused on examining adoption, recent advances in the field are also dealing with evaluating quality of various social Web applications. For instance, Orehovački introduced a set of attributes that contribute to the success of Web 2.0 applications [32], proposed conceptual model together with subjective and objective measuring instrument [30] meant for evaluating pragmatic and hedonic facets of quality in the context various social Web applications including mashups [24], mashup tools [27], services for mind mapping [20, 25, 26], diagramming [25, 32], and collaborative writing when they are employed in their native [20, 22, 30–32] and mobile settings [21] which all resulted in comprehensive evaluation methodology [29]. Finally, Orehovački and Žajdela Hrustek [28] found that learnability, satisfaction, and usefulness are important determinants of the usability of educational artefacts created by means of social Web applications.

All the aforementioned indicates that current studies are mainly focused on exploring the interplay of dimensions adopted from two diverse theories or models. In addition, studies which consider the adoption of different social Web applications employed in educational settings are scarce. Our aim is to introduce a framework whose facets originate from all relevant models and theories on technology acceptance and modelling users' behaviour and thus contribute to the adoption of social Web applications. Details on the proposed framework are provided in the following section.

3   Methodology

Procedure. The study was composed of two main parts: (1) interaction with two social Web applications and (2) the assessment of their adoption by means of the post-use questionnaire. The students' assignment was to collaboratively create an educational artefact. Students were free to choose the topic of the artefact and team members. Each student was asked to complete the aforementioned assignment twice – first with wiki tool integrated in the learning management system (LMS) Moodle and then using the Google Docs (depicted in Figs. 1 and 2, respectively). After completing the assignment with both social Web applications, the participants were asked to fill out the post-use questionnaire. The study was carried out as a part of the cMOOC on Foundations of Informatics.

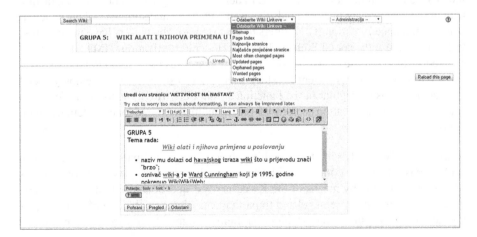

Fig. 1. Wiki tool in LMS Moodle

Fig. 2. Google Docs

Framework. The research framework consists of twelve constructs related to the adoption of social Web applications. Confirmation (CNF) refers to the extent to which social Web application has met users' expectations. Satisfaction (STF) denotes the degree to which users are content with using the social Web application. Perceived Usefulness (PU) signifies the extent to which using the social Web application enhances users' performance in performing assignments. Perceived Ease of Use (PEOU) refers to the degree to which using the social Web application is effortless. Behavioural Control (BCT) represents the extent to which users believe they will be able to conduct assignments by means of social Web application. Self-Efficacy (SEF) denotes the level to which users are self-confident in their abilities to employ social Web application. Anxiety (ANX) refers to a psychological state caused by negative experiences or expectations to lose self-esteem when confronting a situation in which users have to employ social Web application. Playfulness (PLY) denotes the degree to which the interaction with the social Web application holds the users' attention and stimulates their imagination. Continuance Intention (CIN) refers to the extent to which users have the intention to continue to use the social Web application. Hedonic Motivation (HMT) denotes the degree to which the use of social Web application arouses users' emotional responses. Habit (HBT) refers to the extent to which users tend to subconsciously employ social Web applications on regular basis. Functional Suitability (FUS) denotes the degree to which social Web application contains all functionalities required for completing collaborative activities.

Apparatus. The study adopted a within-subjects design comparing two social Web applications. Data was collected with the use of the post-use questionnaire that was administrated online by means of the KwikSurveys[1] questionnaire builder. The questionnaire comprised 13 items related to participants' demography and 55 items meant for measuring the dimensions of adoption. Items assigned to constructs were adopted

---

[1] https://kwiksurveys.com.

from existing models and tailored to the context of the research. Satisfaction and confirmation were measured by items adopted from Bhattacherjee [3], perceived usefulness and perceived ease of use were examined by items adopted from Davis [8] and Venkatesh et al. [41], continuance intention was explored by items adopted from Bhattacherjee [3] and Davis [8], self-efficacy and anxiety were evaluated by items adopted from Venkatesh et al. [41], habit and hedonic motivation were assessed by items adopted from Venkatesh et al. [42], playfulness was measured by items adopted from Moon and Kim [18], behavioural control was examined by items adopted from Taylor and Todd [39] whereas functional suitability was measured by items designed by authors of this paper. Responses to the questionnaire items were modulated on a four point Likert scale (1 – strongly disagree, 4 – strongly agree). Overall preference was assessed directly by an item in which users were asked to choose which of two employed social Web applications is more suitable for performing collaborative educational activities. The sum of responses to items assigned to corresponding construct was used as a composite measure which reflects particular dimension of adoption. Reliability of scales in terms of the internal consistency of introduced adoption constructs was examined with Cronbach's Alpha coefficient values. Differences between wiki and Google Docs were explored with Wilcoxon Signed-Rank Tests. The rationale behind the choice to employ this nonparametric equivalent to the dependent t-test relies on the outcomes of Shapiro-Wilk Tests which revealed that at least one of the variables in a pairwise comparison violates the assumption of normality in data ($p < .05$). Consequently, all the reported results are expressed as the median values. The effect size (r) was estimated as a ratio of Z-value and the square root of number of observations. According to Cohen [6], the values of . 10, .30, and .50 indicate small, medium, and large effect size, respectively.

4   Results

Participants. A total of 190 subjects (48.95% male, 51.05% female) took part in the study. The sample was comprised of 69.47% full-time and 30.53% part-time first year undergraduate students enrolled in various study programmes at Polytechnic of Rijeka including Transport (34.74%), Entrepreneurship (13.68%), Information Science (18.42%) and Occupational Safety (33.16%). The age of students ranged from 18 to 49 years where 75.26% of them had between 18 and 20 years. After having completed collaborative educational activities with social Web applications, 91.57% and 96.74% of students reported that their level of knowledge related to the use of Google Docs and wiki is at least good, respectively. For the purposes of e-learning, 86.53% of students had used different social Web applications (blog, wiki, Google Docs or other) for at least one year. Majority (95.79%) of students are loyal users of Facebook. Finally, the participants use mobile devices (64.21%) and computers (53.68%) for more than three hours a day.

Findings. As outlined in Table 1, the Cronbach's alpha values ranged from .704 to . 903, thus indicating sufficient reliability of scales for exploratory research [11].

Table 1. Reliability of scales

Constructs	Number of items	Cronbach's α[a]	
		Google Docs	Wiki
Anxiety	3	.751	.787
Behavioural control	3	.774	.744
Continuance intention	2	.825	.808
Confirmation	3	.847	.795
Functional suitability	9	.826	.831
Habit	4	.893	.871
Hedonic motivation	3	.877	.812
Perceived ease of use	6	.903	.861
Playfulness	6	.850	.841
Perceived usefulness	6	.886	.858
Self-efficacy	3	.724	.704
Satisfaction	3	.849	.832

[a]Threshold value in exploratory research [11] > .600

The outcomes of data analysis revealed that 28.42% and 30% of study participants are feeling anxious when they have to employ Google Docs and wiki, respectively, for the purpose of performing educational collaborative assignments. It was also discovered that 88.25% and 90.18% of students believe they have everything that is required to complete educational collaborative assignments by means of Google Docs and wiki, respectively. Moreover, it appeared that 72.90% and 66.32% of subjects is willing to continue using Google Docs and wiki, respectively, for collaborative work purposes. Results of data analysis also indicate that 83.33% and 86.49% of students reported that Google Docs and wiki, respectively, have met their expectations in the context of conducting educational collaborative assignments. In addition, 86.20% and 84.85% of study participants believe that Google Docs and wiki, respectively, have all functionalities that are needed for conducting collaborative activities. Only 33.42% and 33.95 of students claim they developed a habit of employing Google Docs and wiki, respectively, for conducting educational collaborative assignments. A total of 79.12% and 75.97% of respondents believe that using Google Docs and wiki, respectively, for educational collaborative activities is fun, interesting, and pleasant.

Data analysis also uncovered that 71.40% and 88.95% users reported that is easy to become proficient in using Google Docs and wiki, respectively. Furthermore, 59.04% and 56.58% of study participants think that interaction with Google Docs and wiki, respectively, can hold their attention for a longer period of time. It also appeared that 85.61% and 72.28% of subjects believe that using Google Docs and wiki, respectively, improves their performance in executing educational collaborative tasks. As much as 49.30% and 50.53% of students reported that they could complete educational collaborative assignments within time frame and without help of any kind when they employed Google Docs and wiki, respectively. Findings of the study also revealed that 85.26% and 87.02% of respondents claimed that interaction with Google Docs and wiki, respectively, represented a positive experience for them. Finally, when overall preference is taken into consideration, 25.26% of students would recommend wiki to their peers, 30.53% of students would recommend Google Docs, while 44.21% of students would recommend both social Web applications for the purpose of conducting educational collaborative activities.

Although reported findings suggest that difference among evaluated social Web applications exist, Wilcoxon Signed-Rank Tests revealed that majority of them are not statistically significant. Namely, it appeared that significant difference between Google Docs and wiki exist only in terms of the construct that explores users' loyalty behaviour ($Z = -3.071, p = .002, r = -.16$). The reported effect is small in size. Results of Wilcoxon Signed-Rank Tests are summarized in Table 2.

Table 2. Outcomes of Wilcoxon Signed-Rank Tests

Constructs	Z	p	r	Median Values	
				Google Docs	Wiki
Anxiety	−1.700	.089	N/A	6.00	6.00
Behavioural control	−1.479	.139	N/A	9.00	9.00
Continuance intention	−3.071	.002	−.16[a]	6.00	6.00
Confirmation	−1.201	.230	N/A	9.00	9.00
Functional suitability	−1.085	.278	N/A	27.00	27.00
Habit	−.084	.933	N/A	9.00	9.00
Hedonic motivation	−1.512	.131	N/A	9.00	9.00
Perceived ease of use	−1.679	.093	N/A	18.00	18.00
Playfulness	−1.935	.053	N/A	15.50	16.00
Perceived usefulness	−.430	.667	N/A	18.00	18.00
Self-efficacy	−1.744	.081	N/A	7.00	7.00
Satisfaction	−.628	.530	N/A	9.00	9.00
Adoption	**−.993**	**.321**	**N/A**	**114.50**	**144.00**

[a]Wiki > Google Docs

5   Conclusions

When constructs that contribute to the adoption of social Web applications are taken into account, Google Docs and wiki are statistically similar environments for performing educational collaborative assignments and can be, therefore, employed as an alternative to one another. Although Google Docs has proved to be better social Web application than wiki with respect to adoption constructs that measure the extent of anxiety, functional suitability, hedonic motivation, playfulness and perceived usefulness, and wiki have reached better students' ratings regarding the constructs that measure the degree of behavioural control, expectations, habit, perceived ease of use, self-efficacy, and satisfaction, significant difference between these two social Web applications was found only in terms of the construct that examines the level of continuance intentions in favour of Google Docs. In addition, results of the item on overall preference indicate that majority of study participants would recommend both application for executing collaborative assignments which further supports the aforementioned findings. Nevertheless, the proposed framework can be employed for exploring adoption of various types of social Web applications used in educational ecosystem.

As in the case of all empirical studies, work discussed in this paper has limitations. The first one is related to the homogeneity of study participants. Although students in our study are representative users of social Web applications, especially since they used these applications for completing educational assignments, heterogeneous sample could have provided importantly different responses. The second one concerns the generalizability of reported findings. Each social Web application has its particularities which might affect adoption constructs. Therefore, reported findings should be interpreted with caution.

In our future work we are planning to conceptualize an interplay of introduced adoption constructs and examine its psychometric features.

References

1. Alraimi, K.M., Zo, H., Ciganek, A.P.: Understanding the MOOCs continuance: the role of openness and reputation. Comput. Educ. **80**, 28–38 (2015)
2. Aparicio, M., Bacao, F.: E-learning concept trends. In: Proceedings of the 2013 International Conference on Information Systems and Design of Communication, pp. 81–86. ACM, Lisboa (2013)
3. Bhattacherjee, A.: Understanding information systems continuance: an expectation confirmation model. MIS Q. **25**(3), 351–370 (2001)
4. Bubaš, G., Ćorić, A., Orehovački, T.: The integration and assessment of students' artefacts created with diverse Web 22.0 applications. Int. J. Knowl. Eng. Soft Data Paradig. **3**(3), 261–279 (2012)
5. Cheung, R., Vogel, D.: Predicting user acceptance of collaborative technologies: an extension of the technology acceptance model for e-learning. Comput. Educ. **63**, 160–175 (2013)
6. Cohen, J.: Statistical Power Analysis for the Behavioral Sciences. Lawrence Erlbaum Associates, Hillsdale (1988)
7. Daradoumis, T., Bassi, R., Xhafa, F., Caballé, S.: A review on massive e-learning (MOOC) design, delivery and assessment. In: Proceedings of the 8th International Conference on P2P, Parallel, Grid, Cloud and Internet Computing, pp. 208–213. IEEE, Compiegne (2013). [27]
8. Davis, F.D.: Perceived usefulness, perceived ease of use, and user acceptance of information technology. MIS Q. **13**(3), 319–340 (1989)
9. Ebner, M., Kickmeier-Rust, M., Holzinger, A.: Utilizing wiki-systems in higher education classes: a chance for universal access? Univ. Access Inf. Soc. **7**(4), 199–207 (2008)
10. Elgort, I., Smith, A.G., Toland, J.: Is wiki an effective platform for group course work? Australas. J. Educ. Technol. **24**(2), 195–210 (2008). [6]
11. Hair, J.F., Ringle, C.M., Sarstedt, M.: PLS-SEM: indeed a silver bullet. J. Mark. Theor. Pract. **19**(2), 139–151 (2011)
12. Kane, G.C., Fichman, R.G.: The Shoemarker's children: using wikis for information systems teaching, research, and publication. MIS Q. **33**(1), 1–17 (2009)
13. Kovačić, A., Bubaš, G., Orehovački, T.: Integrating culture into a business English course: students' perspective on a collaborative online writing project. In: Proceedings of the 23rd Central European Conference on Information and Intelligent Systems, pp. 195–202. Faculty of Organization and Informatics, Varaždin (2012)

14. Krebs, M., Ludwig, M., Müller, W.: Learning mathematics using a wiki. Procedia Soc. Behav. Sci. **2**(2), 1469–1476 (2010)
15. Liu, X.: Empirical testing of a theoretical extension of the technology acceptance model: an exploratory study of educational wikis. Commun. Educ. **59**(1), 52–69 (2010)
16. Mancinelli, E.: e-Inclusion in the information society. In: Information Society: From Theory to Political Practice: Coursebook. Gondolt–Új Mandátum, Budapest (2008)
17. McAuley, A., Stewart, B., Siemens, G., Cormier, D.: The MOOC model for digital practice (2010)
18. Moon, J.W., Kim, Y.G.: Extending the TAM for a world-wide-web context. Inf. Manag. **38**(4), 217–230 (2001)
19. Neumann, D.L., Hood, M.: The effects of using a wiki on student engagement and learning of report writing skills in a university statistics course. Australas. J. Educ. Technol. **25**(3), 382–398 (2010)
20. Orehovački, T., Babić, S., Jadrić, M.: Exploring the validity of an instrument to measure the perceived quality in use of Web 2.0 applications with educational potential. In: Zaphiris, P., Ioannou, A. (eds.) LCT 2014. LNCS, vol. 8523, pp. 192–203. Springer, Cham (2014). doi: 10.1007/978-3-319-07482-5_19
21. Orehovački, T., Babić, S.: Mobile quality of social web applications designed for collaborative writing. In: Zaphiris, P., Ioannou, A. (eds.) LCT 2016. LNCS, vol. 9753, pp. 368–379. Springer, Cham (2016). doi:10.1007/978-3-319-39483-1_34
22. Orehovački, T., Babić, S.: Predicting students' continuance intention related to the use of collaborative Web 2.0 applications. In: Proceedings of the 23rd International Conference on Information Systems Development, pp. 112–122. Faculty of Organization and Informatics, Varaždin (2014)
23. Orehovački, T., Bubaš, G., Kovačić, A.: Taxonomy of Web 2.0 applications with educational potential. In: Cheal, C., Coughlin, J., Moore, S. (eds.) Transformation in Teaching: Social Media Strategies in Higher Education, pp. 43–72. Informing Science Press, Santa Rosa (2012)
24. Orehovački, T., Cappiello, C., Matera, M.: Identifying relevant dimensions for the quality of web mashups: an empirical study. In: Kurosu, M. (ed.) HCI 2016. LNCS, vol. 9731, pp. 396–407. Springer, Cham (2016). doi:10.1007/978-3-319-39510-4_37
25. Orehovački, T., Granić, A., Kermek, D.: Evaluating the perceived and estimated quality in use of Web 2.0 applications. J. Syst. Softw. **86**(12), 3039–3059 (2013)
26. Orehovački, T., Granić, A., Kermek, D.: Exploring the quality in use of Web 2.0 applications: the case of mind mapping services. In: Harth, A., Koch, N. (eds.) ICWE 2011. LNCS, vol. 7059, pp. 266–277. Springer, Heidelberg (2012). doi:10.1007/978-3-642-27997-3_26
27. Orehovački, T., Granollers, T.: Subjective and objective assessment of mashup tools. In: Marcus, A. (ed.) DUXU 2014. LNCS, vol. 8517, pp. 340–351. Springer, Cham (2014). doi: 10.1007/978-3-319-07668-3_33
28. Orehovački, T., Žajdela Hrustek, N.: Development and validation of an instrument to measure the usability of educational artifacts created with Web 2.0 applications. In: Marcus, A. (ed.) DUXU 2013. LNCS, vol. 8012, pp. 369–378. Springer, Heidelberg (2013). doi: 10.1007/978-3-642-39229-0_40
29. Orehovački, T.: Development of a methodology for evaluating the quality in use of Web 2.0 applications. In: Campos, P., Graham, N., Jorge, J., Nunes, N., Palanque, P., Winckler, M. (eds.) INTERACT 2011. LNCS, vol. 6949, pp. 382–385. Springer, Heidelberg (2011). doi: 10.1007/978-3-642-23768-3_38
30. Orehovački, T.: Methodology for evaluating the quality in use of Web 2.0 applications, Ph.D. thesis, Faculty of Organization and Informatics, University of Zagreb, Varaždin (2013)

31. Orehovački, T.: Perceived quality of cloud based applications for collaborative writing. In: Pokorny, J., et al. (eds.) Information Systems Development – Business Systems and Services: Modeling and Development, pp. 575–586. Springer, Heidelberg (2011). doi: 10.1007/978-1-4419-9790-6_46

32. Orehovački, T.: Proposal for a set of quality attributes relevant for Web 2.0 application success. In: Proceedings of the 32nd International Conference on Information Technology Interfaces, pp. 319–326. IEEE Press, Cavtat (2010)

33. Parker, K.R., Chao, J.T.: Wiki as a teaching tool. Interdisc. J. Knowl. Learn. Objects **3**, 57–72 (2007)

34. Rajabi, H., Virkus, S.: The potential and readiness of Tallinn University to establish Massive Open Online Courses (MOOCs). Qual. Quant. Methods Libr. **4**, 431–439 (2013)

35. Rodriguez, O.: The concept of openness behind c and x-MOOCs (Massive Open Online Courses). Open Praxis **5**(1), 67–73 (2013)

36. Saadatmand, M., Kumpulainen, K.: Participants' perceptions of learning and networking in connectivist MOOCs. MERLOT J. Online Learn. Teach. **10**(1), 16–30 (2014)

37. Shiau, W.L., Chau, P.Y.: Understanding blog continuance: a model comparison approach. Ind. Manag. Data Syst. **112**(4), 663–682 (2012)

38. Taylor, C., Hunsinger, D.S.: A study of student use of cloud computing applications. J. Inf. Technol. Manag. **22**(3), 36–50 (2011)

39. Taylor, S., Todd, P.: Decomposition and crossover effects in the theory of planned behavior: a study of consumer adoption intentions. Int. J. Res. Mark. **12**, 137–156 (1995)

40. Venkatesh, V., Bala, H.: Technology acceptance model 3 and a research agenda on interventions. Decis. Sci. **39**(2), 273–315 (2008)

41. Venkatesh, V., Morris, M.G., Davis, G.B., Davis, F.D.: User acceptance of information technology: toward a unified view. MIS Q. **27**(3), 425–478 (2003)

42. Venkatesh, V., Thong, J.Y.L., Xu, X.: Consumer acceptance and use of information technology: extending the unified theory of acceptance and use of technology. MIS Q. **36**(1), 157–178 (2012)

43. Wei, C., Maust, B., Barrick, J., Cuddihy, E., Spyridakis, J.H.: Wikis for supporting distributed collaborative writing. In: Tools and Technology, pp. 204–209 (2005)

44. White, B.J., Brown, J.A.E., Deale, C.S., Hardin, A.T.: Collaboration using cloud computing and traditional systems. Issues Inf. Syst. **10**(2), 27–32 (2009)

45. Wulf, J., Blohm, I., Brenner, W., Leimeister, J.M.: Massive Open Online Courses. Bus. Inf. Syst. Eng. **6**(2), 111–114 (2014)

E-safety in Web 2.0 Learning Environments: A Research Synthesis and Implications for Researchers and Practitioners

Antigoni Parmaxi[1(✉)], Kostantinos Papadamou[1], Michael Sirivianos[1], and Makis Stamatelatos[2]

[1] Cyprus University of Technology, Limassol, Cyprus
antigoni.parmaxi@gmail.com
[2] Innovators Ltd., Athens, Greece

Abstract. This study explores the research development pertaining to safety and security in Web 2.0 learning environments, as well as a review of web-based tools and applications that attempt to address security and privacy issues in Online Social Networks. Published research manuscripts related to safety and security in collaborative learning environments have been explored, and the research topics with which researchers and practitioners deal with are discussed, as well as implications for researchers and practitioners. This paper argues that Web 2.0 learning environments entail threats and challenges in the safety of both students and instructors, and further research needs to take place for handling and protecting the privacy of all involved stakeholders.

Keywords: Security · E-safety · Social media · Web 2.0 · Social web · Social networking sites · OSNs · Literature review

1 Introduction

The advancement of Web 2.0 tools offers a rewarding source of knowledge sharing, inter-action and socialization. Web 2.0 is considered "a catch-all term to describe a variety of developments on the web and a perceived shift in the way the web is used. This has been characterised as the evolution of web use from passive consumption of content to more active participation, creation and sharing – to what is sometimes called the 'read/write' web" [1, p. 9]. This term encompasses technologies that emphasize social networking, collaboration and media sharing such as Facebook, Twitter, Snapchat and MySpace. Amongst the benefits reported in the use of these tools include the development of 21st century skills such as creativity, innovation, team building, critical thinking, information sharing, higher academic achievement and improvement of ICT skills and competences [2–5]. Despite the popularity of Web 2.0 technologies, they still receive concerns by students and teachers with regard to their ability to support learning in a secure environment. Being present in online social networking sites presents particular risks such as exposure to cyberbullying, child abuse, inappropriate material and contact with dangerous strangers. Social Web can facilitate abuse of children by adults - being in place to assume fake

P. Zaphiris and A. Ioannou (Eds.): LCT 2017, Part I, LNCS 10295, pp. 249–261, 2017.
DOI: 10.1007/978-3-319-58509-3_20

identities online, a possible "danger" can intrude a child's private zone leading to violence or even sex crimes [6]. The risks and threats that minors encounter on the internet can be classified under the following five categories [7–9]: (a) content risks: instances or events in which children are exposed to illegal harmful or age inappropriate content and harmful advice; (b) contact risks: instances or events in which children have direct interaction with other children or adults. Frequent threats under this category are cyber-grooming (i.e. adults trying to develop relationships of trust with children with the aim of having sexual intercourse with them) and cyberbullying; (c) Children targeted as consumers: instances or events in which children face the risk of being treated as consumers of products and/or services designed only for adults; (d) Economic risks: instances or events in which children spent money in gambling and other online games; (e) Online privacy risks: instances or events in which children share personal data with inappropriate audience.

A fundamental dilemma that practitioners need to address when considering the use of Web 2.0 tools for minors relates to e-safety and privacy. The question is timely in light of current upsurge of Web 2.0 technologies in educational environments, where researchers and/or instructors attempt to integrate such tools in the learning environment without violating students' safety and personal rights. The question has attracted researchers and practitioners attention as it is evident from research papers and conferences (cf. Special issue of *Computers & Security Journal* on trust in cyber, physical and social computing). Some studies have been guided by the wish to understand students and teachers' concerns in incorporating Web 2.0 technologies in the classroom (cf., for example, [10]) and some by the wish to identify methods for handling e-safety in a cost-effective way (cf., for example, [11]).

This paper provides the state-of-the-art regarding e-safety in the use of online collaborative environments delineating tools and threats dominant in Web 2.0 learning environments; methods and tools for handling these threats, as well as implications for researchers and practitioners.

2   Methodology

With an eye to synthesizing the findings of research regarding e-safety in Web 2.0 learning environments, we followed a three-step approach as demonstrated in Fig. 1. Our approach included: (a) compilation of the e-safety corpus which included research manuscripts related to e-safety from manual search in scientific databases; (b) refinement of the e-safety corpus and (c) synthesis of the research papers.

The methodology of this review was informed by previous studies such as Parmaxi, Zaphiris, Papadima-Sophocleous and Ioannou [4] who reviewed recent research development in Computer-Assisted Language Learning and Parmaxi and Zaphiris [5] who reviewed the use of Web 2.0 tools in Computer-Assisted Language Learning.

2.1   Development of E-safety Corpus

In order to capture scholarly activity in e-safety in Web 2.0 learning environments, we started by selecting appropriate resources which compiled the e-safety corpus.

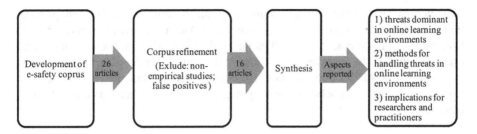

Fig. 1. Flow diagram of the methodology adopted for exploring scholarly activity in e-safety in online collaborative environments.

Appropriate articles for inclusion were selected via manual keyword search in manuscripts' title, abstract and given keywords. The keywords for searching were "security", "safety", "e-safety", "social media", "education", "learning", "threat", "Web 2.0" in the following databases: ERIC, Education Research Complete, Academic Search Complete, Computers & Applied Sciences Complete, Springer Link, Research Starters, Psychology and Behavioral Sciences Collection, Food Science Source, Taylor & Francis Group. The keyword search returned 26 manuscripts which comprised the preliminary e-safety corpus of this review.

2.2 Refinement of E-safety Corpus

The corpus was then refined in order to meet the objectives of this review. Each manuscript was scanned in order to elucidate the aim of each study. This stage facilitated the optimization of the e-safety corpus, as we excluded articles that were incorrectly selected in the search process (false positives) as well as articles reporting on non-empirical studies. The final e-safety corpus included 16 manuscripts.

2.3 Synthesis

Each paper in the e-safety corpus was then examined in depth, extracting information related to the following pre-defined aspects: (1) threats dominant in online learning environments; (2) methods for handling threats in online learning environments and; (3) implications for researchers and practitioners.

3 Findings

Recent debates about students' activities with Web 2.0 technologies strive between their perceived benefits and their potential threats. The social web is seen to have the capacity to foster formal and informal learning, yet students, teachers and parents demonstrate increased concern about the online risks and threats, often related to child sex abusers, and bullying, as well as concerns related to the safe presence of a school community in Online Social Networks (OSNs). Concerns about online safety fit within a broader agenda related to students' e-safety, recognizing the need to develop the skills and competences needed for taking advantage of the benefits that ICTs can provide. Figure 2 provides an overview of e-safety in Web 2.0 learning environments as derived from the e-safety corpus. The classification of the e-safety corpus demonstrated four categories that can be summarized as follows: (a) students' and teachers' attitudes and experiences towards e-safety in OSN, (b) e-safety actions, practices and policies in OSNs, (c) evaluation of schools' e-safety regulations in OSNs and (d) internet safety education.

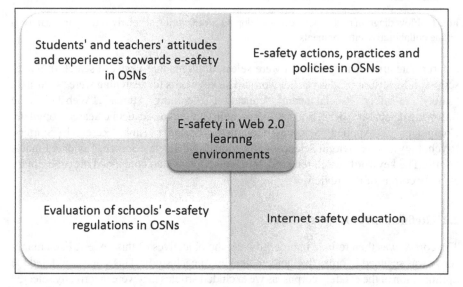

Fig. 2. Overview of e-safety in Web 2.0 learning environments as derived from the e-safety corpus.

3.1   Students' and Teachers' Attitudes and Experiences Towards E-safety in OSNs

This category entails manuscripts that deal with students' and teachers' attitudes and experiences towards e-safety in the use of OSN. For example, Sharples, Graber, Harrison, and Logan [10] report results of a study that explored children's, teachers', parents', managers' and technical staff's understanding of Web 2.0 activities and concerns. Findings demonstrated that a high percentage of the children surveyed (74%) have used social networking sites (SNS), whilst a substantial minority interacted regularly online with people they have not met face-to-face. Although teachers demonstrated the desire to take advantage of the benefits of Web 2.0 for creative and social learning, they reported being limited by a need to show a duty of care that prevents worst-case risk to children, to restrict access to SN sites. The respondents also reported concerns about Internet bullying and exam cheating. Finally, a Policy Delphi process voiced the need for schools to allow access to Web 2.0 sites, but educate children in responsible and creative learning.

3.2   E-safety Actions, Practices and Policies in OSNs

In this category, researchers engage in online safety actions, practices and policies. For example, Searson, Hancock, Soheil, and Shepherd [12] describe the need for developing informed policies and practices that would involve a wide range of sectors of the society. Such practices would inform technology integration in educational settings addressing the following factors: national and local policies, bandwidth and technology infrastructure, educational contexts, cyber-safety and cyberwellness practices and privacy accountability. Two organizations offer examples and set guidelines for digital citizenship in educational settings, that is ISTE (https://www.iste.org/explore/ArticleDetail?articleid=101) and iKeepSafe (http://ikeepsafe.org/). On the same line, Waters [11] highlight the multifarious security challenges that school districts encounter, using as a stepping stone the example of a high school's page that has been hijacked by a former student. The manuscript concludes by suggesting two web browser add ons -Firesheep and BlackSheep- for users on unsecured WiFi networks to identify the social networking sessions of others on that Network. Similarly, the Parent Teacher Association demonstrates its action in educating children and parents about Internet Safety [13]. On the same line, Ramnath [14] discusses how school administrators can protect students' safety while integrating technological advancements in teaching and learning. The study engages in topics such as cyberbullying and cyberstalking, the use of social networking sites for collaboration and the use of Mobile Device Management for the safety of mobile devices within and outside the school network. Similarly, Campbell-Wright [15] examine e-safety in e-learning, the benefits and dangers of online interaction and guidelines for preparing organizations to handle e-safety. Similarly, Wespieser [16], upon a survey distributed in 14,309 young people in London, demonstrated the high percentage of internet usage and social network sites, as well as issues of bullying and exposure to inappropriate material. The British Educational Communications and Technology Agency (BECTA) investigated the use and impact of Web 2.0 technologies in and out of school [10]. Findings demonstrated that at Key Stages 3 and 4, students harness extensively Web 2.0 outside of school, and for social purposes. The major challenge for schools in considering the usage of Web 2.0 technologies is how to support children to engage productively and creatively in social learning while protecting them from potential risk. Most learners demonstrated awareness of internet dangers, though many performed poorly in e-safety (e.g. in practice around password security). Whilst parents are generally positive in the use of technology for learning, yet concerns about e-safety exist. The paper concludes with indicating schools' responsibility in raising children's awareness on safe engagement with Web 2.0 and the internet in general. Triggered by educators' fear to adopt social networking in their teaching, Blazer [17] sets off to review the opportunities and challenges associated with education-based social networking, providing recommendations for schools when they are establishing social networking policies. Despite the risks that schools encounter when exposing students in social networking sites, their use in the classroom can promote academic learning and increase student engagement. Recommendations provided include the formulation of strong policies that address harmful online interactions and provide educators and students with guidance in the use of OSNs. Moreover, non-commercial sites are available and can monitor access to social media. Crook and Harrison [1] also capture the importance to distinguish the current fears of society from evidence of actual risk to children. They demonstrate that the majority of learners in Key stages 3 and 4 are aware of online safety, yet, they demonstrate the need for schools and teachers to have a key role in students' e-safety. Experts participating in the study favored the empower and manage approach, i.e. schools to allow free students' access to public Web 2.0, but children need to be educated on how to use Web 2.0 activities for responsible and creative learning. Children's web activity needs to be monitored for action to be taken against threatening or unsafe online behavior. Similarly, Sutton [18] provides 7 things to know right about campus security: (a) address sexual assaults on campus; (b) develop a social-media network for resources and campus security officials; (c) increase awareness of law enforcement in the higher ed community; (d) provide Web training on current topics; (e) develop crime prevention programs that are customizable; (f) put into place adequate social-media policing policies; (g) understand what the new Violence Against Women Act (VAWA) requirements mean for your campus.

3.3 Evaluation of Schools' E-safety Regulations in OSNs

Being in place to understand and evaluate schools' e-safety regulations is an issue that attracts high interest from researchers. On this line, Lorenz, Kikkas, and Laanpere [19] analyzed the types and sources of safety incidents, the solutions offered, the students' reactions from these incidents and the solutions suggested by students. Findings demonstrated that many students do not understand what e-safety is, assuming that they are not involved in any way in an e-safety episode, even if they have suffered from an online attack. The awareness training about "stop-block-tell" does not work as it is radically different from the way students think and act in real life situations. Blocking unwanted material is the least successful solution for the students, even if current typical awareness training is focusing on it. As findings demonstrated, students seem to be passive reactors to any malicious behavior, thus training focusing on stop-block-tell" or "don't click everywhere" seems unsuccessful. The solution provided by authors "is to include more technical and other practical aspects in the awareness training and distribute step-by-step, common-language how-to-s like how to set one's privacy settings, how to report a page, picture, video or how to behave when someone is being bullied, or what to do when one becomes a victim of fraud or slander. The awareness in these areas is also needed for the adults who are setting the standard how their students or children behave and deal with the problems in the future" [19, p. 336]. Ultimately, it is of major importance for schools to develop policies, strategies and solutions that address the core issues of children.

Following a similar path, Lorenz, Kikkas, and Laanpere [20] explored 201 e-safety related stories presented by students (age 12–16), parents, teachers, school IT managers and police. Through the stories, typical behavioral patterns were mapped, beliefs, regulations and limitations regarding the use of social networks in schools in Estonia. The results demonstrated that few schools hold an explicit policy for e-safety issues. Yet, even these few school-level policy documents fall behind in tackling the topics which were most frequently mentioned in students' stories. Safety incidents related to cyberbullying or exposure to illegal material remain unsolved or even undetected. Schools delegate any safety incidents to parents who in turn look to schools for assistance. As a principle, e-safety policies should focus on topics with which all stakeholder groups agree being important: gaming, fraud, password, harassment, pornography and meeting strangers. Emphasis should be placed in assessing e-safety risks and how they can influence online learning activities. Similarly, Cranmer [21] reports on excluded young people's experiences of e-safety, demonstrating that the strategies they employ to manage their online safety are primitive and insufficient, thus pointing the need for developing further their online strategies and ultimately their digital literacy.

3.4 Internet Safety Education

Internet safety education is a topic that attracts researchers' interest, as advancement of technological systems calls for schools to teach children to protect themselves on the web. Whilst internet safety was introduced with some "special occasion" events or a dedicated "Internet Safety Day", yet these actions seem to serve no purpose and have no real learning impact [22]. On this line, Naidoo, Kritzinger, and Loock [23] present a cyber –safety awareness framework that introduces cyber safety awareness education to primary school children in the South African community. The cyber safety awareness framework offers multifarious benefits for bridging the lack of cyber safety awareness both in schools and in communities. The framework proposes that schools are grouped into clusters, with a cluster coordinator as its head. Cyber safety awareness information is expected to be disseminated through workshops attended by teacher representatives of these school clusters, and distributed back to parents, children, other teachers and ultimately to their communities. On the same line, Orech [22] elaborates on the Digital Citizenship Project that aimed at integrating Internet Safety in the educational curriculum. Through the programme, students learned about cyberbullying and prevention as well as strategies for protecting themselves in case of a cyber-insult. The project had successfully employed social media for engaging middle school teachers and students to discuss about netiquette, digital citizenship, cyber crime prevention and managing digital footprint. Ultimately, sophomore students and teachers become cybermentors engaging in conversations about cyberbullying prevention and protection. Following a somewhat similar path, Moreno, Egan, Bare, Young, and Cox [24] consider internet safety education of vital importance for youth in US, thus they surveyed at what age should such education begin and what group is held responsible for teaching it. Having distributed their survey to 356 teachers, clinicians, parents and adolescents they demonstrated that the optimal age for internet safety education is 7.2 years (SD = 2.5), whilst parents were identified as the stakeholder with the primary responsibility in teaching this topic. Clinician's role was also recognised as vital in providing resources, guidance and support.

3.5 Implications for Researchers and Practitioners

As the usage of Web 2.0 technologies advances, the more instructors and students engage with these technologies in and out of school. Internet usage has changed the way literacy is perceived and taught, raising the crucial need not only for information literacy, but also for digital literacy and specifically e-safety education. In this endeavour, the question of how parents and educators can accommodate children's behaviour on the net still needs to be further investigated. Prohibiting the use of OSNs, blocking the use of unwanted material or even blocking the use of internet in the school environment is the least successful solution. As noted by Lorenz, Kikkas, and Laanpere, [19] there is a need for more technical training; as well as more automated solution that would set one's privacy settings, instructing on how to report a page, picture, video or how to react when someone is being bullied. Taking into consideration the high percentage of internet usage and social network sites, there is a strong need in engaging children productively, responsibly and creatively in social learning while protecting them from potential risks. Whilst children are aware of internet dangers but perform poorly in applying e-safety, rises schools' responsibility in raising children's awareness by providing cyber-safety and cyberwellness practices. Thus, providing online and on-site training for both teachers and parents for confronting the challenges of the new digital era with practical guidelines on e-safety and privacy is vital. With this in mind the next section provides a review of existing web-based tools and mobile applications that attempt to address security and privacy issues in Online Social Networks.

3.6 Security and Privacy Enhancing Web-Based Tools Review

This section provides a review of existing web-based tools and mobile applications that attempt to address the security and privacy issues in Online Social Networks. The tools below are of particular interest to parents and teachers.

Qustodio (https://www.qustodio.com/en/) is a parental/educator control software available in most of the platforms [25]. It enables parents/educators to monitor and manage their kids' web and offline activity on their devices. It also allows parents/educators to track with whom their children is communicating in OSNs and manage their whole OSN activity. In addition, Qustodio can be used as a sensitive content detection and protection tool.

Avira SocialShield (http://www.avira.com/) is a Social Network Protection application developed by Avira [26]. It is a monitoring tool that inform parents/educators of their children's online activities. It monitors and checks their child's social network accounts for any comments, photos etc. that may influence the child's reputation in a negative way or may indicate that the child is in danger. Furthermore, SocialShield is able to protect the children from cyberbullying, to prevent them from participating in online discussions with inappropriate content and it is also able to verify the identities of the child's online friends.

Web of Trust (WoT; https://www.mywot.com/) is a safe browser extension for website reputation rating that helps users to make informed decisions about whether to trust a website or not when browsing online [27]. In order to provide its users an extra layer of security against malicious links posted by malicious users, Facebook uses WoT's reputation data to inform users about low reputation links.

WebWatcher (https://www.webwatcher.com/) is a parental/educator control, cross-platform compatible, monitoring software [28]. It is able to capture the content of emails and instant messages in OSNs, as well as actual keystrokes and screenshots. It assists parents/educators in keeping their children safe online by viewing what is captured in their child's screen from everywhere.

Cloudalc WebFilter Pro (http://www.cloudacl.com/) is a cloud-based content filtering application [29]. Cloudacl monitors billion of web pages to protect families and especially kids from malicious attacks and threats and to ensure a safer Internet surfing. It blocks web pages, spam servers and adult material.

Abuse User Analytics (AuA) is an analytical framework aiming to provide information about the behavior of OSN users [30]. This framework processes data from users' activities in the online social network with the goal to identify deviant or abusive activities through visualization.

FoxFilter - THE Parental control for Firefox (https://addons.mozilla.org/en-US/firefox/addon/foxfilter/) is a free browser add-on produced by Mozilla and is known as the parental control for Firefox browser [31]. It is a personal content filter that helps blocking pornographic and other inappropriate content. A user can block content for an entire site or enter custom keywords filters that will be used to block content for any site that contains these keywords.

Parental Control and Web Filter from MetaCert is a parental control browser add-on that blocks pornography, malware and spyware [32]. It protects kids and adults across multiple categories. It allows users to choose among two main categories (extra strong for kids and strong for adults) while also allows to define the specific categories that you prefer to be protected (such as Bullying, Drugs, Aggressive behavior, Gambling, Sex etc.).

MetaCert Security API (https://metacert.com/) is a Security REST API [33]. It provides a layer of security on top of web applications so the application can protect users from Phishing, Malware and Pornography.

eSafely (http://www.esafely.com/) is a parental/educator control browser add-on that provides kid-safe access to popular web resources, free of adult content [34]. Generally, it offers the following: (a) Kid Safe Facebook that protects children against threat of cyber-bullying by replacing harassing messages with friendly icons in Facebook chat; (b) Kid Safe Images that when a site is identified as hosting adult content it replaces the images with images more suitable for children; (c) Kid Safe YouTube; and (d) Kid Safe Search.

ReThink (http://www.rethinkwords.com/) is an non-intrusive, patented software product that stops Cyberbullying before the damage is done [35]. When a user tries to post an offensive message on social media, ReTHink uses patented context sensitive filtering to determine whether or not it is offensive and gives the adolescent a second chance to reconsider their decision.

PureSight Multi (http://puresight.com/) is a monitoring and filtering cross-platform software that allows children to use the internet without fearing bullies or harassment and keeps parents/educators in the know [36]. It features Facebook/Cyberbullying protection, Web filtering, Reports and alerts, file sharing control and parent/educator portal.

MM Guardian Parental Control app (http://www.mmguardian.com/) is a mobile application that allows you to block incoming calls and texts, monitor alarming texts and control which apps on the device can be used and when on a children's' smartphone [37]. It also allows the parent/educator to locate and lock his childrens' mobiles with a text message, as well as to set time restrictions to limit their use.

Funamo Parental Control app (https://www.funamo.com/) is a mobile applications that allows parents/educators to monitor their childs' mobile devices [38]. Contacts, calls, SMS, browser history, applications and locations will automatically be logged and history data is uploaded to Funamo server each day. It also allows parents/educators to enable safe search engines in the web.

Kids Place is a mobile application that allows parents/educators to choose what their children can do with their mobile device [39]. It requires from the parent/educator to set up a pin when he first login to Kids Place that is then needed to exit the app. This make sure that the kids are restricted to only use apps chosen by the parent/educator. In addition, allows the parent/educator to block incoming calls and disable all wireless signals when the app is running.

AppLock is a parental/educator control mobile application for android platforms [40]. It allows parents/educators to lock SMS, contacts, Gmail, Facebook and any other application to protect their privacy. It also allows them to lock specific photos or videos meaning that they can only access them with a code.

Screen Time Parental Control app is a parental control mobile application that empowers parents to monitor and manage the time spent on their children devices and to set time limits on selected apps, as well as a bedtime curfew, lights out and school time curfews [41]. The app runs in the background of the mobile device and it can be controlled via any web browser.

4   Conclusion

As the Internet and Communication Technologies expand rapidly in many everyday activities, concerns are raised with regard to the safety of a vulnerable group such as children on the web. As noted by O'Brien, Budish, Faris, Gasser, and Lin [42], cybersecurity incidents are reported each year sitting at the top of government policy and boardroom agendas. Our findings demonstrate that recent research activity related to safety in Web 2.0 technologies pertains to: (a) students' and teachers' attitudes and experiences towards e'-safety in OSNs, (b) e-safety actions, practices and policies in OSNs, (c) evaluation of schools' e-safety regulations in OSNs and (d) internet safety education.

The incorporation of OSNs in the classrooms confronts educators with new opportunities and challenges as there is an increasing need for educating children on productive, creative, safe and responsible engagement in the use of OSNs. More work is needed in the provision of online and on-site training of both teachers and parents for confronting the challenges of the new digital era and for putting together a comprehensive e-safety framework in order to include practical guidelines on e-safety and privacy. Blocking the use of OSNs in the school environment provides only a shallow solution to the problem; there is a need for providing students the skills for managing potential risks on the web by properly setting their privacy settings, reporting inappropriate material and reacting to cyber threats.

Moreover, there is an urgent need for designing effective measures against internet risks and threats, as well as for understanding minors' activities online. Most of the existing parental/educational control software rely on monitoring and parent/educator review to detect any abnormal activity. Some of them search for keywords to create alerts, while some others block the usual list of websites. Cyber-bullying, cyber-grooming, and exchange of sensitive content is not intelligently detected by existing web-based tools and this has a negative social effect on the children i.e. they are monitored to an excessive degree and this will probably lead them to find alternative ways to go online. Existing Internet filtering techniques for protecting minors online need to be redesigned and reapplied in a smarter way, by incorporating more sophisticated techniques such as data analytics, advanced content analysis and data mining techniques that could allow for OSN fake account identification and sexual content detection.

5   Limitations

The limitation of the e-safety corpus to the specific databases meant that some manuscripts that relate to e-safety were not included. The aim of this study in not to provide an exhaustive review of the literature pertaining to e-safety in OSNs. The results and implications derive from this particular corpus; however, findings may also reflect both present and future trends.

Acknowledgments. This research has been fully funded by the European Commission as part of the ENCASE project (H2020-MSCA-RISE of the European Union under GA number 691025).

References

1. Crook, C., Harrison, C.: Web 2.0 technologies for learning at key stages 3 and 4: summary report (2008). http://dera.ioe.ac.uk/1480/1/becta_2008_web2_summary.pdf
2. Wright E.R., Lawson A.H.: Computer-mediated communication and student learning in large introductory sociology courses. In: Paper presented at the Annual Meeting of the American Sociological Association, Hilton San Francisco & Renaissance Parc 55 Hotel, San Francisco, CA (2004). http://citation.allacademic.com/meta/p_mla_apa_research_citation/1/0/8/9/6/pages108968/p108968-1.php
3. Green H., Hannon C.: TheirSpace: Education for a Digital Generation. Demos, London (2007). http://dera.ioe.ac.uk/23215/1/Their%20space%20-%20web.pdf
4. Parmaxi, A., Zaphiris, P., Papadima-Sophocleous, S., Ioannou, A.: Mapping the landscape of computer-assisted language learning: an inventory of research. Interact. Technol. Smart Educ. **10**(4), 252–269 (2013). doi:10.1108/ITSE-02-2013-0004
5. Parmaxi, A., Zaphiris, P.: Web 2.0 in computer-assisted language learning: a research synthesis and implications for instructional design and educational practice. Interact. Learn. Environ., 1–13 (2016). doi:10.1080/10494820.2016.1172243

6. Wolak, J., Finkelhor, D., Mitchell, K.J., Ybarra, M.L.: Online 'predators' and their victims: myths, realities and implications for prevention and treatment. Am. Psychol. **63**, 111–128 (2008)
7. Dooley, J., Cross, D., Hearn, L., Treyvaud, R.: Review of existing australian and international cyber-safety research. Child Health Promotion Research Centre, Edith Cowan University, Perth (2009)
8. OECD: The Protection of Children Online: Risks Faced by Children Online and Policies to Protect Them. OECD Digital Economy Papers, No. 179. OECD Publishing, Paris (2011). http://dx.doi.org/10.1787/5kgcjf71pl28-en
9. Tsirtsis, A., Tsapatsoulis, N., Stamatelatos, M., Papadamou, K., Sirivianos, M.: Cyber security risks for minors: a taxonomy and a software architecture. In: 2016 11th International Workshop on Semantic and Social Media Adaptation and Personalization (SMAP), pp. 93–99. IEEE, November 2016
10. Sharples, M., Graber, R., Harrison, C., Logan, K.: E-safety and web 2.0 for children aged 11–16. J. Comput. Assist. Learn. **25**(1), 70–84 (2009)
11. Waters, J.K.: Social networking: keeping it clean. THE J. **38**(1), 52 (2011)
12. Searson, M., Hancock, M., Soheil, N., Shepherd, G.: Digital citizenship within global contexts. Educ. Inf. Technol. **20**(4), 729–741 (2015)
13. A Safer Digital World. Our Child. **39**(5), 5 (2014). ISSN 10833080
14. Ramnath, S.: How schools can keep students safe, and on Facebook. eSchool News **18**(4), 16 (2015)
15. Campbell-Wright, K.: E-safety. NIACE (2013)
16. Wespieser, K.: Young People and E-safety: The Results of the 2015 London Grid for Learning E-safety Survey. National Foundation for Educational Research (2015)
17. Blazer, C.: Social Networking in Schools: Benefits and Risks; Review of the Research; Policy Considerations; and Current Practices. Information Capsule, vol. 1109. Research Services, Miami-Dade County Public Schools (2012)
18. Sutton, H.: Review the top 7 things to know right now about campus security. Campus Secur. Rep. **12**(4), 1–5 (2015)
19. Lorenz, B., Kikkas, K., Laanpere, M.: Comparing children's E-safety strategies with guidelines offered by adults. Electron. J. e-Learn. **10**(3), 326–338 (2012)
20. Lorenz, B., Kikkas, K., Laanpere, M.: Social networks, e-Learning and Internet safety: analysing the stories of students. In: Proceedings of the 10th European Conference on e-Learning ECEL-2011: 10th European Conference on e-Learning ECEL-2011, Brighton, UK, pp. 10–11, November 2011
21. Cranmer, S.: Listening to excluded young people's experiences of e-safety and risk. Learn. Media Technol. **38**(1), 72–85 (2013)
22. Orech, J.: How it's done: incorporating digital citizenship into your everyday curriculum. Tech. Learn. **33**(1), 16–18 (2012)
23. Naidoo, T., Kritzinger, E., Loock, M.: Cyber safety education: towards a cyber-safety awareness framework for primary schools. In: International Conference on e-Learning, p. 272. Academic Conferences International Limited (2013)
24. Moreno, M.A., Egan, K.G., Bare, K., Young, H.N., Cox, E.D.: Internet safety education for youth: stakeholder perspectives. BMC Public Health **13**(1), 543 (2013)
25. Qustodio: Protect, understand and manage your kids internet activity with Qustodio (2016). https://www.qustodio.com/en/
26. The Windows Club: SocialShield: Avira Social Network Protection for your child (2016). http://www.thewindowsclub.com/socialshield-review
27. WOT: Know which sites to trust (2016). https://www.mywot.com/

28. Awareness Technologies Computer & Mobile monitoring software (2016). http://www.webwatcher.com/?refID=lnkshr&siteID=Cty0dj6o3sgGHtU.M9eT5Zlm7qQ5Ms1ig
29. Cloudacl: Web Security Service (2013). http://www.cloudacl.com/webfilter/
30. Squicciarini, A.C., Dupont, J., Chen, R.: Online abusive users analytics through visualization. In: Proceedings of the 23rd International Conference on World Wide Web, pp. 155–158. ACM, April 2014
31. Mozilla add-on: The Parental control for Firefox (2014). https://addons.mozilla.org/en-US/firefox/addon/foxfilter/
32. Chrome web store: Parental Controls & and Web Filter (2016). https://chrome.google.com/webstore/detail/parentalcontrols-web-fil/dpfbddcgbimoafpgmbbjiliegkfcjkmn
33. MetaCert: MetaCert Security API (2009–2016). https://metacert.com/
34. Esafely: eSafely protects you where your Web filter doesn't (2014). http://www.esafely.com/
35. ReThink: ReThink (2016). http://www.rethinkwords.com/
36. Puresight: PureSight Online child safety (2010–2011). http://puresight.com/puresight-prevents-cyberbullying.html
37. Pervasive Group: MM Guardian Parental Control (2016). https://play.google.com/store/apps/details?id=com.mmguardian.childapp
38. Funamo: Funamo Parental Control (2015). https://play.google.com/store/apps/details?id=funamo.funamo
39. General Solutions and Services, LLC: Kids Place - Parental Control (2012). https://play.google.com/store/apps/details?id=com.kiddoware.kidsplace
40. doMobile: AppLock   (2016).   https://play.google.com/store/apps/details?id=com.domobile.applock
41. ScreenTime Labs: Screen Time Parental Control (2016). https://play.google.com/store/apps/details?id=com.screentime.rc&hl=en_GB
42. O'Brien, D., Budish, R., Faris, R., Gasser, U., Lin, T.: Privacy and Cybersecurity Research Briefing (2016)

Pedagogical Voice in an E-Learning System: Content Expert Versus Content Novice

Lincoln Sedlacek, Victor Kostyuk(✉), Matthew Labrum,
Kevin Mulqueeny, Georgina Petronella, and Maisie Wiltshire-Gordon

Reasoning Mind, Houston, TX, USA
lincolnsedlacek@gmail.com,
vkostyuk@reasoningmind.org, mlabrum@gmail.com,
mulqueeny@gmail.com, gpetronella@gmail.com,
maisiewg@gmail.com

Abstract. Studies have shown student performance in virtual learning environments is improved by the presence of a virtual pedagogical agent, particularly when the agent is voiced by a human voice. Furthermore, studies have shown students achieve higher learning outcomes when their teacher is a content expert in the material being taught. This study examines the question at the intersection of these two domains: Do students achieve higher learning outcomes in a virtual learning environment if the actor voicing the virtual agent is a content expert in the material being taught? The analysis found no evidence of such an effect, although more research should be conducted before firm conclusions are drawn.

Keywords: Pedagogical agents · e-Learning · Content expertise · Narration

1 Background

Over the years, a large body of research has accumulated concerning e-learning environments, virtual instruction, and online lessons. Studies have demonstrated positive learning outcomes for students who use e-learning and online instructional programs. At the same time, the computerized nature of these programs allows for easily replicated personalized learning experiences [3, 6].

In studies on the efficacy of e-learning programs, a great deal of attention has been given to the use of on-screen coaches—typically referred to as "pedagogical agents"—to improve learning outcomes. Pedagogical agents are defined in Clark and Mayer's *e-Learning and the Science of Instruction* [3] as "on-screen characters who help guide the learning process during an e-learning episode." The embodiment of a pedagogical agent varies greatly among e-learning programs—some are presented as high-quality talking-head videos, while others may appear as static, cartoon-like characters that "speak" only via printed text.

While research on the effectiveness of pedagogical agents is still in its early stages, multiple studies have shown correlations between the use of embodied pedagogical agents in e-learning programs and improved student learning outcomes [1, 2, 7, 10]. Additionally, studies have shown that, while student performance is not necessarily

P. Zaphiris and A. Ioannou (Eds.): LCT 2017, Part I, LNCS 10295, pp. 262–272, 2017.
DOI: 10.1007/978-3-319-58509-3_21

improved by the agent having a realistic human appearance [10], student performance *is* improved when the agent exhibits human-like behavior, such as gesturing or gazing at relevant material, or speaking in a personalized fashion [7, 9]. Further research has shown that, to improve learning, agents should communicate through speech, rather than through on-screen text [1, 10]; that students perform better when such speech is polite, rather than more direct [12]; and that students perform better when the pedagogical agent has a human voice as opposed to a machine-generated voice [2].

Of course, giving a pedagogical agent a human voice requires a human voice actor. And while there have been several studies on the ideal appearance, sound, and demeanor of a pedagogical agent, there is a dearth of research on what qualities are important in the voice actor voicing a pedagogical agent. The developers of the Reasoning Mind blended learning program for middle school math, *Edifice*, hypothesized that student learning would increase among users of their e-learning software if the voice actors voicing pedagogical agents were content experts in the mathematical subject matter.

1.1 Theoretical Basis

There is some theoretical basis for believing a content-expert voice actor would have a more positive impact on student learning outcomes. Research has shown that, in a real-world mathematics classroom, instructor competency in classroom subject matter greatly affects student learning [5].

However, a pedagogical agent's voice actor is very different from a classroom instructor. Classroom instructors are typically in charge of curriculum construction, lesson content and structure, lesson delivery, one-on-one intervention, classroom management, and a host of other tasks. Voice actors for pedagogical agents typically control a much narrower set of features of their (virtual) classrooms. True, there are examples of virtual learning environments like Khan Academy [4], where Sal Khan originally planned the lesson, wrote the script, and then delivered it in his own voice as an unseen pedagogical agent. Yet many virtual learning environments (Reasoning Mind *Edifice* included) employ curriculum designers who plan, design, and write lessons; have programmers who create the lesson visuals; and recruit voice actors after the lesson is scripted to deliver the lines for the final product. In such settings, voice actors narrate, with limited deviation, pre-written instructional scripts—they do not compose those scripts.

Despite the limited role voice actors have when compared to a more typical course instructor, there are still reasons why their status as a content expert or a content novice may be important when it comes to voicing a pedagogical agent in a virtual or online math lesson:

1. A content novice may not understand the technical vocabulary used in the script, resulting in mispronunciations and disfluencies that are distracting to the student.
2. A content novice may speak without confidence in the delivery, making the student question their understanding and disengage.
3. In an attempt to maintain fluency and confidence, a content novice may deliver lines or modify the script in a way that impedes student understanding, or worse yet, promotes an incorrect understanding of the material.

This last effect may be the most important, and is one that Reasoning Mind *Edifice*'s creators worried might have been occurring within the *Edifice* program.

The following is an example of how line delivery may impede student understanding. During several *Edifice* lessons, students learned about, and completed exercises involving, inverse proportionality. Such lessons would include lines like the following:

> "So, if these quantities are *inversely* proportional, and one of them *increases*, then the other will *decrease*."

A mathematical content expert would understand the importance of distinguishing the words "increases" and "decreases" from each other, which can be done by emphasizing the syllables "in-" and "de-" (highlighting the parts of the words that are different). However, one of the *Edifice* voice actors would consistently emphasize the "-crease" syllable of both words instead, a practice that obscured the meaning of the line by highlighting the *similarity* between the two words.

This, of course, is just one example of line delivery being affected by a voice actor's status as a content novice or content expert. During the *Edifice* creation process, however, several more occurred, such as:

- Word mispronunciations (e.g., pronouncing "multiplicative" as "**muhl**-*tih*-play-*tihv*," which leaves out one full syllable)
- Emphases that obscured the meanings of lines (such as the "*in*crease/*de*crease" vs. "in*crease*/de*crease*" example given above)
- Carelessly paced speech patterns that actively communicated an incorrect meaning of a line (e.g., speaking the line, "The answers are twenty, two, and seven," too quickly, making it sound like, "The answers are twenty-two and seven")
- Emphases that actively communicated an incorrect meaning of a line (e.g., speaking a line like, "You drew a line parallel to line CD. You should have drawn a line perpendicular to line BC," while only emphasizing parallel and perpendicular; such a mistake might lead students to hear "CD" and "BC" as the same, and not recognize that mistake)

As Reasoning Mind curriculum creators, who are content experts in mathematics[1], reviewed lessons in their final form, many felt that these issues were occurring, and may affect student learning outcomes.

All three *Edifice* voice actors had professional experience in voice acting, with each having professional performance credits to their name. However, these voice actors also self-reported having average mathematical competency—they generally understood the material being covered, but wouldn't have considered themselves content experts. Further discussion made it clear that, in many cases where lines were delivered problematically, it was due to a lack of expert-level understanding of the material at hand.

---

[1] Most Reasoning Mind curriculum developers have PhDs or Master's degrees in mathematics or another STEM field.

To better understand the relationship between a pedagogical agent voice actor's mathematical competency and student learning outcomes, we ran an experiment to see if student learning outcomes would be higher with amateur voice actors who were content experts as opposed to professional voice actors who were content novices.

2 Methods

2.1 The Reasoning Mind *Edifice* Platform

Reasoning Mind *Edifice* is a blended learning platform for middle school (Grades 6, 7, and 8) mathematics in which students spend part of their class time learning online, and part learning from teacher-led instruction. Within the online program, students go through a series of over 100 lessons throughout the school year.

Students complete lessons in a "virtual classroom" (See Fig. 1), in which mathematical instruction is delivered through text, illustrations, animations, and voice. Most of the virtual classroom consists of a large "whiteboard" on which information appears in the form of text, formulas, figures, diagrams, problems, animations, and other relevant material.

Also visible in the virtual classroom are two virtual students and a virtual tutor, who go through the lesson with the user. The virtual students act much as a typical student would, asking questions, attempting problems, and contributing to the classroom

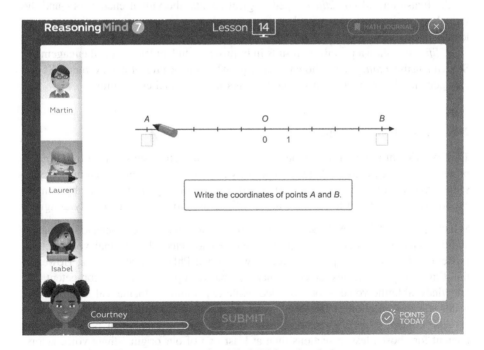

Fig. 1. The Reasoning Mind *Edifice* virtual classroom

discussion of mathematics. The virtual tutor—the pedagogical agent this experiment concerns itself with—leads the lesson much like a traditional teacher would, reviewing homework, introducing the students to new material, explaining concepts, walking students through example problems, leading virtual classroom discussions, asking questions, reacting to students' answers to questions, and reviewing lesson material.

All virtual characters can ask the student user questions; the virtual tutor does this frequently, and the virtual students do occasionally. Student users then respond via one of *Edifice*'s many response tools. A virtual character will give one of several possible reactions to the user's response, depending on what response they gave; a correct response will usually result in some type of congratulatory reaction, while an incorrect response will typically result in course correction coupled with reassuring motivation. If a student user fails to respond to a question for a certain amount of time, a virtual character will continue the lesson, typically with an explanation of the correct answer. Adaptivity occurs at the fine-grained level of individual student answers (e.g., the virtual tutor is programmed to adapt feedback and follow-up questions to answers indicative of particular misconceptions), and at a course-grained level, where stronger students get more challenging problems or less scaffolding during the problem-solving process while weaker students get simpler problems and more scaffolding.

The lessons in *Edifice*'s middle school curriculum house a cast of three virtual tutors and seven virtual students. Virtual tutors and students are rotated through lessons at a rate of two students and one tutor per lesson, providing variety in the virtual characters' genders, races, personalities, portrayed mathematical strengths, etc.

As Reasoning Mind *Edifice*'s pedagogical agents, the virtual characters—and the virtual tutor, in particular—are key features when it comes to promoting positive learning outcomes among student users of the program.

Edifice has shown promising results in improving student learning and engagement. Students using *Edifice* have shown greater growth in measures of achievement [8] and engagement [11] compared to similar students in traditional classrooms.

2.2   Experimental Design

This experiment required one student group to go through lessons voiced by *Edifice*'s professional voice actors (content novices), who had average general competency in school mathematics. Another student group went through lessons voiced by content experts who were not trained voice actors . Students groups were randomly assigned.

Selecting New Voice Actors. Content-expert voice actors were selected using an audition process similar to the process followed to select the original voice actors, moderated by a panel of judges, three of whom had PhDs in mathematics. However, this time, judges were instructed to place a heavy emphasis on how competent and knowledgeable the voice actors sounded while explaining mathematical material. The result was the selection of three new voice actors rated across the board as sounding: (1) like content experts in mathematics, and (2) generally better at performing the content for chosen lesson sections than at least two of our original three voice actors.

The judges also selected another new voice actor that they rated as sounding as close as possible to the original voice actors (a novel content novice). The inclusion of this new content novice voice actor in the experiment was done to investigate the possibility of a novelty effect, as explained in the "implementation" section below.

Implementing New Voice Actors in Lessons. Study designers chose three seventh-grade lessons in which they could implement new voice actors. Each lesson had a different one of the three original professional voice actors who were content novices.

Lesson 105 received two treatment conditions. The version recorded using the original content-novice voice actor was Condition A. Condition B was recorded using the novel content-novice voice actor. Condition C was recorded using the content-expert voice actor. These three conditions allowed for the investigation of a possible novelty effect: if students' performance improved in comparable measure in both Conditions B and C, it would likely be due to a novelty effect. If student performance improved due to the content-expert voice actor in Condition C, student learning outcomes should be significantly higher in Condition C than in Condition B.

Lessons 110 and 112 were each re-recorded once. The version recorded using the original content-novice voice actor was Condition A. Condition B was recorded using the content-expert voice actor. A third version of Lessons 110 and 112 was also created in which the lessons began with the content-expert-voiced virtual tutor being introduced in a short, introductory video. This version was related to another study, and whether students received video or non-video versions of these lessons was randomized for both lessons to mitigate any effects of the third condition.

For every condition with a novel voice actor, virtual tutor avatars were changed, and each new tutor introduced themselves as a new tutor so that students would not be confused by what appeared to be their old tutor suddenly having a different voice. Some lines were also given minor revisions to accommodate new personalities and speaking patterns. (For example, it might distract a student if a new virtual tutor used a catchphrase that was unique to one of the original virtual tutors).

2.3   Participants

Participants in the study were seventh-grade mathematics students from a mid-sized city in Central Texas. Using the experimental setup of the three lessons mentioned above, we conducted a randomized-controlled trial. In the first lesson (Lesson 105), 191 students were included in the experiment, with 65 included in Condition A (content-novice professional voice actor), 59 included in Condition B (content-expert amateur voice actor), and 67 in Condition C (novel content-novice amateur voice actor). The second and third lessons (Lessons 110 and 112) each had 168 students included in the experiment, with 54 students in Condition A and 114 in Condition B.

3 Results

We randomly assigned 191 students into groups that received different versions of Lessons 105, 110, and 112; however, not all students completed every lesson or every outcome measure, due to instances of student absences and other conflicts. For this reason, the sample sizes vary slightly for the homework, quiz, and final exam. In lesson 105, the original content novice was the tutor voice actor for 65 students, the content expert was the tutor voice actor for 59 students, and the novel content novice was the tutor voice actor for 67 students. To establish baseline equivalence of the three groups, we examined the average of scores on two quizzes halfway through the course. The groups did not differ significantly, averaging 54.1 (SD = 27.8), 52.2 (SD = 26.2), and 53.5 (SD = 27.4) for the original content novice, content expert, and novel content novice, respectively (pairwise t-tests between groups had p-values equal to 0.66 for the original content novice and the content expert, 0.89 for the original content novice and the novel content novice, and 0.76 for the content expert and the novel content novice).

Measured outcomes for Lesson 105 are shown in Table 1. Student learning outcomes were determined by measuring lesson accuracy (i.e., the percent of questions answered correctly within the given lesson) and homework accuracy (percent of questions answered correctly on the assigned homework following the lesson), in addition to accuracy on the quiz in Lesson 110 and the Final Exam, both measured as a percentage of questions answered correctly. Number of timeouts (i.e., the number of times a student did not answer a question posed by a virtual character) was used as a measure of student engagement and in-lesson understanding (with the belief being that students who didn't answer questions were less engaged or had trouble understanding the material). Lesson completion time (number of hours it took students to complete the lesson) was also used as a potential measurement for student engagement and in-lesson

Table 1. Lesson 105 ANOVA results

	Condition A: original con. novice M (SD)	Condition B: con. Expert M (SD)	Condition C: novel con. novice M (SD)	F (df)	p-value
Lesson accuracy	63.5 (20.1)	61.3 (20.6)	59.4 (22.5)	0.62 (2,188)	0.54
Lesson completion time	0.79 (.22)	0.83 (.20)	0.88 (.22)	2.66 (2,188)	0.07
Number of timeouts	8.4 (8.6)	6.4 (6.7)	10.5 (12.7)	2.79 (2,188)	0.06
Homework accuracy	41.1 (32.9)	48.5 (32.4)	37.5 (29.9)	1.76 (2,166)	0.18
Quiz accuracy	58.7 (42.8)	49.1 (41.4)	48.3 (45.5)	0.95 (2,163)	0.39
Final exam accuracy	57.0 (29.9)	45.9 (32.5)	44.9 (27.7)	2.08 (2,129)	0.13

understanding (with the assumption that engaged students who had an easier time understanding the material would finish the lesson more quickly). However, this measure should not be over-interpreted: it may also reflect differing voice actor speech speeds.

According to a one-way analysis of variance (ANOVA), the three groups of students did not differ significantly on lesson accuracy, lesson completion time, number of timeouts during the lesson, homework accuracy, Quiz accuracy (in Lesson 110), or Final Exam performance. The number of timeouts and lesson completion time approached significance, with p-values less than 0.1, but pairwise comparisons found no significant differences between any pair of groups. There also did not appear to be any effect of the novelty of the guest tutors.

In Lessons 110 and 112, one group of students received instruction from virtual tutors voiced by the content-novice voice actors (54 students), while the rest were instructed by virtual tutors voiced by content-expert voice actors (114 students). We checked baseline equivalency: the groups did not differ significantly on the average performance of two quizzes halfway through the course, with students who had the content novice averaging 54.1 (SD = 27.8) and those with content experts averaging 52.8 (SD = 26.6, p = 0.73). According to an independent-sample t-test, performance within Lesson 110 was not significantly different between the two groups on lesson accuracy, lesson completion time, number of timeouts, or subsequent homework accuracy. Students with the content-novice voice actors scored 10% points higher on the quiz in Lesson 110 than students with content-expert voice actors, an effect size of 0.23 standard deviations. A similar t-test found performance in Lesson 112 was not significantly different between the two groups, but the content-expert group took significantly longer to complete the lesson. The content-novice group scored significantly higher on the Final Exam in lesson 114, an effect size of 0.39 standard deviations (Tables 2 and 3).

Table 2. Lesson 110 t-test results

	Condition A: content novice M (SD)	Condition B: content expert M (SD)	t (df)	p-value
Lesson accuracy	63.0 (20.8)	60.8 (19.9)	0.66 (161)	0.51
Lesson completion time	0.70 (.14)	0.71 (.16)	−0.66 (161)	0.51
Number of timeouts	3.7 (4.4)	3.9 (3.9)	−0.32 (165)	0.75
Homework accuracy	47.6 (37.6)	44.3 (34.4)	0.51 (136)	0.61
Quiz accuracy	58.7 (42.8)	48.7 (43.3)	1.38 (164)	0.17

Table 3. Lesson 112 *t*-test results

	Condition A: content novice *M (SD)*	Condition B: content expert *M (SD)*	t *(df)*	p-*value*
Lesson accuracy	69.6 (19.3)	68.2 (18.6)	0.43 (147)	0.67
Lesson completion time	0.81 (.17)	0.89 (.20)	**−2.54 (147)**	**0.01***
Number of timeouts	7.7 (7.4)	6.1 (5.8)	1.46 (152)	0.15
Homework accuracy	47.3 (29.5)	47.7 (31.8)	−0.07 (128)	0.94
Final exam accuracy	57.0 (29.9)	45.4 (30.1)	**2.04 (130)**	**0.04***

*a t-test p value of less than 0.05

In all three lessons, there was no significant difference between the groups in each measure of student engagement and student performance after adjusting for multiple comparisons.

4   Discussion

Somewhat surprisingly, the results indicate that the use of content experts as voice actors for pedagogical agents provides no significant effect on either student engagement or student performance. For each group of students (those taking lessons in which the virtual tutor was voiced by the content novice, versus those taking lessons in which the virtual tutor was voiced by a content expert), in each lesson, baseline equivalency was determined by noting the average scores on two quizzes approximately halfway through the course were not significantly different. In all three lessons, there was no significant difference between the groups in each measure of student engagement and student performance after adjusting for multiple comparisons. Prior to the adjustment, two statistically significant (at the 0.05 level) differences were present, in the time taken to complete the last of the three experimental lessons and in the score on the final exam.

Our results may suggest that, unlike in a real-world mathematics classroom, in which instructor quality greatly affects student learning [5], the scripted environment of an e-learning system greatly reduces the effect a tutor voice actor's personal understanding of the material may have on student performance. Therefore, while having a human voice for a pedagogical agent in a virtual learning environment improves student learning outcomes [2], it may not matter whether or not that human voice actor is a content expert.

It is also possible that the mathematical competency of a pedagogical agent's voice actor does have an effect on student learning outcomes, and we simply did not detect such an effect. Such an effect could have gone undetected by us due to an insufficient sample size, or due to difficulties associated with completely isolating variable voice actor characteristics. (For example, voice actors did not differ solely in whether they were a content novice or a content expert, but also in their voiceprints, recording equipment, personal vocal tics, etc.)

Another possibility is that professional voice actors—even ones who are content novices—have developed the skills necessary to deliver material for which they lack a content-expert-level understanding, while amateur voice actors—even content experts—aren't experienced enough in voice acting to deliver all material effectively. This could explain our results, although our lack of an effect on student learning outcomes is still a bit surprising since the presence of Conditions A (content novice, professional voice actor), B (content expert, amateur voice actor), and C (content novice, amateur voice actor) should have controlled for the possibility of this effect. That is, if the advantages of being a professional voice actor and being a content expert were equal, both should have resulted in significantly higher learning outcomes than the content novice, amateur voice actor condition.

It's also notable that, at the time our experimental design was implemented, seventh-grade *Edifice* students had already gone through over 100 lessons with their original seventh-grade virtual tutor voice actors. While three lessons with content expert voice actors may not have resulted in a significant improvement in students' learning outcomes, it is possible that a full year of such lessons would have made a large significant difference. Additionally, the distraction of new virtual tutors, along with the time it took students to get used to them, might have mitigated any benefit students could have gotten from the content expert voice actors' better delivery of mathematical content.

A final possibility is that, while mathematical content experts may have a better idea of how best to explain mathematical content *to another content expert*, voice actors with lower levels of mathematical competency might be more highly attuned to what parts of an explanation students might have trouble with. Therefore, voice actors with lower levels of mathematical competency might better know what parts of an explanation they should emphasize or otherwise set apart when delivering lines to a student. This would result in content novice voice actors fostering higher student learning outcomes, even as they would likely be rated as having poorer voice actor performance by mathematical content experts.

5 Conclusion

In a virtual learning environment, students tend to achieve higher learning outcomes when an embodied pedagogical agent is present in the environment [1, 2, 7, 10]—and they tend to achieve even higher learning outcomes when said virtual pedagogical agent has a natural, human voice [2]. While we theorized that students would achieve even higher learning outcomes if that virtual pedagogical agent was voiced by a content expert, our study found no evidence for this hypothesis. However, while our foray into examining this question may give some guidance to aspiring e-learning designers, more research should be conducted before arriving at firm conclusions.

Acknowledgements. Many thanks to the administrators, teachers, and students who participated in the study. Thanks to our novel virtual tutor voice actors, Khushboo Bansal, Joel Dylong,

Carmel Levy, and Maureen Royce. Thanks also to Leonid Andrulaytis, Olga Ipatova, Alex Khachatryan, Julia Khachatryan, Yulia Konovalova, Victor Kostyuk, Viktoriya Kozyreva, Sergey Makorov, Nikolay Prokopyev, Andrey Romashov, Nathaniel Rounds, Dmitriy Safonov, Yaroslav Vasilyev, Michael Von Korff, Dussy Yermolayeva, and all others who provided guidance, assistance, and other contributions to the project.

References

1. Atkinson, R.K.: Optimizing learning from examples using animated pedagogical agents. J. Educ. Psychol. **94**, 416–427 (2002). doi:10.1037/0022-0663.94.2.416
2. Atkinson, R.K., Mayer, R.E., Merrill, M.M.: Fostering social agency in multimedia learning: examining the impact of an animated agent's voice. Contemp. Educ. Psychol. **30**(1), 117–139 (2005). doi:10.1016/j.cedpsych.2004.07.001
3. Clark, R.C., Mayer, R.E.: e-Learning and the Science of Instruction, 4th edn. Wiley, Hoboken (2016). doi:10.1002/9781119239086
4. Dreifus, C.: Salman Khan turned family tutoring into Khan Academy. The New York Times, 27 January 2014. https://www.nytimes.com/2014/01/28/science/salman-khan-turned-family-tutoring-into-khan-academy.html. Accessed 9 Feb 2017
5. Hanushek, E.A., Rivkin, S.G.: Chapter 18 teacher quality. In: Hanushek, E.A. (ed.) Handbook of the Economics of Education, pp. 1051–1078 (2006). doi:10.1016/s1574-0692(06)02018-6
6. Horn, M.B., Staker, H.: The Rise of K-12 Blended Learning. Innosight Institute, Inc., Mountain View (2011)
7. Lusk, M.M., Atkinson, R.K.: Animated pedagogical agents: does their degree of embodiment impact learning from static or animated worked examples? Appl. Cogn. Psychol. **21**(6), 747–764 (2007). doi:10.1002/acp.1347
8. Mingle, L., Kostyuk, V., Khachatryan, G.: Adapting international math curricula using an online platform. In: Poster to be Presented at The Annual Meeting of the American Educational Research Association in San Antonio (2017)
9. Moreno, R., Mayer, R.E.: Personalized messages that promote science learning in virtual environments. J. Educ. Psychol. **96**(1), 165–173 (2004). doi:10.1037/0022-0663.96.1.165
10. Moreno, R., Mayer, R.E., Spires, H., Lester, J.: The case for social agency in computer-based teaching: do students learn more deeply when they interact with animated pedagogical agents? Cogn. Instr. **19**, 177–214 (2001). doi:10.1207/s1532690xci1902_02
11. Mulqueeny, K., Mingle, Leigh A., Kostyuk, V., Baker, Ryan S., Ocumpaugh, J.: Improving engagement in an e-Learning environment. In: Conati, C., Heffernan, N., Mitrovic, A., Verdejo, M.F. (eds.) AIED 2015. LNCS, vol. 9112, pp. 730–733. Springer, Cham (2015). doi:10.1007/978-3-319-19773-9_103
12. Wang, N., Johnson, W.L., Mayer, R.E., Rizzo, P., Shaw, E., Collins, H.: The politeness effect: pedagogical agents and learning outcomes. Int. J. Hum.-Comput. Stud. **66**(2), 98–112 (2008). doi:10.1016/j.ijhcs.2007.09.003

Adaptive and Cooperative Model of Knowledge Management in MOOCs

María Luisa Sein-Echaluce[1], Ángel Fidalgo-Blanco[2],
and Francisco J. García-Peñalvo[3(✉)]

[1] GIDTIC Research Group, University of Zaragoza, Zaragoza, Spain
mlsein@unizar.es
[2] LITI Laboratory, Technical University of Madrid, Madrid, Spain
angel.fidalgo@upm.es
[3] GRIAL Research Group, University of Salamanca, Salamanca, Spain
fgarcia@usal.es

Abstract. One of the characteristics of Massive Open Online Courses (MOOC) is the heterogeneity of their participants' profiles and, for the most traditional MOOC model, this is an important cause of the low completion rate. The MOOC model presents two apparent antagonistic concepts, globalization and diversity. MOOCs represent globalization (participants have to be adapted to the course) and their participants represent diversity. The authors of this paper argue that both concepts complement each other; that is, a MOOC can adapt the contents and navigation to the diversity of participants; and in turn the participants themselves can increase and improve the contents of the MOOC, through heterogeneous cooperation, to encourage massive learning. To proof it, this paper presents a new model, called ahMOOC, combining the hybrid-MOOC (hMOOC) and the adaptive MOOC (aMOOC). The hMOOC allows integrating characteristics of xMOOCs (based on formal e-training) with cMOOCs (based on informal and cooperative e-training). The aMOOC offers different learning strategies adapted to different learning objectives, profiles, learning styles, etc. of participants. The ahMOOCs continues having a lower dropout rate (such as hMOOC) than the traditional MOOCs. The qualitative analysis show the capacity of participants, with heterogeneous profiles, to create, in a cooperative and massive way, useful knowledge to improve the course and, later, to apply it in their specific work context. The study also shows that participants have a good perception on the capabilities of the ahMOOC to adapt the learning process to their profiles and preferences.

Keywords: Adaptive learning · Massive open online course · Online learning · Learning management system

1 Introduction

The most commonly used Massive Open Online Courses (MOOCs), called xMOOCs, have a structure very similar to academic online courses (with similar platforms, methodologies and objectives).

© Springer International Publishing AG 2017
P. Zaphiris and A. Ioannou (Eds.): LCT 2017, Part I, LNCS 10295, pp. 273–284, 2017.
DOI: 10.1007/978-3-319-58509-3_22

The educational model is based on a traditional academic model (formal learning): content organization into modules with objectives, descriptive videos and evaluation activities (tests and academic works). In spite of this, there are very significant differences with the traditional education models: heterogeneity and overcrowding. A type X MOOC can have thousands of enrolled people with a very heterogeneous profile.

The thousands of participants are multicultural (from dozens of different countries), intergenerational (all age ranges), with different objectives (which do not always coincide with the initials ones), plurality of professions and roles in aspecific context (in education: teachers, students, managers, professionals, retirees, etc.), with different academic grades (from basic levels of studies to doctorate) [1].

In the formal education processes, participants have restrictions and conditions in the courses and the most important are the number of attendees and the required previous knowledge.

The number of attendees is usually predefined in each course, academic area and country. Usually a maximum number of people per course is fixed. This is because overcrowding is an aspect related to learning outcomes.

The other conditioning aspect is the required previous knowledge that is necessary to attend a particular course. This prior knowledge is usually conditioned by academic certifications, which require the passing of certain subjects, or a level of studies such as, for example, to start university studies.

However, in the xMOOCs created by universities these limitations are not contemplated. There is no limit on the number of participants in a MOOC and there are no demands on the required academic levels.

Thus, in xMOOCs use usual platforms and educational methods of online learning, but without the limitations of overcrowding, educational level, age, or even academic degree. These conditions have often been mentioned as the main causes of the very high dropout rate and learning failure associated with MOOCs (between 90% and 95%).

Previous research works seek to improve the success of xMOOCs by combining strategies of cMOOCs (based on connectivism and incorporating cooperative work) with those of type X. These MOOCs are called hybrid MOOCs (hMOOCs) [2].

Other important line is based on personalized learning, one of the important trends in Educational Technology for Higher Education according to NMC Horizon Report: 2017 Higher Education Edition [3], which applies different learning techniques depending on the characteristics of the participants. But to carry out such personalization, the use of a technological systems is essential, taking into account its capabilities regarding adaptability (the participant chooses within the system according to its characteristics) and adaptivity (the system decides depending on the characteristics of the participant) [4, 5].

We are going to denominate Adaptivity to the capacity of a system to facilitate the two previous options. But the educational model must also have these characteristics in order to allow the technology will be effective. This way, an adaptation to the great heterogeneity of the participants is achieved. The MOOCs that present functionalities and adaptive models are called adaptive MOOCs (aMOOCs) [6].

The hMOOCs integrate Learning Content Management Systems (LCMS) platforms with social networks, as well as formal and informal educational methods [7, 8] and learning designs based on instructivism and connectivism [9].

On the other hand, aMOOCs have adaptive platforms that allow different kinds of personalization such as self-assessment training, adapted to the student's learning speed, adaptation of learning to different profiles/skills/interests, contributing and sharing resources among a set of users with a common interest/profile, adapted learning to the acquired knowledge (the results of the activities to be carried on), monitoring student's progress [6].

As a common nexus, the hMOOC and aMOOC proposals aim are intended to provide new models to reduce the dropout rate, taking into account both the over-crowding and the heterogeneity of its participants.

This paper aims to integrate the hMOOC and aMOOC models by adding a new characteristic component of knowledge management: integrating a bureaucratic orga-nization (represented by the common and global aspects of the MOOC) with a creative force type organization (represented by the diversity of profiles, objectives and implementation needs) [10].

The idea behind this research is that overcrowding and heterogeneity can be used as drivers to improve learning. This approach contrasts with the current vision of both face-to-face and on-line education, where overcrowding and heterogeneity are aspects that negatively influence the learning process.

The main objective of this work is to obtain a first prototype where it will be possible to show that the participants in a MOOC, with heterogeneous profiles, can create, in a cooperative and massive way, useful knowledge to improve the course and, later, to apply it in their specific work context.

The main contribution of this paper may be summarized in the following ones:

- A new MOOC model combining hMOOC and aMOOC, called ahMOOC. It pre-sents a technological framework with a prototype.
- An analysis of the participants' capabilities to create knowledge that improves the MOOC itself. This ability to create knowledge would be independent of their academic or professional profile, and their objectives regarding the MOOC.
- The multicultural and heterogeneous perception of the participants, to apply, outside the context of the MOOC, the acquired knowledge in the course itself, as well as the resources created by other participants, even if they do not share the same academic or professional profile or the same objectives about the MOOC.
- The participants' perception about the adaptive characteristics of the ahMOOC, which allow a course with a global design to be adapted to the diversity of par-ticipants' profiles.

The rest of the paper is organized as follows: Sect. 2 describes the proposed model and Sect. 3 presents the context where the prototype was built and the experience was realized. Section 4 includes the results of the experience. Finally, Sects. 5 and 6 include the discussion of the results and conclusions of the work.

2 Conceptual Model of ahMOOC

The proposed model is based on the integration of two already validated models by the authors of this work. The first model is the hMOOC [2] that has been tested on the MiriadaX platform throughout 7 MOOCs (20,000 students). This model includes the characteristics of both xMOOCs and cMOOCs types [1]. The second model, which has been also developed by the authors, is the aMOOC model. This model is experimental and has been validated during the 2015–2016 academic year through 4 aMOOCs interconnected throughout the virtual campus iMOOC [6].

The ahMOOCs are the result of the integration of both models, achievingresource-based MOOCs, supported by social networks and adaptive systems.

2.1 Methodological Model

Figure 1 shows an overview of the model that is composed of four parts, all integrated with each other, but with specific and distinct missions.

Figure 1-a represents the *learning resources* of the course. The organization of the resources is based on xMOOCs. That is, the contents are organized in modules and sections, following a hierarchical structure as an index. The main difference is that in

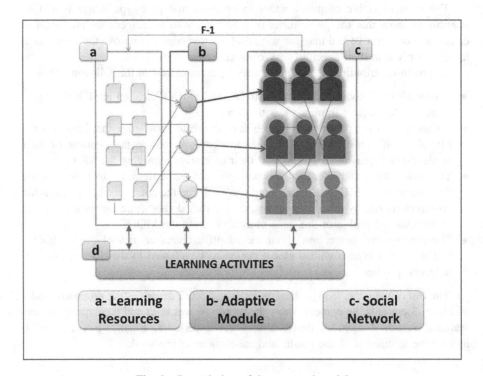

Fig. 1. General view of the proposed model

the proposed model resources are conditioned. Conditional resources are configured as accessible depending on whether a set of conditions are met, resulting from the user's interaction with the course contents.

Figure 1-b represents the *adaptive module*. This module is responsible for interacting with users and, depending on this interaction, selecting the most appropriate resources for each user profile [11]. Thus, it is able to establish different resources and activities based on adaptive processes such as previous knowledge, learning outcome or user profile. This module includes the adaptive indicators of a construct, already validated in a previous work through the perception of participants about the importance of including adaptive actions in the MOOCs [12].

Figure 1-c represents *the students and the social networks*. Unlike other MOOC models, the student profile is taken into account for the realization of the learning process. Both the learning resources and the activities to be carried out may depend on several factors that are associated with the user profile or their educational interests. Also, all users share the same social network, where they can interact with each other, regardless of the profiles.

There exists a duality where, from formal education, they receive specific and concrete resources for each situation, but on the other hand, all of them share a common space where they can exchange resources, information and contacts. The social network remarkable feature is the ability to allow asynchronous communications around the shared resources. For this reason, it can be used from a forum to a social network to carry out this activity.

Figure 1-d represents the*learning activities*. They could be of any type; the remarkable thing is that there are activities that are done specifically by a group of users and whose results are shared in the same group; by the way, other activities are carried out on the social network and these are shared with all users. rivers. The result of the developed activities in the MOOC can be shared in social networks and on the contrary also. That is, the result of activities in social networks can be shared in the MOOC too. This transfer of knowledge is represented by the data flow "F – 1" in Fig. 1. The resources that pass from the social network to the MOOC are reviewed, filtered and selected by the teaching staff.

2.2 Technological Model

The technological model is based on the technological framework presented by the same authors [9] and is based on a technological ecosystem [13, 14], where modules may be added to interact with each other sharing learning resources and integrating technologies. In this case, the proposed ecosystem includes an eLearning platform, an adaptive module, a social web component and a knowledge management system.

The eLearning system is based on the Moodle platform [15], which allows to organize the resources and activities under a classic model of axMOOC. The adaptive module is implemented in the own Moodle through techniques and processes that allow to detect different adaptive processes. The platform where the adaptive module is integrated and the eLearning system is called iMOOC. The social web module is comprised of a social network in Google+, where useful resources and the results of the course activities are provided; also, a blog topost reflections is available.

3 Context of the Experience

The presented research has been carried out from the data obtained in the first edition of the "iMOOC" campus about Educational Innovation, developed during the last quarter of 2015 and the first of 2016.

This campus is made up of four related aMOOCs, since the topics covered in each aMOOC are complementary to the application of educational innovation. The four aMOOCs are as follows:

- PFEI - Practical Fundamentals of Educational Innovation [16].
- FT - Flip Teaching [17].
- LC - Learning Communities [18].
- TWCD - TeamWork Competence Development [19].

PFEI gives the conceptual support to any application of educational innovation, therefore it is related to the rest of the aMOOCs due to it allows to provide the bases of any educational innovation.

FT works with the Flip Teaching methodology, which can be applied to any learning situation, for example with teamwork and with learning communities.

LC allows the use of learning communities as a learning objective or as a complement to other methodologies of educational innovation.

TWCD allows apply teamwork to any other educational methodology.

Thus, MOOCs are related, but can also be done independently.

Below are some results of this implementation, starting with the completion rates in the four aMOOCs and the data collected throughout an opinion survey, filled out by the participants who completed each of the aMOOCs.

4 Results

4.1 Completion Rate

In this edition, 870 people with different profiles and belonging to 27 different countries have been registered, with a majority distribution in Spanish-speaking countries. In addition, participants present a great diversity in terms of profession, academic degree, previous experience and motivation to participate in the MOOC [6, 11, 12].

Table 1 shows the number of participants in each MOOC, ending rate (the completion is obtained when all the evaluation activities have been carried out), and the type of evaluation activity that has been completed in each MOOC.

Evaluation activities include forums or learning communities where interacting, sharing contents or delivering the final project of the course. This final project is an action plan where the participants should apply the acquired knowledge in the MOOC to their future work.

Table 1. Number of participants, completed and surpassed in each aMOOC

aMOOC\Role	Participants	Ending rate (%)	Evaluation activity
LC	203	27.09	Project making and community
TWCD	87	55.17	Forums of opinion and content sharing
FT	162	25.93	Video tuning and project making
PFEI	209	26.32	Project making
Global	661	30.26	

From a global perspective, the 30.26% of enrolled students completed different MOOCs and, individually, the completion rate exceeded 25% in all courses.

4.2 Opinion Poll

A final survey was made to the participants of the different MOOCs based on the modified SEEQ model for MOOC [9], which studies the dimensions: Learning (5 questions), Enthusiasm (4 questions), Contents (3 questions), Organization (5 questions) and Workload (4 questions). Moreover, questions on adaptivity were included in the Organization dimension.

We have chosen a representative question of each of the firsts three dimensions: Learning (Q1), Enthusiasm (Q2) and Contents (Q3) and 3 questions on adaptivity (Q4, Q5 and Q6) that are included in the Organizational dimension. The choice was made based on the initial research work goal (the creation of useful knowledge), application of knowledge and adaptivity indicators.

The answers have been organized based on the Likert 4 scale (1-none agree, 2-somewhat agree, 3-fairly agree and 4 agree). The values (in percentage) of the questions in each aMOOC are included. All the questions that are presented in this work have been made in all aMOOC. The number of valid responses for each aMOOC has been 57 for CA, 57 for TE, 43 for FE and 46 for FPIE, and in all cases, they exceed 100% of participants who completed the activity successfully.

Table 2 shows the percentage of responses for each value of the Likert scale for question Q1: "In this course, I have learned things that I consider valuable", which is representative of the Learning dimension. Table 3 shows the answers for question Q2: "The way of presenting the contents keeps my attention" that represents the Enthusiasm dimension. Table 4 shows the answers to question Q3: "The provided information by the participants in the forums has been useful to assimilate concepts", which is representative of the Content dimension.

Table 2. Percentage of answers to question Q1 for each aMOOC

aMOOC\Likert	1	2	3	4
LC	1.75	1.75	31.58	64.71
TWCD	0	2.17	21.74	76.09
FT	0	0	25.58	74.42
PFEI	0	1.75	29.82	68.42

Table 3. Percentage of answers to question Q2 for each aMOOC

aMOOC\Likert	1	2	3	4
LC	0	12.28	36.84	50.68
TWCD	0	10.87	30.43	58.7
FT	0	4.65	18.6	76.74
PFEI	0	10.53	43.86	45.61

Table 4. Percentage of answers to question Q3 for each aMOOC

aMOOC\Likert	1	2	3	4
LC	5.26	24.56	35.09	35.09
TWCD	6.52	26.09	29.13	28.26
FT	4.65	18.6	32.56	44.19
PFEI	3.51	22.81	52.63	21.05

Table 5. Percentage of answers to question Q4 for each aMOOC

aMOOC\Likert	1	2	3	4
LC	0	5.26	31.58	63.16
TWCD	0	2.17	39.13	58.7
FT	0	2.33	25.58	72.09
PFEI	0	7.02	26.32	66.67

Table 6. Percentage of answers to question Q5 for each aMOOC

aMOOC\Likert	1	2	3	4
LC	0	8.77	24.56	66.67
TWCD	2.17	2.17	17.39	78.26
FT	0	2.33	25.58	72.09
PFEI	3.51	3.51	29.82	63.16

Tables 5 and 6 show the answers for question Q4: "The generation of a course that fits the participant's interests has been well designed" and for question Q5: "Making the resources visible according to my learning pacehas helped me", which are related to adaptivity. Table 7 presents the answers to question Q6: "The proposed activities generate material that is useful after the course ends", which is about the usefulness of the application of the proposed tasks. These three questions are representative of the Organization dimension.

Table 7. Percentage of answers to question Q6 for each aMOOC

aMOOC\Likert	1	2	3	4
LC	0	8.77	29.82	61.4
TWCD	4.35	10.87	34.78	50
FT	4.65	0	25.58	69.77
PFEI	0	8.77	29.82	61.4

5 Discussion

The technological framework is based on the model proposed by the authors in an earlier publication [9]. The supposed flexibility of this model is demonstrated in this work due to it is successfully applied in MOOCs, which integrate innovative features of other models such as hMOOC and aMOOC. Therefore, it demonstrates the versatility and applicability of the proposed technological framework.

Likewise, the proposed model has achieved an average of 30% final results, which represents a considerable difference over the common success rate in xMOOCs, which is between 5% and 10% [1].

Regarding the completion rate, we can compare the results of the PFEI aMOOC with MOOCs with the same contents, which was performed in MiriadaX with an exclusively hMOOC model. The completion mean of the hMOOCs was 25.16% versus 26.32% of the new model performed in this study.

The percentages are similar, however there exists a very important difference. While the evaluation activities in the MiriadaX platform courses are simple tests in each module, in this proposal, the evaluation consisted in the elaboration of a final project the included activities and applied knowledge of each of the modules. Therefore, although the completion rate is very similar, the difficulty and complexity to complete the proposed MOOCs in this model is much greater.

Another comparable aspect is the SEEQ survey about learning. For example, in MiriadaX hMOOC the question about learning was 54.38% "completely in agreement" [9] compared to 68.42% in the equivalent aMOOC performed in this work, which means a considerable difference.

With regard to the original contribution in this work about the participants' ability to create useful knowledge, Table 4 shows that there is a percentage of participants that consider the content contributed are very useful (strongly agree and completely agree) and exceeds 57% in TWCD, while in the other aMOOCs this value exceeds 70%. Therefore, the users consider that they themselves have the capacity to generate useful knowledge. This perception confirms the contents contributed by the participants can improve the MOOC itself [1, 9].

Regarding the perception of the application of the created resources by other participants in their daily activities, Table 7 shows that the vast majority of participants in the MOOC consider that other users' contributions (through the evaluation activities) are useful once the course is completed. Related to this, the 84% of the participants in TWCD select the maximum values of the scale (3 and 4) and exceeds 90% in the rest of the courses, reaching 95% in the case of FT.

The perception about the proposed adaptivity of the MOOCs is highly positive, two types of adaptivity were analyzed: adaptability to the different profiles (Table 5) and adaptation to the learning pace (Table 6).

Table 5 shows that the participants agree or strongly agree that the MOOCs of this project achieved adapting the learning resources to the participants' interests in a percentage higher than 82% in PFEI, while in the rest they exceed 94%. Table 6 shows that more than 90% of the participants (in all aMOOCs) are very or completely agree with the adaptation to the learning rhythm of the MOOC didactic resources, thinking that it helped them in their learning. These results confirm these two indicators as elements of the adaptive construct for MOOCs that was validated in a previous work [12].

This work presents a prototype that has been tested and validated with more than 600 registered users. To implement this model with thousands of users, the analysis, classification, organization and use of the generated resources by the participants would be impracticable, so it is necessary to use a knowledge management system. The proposed technological framework already contemplates this possibility and in other study it has been applied successfully in the management of generated resources by the participants of a course [20].

6   Conclusions

As a general conclusion, it has been demonstrated the feasibility of the integration of MOOCs that allow the adaptivity of learning resources and activities (aMOOC) together with MOOCs that allow cooperation (hMOOC) to define the ahMOOCS. This integration has been shown to be useful for both to reduce dropout rates and to enable heterogeneous participants to produce useful resources to apply in their work context and to improve the learning resources of the ahMOOCs itself.

The ability to generate useful resources by the ahMOOC participants has been proved; thus, the need to use a knowledge management system that is in charge of classifying and organizing those resources has been justified. In this sense, diversity may be considered as a positive value for this kind of courses against the opinions that considered it as a negative issue.

Likewise, it has been demonstrated that the adaptivity in the MOOCs opens a new field of research in the technological and conceptual models. It is shown that axMOOC can combine overcrowding and personalization of learning.

This work has presented a prototype in operation, tested and validated by more than 600 users, but will continue to work on the validation of this work for MOOCs with more than 1000 participants. The work will also continue on integrating the different technologies that make up the different technological modules, extending asynchronous activities to other types of web 2.0 environments such as social networks.

Acknowledgements. This work has been partially funded by the Spanish Government Ministry of Economy and Competitiveness throughout the DEFINES project (Ref. TIN2016-80172-R).

We would like to thank the GATE Service of the Technological University of Madrid, the Government of Aragón andthe European Social Funds for their support. Finally, the authors would like to express their gratitude to the research groups (LITI, http://www.liti.es; GIDTIC, http://gidtic.com and GRIAL, http://grial.usal.es).

References

1. Fidalgo-Blanco, Á., Sein-Echaluce, M.L., García-Peñalvo, F.J.: From massive access to cooperation: lessons learned and proven results of a hybrid xMOOC/cMOOC pedagogical approach to MOOCs. Int. J. Educ. Technol. High. Educ. (ETHE) **13**, 24 (2016)
2. Downes, S.: Stephen's web (2016). http://www.downes.ca/post/65696. Accessed 20 Feb 2017
3. Adams Becker, S., Cummins, M., Davis, A., Freeman, A., Hall Giesinger, C., Ananthanarayanan, V.: NMC Horizon Report: 2017 Higher Education. The New Media Consortium, Austin (2017)
4. Berlanga, A.J., García-Peñalvo, F.J.: IMS LD reusable elements for adaptive learning designs. J. Interact. Media Educ. **11** (2005)
5. Berlanga, A.J., García-Peñalvo, F.J.: Learning design in adaptive educational hypermedia systems. J. Univ. Comput. Sci. **14**, 3627–3647 (2008)
6. Sein-Echaluce, M.L., Fidalgo-Blanco, Á., García-Peñalvo, Francisco J., Conde, M.Á.: iMOOC Platform: Adaptive MOOCs. In: Zaphiris, P., Ioannou, A. (eds.) LCT 2016. LNCS, vol. 9753, pp. 380–390. Springer, Cham (2016). doi:10.1007/978-3-319-39483-1_35
7. García-Peñalvo, F.J., Griffiths, D.: Rethinking informal learning. In: Alves, G.R., Felgueiras, M.C. (eds.) Proceedings of the Third International Conference on Technological Ecosystems for Enhancing Multiculturality, TEEM 2015, Porto, Portugal, October 7–9, 2015, pp. 457–459. ACM, New York (2015)
8. Griffiths, D., García-Peñalvo, F.J.: Informal learning recognition and management. Comput. Hum. Behav. **55A**, 501–503 (2016)
9. Fidalgo-Blanco, Á., Sein-Echaluce Lacleta, M.L., García-Peñalvo, F.J.: Methodological approach and technological framework to break the current limitations of MOOC model. J. Univ. Comput. Sci. **21**, 712–734 (2015)
10. Nonaka, I., Takeuchi, H.: The Knowledge Creating Company. Oxford University Press, New York (1995)
11. Leris, D., Sein-Echaluce, M.L., Hernández, M., Fidalgo-Blanco, A.: Relation between adaptive learning actions and profiles of MOOCs users. In: Fourth International Conference on Technological Ecosystems for Enhancing Multiculturality, TEEM 2016, Salamanca 2–4 Noviembre 2016, pp. 857–863. ACM, New York (2016)
12. Lerís, D., Sein-Echaluce, M.L., Hernández, M., Bueno, C.: Validation of indicators for implementing an adaptive platform for MOOCs. Comput. Hum. Behav. (2016). doi:10.1016/j.chb.2016.07.054. (in press)
13. García-Peñalvo, F.J., Hernández-García, Á., Conde-González, M.Á., Fidalgo-Blanco, Á., Sein-Echaluce Lacleta, M.L., Alier-Forment, M., Llorens-Largo, F., Iglesias-Pradas, S.: Learning services-based technological ecosystems. In: Alves, G.R., Felgueiras, M.C. (eds.) Proceedings of the Third International Conference on Technological Ecosystems for Enhancing Multiculturality, TEEM 2015, Porto, Portugal, October 7–9, 2015, pp. 467–472. ACM, New York (2015)
14. García-Peñalvo, F.J., Hernández-García, Á., Conde, M.Á., Fidalgo-Blanco, Á., Sein-Echaluce, M.L., Alier-Forment, M., Llorens-Largo, F., Iglesias-Pradas, S.: Enhancing education for the knowledge society era with learning ecosystems. In: García-Peñalvo, F.J., García-Holgado, A. (eds.) Open Source Solutions for Knowledge Management and Technological Ecosystems, pp. 1–24. IGI Global, Hershey (2017)

15. Moodle: Moodle web (2017). http://moodle.org. Accessed 20 Feb 2017
16. PFEI: Video presentation (2016). https://prezi.com/glu0pwhpnbc3/fundamentos-practicos-de-la-innovacion-educativa/. Accessed 18 Feb 2016
17. FT: Video presentation (2016). https://www.youtube.com/watch?v=h3W1nOD3FRo&feature=youtu.be. Accessed 18 Feb 2016
18. LC: Video presentation (2016). https://innovacioneducativa.wordpress.com/2015/11/10/como-utilizar-una-red-social-para-construir-una-comunidad-de-aprendizaje/. Accessed 18 Feb 2016
19. TWCD: Video presentation (2016). https://innovacioneducativa.wordpress.com/2015/11/03/como-formar-y-evaluar-en-la-competencia-de-trabajo-en-equipo-de-forma-sencilla-el-metodo-ctmtc/. Accessed 18 Feb 2016
20. García-Peñalvo, F.J., Fidalgo-Blanco, Á., Sein-Echaluce, M.L., Conde, M.Á.: Cooperative micro flip teaching. In: Zaphiris, P., Ioannou, A. (eds.) LCT 2016. LNCS, vol. 9753, pp. 14–24. Springer, Cham (2016). doi:10.1007/978-3-319-39483-1_2

The Quality of MOOCs: How to Improve the Design of Open Education and Online Courses for Learners?

Christian M. Stracke[1,2,3,4(✉)]

[1] Open University of the Netherlands, Heerlen, The Netherlands
christian.stracke@ou.nl
[2] Korean National Open University, Seoul, Korea
[3] East China Normal University, Shanghai, China
[4] ICDE Chair in OER, Oslo, Norway

Abstract. This paper presents the current status of Open Education and MOOCs and discusses their quality following the main question: How can we introduce new design and evaluation methods and personalization strategies to improve the learning quality of Open Education? First, the dimensions of Open Education are differentiated. Then the dimensions of holistic quality development are transferred to Open Education and discussed for the design of MOOCs leading to recommendations for personalization. A new quality indicator for evaluating the quality of MOOCs is introduced: It is proposed not to measure the traditional drop-out rates but the completion of individual goals and intentions by the MOOC learner. It is concluded that Open Education and MOOCs have got the potential for the next revolution in learning experiences.

Keywords: Open Education · MOOCs · Learning quality · Design · Personalization · Evaluation · Learners · Designers · Intention · Personal goal · Quality indicator

1 Introduction

The world is changing and traditional formal education is challenged: New ways of communication and collaboration are asking for innovative learning experiences and environments and for lifelong learning. Opening up education is a holistic approach to facilitate such new learning experiences. This article analyses how we can improve the design of online courses and in particular of MOOCs to increase the learning quality and experience for learners.

2 Open Education: What Is the Current Situation?

The concepts "open" and "openness" are becoming more and more in vogue even though their concepts and descriptions are vague [1]. In many cases it is only referred to "open" and "openness" as general characteristics without any precise definition.

To avoid such confusion just mentioned above, we define Open Education as follows:

© The Author(s) 2017
P. Zaphiris and A. Ioannou (Eds.): LCT 2017, Part I, LNCS 10295, pp. 285–293, 2017.
DOI: 10.1007/978-3-319-58509-3_23

"Open Education covers and addresses all dimensions related to operational, legal and visionary aspects throughout the analysis, design, realization and evaluation of learning experiences to facilitate high quality education meeting the given situation, needs and objectives."

This definition reduces Open Education not only on the open access but includes further legal dimensions such as open licensing and open availability as well as operational dimensions such as open resources, open technologies and open standards as well as visionary dimensions such as open methodologies, open recognition and open innovations. The Fig. 1 presents the overview of the Open Education dimensions:

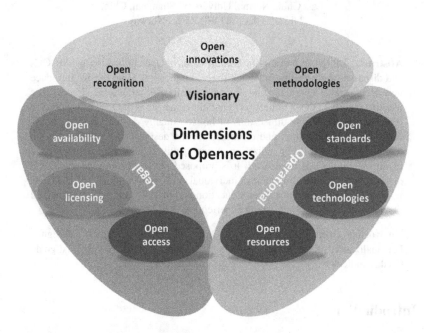

Fig. 1. Dimensions of open education [3]

However, Open Education is not a fad but an increasing requirement due to dramatic changes in societies [2]. The rise of the globalization and the establishment of the worldwide internet have strongly changed communication, business, work and leisure. People as well as organisations, communities and even whole societies are getting under pressure to adopt these changes and to face the arising challenges in business, individual and social life. That leads to new demands for alternative and innovative approaches and concepts in education. Orientation on key (or also so-called "21st century") competences, practical relevance and lifelong learning are three core requests on Therefore, open education is garnering interest as well as spurring adaptations, implementations, and success.

While these Open Education developments were taking root, another phenomenon suddenly appeared and changed the public discussion on open courses: Massive Open Online Courses (MOOCs). Currently the quality of MOOCs is questioned based on the high drop-out and non-completion rates. One main reason is that the concept of quality development is (still) not introduced in the design of Open Education and MOOCs [3] what is ignoring the long-term research and analysis of its relevance for learning processes in general [5].

3   Quality in Open Education

We could conclude in former articles [4, 6] that (learning) quality is most important for learning, education and training. The debates on holistic quality management and on learning quality are very old [7, 8, 9], but discussions and theories on quality development in learning and education only began a few years ago [5].

The concept and philosophy of holistic quality development with a continuous improvement cycle was first introduced in Japan and quickly gained recognition, acceptance, and inspire implementations worldwide [10, 11]: A long-term debate has focused on quality development in general regarding the different quality issues, aspects and approaches [5]. In its broadest sense, quality development can be defined as covering 'every kind of strategy, analysis, design, realization, evaluation, and continuous improvement of the quality within given systems' [6]. Thus, quality development is described formally by the chosen paradigm and adapted approach: Quality is not a fixed characteristic belonging to subjects or systems but rather depends on adapting to specific situations.

Holistic (also called "Total") quality management is divided into three generic quality dimensions: potential, processes and results [12]. Quality assurance is the pure focus on the results (e.g., screws), whereas quality management includes also the processes and their optimization (e.g., the production of screws). The third dimension potential that is addressed by holistic quality management is often not addressed as it requires continuous formative and summative evaluation, needs analysis and improvements based on their results (e.g., new business models and types of screws).

Due to the dramatic changes in societies, openness and open education are becoming not only more and more in vogue, but also vital: It is not a fashion but an increasing requirement [2]. To address and meet the societal challenges, we have transferred and applied the three generic quality dimensions (potential, processes and results) to Open Education by relating them to objectives (from designers as well as from learners), realization (including both, design and learning processes) and achievements (related to both objectives) as illustrated in Fig. 2 [3].

Open Education and learning, education and training in general constitute a special field: Not tangible products are sold but learning opportunities are provided as intangible offers and services that are targeting on learning results as achievements to be built by the learners themselves and not by the learning providers. In consequence, one learning opportunity is not fitting to all potential learners and the quality can only be assessed and measured individually. And in particular in MOOCs with their mass audience there are plenty of different individual motivations, intentions and goals that should be considered already during the design processes before and as well as during the learning processes and experiences themselves [26].

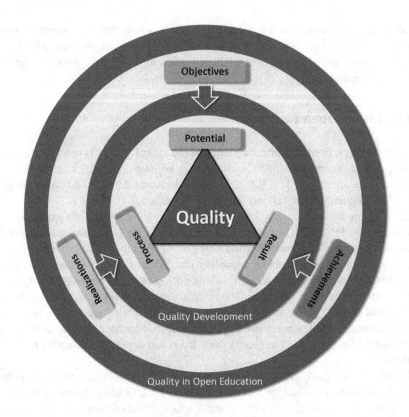

Fig. 2. Quality dimensions in open education [3]

4 Drop-Out Rates and Quality Indicators in MOOCs

In Open Education, the new term MOOC has immediately attracted the masses, despite the fact that it is just another label for a diversity of different online learning scenarios and methodologies that were already developed and implemented many years before [13]. On the one hand, MOOCs can be seen as a product and in this sense they are a special type of Open Educational Resources (OER). On the other hand, MOOCs can also be considered and defined as a learning process or experience and in this sense they are a special type of technology-enhanced learning, also called e-learning, piquing interest anew and offering opportunities to once again reach learners that are attracted toe-learning solutions for many reasons [14]. Discussions of Open Education and e-Learning revealed their historical development and interdependences [3, 4].

Thus, MOOCs can be the facilitators for a renaissance of e-learning and for a broad implementation of online learning even though their completion rates are very low and their general quality is questionable and currently under lively debate [15]. Nowadays, different types of MOOCs (mainly cMOOCs and xMOOCs plus many others) are discussed, but the focus is still on the masses, on technology and promised innovations that are not easy to discover: Most MOOCs lack continuous tutoring and support for all learners who are expected to teach themselves [2, 13]. Having high drop-out rates raised the question of quality regarding MOOCs that currently is discussed heavily [16].

We believe that high drop-out rates are the wrong measure for the success of MOOCs and are only demonstrating the diversity of motivations and personal goals that MOOC learners are bringing with them: In common understanding the drop-out rates are measured against the completion of the MOOC, i.e., fulfillment of all assigned tasks and examinations and of all learning objectives intended and defined by the MOOC designer [25, 26]. But a small online pre-survey (n = 45, the whole results are currently analysed and published soon) has revealed that many MOOC learners do not share the intentions of the MOOC designer and have got their own personal goals like e.g., simple download of all available materials for their self-regulated learning and review. In many cases the MOOC learners have fulfilled their own personal goals and should be considered as successful MOOC completions but are counted as drop-outs as they have not completed the MOOC and its assigned tasks and examinations [25]. Consequently drop-out rates measured in the traditional way against completion should be high indicating the diversity of personal goals and their achievement in many different ways. In addition personalization should be manifold so that MOOC learners can select their own learning pathway according to their individual goals: By facilitation such personalization, MOOCs can pave a path for the future opening up of education to improve the learning quality [3].

Alternatively we propose that another quality indicator for MOOCs is introduced and that the concept drop-out rate should be defined differently. MOOC learners should only be counted as drop-outs if they fail to achieve their personal goals. Consequently the individual goal achievement rate would be the quality indicator for MOOCs that have to offer appropriate personalization to allow such individual learning pathways and results.

Based on our analysis above related to the three dimensions of holistic quality development and the identified need to focus the different individual goals and intentions by the MOOC learners, we can draw consequences and recommendations for MOOC designers to address this variety and to increase the fitting of MOOCs to the learners interests and demands as shown in the following Table 1.

Table 1. MOOC learners' requirements and design recommendations

	Requirements by MOOC learners	Recommendation for MOOC designers
Objectives	Many different individual goals for MOOC registration	Ask for individual learning objectives and their reflection
Realization	Many different learning strategies used in the MOOC	Offer personalization of learning pathways in the MOOC
Achievements	Many different intentions what to achieve in the MOOC	Measure MOOC success according to individual goals and intentions

To research and analyse the details how to evaluate and personalize MOOCS, we have established the European initiative MOOQ for the quality of MOOCs aiming at the development and evaluation of a common Quality Reference Framework and quality indicators for improving, assessing and comparing the quality of MOOCs in close cooperation with all interested MOOC designers, learners, providers and policy makers in

Europe and worldwide [17]: First activity is the launch of three online surveys for the different target groups of MOOC learners, designer and facilitators. Based on their analysis results, semi-structured interviews will ask MOOC designer, facilitator, providers and policy makers for their experiences and demands. Final aim is the validation of design patterns and tools to facilitate and improve the MOOC development for designers and the MOOC learning experiences for learners.

5 Is Open Education the Next Revolution?

According to Marx, a revolution is the complete change of the production relations and means and their new ownership and direction towards changed production power [18]. In relation to open education, the current question is whether open education is indeed a social revolution for individual learners, educational institutions, and global society, or whether MOOCs, the most prominent method of open learning, are only marketing instruments by the traditional educational providers with high reputation. The debate has started immediately after the successful launch and broad recognition of MOOCs in the mass media. The high drop-out rates have led to criticism and currently MOOCs are already declared as dead. Ensuing research on alternative quality indicators and personalization for MOOCs has already started and will provide further findings for future discussion soon.

This paper can only initiate the discussion on the impact of open education that was brought to the mass media and audiences thanks to the appearance of MOOCs. We are convinced that a change of the perspective and of the quality indicators to measure the success of MOOCs as proposed above will demonstrate the potentials that MOOCs can offer. It is necessary for future research and publications to focus on these challenges and provide more MOOC cases with personalization for all MOOC learners for further discussion.

We believe in education as a human right and public good as defined in the Sustainable Development Goal no. 4 by the United Nations [19] and that learning and education need to be changed to keep this status due to major global challenges [2]. The overview of the quality and future of open education and MOOCs has presented the needs and potential approaches to satisfy these requirements, along with how we can achieve higher learning quality by opening up education and introducing open learning innovations [3]. Current main movements in open education such as the global Open Educational Resources (OER) initiative launched with the UNESCO OER Forum (already in 2002) [20] and OER Declaration [21], the International Community for Open Research and Open Education (ICORE) [22] and Opening Up Education by the European Commission [23] are addressing the demand how to change future education. First evaluation frameworks and instruments are developed to assess the importance of open learning and open education for our future and the positive impact on our personal lives and developments as well as on all societies worldwide [24]: Future research should address and investigate the evaluation of Open Education and its impact in innovating learning experiences and quality education and in effects to improve personal development and societies. Then it can maybe be proven that Open Education and MOOCs are introducing the next revolution in learning experiences.

6   Conclusions and Future Work

Open Education and in particular MOOCs have the potential to change and improve future learning experiences. This paper identifies the need for new quality strategies and measures beyond misleading drop-out rates and for looking into all three dimensions of Open Education to meet the learners' requirements and intentions. It is proposed that quality indicators for MOOCs have to take into consideration and evaluate the individual goals and intentions of MOOC learners. And also the MOOC design has to address and facilitate this diversity of different personal motivations, intentions and targeted achievements. That can be realized in MOOCs by asking for individual learning objectives and their reflection, offering personalization of learning pathways in MOOCs and by measuring the success of MOOCs according to individual goals and intentions. Further research is needed to investigate how the different groups of MOOC learners with their specific intentions can be addressed by providing personalized learning experiences in MOOCs as well as to assess the impact of Open Education in the society.

A first step and activity towards this vision and need was the launch of the Global Survey on the Quality of MOOCs [27]. This survey was designed and organized by MOOQ, the European Alliance for the quality of MOOCs [17]. Through the involvement and support by the leading European and international associations and institutions including four United Nation's organizations, the survey has gained a huge recognition and was promoted worldwide. First results will be presented and discussed at the World Learning Summit 2017 [28] as well as in further workshops open for all interested stakeholders.

This debate including all stakeholders will lead to the design of a Quality Reference Framework (QRF). Based on the survey results the QRF draft with quality indicators and tools for MOOCs will be developed and discussed in close collaboration with all interested international stakeholders. It is intended to share and discuss the first draft of the QRF at the Second Open Educational Resources (OER) World Conference by UNESCO taking placing in September 2017 [29]. All discussions, contributions, review and evaluation cycles will lead to valuable instruments for designers and facilitators to improve future MOOCs for all learners worldwide.

Acknowledgments. This article is supported by MOOQ, the European Alliance for Quality of Massive Open Online Courses (www.MOOC-quality.eu). The vision of MOOQ is to foster quality in MOOCs leading to a new era of learning experiences. MOOQ is funded by the European Commission under the project number: 2015-1-NL01-KA203-008950.

References

1. Wiley, D.: Defining "Open" (2009). http://opencontent.org/blog/archives/1123
2. Stracke, C.M.: The need to change education towards open learning. In: Stracke, C.M., Shamarina-Heidenreich, T. (eds.) The Need for Change in Education: Openness as Default?, pp. 11–23. Logos, Berlin (2015). http://www.learning-innovations.eu

3. Stracke, C.M.: Openness for learning quality and change by open education in theory and practice - overview, history, innovations and policies: how can open learning, OER and MOOCs achieve impact for learners, organizations and in society? In: Amiel, T. (ed.) Utopias and Dystopias in Education, Sao Paulo: UNICAMP (2016, in print)

4. Stracke, C.M.: Learning innovations and learning quality: relations, interdependences, and future. In: Stracke, C.M. (ed.) The Future of Learning Innovations and Learning Quality. How do they fit together?, pp. 13–25. Gito, Berlin. http://www.learning-innovations.eu

5. Stracke, C.M.: Process-oriented Quality Management. In: Ehlers, U.-D., Pawlowski, J.M. (eds.) Handbook on Quality and Standardisation in E-learning, pp. 79–96. Springer, Berlin (2006)

6. Stracke, C.M.: Open learning: the concept for modernizing school education and lifelong learning through the combination of learning innovations and quality. In: Stracke, C.M. (ed.) Learning Innovations and Quality: The Future of Digital Resources, pp. 15–28. Logos, Berlin (2013). http://www.learning-innovations.eu

7. Juran, J.M. (ed.): Quality Control Handbook. McGraw-Hill, New York (1951)

8. Deming, W.E.: Quality, productivity and competitive position. MIT, Cambridge (1982)

9. Crosby, P.B.: Quality is Free. The Art of Making Quality Certain. McGraw-Hill, New York (1980)

10. Juran, J.M.: Juran on Quality by Design. The New Steps for Planning Quality into Goods and Services. Free Press, New York (1992)

11. Deming, W.E.: Out of the Crisis. MIT, Cambridge (1986)

12. Donabedian, A.: The Definition of Quality and Approaches to Its Assessment (Explorations in Quality Assessment and Monitoring, vol. 1. Health Administration Press, Ann Arbor (1980)

13. Daniel, J.: Making Sense of MOOCs: Musings in a Maze of Myth, Paradox and Possibility (2012). http://sirjohn.ca/wordpress/wp-content/uploads/2012/08/120925MOOCspaper2.pdf. Accessed 02 Nov 2012

14. Downes, S.: E-learning 2.0. In: eLearn Magazine, October 2005. http://elearnmag.acm.org/featured.cfm?aid=1104968

15. Margaryan, A., Bianco, M., Littlejohn, A.: Instructional quality of massive open online courses (MOOCs). Comput. Educ. **80**, 77–83 (2015)

16. Reich, J.: Rebooting MOOC research. Science **347**(6217), 34–35 (2015)

17. MOOQ. www.MOOC-Quality.eu

18. Marx, K.: Capital. A Critique of Political Economy. Volume I: Book One: The Process of Production of Capital. Progress Publishers, Moscow (1887). http://synagonism.net/book/economy/marx.1887-1867.capital-i.html

19. United Nations: Sustainable Development Goals. New York: United Nations (2016). http://sustainabledevelopment.un.org/sdgs

20. UNESCO: Forum on the Impact of Open Courseware for Higher Education in Developing Countries. Final Report. Paris: UNESCO (2002). http://unesdoc.unesco.org/images/0012/001285/128515e.pdf

21. UNESCO: 2012 Paris OER Declaration. 2012 World Open Educational Resources (OER) Congress. Paris: UNESCO (2012). http://www.unesco.org/new/fileadmin/MULTIMEDIA/HQ/CI/CI/pdf/Events/Paris%20OER%20Declaration_01.pdf

22. ICORE. www.ICORE-online.org

23. European Commission: Opening up Education: Innovative teaching and learning for all through new Technologies and Open Educational Resources. [COM(2013) 654 final] (2013) http://eur-lex.europa.eu/legal-content/EN/TXT/PDF/?uri=CELEX:52013DC0654&from=EN

24. Stracke, C.M.: Evaluation framework EFI for measuring the impact of learning, education and training. 华东师范大学学报(自然科学版). J. East China Normal Univ. **2014**(2), 1–12 (2014). Shanghai: ECNU. doi:10.3969/j.issn.1000-5641.2012.02.012, http://www.opening-up.education

25. Gollwitzer, P.M., Sheeran, P.: Implementation intentions and goal achievement: a meta-analysis of effects and processes. Adv. Exp. Soc. Psychol. **38**, 69–119 (2006)

26. Baek, J., Shore, J.: Promoting student engagement in MOOCs. In: Proceedings of the Third (2016) ACM Conference on Learning @ Scale - L@S 2016, pp. 293–296. ACM Press, New York (2016). http://doi.org/10.1145/2876034.2893437

27. Global Survey on the Quality of MOOCs. www.survey.MOOC-Quality.eu

28. World Learning Summit. www.worldlearningsummit.com

29. UNESCO Second World Open Educational Resources (OER) Conference. http://en.unesco.org/events/2nd-world-open-educational-resources-oer-congress

E-Learning Supported Martial-Arts-Training

Armin Vahidi[✉] and Nicholas H. Müller

Media-Psychology, Faculty of Humanities, Chemnitz University of Technology,
Thüringer Weg 11, 09126 Chemnitz, Germany
armin.vahidi@stabile-ing.de,
nicholas.mueller@phil.tu-chemnitz.de

Abstract. Teaching martial-arts techniques is one of the most time consuming training activities within the domain of sports. Electronic support to teach movements, techniques and correct body postures is already an increasing factor in the martial-arts. One of the main goals of the martial-arts technique WingTsun is obstructing the reach and efficacy of an opponent's weapons (fists, elbows, knees, feet, head) while attempting to incapacitate. The various approaches to achieving this goal are constantly being refined and evaluated. For this project, data will be collected from various test subjects via motion trackerover the course of one year. All test subjects will receive the same amount of schooling from the same instructor. But one group will be equipped with an additional E-learning self-assessment tool. Both groups will be monitored via motion-trackers throughout the entire training interval (approximately 12 months). The data will then by analyzed regarding the efficacy of E-learning pertaining to an overall improvement and/or a faster advance thereof. The paper will detail the training program, the motion-tracker setup as well as future use cases.

Keywords: Martial-arts · Motion-tracking · E-Learning

1 Introduction

In reality, flight should always surpass as a preferred option to fighting. Yet WingTsun also emphasizes the preventive qualities of offensive measures. The goal is to prevent the entire scope of an attack. A proactive approach is recommended in order to familiarize beginners with a swift and realistic minimum capability to defend themselves [3]. Throughout the unfolding of a conflict the preliminary affirmative use of voice and facial expression, especially eye-contact, and the positioning of the entire body are a key to success. Since the opponent may be capable of any kind of physical attack it seems advisable for a student at beginner level to become acquainted with a universal solution, which can pre-emptively circumvent a majority of various attacks. Prerequisites of a universal solution are timing, a powerful kick at knee-height, and powerful striking. These components should suffice to incapacitate the opponent.

Traditional training aims at establishing a body unit, where maximum strength is extracted by utilizing the entire body when kicking and striking. This maximum cannot be accessed by the student without a stable stand, proper muscle tension of the torso, and various strength amplifying factors such as shifting ones weight or rotating the body [3].

© Springer International Publishing AG 2017
P. Zaphiris and A. Ioannou (Eds.): LCT 2017, Part I, LNCS 10295, pp. 294–302, 2017.
DOI: 10.1007/978-3-319-58509-3_24

The e-learning approach enriches this traditional method of teaching by adding another didactical possibility of understanding ones own movement as well as the aspired movement. It can be a visual aid as to what the pre-emptive positioning of the body should look like, how striking and kicking strength can be maximized, and in which way a preventative attack should best be carried out. Certain theories imply that motion sequences are adopted more successfully, if the test person is able to view a demonstration of these sequences repeatedly [4].

Once the aforementioned basics have been established in training, both forms of attack, namely striking and kicking, are to be performed simultaneously. Quite often this is perceived to be a difficult challenge by beginner level students. Flaws within the motion sequences are often perceived more precisely by observers. During a preventative attack, which occurs in an extremely limited time span, the entire body is utilized, different movements are initiated and carried out simultaneously (striking, kicking, pacing, rotating, stabilizing, etc.). A critical self-evaluation of this process is beyond the abilities of a student at beginner level. An observer on the other hand is able to notice whether the preliminary positioning is correct, hand and foot impact simultaneously, core stability is maintained, or the final positioning towards the opponent correlates with his positioning. This guided approach seems necessary until the student has attained an increased level of self-awareness allowing him to make these assessments on his own [5]. A motion-tracker can aid the student in controlling his motion sequences and optimizing his movements by allowing a direct and visual comparison with his trainer's movements [5]. The implementation of a motion tracker [2, 6] enables a time-independent and objective analysis of motion sequences which might be a sufficient way of reducing the time investment necessary to be trained [1].

2 Stances

In WT the universal approach is a preemptive attack in order to undermine a pending attack. It aims at incapacitating the attacker via specific kicking and striking techniques at the exact moment he is about to engage [7]. The main advantage of this approach is that the nature of the attack is of lesser importance. Regarding highly stressful situations an inexperienced participant of a fight cannot be expected to identify the nature of an attack and evaluate the appropriate response [7, 8].

The universal approach features many advantages, but it requires a lot of practice. The deconstruction of the entire process into singular motion exercises enables the correct and effective internalization of the full movement. Partner exercises mainly focus on practicing proper timing, e.g. when should the universal approach be applied. There are several factors that must be regarded in order to provide a holistic and reality-based training such as facial expressions, gestures, language, stress, surroundings, etc. These will not be considered at this point in time regarding the e-learning structure of the universal approach.

2.1 Preliminary Stances

Positioning the entire body is a key factor for a successful universal approach. The following description is based on a right handed person. For a left handed person the stance is vice versa.

The defender has an upright, but not tense, posture (image 1a, image 1b).

Head: The head rests centered between both shoulders, chin slightly pulled inwards, while stretching the crown of the upper head upwards. Image 1c depicts an ineffective posture. The head is set frontally too far beyond the torso. This posture is very common, especially amongst people who spend a majority of time working in a seated position (Fig. 1).

Fig. 1. Image 1a, Image 1b, Image 1c

Shoulders: The shoulders are relaxed beside the torso at equal hight (image 1a, image 1b). They should not be pulled upwards (image 2a) or rotated towards the hips (image 2b).

Arms: The left hand is regarded as the 'ManSao' (Image 1a, image 1b) or 'the searching hand'. The left hand is positioned concetrical to the torso. Both hands are folded upwards, open palms directed at the offender. Both ellbows are set at an angle, one more than the other, yet both pointing towards the floor. The ellbows should not point to the sides (image 2c) (Kernspecht 1994).

The right hand is regarded as the 'WuSao' or 'the protecting hand' (image 1a, image 1b). As the left hand the right one is also concetrical to the torso and at hight of the neck. In comparison to the left the right hand is positioned further back towards the torso in order to protect and also gain more momentum when striking without having to pull back and therefore sacrifice protection (Fig. 2).

The core: The core is engaged and continuously pulled inwards in order to strengthen the stance and avoid bending sideways.

Hip: Hips are parallel to the shoulders, aligning shoulders and hips. The hips should not be inverted or outverted, but placed loosely on the legbones, tailbone pulling towards the floor.

Fig. 2. Image 2a, Image 2b, Image 2c

Legs: The feet are slightly inverted and placed parallel to each other. The space inbetween the midst of the feet is in accordance to one shoulder-length. Ideally the entire body weight is on both feet. The frontal leg should always bear the same amount of weight or less than the back leg.

The entire body is aligned towards the front including eyes and hands. The body should be engaged but not tense and perform each singular movement as an entity [8].

2.2   The Universal Approach Sequences Sans Partner

The left knee is pulled upwards without adjusting the angle between calf and thigh (image 3a). Toes are engaged, pulling towards the knee in order to stabilize the foot and lower leg. The knee is pulled up to the left elbow, hence lower leg and lower arm now protect a large portion of the entire body. The sole of the foot should be visible from the front (image 3b).

Arms and legs should move simultaneously, which will require practice in order to master the correct timing (image 3c). The left hand pushes straight forward while the left foot propels a stomping kick forwards and downwards. Before the left arm is entirely stretched out the right hand surpasses, delivering the next punch, while the left hand is drawn back simultaneously (image 3d). The same process is then initiated with the left hand again, hence delivering three punches/striking/pushing movements and returning to the initial stance of ManSao/WuSao (image 3f). The energy for kicking and stomping is provided by the gluteus maximus and not by the leg muscles. The right leg accelerates the entire body by pushing into the ground and as soon as the left foot touches ground the right one is pulled along, all the while maintaining and coming back to the original stance [8]. The core is constantly engaged keeping the upper body in an upright position (Figs. 3 and 4).

Fig. 3. Image 3a, Image 3b, Image 3c

Fig. 4. Image 3d, Image 3e, Image 3f

Most common mistakes

- The arms are extended too far (image 4a)
- The torso is bent backwards (image 4b)
- The kicking leg is not pulled up to the elbow (image 4c)
- Foot and lower leg are not engaged, the knee is simply pulled upwards (image 4d)
- When kicking the foot is extended and then retracted towards the calf, creating a jerking movement instead of a stomping one
- The core is not engaged allowing the torso to bend backwards while kicking (image 4e)
- The back leg is not locked in with the rest of the movement, hence it does not follow forward. In this case after completion of the movement the entire bodyweight rests on the frontal leg (image 4f)
- Kick and punch are not synchronised, the striking does not occur until after the kick (Figs. 5 and 6).

Fig. 5.   Image 4a, Image 4b, Image 4c

Fig. 6.   Image 4d, Image 4e, Image 4f

2.3   The Universal Approach Sequences with Partner

The body is positioned as mentioned above. The distance between both training partners must be beyond kicking or striking distance (image 5a-d). This requires some experience since each partner has an individual reach [8] (Figs. 7 and 8).

Fig. 7. Image 5a, Image 5b

Fig. 8. Image 5c, Image 5d

The moment the attacking partner is about to curtail the safety perimeter with a step (image 6a) the defending partner initiates the universal approach. An important element of this exercise is reaching the attacking partners knee with the stomping kick just as he sets his foot on the ground (image 6b). It is at this exact moment that the attacker has the least amount of stability and the stomping kick has the maximum effect (Fig. 9).

Fig. 9. Image 6a, Image 6b

Simultaneously the ManSao strikes towards the attackers face. Whether the defending partner's strike reaches the face or the arm is irrelevant at this point.

As the kicking foot touches the ground the right arm takes over and strikes and the right leg is pulled in. At the same time the left lower leg is in contact with the attacking partner's leg ensuring his inability to deliver any kicks (image 6d). While the right leg pulls in, the third strike is executed, hence obtaining the original stance (image 6e) (Fig. 10).

Fig. 10. Image 6c, Image 6d, Image 6e

3   Motion-Tracking Validated E-Learning

The Prime 13 [6] measures 1.3 MP at a Framerate of 240 FPS. It has a horizontal field of view of 56°, and vertically of 46°.

For the validation, the aforementioned instructor poses will be recorded and integrated into a standard web based training software. This software will then present the poses and explain both the practical and theoretical components of each stance. Afterwards, the training process continues.

By using the same setup as for the recordings of the instructors, every two months the students' progress is recorded by the OptiTrack system. By comparing the intended body postures against the recorded ones, progress can be determined for each individual student.

4   Conclusion

Within this paper, the process of an e-learning supported martial-arts-training regiment was described. The traditional form of person-to-person instructions is a well established tradition in martial-arts-training. But while a teacher is only capable of judging correct stances and movements from a position of experience and training, motion-tracking-hardware is far more objective. Especially when studying stances in which balance and a correct weight distribution is of critical importance, the objective eye might be a very influential tool to foster the specificities of each pose.

Our preliminary tests are scheduled for the third quarter of 2017 with the start of new class of martial-arts-students.

Acknowledgements. The authors would like to thank the WinTsun Akademie Tietz and especially Mr. Blanchebarbe for the willingness to pose for this paper as well as the opportunity to work together with their students.

References

1. Burke, D.T., Protopapas, M., Bonato, P., Burke, J.T., Landrum, R.F.: Martial arts: time needed for training. Asian J. Sports Med. **2**(1), 31–36 (2011)
2. Hsu, W.-C., Shih, J.-L.: Applying augmented reality to a mobile-assisted learning system for martial arts using kinect motion capture. In: Blended Learning: Concpets, Methodologies, Tools and Applications (2017)
3. Kernspecht, K.R.: Praxisband Kampflogik! Vom Treffen und nicht getroffen werden, S. 19, pp. 42–44, 57–59 (2014)
4. Kohler, E., et al.: Hearing sounds, understanding actions. Action representation in mirror neurons. Science **297**, 846–848 (2002)
5. Meinel, K., Schnabel, G.: Bewegungslehre Sportmotorik. Abriss einer Theorie der sportlichen Motorik unter pädagogischem Aspekt, S. 179 (2007)
6. Optitrack (2016). http://optitrack.com/products/prime-13/. Accessed 11 Mar 2016
7. Kernspecht, K.R., Beitler, H.: Der Letzte wird der Erste sein- Das Geheimnis effektiver Selbstverteidigung. Wu-Shu-Verlag (2005)
8. Kernspecht, K.R.: Vom Zweikampf – Strategie, Taktik, Physiologie, Psychologie, Philosophie und Geschichte der Waffenlosen Selbstverteidigung. Wu-Shu-Verlag (1994)
9. Kernspecht, K.R.: BlitzDefence – Angriff ist die beste Verteidigung. Wu-Shu-Verlag (2008)

Beyond the Classroom

Security Beyond Secrecy

Practical Strategies to Address Emerging Cybersecurity Paradoxes Through Professional and Stakeholder Education and Co-management Architectures Designed to Cultivate Community-Situated, Non-technical Structures of Group Synthetic Intelligence (aka "Neighborhood Watch")

Scott L. David and Barbara Endicott-Popovsky[✉]

University of Washington, Seattle, WA, USA
{sldavid,endicott}@uw.edu

Abstract. Cybersecurity is changing rapidly as strategies based on secrets are losing traction on the massively interconnected and distributed Internet. This article explores emerging roles for education of cybersecurity professionals and cyber citizens and other new approaches to enhancing security. The article suggests 13 sources of insecurity that prompt new security perspectives, and how each offers an invitation to improve cybersecurity education and operations.

Keywords: Cybersecurity · Information assurance · Synthetic intelligence · Distributed security · Tools and rules

1 Introduction

This paper provides a structured discussion of the cybersecurity implications of the following 13 discreet causes and artifacts of the erosion of secrecy online, and invites responsive innovation by cybersecurity educators and professionals:

1. Death of Secrecy
2. Distributed Information Architectures Blind Hierarchical Organizations
3. The Sovereignty of Complexity
4. Socio-Technical Systems Force Non-Technical Variables Into System Design
5. Information Democratization Collapses Scale and Alters Security Paradigms
6. Data Is a "Dual Use" Technology
7. People are "Data Producers"
8. Big Data Insights Invert (and Re-invent?) Critical Analysis
9. "Synthetic Intelligence" Is a Counterforce to AI
10. The Internet is Privately-Owned/Operated Commercial Space, Not a Public Park
11. Data Is Not Information
12. Power Laws In Bureaucracies Make Security-By-Secrecy Un-Economic
13. AAA Risks Threaten Information Systems

© Springer International Publishing AG 2017
P. Zaphiris and A. Ioannou (Eds.): LCT 2017, Part I, LNCS 10295, pp. 305–323, 2017.
DOI: 10.1007/978-3-319-58509-3_25

Following this Introduction in Sect. 1, Sect. 2 sets forth the 13 issues as security problems, outlines their relationship to the erosion of secrecy, and posits emerging challenges for cybersecurity professionals and educators relating to each of the issues. In Sect. 3, the 13 issues are explored as sources of security system design solutions, and of "workforce ready"-oriented curriculum for security in a post-secrecy world.

2 Problem Statement

Cybersecurity practice and education are struggling, privacy is waning, institutions are losing control of data, individuals feel threatened, and anxiety is running high. A significant cause of these challenges are the artifacts of the habitual application of yesterday's "secrecy-based" security strategies in today's post-secrecy world, and the measurement of system performance against those out-of-date strategies. The transition to post-secrecy security is here explored through 13 different perspectives to help inform future cybersecurity operational and educational approaches. These perspectives are drawn from emerging risk vectors, many of which have not yet been addressed in cybersecurity strategies, operations or curriculum. For each of the 13 perspectives, the authors present:

1. A statement of the issue,
2. An explanation of the issue,
3. An example or description of context, and
4. Notes on impacts of the issue upon cybersecurity analysis, strategy, and education.

2.1 Death of Secrecy

Statement of the Issue. Secrecy died with the rise of the "insight-on-demand" utility we call the Internet. Insight and intrusion are two opposite ends of the information arbitrage formula. With every new insight, the level of collective intrusion deepens; and secrecy further recedes. We all seek greater insight, and tolerate intrusions on others to gain that insight; however, none of us wants to tolerate intrusions on ourselves for the benefit of others. Internet services have not yet offered a choice. Government derives information by legal compulsion; commercial services require information as a precondition for service delivery; insight advances and secrecy erodes.

Explanation of Issue. The effectiveness cybersecurity approaches that depend on secrecy is diminished in a highly distributed, massively interconnected and inter-mediated Internet, operated and used by billions of parties who are all simultaneously engaging in a collective quest for insight. Online secrecy is dead and we all killed it. Further, network security strategies built on secrecy fail to address the sources of system insecurity (i.e., accidents, acts of nature) that are aggravated by secrecy.

Example. Myriad data breaches, news leaks, forwarded emails, insider trades and other unplanned releases of data daily in the news illustrate online secrecy's demise.

Impact on Cybersecurity Analysis, Strategy and Education. The "death of secrecy" concept is offered as an observation, not a suggestion that secrecy-based strategies be abandoned. In the "arms race" of secrecy-as-a-strategy for limiting unauthorized access to data and systems, efforts to maintain secrecy (and enforcement, etc.) help serve to raise the cost of unauthorized access. We should keep working to improve secrecy protections (like cryptography, etc.) to discourage attacks, but should also recognize that secrecy is proving to be a false hope [1], and that attacks are just one set of causes of cyber-insecurity (See "AAA Risks" below).

2.2 Distributed Information Architectures Blind Hierarchical Organizations

Statement of the Issue. Distributed information architectures turn secrecy on its head, rendering hierarchical governance mechanisms (which depend on centralized information flows) blind and ungovernable.

Explanation of Issue. Nearly all human organizations rely on hierarchical governance (and corresponding centralized information flows and decision making), and are rendered blind (and ungovernable) when their institutional communications migrate to distributed information networks. In his work for the RAND Corporation, Paul Baran described a distributed communication system that could resist nuclear attack [2]. His design eliminated a single point of failure. That architecture was applied in building the Internet where that same quality results in a distributed system that resists central control. Where organizations depend on centralized communications for hierarchical decision-making, their migration to the Internet renders them operationally blind.

Example. In Paul Baran's diagrams [3] imagine that each of the dots represents an employee terminal (node) of Company X. Imagine the lines between the dots (edges) to be communications among the employees. In the left-most "centralized" network diagram, all emails pass through a single server on their way to other employees. A CEO can "tap in" to the discussion through the single, central email server. Now imagine those same employees talking about the same issue, but they move the discussion to their personal social network accounts (reflected in the right hand diagram labeled "distributed"). The CEO cannot "tap into" the discussion to inform decision-making, and is effectively blind.

Impact on Cybersecurity Analysis, Strategy and Education. Traditional cybersecurity "controls" are evaporating as Perimeter 1.0 (i.e., the measurable-performance edge of the technical elements of the organization operating system that enabled the measurements of control including secrecy) give way to Perimeter 2.0 (the currently-un-measurable edge of the behaviors of people and institutions on which an organization relies). The Internet rendered hierarchical institutions blind. In a sense, distributed architectures can "hide in plain sight" from hierarchical control structures that depend on centralized information flows. Better cyber education allows for less direct supervision of employees, and empowers neighborhood watch to emerge among citizens.

2.3   The Sovereignty of Complexity

Statement of the Issue.   Information network complexity yields unpredictable system behaviors that confound traditional cyber-risk-mitigation strategies based on historical experience and trends, and make it difficult to teach cybersecurity.

Explanation of Issue.   Mathematically complex systems display non-linear behaviors that cannot be fully predicted based on data about prior system performance. This frustrates traditional approaches to education, training and operations that apply prior experience to guide preparation for future system performance.

Example.   The continuing stream of zero-day exploits is an artifact and cause of system complexity. Other domains (e.g., financial market crises, earthquakes, hurricanes) provide examples of harm from non-linear behaviors of complex systems.

Impact on Cybersecurity Analysis, Strategy and Education.   Cybersecurity practice and teaching focused exclusively on past threats and vulnerabilities will not fully prepare cybersecurity professionals and cyber-citizens/consumers to be able to mitigate future risks. Organizations relying on "normal distribution" models to apply historical data to predict future risks will be surprised by non-linear system behaviors.

2.4   Socio-Technical Systems Force Non-technical Variables into Design

Statement of the Issue.   The reliability and predictability of information network performance depends upon the reliability of behaviors of both technologies *and* people/ institutions that together comprise those networks. Strategies focusing only on security *technology*, without attention to the hybrid "socio-technical" nature of information systems, will fail to address all of the variables that can make them *in*secure.

Explanation of Issue.   Humans have always posed a systems-engineering problem. As biological organisms with socio-psychological behavior patterns, we don't parameterize easily. The same is true of human institutions which reflect, and sometimes magnify, human traits. There are myriad implications of this expanded analysis, e.g., (i) humans and institutions are "informed" when they consume data, creating valuable information; (ii) in the cybersecurity context, *data* networks are *technology* networks, while *information* networks are *hybrid-technology-and-people/institutional* networks (see Sect. 2.6 below); (iii) wholly apart from their role as system "users," people and institutions are also the source of data as the "feedstock" of information networks (See Sect. 2.7 below), and (iv) are also system "operators," (since each has greater access and ability to transfer that information than ever before). The behaviors of people and institutions in these four roles affects cybersecurity performance and analysis.

Example.   Human and institutional behaviors (such as phishing, password sharing, equipment loss, etc.), are a significant cause of data breaches and cybersecurity risks.

Impact on Cybersecurity Analysis, Strategy and Education. Cybersecurity grew from its technical roots in such domains as computer science and engineering. Cybersecurity education and strategies, and CIOs and CTOs backgrounds–still reflect these roots. Technical perspectives are necessary, but not sufficient, for achieving comprehensive cybersecurity in an Internet-dependent world where non-technical elements (such as human psychology, market economics, workplace relations, global politics, regulatory requirements, military strategy, and social trends, etc.) affect performance.

2.5   Information Democratization Collapses Scale, Alters Security Paradigms

Statement of the Issue. The growth of Internet access has progressively democratized information, rendering prior cybersecurity strategies based on maintaining large-scale secrecy too costly and obsolete. Institutions dependent on security through secrecy are witnessing erosion of their power and authority.

Explanation of Issue. All existing institutions (political, commercial, and social) are artifacts of solutions to yesterday's problems, and were built to help leverage and de-risk interactions at the scale of risk that was relevant at their formation. Traditional cybersecurity strategies based on the ability to maintain secrets across large scale organizations has been undermined by rapid advances in communications power and data access for individuals at all levels of information networks. As power migrates to different scales, some institutional solutions become less relevant to their stakeholders. Historical organizations perceive these changes as the "collapse of scale."

Example. Examples of institutional displacement from scale collapse include the existential challenges currently faced by news organizations and library systems, and online auctions that enable global "flea markets." The democratizing information network of libraries was itself dis-intermediated by even-more-ubiquitous mobile devices.

Impact on Cybersecurity Analysis, Strategy and Education. Risks change as scale changes, and risk mitigation strategies at one scale can have negative security consequences at other scales. To encourage "distributed" structures of security, sensitivity to inter-scale impact is important. For example, at larger scales, governance depends on standards, abstractions, and measurement. At smaller scales, those "abstractions" and "standards" are frequently a poor-fit with individual and local needs, yielding a form of "violence of scale" to affected parties. Examples include the standards and rules that are applied to run large scale systems such as telco networks or credit card systems, both of which carry the burden of dealing with many customer complaints that arise from their inability to customize services in a quest for the cost reductions and leverage of scale.

2.6   Data is "Dual-Use" Technology

Statement of the Issue. Data can be used for both good and ill. Cybersecurity strategies that seek to constrain data flow in an effort to prevent bad uses will be undermined by the desire of stakeholders to access the data for good purposes.

Explanation of Issue. A single datum can be used serially, for both good and bad purposes by different data users (See Sect. 2.11). Pervasive reliance on data flow constraints (aka "secrecy") as a "best practice" for preventing bad uses may have the unintended consequence of stultifying good uses. Also, many uses of data will be perceived as "good" or "bad" depending on the parties' perspective in a given interaction. This is a consequence of the nature of information arbitrage - a single data use that is "good" for one party may be "bad" for another. Secrecy is about maintaining information differentials. How might post-secrecy trust frameworks protect against bad uses without dampening good uses?

Example. There are many technologies that have both good and bad uses including firearms, nuclear power, pharmaceuticals, explosives. These "dual use" technologies can provide guidance on programs for cybersecurity.

Impact on Cybersecurity Analysis, Strategy and Education. Since data can be used for good or ill, cybersecurity strategies based on pre-limiting use (aka "secrecy") will be strained by market and social factors. "Neighborhood watch"-based strategies might helpfully monitor distributed use. Education programs should provide tools for cyber professionals and cyber citizens to engage with such ethical use issues.

2.7 People are "Data Producers"

Statement of the Issue. Individual humans are the producers of significant valuable data that is the "feedstock" of many information markets and government applications; however, the absence of a broadly recognized and user-centric analytical and institutional structure for this production activity has the result of undermining individual interests, destabilizing data supplies, and creating harms such as privacy intrusions to people, and risks to institutions that depend on such data.

Explanation of Issue. As they say in politics "If you are not at the table, you are on the menu." The same could be said of humans as "data producers" absented from the networked information rights negotiating "table." In fact, there is no "table" in the absence of a broadly recognized conceptual, legal, economic, or social construction that recognizes people as "data producers." Efforts to stabilize the rights *and* responsibilities of people in data systems are denied the traction of a more formalized structure. This lack of structure is bad for both individual data subjects and for data users, since it results in a defensive posture for privacy and other individual rights, inconsistency of data rights feedstock for users, inability to achieve rights clearances in B2B data transfers, and a default of practices to the narrower goals of commercial online service provider terms of service. Consent is not equivalent to negotiation.

Example. An online book purchaser is the "consumer" of the book. When that book purchaser provides data to the seller (including shipping address, payment card information, etc.), the book "consumer" is also a data "producer."

Impact on Cybersecurity Analysis, Strategy and Education. The absence of frameworks that validate the role of individual data producers enables undesirable relationship dynamics that negatively affect the value of that data-in-use to the detriment of all parties, particularly in the extended secondary information supply chains of "big data." Traditional cybersecurity education (and FIPPs-based regulation) treats consumer and citizen data paternalistically, reflecting last century's dependence upon secrecy – a laudable goal that can nonetheless be contrary to individual interests.

2.8   Big Data Insights Invert (and Re-invent?) Critical Analysis

Statement of the Issue. Correlation does not equal causation. Nonetheless, big data analysis yields many correlations that attract attention and tempt decision-making, producing a secondary source of governance risk.

Explanation of Issue. Mark Twain quoted UK Prime Minister Disraeli as saying that there are three kinds of lies "lies, damn lies and statistics." The exponential increases in global ability to collect, process and transfer data provides us with huge amounts of data. Unfortunately, our ability to generate data correlations vastly exceeds our ability to investigate their underlying value as decision-making fodder. The perceived benefits of raw insight overwhelm our senses, appealing to our instincts which can overwhelm critical thinking.

Example. Correlations are rampant in the news and in organizational decision-making. In legal contexts, they are subject to limitation as "circumstantial evidence." Climate change policy (not scientific) debates pivot on causation-versus-correlation.

Impact on Cybersecurity Analysis, Strategy and Education. Big data systems are new metrics "fire hoses" that produce vast amounts of data. That data deluge presents multiple challenges for cybersecurity professionals and cyber citizens, including how to interpret relationships among that data in risk analysis. There is distinction between causal and correlative relationships, and each may inform risk mitigation analysis.

2.9   "Synthetic Intelligence" Is a Counterforce to AI

Statement of the Issue. Both "Artificial Intelligence" and "Synthetic Intelligence" are forms of non-human thinking the application of which has the potential to threaten human-led sovereignty over human affairs. AI is the source of growing governance fears and existential angst. "SI" describes systems that incorporate and "synthesize" information from multiple sources at scales that are not fully perceptible to humans, and therefore beyond their direct control. SI can be structured to include human needs as a check on potential AI excesses.

Explanation of Issue. AI is feared due to the possibility that AI systems will apply data to gain and apply insights beyond those requested or understood by humans. Knowledge equals power. AI concerns obscure attention to another related form of intelligence, "synthetic intelligence," that is just as potentially detrimental to individual human interests, but might also be recruited to constrain AI excesses. SI is enabled in those systems where people and institutions are joined together by shared rules, norms, goals, language, etc. in units which each display "intelligence" beyond the individual units. SI, as manifested in organizational syntheses of information for decision-making, can strip individuals of discretion (even while providing them a measure of risk reduction and leverage) and threatens notions of participatory engagement.

Example. SI systems include markets, supply chains, commercial and government organizations, and other "hyper-objects" [4], and other structures where insight is derived by multiple parties in excess of that available to any one party.

Impact on Cybersecurity Analysis, Strategy and Education. AI anxiety is focused on technology. SI attention is focused on technology and people/institutions. Cybersecurity strategies being proposed to deal with AI challenges should also start to deal with SI problems, such as the information arbitrage disadvantage of individual stakeholders when dealing with large institutions that enjoy multiple information inputs. AI "control" strategies can also consider SI tools for "neighborhood watch."

2.10   The Internet Is a Privately-Owned/Operated Commercial Space

Statement of the Issue. Cyberspace is mostly owned and operated by commercial organizations, which influences decision-making about its processes, rules and content. Users, cybersecurity professionals and educators who don't comprehend the implications of this commercial omnipresence will find their expectations unmet, resulting in insecurity and a loss of trust.

Explanation of Issue. State law provides that corporations are organized for profit. The Internet is mostly privately owned and operated by corporations, with the result that much of what happens online is affected by monetization goals. Where online monetization goals are inconsistent with other goals (such as security, privacy, social justice, etc.), there is little "public" process infrastructure to support the consideration of those alternative goals. This creates an "agenda gap" paradox on the Internet similar to that affecting other critical infrastructure, i.e., system management and investment decisions driven by profit-enhancement do not always align with social goals.

Example. Decisions motivated by commercial concerns can manifest in harms to individuals and entities in many markets. Examples include environmental accidents from lax maintenance, and the many schemes described in FTC enforcement actions.

Impact on Cybersecurity Analysis, Strategy and Education. Private commercial interests that host and support individual online activity derive value from insights gleaned from data and metadata that traverses the Internet. Each intermediation invites the opportunity for a party to extract value as the data passes by. In the absence of a structure of managed constraints on that activity, each insight is a potential intrusion, and each intrusion is a potential cybersecurity issue. Also, investment in cybersecurity is driven by budgetary considerations supporting profit goals. Cybersecurity risks, like other critical infrastructure failures, often manifest in this "agenda gap."

2.11   Data is not Information

Statement of the Issue.   The failure to distinguish "data" from "information" results in incomplete cybersecurity analysis and ineffective strategy and education/training.

Explanation of Issue.   Data and information are different. Information is created when a party brings meaning to data in the course of its use. Data plus meaning creates information. The failure to recognize this difference raises paradoxes that undermine cybersecurity awareness, strategy and education.

Example.   During flu season Alice and Bob post updates about their "sniffles" in an online social network. The network stores the communication as data with no value to the network until it is used. The network provides the data to a retailer, which is "informed" about the sniffles, and ships tissues to its stores located near Alice and Bob. The data, plus the meaning of that data to the retailer, creates valuable "information" for which the network charges the retailer, achieving 1× data leverage. The network then makes the same data available to a tissue manufacturer. The manufacturer is "informed" about the sniffles, infers a consumer need, and sends discount coupons to Alice and Bob. That is 2× leverage. The network then provides the data to the Center for Disease Control, which is "informed" about the sniffles, and makes an inference about a potential pandemic flu outbreak. That is 3× leverage (non-monetary value in the CDC case). One datum – three separate uses creating valuable information.

Impact on Cybersecurity Analysis, Strategy and Education.   Cybersecurity is difficult to learn and practice, and is made more difficult by ambiguity about what it is that cybersecurity is seeking to protect. Much of the focus of traditional cybersecurity education and practice was on maintaining the secrecy of data, with less regard to its value as information. Some data are more valuable as information than other data. Scarce resources force informed triage of protection of "data" vs. "information."

2.12   Power Laws in Bureaucracies Make Security-by-Secrecy Un-Economic

Statement of the Issue.   The range of interactions that take place over the Internet (and their risks) has increased exponentially. The Internet of Things (IoT) promises to continue that torrid rate of increase. Where the functional interactive "surface" of an organization increases less quickly than the costly/risky bureaucratic interaction "interior," the strain of that difference can sap organizational efficacy, and undermine efforts to regulate/mitigate risk for stakeholders dependent on the system.

Explanation of Issue.   Like an expanding balloon, the functional surface of any system increases less quickly than the volume of the interior that supports it. Distributed information networks supported by ICT technologies made massively interoperable by standards, present a potential attack surface that includes its entire "volume" of bureaucratic interactions. The cost of maintaining security of this massive and growing volume of interactions can only be sustained an equally productive (and growing) functional surface of the bureaucracy. Unfortunately, bureaucracies typically fail to maintain such surface-to-volume growth parity.

Example. Many organizations become challenged by bloated bureaucracies that have grown beyond usefulness compared to their cost. Outsourcing is evidence.

Impact on Cybersecurity Analysis, Strategy and Education. Cybersecurity based on maintaining secrets (i.e. passwords, crypto codes, confidentiality) needs to plug every possible leak in every interaction, since any weak security link breaks the chain. Unfortunately, as the volume of interactions increases exponentially, so too does the cybersecurity risk. Since budgets allocated to security do not increase exponentially, there is a quickly-widening gap. How can any company maintain the secrecy of ALL of its data even as the number of uses of that data is increasing exponentially?

2.13   Attacks, Accidents, Acts of Nature Threaten Information Systems

Statement of the Issue. Security threats are posed by Attacks, Accidents and Acts of Nature (AAA Risks). Security strategies that neglect one or more of these categories of threat are less effective than those that are designed to address a wider variety of threats.

Explanation of Issue. Traditional cybersecurity education and practice that defended data as "secrets," focused on strategies to limit the impact of attacks, typically at the expense of threats of accidents and acts of nature; both of which can also affect system performance and security. AAA risks can also aggravate and compound each other, and maintenance of secrecy can impede response to Accidents/Acts of Nature.

Example. Consider the challenges of accessing HIPAA protected (secret) medical information to identify "at risk" victims following a hurricane (Act of Nature). Also, lack of preparation for hurricanes is an accident that aggravates the hurricane's harm.

Impact on Cybersecurity Analysis, Strategy and Education. Networked information systems can be impacted by multiple threats including Attacks, Accidents and Acts of Nature (and combinations thereof). Cybersecurity strategies that ignore the direct and aggravating consequences of Accidents and Acts of nature are vulnerable to risk. Cybersecurity curriculum should include coverage of all sources of AAA risks.

3   Strategies and Solutions

This section explores some candidate strategies and solutions for improved cybersecurity, operations and education in a post-secrecy world through a compound lens of the 13 perspectives. For each of the 13 perspectives, this Sect. 3 will present:

1. A short statement of a proposed strategy/solution,

2. A description of how that strategy can support cybersecurity beyond secrecy,
3. An example or illustration, and
4. Suggested actions cyber professionals/educators can take to engage with the issue.

3.1   Death of Secrecy

Proposed Strategy/Solution. Cultivate multiple distributed "Neighborhood Watches" in each "cyber-risk-based community-of-interest." Cybersecurity beyond secrecy involves recruiting stakeholders to be part of the security solution through education and appeals to their respective self-interest, starting with those distributed solutions that can mitigate risks in ways that stakeholders cannot achieve unilaterally.

How Can Proposed Strategy Support Cybersecurity Beyond Secrecy? Security beyond secrecy can be enhanced through shared standardized norms, rules and duties that are broadly observed among human and organizational "nodes" in systems that access data and make decisions which affect the performance of the system. Education can spread these shared norms; and incentives and penalties can enforce them.

Example. Examples of security through operation of shared norms and rules includes such common structures as traffic law, markets rules, and "neighborhood watch."

Suggested Actions for Cyber Professionals and Cyber Educators. Reliable data use begins at home. Cybersecurity professionals should work with contract officers to assure that actual data flows to, from and within the organization are accurately reflected in organization contracts, which map and enforce distributed data security. Citizen cybersecurity education efforts can help to build the standard norms that can enable "neighborhood watch" to detect AAA risk.

3.2   Distributed Information Architectures Blind Hierarchical Organizations

Proposed Strategy/Solution. Apply distributed solutions to distributed problems. Distributed security can be improved by creating norms and duties where the interactions take place: the individual stakeholders. The distributed "duties" can be supported by education, and by conditioning stakeholder's rights on their duty conformance.

How Can Proposed Strategy Support Cybersecurity Beyond Secrecy? For distributed cybersecurity, we need to recruit the nodes. In a distributed system, communication between nodes can travel myriad routes, and communications can encounter multiple nodes, any one of which can potentially support or impede the communication. The nodes need to support the network. For device nodes, the question is whether their programming conforms to standard specifications. For people/institution nodes, the question is whether their behavior conforms to rules, policies, and norms. Education is key here, not just for cyber professionals, but also for cyber citizens.

Example. Website terms of service establish standard rules for users, who are interacting nodes in their system. Of course, there is no reason the data/identity space could not be self-regulated by a set of rules that are promulgated from the perspective of the individual data subject (See "people as data producers" below). Credit card systems achieve large scales by offering consumers the convenience and security of using credit cards if they are willing to self-bind to the credit card rules. The distributed architecture is based on an exchange of standard, structured promises relating to system operation. This pre-conditions each of the nodes to act in accordance with standard roles that increases reliability and performance in the system.

Suggestions of Actions That Cyber Professionals and Cyber Educators Can Take to Engage the Issue. Security strategies should include training and user engagement/ incentives for recruitment of system users into distributed "neighborhood watch" strategies for cybersecurity.

3.3 The Sovereignty of Complexity

Proposed Strategy/Solution. The best defense against complexity is joint action. The variety of interactions into which socio-technical, distributed information networks are enmeshed is intrinsically complex, giving rise to emergent, non-linear system behaviors. Thus, catastrophic events from AAA threats should be anticipated in security planning and curriculum. No organization has the resources to fully fund preparations for ALL possible threats, so structures that enable cooperation among similarly-situated stakeholders should be pursued.

How Can Proposed Strategy Support Cybersecurity Beyond Secrecy? Complex problems justify complex explanations and solutions. Systems with many interacting variables display unpredictable behaviors, since it is mathematically intractable to account for all of the variables. Information network technologies present myriad variables. When people and institutions are added to "socio-technical" systems analysis, the number of variables that can affect performance is overwhelming. Cybersecurity professionals and their organizations should recognize that AAA threats will present themselves in a non-linear (unpredictable) fashion, and also consider security solutions (like insurance, indemnities, etc.) that can mitigate harms after the fact.

Example. Stakeholder actions to create and self-bind to behavioral standards (policies, rules, etc.) can reduce the secondary complexity harms caused by lack of coordination, i.e., resource pooling in disaster response, joint defense arrangements; and can spread costs of risks, i.e., forming insurance pools among affected stakeholders.

Suggested Actions for Cyber Professionals and Cyber Educators. Many cybersecurity education programs are starting to emphasize "critical thinking skills" to prepare their students for the unexpected. Cyber professionals and educators should (1) consider chaos theory, and the "fractal" nature of risk and; (2) not assume only "normal" distributions to predict threats and vulnerabilities, but also assume non-linear system behaviors; (3) consider strategies for non-zero-sum solutions to spread risk to affected stakeholders, and standards as a way of directly reducing complexity by decision. Unpack complexity by separating first order risks from second order risks.

3.4   Socio-Technical Systems Force Nontechnical Variables in System Design

Proposed Strategy/Solution. Secure system operation depends on hybrid "specifications" for performance of both technology and people/institutions. Socio technical systems are made reliable by tools AND rules. Tech conforms to standard specifications. People conform to standard laws. "Tools and Rules" are documented in hybrid "Trust Frameworks" that guide predictable performance in information networks.

How Can Proposed Strategy Support Cybersecurity Beyond Secrecy? Anything that helps make people and institutions act more reliably in distributed information networks will help enhance system reliability, a precursor to trusted systems.

Example. PCI-DSS is an example of a system that establishes tools and rules for reliable people and technology. Online marketplaces are an example of how contract (TOU) requirements affects the large-scale behavior of people and institutions.

Suggested Actions for Cyber Professionals and Cyber Educators. Cybersecurity professionals should (1) analyze their existing contracts to confirm that they establish clear duties and rights that are consistent with actual performance expectations for their information networks, (2) identify large-scale system terms that they might normatively cross reference in their contracts, (3) use the CIAC "Atlas of Risk Maps [5]" as a checklist of non-technical elements to consider in security planning.

3.5   Information Democratization Collapses Scale, Alters Security Paradigms

Proposed Strategy/Solution. Tomorrow's resilient and sustainable security solutions will be attentive to and intentional about the scale at which they are deployed and the scales at which they achieve impact, as well as deliberate about addressing the challenges of organizing and operating scale-striding solutions. Fractal-based solutions that display degrees of "scale independence" will prove effective.

How Can Proposed Strategy Support Cybersecurity Beyond Secrecy? The democratization of information access and expression collapsed scale with implications up and down scaled systems. "Upwards" it enables individuals to access both global markets and the eyes, ears, hearts and minds of people worldwide. The increasing intimacy of computing devices (and the crowded ranks of intermediaries offering online services) also collapsed scale "downwards," enabling unprecedented access by organizations to the intimate details about individual the lives. These shifting boundaries of access and insight are not yet reflected in updated institutional structures to reinforce their edges, leading to significant anxiety among stakeholders about reliability. Cybersecurity professionals should consider solutions that are attendant to the effects of actions taken at one scale upon the performance of the system at other scales.

Example. Public health advisories illustrate scale-striding strategies. During flu season they describe multi-level benefits of hand washing to: (1) provide better protection against infection (individual level), (2) support "herd protection" across populations (group level), (3) reduce absenteeism at work (economic level), and (4) conform to courtesy standards (social level). Similar programs can be imagined that advocate for good "data hygiene" by noting the positive effects of individual action at multiple levels. Consider structures that enhance cybersecurity by recruiting individuals to act in a certain way to achieve collective benefit.

Suggested Actions for Cyber Professionals and Cyber Educators. Awareness can permit more intentional engagement to assure that actions (and reactions) at all relevant system levels are recruited into support of a cybersecurity strategy. With incentives and penalties to recruit stakeholder participation, distributed network scan support "neighborhood watch" among members of "communities of interest" convened around shared interests to collectively address risks at multiple scales.

3.6   Data Is "Dual-Use" Technology

Proposed Strategy/Solution. The status of data as a "dual use" technology calls into question security approaches based solely on constraint of data flow, limiting data availability and fostering secrecy.

How Can Proposed Strategy Support Cybersecurity Beyond Secrecy? To the extent that data is made available for "good" uses, it is more exposed to bad uses. Also, a use of data that is good for one party may be bad for another. Both need to be managed rather than ignored. The value of data is in its use as information, so there is continuous pressure to maximize that value and access and use data. Recognizing this pressure, organizational cybersecurity strategies and education should consider approaches to security that do not depend solely upon secrecy. Security controls that focus on managing "use" of data, rather than mere "access" to data can enable flow for good use. That flow of value creation in turn creates a community of interested stakeholders who have a stake in preventing bad uses, and hence can comprise a "neighborhood watch" to help curb "bad" data users.

Example. Pharmaceuticals and explosives are examples of dual use technologies that have co-managed supply chains.

Suggested Actions for Cyber Professionals and Cyber Educators. Cybersecurity strategies and curriculum that focus on Tools and Rules solutions to measure and enable audit and enforcement of shared rules for the "use" of data, will provide the most effective guidance for building resilient future information network architectures. Also, in light of the fact that the discernment of "good" from "bad" uses is bound to context and subjective perspectives, training and education should emphasize exploration and application of ethical and normative elements associated with cybersecurity.

3.7 People Are "Data Producers"

Proposed Strategy/Solution. Security strategies and curriculum that promote the institutionalization of the concept of "people as data producers" can help engender group norms that support the organization of distributed security architectures for open networks, such as "neighborhood watch" approaches.

How Can Proposed Strategy Support Cybersecurity Beyond Secrecy? Security solutions that empower individuals to achieve their personal and professional goals will recruit greater voluntary participation. Incentives for system-consistent behaviors and accounting for value generation from data can yield greater interest in cultivating that value. When stakeholders have something to lose, they are more enthusiastic about defending against that loss.

Example. Civil cases brought by private parties under various securities and intellectual property laws depend on stakeholder diligence in detecting and enforcing rules. The collection of diligent stakeholders in each market is a "neighborhood watch" for that sector.

Suggested Actions for Cyber Professionals and Cyber Educators. Security solutions and curriculum that can build and support systems to recruit stakeholder participation by appealing to their enlightened self-interest can be resilient and scalable.

3.8 Big Data Insights Invert (and Re-invent!) Causation

Proposed Strategy/Solution. Cybersecurity professionals and educators should be wary of the confusion of correlation and causation regarding information network system Tools and Rules performance, but also remain open to treating statistical correlations as "red flags" for investigation. The scientific method *and* correlation-driven analysis are complementary, if handled with intentionality.

How Can Proposed Strategy Support Cybersecurity Beyond Secrecy? The Scientific method starts with a theory which is then tested, generating data that confirms or falsifies the theory. The scientist had to understand the underlying mechanism (described in the theory) to avoid confusing coincidental correlations with causal relationships. Where correlation is confused with causation, efforts to control a system can go astray, and resources can be wasted on false hopes of control. Correlations can, however, provide evidence of causative relationships, and should not be ignored. Correlations can be treated as "phenomenon" to be tested.

Example. The correlation-based advertising services of online social networks generate billions of dollars in market value.

Suggested Actions for Cyber Professionals and Cyber Educators. Security professionals should attend to correlations with skepticism, but maintain a "diligent curiosity" about whether there is a causal link underlying those statistical relationships and, if so, consider how it can inform effective cybersecurity policy. Security curriculum should help train cyber professionals and citizens in critical thinking, providing tools to help navigate a correlation-drenched world.

3.9   "Synthetic Intelligence" Is a Counterforce to AI

Proposed Strategy/Solution. AI and SI offer new tools to cybersecurity professionals, and pose new threats to cybersecurity. AI and SI are artifacts of our quest for insight, and will grow accordingly. SI may provide a mechanism for control over AI.

How Can Proposed Strategy Support Cybersecurity Beyond Secrecy? AI describes a variety of systems that have the potential to make inferences that can intrude on secrecy. The desire for insight shared by individuals and institutions is driving our collective development of AI systems. Efforts are underway to guide its development.

Example AI systems can perceive and analyze phenomena relevant to cybersecurity practice that would elude the most seasoned veteran. SI systems can support emerging "neighborhood watch" models of distributed security. SI systems can also manifest sufficient capacity to provide humans with a potential curb on dangerous "positive feed-back loops" that could cause AI systems to disregard or exceed human controls.

Suggested Actions for Cyber Professionals and Cyber Educators. Security professionals, educators, and organizations should plan for AI and SI-driven systems to generate increasingly independent behaviors and enhanced insight exceeding that of human individuals and institutions. "Neighborhood Watch" models of cybersecurity could morph into the SI-based cybersecurity systems of tomorrow.

3.10   The Internet Is a Privately-Owned/Operated Commercial Space

Proposed Strategy/Solution. Security professionals and educators should recognize that networked information systems are mostly privately owned/operated, and owners and operators will act predictably to maximize revenues.

How Can Proposed Strategy Support Cybersecurity Beyond Secrecy? Internet and online services are mostly owned by commercial enterprises organized for profit. Awareness provides a lens through which Internet activity can be seen as predictable.

Example. Brief reflection reveals how few non-commercial websites attract users.

Suggested Actions for Cyber Professionals and Cyber Educators. Security benefits from the predictable behaviors of system stakeholders. Commercial actors operate and use services over networked information systems – reliably driven by monetary consid-erations. Awareness of this source of reliability can be helpful to designing, developing and deploying cybersecurity solutions that are sustainable and resilient. Cybersecurity professionals should remain aware of the budgetary constraints placed on commercial enterprises, recognizing that commercial actors will act to reduce costs, including cybersecurity expenses, to the minimum necessary for compliance.

3.11   Data Is not Information

Proposed Strategy/Solution. Separating the concept of "data" from "information" is consistent with both information theory and "big data" practice and it provides a compartmentalization that allows cybersecurity to be more readily practiced and taught in a post-secrecy world. Secrecy of *data* may be dead, but interdependent stakeholder co-management of *information* remains viable in a post-secrecy world.

How Can Proposed Strategy Support Cybersecurity Beyond Secrecy? The separation of data and information permits greater solution space in cybersecurity practice and education. The separation enables different security architectures to be applied to different asset classes, and invites consideration of alternative approaches to dealing with different threats and vulnerabilities associated with each.

Example. See sniffles example in Sect. 2.11 above. A single element of data can be used multiple times to "inform" different parties in different contexts.

Suggested Actions for Cyber Professionals and Cyber Educators. Data and information should be separately managed in the security strategy of an organization and separately explored in cybersecurity education. Conflation of the concepts leads to sloppy planning and false sense of security. Awareness of the difference favors security solutions that are able to preserve data's leverage value, while affirmatively guiding its application as information.

3.12   Power Laws in Bureaucracies Make Security-by- Secrecy Un-Economic

Proposed Strategy/Solution. Networked information systems depend upon and serve populations of individuals and entities distributed at different scales of system operation. The most effective cybersecurity solutions will inter-relate stakeholder requirements at multiple system levels.

How Can Proposed Strategy Support Cybersecurity Beyond Secrecy? Networked information systems are depended upon in nearly all domains of human endeavor: becoming as complex as society itself and reflecting an evolving dynamic balance of interests at multiple levels. Sensitivity to differences among stakeholder expectations, needs, duties, rights, obligations at different levels is key to sustainable solutions.

Example. Orange alert systems provide authorities with the equivalent of "1000" eyes to help catch fleeing felons.

Suggested Actions for Cyber Professionals and Cyber Educators. Cybersecurity strategies and curriculum should invite consideration of costs and benefits of cybersecurity strategies at multiple levels. Solutions that can maintain a balance of cost with benefit simultaneously at multiple system levels and among multiple groups of stakeholders interacting at each level will enjoy broader adoption and greater resiliency.

3.13   AAA Risks Threaten Information Systems

Proposed Strategy/Solution. Cybersecurity strategies and curriculum should address all AAA threats: Attacks, Accidents, and Acts of Nature.

How Can Proposed Strategy Support Cybersecurity Beyond Secrecy? Secrecy provided a relevant strategy in a cybersecurity world focused on "Attacks." As secrecy has diminished, cybersecurity has struggled to respond. Security solutions attentive to the different threats, vulnerabilities, assets and risks associated with AAA–attacks, accidents and acts of nature–will be better to address multiple threats. In this new distributed networked world, cybersecurity strategies based on "neighborhood watch" may be the best alternative to offer effective protection. Secrecy can, in fact, be counterproductive in mounting a security response directed to accidents and acts of nature, e.g., by limiting access to needed records, and concealing helpful fixes for accidents.

Example. Following a disaster (Act of Nature), limitations on access (secrecy) under HIPAA to medical records of victims could impede response and recovery

Suggested Actions for Cyber Professionals and Cyber Educators. Cybersecurity professionals and educators should distinguish among the sources of threat in the AAA categories and parse strategies with attention to different risk profile associated with each different threat. These distinctions should be applied in cybersecurity decisions from planning to response.

4   Conclusions

This paper asserts that the death of secrecy in networked information systems signals fundamental changes in cybersecurity practice and education, both of which have long been dependent on secrecy-based strategies. Secrecy is still useful in various forms, but with every day's news come fresh reports of secrecy failures. It is no longer prudent for cyber security professionals to put all of their faith in secrecy as the dominant security paradigm. This paper suggests 13 different paradoxical perspectives on Internet trends that are artifacts or causes of the death of secrecy, and suggests that among those new challenges are the seeds of new approaches and solutions for cybersecurity practice and education.

References

1. Endicott-Popovsky, B.: The probability of 1. J. Cyber Secur. Inf. Syst. **3**(1), 18–19 (2015)
2. Baran, P., et al.: On Distributed Communications, vol. I–XI, RAND Corporation Memos, August 1964

3. Baran   Diagram.   https://docs.switzernet.com/people/emin-gabrielyan/060921-thesis-for-experts/ac43_files/image003.png
4. Morton, T.: Hyperobjects – Philosophy and Ecology After the End of the World. University of Minnesota Press, Minnesota (2013)
5. David, S.: The Atlas of Risk Maps. CIAC, Seattle (2016)

Learning Together with CSCL Tools in the Classroom

Reuma De-Groot[✉]

The Hebrew University of Jerusalem, Jerusalem, Israel
Reuma.de-groot@mail.huji.ac.il

Abstract. The design of CSCL tools has long been a subject of research in the learning sciences community. To this end, theories like dialogic learning and argumentation led to new understandings that see the social context as means to organize learning through collaborative meaning-making. The Metafora and the Collaso learning environments aimed at developing technological tools to afford the smooth integration of inquiry and argumentation to foster learning to learn, L2L, and learning to learn together, L2L2 (in Metafora) and (collaborative) inquiry-based learning (in Collaso). Using three examples of learning activities in one of these environments revealed preliminary understandings and insights on the way tools' design influences group learning in the 21st century. Our preliminary observations show that the two learning environments achieved similar goals despite their different designs. This may shed light on the relevance of educational design for technological environments, suggesting also a closer look at classroom's enculturation and teachers' work when using CSCL co-located in the classroom in order to assess such design work (This paper is partially based on work done by the author and others which was published in Schwarz et al. 2015. The author wish to thank to MinCet Team especially Aviran Mor and Yogev Levy for their dedicated work on Collaso. Many thanks also to Dr. Gil Amit for opening the doors of the Ashkelon College to run our pilots).

Keywords: Dialogic learning · Learning to learn together · Collaborative meaning making · Inquiry based learning · Group reflection · Group agency

1 Introduction

Learning with computers needs a new way of thinking about studying learning. Among other things, Computer Supported Collaborative Learning (CSCL) locates learning in meaning-negotiation carried out in the social world rather than in individuals' heads (Stahl et al. 2006). Theories like dialogic learning (e.g., Hicks 1996) and argumentation (e.g., Andriessen et al. 2003) lead to new understanding of the learning sciences that see the social context as a means to organize meaning constructions (Stahl et al. 2006). The design of software for CSCL, therefore, must be coupled with analysis of the meanings constructed within emergent practices (Koschmann et al. 2006).

Previous work in CSCL suggests that the design of the tools should encourage the practices of reflection and criticism (Fischer et al. 1993). The effectiveness of some of these practices has been widely demonstrated.

P. Zaphiris and A. Ioannou (Eds.): LCT 2017, Part I, LNCS 10295, pp. 324–339, 2017.
DOI: 10.1007/978-3-319-58509-3_26

Learning To Learn (L2L) is a set of capacities and meta-strategies that help the individual learner face challenges for which he/she has to be specifically prepared (e.g., Claxton 2004; Fredriksson and Hoskins 2007; Higgins et al. 2006) These practice/skill were endorsed, recently, by policy makers (e.g., OECD 2003 and 2004)

Practices of inquiry and argumentation stand at the heart of the L2L (Kuhn 2005). These practices learnable but its' integration in classrooms is difficult.

The term *Learning to Learn Together* (L2L2) was first used by Rupert Wegerif based on work done with Marten de Laat (Wegerif and De Laat 2010). They conceived a combination of the space and time of networks ('the space of flows' as defined by Castells, 2004) and of the space and time of dialogues (the 'dialogic space', as defined by Wegerif 2007) towards an overall approach for teaching higher-order thinking skills in the networked society. The Bakhtinian dialogic perspective was applied to networked learning of students to claim that an appropriate pedagogical design can support students learning higher-order skills such as creativity and L2L (Wegerif 2007). This very general claim served as a working hypothesis in the EC-funded *Metafora*R&D project (*Learning to Learn Together: A visual language for social orchestration of educational activities*), led by the author. Metafora focused on the design of a platform for supporting L2L2 in the context of solving problems in mathematics and physics. Our starting point in the project was to clarify the meaning and scope of L2L2, which had been so far an unarticulated concept.

We saw in L2L2 an extension of L2L in the sense that it aims at promoting learning to inquire and learning to argue, as well as collaboration. We experienced that technologies are helpful for integrating inquiry and argumentation. The addition of collaboration as the third tenet of L2L2 naturally led us to posit that CSCL tools should facilitate L2L2 in group learning: Dedicated CSCL tools provide shared space for communication and co-construction of knowledge (Stahl 2006). They also provide constraints and affordances for collaborative behaviors.

At first sight, Scardamalia and Bereiter (1999) already did the job. They showed that with Knowledge Forum, the creation by students of representations of meta-classifications of contributions leads them to an awareness of collective agency. The objectified community knowledge space is necessary for students' ideas to be objectified, shared, examined, improved, synthesized, and used as "thinking devices" (Wertsch, 1998) to enable further advances. The general assumption that in order to take over high levels of social and cognitive responsibility students' ideas must have an "out-in-the-world" existence, and that inventions, models, or plans, should be accessible as knowledge objects to the community (Scardamalia and Bereiter 2006), is broadly accepted.

The two CSCL environments that will be presented here – Metafora (De-Groot et al. 2013) and the Collaso environment (recently under commercial development) aim at developing a technology-based setting to afford the smooth integration of inquiry and argumentation to foster L2L2 (Metafora) and (collaborative) inquiry-based learning (Collaso). Since inquiry and argumentation practices set different goals among participants, we envisaged the interweaving of inquiry outcomes into argumentation practices. Having argumentation and inquiry-based learning in mind with the aim of supporting L2L2, we designed the Metafora and the Collaso tools around two interwoven spaces:

(1) a dialogic, argumentative space and (2) an "open space" to expose ideas and plans to be accessible, negotiable and changed by the group. The different spaces of Metafora & Collaso can be seen in Figs. 1 and 2 (respectively).

In the next paragraphs we will describe the two environments.

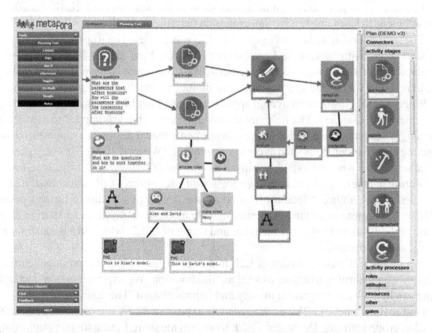

Fig. 1. The Metafora system. Green symbols represent stages of activities, blue symbols represent activities' processes "planning/reflection tool" and the argumentation dialogic space (a detailed description of the other spaces in Metafora may be found in Schwarz et al. 2015) (Color figure online).

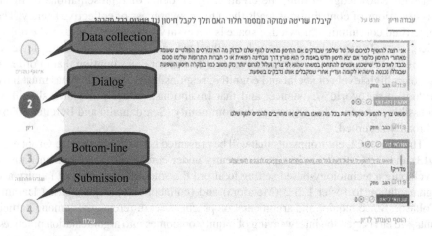

Fig. 2. The Collaso system – the discussion open space –; buttons for the other features appear on the left-hand side.

2   The Metafora Environment for Promoting L2L2

The EU-funded Metafora project (EC/FP6/ICT, 257872; http://www.metafora-project.org/) enabled the development of a system and of an educational environment aimed at promoting L2L2 (De-Groot et al. 2013). The Metafora system comprises (1) a visual tool for planning and reflecting on group work, (2) microworlds for exp riencing phenomena and exploring problem spaces, (3) a space for dialogue and argumentation, and (4) a module for observing group work and possibly intervening by sending messages. In this presentation we will focus on the "planning/reflection tool" and the argumentation dialogic space (a detailed description of the other two spaces may be found in Schwarz et al. 2015).

Space 1. The Planning/Reflection Tool.
The planning/reflection tool offers a visual language that enables students to create and map representations of their work for planning their activities and reflecting on them (see Fig. 1). Cards and connectors are available for this purpose. The cards contain visual symbols and titles, as well as space to insert free text. Some symbols and the titles represent different stages of scientific inquiry learning (e.g., the "explore" card in Fig. 3, or cards for "experimentation", "building models", and "hypothesizing"). A third category of cards represents role assignments within the group (e.g., "evaluator" and "critical" in Fig. 3). The fourth and final set of cards allows access to different resources within the Metafora toolbox (e.g., the card entitled "discussion" in same figure, which allows access to the tool for structured discussion, or cards entitled "Piki" in Fig. 1, which serve as an entry point for a specific microworld, Piki). The connectors (lines and arrows) represent relational heuristics ("is next", "needed for" and "related to") to explicate how the various cards are related in the given plan. The different features of the planning/reflection tool were designed to afford collective reflection on inquiry/problem-solving and collective agency through mutual engagement.

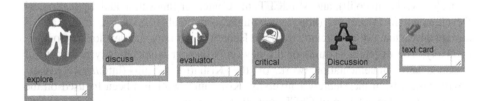

Fig. 3. The visual language in Metafora

Discussion Tool.
Metafora provides tools that allow students to engage in discussion and argumentation. Apart from a chat tool, LASAD (Loll et al. 2012) enables the co-elaboration of argumentation maps (Fig. 4). The LASAD discussion tools promote students' discussions by using labelled cards (e.g. assumption, theory, question) and labeled connectors that define the epistemic nature of the connections between the two labels (e.g. proof and rebuttal). The tool was designed to promote argumentation and collaborative meaning-making.

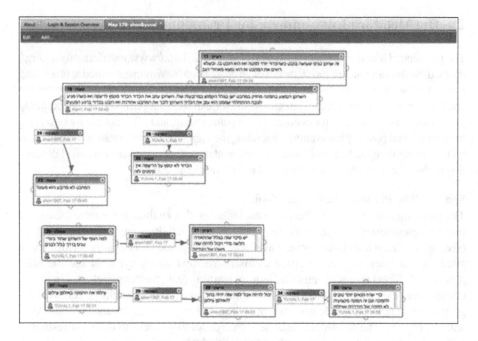

Fig. 4. The Lasad discussion tool

3 Description of the Collaso Tool

The *Collaso* environment - Educational collaborative space for supporting discussion and inquiry-based learning (Fig. 2) is being developed in the framework of a joint initiative between the Hebrew University of Jerusalem's knowledge transfer company, Yissum (http://www.yissum.co.il/), and MindCET, the Center for Innovation and Technological Development in Education, (http://www.mindcet.org/en/about-en/). The tool was co-designed by a team of researchers from the Hebrew University and developers from the company. The different features of the new environment build on 15 years-worth of research and implementation work of the Kishurim Group (http://www.kishur-imgroup.org/) from the Hebrew University. Kishurim's work has been focused on the design and implementation of CSCL tools that foster argumentation and inquiry-based learning in the classroom. The above Yissum-MindCET collaboration resulted in an updated combination of discussion tools co-developed by the Group in various EU-funded R&D projects with a chat-like presentation of discussion contributions that are modern in aspect and appear familiar to the students, and which can also be accessed and read through cellphones and tablets. The other desirable practices (e.g. reflective inquiry and collective agency) that promote L2L and L2L2 are embodied in two additional features: (a) the "bottom-line statement" – a space that enables a collaboratively-created summary of the groups' knowledge accumulated during the discussion, and (b) a "Bird's eye look", allowing teachers and students to see the rates of participation in the discussion. Colla-so's design attempts to provide the necessary substructure for conducting a whole

Fig. 5. The Collaso inquiry and discussion environment. (Color figure online)

sequence of inquiry-based activities (often spanning a few weeks; see Fig. 5), starting from (1) posing a rich research question, through (2) providing a repository for teachers and students of resources related to the problem in case, (3) carrying out a group discussion using (4) the teachers' dashboard, which allows visualizing the rate of participation in the discussion, (5) the *bottom line*, allowing students to collaboratively summarize the most important issues discussed, and (6) the collaborative outcome and results (submitting the joint product – e.g., an essay, a chart, a PowerPoint presentation, a video clip, etc. – to the teacher).

The discussion tool is central to the Collaso environment and we will therefore describe its features more in detail. The tool's user interface is similar to that of WhatsApp, with some additions supporting the dialectical/argumentative affordance needed for our educational purposes (as they appear in the Lasad tool, with different connectors). The additions are symbols of Support (green V), Contra (red X), or Accept (Yellow=), which users can add to each contribution. Furthermore, users may 'tag' the text contributions with a "pin" symbol when they see something that looks important for further elaboration via groups' *bottom line* (e.g., an essay; recall feature 5 above). When a user wishes to react to a specific contribution he/she may click on "react" and that specific contribution is copied into his/her text contribution. This way the chronological sequence of the discussion is kept (the newest contribution is the last one), and users may referrer to others' contributions in more detail. The number of reactions, their nature (Pro, Con, Accept) "Pin" and reactions appear by mouse hover on each contribution.

In the following sections we will show how the different design of the two learning environments influenced the groups' practices related to reflective inquiry (entitled to group reflection) and collective agency which describe the way the individuals in the group takes responsibility as a group. As mentioned above, our approach to L2L was initially based on iterations of argumentation and inquiry learning. A design-based research approach in the design of our tools reveals that the discussion spaces Lasad (see above) and Digalo (Schwarz and Glassner 2007) identified meaning-making through dialogue without interfering too much with the "proper" use of the argumentative terminology suggested (Schwartz and De-Groot 2007). Keeping this in mind, we will present two examples of inquiry-based learning in physics using the Metafora environment and one example of inquiry learning around a dilemma in the social sciences using the Collaso environment.

Although the setting and the issues discussed were taken in a different way in the two environments, some insights related to collective agencies and reflective inquiry that emerge from the different designs of the tools can be detected.

Example 1. The case took place in a high school in a large city in Israel. Twenty-three Grade 9 students participated in the study. They were divided into two groups of 16 and 7 students each. The groups participated in a one-year long course based on weekly 90-minute sessions in which the Metafora environment was used extensively. Typically, students worked in groups of 2–4 peers. In most cases, students in the same group sat close to each other, with each student at an individual computer. Students were introduced to challenges (inquiry problems that were planned to be solved by them in 2–4 lessons) in mechanics around the lever principle and laws of ballistics. We focus here on a group of three students in a challenge related to ballistic motion.

Fig. 6. Stroboscopic picture

Students were first presented with stroboscopic snapshots (Fig. 6) and were asked to describe what they see in the picture. The students were guided to generate concepts relating to motion, in particular the concept of velocity.

Figure 6 shows a tennis player during a serve. The challenge posed by the teacher was "to identify the motion represented in the photograph, and to characterize it". The students split in small groups and began discussing the photograph. After several minutes, the teacher invited the groups to continue their discussion with the LASAD tool. The students did their best to reconstitute the serve, taking into account details such as whether the hand passes between the player and the camera or on the other side of the player, etc. Following the LASAD discussion, students were asked to plan an inquiry activity leading towards a deeper exploration of the photograph: they were asked to follow the ball in the snapshot and to characterize the velocity at each stage. For this endeavor the students were asked to divide the photograph in different parts and to assign roles within the group on how to carry out their work exploring the motions of the ball and the racket. After finalizing their plan the students were asked to share their work with the other groups in a plenary discussion guided by the teacher.

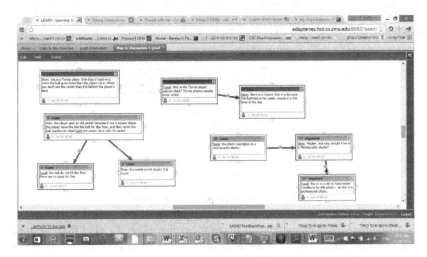

Fig. 7. A Lasad discussion map.

We focus here on the first stages of the work of Ely, Sami and Yaron, discussing their assumptions in the LASAD map. Figure 7 shows a clear disagreement between Yaron and Ely regarding the way the tennis ball reaches the player's racket: Ely thinks that the player first hit the ball on the ground; when the ball bounces to the same height and starts to fall down, he hit it. Yaron claims that the ball does not reach the ground and that the player throws it up, and then hits it. He also challenges Ely's claim that there is no sign that the ball reaches the ground. Interestingly, Ely at this stage does not try to answer Yaron's challenge; rather, he contributes to the ongoing discussion on the lighting conditions that affected the photos of the tennis player and exact measurement of the racket. The Lasad map of the discussion shows that students presented to each other their interpretation of their part of the photo, leading by such doing to the interpretation of the picture as a whole. At some point, Yaron asks Sami whether he also sees the ball jumping on the floor, and Sami answers that he cannot see it. Figure 7 displays a partial view of the map (the full map includes 36 contributions).

Following the LASAD discussion, the students were asked to use their ideas to elaborate a plan for exploring the movement of the tennis ball with the planning tool.

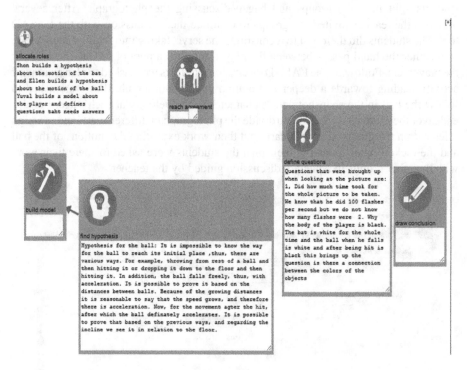

Fig. 8. The initial plan of the group

The triad used three cards only to make their plan (Fig. 8): (1) "Role allocation" (proposed by the teacher), (2) "pose questions" and (3) "find hypotheses". In the "role allocation" card they wrote: "Sami builds a hypothesis about the motion of the racket, Ely builds a hypothesis about the motion of the ball and Yaron builds a hypothesis about the player and poses interesting questions that should be answered". Indeed, Ely raised reasonable hypotheses and Yaron elaborated interesting questions such as "how much time it took for the whole picture to be taken?" Although the students were sitting next to each other, they hardly spoke with each other, but rather filled their planning map to explain what they were about to do. When the teacher saw their plan in the next session, she asked them to turn it to more executive, and asked them to shorten the text in the cards.

The triad then changed the plan to the one shown in Fig. 8. In the "Blank Stage" the triad explains how the photograph was divided in three regions: the trajectory of the ball before it is hit, and after it is hit, and the movement of the hand/racket. This new plan is based on the previous plan. When Eli describes his hypothesis about the movement of the ball he splits it into two phases: first, when the ball falls (he writes "the ball is in free fall, thus accelerates. It is possible to prove it based on the distances between the [stroboscopic captures of the] balls. Because of the growing distances it is reasonable to say that the speed increases"); secondly, when it is hit (he writes "Now for the movement after the hit... the ball accelerates. It is possible to prove it based on previous ways, and regarding the incline we see it in relation to the floor"). The second plan of the group (Fig. 9) shows that Ely beautifully describes the movement through "build a model" cards: the first describes the ball in free fall. The second card is devoted to the movement of the ball after it is hit. The footprints of the role allocation inscribed in the first map are visible in the third and fourth "build model" card: card 3 describes the movement of the racket behind the leg; card 4 describes the movement of the racket to the leg ("We can see that the rocket moved accelerating from the rest of the movement"). This suggests that the group reflected over their previous plan towards the completion of their descriptions.

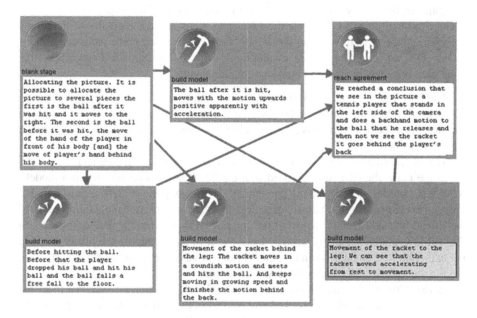

Fig. 9. The second plan of the group

Furthermore we should notice that the students added a "Reach Agreement" card, where they describe their joint explanation regarding what can be seen in the stroboscopic pictures. "We reached a conclusion that we see in the picture a tennis player that stands in the left side of the camera and does a backhand motion to the ball that he releases and when we don't see the racket it goes behind the players' back". Interestingly this explanation does mention the information written in the other cards.

In this example we can detect the move from the discussion tool to the plan supported the group to be more focused on things they should actively carry out together. Although they disagreed on how to interpret the tennis ball's move in their discussion in Lasad, in the plan this dispute does not appear and the group only reports on actions taken with further exploring the picture and the ball's movement. The red arrows put in the plan all point to the final joint agreement of the groups' work. We argue that the plan supported the groups' collective agency with the wish to express their unity with fulfilling their mission together.

Example 2. In this example we present a dyad work, participating in the same activity as above. In the Lasad discussion map the students pose their assumptions regarding what can be seen in the stroboscopic picture. We bring here a few excerpts of their discussion[1].

> Yigal: It's probably a woman tennis player that wears shoes with heals and long skirt; that's why there is a certain segment where you can't see the racket.
> Don: It can be a woman tennis player, how can we really check that? If you have this hypothesis it should be a woman player that wear heals, and this is not logic.
> Yigal: maybe it is a woman model that only takes a pose of a tennis player.
> The dyad continues to elaborate their interpretations about the gender of the tennis player and the reasons why the shoes look the way they look in the picture.
> Don: OK; so according to our assumptions, what do we already know about this picture? Is it possible at all to make assumptions here?

The Lasad discussion we brought here shows that students exchange ideas around one possible interpretation of what was seen in the stroboscopic picture. Their discussion reveals a last move of reflective inquiry cited by Don: "is it possible at all to make assumptions here?"

The Metafora plan of the same dyad showed a different learning behavior[2].

In the map[3] the two students used four cards: 'Role allocation', 'Build a model', 'Check the model' and 'Reaching agreement'. In this map the students report on what they did in the group work. In the 'Allocate role' card they wrote: "Yigal thinks on what we should find and Don writes what the conclusions related to these findings are." In the 'Build a model' card they wrote: "description: in the beginning the player dropped the ball to hit it, than he hit it and we can see the move of the racket to the ball, then we see the movement of the ball after it was hit by the racket."

In the 'Check the model' card they wrote: "the explanations we arrived to fit the pictures as we explained and checked and arrived to the conclusion that the photo was taken in less than a second time as the acceleration fall is 10 m in one second…". In the 'Reaching agreement' card they wrote: "we arrived to the conclusion that what we see in the picture is a tennis player dropping the ball and then hit it with a racket". In this example we see that the move from the discussion space to the planning tool supported the students' move from exchanging general ideas and interpretations of what they see in the picture, to working together on their assignment and reporting on it. Surprisingly,

---

[1] The example we bring here is in Hebrew – and as the Lasad tool is not accessible by us at the moment; we can use only a free translation here.

[2] It should be noted that the students illustrated the map after the teacher asked the group to divide the picture into three parts and explore the movement of the ball in each part separately.

[3] As the Metafora planning tool is not accessible by us at present so we couldn't translate the map.

the agreement they report on "refers"] to their previous discussion on what can be seen in the picture. We may say with some caution that the use of the planning tool supported the dyads' collective agency towards the mission at stake. Their final 'Reach agreement' statement might be seen as the exposure of their wish to show unity or solidarity when reaching a joint understanding after the vagueness of their first session, as it appeared in the discussion space.

Example 3. In this example we present first insights of the use of the Collaso tool as currently undertaken (Winter 2016–2017) with college students in Israel. Collaso was piloted in a computer lab with 2 groups of 32 and 34 students (63 women and 3 men) through two interventions of 1.5 h lesson each, during two weeks. The students were asked to work with the tool as part of their bachelor studies in education as a social sciences discipline. We designed an inquiry-based activity for the pilot dealing with the subject of vaccination. The question we posed was "Should we always take a tetanus vaccination after being wounded by a rusty nail?" As a start, we discussed the vaccination dilemma with the students prior to the discussion in Collaso. After an introduction session the students were divided into groups of 3–5 students each and were asked to start the discussion in the Collaso tool. To inspire their thoughts and arguments we put a few links and relevant references in the Data Collection repository (see Fig. 2 above).

We further asked the students to write a short essay regarding their joint decision whether to vaccinate or not.

We will now follow the thread of one discussion held between 3 students- and follow their conclusions.

S1 - One can't know if this is going to be fine [to get the tetanus vaccination]; there are cases and there are cases. If one gets a deep scratch from a nail I think it is better not to take the chance.

S2 - This vaccination is obligatory so it is very difficult to say if it is necessary – or one can overcome the Tetanus disease without it.

S3 - The main problem with vaccination is that the vaccination contains the bacteria.

S1 - Indeed in our country one cannot trust the doctors anymore.

S3 - [brings an excerpt from a health insurance company about the disease] [...] Tetanus is an infectious disease of the central nervous system. The disease is caused by the bacterium Clostridium Tetani. This bacterium is common in nature, especially in agricultural land cultivated landscapes, but it is also in urban land, house dust, animal intestines and human and animals' stool. The bacterium is anaerobic [...]. The bacterium enters the body through a wound, and after the intrusion secretes a toxin, who is led to the bloodstream, lymphatic system and central nervous system [...]

S3 - So what is the part of the population that is really exposed to the disease?

S2 - It is really interesting [to know] if the body has its own antibodies to struggle with the disease.

S1 - We are all exposed.

S3 - Let's check your question in other sources.

S1 - Tetanus is a serious disease and is often fatal. It is caused by the effect of a toxin produced by the bacterium Clostridium Tetani. Tetanus is a pathogenic bacteria. Infection is usually caused by a wound. Common symptoms are cramping in the muscles of the jaw which are followed by difficulty in swallowing and stiffness of the muscles in the body. Infection can be prevented by a vaccine suitable for prophylaxis after exposure to the bacteria.

S1 - What can be seen here is that in general it is better to be vaccinated. I can't believe that this may cause damage.

S3 - The problem is that all the existing resources were written by agencies that have commercial interests with the vaccination.

S1 - You are right! This is exactly why I chose Wikipedia which is also not 100% reliable.

Bottom Line.
(Following is the content accumulated in the "Bottom Line Space" – see stage 3 in Fig. 2)

We are for Tetanus vaccination; we understand that it is an important vaccine recommended by the ministry of health.

Copied here is the citation from Wikipedia brought in the previous discussion.

"Bottom line" contains what comes up as our main understanding from the information we read and from our discussion on the subject. We understand that it is important not to take the chance, there are many different opinions about the subject but all recommend taking the vaccine. Peoples get the vaccine and call others to be vaccinated more than once in their lives.

From the excerpts we brought here we can see that Collasos' discussion space promoted a coherent thread dealing with the pros and cons of vaccinations. The three students carried out a coherent argumentative discussion, posing questions and searching for more data to support their views (e.g., S3 put a question on the percentage of the population that was really exposed to the disease, S2 put a question regarding people's ability to fight the disease naturally, and S3 suggested to check S2's question in other sources). The discussion in the "Bottom Line space" ("groups' space") was clearly organized by S1, as she went through the discussion and "pinned" what she thought to be the most important contributions. Wisely enough, she brought all pro and con arguments that arose in the discussion[4] - and she actually managed to summarize it shortly with the overall statement that it is better to be vaccinated despite the different opinions that arose. Here she assumed the coordinator's role, summarizing the group's consensus.

4   Discussion

Tackling the relations between software designs and learning outcomes is a difficult task as the effectiveness of collaborative learning depends upon multiple conditions that interact with each other in such way that it is not possible to guarantee learning effects (Dillenbourg et al. 1996). Despite the limitations of the present work (especially because we do not refer to the teachers' role in the classroom and the design of the learning activities) we could identify the role of the planning tool in concretizing the group's work towards reporting on past activities and planning next steps. Furthermore, the use

---

[4] For space limitations we presented only the group's summary without all the annotations from the discussion.

of the plan suggested actions to be taken by the group on the front stage, resolved disagreements and facilitated meaning-making -in the discussion space. We argue that this shift in the group's work occurred because the special design of the plan and the use of the visual language supported that shift also by using scientific concepts like evaluation and exploration, to explore and be an evaluator.

The design the group's space in Collaso (the Bottom Line feature) aimed to allow the crystallization of the group's joint opinion.

In the example we brought above we showed how the discussion space promoted literacy knowing and understanding the joint opinion of the group. In other examples we reviewed from the pilot we could identify different usages. In two examples (out of the 12 groups that reached this stage) the group reflected also on the way they collaborated and on who organized the work and contributed to its success. Our preliminary observation here shows that the Bottom Line space allowed the emergence of group reflection whereas reaching a joint comprehension for the final group's decision was taken by some of the groups as raising collective agency through identifying who did what. We may conclude that the Collaso design supports literacy and the associated collective agency, while Metafora promoted tasks design and role allocation for a work needed to be done.

As for the Discussion Space in Collaso, it served the purpose of carrying out argumentative discussion in a similar fashion to that taking place with the Lasad tool. This observation is interesting, because we know that discussion-supporting tools of the kind of Lasad (e.g., Digalo) usually build on the map-like representation of students' discussions to promote connectivity amongst the discussants. Moreover the Collaso approach allow chronological discussion- (newest contribution appear always in the end of the thread), whereas the Lasad approach allows a- chronological appearance, and therefore focusses users' attention to connect their contributions to others, and by that support the discussions' coherency.

Furthermore, our preliminary observation also shows that users hardly utilized the icons of pro/con and indifference we made available in the Collaso discussion space. Also the PIN was used only after the discussion took place and not during it. This may hint that these orientations are not needed by the users or that they need more time to get used to use them.

Our preliminary observation shows that students use a discussion space with a different representation in a similar way. The underlined assumption that the map appearance would support coherency and thus richer discussions wasn't supported in the present work, having quite similar discussions' threads (in the context of connectivity). These preliminary observations call for further work with the two environments.

What we brought in this paper was actually a partial view of using CSCL tools in the classroom as we did not refer to the teachers' role in the design of the activity. The latter is crucial for the success of the work as it shows also classroom enculturation (Cob 1995) and the impact of the tool's design on its use. Our research on the use of the Metafora tools (see Schwarz et al. 2015) shows how group's collective agency inspired a talented mathematics student to step back with his mathematical solution – waiting for the rest of the group to arrive to the conclusion together. In another example we showed how the teacher mediated the classroom discussion with three students (example

1 above), pushing one of them- to clearly state his mind, which he did by reporting not on his own opinion regarding the balls' movement but on the group's disagreement about the trajectory of the ball in the stroboscopic picture. In both cases the students put the group's collective agency before their own success and individual opinions. These two examples tell also about the classroom orchestration associated with the use of the CSCL tools co-located in the classroom (Asterhan 2016).

To summarize, Metafora and Collaso are two learning environments that were designed with the purpose of combining argumentative discussion with inquiry-based learning. The environments aim at promoting L2L (Collaso) and L2L2 (Metafora), supporting mainly group reflection (reflective inquiry) and collective agency. Our preliminary observations show that the different design of the tools- especially with relation to the discussion space wasn't influential over the students' dialogue. This may shed light on the relevance of educational design to computer mediation of educational goals, suggesting also a closer look on classroom enculturation and teachers' work with CSCL tools co-located in the classroom to assess pedagogical design of such tools.

References

Andriessen, J., Baker, M., Suthers, D.: Arguing to Learn: Confronting Cognitions in Computer-Supported Collaborative Learning Environments. Kluwer, Dordrecht (2003)

Asterhan, C.S.C.: Introducing online dialogues in co-located classrooms: if why and how. In: Asterhan, L.B., Clarke, S. (eds.) Socialization Intelligence Through Academic Talk and Dialogue. Routledge, for AREA books, New York (2016)

Castells, M. (Ed.): The Network Society A Cross-cultural Perspective. Edward ElgarCheltenham, UK Northampton, MA, USA (2004)

Claxton, G.: Teaching children to learn: beyond flat-packs and fine words. Burning Issues in Primary Education No. 11 Birmingham: National Primary Trust (2004)

Cobb, P., Bauersfeld, H. (eds.): The Emergence of Mathematical Meaning: Interaction in Classroom Culture. Lawrence Erlbaum Associates, Hillsdale (1995)

De-Groot, R., Dragon, T., Mavrikis, M., Harrer, A., Pfahler, K., McLaren, B., Wegerif, R., Kynigos, C., Schwarz, B.B.: The Metafora tool: supporting learning to learn together. In: Rummel, N., Kapur, M., Nathan, M., Puntambekar, S. (eds.) See the World at a Grain of Sand: Learning Across Levels of Space, Time and Scale, pp. 392–396 (2013)

Dillenbourg, P., Baker, M., Blaye, A., O'Malley, C.: The evolution of research on collaborative learning. In: Spada, E., Reiman, P. (eds.) Learning in Humans and Machine: Towards an Interdisciplinary Learning Science, pp. 189–211. Elsevier, Oxford (1996)

Fischer, G., Nakakoji, K., Ostwald, J., Stahl, G., Sumner, T.: Embedding critics in design environments. Knowl. Eng. Rev. 8(4), 285–307 (1993)

Fredriksson, U., Hoskins, B.: The development of learning to learn in a European context. Curriculum J. 18(2), 127–134 (2007)

Hicks, D.: Contextual inquiries: a discourse-oriented study of classroom learning. In: Hicks, D. (Ed.) Discourse, Learning and Schooling, pp. 104–141. Cambridge University Press, NY (1996)

Higgins, S., Wall, K., Baumfield, V., Hall, E., Leat, D., Woolner, P.: Learning to Learn in Schools Phase 3 Evaluation: Year Two Report. Campaign for Learning, London (2006). http://www.campaign-for-learning.org.uk/projects/L2L/The%20Project/phase3/year2.htm

Kuhn, D.: Education for thinking. Harvard University Press, Cambridge (2005)

Loll, F., Pinkwart, N., Scheuer, O., McLaren, B.M.: How Tough Should It Be? Simplifying the Development of Argumentation Systems using a Configurable Platform. Bentham Science Publishers, Sharjah (2012)

OECD: Education at a Glance: OECD Indicators. OECD iLibrary (2003)

OECD: Education at a Glance: OECD Indicators. OECD iLibrary (2004)

Schwarz, B.B., De-Groot, R.: Argumentation in a changing world. IJCSCL 2(2–3), 297–313 (2007)

Scardamalia, M., Bereiter, C.: Schools as knowledge building organizations. In: Keating, D., Hertzman, C. (eds.) Today's Children, Tomorrow's Society: the Development of Health and Wealth in Nations. Guilford, New York (1999)

Scardamalia, M., Bereiter, C.: Knowledge building: theory, pedagogy, and technology. In: Sawyer, K. (ed.) Cambridge Handbook of the Learning Sciences, pp. 97–118. Cambridge University Press, New York (2006)

Schwarz, B.B., de Groot, R., Mavrikis, M., Dragon, T.: Learning to learn together with CSCL tools. IJCSCL (Int. J. Comput. Support. Collab. Learn.) 10, 239–271 (2015)

Schwarz, B.B., Glassner, A.: The role of floor control and of ontology in argumentative activities with discussion based tools. Comput. Support. Collab. Learn. 2, 449–478 (2007)

Stahl, G.: Group Cognition: Computer Support for Building Collaborative Knowledge. Acting with Technology Series. MIT Press, Cambridge (2006)

Stahl, G., Koschmann, T., Suthers, D.: Computer-supported collaborative learning: an historical perspective. In: Sawyer, R.K. (ed.) Cambridge Handbook of the Learning Sciences, pp. 409–426, Cambridge, UK (2006)

Wegerif, R.B.: Dialogic, Education and Technology: Expanding the Space of Learning. Springer, New York (2007)

Wegerif, R., De Laat, M.F.: Reframing the teaching of higher order thinking for the network society. In: Ludvigsen, S., Lund, A., Saljo, R. (eds.) Learning in Social Practices: ICT and New Artefacts Transformation of Social and Cultural Practices. Routledge (2010)

Wertsch, J.V.: Mind as action. Oxford University Press, New York (1998)

Yackel, E., Cobb, P.: Sociomathematical norms, argumentation and autonomy in mathematics. J. Res. Math. Educ. 27, 458–477 (1996)

Outdoor Studying System Using Bluetooth Low Energy Beacon—To Feel Cultural Sites

Yuko Hiramatsu[1(✉)], Fumihiro Sato[1], Atsushi Ito[2], Hiroyuki Hatano[2], Mie Sato[2], Yu Watanabe[2], and Akira Sasaki[3]

[1] Chuo University, 742-1 Higashinakano, Hachioji, Tokyo 192-0393, Japan
{susana_y,fsato}@tamacc.chuo-u.ac.jp
[2] Utsunomiya University, 7-1-2 Yoyo, Utsunomiya, Tochigi 321-8505, Japan
{at.ito,hatano,mie,yu}@is.utsunomiya-u.ac.jp
[3] GClue Inc., 134-3 Ikkimachi Turuga, Aizu-wakamatsu-shi,
Fukushima 965-0006, Japan
akira@gclue.jp

Abstract. We investigated outdoor studying using Bluetooth Low Energy (BLE) beacons in Nikko, a world heritage site in Japan, in order to convey traditional cultural information to young students. A BLE beacon can supply information that is related to location. This information is used for many purposes such as e-learning and commercial applications. In this paper, we propose a new style of outdoor studying as a collaboration between outdoor studying and the local economy. Shops in the area supply students with vivid and seasonal information about the area. Over three years of research, we found our application caused students to remember the cultural sites. We also found that they came to value the area. Shop owners hence hope to benefit from this application. However, we also found some tendencies in students' feelings about traveling in this process. This paper describes the results of our research from 2014 to 2016 using BLE beacons in Nikko. We describe several different scenarios using beacons and their results.

Keywords: Outdoor study · Smartphone application · BLE beacon · Cultural site

1 Introduction

There are many new learning materials that use ICT now. Digital texts can show pictures and videos to students with sounds. Some texts involve augmented reality as well [1]. This material is easy to understand for young students, who, from the viewpoint of developmental psychology, still think in concrete terms. Such interesting material makes it seem as if they understand the topic well. However, sometimes, this material is not sufficient for understanding the topic. Using the Internet and convenient tools on a PC, students write and create their reports. However, they do not remember the contents of the course after the class. The complete topic is presented them and they have little chance to think further about the topic inside their heads. The old texts, written using only words, forced students to imagine some elements in their brains in order to understand the topic. Nowadays, students often do not need to be active to understand some new topics. They become so passive that they do not try to imagine any lacking elements.

This tendency makes young students not very active in their travel as well. They visit traditional places and look for the convenience stores that they always go to in their daily lives. Basic social research by the Statistics Bureau in the Ministry of Public Management Home Affairs Posts and Telecommunications in Japan found that the number of young tourists from 15 to 20 years of age as well as those in their 20s and 30s has decreased greatly from 1986 to 2011 [2].

For example, young students in elementary and junior high school in Tokyo used to visit Nikko for their school trips in order to learn the traditions and culture of the old periods. However, according to our research in 2014 (n = 171), many of them did not wish to visit there again when they grew up. Some of them answered that they already knew about Nikko, even though they had visited Nikko by bus and looked at a few famous sights for a short time [3].

We have been studying how such students can begin to learn actively using ICT. We created an application so that they can understand the real world more deeply using smartphones in Nikko. A smartphone is a suitable device for bringing learning material outdoors. Therefore, using a smartphone in the area, students may be more affected when looking at real objects. A smartphone is a tool that can connect an undiscovered real world and their ordinary lives.

The rest of this paper is structured as follows. Section 2 examines related work. Sections 3 and 4 describe our application using Bluetooth low energy (BLE) beacon and explain the results of experiments. Finally, in the conclusion section, we discuss the importance of outdoor study for young students for traditional cultural sites using the smartphone application.

2 Related Work

2.1 Sightseeing Application

Many sightseeing applications exist in Japan that allow tourists to access information about restaurants, souvenir shops, and the local weather as well as to download maps. Augmented reality combines the virtual world with the real world [4]. In addition, a large amount of information has made it possible to make sightseeing location recommendations. The system searches for some locations related to the user's favorites on the basis of some similarity measures [5].

The European Union's TAG CLOUD project (Technologies lead to Adaptability and lifelong engagement with culture throughout the CLOUD) uses smartphone technology to provide information about traditional cultural sites [6]. While TAG CLOUD uses a cloud-based service, our application is designed to work without requiring access to the cloud, since Internet connections may be limited in rural areas.

2.2 BLE Beacons

The global BLE beacon market is expected to grow at a compound annual growth rate of 307.2% from 2015–2020. About 80,000 units were shipped in 2015, and this number is expected to quickly grow to 88.29 million units by 2020 [7]. A new business called Beacon Bank uses beacons that having already been established and is based on a beacon sharing system [8]. BLE beacons are mainly used for indoor location-based services to indicate locations and display information for education scenes. For example, attendance confirmation [9] and information systems in museums [10] are popular. In addition, a BLE beacon library reference system is available at the Sabae Library in Japan [11]. However, we seldom find use cases of BLE beacons for outdoor studying.

2.3 Our Previous Work on School Trips

In 2011, 94% of junior high school students and 97.1% of high school students went on several-day school trips in Japan [12]. While such outdoor activities are valuable, students cannot fully grasp the artistic or cultural value and meaning of the objects or scenery by simply viewing them [13]. To solve this problem, we have developed a learning model for outdoor study [14–17].

Human beings do not always recognize what they are seeing. However, once a particular object is noticed, their attention tends to focus on it. We exploited this concept and developed quiz applications to be used as a trigger to draw attention to a particular object in the scenery that the students were viewing. The quizzes encouraged positive responses. Using the quiz, we encouraged students to notice what they did not understand well and students looked forward to seeing the objects in person in the area.

3 Our Application Using BLE Beacons

3.1 Purpose of the Project

The purpose of this project was to offer local traditional information for an area and interest students in it. In Nikko, some shops have continued for seven generations and one has continued for eight generations. These shop owners live according to the traditional Japanese ways. If they have a chance to tell about their traditional ways of living in a cultural site, students will be interested in them. Tourists who are unaware of the area use an SNS, which offers some information about the area now. Therefore, local seasonal or traditional information is often buried among the numerous photographs and comments left by visitors unfamiliar with the location. Young people have little chance to learn about the effects of traditional ways on daily life.

3.2 New Application Design

We chose BLE beacons in order to create a new application for school trips. We use BLE Beacons (Fig. 1) on the school trip for the following reasons.

- Protection of the environment in the cultural heritage site:
  The world heritage sites have rules to maintain the landscape. Signboards would adversely affect it. Using a smartphone screen as a kind of a personal signboard, we can leave the area unchanged.
- Location serviced and protection of individual privacy:
  The location of students is necessary for teachers. However, such information has to be protected from the viewpoint of security. Using beacons, teachers can know the student locations and timestamps and without needing the data to be sent to the cloud. This system is based on local communication.
- Local and seasonal information:
  Near field communication by Bluetooth provides information at the exact place and time in Nikko. Students can feel the immediacy of this information and will connect with the real place and real season via their smartphones.
- Information of the people living the area:
  The owners of shops on the route install information in the black beacon boxes. Beacons on the poles become a trigger to connect with applications for them. Some tangible signs are useful for prompting a human to perform some action.
- Multi-object use:
  A beacon is an object that can have multiple uses. We present not only messages about traditional places when tourists pass near the beacon, but also seasonal information using push-based information when tourists pass by this application at the station. We install the beacons on local poles. In addition, one member of staff wore a beacon like a watch so that students could find him. The staff then gave students a quiz. A beacon is so small that we can apply it in many scenarios. For example, a lucky dip implemented by a beacon could entertain young students.
  This diversity makes this system a sustainable service. Students have little money and stay in Nikko for only one day or a half day. If this system were useful only for students, it would be difficult to keep it in the area even though it is convenient and interesting. However, if it is useful for people living the area or other tourists in Nikko, it will be continued.

Fig. 1. Beacons (left) on the roadside and (right) with a solar battery

3.3 Design of Our Application

We placed beacons to send short pieces of information about the area to tourists on foot en route to the main shrine in order to create a new traditional road to the main shrine,

Toshogu, in Nikko. It was a necessary effort for pilgrims to walk up the road in past times. There are several little temples and springs on the way to the main shrine, and visitors must travel uphill to visit the Toshogu shrine. The beacons were fitted on lamp posts 100 m apart from each other. Many of the beacons are clustered near Shinkyo Bridge (Fig. 2). Beacons broadcast messages using three channels: 37, 38, and 39, at fixed intervals between 10.24 and 20 s. An important characteristic of BLE is its low power consumption. BLE requires a tenth to a hundredth the power of classic Bluetooth signalling, and a beacon may function for one year or more without a battery change. BLE also requires less power than Wi-Fi. This is the reason we decided to use the BLE beacon for sightseeing, especially for outdoor sightseeing. Figure 3 shows the use case of this application.

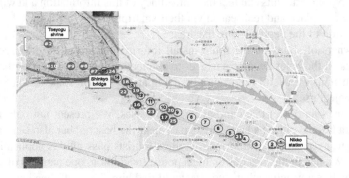

Fig. 2. Beaconmap in Nikko

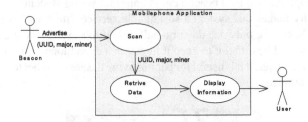

Fig. 3. Usecase of this application

Figure 4 shows some screen shots (the pages of a quiz function) of our application, which is called "Nikkonavi." Figure 4 is a quiz about a sculpture under a temple roof. Immediately before students arrive at the old building, they receive a beacon signal and answer the quiz. Then they go to the temple and confirm the sculpture while looking at the real object. Our quiz courses use the Zeigarnik effect [18], which is a psychological effect in which we, as human beings, remember better an unfinished event or an incomplete one. If students answer a quiz, they might keep thinking about it until they look at the object, that is, the answer of the quiz, near the BLE beacon. Further, teachers can see the locations of their students.

Fig. 4. Screenshots of the quiz function

This application includes a stamp rally in the shopping street, navigation, and bus timetables. Figure 5 shows our service flow. Shop owners can see the customer traffic diagram. We have to consider the merits of the application for people living in Nikko. If we incorporate no advantages for them, the information becomes hollow, and world heritage site becomes an ancient ruin. There are people in Nikko, and they live according to traditional customs even now. They know a large amount of seasonal information about Japanese culture. Their lives create a living stage, and if students learn and feel such living traditional culture, they will maintain an interest in the place. The tangible buildings make students feel as if the architecture is all they have to learn. However, if they catch a glimpse of the spirit of the place, they can hope to understand the place more after their trip. The beacons permit many-sided functions and helps students to appreciate the other people living there or indeed other tourists.

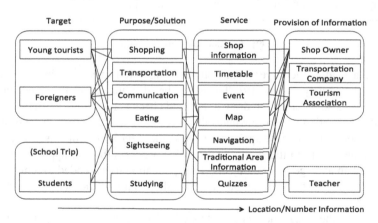

Fig. 5. Service flow

We improved and designed our application with several buttons for several targets: students, foreign tourists, young tourists, and shop owners. Such holistic experiences make the trip come alive. This is an important aspect of the application because we have to preserve not only the buildings of world heritage sites but also its culture for the next generation.

4   Experiments and Results

We performed two experiments to validate the efficacy of our application. One experiment concerns students and the other concerns tourists.

4.1   Quiz Function for Students

In this experiment, 28 students participated in the trial, in which 23 students were required to complete 10 quizzes on the streets and five students walked around without the application for comparison on 26 September 2015. Before looking at some important objects, students were provided with quizzes on the nearby locality, which they answered by viewing objects at the sites. Figure 6 shows an example quiz.

> The height of the place you are standing now is as same as
>   1 Seaside in Tokyo Bay
>   2 Second floor in Nikko Station
>   3 The Five-Storied Pagoda in Kyoto
>   4 Sky Tree, the highest Tower in Japan

> Answer: 4
> Interpretation: you are standing very high place now. Old people built holy places on high place. Pilgrims walked up the hill or the mountain and arrived at holy places with difficulty. Now, you may feel their spirits.

Fig. 6.   Example quiz function

Before and after the experiments, students answered questionnaires. Memory is thought to be largely visual [19]. Therefore, besides answering the questionnaires, students were also requested to draw a map and check some points on the map of the area [20]. Application users drew maps that were more concrete than those of the five students not provided with the application. On average, the application users placed 9.18 objects on the map from the station to the shrine, whereas the non-application participants placed an average of 5.80 objects. The application users tended to remember not only the answers to the quizzes but also the shops around the beacons where they answered the quizzes.

In addition, the maps students drew tended to have certain characteristics. The first area after they arrived at the station was larger than other areas. Figure 7 presents some examples. This effect is considered to be a primacy effect, that is, human beings tend to remember better or more easily the first items of a series [21].

After one month, the same students answered another questionnaire and checked three points in each photograph of the area they walked in Nikko. We constructed heat maps from the students' checks and the results indicate that they remembered the quiz points after a month. After two months, the students answered the same questionnaire presented before the experiments. The results of our experiments show high evaluations.

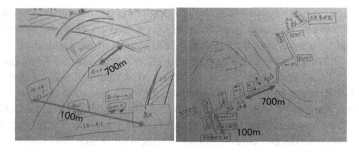

Fig. 7. Maps from the station to the main shrine after the experiment

The students remembered the cultural objects well. In addition, they remembered several shops along the route, and 75% of them hoped to visit there again. Some commented that they had little time to look around the area and hoped to visit Nikko again.

We also analyzed their evaluation of Nikko. There were three clusters. They visited Nikko with high expectations and then, after two months, their evaluation of many subjects was lower than before. However, all of them valued the history and culture in Nikko higher. The students who evaluated the quizzes and maps belonged to cluster 3. They valued several subjects as higher than before (Table 1).

Table 1. Evaluation of our application before and after the experiment (5-point Likert Scale)

Cluster	(A) Before the trip			(B) 2 months fter the trip			(C) Incremental difference (B-A)		
	1	2	3	1	2	3	1	2	3
Nature Landscape	5.00	5.00	3.75	4.43	4.83	4.50	-0.57	-0.17	0.75
History/Culture	4.29	4.71	3.25	4.43	4.80	4.75	0.14	0.09	1.50
Street	4.43	4.29	4.50	4.00	3.83	4.00	-0.43	-0.45	-0.50
Hot Spring	4.14	3.71	3.50	3.57	3.50	3.25	-0.57	-0.21	-0.25
Traditional performing art/ Specialty	3.86	4.00	3.75	3.71	3.83	4.00	-0.14	-0.17	0.25
Food	4.71	4.43	4.25	3.71	3.83	4.75	-1.00	-0.60	0.50
Experience-based tour	3.43	3.57	2.50	3.00	2.83	3.75	-0.43	-0.74	1.25
Shopping	4.14	3.14	3.50	3.00	3.17	3.75	-1.14	0.02	0.25
Night Spot	3.71	3.00	4.50	3.00	2.67	3.00	-0.71	-0.33	-1.50
Relationship with peoplein the area	2.83	3.29	3.00	3.71	3.33	3.00	0.88	0.05	0.00
Easy reservation	4.00	3.29	3.75	3.00	3.17	3.00	-1.00	-0.12	-0.75
Price of hotels	4.57	3.71	5.00	3.00	3.17	3.50	-1.57	-0.55	-1.50
Traffic convenience	4.71	4.43	4.50	3.29	3.50	1.75	-1.43	-0.93	-2.75
Commodity price	4.14	3.57	3.75	3.00	3.83	3.25	-1.14	0.26	-0.50

4.2 Navigation and Shop Information for Tourists (Web Questionnaires)

The sample size for this experiment was 80 tourists (60 Japanese and 20 English-speaking tourists). Nikkonavi is already published and tourists can use it. After using this application, some tourists answered Web questionnaires voluntarily. The impression of our application is "pleasant" and "helpful" for foreigners (Fig. 8). Foreigners and young people who were not familiar with Nikko evaluated the application highly. Of the tourists, 49% of them were visiting Nikko for the first time. Further, 67 tourists looked at our map: 90% of English-speaking users looked at map and 94% of them (17/18) answered that the map was useful. In addition, 38 users looked at the beacon stamps. These stamps were set with some coupons or points, but they were not functioning at that point. Therefore, this function was not useful, but many users paid attention to it. Finally, 14 users did not perceive the sound beacon at all, which is a problem that must be addressed (Fig. 9).

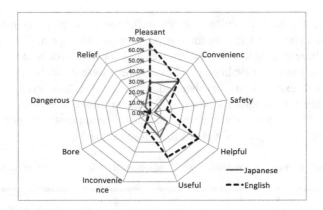

Fig. 8. Impression of the application

Fig. 9. Beacon stamps

4.3   Regional Differences in the Evaluation About Tourism in Nikko

We performed another study in Kobe (n = 80), which is in the Kansai area of Japan and is far from Tokyo. Students in Kobe seldom visit Nikko on their school trips. The questionnaires were the same as before. We compared students in Kobe with students in Tokyo (n = 53). The research objective was to understand users' regional differences. Students in Kobe evaluated Nikko higher than students in Tokyo. Many students in Tokyo had been to Nikko on school trips that lasted a few days. However, they sometimes did not have good impressions of Nikko.

Comparing Tokyo with Kobe (on average), students in Tokyo had higher expectations about "Nature," "History," and "Hot springs." Students from Kobe expected "Shopping," "Nightspots," "Traffic convenience," "Easy reservations," "Commodity prices" and other topics to be higher than the students from Tokyo (Fig. 10). Calculation of a t-test confirmed that there were significant correlations for "Night spot," "Shopping," "Easy reservation," and "Commodity price" between Tokyo and Kobe (α significance level = 0.05). Specifically, the t-test result for "Night spots" obtained a significance probability (two-sided) of 0.003.

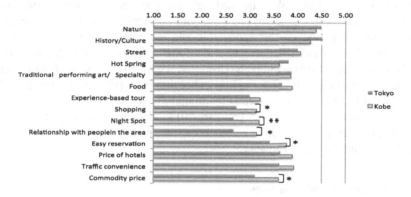

Fig. 10. Expectations about Nikko (5-point Likert Scale)

We believe this can be explained as follows. The students from Kobe belonged to Kobe-gakuin University [22], and its campus is in the city center of Kobe. The night spots are very beautiful in Kobe. In contrast, most of the students in Tokyo belonged to Chuo University (Tama Campus) [23]. Tama campus is located in the suburbs in Tokyo, near the mountains.

The purpose of this study was to define the construct of novelty in the context of tourism [24, 25]. However, the results of our research indicate that students tend to wish for elements in their daily lives. In addition, the students who had been to Nikko on a school trip had lower expectations of the hotels than the others (P = 0.045).

5 Conclusion

5.1 Evaluation of the BLE Beacon: Applications for Sightseeing on School Trips

The evaluation of the BLE beacon application was high, not only for students but also for foreign tourists in Nikko. Students remembered the traditional objects and evaluated the history and culture higher after they visited Nikko. Shop owners have cooperated with us and were prepared to input seasonal and traditional information using this application. Staff in the tourism association use the bus timetables of this application in order to answer inquiries from tourists. Students, tourists, and people in the area have begun to use our application.

We still need to determine how people more people can become aware of the beacon signals and improve the application.

5.2 Inheriting the Culture of World Heritage Sites

Nikko is one of Japan's world heritage sites. It is important for such areas to pass on their culture to younger generations. Not only people who know the area well but also young people should treat the area as a precious cultural resource. If students on school trips use our application and value the region highly, that would be helpful. However, it is not enough. It is important that young people living in the area actively maintain the traditional cultural sites. We requested high school students in Tochigi (some living in Nikko and others living nearby) to walk with our application. They answered the quizzes well. They enjoyed this application and evaluated it more highly than the students in Tokyo. In addition, they gathered information around Nikko Station. We set BLE beacons at about 100 m intervals. However, according the results of our research, the area in front of the station has big impact because of its primary effect (Fig. 7). We hence should to reinforce the information around the station. The junior high school students collected information on 8 February 2017. We will install this information in our application. Such corroboration will encourage the junior high school students living near Nikko to inherit the Nikko area.

5.3 Experiencing Cultural Sites

According to our research, students tended to wish for elements in their daily lives during travel. The characteristic points of traditional cultural areas are different from their daily feelings. Therefore, a smartphone application, which belongs to their daily lives, will be useful for connecting old traditional places with young people.

An application using BLE beacons provideslocal information and connects young and old, from the past to the future. This application has now been modified for Senganen Park for use in Kagoshima, a world industrial heritage site in Japan. In addition, we are now starting to use BLE beacons to support trekking in Senjogahara. In this case, beacons have their own solar power source so that they may be placed in nature without maintenance.

Acknowledgments. We would like to express our gratitude to Mr. Funakoshi (Nikko Tourism Association), Mr. Takamura and Mr. Yoshida (Hatsuishi-kai: an association of Nikko shopping streets), Dr. Kazutaka Ueda (Tokyo Univ.), Dr. Miwa Morishita (Kobegakuin Univ.), Mr. Takanori Kumekawa (Utsunomiya Technical High School), Ms. Kaho Takahashi, Mr. Yukihiro Shimokawabe and Mr. Takao Masuda (Chuo Univ.). This research was performed as a SCOPE (Strategic Information and Communications R&D Promotion Programme) project funded by the Ministry of Internal Affairs and Communications.

References

1. Introduction about AR Text (iPad/iPhone/Android application). Tokyo Shoseki Co., Ltd. https://ten.tokyoshoseki.co.jp/text/hs/math/book001/level5/index.htm
2. White Paper on Land, Infrastructure, Transport and Tourism in Japan. Ministry of Land, Infrastructure, Transport and Tourism (2013). http://www.mlit.go.jp/hakusyo/mlit/h24/hakusho/h25/html/n1236000.html
3. Hiramatsu, Y., Ito, A.: A study of sightseeing support system using ICT based on attitude surveys of visitors to Nikko. The Annual of the Institute of Economic Research Chuo University, No. 46, pp 497–529 (2015)
4. Magazine of Information Processing Society Japan: IPSJ-MGN531103.pdf, October 2012
5. Hisashi, U., Kazutaka, S., Tsutomu, E.: Sightseeing location recommendation using tourism information on the Web. Technical report of IEICE, The Institute of Electronics, Information and Communication Engineers 112, pp. 13–18 (2012)
6. Tag Cloud: Technologies lead to adaptability and lifelong engagement with culture throughout the CLOUD project. http://www.tagcloudproject.eu
7. Tecnavio, J.M.: http://www.technavio.com/blog/bluetooth-beacons-are-teetering-brink-ubiquity-shipment-volume-expected-grow-exponentially-2020#sthash.EqO6arcN.dpuf
8. Beacon Bank HP. https://beaconbank.jp/
9. Mi-Young, B., Dae-Jea, C.: Design and implementation of automatic attendance check system using BLE beacon. Int. J. Multimedia Ubiquit. Eng. **10**, 177–186 (2015)
10. Doljenkova, V., Tung, G.: Beacons: exploring location-based technology in museums. http://www.metmuseum.org/blogs/digital-underground/2015/beacons
11. Sabato Map. https://www.youtube.com/watch?v=EyucY63RVRg
12. Japan Association of Travel Agents HP. https://www.jata-net.or.jp/travel/info/school-trip/excursion01.html
13. The Research Report about usage of ICT devices at junior high school and high school. Study Group on School Trip. http://joyful-shu-gaku.com/
14. Hiramatsu, Y., Ito, A., Sato, F.: The site-specific learning model on mobile phones using Zeigarnik effect. In: Stephanidis, C. (ed.) HCI 2013. CCIS, vol. 374, pp. 43–47. Springer, Heidelberg (2013). doi:10.1007/978-3-642-39476-8_9
15. Hiramatsu, Y., Ito, A., Fujii, M., Sato, F.: Development of the learning system for outdoor study using Zeigarnik effect. In: Zaphiris, P., Ioannou, A. (eds.) LCT 2014. LNCS, vol. 8524, pp. 127–137. Springer, Cham (2014). doi:10.1007/978-3-319-07485-6_13
16. Hiramatsu, Y., Ito, A., Sato, F., Hatano, H., Sato, M., Watanabe, Y., Sasaki, A.: A new model for providing tourism information for traditional cultural sites through ICT. In: ICSIT 2016, Florida, pp. 76–81 (2016)
17. Hiramatsu, Y., Kanbayashi, K., Ito, A., Sato, F.: Evaluation of the new outdoor study scheme using mobile phone based on the Zeigarnik effect. In: Zaphiris, P., Ioannou, A. (eds.) LCT 2016. LNCS, vol. 9753, pp. 320–331. Springer, Cham (2016). doi:10.1007/978-3-319-39483-1_30
18. Zeigarnik, B.V.: On finished and unfinished tasks. In: Ellis, W.D. (ed.) A Sourcebook of Gestalt Psychology. Humanities Press, New York (1967)
19. Haber, R.N., Standing, L.G.: Direct measures of short-term visual storage. Q. J. Exp. Phycol. **21**, 43–54 (1969)
20. Thorndyke, P.W., Hayes-Roth, B.: Individual differences in spatial knowledge acquired from maps and navigation. Cogn. Psychol. **14**, 560–589 (1982)
21. Asch, S.E.: Forming impressions of personality. J. Abnorm. Soc. Psychol. **41**, 258–290 (1946)
22. Kobegakuin University HP. http://www.kobegakuin.ac.jp/english/
23. Chuo University Tama Campus. http://global.chuo-u.ac.jp/english/siteinfo/visit/tama/

24. Lee, T.H., Crompton, J.: Measuring novelty seeking in tourism. Ann. Tourism Res. **19**, 732–751 (1992)
25. Yoshikawa, S.: A psycholinguistic study of tourist motivation. J. Hannan Univ. Humanit. Nat. Sci. **38**, 41–49 (2003). (in Japanese)

Measuring Usability of the Mobile Learning App for the Children

Zahid Hussain[1(✉)], Wolfgang Slany[2], Wajid H. Rizvi[3], Adeel Riaz[1], and Umair Ramzan[1]

[1] Quaid-e-Awam University of Engineering, Science and Technology, Nawabshah, Pakistan
zhussain@quest.edu.pk, adeel12it@gmail.com, umair.sheikh1992@gmail.com
[2] Graz University of Technology, Graz, Austria
wolfgang.slany@tugraz.at
[3] Institute of Business Administration Karachi, Karachi, Pakistan
wrizvi@iba.edu.pk

Abstract. This paper presents findings from the usability study that was conducted for the newly developed mobile learning App for the children. The App facilitates the children aged between 4 and 9 of Class-KG and Class-I to learn English with the help of their native language named Sindhi. After the pilot study, actual usability test was conducted with 100 children. In the study, besides usability tasks performed by the children, Smileyometer and Again-Again Table from the Fun Toolkit were also used to assess user experience. The outcomes disclose that the App was very easy and effective as task accomplishment rate was hundred percent. The results from the Smileyometer and Again-Again Table show that most of the children enjoyed the App. There was no statistically significant difference between the baby girls and the baby boys in terms of task completion time which shows that the App was equally efficient for all the children.

Keywords: Child-Computer Interaction · Usability test · Fun Toolkit · Mobile learning App

1 Introduction

Child-Computer Interaction is very important area that needs to be explored further. Many mobile Apps for children have been developed under various categories, e.g., games, learning apps, etc. Evaluating usability of these mobile Apps is crucial for the success of these Apps. Arain et al. have recently evaluated the usability of mobile learning App. Data was collected through formal experiment and System Usability Scale. Results revealed that App is very effective, efficient and user friendly [1].

Read et al. have measured fun through Fun Toolkit containing (Smileyometer, a Fun-Sorter and an Again-Again Table) with kids having age between 5 and 10 years. They additionally examined relationship amongst fun and usability in three dimensions: Endurability, Engagement, and Expectations. They measured these three dimensions of

P. Zaphiris and A. Ioannou (Eds.): LCT 2017, Part I, LNCS 10295, pp. 353–363, 2017.
DOI: 10.1007/978-3-319-58509-3_28

fun in detail. They concluded that these three measures of fun are useful [2]. The authors provide the guidelines for researchers that how to use Fun Toolkit and other survey methods related with child studies [3]. Two summative evaluation methods have been assessed by [4]: Smileyometer and This or That. Researchers measured reliability and validity of each method with 113 youngsters having age from 3 to 8 years.

Researchers have designed a fun loving interactive Tablet-PC App for playful reading and storytelling for the children. The App was evaluated by 18 children of primary school. Fun Toolkit was used to measure the kids' experience of fun along with usability test [5]. Fun Toolkit has been used to evaluate the children's user experience having age 11–13 years for the prototypes of iPad based game [6]. Smileyometer and Fun-Sorter have been used to evaluate children's experience of fun for the educational software; the children's age was 7–8 years. The authors recommend Fun-Sorter for assessing various products with children [7]. Usability and fun and the relationship between them have been investigated for kids between 7 and 8 years for the educational software [8].

Few learning Apps for children have been developed but not a single App has been developed for learning English-Sindhi Languages. Sindhi language is commonly spoken in Sindh and Balochistan provinces of Pakistan as well as in northern parts of India. We have developed a mobile learning App for the children who are native speakers of Sindhi language to teach them English through the App. Usability test has also been conducted for this learning App and its results are presented in this paper.

The rest of the paper is divided into following sections: Sect. 2 presents overview of the newly developed App. Section 3 describes methodology. Results are shown in Sect. 4 and in Sect. 5 conclusions are given.

2   "Learn English-Sindhi" App

Nowadays children are very accustomed with mobile phones and Tablet-PCs in early age. This provides the chance to teachers and researchers to teach children through interactive mobile leaning Apps. By keeping this fact in mind, we have developed an Android based mobile learning App called "Learn English-Sindhi" for Sindhi speaking children in Pakistan to teach them English through their native language Sindhi. The main objective of the mobile learning App is to provide a dedicated Sindhi Application to Sindhi speaking children so that they themselves can learn English through their native language. There is no such kind of App available yet in the Android market.

The mobile App covers the basic activities that the children use to learn in the early level of the education. These entire activities are presented through the images, text and voice in both languages: English and Sindhi. The target of the App is the children aged between 4 and 9 years.

Figure 1 shows three screenshots of the App, screen (a) shows the main menu of the App which contains seven different learning options (i.e., Alphabets, Numbers, Fruits, Vegetables, Colors, Calendar and Body Parts). Screen (b) shows one of the alphabet "G for Grapes انگور", here text has been written in both languages English and Sindhi with appropriate image and clear voice in both languages, so the children can

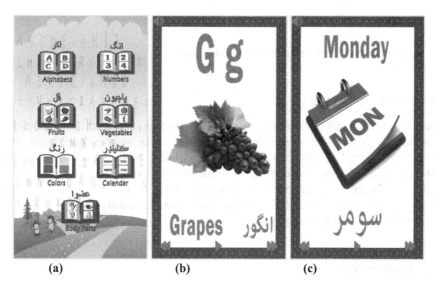

(a)   **(b)**   **(c)**

Fig. 1. Screenshots of **(a)** Menu screen **(b)** G alphabet from Alphabet **(c)** Day Monday from Calendar

easily understand the English word through Sindhi and image. Screen (c) shows one of the calendar's days in English and Sindhi Language.

The App also contains "Numbers" in which there is counting from 1 to 20 in both languages: English and Sindhi. In "Fruits" and "Vegetables" there are some common fruits and vegetables that are used in daily life. "Colors" shows basic colors in both languages and "Body Parts" shows body parts in both languages.

3 Methodology

Demographic questionnaire, usability tasks and Fun Toolkit [2] were used in this research study. As the target audience was children, so Fun Toolkit was used to measure the children's experience of fun after using the App. Before actual usability testing, pilot study was conducted with 10 children and 3 of their teachers with permission from the school administration. Based on the feedback of the pilot study, slight changes were incorporated in the App. Based on the data obtained through demographic questionnaire, hundred students (n = 100) from Class-KG and Class-I having the age group 4 to 9 years were selected randomly, 58% were baby boys while 42% were baby girls. All of the children were well familiar with usage of the smartphone or Table-PC.

The usability test was conducted and then Smileyometer, Again-Again Table and Fun-Sorter from the Fun Toolkit were immediately administered after the children performed the usability tasks. Each child was asked to perform three simple tasks, the tasks were to find out an alphabet, a fruit and a body part from the App. The Samsung Galaxy S4 smartphone was used during the study. For each child, task completion time and task completion rate was recorded. After completing the tasks, the children were asked to give their opinion about the App using the mentioned tools from the Fun Toolkit.

4 Results

The results are presented in the below subsections.

4.1 Demographic Data

According to the results of the demographic questionnaire, 58% participating children were baby boys and 42% were baby girls; having age between 4 and 9 years. 50% children were from Class-KG and 50% were from Class-I. All the participating children had experience of using smartphone or Tablet-PC and were using different mobile Apps. The participating children's usage of smartphone or Tablet-PC was: 59% children spend one hour daily, 30% children spend two hours daily, and 11% children spend three hours daily or above.

4.2 Usability Test

There were three tasks to be performed by the participating children during the usability test. The task completion rate was 100%; this shows that the App is easy and effective as every child completed all the three tasks. Efficiency was measured through task completion time; Fig. 2 shows the average task completion time of the participating baby boys and baby girls.

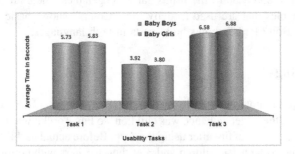

Fig. 2. Average task completion time in seconds

Table 1 shows descriptive statistics of all three tasks in terms of the total task completion time in seconds.

Table 1. Descriptive statistics

S#	Tasks	Mean	Std. Deviation
1	Find out the Letter D (D for Doll) "گڈی"	5.7730	2.8774
2	Find out the Eyes "اکیون"	3.8738	1.7472
3	Find out the Mango "انب"	6.7067	2.3088

Table 2 shows group differences of the participants in categories of gender, education level and smartphone or Tablet-PC usage groups with mean and standard deviation for total task completion time in seconds.

Table 2. Group differences

Group	Category	Mean	Std. Deviation
Gender	Baby boys	5.4114	1.6337
	Baby girls	5.5061	1.9579
Education level	Class-KG	5.4448	1.7386
	Class-I	5.4575	1.8149
Smartphone or tablet-PC usage	1 h daily	5.5126	1.7184
	2 h daily	5.7438	1.9962
	3 h daily or above	4.3236	0.7684

Table 3 shows regarding the participating children that there is no statistically significant difference between gender, education level and smartphone usage groups in terms of total task completion time. The t value of gender group is $t(98) = -0.263$ and $p = 0.793$, so there is no statistically significance difference between baby boys and baby girls. Similarly, in second group education level t value is $t(98) = -0.036$ and $p = 0.973$ and in third group one-way ANOVA has been applied where $F(2, 97) = 2.779$ and $p = 0.067$. The results show that the App is equally efficient for all the participating children regardless of their gender, education level or daily usage time of smartphone or Tablet-PC.

Table 3. Independent samples t-test and one-way ANOVA

Test type	Testing variable	Value	Probability
Independent samples t-test	Gender	$t(98) = -0.263$	$P = 0.793$
Independent samples t-test	Education level	$t(98) = -0.036$	$P = 0.971$
One-way ANOVA	Smartphone or tablet-PC usage	$F(2, 97) = 2.779$	$P = 0.067$

4.3 Fun Toolkit

Fun Toolkit has been used to measure the participating children's experience of fun after completing the tasks.

4.3.1 Smileyometer

Smileyometer from Fun Toolkit has been used to measure the children's experience of fun that how much fun it was to use the various activities of the App. Figure 3 shows a five-point scale (Awful, Not very good, Good, Really good, Brilliant) which is used to record the response from the participating children for the Task 3.

3. **Find out the Mango "انب".**

How much fun was it to use this activity?

Mango

انب

Awful Not very good Good Really good Brilliant

Fig. 3. Smileyometer

Figure 4(a) shows the response of the participating children for Task 1: The total response for Brilliant and Really good is 78%, while the rest of the participants' response is Good. Figure 4(b) shows the response of the participating children for Task 2: The total response for Brilliant and Really good is 79%, while the rest of the participants' response is Good. Figure 4(c) shows the response of the participating children for Task 3: The total response for Brilliant and Really good is 81%, while the rest of the participants' response

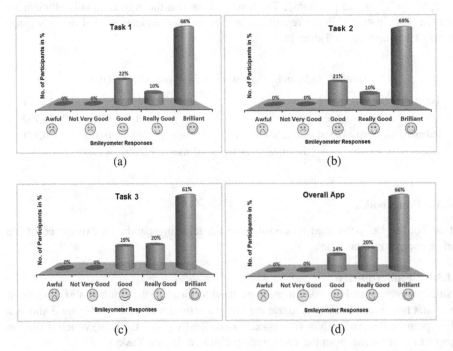

Fig. 4. Smileyometer response of the participating children for (a) Task 1 (b) Task 2 (c) Task 3 (d) Overall App

is Good and Fig. 4(d) shows the response of the participating children for the overall App: the participating children's experience regarding the App was enjoyable as the total response for Brilliant and Really good is 86%, while the rest of the participants' response is Good.

Table 4 shows group differences of the participating children in categories of gender, education level and smartphone or Tablet-PC usage groups with mean and standard deviation for the response of Smileyometer regarding all the tasks.

Table 4. Group differences

Group	Category	Mean	Std. Deviation
Gender	Baby boys	4.4713	0.6609
	Baby girls	4.4286	0.6799
Education level	Class-KG	4.4933	0.6538
	Class-I	4.4133	0.6820
Smartphone or tablet-PC usage	1 h daily	4.5141	0.6818
	2 h daily	4.3889	0.5746
	3 h daily or above	4.3030	0.8227

Table 5 shows that regarding the participating children, there is no statistically significant difference between gender, education level and smartphone or Tablet-PC usage groups in terms of Smileyometer response regarding all three tasks. The t value of gender group is $t(98) = 0.315$ and $p = 0.753$, so there is no statistically significance difference between the baby boys and the baby girls. Similarly, in second group education level, t value is $t(98) = 0.599$ and $p = 0.551$ and on third group one-way ANOVA has been applied where $F(2, 97) = 0.662$ and $p = 0.518$. The results show that the participating children's reported experience of fun about the App is equal regardless of their gender, education level or daily usage time of smartphone or Tablet-PC.

Table 5. Independent samples t-test and one-way ANOVA

Test type	Testing variable	Value	Probability
Independent samples t-test	Gender	$t(98) = 0.315$	$P = 0.753$
Independent samples t-test	Education level	$t(98) = 0.599$	$P = 0.551$
One-way ANOVA	Smartphone or tablet-PC usage	$F(2, 97) = 0.662$	$P = 0.518$

4.3.2 Again-Again Table

Again-Again Table is used to ask the opinion of children whether they want to use the App or to do the activity (task) again or not, for capturing an idea of engagement, as illustrated in Fig. 5.

Would you like to use "Learn English - Sindhi" App again?			
	Yes	**May be**	**No**

Fig. 5. Again-Again table

Figure 6(a) shows the response of the participating children for Task 1 in terms of Again-Again Table: The total response for YES is 86% and response of MAYBE is 14%, while participants' response for NO is 0%. Figure 6(b) shows the response of the participating children for Task 2 in terms of Again-Again Table: The total response for YES is 90% and response of MAYBE is 10%, while participants' response for NO is 0%. Figure 6(c) shows the response of the participating children for Task 3 in terms of

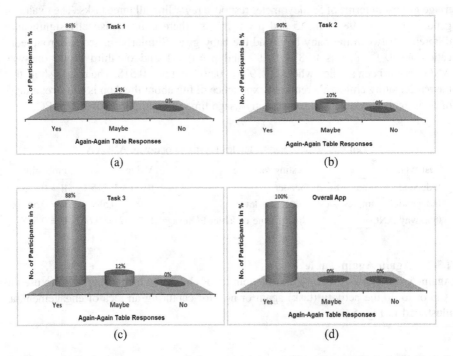

Fig. 6. Again-Again table response of the participating children for (a) Task 1 (b) Task 2 (c) Task 3 (d) Overall App

Again-Again Table: The total response for YES is 88% and response of MAYBE is 12%, while participants' response for NO is 0%. Figure 6(d) shows the response of the participating children for the overall App in terms of Again-Again Table: The total response for YES is 100% which shows that all the participating children want to use this App again.

Table 6 shows group differences of the participants in categories of gender, education level and smartphone or Tablet-PC usage groups with mean and standard deviation for the response of Again-Again Table regarding all the tasks.

Table 6. Group differences

Group	Category	Mean	Std. Deviation
Gender	Baby boys	2.9078	0.2240
	Baby girls	2.8412	0.2878
Education level	Class-KG	2.9266	0.2265
	Class-I	2.8330	0.2723
Smartphone or tablet-PC usage	1 h daily	2.8814	0.2821
	2 h daily	2.8667	0.2850
	3 h daily or above	2.9091	0.3015

Table 7 shows that there is no statistically significant difference between gender, education level and smartphone or Tablet-PC usage groups in terms of Again-Again Table response regarding all three tasks. The t value of gender group is $t(98) = 1.300$ and $p = 0.197$, so there is no statistically significance difference between baby boys and baby girls. Similarly, in second group education level, t value is $t(98) = 1.869$ and $p = 0.065$ and on third group one-way ANOVA has been applied where $F(2, 97) = 0.091$ and $p = 0.913$. The results show that the App would be equally used again by the participating children regardless of their gender, education level or daily usage time of smartphone or Tablet-PC.

Table 7. Independent samples t-test and one-way ANOVA

Test type	Testing variable	Value	Probability
Independent samples t-test	Gender	$t(98) = 1.300$	$P = 0.197$
Independent samples t-test	Education level	$t(98) = 1.869$	$P = 0.065$
One-way ANOVA	Smartphone or tablet-PC usage	$F(2, 97) = 0.091$	$P = 0.913$

4.3.3 Fun-Sorter

Figure 7 shows the Fun-Sorter response of the participating children about three tasks.

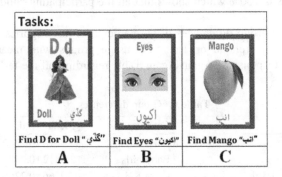

Fig. 7. Fun-Sorter

According to the participating children's reported opinion, Task 1 is the easiest task to do. The participating children found Task 2 as the most enjoyable activity as compared to two other activities.

5 Conclusions

This paper shows results from the usability study that was conducted for the newly developed mobile learning App for the children aged between 4 and 9. The findings show that the App was very easy and effective as task accomplishment rate was hundred percent. There was no statistically significant difference between the baby girls and the baby boys in terms of task completion time which shows that the App was equally efficient for all the children regardless of their gender, education level or daily usage time of smartphone or Tablet-PC. According to the results most of the children enjoyed the App and all the participating children want to use this App again. Future work would include the observation of the children while using the App and comparing the observational data with the children's reported experience of fun.

References

1. Arain, A.A., Hussain, Z., Rizvi, W.H., Vighio, M.S.: Evaluating usability of m-Learning application in the context of higher education institute. In: Zaphiris P., Ioannou A. (eds.) Learning and Collaboration Technologies. LNCS, vol. 9753, pp. 259–268. Springer, Cham (2016). doi:10.1007/978-3-319-39483-1_24

2. Read, J.C., MacFarlane, S.J., Casey, C.: Endurability, engagement and expectations: measuring children's fun. In: Interaction Design and Children, vol. 2, pp. 1–23. Shaker Publishing, Eindhoven (2002)

3. Read, J.C., MacFarlane, S.: Using the fun toolkit and other survey methods to gather opinions in child computer interaction. In: Proceedings of the 2006 Conference on Interaction Design and Children, pp. 81–88. ACM (2006)

4. Zaman, B., Abeele, V.V., De Grooff, D.: Measuring product liking in preschool children: an evaluation of the Smileyometer and this or that methods. Int. J. Child-Comput. Inter. 1(2), 61–70 (2013)

5. Alaamri, F., Greuter, S., Walz, S.P.: Trees of tales: a playful reading application for Arabic children. In: International Conference on Entertainment Computing, pp. 3–10. Springer, Heidelberg (2014)

6. Sim, G., Cassidy, B.: Investigating the fidelity effect when evaluating game prototypes with children. In: Proceedings of the 27th International BCS Human Computer Interaction Conference. British Computer Society (2013). Article no. 53

7. Sim, G., MacFarlane, S., Read, J.: All work and no play: measuring fun, usability, and learning in software for children. Comput. Educ. 46(3), 235–248 (2006)

8. MacFarlane, S., Sim, G., Horton, M.: Assessing usability and fun in educational software. In: Proceedings of the Conference on Interaction Design and Children, pp. 103–109. ACM (2005)

An Analysis of the Note-Taking Function of the Audience Response System

Toshikazu Iitaka[✉]

Kumamoto Gakuen University, 2-5-1 Oe, Chuo-ku, Kumamoto 862-8680, Japan
iitaka2@yahoo.co.jp

Abstract. This paper analyzes the note-taking function of the Audience Response System. The analysis shows the positive effects of the note-taking function and it shows that the note-taking function interacts with other ARS functions. Studying these features will help design more interactive lectures.

Keywords: Digital-note-taking · ARS · e-learning

1 Objective

Note taking using electronic instruments is gaining popularity. To improve interactions with their audiences, presenters use systems that record audience responses, such as the Audience Response System (ARS). The note-taking function of ARS is examined in this paper. ARS introduced by this paper is a module of Xoops, an open-source content management system (CMS). This paper has two objectives. First, it will introduce the features of the note-taking function. Second the effect of the note-taking function will be analyzed.

Note taking is one of the most common ways of learning. Therefore, the importance of note taking is often pointed out by educational technology research. Some researchers such as Nakayama et al. [6, 7] investigated the digital note-taking system, which is suitable for the network age. The system introduced by this paper seeks to reinforce ARS by using the note-taking system. ARS allows us to conduct interactive lectures in which the audiences use devices like clickers to respond to questions posed by the lecturer. In addition, ARS has also been developed as a web application that can be accessed using a mobile phone [3]. Iitaka [3] introduced one such application, which also has the note-taking function.

This paper focuses on the note-taking function of the ARS module. First, related literature is analyzed. Then, the note-taking function will be explored. After that, we analyze the data for which the ARS module was implemented. We obtained statistically significant results that enabled us to estimate the positive effect of the note- taking function.

© Springer International Publishing AG 2017
P. Zaphiris and A. Ioannou (Eds.): LCT 2017, Part I, LNCS 10295, pp. 364–374, 2017.
DOI: 10.1007/978-3-319-58509-3_29

2 Background

We first analyzed similar studies from literature. Note taking has a positive effect on learning. Previous studies such as Weener [8] have described these positive effects. Digital note taking has also been investigated in the network age [6]. According to Nakayama et al. [7], the positive effect of digital note taking has been confirmed. Nakayama also predicted the possibility of sharing digital notes online.

This paper is based on these arguments. The note-taking function described in this paper is a function of the online e-learning system. The online e-learning system here is the ARS module of CMS.

The typical ARS is realized by using special instruments such as a clicker. When lecturers ask questions during lectures, the audiences can answer using such instruments. The ARS that does not depend on such special instruments has also been investigated. Web applications that are accessed by mobile phones can also be used for note taking. We developed an ARS that is a module of CMS, which is already being used in various universities. If we take advantage of such circumstances, we can use course data and student data to make the system more useable. Besides, the ARS module shares the question data with the online drill module introduced by Iitaka [1, 2]. Data sharing makes the ARS module more useful.

The ARS module introduced by Iitaka [3] also has a note-taking function. Like ARS, the note-taking function is often used during lectures. Therefore, we can expect further usability.

This note-taking function has already been introduced by Iitaka [4, 5], who tried to evaluate its applicability. However, it could not be fully determined because very few individuals in the audience chose to implement this notebook function. Therefore, a lecture had to be designed to encourage audiences to use the note-taking function.

3 Method

3.1 Features of Note-Taking Function

This section shows the structure of the note-taking function. Then, we will see how to use the function.

Figure 1 shows the possible applications of the note-taking function.

A major advantage of this ARS module is that it enables audiences to share and evaluate notebook data with other groups. The common evaluation of the notebook data promotes data sharing, which, in turn, encourages the audience to learn harder.

The ARS module allows us to set keywords that can be used to check the audiences' understanding of lectures. The system determines whether the keywords appear on the notes taken during the lectures. If keywords are present in the notebook data, we can assume that the audience has understood the lecture content (Fig. 2).

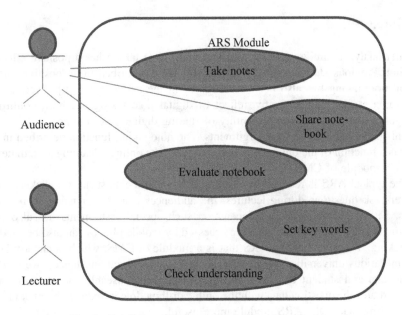

Fig. 1. Possible applications of the note-taking function

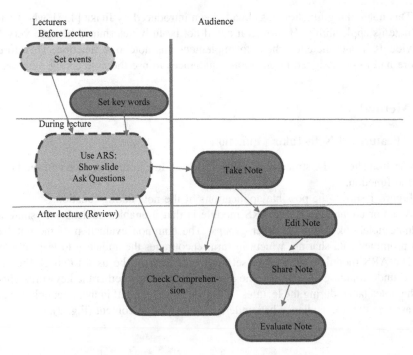

Fig. 2. How to use the note-taking function

Then, we show the data structure of the note-taking function (Fig. 3).

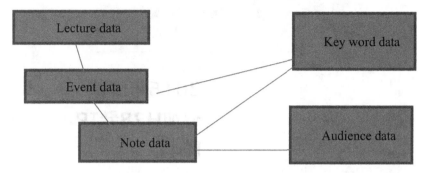

Fig. 3. Data structure of the note-taking function

Keyword data is a characteristic of the note-taking function; it corresponds to event data. An event such as a slide or a quiz, which is shown during a lecture, has multiple keywords. The notebook data of each user also corresponds to the event data. This structure allows us to check whether the keywords appear in the notebook data. Hence, we can check whether a user has understood the event about which notes were taken. This feature and the sharing of notebook data are two big advantages of digital note taking.

Subsequently, we provide some more concrete descriptions. First, we show how to set keywords.

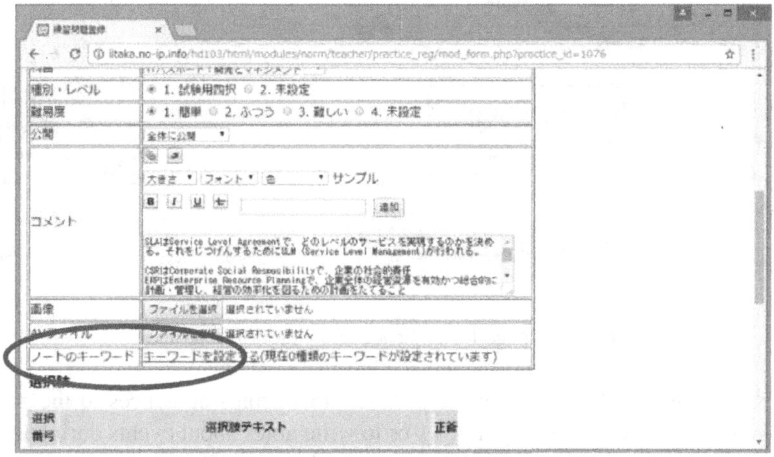

Fig. 4. Page for EventSetting

As shown in Fig. 4, each event that has been set has hyper texts that allow us to access the page for setting key words (Fig. 5).

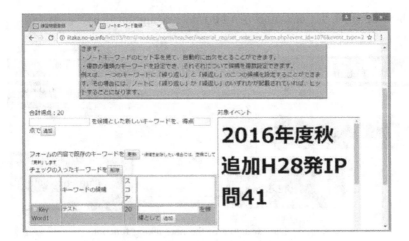

Fig. 5. Page for setting keywords

We can set multiple keywords for each event on this page. Besides, we can set the importance of each keyword. Notebook data with more important keywords can have a higher evaluation.

Audiences can access the following pages during the lectures (Fig. 6).

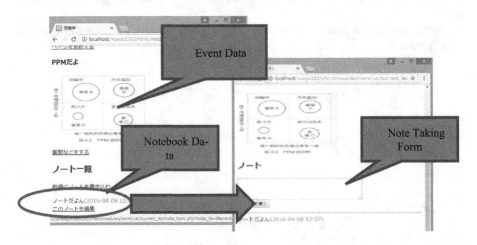

Fig. 6. ARS page for audience and page for note taking

This ARS answer form also has hyper texts that brings audiences to the page for note taking. This note-taking page allows us to write notes about events during lectures. Notebook data always relates to the event data of lectures. Therefore, by checking the notebook data, we can determine whether the listeners are concentrating on the lectures and understanding the contents. If keywords occur in a person's notebook data, we could conclude that he or she has understood the contents and is able to concentrate on the lectures.

Besides, we can use this ARS after lectures. Audiences can review events of the lectures using the following page (Fig. 7).

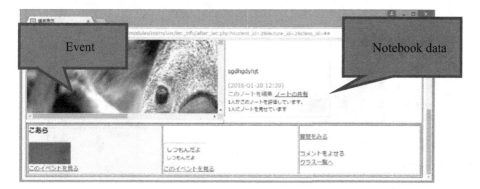

Fig. 7. Review page

The audiences can read the note on each event using this review page. This page also enables the audiences to edit the note. CKEditor is implemented to realize this function.

This system is designed to share the edited note data using the pages shown in Fig. 8.

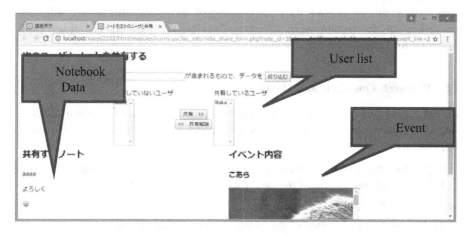

Fig. 8. SharedNotebookData

The review page displays not only the user's own notebook data but also the shared notebook data that is written by other users. The user who is allowed to access another person's notebook data can evaluate that data. This feature of the note-taking function can promote peer learning.

Besides, both lecturers and audiences can check how many keywords appear in the notebook data when they access the following page (Fig. 9).

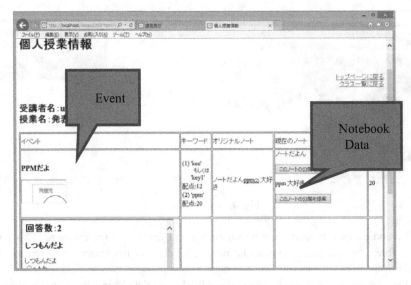

Fig. 9. Review notebook page

Using this page, we can check whether there are keywords in the notebook data, which will enable us to grasp the understanding of audiences. This feature will make our review of the lecture more effective. Besides, the lecturers can teach easily according to the audience's understanding.

3.2   Research Questions and Hypothesis

The effect of digital note taking has already been proven [7]. Therefore, the note-taking function of this paper must also have a positive effect. We phrase our research question (RQ) and hypothesis (H) as follows:

RQ1. Does the note-taking function have a positive effect on the examination score?
H1. The audience that used the note-taking function tends to obtain higher scores than the audience who did not use it.

If the note-taking function of this paper is correctly developed, the hypothesis H1 must be proven because Nakayama [7] has already shown the positive effects of note taking.

The note-taking function of this paper must have additional effects. It is intended to be more effective in combination with various other functions of the ARS module. Therefore, we phrase the second research question as follows:

RQ2. Does the note-taking function have a positive effect in combination with other functions of ARS?

We will verify the above research questions in the following section.

3.3 Use of the Note-Taking Function During Lectures

As shown in Sect. 2, the lecture needs to be designed to encourage audiences to use the notebook function. Therefore, we considered designing the study to attract new users. In particular, the use of the note-taking function was announced and recommended to the audiences at the beginning of the lecture.

ARS was implemented in the lecture as shown in Table 1.

Table 1. Lecture characteristics with ARS implemented

Lecture objective	Introduction to Informatics: Preparing for a qualifying examination on information technology
Type of audience	Students at the Faculty of Economics
Period	April–July 2016
Number of attendants	250
Number of note-taking function users	47

As shown in Table 1, the lecture was designed to help the audiences pass a qualifying examination on information technology. The lecturer explained some issues on information technology and provided related questions from past examinations. Then, the audiences answered the questions using cell phones and ARS. There were 250 attendants, and 47 of them (18%) used the note-taking function. In contrast, only 5% of the participants used the function in the lecture studied by Iitaka [5]. Therefore, this analysis can be considered more reliable than that of Iitaka [5].

Next, the effect of the note-taking function was examined based on the scores achieved by participants during the periodic examination of the lecture.

As shown in Table 2, both skewness and kurtosis are not extreme. Therefore, we consider the distribution of the score data as a normal distribution.

Table 2. Scores on the periodic examination

Average score of all participants	26.46
Average score of the function users	28.30
Average score of participants who did not use the function	26.03
Skewness	-0.427
Kurtosis	-0.466

Then, we checked RQ1. We analyzed the effect of the note-taking function. The average score of all the participants was 26.46. The average score of the function users was 28.30 points; the participants who did not use the function had an average score of 26.03 points. Therefore, the average score of the function users was higher than that of the participants who did not use the notebook function. The t-test proved that the difference is statistically significant ($t(248) = 2.005$, $p < 0.05$). Therefore, we can say that H1 is proven.

These results find support in literature [7]. This paper further studied the effect of the note-taking function in combination with other functions of ARS, which is RQ2. We examined the research question by interacting with other functions of ARS. When we examined the interactions, we found statistically significant interactions between the use of the note-taking function and the use of the comment function. The ARS module has many side functions. The comment function is one of them; it allows the audience to write comments during lectures. The comments are displayed on the screen along with the events (Fig. 10).

Fig. 10. Comments during lectures

To check the interaction, we divide the users of ARS into three groups based on the frequency of use of the note-taking function.

Table 3. User groups

	Frequency	Number
Group 1	0	198
Group 2	1–5	36
Group 3	6–	16

As shown in Table 3, the 198 users who never used the note-taking function formed Group 1; the 36 users who used the function 1–5 times formed Group 2; and the 16 users who used the function more than six times formed Group 3. Though comment writing itself did not have any effect on the examination score ($t(248) = 0.466$, n. s.), it could reinforce the effect of the note-taking function. We could confirm interactions between comment writing and note-taking. ANOVA proved that the interaction is statistically significant ($F(2, 244) = 3.08$, $p < 0.05$).

Table 4. Result of analysis of the interactions (1)

Comment writing		Mean	Std. Error	95% Confidence Interval	
				Lower bound	Upper bound
Not used	Group 1	26.364	.581	25.219	27.509
	Group 2	27.762	1.501	24.806	30.718
	Group 3	27.750	2.432	22.960	32.540
Users	Group 1	25.362	.903	23.583	27.141
	Group 2	24.667	1.776	21.169	28.165
	Group 3	34.750	2.432	29.960	39.540

Table 5. Result of analysis of the interactions (2)

Comment writing			Mean Difference (I − J)	Std. Error	Sig.[a]	95% Confidence Interval for Difference[a]	
						Lower bound	Upper bound
Group 1	Not used (I)	Users (J)	1.002	1.074	.352	−1.113	3.118
	Users (I)	Not used (J)	−1.002	1.074	.352	−3.118	1.113
Group 2	Not used (I)	Users (J)	3.095	2.325	.184	−1.485	7.675
	Users (I)	Not used (J)	−3.095	2.325	.184	−7.675	1.485
Group 3	Not used(I)	Users (J)	−7.000[*]	3.439	.043	−13.774	−.226
	Users (I)	Not used (J)	7.000[*]	3.439	.043	.226	13.774

[*]$p < 0.05$
[a]Adjustment for multiple comparisons: Bonferroni.

Tables 4 and 5 show the significant differences within Group 3. The users of the comment function of Group 3 obviously obtained higher scores than other members of Group 3. The average score of the users in Group 3 was 34.75, whereas the average score of other members in Group 3 was 27.75. Therefore, we obtained results that allowed us to estimate the interactions between the comment function and the note-taking function. These results show how to design a better lecture by using ARS.

4 Discussion of Results

This paper first described the features of the note-taking function. Then, the effect of the function was analyzed. Though the positive effect of note-taking itself had already been confirmed, the effect of the system developed in this paper had not been confirmed [5]. Iitaka [5] stated that this happened because not enough users used the note-taking function. Therefore, this paper tried to obtain more users. As a result, we can confirm statistically significant results that allow us to estimate the positive effect of the note-taking function on the examination scores.

Besides, we also confirmed the interactions between the note-taking function and other ARS functions. We can estimate that the note-taking function interacts with the comment function. If this interaction is investigated more deeply, it will help us design more interactive lectures. We are now building the recommendation engine that suggests better learning plans based on various CMS data. This interaction may help us to create data for such recommendation engines.

However, even this study has a serious limitation. As a reviewer of this paper correctly pointed out, the number of users of the note-taking function is still not enough to perform an in-depth analysis. Actually, an important characteristic of the function is checking keywords and sharing note data. However, there were too few users who had used these sub-functions.

Therefore, we need to design lectures that motivate more audiences to use the note-taking function. Then, we will be able to analyze the effects of the sub-functions (e.g., checking keywords and sharing notes). This analysis will contribute to providing more effective lecture designs using ARS.

Acknowledgement. This work was supported by JSPS KAKENHI Grant Number JP 15K12175.

References

1. Iitaka, T., Hirai, A.: CMS module for online testing. IEICE technical report, Tokyo, vol. 107, no. 462, pp. 25–29 (2008)
2. Iitaka, T.: Mobile practice system using web item databank. IEICE technical report, Tokyo, vol. 111, no. 237, pp. 31–36 (2011)
3. Iitaka, T.: ARS module of contents management system using cell phones. In: Marcus, A. (ed.) DUXU 2013. LNCS, vol. 8015, pp. 682–690. Springer, Heidelberg (2013). doi:10. 1007/978-3-642-39253-5_76
4. Iitaka, T.: On the note-taking function of ARS module. IEICE technical report, Tokyo, ET2014-74, vol. 114, no. 441, pp. 11–16 (2015)
5. Iitaka, T.: An analysis on note making function of a system for interactive lectures. IEICE technical report, Osaka, ET2015-90, vol. 115, no. 444, pp. 29–34 (2016)
6. Nakayama, M., Mutsuura, K., Yamamoto, H.: Impact of note-taking activity for a performance in online learning. IEICE technical report, Tokyo, ET2010-88, vol. 110, no. 405 (2010)
7. Nakayama, M., Mutsuura, K., Yamamoto, H.: Relationship between factors of note-taking activity and student notes assessment in fully online learning environment. IEICE technical report, Tokyo, ET2011-49, vol. 111, no. 237 (2011)
8. Weener, P.: Note taking and student verbalization as instrumental learning activities. Instr. Sci. **3**, 51–74 (1974)
9. Ito, K., Okamoto, T., Isomoto, I., Watanabe, N., Fukuhara, M., Nagaoka, K.: 教育工学研究会の果たすべき役割(教育工学研究の歴史と未来-40周年記念研究会-). IEICE technical report, Tokyo, vol. 107, no. 462, pp. 25–29 (2008)
10. XoopsCube Web Page. http://xoopscube.jp/
11. Xoops Module E-frit Web Page. http://iitaka.no-ip.info
12. Xoops Module Nome Web Page. http://iitaka.no-ip.info/norm/

Measuring User Engagement in Mobile Classroom Response System: A Case Study

Tek Yong Lim[1(✉)], Chia Ying Khor[1], and Yin Bee Oon[2]

[1] Multimedia University, Cyberjaya, Malaysia
{tylim, cykhor}@mmu.edu.my
[2] Universiti Malaysia Sarawak, Kota Samarahan, Malaysia
yinbee@unimas.my

Abstract. Mobile classroom response system, formerly known as clicker, is a promising technology to engage students in a lecture hall. Previous studies reported the positive effects of clickers on student engagement. However, most studies focused on patterns of cohort transitions using clickers during peer-instruction activities. This paper describes a mixed method approach to explore the dynamic of user engagement among undergraduate students in a local Malaysian university. Both interaction log and diary study were selected to track the pattern of ninety five registered students using mobile classroom response system across seven lecture weeks. Interaction logs were used to profile user type, participation type and submission type. The analysis of interaction logs revealed that seven visitors participated during lecture, only around 18% of registered students participated actively, registered students were more likely to answer all questions at the end of lecture compared to the beginning of lecture and middle of lecture. On the other hand, the analysis of diary entries provided qualitative information about user engagement attributes such focused attention, felt involvement, endurability, perceived usability and novelty. Both interaction log and students diary indicated that two registered students had positive engagement using mobile classroom response system during lecture.

Keywords: User engagement · Mobile classroom response system · Interaction log · Diary study

1 Introduction

Technologies have been used to transform the students' learning experience in a lecture hall. For example, instructors adopted television and radio to capture the students' attention in the early days [1]. Then, computer and projector became the necessary tools in every lecture hall. However, these technologies are not design to encourage student participation in traditional lecture hall and the students are more likely to sit passively for entire lecture session. New mobile classroom response system has emerged as a promising technology to engage large audience using mobile devices [2].

Mobile classroom response system, formerly known as clicker [3], is a management tool for instructors to deliver an interactive lecture especially in a large classroom setting. This system is known under various names such as personal response system [4], student

© Springer International Publishing AG 2017
P. Zaphiris and A. Ioannou (Eds.): LCT 2017, Part I, LNCS 10295, pp. 375–388, 2017.
DOI: 10.1007/978-3-319-58509-3_30

response system [5], audience response system [6], electronic voting system [7], wireless keypad [8], and classroom communication system [9]. Throughout this paper, the term mobile classroom response system will refer to an evolution of clicker that works on mobile platform and has enhanced capabilities of a typical clicker.

There are three main components of a mobile classroom response system, namely (1) questioning and presentation, (2) response and display, and (3) data management and analysis [10]. So, this system allows an instructor to post a question, the students submit their responses using their mobile devices and an overview of students' answer is instantly made available on a main projector screen for entire class discussion. After the session ended, the instructor can save every student responses for future analysis, especially to review each student performance.

A considerable amount of literature has been published on the positive impacts of clickers [3, 11, 12]. For examples, acquisition of advanced reasoning skills [13], improvement in student attendance [14], and greater positive enjoyment among students [15]. From the education perspective, these impacts can be categorized into three types of engagement such as cognitive engagement, behavioral engagement and emotional engagement [16]. In short, cognitive engagement can be defined as student psychological investment in learning, the term behavioral engagement refers to student participation in classroom activities, and emotional engagement can be described as student affective reaction in classroom.

On the other hand, user engagement can be viewed as both an outcome of experience and a process during an interaction [17]. Several studies had shown temporal dynamics of user engagement in different contexts such as reading online news [18], writing documents [19], viewing television [20], learning in blended classroom [21] and participating in face-to-face classroom [22]. Most studies, as far as the authors are aware, only focused on patterns of cohort transitions when using clickers [23] and their studies are applicable for peer-instruction activities [24]. This study seeks to explore alternative patterns of user engagement during mobile classroom response system session over a prolonged period of time. This study intends to unravel the dynamic interaction between students and mobile classroom response system. Thus, this study employs a mixed-methods approach to gain an in-depth understanding of user engagement across time.

The remainder of this paper is organized as follows: Sect. 2 reviews the user engagement. In Sect. 3, the methodology used for this study are described. Section 4 presents the findings of the study. The paper concludes in Sect. 5.

2 User Engagement

One of the challenges for user experience researchers is to engage a person using a particular system in a specific context [25]. Different contexts have different user engagement measurements. For example, attendance is one of the common measurements for user engagement in mobile classroom response system. However, attendance may not be a good indicator because certain educational institutions imposed exam barring based on student's poor attendance. Thus, these students are more likely to maintain a good record of their attendance with or without using mobile classroom response system.

In this paper, user engagement can be defined as a quality user experience when a person was pleased using a particular technology and a desire to use the technology more frequently. The user experience can be divided into four types of time span, namely anticipated user experience, momentary user experience, episodic user experience and cumulative user experience [26]. In other words, a user experience may refer to a user imagination before first usage (anticipated user experience), a user feeling during an interaction (momentary user experience), a user appraisal after a particular usage (episodic user experience) or a user view on a technology as a whole over multiple periods of usages (cumulative user experience). Hence, different methods are required to uncover user experience at different time spans. This paper reviews longitudinal methods from human computer interaction perspective because this study attempts to discover the changes of user engagement over time.

2.1 Interaction Log

Interaction log involves tracking a student's behavior automatically when he/she using a mobile classroom response system. The interaction log can reveal students' usage patterns through the whole lecture session and even across an entire trimester. This technique is easy because the instructor can retrieve interaction log directly from the mobile classroom response system. In addition, this method is more scalable compared to human observer because human may not able to track all behavior changes manually in a lecture hall [22]. However, interaction log is also considered as an implicit feedback because an inference is made based on user actions and it may not tell whether a student is really engaged or not. Thus, diary study can be used to complement the findings of interaction log.

2.2 Diary Study

Diary study is another form of logging methods where participants are asked to write an entry about their personal experiences using a particular technology. The diary may contain facts as well as subjective assessment such as feelings and impressions. Diary can help to reveal real student issues and needs in the context of mobile classroom response system. There are three types of diary entry such as interval-contingent protocol, signal-contingent protocol, event-contingent protocol [27]. So, students are required either to document their experiences at fixed intervals (interval-contingent protocol), to make entry when prompted by a signaling device (signal-contingent protocol) or to report each time a particular event occur (event-contingent protocol).

Due to the nature of lecture hall setting, this study employs interaction log based on mobile classroom response system and diary study in order to measure user engagement over time. Both techniques allow researchers to track students' activities indirectly and students can participate in lecture activities without any distraction.

3 Methodology

A case study was conducted in Multimedia University, Malaysia and based on the university database, ninety five undergraduate students registered officially for software requirements engineering in Trimester 2 (2015/2016). Software requirements engineering is considered one of the challenging computing subjects. This subject covered multidisciplinary fields ranging from social sciences to computer science concepts [28].

Various mobile classroom response systems (such as Formative, Pear Deck, Unitag and Kahoot) were introduced and used during lecture. Each mobile classroom response system has its own unique feature. For example, Formative enables students to pick a correct option under multiple choice question and true/false question. Besides that, students can type short answer and show their drawing in Formative. Pear Deck allows students to response by dragging an icon toward the answer area and enables instructor to see the pattern of all students' responses on the projector view. On the other hand, Kahoot plays music sound and displays a countdown timer to encourage students to compete with others. Unitag can generate free quick response code and provides instructor with the ability to track student participation in lottery and scratch card games.

For each lecture week, the instructor had carried out three short clicker sessions (beginning of lecture, middle of lecture and end of lecture) using mobile classroom response system. Different types of questions were posed to students during lecture such as probing students' pre-existing level of understanding, assessing students' ability to apply lecture material to a new situation, and polling student opinions. Only three questions were posed for each clicker session. After each lecture ended, the students were encouraged to post their learning experiences within three days on a social networking website. There is no limit on the number of words. The students can write their diary entry using English language or create multimedia diary such as images or videos. Figure 1 presents the overview of data collection for each lecture week.

Students were rewarded with additional experience scores for their participation using mobile classroom response system and diaries submission. Those additional experience scores accounted for five marks in their coursework grade. Thus, the students were asked to enter their real name and student identification number for every submission.

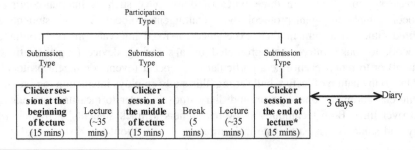

Fig. 1. Overview of data collection for each lecture week

Table 1. Metrics used in this study

Metrics	Description
Type of user	(participate for a particular lecture week)
#User	Number of distinct users
#Registered	Number of registered students
#Visitor	Number of visitors
Type of participation	(for a particular lecture week)
#Active	Number of registered students participated actively in all three consecutively clicker sessions
#Inconsistent	Number of registered students participated inconsistently in certain clicker sessions
#Passive	Number of registered students did not participate in all three consecutively clicker sessions
Type of submission	(for a particular clicker session)
#Complete	Number of registered students submit answers to all questions posed
#Partial	Number of registered students missed out certain questions posed
#None	Number of registered students did not submit any answer for all questions posed

The interaction log of mobile classroom response system was used to profile each student and their level of engagement (see Table 1). A user is refers to the distinct user participates during a particular lecture week and can be divided into two sub-types, namely registered student and visitor. A registered student refers to a student who register officially for the software requirements engineering subject in university database and those with non-registered status are classified as visitors.

An active participation is counted when a student participated with complete submission in all three consecutively clicker sessions for a particular lecture week. An inconsistent participation is considered when a student participated inconsistently in certain clicker sessions due to partial submission or non-submission. A passive participation is recorded when a student did not participate in all three consecutively clicker sessions due to non-submission.

A complete submission is counted when a student submitted his/her answer for all questions posed during a particular clicker session. A partial submission is considered when a student failed to submit his/her answer for certain question(s) during a particular clicker session. A non-submission is recorded when a student did not submit his/her answer for all questions posed during a particular clicker session.

4 Result

Some of lecture weeks were postpone due to public holidays and other lecture weeks required a paper-and-pencil approach because majority students had difficulty to draw requirements models using mobile classroom response system. Thus, this paper only reported seven lecture weeks where mobile classroom response system was used.

4.1   User Types

There were 102 users found in the result across seven lecture weeks. Ninety five of 102 users were registered students and the remaining were seven visitors. Table 2 summarizes the number of distinct users participated in lecture using mobile classroom response system. The trend showed that the number of distinct users participated at the beginning of trimester was higher (Week 1, Week 2, Week 3) but the distinct users' participation decreased at the end of trimester (Week 13).

Although the number of distinct users did not exceed the actual registered students for each week, but there was a small number of visitors participated in clicker sessions (except on Week 3) and a further analysis revealed that there was one visitor participated in four out of seven lecture weeks.

Table 2. Summary of user types

Lecture week	Week1	Week2	Week3	Week4	Week6	Week12	Week13
#User	84	89	93	89	90	79	66
#Registered	83	87	93	87	88	78	64
#Visitor	1	2	0	2	2	1	2

4.2   Participation Types

For this section, we reported findings on ninety five registered students only and excluded all visitors from the analysis. Figure 2 shows the participation types of registered students for seven lecture weeks. The trend showed that registered students

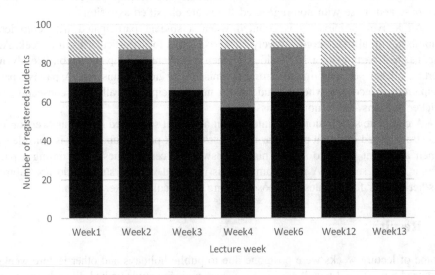

Fig. 2. Overview of participation types over seven lecture weeks

participated more actively using mobile classroom response system in the early of trimester (74% in Week 1 and 86% in Week 2) compared to the end of trimester (42% in Week 12 and 37% in Week 13). In other words, more than 50% of registered students shown either inconsistent or passive participation during clicker sessions at the end of trimester. However, we cannot make an assumption that a registered student had the same participation pattern throughout the whole trimester.

Thus, a further analysis was performed at individual level and revealed that only around 18% of ninety five registered students were participated actively across seven lecture weeks. The remaining registered students (82%) had inconsistent participation. From the interaction log analysis, we selected two students who participated actively (Learner#45) and inconsistently (Learner#85) during clicker sessions. Figure 3 compares the participation types between Learner#45 and Learner#85. Learner#85 had one active participation (Week 3), five inconsistent participation (Week 1, Week 2, Week 4, Week 6, Week 12) and one passive participation (Week 13). On the other hand, Learner#45 had active participation consistently across seven lecture weeks.

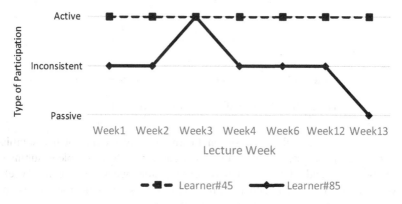

Fig. 3. Comparison of Learner#45's and Learner#85's participation types

4.3   Submission Types

In this section, only the active and inconsistent participations of registered students were analyzed to recreate the sequence of behavioral actions that occurred during clicker sessions. Figure 4 provides the submission types of registered students for each clicker session (beginning of lecture, middle of lecture and end of lecture).

With a total of 1740 submissions over seven lecture weeks, the analysis showed that the number of complete submissions gradually increased per clicker session (27% at the beginning of lecture, 30% at the middle of lecture and 31% at the end of lecture). On the other hand, the number of non-submissions were highly occurred at the beginning of lecture (5%) compared to at the middle of lecture (1%) and at the end of lecture (1%). The number of partial submissions were frequently happened at the middle of lecture (3%) compared to at the beginning of lecture (1%) and at the end of lecture (1%).

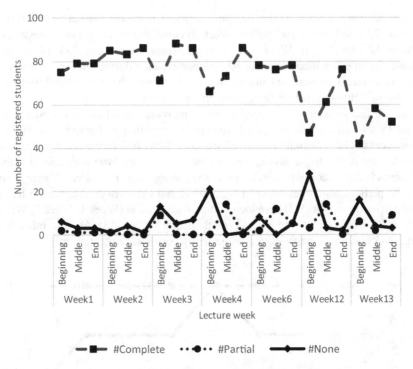

Fig. 4. Overall submission types over seven lecture weeks

We performed a granular analysis on Learner#85 by looking at her submission types for each clicker session (see Fig. 5). Learner#85 had complete submissions consistently at the end of lecture across seven lecture weeks except for Week 13. However, she tend to have either partial submissions or non-submissions at the beginning of lecture except for Week 3 and Week 6.

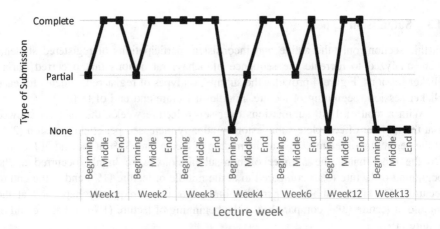

Fig. 5. Submission types for Learner#85

4.4   Diary Entries

The students' diary went through two iterative examinations. The first pass through the data focused on identification of emotional responses related to mobile classroom response system. Then, each excerpt was analyzed using user engagement attributes categorization scheme derived from [29]. The model of user engagement consists of six factors, namely aesthetic appeal, focused attention, perceived usability, novelty, felt involvement and endurability. However, aesthetic appeal was not found in the student diary entries. From the systematic analysis approach, we describe the findings according to the five attributes of user engagement.

Focused Attention. Focused attention is refers to student concentration on one stimulus only and ignoring others. Sometimes, the student become absorbed with learning activities and surprised at how much time passes. The diary entries revealed that some students put their full attention by listening to lecture so that they can answer those questions posed by instructor using mobile classroom response system.

"Then, coming to the lecture class, same old boring lecture class is not the same anymore. During the first session I almost fell asleep.. sorry. But surprise surprise, 3 super simple questions to answer after every session, when I say super simple I mean provided that you pay attention in class. Well, it's a really good way to help me focus in class honestly, especially by using goformative, it makes it so simple and easy for us to access and answer the questions." (Learner#28)

"With every segments of the lecture, we are provided with a set of questions based on what was taught on Formative. This kind of new learning environment made me somewhat excited towards the lecture and what was taught, I began to listen more attentively instead of staring down the table to my phone screen like I used to do... As we transitioned from lecture to answering question in Formative from time to time, I didn't even realized that two full hours have passed. With this new learning experience that I had, I hope that it will continue enriching me throughout this semester." (Learner#26)

Novelty. Novelty can be defined as a new, interesting or unexpected situation that increases students' curiosity and rouses their inquisitive behavior. In other words, those sudden and surprising changes evoke a positive reaction, such as excitement and joy, from the student. The students highlighted the uniqueness of each mobile classroom response system being introduced in different lecture and how these mobile classroom response systems are effectively blended in lecture.

"Class activity in this week we are using a website call "Peardeck". "Peardeck" are different from goformative, the way to answer some of the question in "Peardeck" are different, we using the red-dot to point to the answer instead of typing the text to answer." (Learner#72)

"In the end of this lecture, the lecturer asked us to vote for the date and duration for the replacement class and for the midterm test and presentation by using Kahoot. The Kahoot is good as it is new to us and voting will show more democratic results." (Learner#88)

Perceived Usability. Perceived usability is defined as cognitive and affective aspects when dealing with mobile classroom response system. Sometimes, students may experience frustration when they could not complete certain tasks using mobile classroom response system. The students shared their negative experiences such as difficulty to draw requirements model on their mobile device due to small screen size. Some students highlighted that they could not participate because their mobile phone were out of battery or exceeded mobile data quota. A high rate of inconsistent participation in a particular lecture supported these students' comments.

"Although we are using back the GoFormative but the method that used to answer the question seriously difficult for the big-hand person. The mobile phone's screen so small and my hand so big (T^T) I have try to write the answer on the blank box for more than twice. And the most important is the system did not provide the erase to users which mean if you write wrongly then you have to "re-draw" it." (Learner#68)

"The goFormative activity today caused some problems for a few students. (Phone cannot snap photo, cannot upload photo, phone no battery) ... Not sure if goFormative or their phone is at fault." (Learner#87)

Felt Involvement. Felt involvement can be described as student's feeling of the overall learning experience as fun. In other words, the students are enjoyed with learning experience using mobile classroom response system during lecture.

"Software Requirement Engineering (TSE2451) it sounds like a dull and boring subject, but it is quite fun when I attended the first class. First, this is not the first subject that use online assessment platform to evaluate students, but this is a first class that give me a chance to get bonus marks by earning experience marks from the online assessments. Second, I like the teaching style of the lecture. Lecture will prepare an online assessment about the topic after each lecture." (Learner#37)

"Waw....I-nigma, the QR code scanner is the best. It just take less than one second to bring me to the web page. Fantastic! With all the interesting activities in the class, I have never falling asleep in the class. I'm so scare that I will miss the fun games." (Learner#35)

Endurability. Endurability is refers to likelihood to remember things that students have enjoyed and a desire to repeat a fun activity. Thus, a positive past experience using mobile classroom response system would encourage the students to do the same activity again in the future. Some students indicated in their diary that they were excited and eager to come again for the next lecture.

"The past two week class for this subject was quite fun with the use of goformative.com. I really love the way the lecturer conducting the class by providing us short quizzes every time we finish a subtopic. This method is actually quite efficient because it helps me to understand better on what the lecturer teaching us. So far I scored well in the quizzes and that really helps my confidence level and make me feel that I can do

really well for this subject for this semester. I'm looking forward for next week lecture class." (Learner#81)

4.5   Holistic View on User Engagement Patterns

By connecting the two students' diary entries with their interaction logs, we were able to understand that both students (Learner#45 and Learner#85) had positive engagement using mobile classroom response system. As shown in Table 3, six diary entries shared by Learner#45. In Week 1 and Week 2, Learner#45 highlighted that she was actively thinking when answering those questions posed using mobile classroom response system (Formative). She also had fun time with her friends during Week 3. On Week 4, she had a new experience using a different mobile classroom response system (Unitag)

Table 3. Diary entries of Learner#45

Week	Diary excerpt	Identified engagement attributes
Week 1	*"Great in motivation but brain teasing in answering goformative session, must squeeze a lot of 'brain juice'!"*	Focused attention
Week 2	*"Answering goformative question significantly developed my understanding of the subject although I mentioned 'twisting my brain' from the 1st journal but honestly it really did a brush up what we had learned from the class and figure out the reason for the answer. In addition, [instructor] had discussed the answer immediately after the quiz and this makes me understand better and not easy to forget."*	Focused attention
Week 3	*"Overall, it was quite fun and student may have better understanding involving themselves in the activity rather than reading the textbook word by word."*	Felt involvement
Week 4	*"Lastly, QR reader has been introduced in the questionnaire activity. It was a new experience for me and interesting as well."*	Novel
	"I am excited and looking forward new technology introduced in the class."	Endurability
Week 6	*"Yet, Kahoot! another fun apps introduced in the class. I very appreciated [instructor] effort on finding and introduced us new apps to experience and learn the new technology."*	Novel
Week 13	*"Thanks to [instructor] on interesting learning experience on variety of class activities, and quizzes e.g. kahoot, Pear Deck, goformative, bingo, MTSB quiz and so forth. Amazing computerized mid-term test that you immediately know your score after the test."*	Novel

Table 4. Diary entries of Learner#85

Week	Diary excerpt	Identified engagement attributes
Week 2	*"I wasn't able to do last week's journal as everything was haywire with the first week drama, but I told myself to start this week onwards. It's better to be late than never."*	
	"I came late to yesterday class because I only had a one hour break to have lunch and in that hour, it was lunch hour so practically everywhere was in a mess. Though I came late, I sat in front and learned three facet's."	
	"I was able to answer the six questions as well in goformative so I felt yesterday class was good to me. I don't feel quite lost anymore and I feel pretty confident about this subject."	Focused attention
Week 3	*"This week was fun during lecture. I had so much fun and made new friends in class."*	Felt involvement
Week 4	*"This week was another interesting lecture. We used QR code scanner to answer questions instead of goformative."*	Novel
	"I enjoyed this week lecture and tutorial we did exercise which made me learn a lot."	Felt involvement
Week 6	*"This week class was rather exciting, we had to draw in GoFormative, and using my tiny phone, I managed to do so it was really funny though because not only that, MMU wifi was another problem, so face problem did strike here and there."*	Perceived usability
	"Besides that, we did votes and yaaaay my votes were all on the winning side tongue emoticon"	Felt involvement
Week 12	*"Answering the questions at goformative was fun as usual though my phone wasn't working well."*	Perceived usability
	"But most of all, opening the ang pow at the end was the main highlight, 10 XP yaaaay! grin emoticon"	Felt involvement

and excited to attend the next lecture. She highlighted a new mobile classroom response system (Kahoot) in Week 6 and shared her overall positive learning experience using various mobile classroom response systems in Week 13.

Learner#85 also submitted her diary entries in this study (see Table 4). On Week 2, she indicated her reason for being late (inconsistent participation) but she was satisfied with her own performance using mobile classroom response system (Formative). She also shared her positive engagement with her new friends in Week 3. She highlighted a new mobile classroom response system (Unitag) on Week 4. For Week 6 and Week 12, she faced some challenges such as wireless local area network and drawing on mobile device (inconsistent participation) but she was happy with voting result (Kahoot) and electronic lucky draw (Unitag) using mobile classroom response system.

5 Conclusion

In general, this paper has shown a different insight on user engagement by employing both interaction log and diary study methods. This mixed-methods approach unravels the temporal dynamic of user engagement using mobile classroom response system. The results of this study allow researchers to understand why students were engaged during lecture. These student behaviors may not be obvious in a large classroom setting because the lecturer's goal is to deliver knowledge and share the knowledge in an engaging setting. This information could help lecturers to deliver an engaging lecture by using appropriate mobile classroom response system in the future.

Acknowledgement. This work was supported by Ministry of Education Malaysia under the Fundamental Research Grant Scheme (FRGS/1/2016/SS06/MMU/02/1).

References

1. Cuban, L.: Teachers and Machines: The Classroom Use of Technology Since 1920. Teachers College Press, New York (1986)
2. Dunn, P.K., Richardson, A., Oprescu, F., McDonald, C.: Mobile-phone-based classroom response systems: students' perceptions of engagement and learning in a large undergraduate course. Int. J. Math. Educ. Sci. Technol. **44**, 1160–1174 (2013)
3. Caldwell, J.E.: Clickers in the large classroom: current research and best-practice tips (2007). http://www.lifescied.org/content/6/1/9.short
4. Gauci, S.A., Dantas, A.M., Williams, D.A., Kemm, R.E.: Promoting student-centered active learning in lectures with a personal response system. Adv. Physiol. Educ. **33**, 60–71 (2009)
5. Aljaloud, A., Gromik, N., Billingsley, W., Kwan, P.: Research trends in student response systems: a literature review. Int. J. Learn. Technol. **10**, 313 (2015)
6. Schackow, T.E., Chavez, M., Loya, L., Friedman, M.: Audience response system: effect on learning in family medicine residents. Fam. Med. **36**(4), 496–504 (2004)
7. Draper, S.W., Brown, M.I.: Increasing interactivity in lectures using an electronic voting system (2004). http://onlinelibrary.wiley.com/doi/10.1111/j.1365-2729.2004.00074.x/full
8. Burnstein, R.A., Lederman, L.M.: Using wireless keypads in lecture classes. Phys. Teach. **39**, 8 (2001)
9. Dufresne, R.J., Gerace, W.J., Leonard, W.J., Mestre, J.P., Wenk, L.: Classtalk: a classroom communication system for active learning. J. Comput. High. Educ. **7**, 3–47 (1996)
10. Deal, A.: Classroom Response Systems: A Teaching with Technology White Paper
11. Fies, C., Marshall, J.: Classroom response systems: a review of the literature (2006). http://link.springer.com/article/10.1007/s10956-006-0360-1
12. Kay, R.H., LeSage, A.: Examining the benefits and challenges of using audience response systems: a review of the literature. Australas. J. Educ. Technol. **25**, 235–249 (2009)
13. DeBourgh, G.: Use of classroom "clickers" to promote acquisition of advanced reasoning skills. Nurse Educ. Pract. **8**(2), 76–87 (2008)
14. Greer, L., Heaney, P.: Real-time analysis of student comprehension: an assessment of electronic student response technology in an introductory earth science course. J. Geosci. Educ. **52**, 345–351 (2004)

15. Stowell, J.R., Nelson, J.M.: Benefits of electronic audience response systems on student participation, learning, and emotion. Teach. Psychol. **34**, 253–258 (2007)
16. Fredricks, J.A., Blumenfeld, P.C., Paris, A.H.: School engagement: potential of the concept, state of the evidence. Rev. Educ. Res. **74**, 59–109 (2004)
17. O'Brien, H.L., Maclean, K.E.: Measuring the user engagement process. In: Engagement by Design, Pre-Conference Work, CHI 2009, pp. 1–7 (2009)
18. Lagun, D., Lalmas, M.: Understanding user attention and engagement in online news reading. In: Proceedings of the Ninth ACM International Conference on Web Search and Data Mining - WSDM 2016, pp. 113–122. ACM Press, New York (2016)
19. Liu, M., Calvo, R.A., Pardo, A., Martin, A.: Measuring and visualizing students' behavioral engagement in writing activities. IEEE Trans. Learn. Technol. **8**, 215–224 (2015)
20. Hernandez, J., Liu, Z., Hulten, G., Debarr, D., Krum, K., Zhang, Z.: Measuring the engagement level of TV viewers. In: 2013 10th IEEE International Conference and Workshops on Automatic Face and Gesture Recognition, FG 2013 (2013)
21. Henrie, C.R., Bodily, R., Manwaring, K.C., Graham, C.R.: Exploring intensive longitudinal measures of student engagement in blended learning. Int. Rev. Res. Open Distrib. Learn. **16**, 131–155 (2015)
22. Lane, B.E.S., Harris, S.E.: a new tool for measuring student behavioral engagement in large university classes. J. Coll. Sci. Teach. **44**, 83–91 (2015)
23. Majumdar, R., Iyer, S.: Beyond clickers: tracing patterns in students' response through iSAT. (2015)
24. Kushnir, L.P.: The clicker way to an "A"! New evidence for increased student learning and engagement: understanding the pedagogy behind the technology. World Conf. Educ. Multimedia, Hypermedia Telecommun. **2013**, 2212–2221 (2013)
25. O'Brien, H.: Theoretical perspectives on user engagement. In: Why Engagement Matters: Cross-Disciplinary Perspectives of User Engagement in Digital Media, pp. 1–26 (2016)
26. Roto, V., Law, E., Vermeeren, A., Hoonhout, J.: User experience white paper: bringing clarity to the concept of user experience. Semin. Demarcating User Exp. **12**, 1–12 (2010)
27. Wheeler, L., Reis, H.T.: Self-recording of everyday life events: origins, types, and uses. J. Pers. **59**, 339–354 (1991)
28. Portugal, R.L.Q., Engiel, P., Pivatelli, J., do Prado Leite, J.C.S.: Facing the challenges of teaching requirements engineering. In: Proceedings of the 38th International Conference on Software Engineering Companion - ICSE 2016, pp. 461–470. ACM Press, New York (2016)
29. Brien, H.L.O., Toms, E.G.: The development and evaluation of a survey to measure user engagement. J. Am. Soc. Inf. Sci. Technol. **61**, 50–69 (2010)

Higher Education Disruption Through IoT and Big Data: A Conceptual Approach

Fernando Moreira[1,2(✉)], Maria João Ferreira[3,4], and Abílio Cardoso[1]

[1] DEGI, Portucalense Institute for Legal Research–IJP, Univ. Portucalense, Porto, Portugal
{fmoreira,Abilio.Cardoso}@upt.pt
[2] IEETA, Universidade Aveiro, Aveiro, Portugal
[3] Univ. Portucalense, Porto, Portugal
mjoao@upt.pt
[4] Algoritmi, Universidade do Minho, Braga, Portugal

Abstract. The emergence of new technologies such as IoT and Big Data, the change in the behavior of society in general and the younger generation in particular, require higher education institutions to "look" for teaching differently. This statement is complemented by the prediction of the futurist Thomas Frey, who postulates that *"in 14 years it will be a big deal when students learn from robot teachers over the internet"*. Thus, it is necessary to urgently begin a disruption of current teaching models, to be able to include in these processes the new technologies and the daily habits of the new generations. The early usage of mobile devices and the constant connection to the Internet (social networks, among others) mean that the current generation of young people, who are reaching higher education, has the most technological literacy ever. In this new context, this article presents a disruptive conceptual approach to higher education, using information gathered by IoT and based on Big Data & Cloud Computing and Learning Analytics analysis tools. This approach will, for example, allow individualized solutions taking into account the characteristics of the students, to help them customize their curriculum and overcome their limitations and difficulties, throughout the learning process .

Keywords: Education · Disruption · IoT · Big Data · Higher education institutions

1   Introduction

According to [1], educational systems in general and those of higher education in particular have not had the expected evolution in terms of the potential introduced by the adoption of technology and virtual teaching/learning approaches, e-learning, m-learning [2], u-learning [3]. Although these tools are used, educators do not sufficiently exploit their great potentialities and the objectives for which they were proposed. In this context, it is possible to specify u-learning, which theoretically has great potential, since it allows the expansion of access to learning contents and collaborative learning environments, anytime and anywhere, combining physical and virtual spaces. With the stated purpose, the Massive Open Online Courses (MOOCs) and some alternative approaches (Flipped

© Springer International Publishing AG 2017
P. Zaphiris and A. Ioannou (Eds.): LCT 2017, Part I, LNCS 10295, pp. 389–405, 2017.
DOI: 10.1007/978-3-319-58509-3_31

Classroom, Class-wide Discussion, …) were some of the innovations introduced in the training processes of students [4] that they intended to implement disruption, but without the expected success. However, it is clear that, within the current technologies, some are beginning to reveal a significant and increasing role in the education area. For example, whenever students obtain online learning materials and need to work actively with them, it may be beneficial to observe their behavior in order to apply adjustments or corrective measures. The teacher, when asking questions such as, are students solving the tasks in the correct order? or How many times have students viewed the video or heard the podcast? Can provide the teacher with data that enable him to make a curriculum adaptation according to the students characteristics concerning the required pace of work, materials available, among others.

As previously noted, the use of observation and correction measures, Internet of Things (IoT), Big Data and Learning Analytics will play a key role in education as more and more students expect to have their "… *personalized Curriculum delivered to their desk*" [1].

Understanding both the technical support and the social impact of IoT is, and will be, crucial for the future digital professionals [5]. According to [6, 7] "*The global accessibility of education may be provided through the use of Internet of Things*". This is justified by the predictions found in the literature about the number of sensors that will be linked up to 2020. For example, Boche [8] indicates that there will be about 14 billion devices; Cisco assumes that about 50 billion will be connected and Morgan Stanley indicates that the number may currently be over 75 billion [9]. However, all the authors agree that most of these will be smart wearables, which are the latest technological trends. The increasing distribution of sensors provides a massive amount of data sources, and thus new possibilities for applications and services for higher education will emerge.

In this context, learning in the future will be determined by personalization and creativity as indicated in [10]. With the same perspective, in an interview in 1988 [11] Isaac Asimov predicted that, "*computing could allow such a personalized, one-teacher-one-student experience to be available to the masses, replacing or supplementing the one-teacher-many-students Experience of most classrooms*."

Personalization, because smart wearables will collect enough data to "*know*" well the habits and preferences of their users and, in the case of education, to provide the means for quality training, planned and controllable, so that it is possible to perceive the advantages, conditions and limits of learning in an intelligent context. Thus, the gathering, storage and processing of data will be critical, and therefore the crucial need to use Big Data techniques.

Big Data has a comprehensive application [12], covering a wide range of areas, including science, engineering, medicine, healthcare, finance, business, education, transportation, retail and telecommunications, and organizations such as small and large companies, Government departments, human-machine interaction, etc.

Nowadays, the market already provides a considerable set of tools and techniques [13] for monitoring and analysis of automatically collected data on students' activities. In this way, it is possible to use these powerful features to integrate a large amount of data from multiple sources and use them to extract useful behavioral information. In addition, according to the Horizon report [14], the data gathered from the learning actions in conjunction with Learning Analytics allows to enhance the curricula adequacy with the student's profile [15]. However, behavioral analysis is a complex endeavor, given the existence of several factors that may influence students' behavior. These factors include, but are not limited to, family, friends, habits and interests, and data regarding those factors are not readily available and may raise ethical and/or legal issues in the way that they are collected and used.

Notwithstanding the above, the gather of data regarding students from higher education can be facilitated, since universities already monitor, and have available some student behavioral data. According to [16] they are: (i) Institutional databases; (ii) Personal data that may be in digital format (e-mails, digital photographs, videos, etc.), or not digital (paper documents, notes, paper photographs, etc.); (iii) Digital track on the web, if the students are connected through the university network or Wi-Fi network areas, individually or collectively. In addition, it is also possible to monitor outdoor activities, in particular the various sources of information that the university has at its disposal: (i) Data related to the entrance and exit of cars in the institution; (ii) Video surveillance data; (iii) Information on various areas of the university (canteen, bar, library, etc.) and (iv) IoT data.

With all this data, the next phase is its integration so that it is possible to extract models of behavior. In this context monitor students based on their background training, profile, performance history, demographics current interests and activities. Long and Siemens [17] show that listening to a teacher in a traditional classroom or reading a book leaves a very limited track that can be harnessed for monitoring and/or intervention. However, students produce data with *"every click, every tweet or Facebook status update, every social interaction and every page read online,"* along with students' digital records, "online learning, Happening in the learning process." In this context and according to Oracle [18] through knowledge *"student's work, social, and eating habits"* it is easier to anticipate problems in the teaching-learning process (TLP) and to initiate actions to correct them.

The proper evaluation of all data, as well as the information collected from IoT objects related to a variety of physical characteristics of didactic interest, lead teachers to raise some important questions that may be decisive to choose the most appropriate curriculum, (e.g., corrective measures) to be applied to a particular student.

This article presents a disruptive conceptual approach aimed at higher using information gathered by IoT and based on Big Data & Cloud Computing analysis tools and Learning Analytics, which, for example, will allow individualized curricula solutions taking into account the students' characteristics to help them customize their curriculum and know their limitations and difficulties throughout the learning process.

2 Background

In this section, the relevant concepts are presented for a better understanding and analysis of the issues under discussion.

2.1 Main Concepts

Disruption. Disruption can be considered as an enabler for the transformation of any activity sector from the retail to the computers, through education, and one of its objectives is the quality and cost reduction of goods and services [19].

According to the Oxford Dictionary [20], disruption is defined as a *"Disturbance or problems which interrupt an event, activity, or process"*, and at [21] is *"the mechanism that ignites the true power of capitalism in two ways: And creative construction."*

Disruption can be oriented in two ways: (1) creation of a completely new market, or (2) creation of alternative, profitable business models for less demanding customers [21]. It is in the first strand where the most disruptive innovations are found, for example, the telephone, the computer, etc.

In education, the problem of disruption is more complex, as indicated in [22] *"The last technological disruption in teaching happened more than 500 years ago. Until then, the role of the 'lecturer' had been clear—the word's source being the Latin 'lectura', meaning to 'read'."* The same authors point that the role of educators has not evolved, since most use the same instruments (lessons, homework, tests, etc.) in the TLP. However, a set of paths are provided to overcome resistance to change and create a disruption in TLP, namely the possibility of having customized curricula, introducing technologies that enable Learning Analytics and Adaptive Learning, the use of artificial intelligence techniques, recommendation agents, among others. Finally, there is still, according to [22] a fundamental point, the *"universities have such an investment in their existing structures that they are unwilling to change."*

IoT. Kevin Ashton in 1999 [23] introduced the term Internet of Things (IoT) in the context of supply chain management. However, its use has become more comprehensive and inclusive in relation to several areas of activity (health, transport, etc.) [24], and integrated into our daily lives by any citizen [25]. IoT [26] has gained drive due to the advancement of telecommunications, with the growth of broadband networks, integrated in a wide variety of devices (mobile devices, vehicles, etc.) that can be managed via web providing data in real-time [27]. This data can be placed in the cloud [24] for processing, with the necessary protection, since in many cases it is related to people, that is, personal data such as location, health, etc.

Given the disruption of IoT, its definition is still not consensual, and there are several definitions in the literature. In [28] IoT is defined as *"The worldwide network of inter-connected objects uniquely addressable based on standard communication protocols."* The IoT European Projects Cluster [24] defines IoT as *"'Things' are active participants in business, information and social processes where they are enabled to interact and communicate among themselves and with the environment by exchanging data and information sensed about the environment, while reacting autonomously to the real/physical world events and influencing it by running processes that trigger actions and create services with or without direct human intervention."* Moreover, Gubbi, et al. [26] defines IoT as an *"Interconnection of sensing and actuating devices providing the ability to share information across platforms through a unified framework, developing a common operating picture for enabling innovative applications. This is achieved by seamless ubiquitous sensing, data analytics and information representation with Cloud computing as the unifying framework."*

With the emergence of these sensors, their application in TLPs is still at a very embryonic stage, due to the lack of adaptability of HEIs infrastructures, namely the investment needed and, on the other hand, the ethical and legal issues of collection, storage and treatment of personal data. In this context, the use of the definition introduced in [26] is appropriate for adaptation to the education sector.

Big Data. According to the International Data Corporation (IDC), in 2011 were created and copied 1.8 ZB, and projected that this data volume will grow about nine times in the next five years [29]. In this context, the term Big Data is used to describe large data sets, including unstructured data and their analysis in real time. To illustrate this growth it is possible to point out examples of internationally known organizations: Google processes thousands of Petabyte (PB), Facebook stores about 10 PB per month, YouTube receives from upload 72 h of videos per minute [30]. Additionally, with the growth of cloud computing and IoT, the amount of data generated will be even greater. The very strong growth in data generation, storage and analysis raises a number of issues, including how to store and manipulate heterogeneous data, the scalability of systems, complexity, and privacy that are yet to be addressed.

The definition of Big Data presents the same problem of cloud computing in its initial phase, that is, the existence of several definitions, because Big Data is an abstract concept. The definition/concept of Big Date has been a source of great discussion both in industry and academia [31, 32].

In 2010 Apache Hadoop defined Big Data as "*datasets which could not be captured, managed, and processed by general computers within an acceptable scope.*" However, Big Data was already defined in 2001 by Doug Laney as the 3Vs model (Volume, Velocity, and Variety) [33]. In the "3Vs" model, Volume means, with the generation and collection of masses of data, data scale becomes increasingly big; Velocity means the timeliness of big data, specifically, data collection and analysis, etc. Must be rapidly and timely conducted, only to use the commercial value of big data; Variety indicates the various types of data, which includes semi-structured and unstructured data such as audio, video, webpage, and text, as well as traditional structured data. On the other hand, others have different opinions, including IDC, that in 2011, defined Big Data as "*big data technologies describes the new generation of technologies and architectures, designed to economically extract value from very large volumes of a wide variety of data, by enabling the High-velocity capture, discovery, and/or analysis*" [29]. After this definition, a fourth V was added, with Big Data being applied as a 4Vs model, i.e. Volume (great volume), Variety (various modalities), Velocity (rapid generation), and Value (very low but very low density). Facebook's Jay Parikh says, "*You could only own a bunch of data other than big data if you do not use the collected data*" [30].

As a complement, NIST defined Big Data as "*the data of which the data volume, acquisition speed, or data representation limits the capacity of using traditional relational methods to conduct effective analysis or the data which may be effectively processed with important horizontal zoom technologies*".

In the proposed disruptive conceptual approach, the definition presented by NIST is sufficiently broad to be assumed as the most adequate.

Learning Analytics. Learning Analytics (LA) is defined as "*the measurement, collection, analysis and reporting of data about learners and their contexts, for purposes of understanding and optimizing learning and the environments in which it occurs*" [34].

Different authors have complemented this definition over time: Campell [35] shown that an analysis process is composed of five steps: (i) capture, (ii) report, (iii) predict, (iv) act, and (v) refine. Later the concept of closed loop in the process was introduced to create an interactive effect [36]. In a next phase, the stakeholders are included in the previous cycle according to their visions and missions [37], complemented by anonymization in order to preserve students' privacy [38].

In this context, and for students, all the information that is collected regarding their activity is processed in order to carry out an analysis to support the actions to be taken by both teachers and students [39]. The authors [40, 41] show that, in addition to the above analysis, it is necessary to take into account how information is presented to the stakeholders in this process information, that is, system feedback. Finally, the study of students' behavior patterns can be very useful in order to adopt strategies to improve the learning process [42, 43].

2.2   Related Technologies

Technologies presented and discussed above, as can be concluded, are directly related among each other. Cloud Computing is related to Big Data since its main purpose is to use the great capacity of computing and storage. Thus, Cloud Computing provides solutions for storing and processing Big Data. However, the two technologies have different concepts and different audiences.

The evolution of Big Data was driven by the rapidly growing demand for Cloud Computing applications built on virtualized technologies. Consequently, Cloud Computing not only provides computation and processing for Big Data, but also itself is a mode of service; in this way, advances in Cloud Computing promote the development of Big Data, since they complement each other.

As far as IoT is concerned, there is and will be a large set of sensors embedded in networked devices around the world. According to HP, in 2030, the number of sensors will reach a trillion, and IoT data will be the "*supplier*" of Big Data's most important data, since they include heterogeneity, variety, unstructured, etc. These sensors have as main function to collect the various types of data, from environmental data to logistic data, practically passing crossing through all sectors of activity and society. According to Intel the Big Data, in IoT, has three essential characteristics: (i) many terminals generate large amounts of data; (ii) the data generated is semi-structured and unstructured, and (iii) the data is useful only when analyzed.

The data generated by IoT presents a set of characteristics that, in addition to its importance, have to be taken into account for its use: (i) large scale data (e.g. location, video surveillance); (ii) heterogeneity; (iii) strong correlation between space and time (important dimensions for statistical analysis); (iv) Effective data represents only a small part of Big Data (during traffic video surveillance, only serving frames, or rule violations or accidents).

As a conclusion, one of the biggest problems with the data generated by IoT is its heterogeneity and the complexity that has not existed until up to now [44].

3   State of the Art

The need to find solutions to the problems previously analyzed is possible, at an initial stage, by the analysis of works carried out in the area and in related areas. Almost all HEIs live today with pedagogical models of teachers and students. In the first case, teachers follow the classical model (pedagogies used from the 14th century) and mostly with face-to-face teaching. While students already follow a more "hybrid" model, since many of the materials needed for their study are already online and therefore, which fit into a b-Learning model.

One of the attempts, with greater visibility, to induce a disruption in higher education is the MOOCs in the sense of being able to challenge the education scale, but with "old" pedagogies that led to its failure [45]. However, MOOCs have left a set of clues for the future, since (i) audiences are increasingly heterogeneous, (ii) with involvement in face-to-face, virtual or mixed activities, (iii) controlled by teachers and/or by software and (iv) skills for the present century are changing [45]. With regard to the skills to be acquired by the 21st century students, according to [45], autonomy is the most critical competence, since it requires pedagogy of autonomy and initiative.

In [46] the authors propose a model to teach topics related to IoT based on a platform in the cloud web-service oriented. This model aims to provide university students with knowledge about IoT regarding concepts, possibilities and business models that allow the development of prototypes using micro devices and cloud. The model is based on traditional lessons in a Short Message Service (SMS) system. The authors suggest that educational institutions should provide students with the greatest number of didactic approaches to increase their motivation. The proposed model, given the small number of participants, did not allow significant results to be obtained on its feasibility.

The need to obtain information on how students interact with e-learning platforms is the subject of study [47]. In this article, the authors present a service-based architecture and deployed in the cloud to obtain, analyze and present information obtained from distance learning environments, for example Virtual Worlds. Teachers with the information collected regarding students' interactions with the system have extracted the necessary information to identify behaviors and/or practices that can lead to poor results and thus implement corrective procedures.

The projects used in the TLP, in several areas, using virtual worlds, such as Second Life, is a reality [48–50]. However, the important issue that raises one or more problems is how to extract data from participants' activities and how they can be used to improve TLP and students' assessment.

One of the current trends to support TLP is Learning Analytics [51–54]. This field of research is very broad and can be applied to many areas of science, according to [49] *"for example it includes issues related to software engineering architectures, data retrieval, knowledge discovery, etc."* Beyond the coverage is an important area of research, since its integration can – on analysis of information from various sources (LMS sensors, institutional databases, etc.) – to support the definition of the custom curriculum, and student orientation and motivation during TLP. These information flows from various sources are important in decision making in learning systems that allow a disruption of current TLPs, if it is possible to have solutions that go along with all phases (data retrieval, data storage, data discovery, knowledge discovery, knowledge Representation), as indicated in [51].

The identification and validation of behaviors using standards allow students to perceive their usage trends in order to understand the knowledge and proficiency regarding the resources available for TLP [55–58]. This knowledge – to see whether students value and motivate themselves in TLP based on technology or content, or both – is fundamental to the introduction of new teaching models, namely when students have individualized curricula and can perform autonomously, and anywhere.

The increasing use in the development of IoT scenario's tests has been a reason for recent research. In [1] a project is presented using IoT with Arduino boards whose objective is to show that the latest technologies can be introduced successfully in TLP. This success must be guaranteed using, on the one hand, mechanisms of collection, storage, representation of knowledge, etc., in order to have as much in-depth knowledge as possible of the actions taken by the student during the learning activity and, on the other hand, these Innovations are accompanied by the evolution of teaching-learning methodologies [51]. Gomez et al. [59] present a project where the focus is the use of IoT to create more learning spaces, allowing students to interact with physical objects that surround them and that are associated with the learning activity that they are doing. The obtained results were very promising, showing that students improved their learning. However, the authors state that *"The road in front of the Internet of Objects and their applications in education is just beginning…"*

In short, no solution or project described in this section integrates all the components discussed in Sect. 2, that is, IoT, Big Data & Cloud Computing and Learning Analytics. In this context, disruption in education in higher education will only be possible if these components are used together and in an integrated manner, including the skills required for the present century as defined in [45].

4   Conceptual Approach Proposal

In this section, we present our approach to a disruptive solution using IoT, Big Data & Cloud Computing and Learning Analytics in the context of HEI.

4.1   Rational

According to Lenz et al. [60] information about people can be collected through a variety of devices, including smartphones, wearables or even other types of sensors, and therefore reflect the distinctive behavior and personality of those people. In parallel, according to [61], current HEIs receive data from various sources, namely LMS, social networks, digital libraries, student surveys and Internet logs [62]. All of these data provide a "global" digital trend in the HEIs environment. At the same time as students work in an increasingly digital environment, using their smart devices equipped with sensors, data sources are expanding on a large scale [63]. In this context, data can be related to the TLP and can be processed in order to obtain significant information and reflected in the same process. At the same time, it is also possible to use data collected from several sources other than those referred to, such as documents, audit registers, CCTV images, biometric devices, etc., [65] and in an integrated way, to obtain information to take the necessary measures in order to improve the performance of students in their academic life.

Based on all available data sources, the way traditional database systems are processed is not keeping up with the growth and complexity of current data. Thus, according to [64] the huge amount of unstructured data available does not have adequate use. This situation occurs because most HEIs do not have the appropriate mechanisms to convert this data into useful information. After due treatment of this data, its impact on management policies, and LTP may be significant, allowing the implementation of preventive actions, giving insights on the information not yet explored, which may be fundamental for institutional success. This information can be useful, through its analysis, using methods in the context of Big Data, for the personalization of curricula, for student performance, among other issues. The Big Data methods, according to [60], are determined by two basic requirements: "*(i) the ability of a multilayer information system to bring together all these different heterogeneous data and provide methods for a combined analysis of collected information. (ii) The ability of devices to collect user-specific data such as movements, gestures, eye movements and so on.*" However, there is still very little research on the use of Big Data, IoT, and learn analytics working together within HEIs, as discussed in Sect. 3.

4.2 Conceptual Approach

As argued in the previous section, it is inevitable the junction of the various technologies. The data generated, its collection, treatment, presentation of results, and suggestions that enhance the improvement of TLP, make the combination of IoT, Big Data & Cloud and Learning Analytics inseparable from the construction of a disruptive approach to higher education. Its main objective is to allow the creation of individualized solutions taking into account the characteristics of the students to help them define their personalized curriculum and overcome their limitations and difficulties throughout the learning process.

All data generated, stored, analyzed and presented will have different meanings whenever the angle of observation is changed, that is, they depend on the observer group. In this proposal, three major groups are considered within HEIs: (i) Governance; (ii) Students; and (iii) Professors.

The various possible interceptions between the technological solutions and the defined groups will allow, on the one hand, the necessary knowledge for the elaboration of policies of institutional and scientific-pedagogical management of HEIs. On the other hand, allow the students to be monitored appropriately to their profile and teachers develop teaching strategies for new audiences with very different skills from the last century. The competences for the 21st century, according to [45] are: "*(i) Foundational Literacies (How students apply core skills to everyday tasks) (How students approach their changing environment).*" In this context, it can be said that these competences will play an important role in inducing disruption, which is necessary in higher education.

Figure 1 shows a conceptual approach, in its initial phase, which will serve for a disruption of education in HEIs.

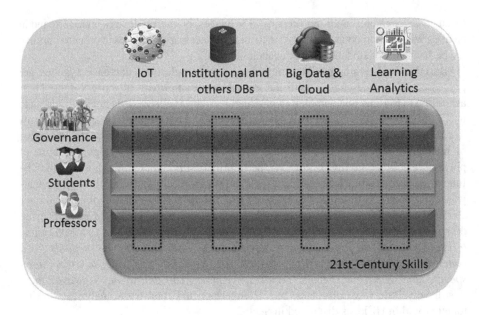

Fig. 1. Conceptual approach.

The proposed approach is composed of four components and three groups of inter-locutors, the components are: IoT, Institutional and others DBs, Big Data & Cloud, and Learning Analytics; and, the groups: Governance, Students, and Professors, with all interceptions based on 21st-century skills. In the following subsections are presented and discussed the groups listed and how they are influenced or influence each of the other components.

Governance. The constitution of the governance board is always the most critical step for the success of a change like this. This entity will set objectives, goals, develop exchange programs, among others, based on data collected from various information sources (IoT, Institutional and others DBs) and evaluated (Big Data & Cloud and Learning Analytics), related to students. This governance board will also be responsible for selecting the type of infrastructure and software needed among other important technical issues to enhance change. For example, governance will have to decide whether the infrastructure will be supported by a private cloud, or a public provider, by analyzing the advantages and disadvantages of each option. In a pragmatic view, starting a project of this size, non-investment in private infrastructure may be a good option not to consume monetary resources related to its maintenance, thus releasing those same resources to other areas of intervention. From this perspective, the team can focus on the appropriate strategy to achieve the stated objectives, using existing services [66].

When students arrive at HEIs, they generally do not have a clear view of what they want and what they can find. Therefore, at an early stage, the use of Big Data can play an important role in the analysis of previous trends provided by the students (profile study, previous knowledge about the area, activity in social networks, etc.), designing predictive models and performing Analysis of feelings and behavior. The intelligent combination of this data with the Institutional and others DBs can be used to make forecasts, projections or to trigger actions in different areas [61].

Finally, this body will be responsible for the introduction of policies to be followed within the HEIs facilities. These policies serve to maintain control of the premises so that they are protected and safe, avoiding any kind of threats [67].

Students. The time of reaction to the evolution of society is taken into account in different rhythms, depending on the groups and institutions in general. Students are one of the groups that have a higher rate adaptation within the universe of HEIs, and there are factors that determine students' success or failure. Therefore, motivation, relevance of content, always in line with new skills [45], pedagogical methods and systems involving the whole TLP serve to avoid three difficult situations: absenteeism, retention, and dropout.

Student absenteeism can be measured and a knowledge base built to predict which underlying causal factors. For example, these factors may include: (i) Academic (inadequate preparation, disinterest with content, etc.); (ii) Motivational (low level of commitment to the institution, etc.); (iii) Psychosocial (social factors, emotional issues); and (iv) Financial (inability to pay school fees, etc.) [68].

With regard to retention, and dropout, it is necessary to identify student retention patterns and seek to assess the underlying reasons that lead students to leave a given particular curricular unit, or a course in general [69]. Based on the information provided, it is possible to construct and propose actions to solve these issues in a preventive manner. In both cases, according to [61], the use of Big Data, IoT and Institutional and others DBs to monitor students' learning process and performance will help to detect potential problems in advance, more efficiently and accurately than Traditional data systems. An early identification of the possibility that a student may be at risk of failing a subject or program of study should lead to corrective action by the teacher to help reduce risk. Big Data analytical tools can produce instant alerts and provide feedback to faculty and students on academic performance by analyzing complex data patterns.

Conventional information models currently used in the HEIs do not take into account the feelings and skills related to behavior. According to [70, 71] the analysis of feelings and behavior data (social networks, notes of student-teacher meetings, and so on) of students in online courses showed the differences between successful and unsuccessful students. In this context, the tools of Big Data analysis and Learning Analytics, according to [72] can reveal the true behavior of the students in a more precise way.

Finally, in addition to concerns about absenteeism and retention and drop-out, it is necessary to motivate students, who are on the right track and have a profile of researchers, to be integrated as early as possible into research projects.

Professors. Teachers will be able, according to [60] to observe the behavior of the students during the classes, as well as throughout the training time, with the help of IoT. For example, authors highlight the use of speech recording devices, reading progress recording tablets or wearables to record heart rate, student eye movement, among others, which will enable the teacher to obtain a more complete view of the students' behavior.

In addition, it is still possible to use the data collected by IoT to be used in combination with other data collected context-oriented data to improve TLP [72].

One aspect not to be overlooked by teachers is the mistaken assumption that all students begin at the same time, and follow practically the same course, and at the same rate [61]. This behavior can be overcome as presented in Sect. 3. These examples show that data collection from various sources of information (from institutional databases and unstructured data collected from sensors), and with the help of Big Data and Learning Analytics, gives these differences, often significant. These differences lead to the need, for a disruption of the current models, of learning to be increasingly personalized. With this type of learning the teacher can observe the students in order to realize which area within a program of study is that they find it difficult and spend most of the time, the sections they recommend to their peers, learning styles Which they prefer, and the time of day that they learn best [69].

Learning can be increasingly personalized and the teacher should be able to observe his/her students in order to perceive which area, within a curriculum is considered more difficult and concentrate most of the time to overcome these difficulties, or which curriculum sections need adjustments, what learning styles they prefer, as well as the time of day that they learn best [72].

Another very relevant aspect is the form of evaluation of the contents taught, i.e. whether the evaluation should be at the end of the lecture of all the contents, or if a formative and phased assessment should be carried out. In [61] it is suggested that with the help of Big Data and Learning Analytics, it is possible for the teacher to formulate appropriately challenging or demanding formative assessments according to each student's talent and learning ability. The same authors suggest the creation of groups based on the capacity within the system and/or the assignment of a student to an appropriate group, as well as, according to [64] teachers can calculate student attention levels and prepare more interesting sessions, to increase levels of attention. In this context, the results obtained will be indicators of the next steps (more advanced learning, or different or more practical content on the same topic), allowing the implementation of a continuous improvement of individual TLP.

5   Conclusions

With the advent of IoT, Big Date, Learning Analytics, among other technologies, changing the behavior of society in general and the younger generation in particular, how to "look" for higher education, has to adapt urgently. This change requires a disruption of current TLP models in order to be able to include in this process the technology and habits of the daily lives of the generations that are coming year after year to higher education. With IoT devices, almost all data and services are now in the cloud. The data that used to be considered "waste" is now having more value to decision-making in different areas of activity and in particular in education through Big Data Analytics and Learning Analytics, allowing a more effective analysis of student learning. With these analyses and their results, investment issues in the education sector require effective use of "new" resources.

These technologies will allow the development of new decision support systems that will be based on evidence of analysis of the behavior and feelings of students and teachers, by analyzing their behavior and activity patterns and adapting them to students, avoiding absenteeism, retention, and dropouts.

In order to respond to the issues discussed above, a disruptive conceptual approach directed to higher education TLPs is proposed, using information gathered by IoT and based on Big Data & Cloud Computing, Institutional and others DBs and Learning Analytics. The result is the definition of individualized solutions taking into account the characteristics of the students, including a personalized curriculum in order to meet their limitations and difficulties throughout the TLP.

The proposed approach, still in its embryonic phase, assumes that we are not all equal and, as a result, there will be different variables for different people that can be analyzed, in order to construct meaningful behavioral patterns that can be used. For a personalized system, behavior has to be analyzed and training must be provided to all, that is, to meet the needs and desires of society. In this context, it is possible to defend the idea that the education system could benefit from IoT data collection, based on Big Data & Cloud Computing analysis tools, Institutional and others DBs and Learning Analytics, so that HEIs can conduct their activities to train better professionals and citizens.

References

1. Gomez, J., Huete, J.F., Hoyos, O., Perez, L., Grigori, D.: Interaction system based on Internet of Things as support for education. Procedia Comput. Sci. **21**, 132–139 (2013)
2. Sharples, M., Taylor, J., Vavoula, G.: A theory of learning for the mobile age (2007)
3. Bomsdorf, B.: Adaptation of learning spaces: supporting ubiquitous learning in higher distance education (2005)
4. Mayer-Schönberger, V., Cukier, K.: Learning with Big Data: The Future of Education. Eamon Dolan/Houghton Mofflin Harcourt, London (2014)
5. Kortuem, G., Bandara, A., Smith, N., Richards, M., Petre, M.: Educating the Internet-of-Things generation. Computer **46**(2), 53–61 (2013)
6. Jeffords, J., Kane, P., Moghaddam, Y., Rucinski, A., Temesgen, Z.: Exponentially disruptive innovation driven by service science and the Internet of Things as a Grand Challenge enabler in education. In: 2014 International Conference on Interactive Collaborative Learning, pp. 1021–1025 (2014)
7. IEEE Project: P2413 Standard for an architectural framework for the Internet of Things (IoT). http://standards.ieee.org/develop/project/2413.html
8. Bosch: Market size and connected devices: Where's the future of IoT? (2014). http://blog.boschsi.com/categories/internetofthings/2014/05/marketsize-and-connected-devices-wheres-the-future-of-iot/
9. Danova, T.: Morgan Stanley: 75 billion devices will be connected to the Internet of Things by 2020 (2013). http://www.businessinsider.com/75-billion-deviceswill-be-connected-to-the-internet-by-2020-2013-10
10. Bulger, M.: Personalized learning: the conversations we're not having. Working Paper, 22 July 2016. https://datasociety.net/pubs/ecl/PersonalizedLearning_primer_2016.pdf
11. Asimov, I.: The promise of personalized learning. Interview with Bill Moyers, PBS (1988). Chen, M., Mao, S., Liu, Y.: Big Data: a survey mobile. Netw. Appl. **19**, 171–209 (2014). doi10.1007/s11036-013-0489-0

12. Sharda, R., Delen, D., Turban, E.: Business Intelligence and Analytics: Systems for Decision Support, 10th edn. TLPrson/Prentice Hall, Englewood Cliffs (2015)
13. Johnson, L., Adams Becker, S., Estrada, V., Freeman, A., Kampylis, P., Vuorikari, R., Punie, Y.: Horizon Report Europe, 2014 Schools edn. Publications Office of the EuroTLPn Union, Luxembourg, The New Media Consortium, Austin (2014)
14. Horizon Report: The NMC Horizon Report, Higher Education edn. (2016). http://cdn.nmc.org/media/2016-nmc-horizon-report-he-EN.pdf
15. Baig, A.R., Jabeen, H.: Big Data analytics for behavior monitoring of students. Procedia Comput. Sci. **82**, 43–48 (2016)
16. Siemens, G., Long, P.: Penetrating the fog: analytics in learning and education. EDUCAUSE Rev. **46**(5), 30 (2011)
17. The Oracle Corporation: Improving higher education performance with Big Data - architect's guide and reference architecture introduction (2015). http://www.oracle.com/us/technologies/big-data/big-dataeducation-2511586.pdf
18. Kennedy, J.V., Castro, D., Atkinson, R.D.: Why it's time to disrupt higher education by separating learning from credentialing, pp. 1–19. Information Technology & Innovation Foundation (2016)
19. Oxford: Disruption (2016). https://en.oxforddictionaries.com/definition/disruption
20. Christensen, C.M., Aaron, S., Clark, W.: Disruption in education, pp. 19–44 (2003). https://net.educause.edu/ir/library/pdf/ffpiu013.pdf
21. Buckley, R.: Why the education sector is ripe for digital disruption (2015). http://www.i-cio.com/management/insight/item/why-education-sector-is-ripe-for-digital-disruption
22. Ashton, K.: Internet of Things. RFiD J. **22**, 97–114 (2009)
23. Sundmaeker, H., Guillemin, P., Friess, P., Woelfflé, S.: Vision and challenges for realising the Internet of Things. In: Cluster of EuroTLPn Research Projects on the Internet of Things —CERP IoT (2010)
24. Atzoria, L., Ierab, A., Morabito, G.: The Internet of Things: a survey. Comput. Netw. **54**, 2787–2805 (2010)
25. Shi, Z., Liao, K., Yin, S.: Design and implementation of the mobile Internet of Things based on TD-SCDMA network. In: 2010 IEEE International Conference on Information Theory and Information Security, pp. 954–957 (2010)
26. Kortuem, G., Kawsar, F., Sundramoorthy, V., Fitton, D.: Smart objects as building blocks for the Internet of Things. IEEE Internet Comput. **14**, 44–51 (2010)
27. Ma, Y., Rao, J., Hu, W., Meng, X., Han, X., Zhang, Y., Chai, Y., Liu, C.: An efficient index for massive IoT data in cloud environment. In: Proceedings of the 21st ACM International Conference on Information and Knowledge Management, CIKM 2012, Hawaii, USA, pp. 2129–2133 (2012)
28. Gantz, J., Reinsel, D.: Extracting value from chaos. In: IDC iView, pp. 1–12 (2011)
29. Mayer-Schonberger, V, Cukier, K.: Big Data: A Revolution that will Transform How We Live, Work, and Think. Eamon Dolan/Houghton Mifflin Harcourt, Boston (2013)
30. O'Reilly Radar Team: Big Data now: Current Perspectives from OReilly Radar. OReilly Media (2011)
31. Grobelnik, M.: Big Data tutorial (2012). http://videolectures.net/eswc2012grobelnikbigdata/
32. Laney, D.: 3-d data management: controlling data volume, velocity and variety. META Group Research Note, 6 February 2001
33. Siemens, G., Gasevic, D.: Guest editorial - learning and knowledge analytics. Educ. Technol. Soc. **15**(3), 1–3 (2012)
34. Campbell, J.P., DeBlois, P.B., Oblinger, D.G.: Academic analytics: a new tool for a new era. EDUCAUSE Rev. **42**(4), 40 (2007)

35. Clow, D.: The learning analytics cycle: closing the loop effectively. In: Buckingham Shum, S., Gasevic, D., Ferguson, R. (eds.) Proceedings of 2nd International Conference on Learning Analytics and Knowledge, LAK 2012, New York, USA, pp. 134–138 (2012)

36. Khalil, M., Ebner, M.: Learning analytics: principles and constraints. In: Proceedings of World Conference on Educational Multimedia, Hypermedia and Telecommunications, EdMedia 2015, pp. 1326–1336. AACE Waynesville (2015)

37. Khalil, M., Ebner, M.: De-identification in learning analytics. J. Learn. Anal. 3(1), 129–138 (2016)

38. Siemens, G.: Learning analytics: envisioning a research discipline and a domain of practice. In: Proceedings of the 2nd International Conference on Learning Analytics and Knowledge, pp. 4–8. ACM (2012)

39. Baker, R.S.J.D., Duval, E., Stamper, J., Wiley, D., Buckingham Shum, S.: Panel: educational data mining meets learning analytics. In: Buckingham Shum, S., Gasevic, D., Ferguson, R. (eds.) Proceedings of 2nd International Conference on Learning Analytics and Knowledge, LAK 2012, New York, USA, p. 20 (2012)

40. Neuhold, B.: Learning Analytics-Mathematik Lernen neu gedacht, BoD–Books on Demand (2013)

41. Taraghi, B., Saranti, A., Ebner, M., Müller, V., Großmann, A.: Towards a learning-aware application guided by hierarchical classification of learner profiles. J. Univ. Comput. Sci. 21(1), 93–109 (2015)

42. Taraghi, B., Frey, M., Saranti, A., Ebner, M., Müller, V., Großmann, A.: Determining the causing factors of errors for multiplication problems. In: Ebner, M., Erenli, K., Malaka, R., Pirker, J., Walsh, Aaron E. (eds.) EiED 2014. CCIS, vol. 486, pp. 27–38. Springer, Cham (2015). doi:10.1007/978-3-319-22017-8_3

43. Bhatotia, P., Wieder, A., Rodrigues, R., Acar, U.A., Pasquin, R.: Incoop: MapReduce for incremental computations. In: Proceedings of the 2nd ACM Symposium on Cloud Computing, p. 7. ACM (2011)

44. World Economic Forum: New Vision for Education: Fostering Social and Emotional Learning Through Technology (2016). http://www3.weforum.org/docs/WEF_New_Vision_for_Education.pdf

45. Bogdanović, Z., Simić, K., Milutinović, M., Radenković, B., Despotović-Zrakić, M.: A platform for learning Internet of Things. In: International Conference e-Learning 2014, pp. 259–266 (2014)

46. Cruz-Benito, J., García-Peñalvo, F.J., Therón, R., Maderuelo, C., Pérez-Blanco, J.S., Zazo, H., Martín-Suárez, A.: Using software architectures to retrieve interaction information in eLearning environments. In: Rodríguez, J.L.S., Beardo, J.M.D., Burgos, D. (eds.) International Symposium on Computers in Education (SIIE), pp. 117–120 (2014)

47. Cruz-Benito, J., Maderuelo, C., García-Peñalvo, F.J., Therón, R., Pérez-Blanco, J.S., Zazo Gómez, H., Martín-Suárez, A.: Usalpharma: a software architecture to support learning in virtual worlds. IEEE Revista Iberoamericana de Tecnologias del Aprendizaje 11(3), 194–204 (2016). doi:10.1109/RITA.2016.2589719

48. Chen, J.C.: The crossroads of English language learners, task-based instruction, and 3D multi-user virtual learning in Second Life. Comput. Educ. 102, 152–171 (2016)

49. Gallego, M.D., Bueno, S., Noyes, J.: Second Life adoption in education: a motivational model based on uses and gratifications theory. Comput. Educ. 100, 81–93 (2016)

50. Cruz-Benito, J., Therón, R., García-Peñalvo, F.J.: Analytics of information flows and decision making in heterogeneous learning ecosystems. In: García-Peñalvo, F.J. (ed.) Proceedings of the Second International Conference on Technological Ecosystems for Enhancing Multiculturality, TEEM 2014, pp. 703–707 (2014)

51. Gašević, D., Dawson, S., Rogers, T., Gasevic, D.: Learning analytics should not promote one size fits all: the effects of instructional conditions in predicting academic success. Internet Higher Educ. **28**, 68–84 (2016)
52. Dodero, J.M., González-Conejero, E.J., Gutiérrez-Herrera, G., Peinado, S., Tocino, J.T., Ruiz-Rube, I.: Trade-off between interoperability and data collection performance when designing an architecture for learning analytics. Future Gener. Comput. Syst. **68**, 31–37 (2016)
53. Serrano-Laguna, Á., Martínez-Ortiz, I., Haag, J., Regan, D., Johnson, A., Fernández-Manjón, B.: Applying standards to systematize learning analytics in serious games. Comput. Stand. Interfaces **50**, 116–123 (2016)
54. Cruz-Benito, J., Therón, R., García-Peñalvo, F.J., Pizarro Lucas, E.: Discovering usage behaviors and engagement in an educational virtual world. Comput. Hum. Behav. **47**, 18–25 (2015). http://dx.doi.org/10.1016/j.chb.2014.11.028
55. Qian, M., Clark, K.R.: Game-based learning and 21st century skills: a review of recent research. Comput. Hum. Behav. **63**, 50–58 (2016)
56. Howard, S.K., Ma, J., Yang, J.: Student rules: exploring patterns of students' computer-efficacy and engagement with digital technologies in learning. Comput. Educ. **101**, 29–42 (2016)
57. Hermsen, S., Frost, J., Renes, R.J., Kerkhof, P.: Using feedback through digital technology to disrupt and change habitual behavior: a critical review of current literature. Comput. Hum. Behav. **57**, 61–74 (2016)
58. Salis, C., Murgia, F., Wilson, M.F., Mameli, A.: IoT-DESIR: a case study on a cooperative learning experiment in Sardinia. In: Proceedings of 2015 International Conference on Interactive Collaborative Learning (ICL), pp. 785–792 (2015)
59. Lenz, L., Pomp, A., Meisen, T., Jeschke, S.: How will the Internet of Things and Big Data analytics impact the education of learning-disabled students? A concept paper. In: Proceedings of 3rd MEC International Conference on Big Data and Smart City (2016)
60. Riffai, M., Edgar, D., Duncan, P., Al-Bulushi, A.: The potential for Big Data to enhance the higher education sector in Oman. In: Proceedings of 3rd MEC International Conference on Big Data and Smart City (2016)
61. Rossi, B.: Top 4 ways to apply Big Data in higher education (2015). http://www.information-age.com/it-management/strategy-andinnovation/123460114/top-4-ways-apply-big-data-higher-education
62. Timms, M.J.: Big Data in Education: A Guide for Educators. Centre for Strategic Education (CSE) (2015)
63. Bhat, A., Ahmed, I.: Big Data for institutional planning, decision support and academic excellence. In: Proceedings of 3rd MEC International Conference on Big Data and Smart City (2016)
64. Drysdale, R.: University data can be a force for good (2013). http://www.theguardian.com/higher-educationnetwork/blog/2013/nov/27/university-data-studentengagement-retention
65. Richard, S.J.: Governance strategies for the Cloud, Big Data and other technologies in education. In: TEEE/ACM 7th International Conference on Utility and Cloud Computing (2014)
66. O'sullivan, P.: A critical evaluation of the strategic governance issues involved in implementing social networking technologies into university teaching and learning. In: Mawhinney, L., Self, R.J. (eds.) Sustainable Governance Strategies, vol. 1. University of Derby (2014)
67. Cuseo, J.: The "BIG PICTURE": key causes of student attrition & key components of a comprehensive student retention plan (2008). http://web.ysu.edu/gen/ysu_generated_bin/documents/basic_module/Key_Causes_of_Student_AttritionComprehensive_Retention_Plan.pdf

68. Burley, K.: Data mining techniques in higher education research: the example of student retention. In: 29th Annual EAIR Forum, Innsbruck, Austria, 26–29 August 2007
69. Macfadyen, L.P., Dawson, S.: Mining LMS data to develop an "early warning system" for educators: a proof of concept. Comput. Educ. **54**(2), 588–599 (2010)
70. Schmarzo, B.: Big Data: Understanding How Data Powers Big Business. Wiley, Indianapolis (2013)
71. Pietrosanti, K.: When E-learning technologies embrace Big Data (2013). https://www.docebo.com/2013/12/06/when-elearning-technologiesembrace-big-data-2/
72. IBI: Smart education (2015). http://www.ibigroup.com/new-smart-cities-landingpage/education-smart-cities/

Connectivist, Context-Aware Communication Channels - Peer Finding Algorithm for Distributed Learning Networks

Ingolf Waßmann[1(✉)] and Ebram Sherif[2]

[1] University of Rostock, Rostock, Germany
ingolf.wassmann@uni-rostock.de
[2] German University of Cairo, New Cairo, Egypt
ebramsherif@gmail.com

Abstract. Digital Age is characterized by an increasing complexity of IT systems on the one hand, and a Web 2.0 caused information overload on the other hand. As a solution, Connectivism states the finding of nodes, for example other people having specific knowledge, in order to share required information. Based on mathematical models, this contribution presents a generic solution to support these processes. So-called Co^3 channels automatically connect people within communication channels according thematic relation (For example, does the user has general or specific interest about the topic?) and thematic competence (Does the user has any experiences and achievements in this area?), tutor competence (How active is the user within the system and has he ever helped other people?), and seeker relation (Does the user fit seeker's preferences according social connection, communication type, and others?). The practical realization of the concept is shown by means of a live chat tool that is embedded into a learning environment.

Keywords: Peer finding · Learning Networks · Connectivism · Live chat

1 Introduction

George Siemens discussed in his article "Connectivism: A Learning Theory for the Digital Age" [1] how current learning theories have become influenced and limited by the rapid advancements in human technology. The increasing integration of information technology (IT) in production phases of nearly every industry section leads to a growing complexity of corresponding working processes. Consequently, employees have to update their knowledge and skills on a regular basis. Facing the challenges of the up-coming fourth Industrial Revolution ("Industry 4.0"), a user-centered, just-in-time, on-demand and extra-occupational lifelong learning procedure is needed [2].

At the same time, the Web 2.0 credo of so-called "prosumers" - people being consumer *and* producer of content - plus technologies like social networks, forums

© Springer International Publishing AG 2017
P. Zaphiris and A. Ioannou (Eds.): LCT 2017, Part I, LNCS 10295, pp. 406–419, 2017.
DOI: 10.1007/978-3-319-58509-3_32

and blogs furnish a huge amount of data each day, which results in an information overload. Individuals are no longer capable of independently filtering and converting all available information into required knowledge. According to the statement "collecting knowledge through collecting people" by Karen Stephenson [3], Connectivism theory views the learning process as networking with other people having specific knowledge in order to exchange required information. For acquiring new knowledge, *know-where* is more important than know-what and know-how: "the pipe is more important than the content within the pipe" [1].

The Open University of Netherlands have done research in this field and developed a solution [4] that finds fitting peer tutors concerning a given question of a user and connects the participants on a wiki page in order to find a solution collaboratively. For this, the underlying algorithm analyzes:

- *thematic competence* that takes into consideration if the user has successfully finished any question-related courses within the learning environment, the time expired since completion, and the whole study time of that course(s);
- *tutor competence* that is derived from activity within the system and ratings of given answers;
- *eligibility* that gives an evaluation of the similarity according expertise and knowledge background of the learners;
- and *availability* that depends on the workload of a user taking into account the number of past participations in answering questions.

This approach is characterized by some major deficits that don't fulfill the previously mentioned demand of a user-centered lifelong learning procedure. Individual preferences according specific situations (learning, authoring, tutoring, etc.), learner types, social connections and more are not considered here. Furthermore, it's just an indirect type of asynchronous, text-based communication via a wiki page. Both synchronous communication methods and different transmission data like audio and video are not part of the above concept.

Consequently, we introduce a solution that overcomes these deficits. Required background information according basic models are given in the following Sect. 2. Subsequently, the algorithm is depicted and afterwards a prototype in terms of a live chat tool will be presented. The last chapter summarizes the outcomes of this contribution and gives an outlook for future work.

2 Basic Models

This contribution presents an approach that supports the essential tasks of Connectivism by automatically connecting users of a social learning environment who are familiar to a specific topic in so-called "Connectivist Context-Aware Communication (Co^3) Channels". For this, the fundamental understanding of *contents*, *users*, *context* respectively *context-awareness* and *communication channels* are clarified in the following sections.

2.1   Content Model

Based on the ideas of [5], a hierarchically structured content model is used to depict semantically linked learning materials (Fig. 1). At the lowest level, an object consists of one content (text, audio, video, etc.) and a set of descriptive keywords. One level higher, an ordered list of objects and a set of comprehensive topics form a unit. Finally, at least one unit and a set of overall learning objectives are the basis for one module, which is also described by all keywords attached to the included units and objects.

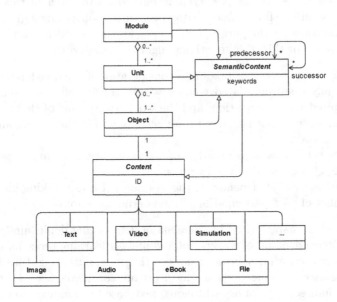

Fig. 1. Content diagram

In the derived mathematical model there're sets of IDs (encoded as natural numbers) for contents $CONS$ (Eq. 1), objects $OBJS$ (Eq. 2), units $UNIS$ (Eq. 3) and modules $MODS$ (Eq. 4), as well as keywords $KEYS$ (Eq. 5). Thus, a single object Obj (Eq. 6), unit Uni (Eq. 7) and module Mod (Eq. 8) are depicted by 5-tuples including an ID, one content ID (in case it's an object) respectively a tuple of object IDs (in case it's a unit) or a tuple of unit IDs (in case it's a module), a set of predecessors and successors, and a set of keywords. Consequently, learning modules are described by an ordered list of units, that in turn consists of ordered lists of objects. In this way, *learning paths* are modeled.

$$CONS = \{ c \in \mathbb{N} \mid c \text{ is content ID } \} \tag{1}$$

$$OBJS = \{ o \in \mathbb{N} \mid o \text{ is object ID } \} \tag{2}$$

$$UNIS = \{ u \in \mathbb{N} \mid u \text{ is unit ID } \} \tag{3}$$

$$MODS = \{ m \in \mathbb{N} \mid m \text{ is module ID } \} \tag{4}$$

$$KEYS = \{ k \in \mathbb{N} \mid k \text{ is keyword ID } \} \tag{5}$$

$$Obj = (o, c, PREO, SUCO, KEYO| \tag{6}$$

$o \in OBJS$, object ID

$c \in CONS$, content ID

$PREO \subseteq OBJS$, predecessor objects

$SUCO \subseteq OBJS$, successor objects

$KEYO \subseteq KEYS$, object's keywords)

$$Uni = (u, (o_r), PREU, SUCU, KEYU| \tag{7}$$

$u \in UNIS$, unit ID

$o_r \in OBJS, r \in \mathbb{N}$, object IDs

$PREU \subseteq UNIS$, predecessor units

$SUCU \subseteq UNIS$, successor units

$KEYU \subseteq KEYS$, unit's keywords)

$$Mod = (m, (u_s), PREM, SUCM, KEYM| \tag{8}$$

$m \in MODS$, module ID

$u_s \in UNIS, s \in \mathbb{N}$, unit IDs

$PREM \subseteq MODS$, predecessor modules

$SUCM \subseteq MODS$, successor modules

$KEYM \subseteq KEYS$, module's keywords)

2.2   Context and Context-Awareness

Abowd et al. name a system *context-aware* "if it uses context to provide relevant information and/or services to the user, where relevancy depends on the user's task" [6]. Furthermore, the authors describe *context* in terms of two general categories: *primary* and *secondary* context information. The first one includes four basic information that are required to clearly describe a situation: identity (Who?), location (Where?), activity (What?), and time (When?). Secondary context information includes all other information about entities and the situation that can be derived from primary ones, for example getting a telephone number by looking up a name (identity) in a directory. Our derived definition of context C_e (Eq. 9) includes all primary and secondary information of an entity e as an ordered list regarding a specific time.

$$C_e(t) = C_e = (C_1, \ldots, C_n) \tag{9}$$
$$\forall c \in C_j \in C_e, j = 1 \ldots n : c \in \mathbb{N}$$

Each information is modeled as a set or a tuple C_j, which encodes the information as natural numbers. For instance, the location of an entity could be described by longitude and latitude given as a decimal number in degree which in turn could be represented as a natural number by separating mantissa and exponent.

2.3   User Model

In analogy to the content model, the set $USRS$ (Eq. 10) consists of all existing user IDs. A single user Usr is described by a 2-tuple including a user ID (Who?) and context information (Eq. 11). The latter one is composed of different user data (Eq. 12):

- C_{Sit}: situation including current activity (What?) and cyber location (Where?);
- C_{His}: last consumed learning objects;
- C_{Mod}: progress, time, and evaluation of registered learning modules;
- C_{Exp}: experiences and skills;
- C_{Int}: general interests;
- C_{Tar}: specific learning targets;
- C_{Rat}: general activity rating within the learning environment;
- C_{Rev}: community reviews of given answers;
- C_{Lan}: spoken languages;
- C_{Rol}: activity ratings of specific learning objects regarding different roles;
- C_{Soc}: social connections within the learning environment;
- C_{Com}: preferred communication types.

$$USRS = \left\{ u \in \mathbb{N} \,\middle|\, \text{u is user ID} \right\} \tag{10}$$

$$Usr = \left(u, C_u \,\middle|\, \begin{array}{l} u \in USRS, \text{ user ID} \\ C_u, \text{ user's context} \end{array} \right) \tag{11}$$

$$\begin{aligned} C_u = (&C_{Sit}, C_{His}, C_{Mod}, C_{Exp}, C_{Int}, C_{Tar}, \\ &C_{Rat}, C_{Rev}, C_{Lan}, C_{Rol}, C_{Soc}, C_{Com}) \end{aligned} \tag{12}$$

2.4   Communication Channel Model

Following Shannon's mathematical theory of communication [7], a simplified model is derived. A communication channel is a 2-tuple Co (Eq. 13) that includes a set of participating entities ENT (Eq. 14) and a set of the connections $LINK$ (Eq. 15) between them. In analogy to the term "nodes" that is used in Connectivism [1], an entity could be a user but also non-human things like a database or a software agent.

$$Co = (ENT, LINK) \,\middle|\, \begin{array}{c} \forall e_i, e_j \in ENT: \\ \exists (e_i, e_j) \in LINK \wedge \exists (e_j, e_i) \in LINK \end{array} \tag{13}$$

$$ENT \subseteq \left\{ e \in \mathbb{N} \,\middle|\, \forall e_i, e_j \in ENT : e_i \neq e_j \wedge i \neq j \right\} \tag{14}$$
$$|ENT| \geq 2 \implies ENT \neq \emptyset$$

$$LINK \subseteq \left\{ (u,v) \,\middle|\, u,v \in ENT, u \neq v \right\} \tag{15}$$
$$|LINK| \geq 2 \implies LINK \neq \emptyset$$

All entities are connected to each other in order to exchange information in duplex mode in a directed, connected graph. One example of such a communication channel are public online chats like Chatting.com [8]. Each user of the service is connected to each other and can share textual information.

2.5   Co³ Channel Model

Based on the above definitions and taking into account the specific requirements of Connectivism theory that were explained in the first chapter, so-called "Connectivist, Context-Aware Communication (Co³) Channels" connect entities within a communication network in order to support individual learning processes.

As an extension of a regular communication channel Co (Sect. 2.4), a Co^3 channel (Eq. 16) is a 3-tuple including a set ENT^C (Eq. 17) of participating entities e plus attached context information C_e, a set $LINK$ of connections between them (Eq. 18), and a membership function ω (Eq. 19) that determines if an entity is included in ENT^C.

$$Co^3 = \left(ENT^C, LINK, \omega\right) \left| \begin{array}{l} \forall (u, C_u), (v, C_v) \in ENT^C : \\ \exists (u, v) \in LINK \wedge \exists (v, u) \in LINK \end{array} \right. \tag{16}$$

$$ENT^C \subseteq \left\{ (e, C_e) \left| \begin{array}{l} \forall u, v \in ENT^C : \\ u \neq v \wedge C_u \neq C_v \end{array} \right. \right\} \tag{17}$$
$$ENT^C \neq \emptyset, |ENT^C| \geq 2$$

$$LINK \subseteq \left\{ (u, v) \left| u, v \in ENT, u \neq v \right. \right\} \tag{18}$$
$$LINK \neq \emptyset, |LINK| \geq 2$$

$$\omega(C_e) : C_e \longmapsto [0, 1] \tag{19}$$
$$\forall (e, C_e) \in ENT^C : \omega(C_e) > 0$$

In contrast to classical sets, ENT^C is a fuzzy set, because ω calculates a degree (a real number in the interval from 0 to 1) of belonging to this set for each entity. Here, ENT^C is called a "Connectivist Communication Network (CCN)" [9]. The presented approach by van Rosmalen et al. [4] is one solution to build a CCN. In the following chapter, a new one is introduced.

3   Peer Finding Algorithm for Co³ Channels

For connecting entities within CCNs, this chapter presents the individual components of the membership function ω. Although, there're a lot of use cases in learning environments for such a solution [10], this contribution focuses on a peer finding strategy that overcome the mentioned disadvantages of the solution by van Rosmalen et al. [4].

The function ω in Eq. 20 calculates for every individual within a learning network a value between 0 and 1 by dividing every value by the maximum (Eq. 21). The result represents a kind of helpfulness probability. The higher this value is the higher the probability is that this user might help the person asking for peer support. For this, different context information of the network participants are considered in the individual evaluations of four major categories (Eq. 22) that are depicted in the following sections.

$$\omega(C_u) = \frac{\omega'(C_u)}{\omega'_{MAX}} \tag{20}$$

$$\omega'_{MAX} = \omega'(C_a) \Longleftrightarrow (a, C_a) \in ENT^C \wedge \tag{21}$$
$$\forall (b, C_b) \in ENT^C : \omega'(C_b) \leq \omega'(C_a)$$

$$\omega'(C_u) = \omega'_{ThCo}(C_u) + \omega'_{TuCo}(C_u) + \omega'_{ThRe}(C_u) + \omega'_{SeRe}(C_u) \tag{22}$$

3.1   Thematic Competence

Similar to the described approach by van Rosmalen et al. [4], the evaluation of the thematic competence of a user is one aspect of the membership function. Based on the introduced content model (Sect. 2.1), a person seeking for help can directly initialize the Co^3 channel while consuming a specific learning object o. Then, the thematic competence of each user u will be evaluated using Eq. 23. The first part of the formula checks if the learning object o, which is the basis of the seeker's question, has already visited by the user. In other words, it's determined if o is part of the history C_{His} (Eq. 25) by using the helping function f_{incl} (Eq. 24). This returns 1 if it's included, 0 else. Any longer, the learner's registered modules C_{Mod} (Eq. 26) are analyzed. Here, the individual progress (between 0 and 100), totally spent time (stated in hours) and evaluation grade (between 0 and 100) are summed. The time being absent from learning the content (stated in months) is subtracted.

$$\omega'_{ThCo}(C_u, o) = \alpha_{His} * f_{incl}\left(C_{His}, \{o\}\right) \tag{23}$$
$$+ \alpha_{Mod} * \sum_{i=0}^{n} \left(\left(\alpha_{Pro} * p_i + \alpha_{Tim} * t_i - \alpha_{Abs} * a_i + \alpha_{Eva} * e_i \right) \right.$$
$$\left. * f_{incl}\left(OBJ(m_i), \{o\}\right) \right)$$
$$+ \alpha_{Exp} * \sum_{i=0}^{n} \left(f_{incl}\left(KEYS(m_i), C_{Exp}\right) * f_{incl}\left(OBJ(m_i), \{o\}\right) \right)$$

$$f_{incl}(M, N) = \begin{cases} 1 : \exists x \in M \land \exists y \in N \land x = y \\ 0 : else. \end{cases} \tag{24}$$

$$C_{His} = \{ h \in OBJS \,|\, h \text{ is an object ID, u visited} \} \tag{25}$$

$$C_{Mod} = \left(m_n, p_n, t_n, a_n, e_n \,\middle|\, \begin{array}{c} m \in MODS, \text{ module ID} \\ p : \text{progress of module } m \\ t : \text{time spent for module } m \\ a : \text{time absent from module } m \\ e : \text{evaluation grade of module } m \\ p, t, a, e, n \in \mathbb{N} \end{array} \right) \tag{26}$$

Only modules that include the object o are considered. For this, f_{incl} checks if o is included in the set $OBJ(m)$ (Eq. 27) that consists of all objects that are part of module m's units. As a third component of this category, individual experiences C_{Exp} (Eq. 29) given as keywords are taken into account by comparing them with all keywords $KEYS(m)$ (Eq. 28) that describe a module, also including keywords of attached units and objects.

$$OBJ(m) = \left\{ o \in OBJS \,\middle|\, \begin{array}{c} o \in Uni_2 \land u = Uni_1 \land \\ u \in Mod_2 \land m = Mod_1 \end{array} \right\} \tag{27}$$

$$KEYS(m) = KEYM \bigcup_{i=0}^{s} KEYU_i \bigcup_{j=0}^{r} KEYO_j \tag{28}$$

$$m = Mod_1 \land KEYM = Mod_5 \land$$
$$\Leftrightarrow Uni_1 \in Mod_2 \land KEYU_i = Uni_5 \land$$
$$Obj_1 \in Uni_2 \land KEYO_j = Obj_5$$

$$C_{Exp} = \{ e \in KEYS \,|\, e \text{ is keyword ID of an experience of u} \} \tag{29}$$

3.2   Thematic Relation

In contrast to the approach by van Rosmalen et al. [4], our algorithm not only takes into account the thematic competence, but also user's interest about the content. We assume a higher intrinsic motivation to help, because both learners share a common desire.

According to the general distinction between coarse- and fine-grained objectives during learning processes [11], user's general interests C_{Int} (Eq. 31) and specific learning targets C_{Tar} (Eq. 32) are analyzed by doing a keyword matching (Eq. 30). For this, the set of keywords $KEYO$ that describe the object o are used.

$$\omega'_{ThRe}(C_u, KEYO) = \alpha_{Int} * f_{incl}\left(C_{Int}, KEYO\right) \tag{30}$$
$$+ \alpha_{Tar} * f_{incl}\left(C_{Tar}, KEYO\right)$$

$$C_{Int} = \left\{i \in KEYS \,\middle|\, i \text{ is keyword ID of an interest of u} \right\} \tag{31}$$

$$C_{Tar} = \left\{t \in KEYS \,\middle|\, t \text{ is keyword ID of a target of u} \right\} \tag{32}$$

3.3   Tutor Competence

In analogy to the concept by van Rosmalen et al. [4], user's tutor competence (Eq. 33) is evaluated by an activity rating C_{Rat} (Eq. 34) plus a reviews rating C_{Rev} (Eq. 35). While the former one is determined by specific points for different interactions with the learning system (for example being online, editing content, sharing materials, etc.), the latter one is based on a crowd ranking for previously given answers within CCNs.

$$\omega'_{TuCo}(C_u) = \alpha_{Rat} * C_{Rat} + \alpha_{Rev} * C_{Rev} \tag{33}$$

$$C_{Rat} = \left\{a \in \mathbb{N} \,\middle|\, a \text{ is general activity rating of u} \right\} \tag{34}$$

$$C_{Rev} = \left\{r \in \mathbb{N} \,\middle|\, r \text{ is review rating of given answers} \right\} \tag{35}$$

3.4   Seeker Relation

The major difference between our solution and the approach by van Rosmalen et al. [4] is the consideration of individual preferences of the seeker who is asking for help. For this, the evaluation function (Eq. 36) gets additional context information C_S (Eq. 37) of the seeker.

$$\omega'_{SeRe}(C_u, C_s, o) = \alpha_{Lan} * f_{incl}\left(C_{Lan}, \{l_s\}\right) \tag{36}$$
$$+ \alpha_{Rol} * \sum_{i=0}^{m} \left((au_i * r_{au} + tu_i * r_{tu} + as_i * r_{as})\right.$$
$$\left. * f_{incl}(\{o_i\}, \{o\})\right)$$
$$+ \alpha_{Soc} * f_{incl}\left(C_{Soc}, \{u_s\}\right)$$
$$+ \alpha_{Com} * f_{incl}\left(C_{Com}, \{c_s\}\right)$$
$$+ \alpha_{Sit} * \left(f_{incl}(\{lo\}, \{lo_s\}) + f_{incl}(\{ac\}, \{ac_s\})\right.$$
$$\left. + f_{incl}(\{on\}, \{on_s\})\right)$$

$$C_S = \left(\{l_s\}, (r_{au}, r_{tu}, r_{as}), u_s, \{c_s\}, lo_s, ac_s, on_s \right) \tag{37}$$

This tuple includes the following data:

- $\{l_s\}$: a set of languages that are preferred by the seeker;
- (r_{au}, r_{tu}, r_{as}): a tuple including preferred roles (for example: (1, 0, 1) means that the seeker prefers authors and assessors);
- u_s: the seeker's user ID to check social connection;
- $\{c_s\}$: preferred communication types;
- lo_s: current cyber location of the seeker;
- ac_s: preferred activity of the user;
- on_s: preferred online status of the user (0 – offline, 1 – online).

At first, speech comprehension is validated by comparing the preferred languages l_s of the seeker with all languages C_{Lan} (Eq. 38) that are spoken by user u. If the seeker only wants specific user roles to join, C_{Rol} (Eq. 39) of the user is analyzed. Based on a similar approach like for evaluating tutor competence (Sect. 3.3), a user gets a rating for author, tutor and assessment activity concerning every learning object.

$$C_{Lan} = \{l \in \mathbb{N} \,|\, l \text{ is language ID, u speaks} \} \tag{38}$$

$$C_{Rol} = \left(o_m, au_m, tu_m, as_m \left| \begin{array}{c} o \in OBJS, \text{ object ID} \\ au : \text{author rating regarding } o \\ tu : \text{tutor rating regarding } o \\ as : \text{assessment rating regarding } o \\ au, tu, as, m \in \mathbb{N} \end{array} \right. \right) \tag{39}$$

Assuming the seeker only wants to communicate with known people, social connections C_{Soc} (Eq. 40) within the learning environment are analyzed. It's checked, if the seeker's user ID u_s is included in the social connections C_{Soc} of the user.

$$C_{Soc} = \{s \in USRS \,|\, s \text{ is user ID, connected with u} \} \tag{40}$$

Based on the selected communication type of the Co^3 channel (Fig. 2) only users who also prefer this type are selected (C_{Com}, Eq. 41).

$$C_{Com} = \{c \in \mathbb{N} \,|\, c \text{ is communication type ID, preferred by u} \} \tag{41}$$

In addition, the current situation C_{Sit} (Eq. 42) of the user might play an important role. This includes the current location of the user represented as the underlying content (cyber location), the current activity (for example reading or editing the content) and the current online status (online or offline).

$$C_{Sit} = \left(t, lo, ac, on \left| \begin{array}{c} t \in \mathbb{N}, \text{ timestamp} \\ lo \in CONS, \text{ location of u at t} \\ ac \in \mathbb{N}, \text{ activity ID of u at t} \\ on \in \{0,1\}, \text{ online status of u at t} \end{array} \right. \right) \tag{42}$$

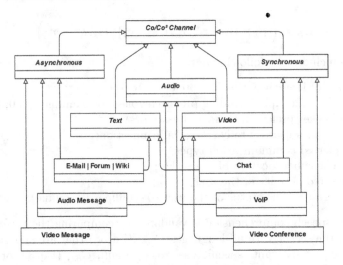

Fig. 2. Different communication types

3.5 Weight Parameters

Each of the presented evaluation functions ω' includes weight parameters α that are necessary to balance the membership function ω. In order to determine these values, an empirical study was carried out in terms of a questionnaire asking about the importance of different points regarding *computer-supported collaborative work/learning (CSCW/L) in peer networks*. Each element was rated by over 700 participants on a scale from 0 ("unimportant" or "not true at all")

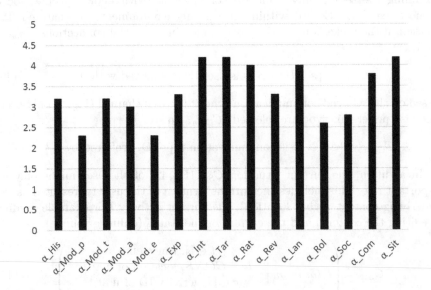

Fig. 3. Weight parameters based on an empirical study

to 5 ("very important" or "very true"). As a result, Fig. 3 reveals derived values for the weight parameters. While the progress and evaluation of a related learning module, as well as the user's role regarding a specific content were evaluated as rather unimportant, besides to a same language level the current situation of users, especially concerning interests and targets, play the most important roles.

4   Live Chat Prototype

Based on the introduced mathematical model, a first prototype was realized in terms of a live chat tool [9,10] that is fully embedded into the web 3.0 teaching and learning environment *Wiki-Learnia* [12]. If a user has a problem regarding the underlying content, a live chat can be initialized by clicking on "Dynamic Chat" in the help menu (upper screenshot in Fig. 4).

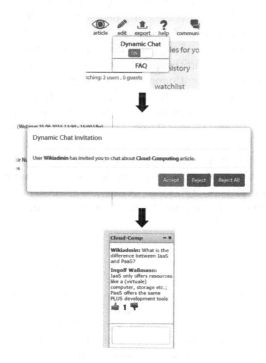

Fig. 4. Live chat prototype

Subsequently, a pop-up window appears in which the seeker can check different options:

- *friends-only*: add users being in seeker's social connections;
- *authors-only*: add users who were active as author regarding this object;
- *tutors-only*: add users who were active as tutor regarding this object;
- *assessors-only*: add users who were active as assessor regarding this object;

After defining the target audience (default: all), the peer finding algorithm is executed. According the current situation of a user (C_{Sit}), online users being on the same content page and doing the same activity (either reading or editing the content) are invited by the tool. The algorithm doesn't evaluate the workload of a user like it's done by van Rosmalen et al. [4]. Every user can decide for themselves to join the live chat (middle screenshot in Fig. 4). If the invitation is accepted, a chat pop-up window appears on the current page. Given answers can be rated by the chat participants (lower screenshot in Fig. 4). At the end, the question of the seeker plus the highest ranked answer are automatically attached to a frequently asked questions (FAQ) section under the corresponding content.

5   Summary and Outlook

As an extension of the existing approach by van Rosmalen et al. [4], a user-centered model for finding and connecting people within CCNs was introduced. The abstract mathematical model allows several practical realizations of the idea, which is independent of the communication type. Indeed, a live chat tool was implemented as a first prototype of the concept, that will be tested with about 200 participants of the Junior Studies project [13] at the University of Rostock in Winter 2017. While the solution by van Rosmalen et al. [4] only considers an asynchronous communication via a wiki page, our model supports all possible ways of information exchanges within social learning environments.

Since everybody has own preferences according the weights of each part of the algorithm, a machine learning approach should be included that automatically adapt the α values for every user. Furthermore, a dynamic variant of Co^3 channels will be developed. By means of latent semantic analysis mechanisms, the solution will react to changing discussion topics within the communication channel.

References

1. Siemens, G.: Connectivism: a learning theory for the digital age. Int. J. Instr. Technol. Distance Learn. **2**(1), 3–10 (2005)
2. German Federal Ministry for Economic Affairs, Energy: Digitale Bildung - Der Schlüssel zu einer Welt im Wandel (2016). https://www.bmwi.de/
3. Stephenson, K.: What knowledge tears apart, networks make whole. Intern. Commun. Focus **36**, 1–6 (1998)
4. Van Rosmalen, P., Sloep, P., Kester, L., Brouns, F., De Croock, M., Pannekeet, K., Koper, R.: A learner support model based on peer tutor selection. J. Comput. Assist. Learn. **24**(1), 74–86 (2008)
5. Niegemann, H.M.: Digitale Lerninhalte und Autorenwerkzeuge. Kompendium multimediales Lernen, pp. 557–601 (2008)
6. Abowd, G.D., Dey, A.K., Brown, P.J., Davies, N., Smith, M., Steggles, P.: Towards a better understanding of context and context-awareness. In: Gellersen, H.-W. (ed.) HUC 1999. LNCS, vol. 1707, pp. 304–307. Springer, Heidelberg (1999). doi:10.1007/3-540-48157-5_29

7. Shannon, C.E.: A mathematical theory of communication. ACM SIGMOBILE Mob. Comput. Commun. Rev. **5**(1), 3–55 (2001)
8. Chatting.com. http://www.chatting.com/
9. Waßmann, I., Nicolay, R., Martens, M.: Connectivist communication networks. In: 13th International Conference on Cognition and Exploratory Learning in Digital Age (CELDA) Proceedings, pp. 279–282 (2016)
10. Waßmann, I., Tavangarian, D., Forbrig, P.: Context-aware communication channels in e-learning. In: International Technology, Education and Development Conference Proceedings, pp. 4099–4109 (2016)
11. Mayer, H.O., Hertnagel, J., Weber, H.: Lernzielüberprüfung im eLearning. Walter de Gruyter GmbH & Co. KG (2009)
12. Waßmann, I., Versick, D., Thomanek, A., Tavangarian, D.: Learning through life. eleed (2014). Issue 10
13. Versick, D., Rücker, M.L., Waltemath, R., Tavangarian, D.: Online-gestützte Lehrveranstaltungen: Management: Organisation und Erfahrungen. DeLFI Conference Proceedings 2015, pp. 195–207 (2015)

Games and Gamification for Learning

CodeAdventure: An Adventure Game for Computer Science Education

Panayiotis Andreou[1]([⊠]), George Nicou[1], Irene Polycarpou[1], Panagiotis Germanakos[2], and Nearchos Paspallis[1]

[1] University of Central Lancashire, Larnaka, Cyprus
{pgandreou,gnicou,ipolycarpou,npaspallis}@uclan.ac.uk
[2] SAP SE, Walldorf, Germany
panagiotis.germanakos@sap.com

Abstract. Among the most fundamental concepts of computer science education is introductory programming, and, many effective approaches were proposed to teach programming to novice learners. Despite all efforts, students still show poor performance with course assessments, which can then lead to dropping out of their studies after their first experience with programming. In the last few years, a number of interventions were suggested, including the utilization of educational games that can motivate, stimulate and engage students far better than conventional approaches. In this paper, we present CodeAdventure, an educational adventure-like game that has been designed for learning and practicing introductory programming concepts. CodeAdventure adopts an integrated design approach that employs various mechanisms and techniques to achieve a truly immersive game learning experience while in parallel provides a fun way to practice and apply various programming concepts. CodeAdventure uses compelling graphics and incorporates different learning techniques that have been shown to be effective for students' learning, such as providing hints and clues on how to solve puzzles, referencing instructional material, and immediate feedback on students' performance .

Keywords: Game-based learning · Educational technologies · Learning · User experience · Programming concepts

1 Introduction

Among the most fundamental concepts of computer science education is introductory programming, and thus, many different approaches were proposed on efficient and effective ways to teach programming to novice learners. Despite all the efforts, it has been well documented that students have difficulties learning introductory programming and as a result, many of them have poor performance with course assessments, which can then lead to dropping out of computer science studies after their first experience with programming [2, 12]. In [2], the authors present the results of study which suggest that the main sources of student-reported learning difficulties are the lack of previous knowledge, the lack of effort or personal persistence, and the lack of motivation.

© Springer International Publishing AG 2017
P. Zaphiris and A. Ioannou (Eds.): LCT 2017, Part I, LNCS 10295, pp. 423–432, 2017.
DOI: 10.1007/978-3-319-58509-3_33

In the last few years, a number of interventions have been suggested [4, 15–17], including the utilization of educational software [1, 9–11], and more specifically, educational games [3, 6, 13] that can provide students with a non-traditional learning environment in which they can learn and practice in a fun and intuitive way. Many researchers argue for the appeal of educational games to students of all ages and their potential to enhance the educational experience, including motivating, exciting and engaging the students in the learning process [5, 7, 8, 14]. Educational games can enable self-paced interactive learning; allow students to make mistakes and re-attempt problems without negative outcomes; support various modes of level difficulty and achievements to accommodate for mixed ability classes and personal student goals; and enhance the development of understanding through immersive environments and their reflective nature [3]. Furthermore, educational games can take advantage of students' enthusiasm about video games and serve as an additional motivational and inspirational factor. Given the demanding curriculum and the limited amount of time available for instructors to convey the rather complex (for novice learners) concepts of programming, an educational game can provide an additional resource of information and practice problems that students can use on their own time and pace as well as provide the opportunity to spend additional time to focus on the material that is more challenging for them.

In this paper, we present an educational game, called CodeAdventure, which has been designed for computer science students to learn and practice introductory programming concepts. CodeAdventure is an adventure game where the player assumes the role of the protagonist exploring the game environment, and in the process, solving puzzles, and overcoming challenges in order to discover and acquire certain items. In terms of educational value, in addition to providing a fun way to practice and apply various programming concepts, CodeAdventure incorporates different learning techniques that have been shown to be effective for students' learning, such as providing hints and clues on how to solve puzzles referencing instructional material, and immediate feedback on students' performance [6].

The remainder of this paper is organized as follows: Sect. 2 reviews the literature. Next, Sect. 3 presents the CodeAdventure educational game and finally Sect. 4 concludes the paper.

2   Background and Related Work

In the last few decades there has been a reform movement in higher education to shift from the traditional paradigm, the positivist approach, towards the constructivism paradigm. This emerged in a wide range of academic areas such as philosophy, the arts, education, politics, religion, medicine, physics, chemistry, ecology, evolution, psychology, linguistics, and sciences [25, 26]. Following the constructivist approach, educators serve as the main teaching instrument. According to [27], constructivist knowledge "is knowledge that human reason derives from experience. It does not represent a picture of the 'real' world but provides structure and organization to experience" (p. 5). For the educators the facilitation of understanding is a process of co-construction of multiple meanings in which they accommodate their own understanding to fit students' own experiences. To be able to construct their own understanding, students should be actively involved and engaged in the learning process, rather than being passive recipients of knowledge. This turns to be one of the most challenging principles of constructivism and the one that educators struggle to accommodate.

Educators from different disciplines are investigating ways to enhance the way they design and develop their teaching material and activities, so that they are more motivational and engaging for the students. According to [20], failure of students to actively engage with the taught material can lead to poor understanding and performance with the course (e.g., low marks on the course assessments). Students learn best when they feel that they enjoy learning and are engaging in the learning process. Furthermore, the results of a study conducted by [22] suggest that the higher the student engagement, the higher the student learning. There are many suggestions in the literature on how to motivate and engage students in their own learning, especially as they relate to sciences. As reported in [20] students can be motivated when the material is presented within a real life context, in relation to students' needs, as well as when they are provided with constructive feedback, valuable reward for their efforts, and clear expectations.

One way to engage students is to provide an enjoyable learning environment through play and fun activities, a concept that many times is referred to as edutainment (entertainment which is specifically designed to be educational, i.e., educational entertainment). As with entertainment, edutainment can have many different forms, ranging from media (e.g., video productions, audio productions, computer software, etc.) to physical places (museums, educational centres, parks and exhibits, etc.), all with the aim to attract learners and keep their interest on specific subject areas. Of special interest to this paper, are educational software, and specifically, educational video games. Many researchers argue that educational video games, as opposed to other edutainment elements, have a greater appeal to students of all ages and can potentially enhance the educational experience. While edutainment is being grounded on only didactical purposes and allows for static linear progressions, [29], it does not allow for exploration or consideration of alternative routes, thus decreasing the overall motivation and engagement of the student. In contrast, the immersive environments supported by educational video games use compelling graphics, sound, and physical interaction that can significantly enhance the educational experience, motivate, excite and engage the students [5, 7, 8, 14, 18, 19, 24]. Additionally, allowing users to roam freely large spaces and explore different scenarios, which they can connect to their learning experience, increases the cognitive curiosity of the student and offers an intrinsic reward.

On the other hand, the majority of games also employ a number of extrinsic rewards for their end-users to further increase motivation, participation and engagement. This includes game components like points, levels, badges and quests that can be used also for tracking the players' progress. Allowing the user to reflect on his/her progress is also a very important element of active learning. In particular, educational games use concrete goals to make learning through reflection possible. In particular, by placing specific goals that the user must meet (e.g., quizzes and puzzles that assess the level of knowledge) the game ensures that essential skills are acquired before he/she can continue in more complex areas.

Educational games have gained increasing popularity in the last years and there has been a rapid growth in their development and effective use as non-traditional learning environments for independent learning as well as a supplement of traditional instruction, along with other pedagogical methods [5, 19]. They have become part of the modern culture and the everyday life of the young generation of learners, since they become familiar with them as early as preschool when they use them to learn numbers, letters, colours, shapes, etc. [5]. Computer Science and more specifically, introductory programming, is no exception. There is a vast literature on educational games and how they can be used to enhance instruction of introductory programming as well as to motivate and engage young learners with introductory programming [21, 23].

3   Code Adventure

CodeAdventure is an adventure game where the player assumes the role of the protagonist exploring the game environment, and in the process, solving puzzles, and overcoming challenges in order to discover and acquire certain items. CodeAdventure adopts an integrated design approach by employing various mechanisms and techniques to achieve a truly immersive game learning experience. In particular, the game has an attractive storyline and offers a highly interactive 3D environment that allows the user to explore different levels, which are composed of multiple rooms, each one containing a diverse set of puzzles. Each room has specific objectives and includes various encyclopaedic interactive elements that convey the required knowledge to meet the objectives as well assessment methods that allow the user to reflect on his/her current status and progress. Moreover, achievements, rewards and secret items provide a feeling of challenge and increase overall engagement.

In the following sections we thoroughly describe the design aspects of CodeAdventure.

3.1   Storyline

The game story takes place in the year 2500, where the player, who is a time-traveller, detects a strong ripple in the fabric of space-time caused by another time-traveller. This nemesis, who travelled back in time to steal the six rotors of the Enigma machine, has a mission to prevent Alan Turing from breaking Enigma ciphers, thus allowing the Nazi to win World War II. The player traces that the nemesis has travelled back in 1939, and hid the rotors in different rooms. The game starts at the point in time where the player has travelled back in time, and is searching to find the six rotors. The player is required to solve specific programming puzzles and overcome specific challenges (e.g., unlocking doors and chests) in order to explore all the rooms and discover the hidden rotors.

3.2   Level Design

Code Adventure features 4 distinct levels representing different "subject areas" for introductory programming. In particular, there are four levels incorporated in the current version of the game: (i) Introduction to the JAVA language; (ii) Object-oriented

Programming; (iii) Data Structures and Algorithms; and (iv) Advanced Topics. As illustrated in Fig. 1(left), each level is composed of multiple rooms that may have one or more doors[1] each posing unique challenges (e.g., quizzes, puzzles) that must be met in order to allow to the user to continue to next one. Each room has a specific theme that represents one or more related programming topics (e.g., introduction to data types) as can be seen from the superimposed overlay in the middle of Fig. 1(right).

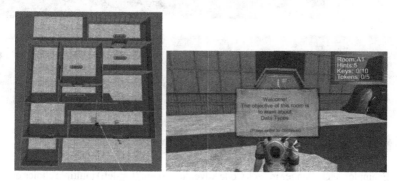

Fig. 1. (left) One of the CodeAdventure levels showing the configuration of multiple rooms; (right) One of the rooms of CodeAdventure that introduces data types

3.3   Room Design

Each room of CodeAdventure focuses on one or more related introductory programming topics. At the entrance of the room, the user is informed about the learning objective(s) using an overlaid message, as illustrated in Fig. 1(right). When the user enters the room, he/she need to explore and find the entrance to the next room by finding specific coloured key cards. In order to acquire these cards, the user must explore the room, discover their location and solve specific challenges to get them.

Examples of challenges are illustrated in Fig. 2, where the user is asked to: (i) (top-left) solve a multiple choice question; (top-right) rotate a wheel to solve a puzzle; (iii) (bottom-left) rotate boxes with operators to validate a mathematical expression; and (iv) (bottom-right) pull/push levers to form the bit representation of a number.

In order to solve the challenges the user can participate in a number of learning of active and passive learning activities. These activities currently include: (i) static overlaid visual elements (e.g., banners in corridors, wall papers); (ii) interactive visual elements (e.g., movable boxes, push buttons, levers); (iii) animated elements (e.g., moving rotors, small toy vehicles); and (iv) reference points (e.g., question mark icons that link to external documentation). In order to facilitate our description, consider the gameplay screenshots in Fig. 3. As was mentioned before, each room has a specific theme that represents one or more related programming topic (e.g., introduction to data types, casting, operator precedence). As can be seen in Fig. 3(left) and (right) has an overlaid label that shows the type of each box. For example, Additionally,

---

[1]   Doors include traditional doors, automatic doors, electric fences, etc.

Fig. 2. Examples of challenges in each CodeAdventure room: (top-left) multiple choice question; (top-right) mechanical wheel puzzle; (bottom-left) rotating operator boxes mathematical challenge; and (bottom-right) pulling/pushing levels for bit representation of numbers

Fig. 3. (left) static visual elements: (a) boxes with overlaid data type name. (b) Quantified visual representation of data types: a single box represents a byte-sized data type such as byte and boolean. Boxes are grouped to form larger data types (e.g., two boxes form a two-byte data type such as short, four boxes form a four-byte data type such as int); (right) expressions embossed on corridor tiles.

3.4   End-User Monitoring

The monitoring of the end user interaction is being performed in a multi-modal way as illustrated in Fig. 4. All the actions of the user are recorded and time stamped for further analysis and understanding of how much time a student spent on a specific activity learning or practicing. This sets the foundation on understanding the user's behaviour and assessing the effectiveness of the software.

Additionally, we have also incorporated components to collect continuous streams of sensor data (e.g., Accelerometer, Galvanic Skin Response and Heart Rate) through smart wearable devices and to expose them in a unified way for further processing. These

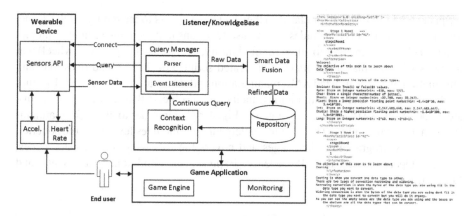

Fig. 4. (left) The monitoring architecture of CodeAdventure (right) XML representation of the information utilized for room configuration

mechanisms will in the future augment the data received from the aforementioned monitoring of activities to infer knowledge about a user's affective state during game play, eventually leading to an enhanced understanding of his behaviour and experience.

3.5 Feedback

Allowing the user to reflect on his/her progress is a very important element of active learning. To this end, CodeAdventure provides a variety of feedback mechanisms that allow the student to be informed on his progress and assess his current level of knowledge.

On the top right corner, the user is always aware of his location (i.e., level and room code), number of available hints, and number of keys and tokens acquired. Before entering the room, an overlaid message displays the objective of the room (i.e., the programming topic that will be covered with the visual elements and objects). When the user enters the room, there are one or more tokens that provide information about the theory behind the topic. This information is provided as a link to specific content (e.g., links to lecture notes, to oracle website with JAVA documentation, etc.). Additionally, an object may have a label that signifies something related to the theory (e.g., box labelled as Boolean). Furthermore, when the user is in close proximity of an object, the object may change colour if there is an interactive activity related to it. Finally, during the answering of questions, the system illuminates a green light for every correct answer and a red for incorrect ones.

3.6 Prototype Implementation

CodeAdventure was implemented with Unity 5.5[2] using C# scripts. It uses only unity libraries and in order to facilitate access into the scene, the majority of the developed

---

[2] Unity game development platform, https://unity3d.com/learn.

scripts extend monoBehavior class[3] so they can have access to the models in the scene. The monoBehavior class includes easy to use functions that facilitate seamless interaction in each frame. In order to allow for modularity, every object (e.g., lever, wheel) that interacts with the player has its own dedicated script. For the overlaid questions and information, we have utilized XML manipulation and IO libraries from the .NET framework. Finally, all room configurations, including all objects that reside inside rooms, are loaded from XML files as illustrated in Fig. 4(right) in order to allow for maintainability and expandability. The current implementation includes level one: Introduction to the JAVA programming languages and covers the following topics: Data Types, Casting, Operators and their Precedence, Expressions, Conditional Statements, and Loop Structures.

4   Conclusions and Future Work

In this paper, we have presented CodeAdventure, an educational game for learning and practicing introductory programming concepts. Inside CodeAdventure, players need to solve specific programming puzzles and overcome specific challenges (e.g., unlocking doors and chests), in order to explore different rooms and discover hidden items. Throughout the game, players are exposed to theory related to specific programming concepts, while at the same time they can practice and apply the concepts in a fun and engaging way. CodeAdventure incorporates different effective learning techniques, such as providing hints and clues on how to solve puzzles and providing immediate feedback on students' performance.

Since our game-based learning environment is still at a functional prototype level, we have conducted a qualitative exploratory study to evaluate its usability and accept-ability using a small group of students. In the format of focus groups and following the open-ended questions protocol, we tried to derive insights regarding students' thoughts and feelings while interacting with the environment. At this stage our main concern was to understand whether the objectives of the game were clear for them and the scenario structured and motivating. Also, special emphasis placed on the visual representation and navigation over the various elements of the game. In this respect, our understanding focused on the challenges and difficulties they had to encounter while tackling the proposed learning activities as well as on their overall experience during their interaction. Even though a detailed analysis of the data collected is still pending, the preliminary results indicate that CodeAdventure visually communicates fundamental programming concepts in a fun, stimulating and engaging manner, leading to increased student comprehension.

To further validate the impact of CodeAdventure on learning, during the next academic year (i.e., 2017/18), we plan to conduct a larger user study, using first year undergraduate computer science students taking Introduction to Programming with JAVA. In addition to the regular lecturing hours and use of provided learning material, participants will be given access to CodeAdventure as an auxiliary tool that would support their learning, will be asked to play the game on their own time and undertake particular tasks that refer to specific sections of the course. At the end of each semester, a survey questionnaire will be

---

[3] Creating and Using Scripts, https://docs.unity3d.com/Manual/CreatingAndUsingScripts.html.

administered to all participants, with questions for identifying specific behavioral and usability factors such as motivation, engagement into the learning objectives, ease of use. In addition, focus groups will be organized, so as to take advantage of group interaction for acquisition of supplementary information and insights into participants' thoughts and perceptions about the game.

References

1. Efopoulos, V., Dagdilelis, V., Evangelidis, G., Satratzemi, M.: WIPE: a programming environment for novices. In: 10th Annual SIGCSE Conference on Innovation and Technology in Computer Science Education (ITiCSE 2005), pp. 113–117. ACM, New York (2005). doi: 10.1145/1067445.1067479
2. Gomez, A., Santos, A., Mendes, J.A: A study on students' behaviours and attitudes towards learning to program. In: 17th ACM Annual Conference on Innovation and Technology in Computer Science Education (ITiCSE 2012), pp. 132–137. ACM, New York (2012). doi: 10.1145/2325296.2325364
3. Hijón-Neira, R., Velázquez-Iturbide, A., Pizarro-Romero, C., Carriço, L.: Game programming for improving learning experience. In: 2014 Conference on Innovation and Technology in Computer Science Education (ITiCSE 2014), pp. 225–230. ACM, New York (2014). doi:10.1145/2591708.2591737
4. Isomottonen, V., Nylen, A., Tirronen, V.: Writing to learn programming? A single case pilot study. In: Koli Calling, pp. 140–144. ACM, New York (2016)
5. Mach, N.: Gaming, learning 2.0, and the digital divide. In: Siemens, G., Fulford, C. (eds.) EdMedia: World Conference on Educational Media and Technology 2009, pp. 2972–2977. Association for the Advancement of Computing in Education (AACE) (2009)
6. Miljanovic, M., Bradbury, J.: Robot ON!: A serious game for improving programming comprehension. In: 5th International Workshop on Games and Software Engineering (GAS 2016), pp. 33–36. ACM, New York (2016). doi:10.1145/2896958.2896962
7. Pierce, N., Conlan, O., Wade, V.: Adaptive educational games: providing non-invasive personalized learning experiences. IEEE Computer Society (2008)
8. Prensky, M.: Digital Game-Based Learning. McGraw-Hill, New York (2001)
9. Rajala, T., Laakso, M., Kaila, E., Salakoski, T.: VILLE – a language-independent program visualization tool. In: Seventh Baltic Sea Conference on Computing Education Research (Koli Calling 2007), vol. 99, pp. 151–159. ACM, New York (2007)
10. Saloun, P. Velart, Z.: Adaptive hypermedia as a means for learning programming. In: Adaptive Hypermedia as a Means for Learning Programming (ICWE 2006 Workshop). ACM, New York (2006). Article 11, doi:10.1145/1149993.1150006
11. Schoeman, M., Gelderblom, H.: The effect of students' educational background and use of a program visualization tool in introductory programming. In: Annual Conference of the South African Institute of Computer Scientists and Information Technologists (SAICSIT 2016). ACM, New York (2016). Article 37, doi:10.1145/2987491.2987519
12. Shuhindan, S., Hamilton, M., Souza, D.: A study of the difficulties of novice programmers. In: 10th Annual SIGCSE Conference on Innovation and Technology in Computer Science Education (ITiCSE 2005), pp. 14–18. ACM, New York (2005). doi:10.1145/1067445.1067453
13. Tillmann, N., de Halleux, J., Xie, T., Gulwani, S., Bishop, J.: Teaching and learning programming and software engineering via interactive gaming. In: 2013 International Conference on Software Engineering (ICSE 2013), pp. 1117–1126. ACM, New York (2013)

14. Van Eck, R.: Digital game-based learning: it's not just the digital natives who are restless. EDUCAUSE Rev. **41**(2), 16–30 (2006)
15. Wirth, M., McCuaig, J.: Making programs with the Raspberry Pi. In: Western Canadian Conference on Computing Education (WCCCE 2014). ACM, New York (2014). Article 17, doi: 10.1145/2597959.2597970
16. Wulf, T.: Constructivist approaches for teaching computer programming. In: Constructivist Approaches for Teaching Computer Programming (SIGITE 2005), pp. 245–248. ACM, New York (2005). doi:10.1145/1095714.1095771
17. Xinogalos, S., Malliarakis, C., Tsompanoudi, D., Satratzemi, M.: Microworlds, games and collaboration: three effective approaches to support novices in learning programming. In: 7th Balkan Conference on Informatics Conference (BCI 2015). ACM, New York (2015). Article 39, doi:10.1145/2801081.2801094
18. Bitter, G., Legacy, M.: Using Technology in the Classroom, 7th edn. Pearson Education Inc., Upper Saddle River (2008)
19. Bodnar, C., Anastasio, D., Enszer, J., Burkey, D.: Engineers at play: games as teaching tools for undergraduate engineering students. Res. J. Eng. Educ. **105**, 147–200 (2015)
20. Chan, E.: Motivation for mandatory courses. **7**(3) (2004). Centre for Development of Teaching and Learning
21. Eagle, M., Barnes, T.: Experimental evaluation of an educational game for improved learning in introductory computing. ACM SIGCSE Bull. **41**(1), 321–325 (2009)
22. Grissom, S., McNally, M.F., Naps, T.: Algorithm visualization in CS education: comparing levels of student engagement. In: Proceedings of the 2003 ACM Symposium on Software Visualization (2003)
23. Hijon-Neira, R., Velazquez-iturbide, A., Pizarro-Romero, C., Carrico, L.: Game programming for improving learning experience. In: The 2014 Conference on Innovation and Technology in Computer Science Education (ITiCSE 2014), pp. 225–230. ACM, New York (2012). doi: 10.1145/2591708
24. Ireland, A., Kaufman, D., Sauvé, L.: Simulation and Advanced Gaming Environments (SAGE) for learning. In: Reeves, T., Yamashita, S. (eds.) World Conference on E-Learning in Corporate, Government, Healthcare, and Higher Education, Cheasapeake, VA, pp. 2028–2036 (2006)
25. Oblinger, D.: Simulations, games and learning, pp. 1–6. EDUCAUSE Learning Initiative (2006). http://net.educause.edu/ir/library/pdf/ELI3004.pdf
26. Lincoln, Y.S., Guba, E.G.: Naturalistic Inquiry. Sage Publications, Newbury Park (1985)
27. Schwartz, P., Ogilvy, J.: The emergent paradigm: changing patterns of thought and belief (SRI International). (1979). Cited in [26]
28. Von Glasersfeld, E.: Learning as a constructive activity. In: Janvier, C. (ed.) Problems of Representation in the Teaching and Learning of Mathematics, pp. 3–18. Lawrence Erlbaum Assoc., Hillsdale (1987)
29. Denis, G., Jouvelot, P.: Motivation-driven educational game design: applying best practices to music education. Paper presented at the 2005 ACM SIGCHI international conference on advances in computer entertainment technology, Valencia, Spain (2005)

Using Mental Models to Design for Learning: Lessons from Game Development

Aleshia Hayes[(✉)]

Purdue University, Fort Wayne, IN, USA
hayesa@ipfw.edu

Abstract. Of the many approaches game designers take to understand the way their experiences and messages will be perceived, a good deal of these approaches include explicitly or implicitly evaluating user mental models. These mental models are formed implicitly and explicitly during a range of activities from mundane to game play. Individuals hold mental models that they use to interpret the world and experiences. When one's mental model is incorrect or incomplete they may or may not have success on the execution of an intended action, similarly, the action may not have evaluated the situation appropriately, so their action may be ineffective or even detrimental. This phenomenon can be seen manifested in the actions in the physical world, in interaction with software applications, in interaction with various hardware, and in games. Because many solutions to real world problems that can be solved by simple shifts in mental models, this paper highlights the activities that games do well to train users (players) to grow and evolve their mental models through game play that is designed for interaction.

The process of designing an interface for interaction is a communication process that involves the designer conveying messages and experiences to elicit emotion, behavior or cognition and in order to guide users to desired actions. During this process the designer must consider the motivations and preconceived perspectives of what to expect from and experience and how to engage with that experience. This paper highlights strategies to teaching players how to play video games and the approaches game designers take to understand and shift mental models that have been employed in games. These strategies and approaches are then used to make recommendations on how to transfer those lessons about humans and mental models to other learning software systems.

Keywords: Mental models · Human computer interaction · Games · Gamification · UX · Motivation · Peripherals · Game controllers · Contextual analysis

1 Introduction

There are many solutions to real world problems that can be solved by simple shifts in mental models, or the framework that individuals make sense of their experiences in relationship to affect, behavior, and cognition. They go on to apply mental models in their evaluation of experiences in the world [1, 8] to determine appropriate actions. Finally, individuals execute actions based on mental models of how actions will impact

© Springer International Publishing AG 2017
P. Zaphiris and A. Ioannou (Eds.): LCT 2017, Part I, LNCS 10295, pp. 433–442, 2017.
DOI: 10.1007/978-3-319-58509-3_34

the perceived situation. When one's mental model is incorrect or incomplete they may or may not have success on the execution of an intended action, similarly, the action may not have evaluated the situation appropriately, so their action may be ineffective. This phenomenon can be seen manifested in the actions in the physical world, in interaction with software applications, in interaction with various hardware, and in games.

While the term mental model is not referenced as frequently in game design, the game industry has distinguished itself by its effectiveness in adapting to existing mental models and the evolution of those models to create uniform play experiences. This paper discussed the findings of research designed to explore the employment of mental models in the game industry. The process of gaining a baseline understanding on player intuition leads game designers to exploit the players mental framework through which they assign meaning to an interaction. Once the user engages through exploitation of existing mental models, the design of the game can implicitly or explicitly teach the user a new piece of information that the user can integrate with existing mental models.

The lessons from reviewing the efficient process of changing mental models in games can be applied to shifting user mental models across multiple industries. The lessons that can most directly be extrapolated from the research are the implicit and explicit cues used to affect user mental models. The process of designing an interface for interaction is a communication process. The designer is communicating experiences to elicit emotion, behavior or cognition and in order to guide users to desired actions, the designer must consider the motivations and preconceived perspectives of what to expect from and experience and how to engage with that experience (mental models).

1.1   What Is a Mental Model?

Human consciousness is largely concerned with making sense of the world. The concept of mental models was introduced by Craik in 1943 as a mental "small scale model of external reality and its own possible actions [8]. These models are used to interpret and evaluate elements in the world, make predictions, and formulate action plans to act in the world. Evolutionary theories suggest this has evolved as our motivations have changed. "Informational states such as being lost, confused, or disoriented not only have affective consequences in terms of their adaptive implications. The evolutionary advantage to understanding one's environment is clear." [5, p. 2] Hence, humans are compelled to controlled exploration not only as a ludic expression, but also as an evolved human trait. Psychologists have theorized that a significant part of the process of interpretation of the way things work in the world relies on the internal models that represent reality to an individual. These models are frequently adjusted subconsciously, they are unseen and often forgotten. In fact, the very act of explicitly addressing an implicit mental model is to present possible change to it [5].

1.2   Mental Models in Games

Boyan and Sherry [1] identified process of learning the game environment is a process of creating a mental model of the game that is similar or identical to the programmed computer model of the game. Designer's do this to decrease the gap between existing and new knowledge. In games, the conceptual model created by the designer can be frequently matched with the player mental model. Part of this phenomenon is supported by the fact that there is a context that gamers share. Knowing this context empowers the designer to design based on elements of an experience that are shared and commonly known in the context.

2 How Mental Models Are Constructed

Mental models are constructed as human minds interpret and make sense of the world around them. Mental Models are constructed both implicitly and/or explicitly. In some events mental models are naturally developed and are theorized to evolve with a species. Inversely, most mental models that we hold are learned from implicit and explicit cues from the environment. In the case of games, game developers make a practice of understanding how mental models manifest themselves and how to engage those models. Piaget referenced a central element of mental models as being the object through which individuals organized new information with existing knowledge, citing application of laws of inference a human specific capability [16]. When new information is synthesized with existing information, learning occurs [19]. An important consideration with mental models is that learning must be monitored as well there is frequent inappropriate application of mental models.

Because mental models build upon prior knowledge, there is no end to the evolution of these models. This provides us with an opportunity to iterate on efforts to impact user mental models in games.

3 Implicit Construction of Mental Models in Games

The primary and most prominent factor impacting mental models are affordances. Affordances include the capabilities an element is able to perform. The goal of designers is to make affordances discoverable by making the capacity perceivable. One example is that when a player moves his or her character up to an object in a game, the developers must program the element and character model to give feedback that *indicates* that the object may be acted upon. The cues that communicate the capability are *signifiers*.

How do games signify an affordance? Affordance signifying can occur through mapping, symbols, feedback, and constraints. When used effectively the interaction between the game and the player is natural, intuitive, transparent and consistent with existing interfaces.

3.1 Mapping

When referring to mapping in the strict interface design sense, mapping refers to matching controls to the physical object controlled. This direct mapping is not relevant in the same sense to the mapping of a game controller, "The relationship between design controls, their movements, and their effects on the element(s) they control. Moving a joystick to the left should result in something moving left." This mapping can become more complex as there are multiple platforms that a single game can be played on, such as a game released for XBOX, Playstation 4, and PC. Controller mapping must be done for each of these interfaces. UI designers and programmers work together to ensure that the mental models of the users of each kind of device are taken into account for effective design across platforms.

3.2   Feedback

In addition to signifiers, punishment, rewards, and constraints are used in game to shape behavior and affect. Video games are so effective at harnessing these tools that they frequently run the risk of addiction among a subset of players [9]. To exemplify the strategy in giving structured feedback, video game designers systematically use the color red to convey multiple messages. This is effective because of the implicit impact of the color red on cognition. "Red is hypothesized to impair performance on achievement tasks, because red is associated with the danger of failure in achievement contexts and evokes avoidance motivation" [4, p. 155].

A key example of introducing a need for a new mental model is the MS Kinect. The voice recognition technology of the Kinect works better than many other developments, but the voice recognition doesn't always pick up on the intended messages. When the interaction doesn't go the way the player intended, players revert to their mental models on how to convey messages verbally. Players then evaluate the situation and form a plan of action to effectively manage the interaction. This assessment of the problem and solution are then reinforced when the repetition of the original command appears to be executed. This process exemplifies why many people hold largely skewed mental models that don't align with the systems in the physical world.

3.3   Physical Examples

Video game controllers serve as a great example of the evolution of technology and the human tendency to revert to mental models that players understand. The original pong controller has both physical and cognitive mapping to signify the affordances of the game pong by looking at the controller. Each one of these controllers is built upon existing perspectives about controllers. The original one button Atari controller communicated the affordances clearly. While the affordance of pushing the button and moving the joystick, it was up to the designer to design an interface that was intuitive, transparent, and natural.

Consistency of button use from the original buttons for which people have existing models is not only a design principle, but also a strategy for smoothly shifting from one mental model to another. If "X" for instance is the button used to jump with the older version of the controller, there is no reason to change the jump button for the next experience. Training on the controllers differs, depending on the selected user mental model. If the end user has some experience with some element of the controller, the next step is to test the UX. The development of each subsequent video game controller has build upon the feedback from users, but also upon the existence of it's predecessors. Iteration between controllers included changes to ergonomic design, number and position of buttons, and even tactile and haptic feedback, largely based on player feedback (Fig. 1).

a) Atari Pong Controller (1975)

b) Atari 2600 Controller (1977)

c) Atari Jaguar Controller (1993)

d) Nintendo Controller (1989)

e) Nintendo 64 Controller (1996)

f) Nintendo Switch Controller (2017)

g) Original XBOX Controller (2001)

h) XBOX 30 Controller (2005)

i) XBOX ONE Controller (2013)

j) Sony Playstation Controller (1994)

k) Playstation 3 Controller (2006)

l) Sony PS4 Controller (2014)

Fig. 1.

The designs of the more recent controllers support more implicit feedback. The vibro-tactile feedback afforded by the PS4 controller and the XBOX one controller and the Nintendo Switch controller allow the game to signify possibilities, constraints, and even negative feedback, such as being wounded by a weapon or environmental factor.

4   Explicit Construction of Mental Models in Games

4.1   Tutorials

In game tutorials are the explicit approach to teaching a user how interaction will be navigated. The Mario tutorial below explicitly describes the elements of the game play, whereas the original Mario game required very little reading to effectively engage the mental models.

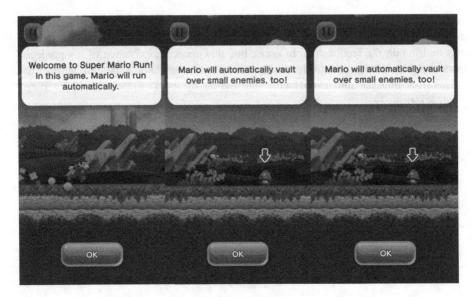

Fig. 2.

Visual Cues. Visual Cues include blinking, flashing, directing with arrows, lights, patterns, emphasis, and color. These can be seen in the example above (Fig. 2) from Mario Run. In addition to the text based tutorial, the designers employed arrows to draw attention to the enemy and obstacles (Fig. 3).

Fig. 3. Original Mario allowed for more exploration of the control layout.

5   Revealing Mental Models

Researchers often extrapolate the mental models around the games they design from introspection on their own experiences in gaming. While there are many psychological approaches that have been employed over the last decades, for the purposes of human computer interaction, we can take a more practical and applied approach to uncovering mental models. User experience professionals have honed the use of various tools, including: play-testing, questionnaires, Observations, basic informational interviews, and contextual inquiry.

Some mental models are collaborative. Teammates share knowledge about events and situations that allows them to better adapt to new challenges and environments by being able to predict their teammates' needs [18]. While this is useful in game, it is critical to saving resources and optimizing the work done by serious softwares for training and daily living.

5.1 Strategies to Reveal Mental Models

Contextual Inquiry is an ethnographic practice that includes exploration of the user's natural environment, perspectives, and thought processes to gain insight into their identity. The purpose of the contextual inquiry is to gain a richer more robust understanding of a target group. 2016 research [17] found that contextual inquiry to support participatory design of a serious game to assist hospitalized children in learning was highly effective in developing a game that satisfied the wishes and goals of the target audience (Table 1).

Table 1. Strategies to discover player mental models

Practice	What is done?	Purpose
Interviews	Ask users about their expectations of the proposed product. Ask user their previous experiences with similar products. Ask user about their perspective on the proposed product. Ask the user if any part of the product violates expectations	Gain insight into the mental models of the motivations for using existing products. Gain insight into the perspective on the proposed product
Play testing	Watch user interact with the proposed software. Give no guidance to the user, as they bias the user. (This is often observed from the other side of a one way mirror or live stream or play video)	Gain Insight into the user's mental model. Observe manifestations of the users mental models
Think aloud	User is asked to use the software and speak their thought process as they engage [3, 10–12].	Reveals mental models that relate to both evaluation and execution stages of action in software use
Contextual inquiry	Observe users performing related tasks in the field. Accompany the user in natural (e.g. work or home) environment and talk to them to learn their perspectives	Explore the user's natural process doing the. Expose the context of the target behavior. Gain empathy for the user's mental model
Questionnaires	Directed questionnaires asking targeted questions about proposed mental models	Add clarity to the understanding of the theorized mental models. Revise mental models. Create new categories of user persona mental models

6 Applying Mental Models Game Design for Learning

Mental models are shaped in the physical world to shape shape affect, behavior, or cognition, which many would call learning [15, 17] Ideally, the process of applying mental models begins with examination of current mental model, as highlighted in the previous section (Sect. 5).

Training. One of the first obvious applications for shaping behavior through mental models would be training. In video games designers can communicate to a player to follow a very specific, complex, and counterintuitive process to achieve some desired game state. How can designers use what we know about mental models to design for learning outside of game.

To begin with the process of shaping, wherein a target is rewarded for approaches to a target behavior. This process is frequently completed in games in combination with audio and visual feedback. This is frequently done to encourage a target behavior. The completion of such a task is the validation of the theorized mental model. An example of this is when a player approaches an area that they need to explore, music may get more pronounced, lights may flash, some artifact may appear, and there may be a text or verbal cue encouraging their actions.

Motivation. Knowledge of the intrinsic semantic constraint elicited by the color red is used frequently in design to implicitly communicate emotional states of violence and danger. For another example, while developers of horror games do not formally study fear, they do understand the elements of an experience that create sensations of terror and foreboding. Finally, the motivation that each user has to stay engaged with a game can be explored in terms of mental models. Richard Bartle established Bartle's player types which highlight the competing motivations that may lead an individual [2]. Bartle's player types consist of Killers, Achievers, Socializers, and Explorers. The player type reveals their central motivating factor for playing video games.

7 Conclusion: Transfer to User Centered Design Practice

In 2011 Boyan and Sherry asked if mental models developed in games would transfer to effect real life behavior. Since then, many studies have demonstrated the transfer of mental models gained in gaming and other digital entertainment contexts to action in the physical and practical world. Not only are there many games that have already demonstrated transfer of learned skills to the real world [6, 7] Given this transfer is established as an outcome of learning in game, how do teams design with this goal in mind?

To design UX in a User Centered Approach with learning in mind:

1. Determine the mental model(s) held by target users regarding the project.
2. Determine your experience conceptual model.
3. Determine target conceptual model.
4. Determine the learning goals or behavioral goals.
5. Review obstacles to the goal.
6. Determine in advance how learning outcome will be measured.

The lessons that can most directly be extrapolated from the research are the implicit and explicit cues used to affect user mental models. The process of designing an interface for interaction is a communication process. The designer is communicating experiences to elicit emotion, behavior or cognition and in order to guide users to desired actions, the designer must consider the motivations and preconceived perspectives of what to expect from and experience and how to engage with that experience (mental models).

References

1. Boyan, A., Sherry, J.L.: The challenge in creating games for education: aligning mental models with game models. Child. Dev. Perspect. **5**, 82–87 (2011). doi:10.1111/j.1750-8606. 2011.00160.x
2. Bartle, R.: Hearts, clubs, diamonds, spades: players who suit MUDs. J. MUD Res. **1**(1), 19 (1996)
3. Tan, C.T., Leong, T.W., Shen, S.: Combining think-aloud and physiological data to understand video game experiences. In: Proceedings of the SIGCHI Conference on Human Factors in Computing Systems (CHI 2014), pp. 381–390. ACM, New York (2014). https://doi.org/10.1145/2556288.2557326
4. Elliot, A.J., Maier, M.A., Moller, A.C., Friedman, R., Meinhardt, J.: Color and psychological functioning: The effect of red on performance attainment. J. Exp. Psychol. Gen. **136**(1), 154–168 (2007). http://dx.doi.org/10.1037/0096-3445.136.1.154
5. Hanke, U., Baraldini, M., Pfaeffle, U.: Teacher models about the knowledge of their students (2008)
6. Hayes, A.T., Hardin, S.E., Hughes, C.E.: Perceived presence's role on learning outcomes in a mixed reality classroom of simulated students. In: Shumaker, R. (ed.) VAMR 2013. LNCS, vol. 8022, pp. 142–151. Springer, Heidelberg (2013). doi:10.1007/978-3-642-39420-1_16
7. Hayes, A.T., Straub, C.L., Dieker, L.A., Hughes, C.E., Hynes, M.C.: Ludic learning: exploration of TLE TeachLivE™ and effective teacher training. Int. J. Gaming Comput. Mediat. Simul. (IJGCMS) **5**(2), 20–33 (2013). Chicago
8. Johnson-Laird, P.N.: Mental models and thought. In: Holyoak, K.J., Morrison, R.G. (eds.) The Cambridge Handbook of Thinking and Reasoning, pp. 185–208. Cambridge University Press, New York (2005)
9. King, D., Delfabbro, P., Griffiths, M.: Video game structural characteristics: a new psychological taxonomy. Int. J. Ment. Health Addict. **8**, 90 (2010). doi:10.1007/s11469-009-9206-4
10. Nielsen, J.: Estimating the number of subjects needed for a thinking aloud test. Int. J. Hum. Comput. Stud. **41**(3), 385–397 (1994)
11. Nielsen, J.: Evaluating the thinking aloud technique for use by computer scientists. In: Hartson, H.R., Hix, D. (eds.) Advances in Human-Computer Interaction. Ablex, Norwood (1992)
12. Nielsen, J., Clemmensen, T., Yssing, C.: Getting access to what goes on in people's heads?: reflections on the think-aloud technique. In: Proceedings of the Second Nordic Conference on Human-Computer Interaction (NordiCHI 2002), pp. 101–110. ACM, New York (2002). http://dx.doi.org.ezproxy.library.ipfw.edu/10.1145/572020.572033
13. Norman, D.: The Design of Everyday Things. Basic Books Inc., New York (2002)

14. Nunes, E.P.S., Luz, A.R., Lemos, E.M., Nunes, C.: Approaches of participatory design in the design process of a serious game to assist in the learning of hospitalized children. In: Kurosu, M. (ed.) HCI 2016. LNCS, vol. 9733, pp. 406–416. Springer, Cham (2016). doi:10.1007/978-3-319-39513-5_38
15. Piaget, J.: Equilibration of Cognitive Structures: The Central Problem of Cognitive Development. University of Chicago Press, Chicago (1985)
16. Rigas, G., Elg, F.: Mental models, confidence, and performance in a complex dynamic decision making environment. Uppsala University, Sweden (1997)
17. Swain, K., Mills, V.: Implicit communication in novice and expert teams (No. DSTO-TN-0474). Defence Science and Technology Organisation Salisbury Systems Sciences Lab, Australia (2003)
18. Vygotsky, L.: Interaction between learning and development. Read. Dev. Child. **23**(3), 34–41 (1978). Chicago

Strategic Design: Breaking Mental Models Initiates Learning in Video Games

Jay Dee Johns III[1,2(✉)]

[1] IUPUI School of Informatics, Indianapolis, IN, USA
[2] 3r Interactive, LLC, Fort Wayne, IN, USA
jay@3rinteractive.com

Abstract. An important part of all digital design is effective communication with users. Video game designers, compared to other types of digital designers, have much that they need to communicate within games. As a game progresses, there are often more incrementally challenging mechanics for the player to encounter and experience. By briefly explaining the more traditional methods of educating game players, I will explain how game designers can draw from user experience frameworks to improve gameplay by teaching players in both subtle and dramatic ways with the use of mental models. Perhaps most commonly, mental models have been used to describe and analyze user satisfaction, particularly among digital technologies such as websites. Although there are some key similarities between these types of technologies and video games, significant differences do emerge, although many parallels can still be drawn. I will first explain how video game designers can strategically utilize the lessons learned from previous design researchers. Then, I will explain how and when these models should be broken. By drawing on expectancy violation theory and game design strategies, I argue that purposely violating a player's mental models can prime the player for learning in order to expand his understanding of the game world. After several case studies, I will then provide guidance to game designers who want to implement a disruptive mental model approach to educating players.

Keywords: Mental model · Game design · Expectancy violation theory

1 Designing to Communicate

Every video game designer has a challenge of effectively communicating with the user. When a user plays a game for the first time there can be a lot to learn. Every game has mechanics that need to be understood, and, depending on the game, a story will be in place that gives the user a greater understanding of the universe the player character inhabits. Compared to other forms of digital content, the amount of information available to learn, understand, and eventually utilize can be overwhelming. Game designers strive to communicate the intricacies of the game universe in a way that is efficient enough that the player can enjoy the game and not be frustrated or confused about how to play, but also is not boring or disruptive to gameplay.

© Springer International Publishing AG 2017
P. Zaphiris and A. Ioannou (Eds.): LCT 2017, Part I, LNCS 10295, pp. 443–461, 2017.
DOI: 10.1007/978-3-319-58509-3_35

Throughout the history of video games, many teaching methodologies have been applied to situations where the user needs to learn something new. Neither Pong, arguably the very first video game, nor Super Mario Bros, perhaps the first widely known video game in the traditional sense, spent any time explaining different mechanics [1]. Everything the user learns in Super Mario Bros is through experimentation. For example, the first section of the first level teaches the user that moving right is the primary direction because there is no other direction the game will allow the character to go. It teaches the player to jump by introducing a mushroom shaped enemy creature that kills the player's character on contact with no other way to avoid it. With the ability to jump, the player learns that hitting boxes with question marks on them gives the player coins. Each new game mechanic is taught passively and builds upon what the player has clearly already learned.

Modern high profile video games, generally, have taken the approach that people who play video games need to have their hands held and led through the game. Every action or experience is told to the user through voice over or a pop-up text box. The concept of teaching through intentional design rather than force feeding the user has not been a common practice for many years. With the rise of independent developers and the growing understanding of user experience, the game industry has recently seen a variety of design experimentations. For example, *Papers Please* and *Her Story* both focus on allowing the user to sift through documents or other types of evidence to determine the course of the game without any need for traditional character movement. This type of creativity is encouraging for the future of video games.

By understanding how users learn and absorb information during gameplay, game developers can design games in a way that improves players' experiences. Recently, designers have looked to psychological principles to improve user experience. For example, by understanding player motivation a designer can create a more engaging game, or by understanding what makes a player emotionally connect to a character, a designer can create a more impactful story [2–4]. In a similar fashion, psychology and education can provide designers with tools on how to better present information about the game's universe in a way that is purposeful—either in a way that conforms to what the player expects, or surprises the player with something unexpected.

Psychologists have documented how finicky human attention, observation, perception, and memory can be. For example, the alarming rates of false eye witness identification are well known. In simulated crime research, some studies resulted in only false identification only a few percent of the time, but in other studies the false identification rate was greater than 90% [5]. During 1996 a study was done on exonerated individuals. The study consisted of 40 convicted individuals that were exonerated by DNA evidence—36 of these "involved eyewitness identification evidence in which one ore more eyewitnesses falsely identified the person. One person was identified by five separate eyewitnesses" [6]. Researchers have not figured out *exactly* why humans sometimes think they see people that they do not, but being aware of the vulnerabilities of human observation is the first step to designing to communicate. Similar problems of perception can befall a player in a game world. Once a player has established a basic understanding of how a game works, the user becomes less attuned to all the facets of the game. The player's thoughts concentrate on the tasks at hand to win the game or solve the next puzzle. This phenomenon was best illustrated in Simons and Chabris 1999 experiment "gorilla." Subjects had to watch a video in which two teams of people, three wearing black shirts three wearing white shirts, were moving around and passing basketballs. The subjects had to count basketball passes made by players wearing white shirts. During the video, a person in a black gorilla suit walked into the scene, thumps its chest, and then walked off the scene. The person in the gorilla suit was on the screen for nine seconds. The results showed that most subjects, with their attention focused on counting the basketball passes from the white team, missed seeing the gorilla. This study shows that users, when focused on a task, can miss information developers are trying to convey [7].

It seems to make no sense that a user would fail to see a gorilla; however, if you understand mental models and working memory, it makes perfect sense. A person sets up a model to make sure he or she understand and executes the task. "Gorillas are irrelevant and would displace the task in working memory. So the brain, efficient system that it is, filters out the gorilla so that you can keep counting. Seeing the gorilla would be a mistake. You'd lose count" [8]. Given this study it is not hard to see that learning new information about a video game can easily be ignored while a user is deeply engaged.

A different, but equally important, lesson game designers can learn from psychology relates to how individuals' ability to learn new information corresponds to their expectations about that new information and their mind state as to whether they believe they already know the information. Many of us remember succumbing to the classic "Can You Follow Directions?" worksheet as a child [9]. This worksheet, although it has many variations, begins by telling the reader to read all the instructions first, and then at the end of the instructions tells the reader to only complete a certain portion of the instructions. Needless to say, the first time many children encounter this type of worksheet, they complete the instructions that the worksheet tells them to skip. When game designers are aware of how individuals may skip full instructions, they can take steps to prevent these types of mishaps.

A game designer should consider the mental state of the player and ensure that any new or important aspects of the game are not introduced in a way that will be overlooked. One way to do this is to intentionally break a user's mental model.

2   Using Mental Models to Better Understand User State of Mind

A mental model is a psychological representation of what someone believes something is or what someone believes will happen, or, in other words, "Mental models are psychological representations of real, hypothetical, or imaginary situations" [10]. Belief is the important part of this definition, as a mental model is not factual. The person is trying to predict what is to come based on the information that they have. Since mental models are predictions, users can have different mental models of an interaction due to previous experiences. People form mental models as they interact with their environments and reflect on causes and effects [11]. Humans have mental models of nearly everything. For example, an American person's mental model of a traditional restaurant might entail a process of waiting to be seated, ordering off a menu, and having food brought out to the table, among other things. Or, for another example, a person could have a mental model of a pizza that includes crust, then sauce, and then cheese - many would be surprised if the pizza came out with the sauce on top of the cheese.

The concept of mental models goes back to 1943 when the Scottish psychologist, Kenneth Craik, suggested that "perception constructs 'small-scale models' of reality that are used to anticipate events and to reason" [12, 13]. Psychologists have since used mental models when explaining cognitive development. The term 'schema' is now more common in psychology than the term 'mental model' although the usages are similar. Piaget, in 1954 defined a schema as the basic building block of intelligent behavior, a way of organizing knowledge. "Young children assimilate new observations to schemas derived from their own actions and experiences" [14]. A more defined understanding of a schema was given in the early 2000's by Wadsworth, "schemata (the plural of schema) be thought of as 'index cards' filed in the brain, each one telling an individual how to identify and react to incoming stimuli or information" [15].

Although the concept of a mental model has been used in psychology since 1943, it was not commonly discussed by software designers until the late 1980s. Don Norman's book *The Design of Everyday Things*, released in 1988, was one of the first books focused on design that mentioned the term mental model. Software developers and website designers have used Norman's book as a benchmark ever since.

Software developers and website developers have made it a practice to build on Norman's design concepts. With the rise in popularity of computers and internet use, the main aspiration for a software developer is to create an intuitive experience for the user. Users will describe an experience as intuitive when a design matches their mental model [16]. Every new user to a website or a piece of software will have expectations, mental models, based on their prior similar experiences. "Given that we all have mental models of interaction – it is a good rule of thumb to assume that wherever possible; users will form their mental models based on interactions with existing applications" [17]. For example, if a user is asked to find a particular product on an e-commerce website, today's user would expect a search function and might be frustrated if such a function was not available. When developers understand the mental models of an average user, they will be better able to generate quality designs that are pleasant to use.

Utilizing a user's mental models in the design phase has only recently become a common practice throughout the video game industry. This does not mean that companies had not previously employed mental model design techniques, only that the terminology was not universally used. This could be hard to measure, however, since video game companies rarely shared development strategies in an attempt to retain competitive advantages. It was not until the rise of the independent developers in the mid-2000's, and the communities that grew with them, that development strategies began to circulate. Independent developers started to share the development process to gain attention from potential users and to learn from other game developers. Around this same time, books and articles started being published regarding the use of psychology in the development of video games.

Similarly, due to the growth of user experience research, video game developers have begun to understand the benefits of studying a typical user's mental model. One advantage is better-designed games with fewer iterations needed near the end of a development cycle. Understanding user expectations assists a developer in determining when the game plays smoothly or when a user may become frustrated or confused.

The lessons that have been learned from web and software technology clearly have some application in the video game world as well. For example, by ensuring that default button controls are consistent within the gaming platform (whether specific console, PC, handheld, or mobile device), a gamer is more easily able to both try and enjoy a new game if basic functions work as expected. New users expect certain button control functionality consistencies based on previous experiences. For instance, if the game has a shooting mechanic and is being developed for a Microsoft or Sony console it is a best practice to set the Right Trigger button on the controller as the fire button. The results of changing up button controls may not be as catastrophic as, for example, changing the gas pedal and the break pedal in a new car; however, game developers need to ensure that new users can be quickly drawn into the game. The user already has a lot to learn about the new game, conforming to these basic criteria allows the game to feel more intuitive. The user will have an easier time jumping in and learning the different facets of your game. "Exploiting standard mappings of input to response leverages assumable common knowledge to avoid making the player learn something new. A steering wheel turning a car; a mouse moving a cursor; and the W, A, S, D keys moving an avatar are examples of established cultural standards for control" [18].

Even though there are good reasons for keeping certain default mental models intact, there are also reasons that a game developer should break the mental model of a user - particularly at a time in the game when the developer wants the user to be paying attention.

3   Another Way to Utilize Mental Models: Intentionally Breaking Them

Many times video game users ignore information that is displayed or narrated. At the heart of this problem is modern high profile video game design. A user can get the feeling that the video game is holding the user's hand by giving a tour of the game rather than allowing the user to explore. The biggest culprit is the use of tutorials in the form of text displayed on the screen. Users tend to skip or ignore information the game tries to force on them in text [19]. By ignoring these forced teaching moments, user's attempt to simulate the feeling of exploration. However, there are other ways to ensure that users are taught important gameplay information, such as gaining the users attention by breaking their mental models.

Although a user's initial mental model when beginning a game would be based on their similar, outside, real world experiences, the user develops a mental model of each specific game through reinforcement during play [20]. After enough reinforcement, the mental models evolve from predictions to stronger expectations. At this point, we can look to Social Psychology's Expectancy Violation Theory to understand how breaking a user's expectation, or mental model, can create a teaching moment.

"Expectancy violation theory (EVT) was developed by Judee K. Burgoon and several colleagues to predict and explain the impact of unexpected communication behavior" [21]. Burgoon's research initially focused on the communication that occurs between individuals when a personal space violation occurs. She explains that unexpected behavior causes "arousal" and "influences communication outcomes," or in other words, that individuals attempt to explain unexpected behavior [22]. Further study of interpersonal communication has confirmed that "when expectations are violated, there is a heightened awareness which is arousing and distracting. This heightened state causes one to regard another person's communication more carefully" [23].

Although EVT has mainly been used to describe interpersonal communication, the theory can also be used to describe communication between person and object. Although there are not exactly social norms related to human-object communication, most individuals have mental models surrounding how certain objects should behave and/or communicate. For example, individuals who maintain a router for wifi in their homes, expect that their connectable electronic devices will automatically connect to the internet. They maintain mental models regarding not only that the wifi will connect, but also how quickly they will able to receive data. When the wifi is working, there is little thought or attention given to the router. It likely sits in a corner collecting dust. However, as soon as the router behaves unexpectedly, such as slowing data download speeds, the individuals begin to pay a significant amount of attention to it as they attempt to figure out why the device is not acting as expected.

These same concepts can be utilized to explain how some interactions between video games and users take place. It is not beyond the pale to consider the user is in communication with the game. For example, when the user presses a button, they are expecting the game to do something, or, in other words, to give the user feedback. When a user first begins a game, the mental model of what is expected has not been fully formed. One could compare this more open state of mind to visiting another country and being unsure what societal norms to expect. An individual may know, to some degree, when he does not know what to expect. When starting new games, users are open to learning new information; the designer does not have as hard of a time teaching the user, as long as teaching is done in small chunks because users can easily be overloaded with information. At the beginning of the game, the user is in a frame of mind to learn new things because the mental models have not yet been fully established. However, as has been discussed, mental models are formed and strengthened with repetition. As mental models are reinforced the user builds an expectancy on how the interactions should take place and begins to act out of habit.

Particularly near the middle or the end of the game, there is a higher chance that the user will not be paying much attention to the gaming environment. Information may be glossed over, especially when presented in the form of text boxes or slow narration, and the user will not commit important information to long-term memory, if the information is acknowledged at all. Do you remember the man in the gorilla suit? However, when expectancy, formed from the mental model, is broken, it will be jarring and cause temporary confusion distracting from what they were trying to achieve. The user now has a focused interest, seeking information on why expectations are not met. The designers have a captive audience to the information the designer is trying to convey.

Jesse Schell, in the book *Art of Game Design*, talks about mental models and magicians. His point is that magicians break a viewer's mental model in order to complete the magic trick. "The audible gasp that comes from an audience at the culmination of a magic trick is the sound of their mental models being torn asunder" [24]. A similar effect is happening when breaking the mental model in a video game. Hopefully, if done well, the user will be inspired to seek out information rather than be entirely stunned by an illusion. The aroused user will be more attentive and likely more inspired to actively interact and communicate with the game.

I am not proposing that this is the only or best way to communicate with or teach the user. I am simply suggesting that intentionally breaking a user's mental model is simply one design methodology to add to the game designer's toolbox. There are clearly many different styles and ways of learning, and depending on the type of information your user needs to learn, as well as who your learner is, a different methodology might work better. For example, a complicated task that builds on information previously learned might be better suited by using scaffolding instruction, which is a method of teaching that assists the learner only when support is needed for tasks that the learner would not otherwise be able to complete [25].

However, although further research is needed, breaking the user's mental model likely has several benefits that other forms of instruction do not, particularly when considering the lack of attention some game designers give to methods of learning and the commonplace use of disruptive pop-up text boxes as a method of instruction. For example, breaking a user's mental model may be able to keep a user in a flow state and teach the player at the same time. A flow state is when skill and difficulty are roughly proportional, and the user becomes immersed in the game. In the 1970s Mihaly Csikszentmihalyi found that the difficulty of a task and the person's skill result in different cognitive and emotional states. "When skill is too low and the task too hard, people become anxious. Alternatively, if the task is too easy and skill too high, people become bored" [26] (Fig. 1).

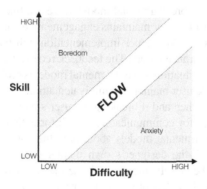

Fig. 1. Flow, boredom, and anxiety as they relate to task difficulty and user skill level. (Source: *Baron, S. (2012)*)

Additionally, by breaking the mental model and encouraging the user to find out why the game is not acting as expected, the user will be more likely to test different functionalities within the established game mechanics and further explore the game world. This should keep the user in a flow state leading to interesting experiences and more enjoyment for the user during play.

A designer might also consider employing multiple instructional methods together by first breaking the user's mental model and thus generating an optimal learning state of the user before further employing another teaching technique. Breaking the user's mental model is an educational technique that can be helpful on its own or in conjunction with other teaching strategies.

4   How Game Designers Can Successfully Apply These Theories

Breaking a user's mental model is not a methodology that can be used every time you want to teach the user something about the game. It should be applied once the user established the mental models that are specific to the experience the game provides.

An excellent way to help the user establish mental models in the beginning of the game is to be aware of the onboarding process. Onboarding is a term the user experience field took from the field of human resources that describes getting a new user (or employee, in HR) up and running. "The onboarding process is a critical step in setting your users up for success with your product" [27]. A common mistake by developers of all disciplines, not just game design, is to overload the user with information during the onboarding process. This leads to the user feeling overwhelmed and frustrated. Celia Hodent, the Director of User Experience at Epic Games, recommends that only small amounts of information be taught at one time in order to ensure smoother onboarding. During a lecture at the 2016 Game Developer Conference, Hodent stated, "I suggest you to remember that 3 items to process at the same time is THE MAXIMUM when in learning mode (discovering every-thing) because new tasks have a much higher cognitive load than familiar or automated ones" [28].

When the time comes to break a mental model, there is a fine line between breaking a mental model in a way that the user maintains engagement versus user disappointment, or worse, user disengagement [29]. Proper implementation will happen after testing with users as well as quality assurance testers. The feedback received will give great insights on how the user interprets the situation when the mental model is broken. It may require a few iterations to ensure that the user maintains a motivated attitude.

In order to determine when and if breaking the user's mental model will be an effective development strategy for communicating new information, the designer must first understand his or her own mental models about how the game operates, given that the design itself was built off the designer's own mental models. The designer's mental models may or may not be closely aligned with the mental model's of the game's eventual users. Both the mental models of the designer and of the users are built from interacting with the game and reliance on prior experiences [30].

Understand the Game's Genre and Pick a Target Audience. Before a designer can attempt to accurately predict the mental models that a user will bring to the game, and those that the user will develop within the game, the designer should first consider the genre of the game and the genre's target demographic. Video game genres can be very nuanced, which leads to a very long list of different genre types. In the book, *The Medium of the Video Game*, Mark Wolf, lists 42 categories of video game genres [31]. Some of the most common genres of video games include: Action, Fighting, Platformers, Puzzle,

Racing, Strategy, Sports, and Shooter [32]. Keep in mind that just because a genre is chosen does not mean that the designer should copy and paste interactions, "it must be noted that players of games—that is, their audience—are not necessarily satisfied with the same generic conventions being endlessly repeated. The expectation is that the stability of genre will be tempered by innovation; this innovation may be technical, not necessarily stylistic" [33]. For a designer, a video game genre is a roadmap, not a blueprint. However, without understanding the breadth and scope of the genre of your game, a designer will not be able to properly understand what mental models players will be bringing to the game from prior experience.

Even within a singular genre a demographic-or a target audience-should be established. The International Academy of Design & Technology blog suggests that, in order to identify and understand the demographic of your audience, a game designer should consider questions such as, "Who will enjoy my game, what other types of games do these gamers enjoy, and what kinds of challenges or narratives do they like?" [34]. Another aspect to consider is the segment of the demographic that the game aims to target. Jason VandenBerghe, a Creative Director at Ubisoft, during a presentation at the 2016 Game Developers Conference, talks about the concept of taste mapping. Customers will have different reasons for playing a game. Those reasons can end up graphed in a bell curve starting with "Care a lot" to "Meh." The curve represents the users likely investment in your game (Fig. 2).

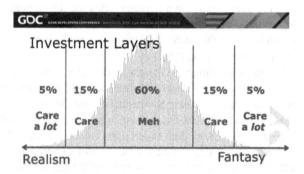

Fig. 2. Investment layers slide from 2016 game developers conference talk by Jason VandenBerghe

VandenBerghe took the investment layers graph and applied it to a taste map with the same realism/fantasy scale but also added the reasons building things versus exploring. A taste map can be made with any type of reasons a user may play a game. Another example of a taste map may show mechanics vs context and combat vs cooperative play. The 5% of people that are really invested will be advocates of the game and do what they can to talk about the game to other users. This segment of high investment users are unfortunately a low percentage of the total user population. The middle of the chart show the users with low investment in certain aspects, but there are a lot of users. Choosing which segment of the demographic to design for can be a challenge [35] (Fig. 3).

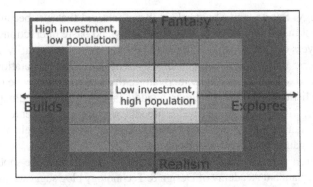

Fig. 3. Taste mapping slide from 2016 game developers conference talk by Jason VandenBerghe

Create a Persona of a Typical User. Once the genre and target audience has been established, the designer should create a persona of a typical user. A persona is a fictional character designed to represent a typical user. "Personas not only make the target audience more real to designers and engineers, they also ensure that requirements are prioritized to specifically meet the needs of high-value users" [36]. Personas should be created at the beginning of a project because they can inform game functionality, help uncover gaps, or highlight new opportunities [37]. It is important to understand that a persona acts as the voice of the user. Applying a persona helps the developers understand the user's context, pain points, behaviors, goals, motivations, needs, and attitudes. Additionally, personas can be used to validate or disprove design decisions, vet and prioritize feature requests, and inspire ideation [38].

Personas are ideal for determining the mental models of a typical user. When a game developer understands a user's motivations and strategies, which are revealed through the creation of a persona, designing teaching moments become clearer [29]. Often multiple personas are created; common choices are to create a novice and an expert user persona. There is always a design balance regarding expert users and novice users. If too much time is spent explaining game mechanics, the expert users will feel bored and uninterested. If not enough information is given, the novice players will become frustrated. The term expert does not mean users that have already played the game and are now proficient. In this case, the term expert is used for new players that have strong expertise in the genre. "When a productivity interface exploits the existing skills of users, even those who are new to the interface can perform tasks rapidly and with few errors" [39]. A small example of a common design theme among genres is the use of the exclamation marks and question marks over the head of a non-player character (NPC) in role-playing games.

An expert user in the genre will instantly know that an NPC with an exclamation mark will have valuable information and or give the user a quest. If a user sees an NPC with a question mark, then the user has satisfied the requirements to complete a given quest. Speaking with the NPC with a question mark will allow the user to earn rewards for the completion of the quest (Fig. 4). As mentioned, this was a small example and is not implied that it would be hard for a novice user to learn the meaning of the exclamation marks and question marks. A series of steps can be taken to implement the methodology of breaking a user's mental model within a video game.

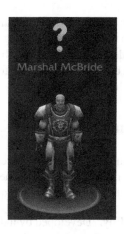

Fig. 4. Images from the game World of Warcraft

Figure Out the Mental Models That Will Be Created When the User Plays the Game. Every video game will create a user experience that impacts the development of its users' mental models. The designer cannot attempt to break a user's mental model if the basic mental models of the game have not been well established or if the developer has not taken the time to understand how the game experience is impacting the players. It will, of course, be impossible to know each potential user's exact mental models, as each person experiences the world differently, but, by utilizing personas and paying attention to the details of the game, the designer can likely predict the most common mental models with some accuracy.

Mental models are commonly established when the user learns the game mechanics. Super Mario Bros. establishes the mental model that the player character runs and jumps. Game mechanics establish the rules of the game and actions that can be performed. "These actions are most often related to character movement, vulnerability to threat, sense knowledge, and interaction (e.g., speaking, shooting, fighting). Each of these character mechanics has parameters that delimit a particular ability" [40].

Determine the Information That You Want To Teach and Disrupt the User's Mental Model. Very often a video game will need to teach a user something in the middle or near the end of the game, perhaps a new ability, a new location that is now available, or a new enemy that appears. Understanding what information is required to teach the user during the design phase will allow more creative solutions to breaking the users mental model. To effectively teach important information, the designer can strategically break the user's mental models and establish a captive audience.

Once a mental model is generated, the designers will have information regarding the best places to implement the intentional use of breaking the user's mental model. There are at least two things the designer must consider when implanting this type of learning strategy: first, how is this new information entirely different from the mental models already established, and second, how can the game cause the player to try or utilize this new information? If the answers to these questions can be clearly answered, hopefully, the game will break the user's mental model, creating a teaching moment where the user will be more likely to retain the information in long term memory and have better engagement.

A few video games that have broken the mental model are listed below. These examples can be used as inspiration for when to apply the method of breaking the mental model to teach.

5   Breaking Mental Models: Case Studies of an Effective Practice

Intentionally using the method of breaking a user's mental model for teaching purposes is not widely used in the video game industry. However, there have been examples of video games that employ the technique, whether meaningful or not.

Super Meat Boy. Developed by independent developers Team Meat, Super Meat Boy is a challenging 2D video game in the platformer genre (Fig. 5). At the beginning of the game, the user builds a mental model around the jump mechanic. The user jumps to avoid saw blades and jumps from one platform to another avoiding falling into large gaps. When the creators of Super Meat Boy want to teach the user the "wall climb" mechanic, they load the user into a level with only a large wall on the right side of the screen; no platforms are available in range to jump on. The lack of platforms in the level breaks the user's mental model of the jump mechanic, forcing the player to solve a problem not yet encountered.

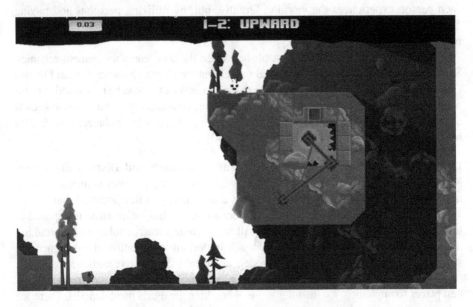

Fig. 5. Gameplay screenshot of Super Meat Boy.

Before this point in the game, users understood that to get around tall obstacles, they needed to jump on platforms in a stair-step motion. With the jump mechanic mental model broken, the user has naturally become willing to learn. During problem-solving, the user will eventually jump onto the large wall on the right side of the screen, in an effort to make use of the jumping mental model already established. Once players jump on the wall. They will notice the ability to "wall climb."

Uncovering the "wall climb" mechanic and solving the problem of completing the level gives the user a great deal of satisfaction because the user is self-taught. Additionally, because the user was self-taught he will be more likely to apply this teaching moment to long term memory. Being able to recall the ability will be helpful in later levels of the game. If the developers had taken a traditional route to teaching the player about the "wall climb" ability, a text box would have appeared once the player loads into the level, explaining the new mechanic. Users would have either ignored the text box or, at the very least, felt half-hearted about the "wall climb" ability because they would not have experienced a sense of discovery.

Final Fantasy X. Developed by Squaresoft, Final Fantasy X breaks the mental model of how healing and damage dealing effects can be applied (Fig. 6). This section is written based on my experience playing Final Fantasy X. Admittedly, the status effect Zombie could have appeared in previous Final Fantasy games and lovers of this Role Playing Game (RPG) series may have learned of it before Final Fantasy X. At the time, this was my first attempt at a Final Fantasy game, so I am commenting from that perspective. I was fighting the boss Lady Yunalesca, and a status effect Zombie was placed on all of the player characters in my party. I had not encountered the Zombie effect previously in the game and was unsure what to expect. Lady Yunalesca attacked one of my characters and lowered the health to nearly zero. I attempted to heal the character by using a healing potion to save her from death. My mental model of healing was broken when the healing potion dealt damage and killed the character rather than healing. Along with the mental model of healing, my mental model of how to complete a boss battle was now broken. Lady Yunalesca was still able to inflict melee damage, and I needed to figure out different steps to take to keep my characters alive while fighting a boss battle.

Now with full engagement, I was willing to learn all I could about the Zombie effect. Ultimately, I discovered that there are ways to heal a Zombie status effect, using a Holy Water potion or Remedy spell for example. However, during this boss battle, I found out that while inflicted with Zombie, characters would be immune to Instant Death attacks. Lady Yunalesca uses a spell called Mega Death which would kill all of the player characters not affected by Zombie. The developers made sure to show different facets of this one effect during the boss battle.

With my healing mental model broken and more knowledgeable on how the Zombie effect works, I am now inspired to be creative with the Zombie effect in the future. One of the player characters, Auron will eventually have the option to learn the Zombie ability and use it on enemies. Being creative, I found out that I could inflict enemies with Zombie and then use the potion Phoenix Down, which normally resurrects fallen player characters, and instantly kill the infected enemy. A whole new world of possibilities opened up on how I could inflict damage.

Fig. 6. Gameplay screenshot of Final Fantasy X.

World of Goo. Developed by 2D Boy, World of Goo is a physics-based puzzle game in which players construct structurally sound platforms out of black balls of goo. The goal is to build "bridge like" structures that can get from one part of the level to another. However, when the user gets to Chapter 4 the mental model is broken regarding the balls of goo and how they work. When loading into Chapter 4 the balls of goo change from the color black to the color green and are accompanied by green square blocks of goo (Fig. 7). Not only does the color change for the balls of goo, but they are no longer used

Fig. 7. Gameplay screenshot of World of Goo (Color figure online)

for building structures. Instead, they jump to other formed structures when the user interacts with them. Due to the broken mental model, the user experiments with the new functionality of the balls of goo as well as the green square blocks. After experimentation, the user learns that the green square blocks take the place of the previous balls of goo and are used for constructing structures the green balls of goo can jump on too.

Snapshot. Developed by Retro Affect, Snapshot is a 2D platform game in which the user takes photos of objects and can drop the photographed objects in different parts of the level. The player's mental model of getting over a high platform is taking photos of the objects, mainly boxes, and stacking them up. The goal is to be able to stand on the stacked objects like a step stool in order to jump onto the high platform. The developers took a similar approach to teaching the player a new ability as the designers of Super Meat Boy in this example. The user loads into a level with a high platform, they do not have access to an object that can be stacked. With the mental model broken, the users starts to take a second look at the environment around them to solve the problem.

Snapshot does not have a "wall climb" mechanic like in Super Meat Boy. Instead, the developers are trying to teach the players that elephants will act like trampolines. Walking along the ground at the bottom of the level is an elephant. At first the elephant seems like an interesting artistic asset to make the world appear more real. If users attempt to interact with the elephant, they will notice the trampoline effect and can then get over the high platform (Fig. 8).

Fig. 8. Gameplay screenshot of Snapshot.

Hearthstone. Developed by Blizzard Entertainment, Hearthstone is an online collectible card game, similar to Magic: the Gathering. Near the end of Hearthstone tutorial is an example of a mental model being broken. Each player has the same set of cards to make a card deck and the rules apply to both users equally. Up until this point, the only way to play was to make decisions based on the cards in the player's hand or the cards that are still on the board from a previous turn.

The developers want to teach the player a new mechanic in which the player character gains a Hero Power. To do this, the user is introduced to the new mechanic by seeing the hero ability given to the computer opponent first. This different ability draws attention and breaks the mental model of standard gameplay because the players are no longer equal in types of choices to make. The user is paying close attention to how the computer opponent is using the new ability in order to learn how to play against it. Additionally, suspense builds as the user becomes curious if they will get a similar ability. Once the computer opponent uses the Hero Ability to attack the player the turn ends and it is now the user's turn. During this turn, the Hero Ability is applied to the player. The player paid close attention to how the opponent used the ability and will not need much training on how to apply it (Fig. 9).

Fig. 9. Gameplay screenshot of Hearthstone.

Mega Man X. Developed by Capcom, Mega Man X has one of the best examples of breaking the mental model. In the first level, the player is introduced to nearly all the mechanics of the game. The user learns that they have the ability to shoot a weapon, shoot while jumping, wall climb, and some enemies exist with "sweet spots" meaning the weapon can hit only certain areas, otherwise no damage will take place to these enemies. At the end of the first level the player encounters the boss, none of the abilities the player has learned deal damage to the boss character. The user's mental model regarding attacks are broken, and the user starts to feel defeated as the player characters health bar is nearly depleted.

The mental model has been broken since the start of the boss battle. However, near the end of the encounter is when the teaching moment takes place. A friendly nonplayer character (NPC) named Zero appears and uses a charge effect shot on the boss, doing enough damage it causes the boss to escape (Fig. 10). Through this interaction, the player learns that they can charge their shoot ability to use a stronger attack. The game did not have to stop gameplay to teach this ability, and the players learned on their own.

Fig. 10. Gameplay screenshot of Mega Man X.

6 Conclusion

Users have a surplus of video game options in today's market. A user's time has become the most important element to the decision of purchasing a game. Understanding that competition among video game developers is high, it is important to be able to communicate effectively to the users. Developers can turn users into evangelists for their game when a user has an immersive, enjoyable experience. An important factor of immersion is how the user absorbs information and can apply the lessons appropriately. Employing the teaching technique of breaking the user's mental model will ensure that the user is open, in that moment, to learning new things about the world created by the development team.

References

1. Pedersen, C., Togelius, J., Yannakakis, G.N.: Modeling player experience in super Mario Bros. In: IEEE Symposium on Computational Intelligence and Games, CIG 2009, pp. 132–139. IEEE, September 2009
2. Yee, N.: The gamer motivation profile: model and findings. In: Lecture presented at 2016 Game Developers Conference (n.d.)
3. Murphy, C., Chertoff, D., Guerrero, M., Moffitt, K.: Design Better Games: Flow, Motivation, and Fun. Design and Development of Training Games: Practical Guidelines from a Multidisciplinary Perspective, p. 1773 (2014)

4. Ghozland, D.: Designing for motivation. http://www.gamasutra.com/view/feature/1419/designing_for_motivation.php?print=1. Accessed 07 June 2007

5. Wells, G.L.: What do we know about eyewitness identification? Am. Psychol. **48**(5), 553 (1993)

6. Wells, G.L., Small, M., Penrod, S., Malpass, R.S., Fulero, S.M., Brimacombe, C.E.: Eyewitness identification procedures: recommendations for lineups and photo- spreads. Law Hum Behav. **22**(6), 603 (1998)

7. Simons, D.J., Chabris, C.F.: Gorillas in our midst: sustained inattentional blindness for dynamic events. Perception **28**(9), 1059–1074 (1999)

8. Gonzales, L.: Deep Survival Who Lives, Who Dies, and Why. W.W. Norton, New York (2005)

9. Can You Follow Directions? Learning and Academic Skills Center. http://blogs.scholastic.com/files/followdirection.pdf. (n.d.)

10. What are mental models?\Mental Models and Reasoning Lab (n.d.). http://mentalmodels.princeton.edu/about/what-are-mental-models/. Accessed 10 Feb 2017

11. Halevy, N., Cohen, T.R., Chou, E.Y., Katz, J.J., Panter, A.T.: Mental models at work: cognitive causes and consequences of conflict in organizations. Pers. Soc. Psychol. Bull. **40**(1), 92–110 (2014)

12. Johnson-Laird, P.N.: Mental models and deduction. Trends Cogn. Sci. **5**(10), 434–442 (2001)

13. Craik, K.: The Nature of Explanation. Cambridge University Press, Cambridge (1943)

14. Beard, R.: An Outline of Piaget's Developmental Psychology. Routledge, London (2013)

15. Tuckman, B., Monetti, Z.: Educational Psychology. Cengage Learning, Wadsworth (2010)

16. Weinschenk, S.: The secret to designing an intuitive UX (n.d.). http://uxmag.com/articles/the-secret-to-designing-an-intuitive-user-experience. Accessed 10 Feb 2017

17. Crawford, N.: A very useful work of fiction – mental models in design (n.d.). https://www.interaction-design.org/literature/article/130558. Accessed 10 Feb 2017

18. Swink, S.: Game Feel: A Game Designer's Guide to Virtual Sensation. Morgan Kaufmann/Elsevier, Amsterdam (2009)

19. Extra credits: tutorials 101. https://www.youtube.com/watch?v=BCPcn-Q5nKE. Accessed 19 Apr 2012

20. Nielsen, J.: Mental models and user experience design (n.d.). https://www.nngroup.com/articles/mental-models/. Accessed 10 Feb 2017

21. Littlejohn, S.W., Foss, K.A.: Encyclopedia of Communication Theory. Sage, Los Ange- les, CA (2009)

22. Burgoon, J.K.: A communication model of personal space violation: explication and an initial test. Hum. Commun. Res. **4**, 129–142 (1978)

23. Mooradian, B.L.: Going home when home does not feel like home: reentry, expectancy violation theory, self-construal, and psychological and social support. Intercult. Commun. Stud. **13**, 37–50 (2004)

24. Schell, Jesse: The Art of Game Design: A Book of Lenses. Elsevier/Morgan Kaufmann, Amsterdam (2008)

25. Loparev, A., Egert, C.A.: Scaffolding in educational video games: an approach to teaching collaborative support skills. In: Frontiers in Education Conference (FIE), vol. 32614, pp. 1–5. IEEE, October 2015

26. Baron, S.: Cognitive flow: the psychology of great game design. Gamasutra-The Art & Business of Making Games (2012)

27. Plank, T.: Up & Running: 3 Tips For An Awesome Onboarding UX. https://blinkux.com/blog/up-running-3-tips-for-an-awesome-onboarding-ux/. Accessed 05 May 2015

28. Hodent, C.: The gamer's brain, part 2: UX of onboarding and player engagement. In: Speech Presented at 2016 Game Developer Conference (n.d.). http://celiahodent.com/the-gamers-brain-part-2-gdc16/#more-610

29. Ballav, A.: Mental models and user experience, May, June 2016. http://www.uxmatters.com/mt/archives/2016/05/mental-models-and-user-experience.php

30. Norman, D.A.: The Design of Everyday Things. Basic Books, New York (2013)

31. Wolf, M.J.: Genre and the video game. The Medium of the Video Game, pp. 113–134 (2001)

32. Clements, R.: http://www.ign.com/articles/2012/12/12/rpgs-took-over-every-video-game-genre

33. Apperley, T.H.: Genre and game studies: toward a critical approach to video game genres. Simul. Gaming 37(1), 6–23 (2006)

34. Targeting your audience: 3 important tips for designing games, May, June 2013. http://www.iadt.edu/student-life/iadt-buzz/may-2013/tips-for-designing-games-audience

35. VandenBerghe, J.: Engines of play: how player motivation changes over time (powerpoint slides) (2016). http://www.gdcvault.com/play/1023329/Engines-of-Play-How-Player

36. Lidwell, W., Holden, K., Butler, J.: Universal Principles of Design (2010). Rockport Publishers, ISBN 978-1-61058-065-6

37. Personas - https://www.usability.gov/how-to-and-tools/methods/personas.html

38. Ilama, E.: Creating Personas. Retrieved from http://www.uxbooth.com/articles/creating-personas/

39. MacDorman, K.F., Whalen, T.J., Ho, C.C., Patel, H.: An improved usability measure based on novice and expert performance. Int. J. Hum. Comput. Interact. 27(3), 280–302 (2011)

40. Boyan, A., Sherry, J.L.: The challenge in creating games for education: aligning mental models with game models. Child. Dev. Perspect. 5(2), 82–87 (2011)

Gamifying the Eating Experience: An Interactive Companion for Children's Nutrition Education and Behavior

Erin Lew, Jevrin Alviando, EunSook Kwon, and Jorge D. Camba[✉]

Gerald D. Hines College of Architecture and Design, University of Houston, Houston, TX, USA
{eplew,jalviando,ekwon,jdorribo}@uh.edu

Abstract. We present an interactive companion for children's nutrition education that capitalizes on digital technology to promote mental and physical stimulation by adding game-like elements to the eating experience. Our device allows children to manage portion sizes easily and promotes the practice of healthy eating habits by interacting with "Cibo," a healthy kid metaphor that encourages children to learn how different food groups benefit the body. Different parts of the device provide active feedback as the child eats his/her meal. The combination of physical and digital interaction gamifies the eating experience and redefines "playing at the dinner table" into a positive event that nourishes children physically, cognitively, and emotionally.

Keywords: Nutrition education and training · Playful interfaces · Educational technology · Child development

1 Introduction

For the past three decades, the prevalence of childhood obesity has significantly risen worldwide (see Fig. 1) [1]. According to recent statistics, nearly one out of every three children in the United States between the ages of two and nineteen is now overweight or obese [1, 2]. Childhood obesity occurs when the child's body mass index is equal to or greater than the ninety-fifth percentile [2]. Obese and overweight children are at risk of developing type-two diabetes, asthma, and heart disease later in life [3–5]. Being obese as a child is also a major risk factor for being obese as an adult [6].

The main contributing factors for childhood obesity include the increased access to processed foods, lack of physical activity, social and cultural factors, and an increase in portion sizes [7]. Consequently, most intervention studies for child obesity prevention involve strategies that focus on developing healthy eating habits and promoting active classroom activities such as sports and physical play. Researchers agree that successful interventions should involve home, school or kindergarten, and community participants [8–10].

In recent years, the idea of giving children more independence starting at a younger age is gaining popularity among many parents. In the Baby-Led Weaning approach (BLW), for example, parents encourage their infants to feed themselves so they can

© Springer International Publishing AG 2017
P. Zaphiris and A. Ioannou (Eds.): LCT 2017, Part I, LNCS 10295, pp. 462–473, 2017.
DOI: 10.1007/978-3-319-58509-3_36

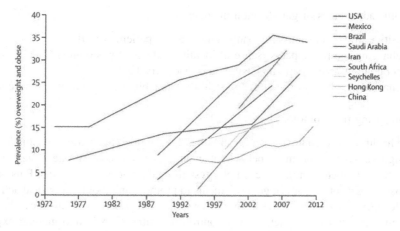

Fig. 1. Prevalence trends for childhood obesity in the USA and other countries [1]

proactively explore foods and develop their motor skills and independence [11]. During the preschool stage between three and six years old, children are naturally curious and inclined to do tasks without the assistance of their parents. The Montessori method of education uses the "whole child approach" which allows the child to experience the joy of learning and develop self-esteem through their experiences, which create their knowledge [12].

Montessori's holistic approach to school curriculum was greatly influenced by Piaget's theory of cognitive development [13] and Dewey's theory of childhood education [14]. Both theories stress the importance of children interacting with their environments to discover the world for themselves [15]. In the context of nutrition, if children could learn about the importance and the nutritional benefits of foods in relation to their bodies, healthy eating habits could be promoted at an earlier age.

In this paper, we describe the development of an interactive eating companion for children that uses gamification strategies to promote behavioral change. The device is designed to stimulate healthy eating by practicing portion control and familiarizing children with the nutritional benefits of the different food groups while encouraging independence.

2   Related Work

The terms "gamification" and "serious games" refer to the application of game-design principles to non-game contexts with the goal of improving user experience and engagement [16]. Simple game-like elements such as challenges, gratification and reward points, badges, and social encouragement have been applied to almost any situation that involves user interaction, including education [17], marketing and advertising [18], and business management [19], among others.

Some advantages of gamification include:

- Positive impact on the participants' emotional experiences [20].
- Enhancing the participants' sense of identity and social positioning [20].
- Encouraging active experimentation and discovery [20].
- Enhancing high-level social skills such as leadership, communication, and collaboration [21].
- Enhancing psychomotor skills [22, 23].

In health-related contexts, gamification has been applied to a variety of situations as a design strategy to promote behavioral change (i.e, promote wellness and reduce unhealthy/risky behaviors). For example, systems and devices such as Nike Plus or the Microsoft's Kinect sensor use game elements to promote and monitor physical activity. Mobile apps such as Slimkicker (http://www.slimkicker.com) or Fitocracy (https://www.fitocracy.com) turn diet, weight control, and fitness goals into gaming experiences. Many game-like applications have been developed to encourage personal hygiene [24] and good tooth brushing habits [25]. Significant efforts have also been made in the area of medication adherence and patient engagement [26, 27] as well as medical training and education [28].

Some schools and educational programs are making an effort to emphasize the importance of nutrition. However, the role of the parents is a large contributing factor as to why children are unaware of a healthy lifestyle. There is evidence that suggests that family rules have a significant effect on healthier eating habits and may serve as an intermediary mechanism to curb childhood obesity [29]. If healthy eating habits are reinforced and children appreciate the benefits of healthy foods, the habits will likely be sustained into adulthood.

Popular examples of the application of gamification strategies for promoting a healthy lifestyle among children include the Nintendo Wii console, which facilitates physical exercise through active gameplay [30], and the U.S. Department of Agriculture's 2013 initiative "Apps for Healthy Kids Competition." The competition "challenged software developers, game designers, students, and others to develop fun and engaging software tools and games that drive children to eat better and be more physically active" [31]. Winning submissions such as *Pick Chow!*, *PapayaHead*, or *The Snack Neutralizer* used game elements to motivate children to eat healthy and teach about the nutritional values of different foods.

Gamified systems that bring technology to the dining environment have also been proposed. For example, technology-based dining tables and plates have proven successful in helping children improve their eating habits [32, 33]. Similar approaches such as the computer-augmented tableware "EducaTableware" [34] provide auditory feedback when a user eats or drinks.

Commercially, one of the most well-known examples of technology-based hardware to train better eating habits is the "HAPIfork" [35], a smart fork that provides haptic feedback for the rate at which the user eats.

In this paper, we focus on the incorporation of digital elements to a children's dining tray. The goal is to teach correct portion sizes and allow precise measurements for extreme users that may have health and dietary restrictions. The target age range for our study is three to six year olds or the preschool range, as this is when children can start developing lifetime habits. Our concept seeks to provide an engaging mechanism to motivate the youth to learn proper portion control for developing better eating habits in the future.

3 Design Concept

A number of informal interviews were conducted with a group of parents and their elementary school age children to gain a better understanding of the most common approaches to nutrition education at the dining table from a parent perspective. Three key ideas were reoccurring in these conversations. In general, parents want their children to (1) finish the food on their plates, (2) eat a moderate pace, not too fast or too slow, and (3) keep their attention at the dinner table. In many cases, solutions to these problems involve negative actions such as bargaining, punishment, and letting the children have their way for having toys at the dinner table.

Additionally, registered dietitians and certified nutritionists were also interviewed about recommended portion sizes for children and the tools used to teach those measurements. According to these professionals, a typical child's plate is approximately seven inches in diameter. The recommended serving size for protein is the size of a deck of cards, which occupies one fourth of the plate. Grains should also occupy one fourth of the plate, whereas fruits and vegetables will fill half the plate. Although the market is crowded with children's plates that are divided into these three sections (which are generally a good way to start teaching proper portioning to children), it is too easy to pile the food high while still having the three divisions.

The data collected from the interviews was used to guide the development of "Cibo," a tool for child nutritional education that gamifies eating and incorporates physical interactions with a digital interface. Our first design concepts were inspired by traditional segmented plating to emphasize the visual aspect of managing food proportions, and popular child feeding practices such as the use of transportation vehicle metaphors (e.g. planes or trains). However, to emphasize the educational and teaching aspects of the design, a decision was made to make the final concept resemble a traditional storybook; one page with an interaction (e.g., reading) and the other page with visual feedback (e.g., pictures). As the child interacts with the food, the image on the left part of the board will display how the child's action and participation are being rewarded.

Our proposed device takes the form of an interactive tray or dining board that mimics a digital scale which is inspired by the well-known saying, "eat a balanced meal." The board is controlled by an Arduino microcontroller and is battery powered so it is portable and can be used when there is no outlet available. Settings on the board allow the parent to specify the desired age group for the child.

Visual feedback is provided by a group of LEDs inside "Cibo's" silhouette. The LEDs are based on the WS2812 integrated light source, which uses a built-in driver and a single-wire control protocol to allow each pixel to be uniquely addressed. The light emitted by the LEDs is diffused by a plastic cover to create smoother light transitions.

The board is divided into two main areas. The right side of the board accommodates four force sensitive resistors calibrated to detect a range of values that correlates to the appropriate weights of a healthy serving size of the four main food groups. The left side provides a visual representation of our character "Cibo" which represents a healthy and happy kid that gives real-time feedback as the child is eating his or her meal. The character's happy face and raised arms show strength and excitement. The idea is to incentivize children to finish their meals by presenting "Cibo" as a friend that

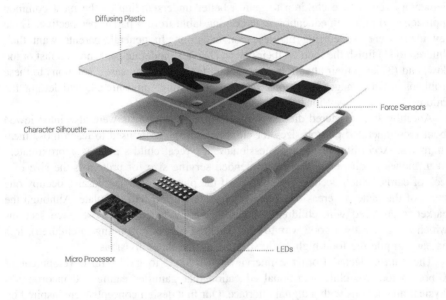

Fig. 2. Main components of the interactive board

needs to be taken care of. In order to see "Cibo's" happy face and complete body systems, the child will need to eat the entire servings.

The left part of the board is slightly elevated with respect to the right side in order to separate the two main areas and bring the feedback interface closer to the child. The interface is comprised of four indicator lights, the character silhouette and body systems, and a button to begin the interaction. The main components of the device are shown in Fig. 2.

Four plastic bowls are used as food containers. All bowls have the same dimensions (3″ × 3″ × 2″) to encourage experimentation. Rather than visually showing which

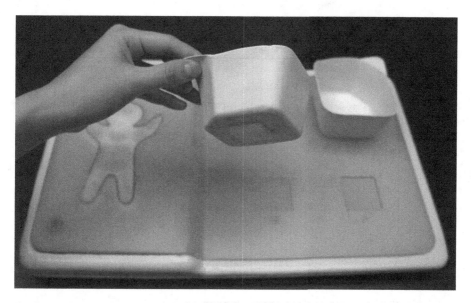

Fig. 3. Interactive board with "Cibo" character (left) and serving containers with flat bottom piece to facilitate contact with force sensors (right)

portions need to be bigger, children can explore and test different amounts as they serve themselves, thus training their eyes to recognize and estimate food sizes and serving amounts, which can help develop good habits as they grow older.

The bottom of each bowl has a flat square piece that makes contact with the force sensors and allows for an even weight distribution, which results in a more accurate reading (see Fig. 3). Graphic icons of the four food groups (fruit, vegetables, protein, and grains) are provided on the board to indicate the proper location of each bowl on the surface.

4   User Interface

The main interface elements of the board are shown in Fig. 4. The measurement indicator lights are mapped to the corresponding force sensitive resistor located on the right side of the board (e.g., the top left indicator informs about the status of the top left force sensor). The indicators are used to guide the serving process by providing feedback regarding the amount of food placed in each container. When the child does not serve enough food of a particular food group (i.e., in the appropriate container), the indicator will turn yellow. The light will change to red when the child has served too big of a portion. Only when the amount served in a particular container falls inside the calibrated range of a properly sized serving, the indicator will turn green. When all lights are green, the child can begin to eat and help "Cibo" grow healthy.

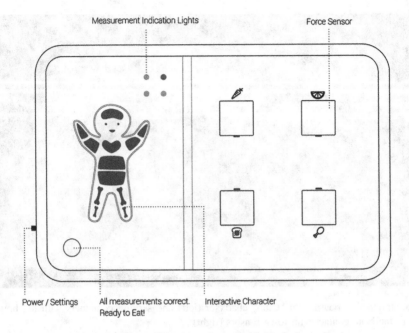

Fig. 4. Main user interface elements (Color figure online)

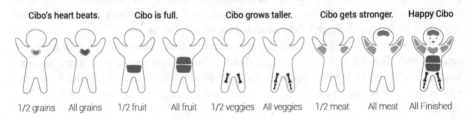

Fig. 5. Visual feedback provided by "Cibo"

The different feedbacks of "Cibo" are illustrated in Fig. 5. The bones, digestive system, muscles, heart, and brain glow as the child eats different foods. Eating grains from the grain container will start "Cibo's" heart and make it beat. Eating fruit from the corresponding container will help fill up "Cibo's" tummy. Eating vegetables will let "Cibo's" bones grow. Eating protein will let "Cibo" gain muscle in his arms and also feed his brain.

The type of interactive behavior and responses described above let the child learn what foods are good for the various parts and systems of the body. In addition, by having to complete "Cibo," the child is given an incentive to finish his/her meal. They can also eat to make "Cibo" a healthy kid as they nourish their own bodies.

5 Software

The two main components of the system in terms of software are the serving calibration process, which is required to establish a baseline for tracking how much the child is going to eat from each group; and the tracking process, which involves monitoring the force sensitive sensors and provide proper feedback mechanisms. Naturally, the serving calibration process will be performed first, before the tracking process. The predefined serving weights (MAX and MIN, in the algorithm) were portioned and recorded from a digital scale according to the serving sizes recommended by professionals.

The pseudocode for the main algorithms implemented in our prototype is provided.

```
Function Calibration() {
  For each Force Sensor Do {
    //initialize corresponding Indication Light(IL)
    TurnOff (IL);
    readyToEat = false; //proper weight reached?

    while (!readyToEat){
      ReadForceSensor(); //weight of the filled container

      if (ForceSensor <= MAX &&  ForceSensor <=MIN) {
      //Proper amount of food in the container
       readyToEat = true; //exit loop
       TurnOn (IL, "Green"); //notify user
      }
      else if (ForceSensor < MIN
             //Not enough food in the container
            TurnOn (IL, "Yellow"); //notify user
         else if (sensorValue > MAXIMUM VALUE
             //Too much food in the container
             TurnOn (IL, "Red"); //notify user
  }
}
```

When all measurement indication lights are green, the child can begin to eat. The tracking algorithm is responsible for monitoring the weight of each container and updating the "Cibo" character accordingly.

```
Function Tracking {
  For each Force Sensor Do {
    containerEmpty = false; //is the child done eating?

    while (!containerEmpty){
      ReadForceSensor(); //weight of the container

      if (ForceSensor = weightOfEmptyContainer) {
        //child has finished eating
        containerEmpty = true; //exit loop
        updateciboStatus(COMPLETE);
      }
      else if (ForceSensor = weightOfFullContainer / 2
        //container is half empty
        updateCiboStatus(HALF); //notify user
    }
  }
}
```

6   Process of Use

The proposed device constantly monitors input from the force sensitive resistors located on the right side of the board. When the weight of each individual container filled with a specific type of food reaches a predefined limit (triggering the force sensitive resistors), the device will inform the child that "Cibo" is ready to be used.

The use cycle of the device is described in Table 1.

Table 1. Sequence of stages and actions in the use cycle of the interactive board.

Step	Action	Description
1	System setup	With the help of the parent, the board is switched on to a setting based on the age and size of the child
2	Food serving	Child will serve him or herself food from the different food groups into separate bowls
3	Container placement	The bowls are placed onto the correlating food group sensor indicated by the etched icons on the board surface
4	Initial feedback	Measurement indicator lights are shown over the Cibo character
5	Begin interaction	When all four indicator lights are green, they will flash indicating success in their first goal. The child will push the start button to begin eating and interacting with Cibo
6	Eating process	Force sensors will constantly read the current weight in the bowls. When the values drop to a range that indicates a half full bowl or an empty bowl, different body systems of Cibo will illuminate in response to the food group
7	Reset	When all the food is consumed, Cibo's face will light up, which completes the process

7 Conclusions and Future Work

In this paper, we presented an interactive device for children nutrition education. The features combine physical nourishment, nutritional education, and playing at the table. The incorporation of a friendly character and game-like elements in the device encourages empathy and gives the child incentive to finish her meal and see her friend grow healthy and happy. The interaction between the child and the device helps the child understand the benefits of eating healthy while practicing independence.

Although informal evaluations and expert reviews suggest our approach might be an effective tool to encourage healthy eating habits in young children, the device remains untested with large sample sizes. Future testing will include wider studies across a broad demographic, both in home environments and educational settings such as schools and day cares. Testing is also needed to refine the interface, as the abstraction of the character may be confusing to younger children who have yet not learned general anatomy. A simple solution could include the visual customization of "Cibo" through interchangeable character silhouettes.

As future work, we would like to provide higher levels of adaptability to the device, as different children have different nutritional needs. For example, the two settings used to define the portion sizes (child age and size) could be accompanied by an additional option for snacks or for children with dietary restrictions such as a setting that does not activate the sensor responsible for the protein container for a vegetarian child.

Finally, it would be interesting to test the conditions under which the board and/or the interactions could be modified for children who are overweight, underweight, or have an eating disorder and need a strict diet or an activity to encourage healthy habits and bring delight, if eating is a difficult task.

References

1. Lobstein, T., Jackson-Leach, R., Moodie, M.L., Hall, K.D., Gortmaker, S.L., Swinburn, B. A., James, W.P.T., Wang, Y., McPherson, K.: Child and adolescent obesity: part of a bigger picture. The Lancet **385**(9986), 2510–2520 (2015)
2. American Heart Association: Overweight in Children (2016). http://www.heart.org/ HEARTORG/HealthyLiving/HealthyKids/ChildhoodObesity/Overweight-in-Children_ UCM_304054_Article.jsp. Accessed Mar 2016)
3. Lloyd, L.J., Langley-Evans, S.C., McMullen, S.: Childhood obesity and risk of the adult metabolic syndrome: a systematic review. Int. J. Obes. **36**(1), 1–11 (2012)
4. Mohanan, S., Tapp, H., McWilliams, A., Dulin, M.: Obesity and asthma: pathophysiology and implications for diagnosis and management in primary care. Exp. Biol. Med. **239**(11), 1531–1540 (2014)
5. Bacha, F., Gidding, S.S.: Cardiac abnormalities in youth with obesity and type 2 diabetes. Curr. Diab. Rep. **16**(7), 62 (2016). doi:10.1007/s11892-016-0750-6
6. Goldschmidt, A.B., Wilfley, D.E., Paluch, R.A., Roemmich, J.N., Epstein, L.H.: Indicated prevention of adult obesity: reference data for weight normalization in overweight children. Arch. Pediatr. Adolesc. Med. **167**, 21–26 (2013)

7. Centers for Disease Control and Prevention (CDC): Childhood Obesity Causes & Consequences. https://www.cdc.gov/obesity/childhood/causes.html. Accessed Mar 2016

8. Wang, Y., Wu, Y., Wilson, R.F., Bleich, S., Cheskin, L., Weston, C., Showell, N., Fawole, O., Lau, B. Segal, J.: Childhood obesity prevention programs: comparative effectiveness review and meta-analysis. Comparative effectiveness review no. 115. Agency for Healthcare Research and Quality, Rockville (2013)

9. Nixon, C.A., Moore, H.J., Douthwaite, W., Gibson, E.L., Vogele, C., Kreichauf, S., Wildgruber, A., Manios, Y., Summerbell, C.D.: Identifying effective behavioural models and behaviour change strategies underpinning preschool- and school-based obesity prevention interventions aimed at 4–6-year-olds: a systematic review. Obes. Rev. **13**, 106–117 (2012)

10. Khambalia, A.Z., Dickinson, S., Hardy, L.L., Gill, T., Baur, L.A.: A synthesis of existing systematic reviews and meta-analyses of school-based behavioural interventions for controlling and preventing obesity. Obes. Rev. **13**, 214–233 (2012)

11. Rapley, G., Murkett, T.: Baby Led Weaning: The Essential Guide to Introducing Solid Foods and Helping Your Baby to Grow Up a Happy and Confident Eater. The Experiment, LLC, New York (2005)

12. Montessori, M.: The Montessori Method. Transaction publishers, Chicago (2013)

13. Piaget, J.: The Child's Conception of the World, vol. 213. Rowman & Littlefield, New York (1951)

14. Dewey, J.: Experience & Education. Kappa Delta Pi, New York (1938)

15. Mooney, C.G.: Theories of Childhood: An Introduction to Dewey, Montessori, Erikson, Piaget & Vygotsky. Redleaf Press, Little Canada (2013)

16. Deterding, S., Dixon, D., Khaled, R., Nacke, L.: From game design elements to gamefulness: defining gamification. In: Proceedings of the 15th International Academic MindTrek Conference: Envisioning Future Media Environments, pp. 9–15. ACM. Chicago (2011)

17. Dicheva, D., Dichev, C., Agre, G., Angelova, G.: Gamification in education: a systematic mapping study. Educ. Technol. Soc. **18**(3), 75–88 (2015)

18. Terlutter, R., Capella, M.L.: The gamification of advertising: analysis and research directions of in-game advertising, advergames, and advertising in social network games. J. Advertising **42**(2–3), 95–112 (2013)

19. Robson, K., Plangger, K., Kietzmann, J.H., McCarthy, I., Pitt, L.: Game on: engaging customers and employees through gamification. Bus. Horiz. **59**(1), 29–36 (2016)

20. Lee, J.J., Hammer, J.: Gamification in education: what, how, why bother? Acad. Exch. Q. **15**(2), 2 (2011)

21. Read, J.L., Shortell, S.M.: Interactive games to promote behavior change in prevention and treatment. JAMA **305**(16), 1704–1705 (2011)

22. Biddiss, E., Irwin, J.: Active video games to promote physical activity in children and youth: a systematic review. Arch. Pediatr. Adolesc. Med. **164**(7), 664–672 (2010)

23. McConville, K.M.V., Virk, S.: Evaluation of an electronic video game for improvement of balance. Virtual Reality **16**, 315–323 (2012)

24. Lapao, L.V., Marques, R., Gregorio, J., Mira-da-Silva, M.: Nurses' self-improvement hand-hygiene compliance in a hospital ward: combining indoor location with gamification data presentation. Antimicrobial. Resist. Infect. Control **4**(1), I11 (2015)

25. Lee, N., Jang, D., Kim, Y., Bae, B.C., Cho, J.D.: DenTeach: a device for fostering children's good tooth-brushing habits. In: Proceedings of the 15th International Conference on Interaction Design and Children, pp. 619–624. ACM (2016)

26. Miller, A.S., Cafazzo, J.A., Seto, E.: A game plan: Gamification design principles in mHealth applications for chronic disease management. Health Inf. J. **22**(2), 184–193 (2016)

27. Theng, Y.L., Lee, J.W., Patinadan, P.V., Foo, S.S.: The use of videogames, gamification, and virtual environments in the self-management of diabetes: a systematic review of evidence. Games Health J. **4**(5), 352–361 (2015)
28. Graafland, M., Schraagen, J.M., Schijven, M.P.: Systematic review of serious games for medical education and surgical skills training. Br. J. Surg. **99**, 1322–1330 (2012)
29. Lederer, A.M., King, M.H., Sovinski, D., Kim, N.: The impact of family rules on children's eating habits, sedentary behaviors, and weight status. Child. Obes. **11**(4), 421–429 (2015)
30. Graf, D.L., Pratt, L.V., Hester, C.N., Short, K.R.: Playing active video games increases energy expenditure in children. Pediatrics **124**(2), 534–540 (2009)
31. U.S. Department of Agriculture: Let's Move! The Apps for Healthy Kids. http://appsforhealthykids.challengepost.com. Accessed Jan 2016
32. Lo, J.-L., Lin, T.-Y., Chu, H.-H., Chou, H.-C., Chen, J.-H., Hsu, J.Y.-J., Huang, P.: Playful tray: adopting Ubicomp and persuasive techniques into play-based occupational therapy for reducing poor eating behavior in young children. In: Proceedings of the 9th International Conference on Ubiquitous Computing, UbiComp 2007 (2007)
33. Mori, M., Kurihara, K., Tsukada, K., Siio, I.: Dining presenter: augmented reality system for a dining tabletop, In: Proceedings of the 11th International Conference on Ubiquitous Computing, UbiComp 2009 (2009)
34. Kadomura, A., Tsukada, K., Siio, I.: EducaTableware: computer-augmented tableware to enhance the eating experiences. In: CHI 2013 Extended Abstracts on Human Factors in Computing Systems, pp. 3071–3074. ACM (2013)
35. HapiFork: HAPI.com. https://www.hapi.com/product/hapifork. Accessed Mar 2016

Gamification Methods in Higher Education

Lila A. Loos[✉] and Martha E. Crosby[✉]

University of Hawaii at Manoa, 1680 East-West Road POST 305D,
Honolulu, HI 96822, USA
{Lila7194,Crosby}@Hawaii.edu

Abstract. Gamification impacts the classroom through the integration of personal and social elements, creating an immersive learning environment. Rooted in the motivational framework of flow experiences, gamification is a contemporary educational approach that leverages the characteristics of gaming culture. This study examined how gamification techniques were operationalized by eight professors and one director of instructional technology. The results of interviews among a purposive sample show that gamification improves learning outcomes. Subjects ranging from computer science and technology to languages and multimedia journalism are taught in classrooms on campus, online, and in hybrid settings. Game design mechanics such as points, challenges, and collaboration rank as the top three elements of gamification. Professors noted increases in student coursework completion and discussion participation; students were exposed to real life situations and had fun learning. This study addresses the gap in educational perspectives through gamification to encourage desirable behavior for the benefit of the learner community.

Keywords: Gamification · Flow · Engagement · Interaction · Higher education

1 Introduction

The use of gamification to promote student engagement embodies an evolving approach to learning in higher education. The application of digital game playing represents a shift in the information culture to the Internet and is especially relevant to those born after 1990 because this method intensifies engagement and active participation [1]. Gamification fosters critical thinking about real world topics, prepares students to enter a technical workforce [2], and provides solutions to help schools solve difficult motivation and engagement problems [3]. Irrespective of the application of gamification to enhance or resolve educational concerns, skills necessary for gaming, such as anticipating, thinking recursively, and organizing information within time constraints, align with preferred educational abilities and skills [4]. Based on the concept of active learning, gamification techniques are an alternative to the passive classroom and a driver of student engagement. In this study, experts are interviewed to discover the methods and the impact of gamification, revealing an adoption of concept-mastery-based learning. The following sections strengthen educators' foundational knowledge of gamification: diverse definitions of gamification in the non-game context of education, framework of flow, method, results and discussion, and conclusion.

© Springer International Publishing AG 2017
P. Zaphiris and A. Ioannou (Eds.): LCT 2017, Part I, LNCS 10295, pp. 474–486, 2017.
DOI: 10.1007/978-3-319-58509-3_37

2 Diverse Definitions of Gamification in the Non-game Context of Education

Gamification is defined as the use of game elements to create an active learning environment by engaging students in the process of knowledge acquisition. Although the term was first used in 2008, gamification's popularity was established in 2010 and its definition has since come under dispute [5]. Deterding, Dixon, Khaled, and Nacke [5] define gamification as "the use of game design elements in non-game contexts" (p. 12). The power of game-like techniques in the context of learner behavior has been explored and defined by researchers studying subjects in the educational domain. Kapp's [6] multifaceted integration of game-like elements combines elements such as narrative, challenge, sense of control and mastery, and decision-making in a non-game environment. As educators integrate game elements into the classroom, the gamification dialog evolves and its definition develops.

Although learning from game elements is dissimilar from playing a game designed to promote the mastery of a specific concept, educators may include games in their methodological approach to gamification. One example of game integration is Fink, Best, Manz, Popovsky, and Endicott-Popovsky's [7] presentation of security scenarios to assess learner responses. The observational experiment measures cyber defense situational awareness by scoring teams based on the conditions for each requirement. In this instance, incorporating games to improve readiness for real world cyber defense provides an immersive simulation similar to Reiners et al.'s [8] authentic problem solving environment, in which student "learning should be about fun, play, and passion" (p. 7). Huang and Soman [9] suggest distinguishing games from gamification because the latter utilizes game elements, such as points and leaderboards, in the learning process to accomplish an action that increases skill and knowledge and stimulates engagement and motivation. Based on outcomes, gamification includes games because they activate learning in the classroom, suggesting a more grounded definition of gamification.

Gros [10] focuses on the integration of the structural aspects of games, such as icons and imagery, to "promote conceptual learning, problem solving skills, co-operation, and practical participation" (p. 30). The team-based element harnesses student competitiveness to enhance learning. Likewise, Burke's [11] method of using game mechanics such as challenges, points, badges, and leaderboards to track students' progress through levels of skill development and autonomy encourages motivated players toward goal achievement. Alternatively, Lee and Hammer [3] emphasize the design of gamification targets to meet the specific needs of schools and achieve effective results, distinguishing gamification from its normal classroom counterparts such as grades, tests, group projects, and extra credit. The authors propose that game elements do not automatically produce student engagement; rather, they represent an intervention for addressing cognitive, emotional, and social problems. Although not defined by a specific pedagogy, the structure of gamification supports techniques for enhancing student learning experiences, supporting Kapp's [6] application of game elements that activate desirable learning behavior or offer solutions to problematic learning issues. The evolving phenomena are examined through current methods of gamification and their potential for promoting constructive learning in higher education.

3 Framework of Flow

The cultivation of motivation and engagement through gamification is foundational to Csikszentmihalyi's [12] theoretical framework of flow. Positive psychology recognizes the subjective experience of flow as it is conditioned by goals and the adjustment of responses based on feedback [13]. Empirical evidence suggests that the integration of flow has a positive influence in higher education contexts.

Csikszentmihalyi [12] describes flow as a powerful force, a "state of concentration so focused that it amounts to absolute absorption in an activity" (p. 1). Csikszentmihalyi's [12] studies of interviewees report similar experiences of flow, including the ability to complete tasks, concentrate deeply, have clear goals, receive immediate feedback, achieve effortless involvement, control one's actions, and have no concern for self or sense of the passage of time during the activity. These common flow characteristics produce states of enjoyment represented by deep concentration on an activity that, based on a student's skill level, is sufficiently challenging. Csikszentmihalyi [14] argues that these relevant components allow flow to be experienced during "almost any activity" (p. 2), and he advocates flow-augmented creativity in the student and teacher domain.

Flow experiences require a combination of "well-presented knowledge, interested students, and stimulating teachers" [15] p. 181. The intrinsic characteristics of flow are argued to be present in gamification, affecting learners by encouraging engaged behavior. Contrary to the standard approach of memorization-based classroom teaching, Khan [16] suggests, "the most effective way to teach would be to emphasize the flow of a subject, the chain of associations that relates one concept to the next and across subjects" (p. 48). The association between flow and the integration of game mechanics motivates student learning. Steele and Fullagar [17] studied engagement in college coursework mediated by flow. A positive association was found between flow and instructor support of autonomy defined by goals and tasks. Feedback from a teacher or from the task itself is a predictor of progress toward goals and a state of flow. Gammon and Lawrence [18] studied the effect of feedback and self-assessment on flow analytics, focusing on test-taking experiences. They found that student feedback and self-assessment experiences presented supplementary opportunities for teachers to enhance learning material, thus supporting learner performance.

Similar studies suggest that the flow condition of engagement occurs when the task is at a level appropriate to one's capabilities. Nakamura and Csikszentmihalyi [13] describe two empirical studies. The first examined recreational activities, emphasizing the intrinsic rewards of play and games, and the second studied surgeons who are rewarded extrinsically. In both groups, the results demonstrate a sense of engagement perceived by the participants while participating in activities at levels appropriate to their individual abilities. Csikszentmihalyi [14] emphasizes the importance of balancing challenges and skills to avoid the distraction of more ambitious tasks and to encourage concentration, interest, and enjoyment, which result in flow. In a subsequent study, D. Shernoff, Csikszentmihalyi, Shneider, and E. Shernoff [19] encouraged instructors to engage learners through incremental skill-building and immediate feedback to match student ability to skill level.

Beylefeld and Struwig [20] argue that the "relationship between flow and motivation is highly relevant in higher education environments" (p. 933). Their study investigates students' ability to master medical microbiology through game-based learning strategies by documenting the impact of flow on student engagement in skill development. The results showed that students responded positively to the flow-inducing game-based learning used to promote engagement with and mastery of microbiology content, describing it as an "invigorating teaching device" (p. 938). Kiili's [21] study of flow experiences through content creation in educational games reports student satisfaction with appropriate challenges, problems, and a story line. The author recognizes the benefit of flow in the design of educational games: "the reward of flow is obvious: it has a positive effect on learning" (p. 196). Flow is argued to have a positive effect on learner attentiveness, thereby increasing engagement with bodies of knowledge. This study describes relevant approaches, encompassing both games and game mechanics, to enhancing learner outcomes.

4 Method

The purpose of this study is to discover how gamification techniques are used in higher education to engage students and improve learning outcomes (Table 1). Game-based techniques are examined through discussions with eight university professors and an instructional technology designer, all of whom apply immersive methods to improve learning outcomes. The interview questions were designed to capture emergent themes that deepen our understanding of gamification processes and learner impact. The research instrument consisted of nine open-ended questions and three closed-ended questions (Appendix). The questions gave respondents maximum flexibility in structuring their responses [22] and allowed paths of discovery to reveal themselves for comparative induction. The interview focused on the selection and implementation of gamification elements, methodology, and classroom results. The comprehensive data collected through participant perspectives and experiences revealed a variety of design methods and prompted in-depth discussions of the implementation of gamification in higher education.

Table 1. Research questions

RQ1: What gamification techniques do educators employ as an approach to higher education learning?
RQ2: How do educators use gamification-based learning to engage students in higher education?
RQ3: What is the impact of gamification on the learning outcomes of higher education students?

The responses were recorded, transcribed and analyzed to discover the emergent themes. Similarities and differences were compared to increase the validity of the findings [23]. Through inductive comparisons, descriptive connections were made by categorizing and delineating the themes used in the coding process [24]; the core interview themes are formulated and presented in the following sections.

5   Results and Discussion

A sample of nine professionals utilizing gamification in education participated in the interview process. The data gathered in 2014 was collected from various United States universities and a private organization in England. Pseudonyms are used to protect interviewees' identities. Table 2 provides a summary of the interviewees.

Table 2. Participants

Pseudonym	Occupational title	Academic specialty or industry specialty	University or company name
P1	Professor	Computer science	University of Washington
P2	Professor	Sports education	University of Idaho
P3	Professor	Communications	University of Hawaii
P4	Lecturer, manager	Learning technologies	University of Brighton
P5	Technology director	Instructional technology design	Rosetta Stone
P6	Professor	Game design	Carnegie Mellon University
P7	Professor	Information systems	University of Michigan
P8	Professor	Journalism	University of Hawaii
P9	Professor	Social interactions	Syracuse University

The courses taught by the respondents range from technology to languages. Four of the respondents with fewer than ten years of teaching experience use gamification in language, social media innovation, multimedia journalism, news writing, introduction to mass communications, and introduction to information courses. Seven of these courses are located on university campuses and one course is offered online. One respondent has ten years of teaching experience in a variety of venues (campus, online, and in hybrid settings) and applies gamification in computer science and information assurance courses.

Burke [11] argues that the value of gamification becomes a reality through educators who understand its importance and reports that the most significant barrier to success is the lack of gamification design skills. The participants discussed how they define, drive, measure, design, determine, and personalize game mechanics in their approaches to implementing gamification.

5.1 Defining Gamification

Participants consistently described gamification as an interactive and immersive mechanism aimed at challenging students and activating classroom participation. Table 3 lists definitions focused on the design aspect of gamification.

Table 3. Gamification definitions

Definition	Participant
"The use of design principles commonly used in games for purposes other than games"	P6
"Game-like features such as a point system, competitive ranking, or badging"	P5
"An educational process for the purpose of activation of student learning and transferring them from a productive to more creative thinking and approach to the learning process and application of this knowledge to real life"	P2
"Ways to bring real work activity into the classroom to help students learn beyond just reading and listening to lectures"	P1
"Choose the way they want to learn including the modes of learning and much of the significant attributes of assignments and activities"	P8
"Meaningful changes in the system that are equally valuable yet tailored to what the student wants to learn"	P8
"Giving people compelling choices in which they can pick their path to learning and success"	P8

Participants emphasized structural definitions of gamification. Similarly, Werbach [25] describes gamification as an academic expansion beyond points and badges to aligning learning experiences with game mechanics. Similar to the description of student agency advocated by P8, flow studies [6, 12, 17, 26, 27] suggest that gamification supports autonomy and personal control. All participants described game-like principles in their approach to active education.

Table 4. Gamification drivers

Driver	Participant
"Ways to activate a student so they become involved in their learning process so that learning becomes more than just memorization"	P1
"As the material becomes more interactive, it becomes more engaging"	P3
"Commonly used as a method of giving feedback about performance and for incentivizing performance"	P4
"Fundamentally and the most important part of learning is developing a love for learning and if you can develop that love about the topic you're teaching, then the students will embrace that and gravitate toward that the rest of their lives"	P8
"Provided feedback in a complex social system"	P9

5.2   Gamification Drivers

Identified as motivational experiences, the gamification drivers mentioned by the participants are shown in Table 4. The informants reported increased student involvement, social interaction, and feedback as factors that supported improved learning outcomes. Several studies [9, 12, 17–19, 27, 28] have reported that feedback is a motivational tool that can be used to align student abilities with skills.

5.3   Measuring Student Learning Outcomes with Gamification

Measuring learning outcomes using a point system was the most common form of student assessment. Although the majority of respondents gamified specific course content, P8 applied gamification to the entire classroom structure and observed that grades are at the forefront of students' minds. In a gamified course, grades begin at zero and students gain points through the point system. Alternatively, P5 proposed a virtual interactive game environment in which an avatar drives engagement and allows students to demonstrate their mastery of the learning objectives. P3, like P4, uses gamification as a motivator but uses exams and grades to assess the quality of student work. Table 5 lists participant measures of gamification.

Table 5. Measuring student learning outcomes with gamification

Measurement by gamification	Participant
"Can be done inside or outside of a game system"	P6
"Learning outcomes cannot be measured using gamification"	P5
"Think it is inappropriate to use gamification to measure learning outcomes"	P7
"Game is really just there to deliver the lesson"	P3
"Allocated points to a rubric for student evaluation"	P1

5.4   Gamification Pedagogy

De Byl's [29] study of student enjoyment and engagement in a gamified curriculum suggests that "educators are always seeking a new pedagogy or technology that might engage and immerse their students" (p. 256). Although more than half of the respondents have not applied pedagogy to gamification methods (Table 6), P2 identified pedagogy as necessary for effective implementation: "gamification is not a system by itself, it has to be treated as a pedagogical system." P1 uses the high-level Kuzmina-Bespalko-Popovsky (KBP) model, which is based on American and Russian pedagogical approaches [30] and modifies content and delivery methods to gamify education. This system-centered process produces creative problem solvers through interconnected and dynamic elements comprising the "student, teacher, goals, content, and didactic processes of the curriculum" (p. 59). Like Csikszentmihalyi's [12] match between student ability and skill level, Vygotsky [31] suggests a relationship between learning and development in which levels should be matched; an approach identified by P7. Vygotsky's [31] theory on the zone of proximal development is the "distance

Table 6. Gamification pedagogy

Pedagogy	Participant
Pedagogy contains elements of a method, organization, and remedy	P2
Kuzmina-Bespalko-Popovsky (KBP) model	P1
Vygotsky's zone of proximal development and Csikszentmihalyi's concept of flow	P7

between the actual developmental level as determined by independent problem solving and the level of potential development as determined through problem solving under adult guidance or in collaboration with more capable peers" (p. 40). Shernoff, Hamari, and Rowe [32] propose a similar viewpoint in which flow is achieved by increasing the level of skill to the next, more challenging, level.

5.5 Gamification Elements

Table 7 provides a list of gamification elements employed in the classroom. Ten mechanisms are arranged in descending order according to the frequency with which they were mentioned by the participants.

The use of game design characteristics such as points, the addition of new challenges, collaboration, and games were the four most frequently used mechanisms of gamification. A notable exception is illuminated by P6, who does not believe gamification exists:

> If it does exist, every classroom is already gamified as students already receive points, grades. The only question worth discussing is where the designs of the systems are good ones or not, whether they are gamified is unimportant and misleading.

This participant claims that gamification elements are already present in schools but under different labels. Examples of game elements that parallel existing classroom components are the use of points to determine grades, bonuses taking the place of extra

Table 7. Gamification elements

Gamification elements	Participant
Points increase your level	P1, P2, P3, P4, P5, P7, P8, P9
Addition of new challenges	P1, P3, P4, P5, P7, P8, P9
Collaboration and/or interaction	P1, P3, P4, P5, P8, P9
Games in the educational process	P1, P2, P3, P4, P5
Achievements earn recognition	P3, P5, P7, P8
Leaderboard displays levels in descending order	P4, P5, P7, P8
Master one level before moving to the next level	P1, P2, P5, P7
Bonuses received as extra reward	P7, P8, P9
Flexibility of path selection	P1, P8, P9
Countdown for time limits or deadlines	P8, P9

credit, countdowns to deadlines, or additional challenges replacing surprise quizzes. Although de Byl [29] recognizes the existing alignment between gamification and the educational system, the author acknowledges differences, including increased engagement and the transparency of points, levels, and status, between a gamified setting and the traditional classroom's system of weighted assignment and test grades.

P5 considers the learning goal prior to selecting the appropriate gamification elements. Although studies have found that feedback is a motivational tool that produces positive results [9, 12, 17–19, 27, 28], it was not mentioned as an element employed by the participants. Feedback was used to define gamification by one respondent, however, and was another respondent's reason for employing gamification.

5.6 Personalizing Gamification Techniques

Five respondents reflected on the benefits of tailoring gamification techniques to students' personality or cognitive ability, as shown in Table 8. P9 feels that personalization is risky and would not apply it when instructing a classroom of 250 students, arguing instead that teaching options should be aligned with learning goals. P1 uses the KBP pedagogical model to understand the student and adjust course content accordingly.

Table 8. Personalizing gamification techniques

Personalization	Participant
"I give them options so the students themselves can kind of adjust their learning based on the topic that they pick"	P1
Aligns student physiology with athletic activity	P2
"Always get to know the student and then tailor each assignment to that student's needs and talents"	P8
"Adapt techniques from semester to semester based on student feedback and I try to be sensitive to a full range of student needs and motivations"	P7
"I don't personalize techniques based on personality other than the idea that there are different learner styles and I try to match the literature"	P9

6 Evaluation of Gamification

Participants' ability to effectively address classroom difficulties necessitates the continuous modification and improvement of their gamification design methods. To maximize learner engagement, educators evaluated the appropriate selection of subject matter delivery methods and experiences, as shown in Table 9. Instructors' methods emphasized gamification as a positive accompaniment to lectures that accommodates various learner types. Furthermore, student feedback and outcomes improve the implementation of gamification in the classroom. The participants reported no major problems, with the exception of the barrier created by cultural expectations of the lecture format in higher education.

Table 9. Evaluation of gamification

Evaluation	Participant
Applications to real world scenarios	P1
Students work harder with games compared to regular assignments	P1
Hands-on work	P3
Well-designed teacher and student assessments	P3
Potential inability of students to get along in their particular groups	P3
Flexibility in assignments and higher student ratings for the gamified class	P9
Can be disruptive and alienating when rules change	P4, P9
Creates a sense of fairness by accommodating highly attentive and mediocre learners	P9
Some students prefer to have content delivered via lecture	P1, P8
Effective processes defined by pedagogy	P1, P2, P8
Well-designed teacher and student assessments	P3, P5, P7
Build layers of gamification to understand what works best	P5, P7

7 Conclusion

The results indicate that gamification's use of game mechanics activates student involvement, engagement, and motivation. Desiring to enrich student engagement in higher education, the participants leveraged students' ubiquitous exposure to the intense state of game technologies to create an intensified exploration of their course's subject matter. Through the practical application of gamification elements characterized by personal and social combinations of classroom activities, including exposure to real life work activities, optimal learner experiences were observed to produce increased student discussion, higher coursework scores, and more enjoyment for learners.

Gamification is an incentivizing technique that explains, reshapes, and brings attention to immersive learning methods. Games are an element of gamification that supplement active learning and do not replace teacher instruction. Research indicates [28, 33] that gamification has yet to become a mainstream program of study in higher education. Some studies, however, suggest it has the potential to become a conventional method in less than five years [34]. This study advances gamification's role as a game-based learning tool for higher education by identifying methods and exploring educators' successes and challenges. Arnab et al. [35] suggest a gap in the research findings regarding the assimilation potential for education adoption. In response to these obstacles, this research contributes to the future development of more complex gamification design approaches that integrate game elements for more effective implementation.

Additionally, future research in pedagogy should systematically develop a gamification discourse and assess the impact of gamification on the learning environment. Ignoring the gamification movement may deprive students of the opportunity to discover information and ideas through active involvement.

Appendix

Interview Questions

Closed-ended questions	Link to research question Table 10
1. What is your title?	
2. What is your academic specialty?	
3. What classes have you recently taught that contain gamification elements? a. What was the subject of the class? b. Was the class on-campus, online, or hybrid? c. How long have you taught the class?	1
Open-ended questions	Link to research question Table 10
1. How do you define gamification?	1, 2, 3
2. What is the purpose of employing gamification in the classroom?	2, 3
3. How do you measure student learning outcomes utilizing gamification?	3
4. Is there any gamification pedagogy that you particularly identify with?	2
5. How do you select gamification elements?	1
6. Have you ever personalized gamifying techniques based on student personality or cognitive ability?	1
7. Could you reflect on the positive results, if any, that you have experienced using gamification in the classroom? Were the results quantified?	3
8. Have you experienced any problems using gamification in the classroom? Were the results quantified?	3
9. Is there any general advice or best practices that you would like to elaborate on?	2, 3

Table 10. Research questions

1. What gamification techniques do educators employ in higher education learning?
2. How do educators use gamification-based learning to engage students in higher education?
3. What is the impact of gamification on the learning outcomes of higher education students?

References

1. McGonigal, J.: Reality is Broken: Why Games Make Us Better and How They Can Change the World. Penguin, Jonathan Cape (2011)
2. Sardone, N.B., Devlin-Scherer, R.: Teacher candidate responses to digital games. J. Res. Technol. Educ. **42**(4), 409–425 (2010). doi:10.1080/15391523.2010.10782558
3. Lee, J.J., Hammer, J.: Gamification in education: what, how, why bother? Acad. Exch. Q. **15** (2), 146 (2011). https://dialnet.unirioja.es/servlet/articulo?codigo=3714308
4. Pillay, H.: An investigation of cognitive processes engaged in by recreational computer game players: implications for skills of the future. J. Res. Technol. Educ. **34**(3), 336–350 (2002). doi:10.1080/15391523.2002.10782354
5. Deterding, S., Khaled, R., Nacke, L., Dixon, D.: Gamification: toward a definition. In: Paper Presented at the Gamification Workshop Proceedings of ACM CHI 2011 Conference on Human Factors in Computing Systems, Vancouver, BC, Canada: ACM (2011). http://gamification-research.org/wp-content/uploads/2011/04/02-Deterding-Khaled-Nacke-Dixon.pdf
6. Kapp, K.M.: The Gamification of Learning and Instruction: Game-Based Methods and Strategies for Training and Education. Wiley, San Francisco (2012)
7. Fink, G., Best, D., Manz, D., Popovsky, V., Endicott-Popovsky, B.: Gamification for measuring cyber security situational awareness. Found. Augmented Cogn. **8027**, 656–665 (2013). doi:10.1007/978-3-642-39454-6_70
8. Reiners, T., Wood, L.C., Chang, V., Guetl, C., Herrington, J., Gregory, S., Teräs, H.: Operationalising gamification in an educational authentic environment. In: Kommers, P., Issa, T., Isaías, P. (eds.) International Conference on Internet Technologies and Society, pp. 93–100. IADIS Press, Perth (2012)
9. Huang, W.H.-Y., Soman, D.: Gamification of education. In: Paper Presented at Research Report Series: Behavioural Economics in Action. Rotman School of Management, Toronto, Canada (2013)
10. Gros, B.: Digital games in education: the design of games-based learning environments. J. Res. Technol. Educ. **40**(1), 23–38 (2007)
11. Burke, B.: Gamify: how gamification motivates people to do extraordinary things. Bibliomotion, Brookline (2014)
12. Csikszentmihalyi, M.: Flow: The Psychology of Optimal Experience. Harper-Perennial, New York (1990)
13. Nakamura, J., Csikszentmihalyi, M.: The concept of flow. In: Snyder, C.R., Lopez, S.J. (eds.) Handbook of Positive Psychology, pp. 89–105. Oxford University Press, New York (2002)
14. Csikszentmihalyi, M.: Finding Flow: The Psychology of Engagement with Everyday Life. HarperCollins, New York (1997)
15. Csikszentmihalyi, M.: The Systems Model of Creativity: The Collected Works of Mihaly Csikszentmihalyi. Springer, Dordrecht (2015)
16. Khan, S.: The One World Schoolhouse: Education Reimagined. Hachette Digital, New York (2012)
17. Steele, J.P., Fullagar, C.J.: Facilitators and outcomes of student engagement in a college setting. J. Psychol. **143**(1), 5–27 (2009). doi:10.3200/jrlp.143.1.5-27
18. Gammon, S., Lawrence, L.: Improving student experience through making assessments 'flow'. In: Bryan, C., Clegg, K. (eds.) Innovative Assessment in Higher Education, pp. 132–140. Routledge, New York (2006)

19. Shernoff, D.J., Csikszentmihalyi, M., Shneider, B., Shernoff, E.S.: Student engagement in high school classrooms from the perspective of flow theory. School Psychol. Q. **18**(2), 158–176 (2003). doi:10.1521/scpq.18.2.158.21860

20. Beylefeld, A.A., Struwig, M.C.: A gaming approach to learning medical microbiology: students' experiences of flow. Med. Teacher **29**(9), 933–940 (2007). doi:10.1080/01421590701601550

21. Kiili, K.: Content creation challenges and flow experience in educational games: the IT-emperor case. Internet High. Educ. **8**(3), 183–198 (2005). doi:10.1016/j.iheduc.2005.06.001

22. Aberbach, J.D., Rockman, B.A.: Conducting and coding elite interviews. Polit. Sci. Polit. **35** (04), 673–676 (2002)

23. Boeije, H.: A purposeful approach to the constant comparative method in the analysis of qualitative interviews. Qual. Quant. **36**(4), 391–409 (2002). doi:10.1023/a:1020909529486

24. Mayring, P.: Qualitative Content Analysis: Theoretical Foundation, Basic Procedures and Software Solution. Springer, Klagenfurt (2014)

25. Werbach, K.: (Re)Defining gamification: a process approach. In: Spagnolli, A., Chittaro, L., Gamberini, L. (eds.) Persuasive Technology, pp. 266–272. Springer, Switzerland (2014)

26. Agarwal, R., Karahanna, E.: Time flies when you're having fun: cognitive absorption and beliefs about information technology usage. MIS Q. **24**(4), 665–694 (2000). http://misq.org/cat-articles/time-flies-when-you-re-having-fun-cognitive-absorption-and-beliefs-about-information-technology-usage.html

27. Kiili, K.: Digital game-based learning: towards an experiential gaming model. Internet High. Educ. **8**(1), 13–24 (2005). doi:10.1016/j.iheduc.2004.12.001

28. Hamari, J., Koivisto, J., Sarsa, H.: Does gamification work? A literature review of empirical studies on gamification. In: Paper Presented at the Proceedings of the 47th Hawaii International Conference on System Sciences, pp. 3025–3034. Computer Society Press, Honolulu, January, 2014. http://people.uta.fi/~kljuham/2014-hamari_et_al-does_gamification_work.pdf

29. De Byl, P.: Can digital natives level-up in a gamified curriculum? In: Brown, M., Hartnett, M., Stewart, T. (eds.) Future Challenges, Sustainable Futures, pp. 256–266. ASCILITE, New Zealand (2012)

30. Endicott-Popovsky, B.E., Popovsky, V.M.: Application of pedagogical fundamentals for the holistic development of cybersecurity professionals. ACM Inroads **5**(1), 57–68 (2014). doi:10.1145/2568195.2568214

31. Vygotsky, L.: Interaction between learning and development. In: Gauvain, M., Cole, M. (eds.) Readings on the Development of Children 2004, pp. 34–41. Worth Publishers, New York (1978)

32. Shernoff, D.J., Hamari, J., Rowe, E.: Measuring flow in educational games and gamified learning environments. In: World Conference on Educational Media and Technology. AACE, Tampere, Finland (2014). https://www.researchgate.net/publication/264046054_Measuring_Flow_in_Educational_Games_and_Gamified_Learning_Environments

33. Park, H.J., Bae, J.H.: Analysis and survey of gamification. In: Paper Presented at the Science and Engineering Research Support Society, Current Research on Game and Graphics (2287-1233), International Workshop on Game and Graphics Tasmania, Australia. SERC (2013)

34. Johnson, L., Adams, B.S., Cummins, M., Estrada, V., Freeman, A., Ludgate, H.: NMC Horizon Report: 2013 Higher Education. The New Media Consortium, Austin (2013)

35. Arnab, S., Berta, R., Earp, J., De Freitas, S., Popescu, M., Romero, M., Stanescu, I., Usart, M.: Framing the adoption of serious games in formal education. Electron. J. e-Learning **10** (2), 159–171 (2012)

Subliminal Learning. What Do Games Teach Us?

Vicente A. Quesada Mora[1], Francisco J. Gallego-Durán[2],
Rafael Molina-Carmona[2(✉)], and Faraón Llorens-Largo[2]

[1] Inverge Studios, Alicante, Spain
vicenteq@invergestudios.com
[2] Cátedra Santander-UA de Transformación Digital,
University of Alicante, Alicante, Spain
{fgallego,rmolina}@dccia.ua.es, faraon.llorens@ua.es

Abstract. In video games, organic tutorials are first levels of the games, designed to teach their basic controls while the player plays. They provide some kind of subliminal learning, are very effective and natural and teach without losing the fun, but they are not easy to be properly designed. The purpose of this research is assisting the designers in the task of defining organic tutorials by proposing a guide of design principles and patterns. After reviewing the learning theories and design techniques for organic tutorials, an analysis of some representative video games is performed. Then, a guide made of ten principles is proposed. This guide helps the developers to clearly understand the fundamentals of organic tutorials and sheds light on what games teach us. It helps to understand some kind of subliminal learning and opens the way to design other learning experiences based on the proposed principles.

Keywords: Organic tutorial · Videogame tutorial · Subliminal learning

1 Introduction

Video games are one of the most important industries nowadays. Thousands of video games, with millionaire budgets, are published every year, but not all of them reach success. One of the key factors in a game's success is the way its rules are learned. Nowadays, the use of manuals has declined mainly due to the digital format boom, the high printing costs and the high complexity of the current video games. This is how the tutorials come up. The function of the tutorials is giving some guidelines during the first stages of the game so that the player acquires enough knowledge to be able to overcome the rest of the game. A tutorial is a first level that teaches the player the basic controls and mechanics of the video game. The more complex mechanics are introduced, progressively, throughout the game. In spite of being the first level to be played, the tutorial is usually the last level to be developed.

In broad outline, there are two main types of tutorials: direct and organic tutorials. Direct tutorials are based on text and images that explain in detail what actions players can take. Organic tutorials, on the contrary, indirectly teach

© Springer International Publishing AG 2017
P. Zaphiris and A. Ioannou (Eds.): LCT 2017, Part I, LNCS 10295, pp. 487–501, 2017.
DOI: 10.1007/978-3-319-58509-3_38

the players while they play the tutorial level. They are characterized by proposing a controlled and limited environment where the player learns by trying the mechanics and has the feeling of advancing with no external help but with ones own merit. There fore, this type of tutorials provides some kind of subliminal learning, which is very effective and natural. While being part of the video game, they fulfil the dual purpose of teaching without losing the fun. Unfortunately, organic tutorials are very extremely difficulty to be properly designed and implemented.

This research work arises to assist in the task of designing organic tutorials. Its objectives are:

- Analyse the psychological, behavioural and learning theories, and the design techniques used to indirectly guide and teach the player in video games with organic tutorials.
- Analyse a set of video games, of different genres and time that teach players the playable mechanics through level design.
- Develop of a guide of design principles and patterns of organic tutorials for future designers.

The first objective is developed in Sect. 2, Context, which presents a deeper study about the relationship between video games and learning, the previous studies about organic tutorials and an analysis of the concept of subliminal learning. Section 3 describes the methodology used to perform the analysis of the first level of different video games, to be able to extract some principles for the design of organic tutorials. Since the amount of video games that use organic tutorials is too large, a selection of 8 representative video games has been chosen to make the study. The guide of design principles is described in Sect. 4, made of three fundamental features of a well-designed organic tutorial that are decomposed, in turn, in 10 techniques for level design and gameplay. Finally some conclusions and future lines of research are presented in Sect. 5.

2 Context

2.1 Learning and Video Games

The twentieth century is considered the century of the cinema, because of its technical and artistic evolution and the imprint left in society, establishing the concept of seventh art. It is very likely that the 21st century is the century of digital interactive entertainment, that is, the century of video game. Hundreds of video games with multi-million dollar production costs and thousands of video games of medium and independent studios are published every year. In addition, more and more people, of any age or sex, play video games on the wide variety of available devices.

Video games have changed the way young people (and also adults) conceive reality and interact with each other [15,24]. One can say that good video games have the ability to optimally convey much information of a particular type, causing the player to pursue more information. According to Prensky [17,18] video games attract players for several reasons: they encourage participation, motivate users to gradually achieving small goals, offer rewards or immediate punishments, and difficulties of each level are adjusted according to the players skills. Hamari et al. [10] have investigated the impact of flow, engagement and immersion in game-based learning environments. Although most psychological studies focus on the negative effects of video games on adolescents, there are other studies that argue and document the benefits: voluntariness, competitiveness and cooperation, immersion, sense of control, achievement of goals (objectives), but especially satisfaction. Granic et al. [9] have conducted an extensive review of the literature on the benefits of video games and their potential.

Playing is inherent to human beings [11] and the game is a driving element of mental development [25], it improves learning and arouses curiosity, so the games are a great teaching tool. Fun involves new information fixed in the brain, so that the secret of optimal learning lies in the fun [13]. Good games get this fun, while the player learns their contents [6,7,12]. Analysing how games achieve the objective of fun is essential to design similar strategies in other areas and get to convey the information we want to be learned and fixed [14]. The principles of video games can help us achieve an innovative and effective training model, that particularly enhances student motivation, and the mechanisms to measure real progress in learning, that is, a truly continuous formative evaluation [8,16].

2.2   Organic Tutorials

During the development of a video game, one of the most important problems that designers must solve is teaching users to play their game. A video game, unlike cinema or music, is an interactive and immersive product so, for the player to fully enjoy it, he or she needs to know its rules: what you can and cannot be done in that new virtual environment. Currently, teaching players through printed manuals is not feasible because of the high complexity of video games. This is way the most common solution is the use, during the game, of tutorials that teach the player the controls and mechanics of the video game. The function of a tutorial is achieving that, once completed during the first levels of the game, the player has the knowledge necessary to overcome the rest of the game. The more complex mechanics will be progressively introduced throughout the game.

The wide variety of video game genres derives in diverse types of tutorials. Keep in mind that there is no tutorial that is valid for all genres: an inappropriate tutorial for an action game can be excellent for a complex strategy game. In general terms, two types of tutorials can be differentiated: direct and organic tutorials. The direct ones are those that use pop-up windows with text and images to explain in detail what actions players can take. On the contrary, the organic ones avoid the use of text and integrate the rules in a specific level so that the player can learn the mechanics in a more natural fashion. The organic tutorials are most appreciated by players since they indirectly teach through an intelligent design of the level.

The organic tutorial term has been coined by game design specialist Josh Bycer [2], referring to the organic game design, which in turn comes from the concept of organic architecture. It is a philosophy created by the architect Frank Lloyd Wright [27] to refer to fully integrated constructions in their natural surroundings. They are also called non-tutorials, integrated tutorials or invisible tutorials because, at first glance, they may seem not to exist. However, it is quite the opposite: these tutorials are so well designed that they are completely merged with the level and flow of the game. The main problem of organic tutorials is the high difficulty to properly design and implement them, as well as the risk they entail. A poorly designed organic tutorial can frustrate the player by not correctly teaching the mechanics, causing him to leave the game. Although difficult to implement, they are very effective, since what is naturally learned, while playing and having fun, is better recorded in memory. A good organic tutorial should not be obvious to players.

The fun in video games, as in other conventional games, comes from the action of playing them, not from learning how they work. A tutorial that is not evident, and that is part of the video game, fulfils the dual purpose of teaching without losing the fun. The environment of an organic tutorial is controlled and limited so that the player can learn by testing the actions that designers planned during the game conception. Moreover, these tutorials allow the players to feel that their progress is an achievement made by themselves, without outside help from the developers. Since there is no direct guide, the rules are learned by trial-and-error. This method requires a well-studied learning curve so that the player improves his skills while the challenges increase in difficulty, preventing him from becoming frustrated or bored, and leaving the game therefore.

2.3 Subliminal Learning

Humans are able to unconsciously perceive stimuli. Subliminal stimulation and subconscious power have been widely studied in the field of psychology [1,20]. Nowadays it has recovered a new impetus even talking about the rebirth of the subliminal [5]. Subliminal learning would occur as a result of exposure to a subliminal stimulus, with no conscious attention from the subject, although this type of learning is far from being passive and requires high level processing, as Seitz and Watanabe state [23]. They consider that diffuse reinforcement and learning signals are complementary to focused attention in subliminal learning. In reinforcement learning, a reward signal links the neural response with task performance, whereas focused attention allows knowledge to bias the neural response and involves cortical processing. They show that presenting a stimulus that is relevant to a task can give rise to an internal reward that works like an external reward in reinforcement learning [23]. Moreover, subliminal learning may involve attentional processing, but attention does not need to be directed to a feature for that feature to be learned [22]. Among other fields, subliminal actions have been extensively treated in the world of advertising, even talking about subliminal advertisements in electoral campaigns, fully entering into the field of political communication [21]. The aim of our work is trying to transfer this concept to the field of education.

A similar term, from the point of view of our purpose, is that of invisible learning of Cobo and Moravec [3], in the sense that invisible is what exists, but cannot be observed. It is based on three axes: sharing experiences and innovative perspectives, aimed at rethinking strategies for continuously learning and unlearning; promoting critical thinking about the role of formal, informal and non-formal education at all educational levels; and contributing to the creation of a sustainable and permanent learning process, by innovating and designing new cultures for a global society. This work analyses the impact of technological advances and changes in formal, non-formal, and informal education, and the meta-spaces in between. The authors offer the reader an overview of options for the future development of education that is relevant for this century. The invisible learning project analyses the role that technological advances play in transforming the learning process and it goes beyond the traditional distinctions between formal, non-formal and informal education, reflecting how it is possible to learn in the 21st century.

It is in this sense that we use the term subliminal learning in this research: that formal or informal learning that occurs without the conscious attention of the individual to such learning. And it is in this sense that we look at the world of video games to see how they incorporate this subliminal learning into their games to give their instructions.

3   Analysis of Level Design in Video Games

3.1   Methodology

Although the use of organic tutorials is not a very common practice, there are a high number of titles that use them. Therefore, the first step for the analysis of video games is selecting an affordable and representative number of games. To select a representative sample of this population, we started with an initial set of 74 video games (14 obtained from our experience as players and 60 recommended through a petition in social networks). This number was still high for a detailed analysis, so different filters were applied to reduce the number of video games to be analysed: votes in social networks, adaptation to the study objective and variety in terms of generations, genre and technology. Finally the following eight video games were selected for analysis [19]:

- *Super Mario Bros.* (Nintendo, 1985).
- *Mega Man X* (Capcom, 1993).
- *Super Metroid* (Nintendo, 1994).
- *Half-Life 2* (Valve Corporation, 2004).
- *BioShock* (2K Games, 2007).
- *Portal* (Valve Corporation, 2007).
- *Dark Souls* (From Software, 2011).
- *Jouney* (ThatGameCompany, 2012).

In the final sample, there is little presence, even absence, of strategy, resource management, board, sports, simulation and role-playing games. This is due to the fact that in these genres it is not advisable to use organic tutorials, due to its high complexity, abstraction and randomization.

3.2 Analysis Elements of Organic Tutorials

The design of video games, their levels and their tutorials, is closely linked to psychology, since the objective of any interactive entertainment product is producing some reaction of the player. When developing video games, some design techniques based on previous studies of human behaviour and learning are used to guide and teach the player and transmit what they want. An example is the shift from left to right in 2D environments. In most 2D platforms video games the character moves to the right to reach the end of the level. This largely accepted convention was considered to be due to the success of *Super Mario Bros.* game, but the movement from left to right seems to be an intrinsic preference to the human being [26].

Specifically, the elements to be studied in this analysis of the initial levels of video games are:

1. *Guidance and direct navigation.* One of the biggest challenges that designers must overcome is to guide the player through the video game so that he follows the correct path and meets the objectives in the established order. However, the player must not become aware of this guidance since a perception of freedom must be achieved. The direct way to keep the player on the road is to create obstacles, points of no return, restrictions and artificial rules that force him to follow the pre-established route to the goal (what is called *railroading*).

2. *Guidance and indirect navigation.* In addition to direct ways of guiding the player through the level, there are more subtle forms that can be used together to obtain a better result: tactical elements, focal points that draw the player's attention, scene composition (foreground, centre of interest and background), views, landmarks, guide lines, lighting, colours, coherent shape language, information silhouettes, level of detail, animated elements or audio tracks.

3. *Teach through contextual practice.* When a player learns a new skill, it must be put into practice immediately, but allowing the player to decide where and when. For example, subtly placing obstacles that can only be overcome with the latest mechanics learned, so that players immediately practice a new action in its context. The effect is a natural and fluid way of learning.

4. *Antepiece, Setpiece and Conveyance.* The *antepiece* is an initial section that prepares the player through practice, without being aware, for a greater challenge, usually called the *setpiece*. Overcoming simple obstacles, mechanically similar, with an appropriate and increasing difficulty curve, allows the player to develop his skill and obtain the necessary clues to overcome the *setpiece*. The *conveyance* is the fact of learning simple lessons that are then

used for more complex problems. The result is that the process of in-depth understanding the video game is the same as the one of learning to play it.

5. *Teaching through failing.* In a video game, failing usually results in a loss (loss of resources, time, progress...). As a consequence, the player learns a lesson that will last in his memory depending on the importance he gives to the lost resource and its ability to take on failure.

6. *Teaching through accident.* It is when the video game incites the player to accidentally perform some action, allowing him to learn something new in the process. Making an accidental discovery causes surprise, so the player will remember what was learned during that discovery better than if he had read it.

7. *Safe areas.* It is imperative that the first area of the game is free of hazards, such as enemies or pernicious scenery elements. However it must have enough elements for the player to learn the basics of the game and test the controls on their own. They are also often used to introduce new enemies and dangers: in safe areas the player can observe and learn their patterns before confronting them.

8. *Short iteration cycles.* The tutorial is the first contact of a player with the video game and it is essential prevent him from getting to the point of frustration and abandon the game. The earlier he leaves, the higher the possibility of definitive withdrawal. Checkpoints and savepoints are usually closer in the initial levels and they are more separated as the game progresses. Short iterations are essential for trial-error learning.

9. *The flow.* Another concept of great importance within the anti-frustration features is *Cognitive Flow* [4]. When the skill required to perform a task is too high, the person becomes frustrated. On the contrary, if the task is too easy for the skill the person has, he or she gets bored. When the required skill and difficulty are in accordance, the person is in a state of flow. A video game, and especially his tutorial, should keep the player within the flow zone as long as possible, because boredom or frustration will lead him to leave the game.

10. *Reward the observant player.* Organic tutorials teach while playing so it is indispensable that the player pays attention to every detail in the scenario left by the developers. For instance, to avoid the frustration of a player the obstacles do not necessarily have to be easy: they can be difficult but fair. That is to say, an observant player should have the possibility to overcome it thanks to the tracks previously left. This type of support is a reward for the most attentive players. It is common to reward the good explorer, through improvement items, to encourage him to go all the corners of the stage in search of more objects, shortcuts, argument pieces, Easter Eggs or secret areas.

3.3   Comparative analysis of organic tutorials

The theoretical basis to understand the design of organic tutorials introduced in Sect. 2, the sample of games defined in Sect. 3.1, and the items to properly analyse levels identified in Sect. 3.2, provide the elements to perform the study of video games to obtain design patterns. The process to perform this analysis for each video game is made of the following steps:

1. Play the tutorial.
2. Read the studies and essays about design concepts made by other authors,.
3. Replay the tutorial, considering the design concepts.
4. Match the elements of the game with design concepts.

After analysing all the video games in the sample, we made the last step of this research: a comparative analysis of the two best examples of organic tutorials in the sample. Specifically, the organic tutorials to be compared are those belonging to *Super Mario Bros.* (SMB) and *Dark Souls* (DS) video games, two completely different games (see Table 1 with the main features of the games) whose organic tutorials are recognized for their quality. Each analysis element has been studied, checking whether they are fulfilled by both games. The results will help to demonstrate that these elements of design give rise to exceptional tutorials, regardless of the genre and the time of the game, if they are well implemented.

Table 1. Main features of *Super Mario Bros.* and *Dark Souls*

	Super Mario Bros.	*Dark Souls*
Genre	Platforms	Action-Role
View	2D	3D
Year	1985	2011
PEGI	+3	+16
Actions	3	12

The review of the ten analysis elements for organic tutorial design (Sect. 3.2) is presented in Tables 2 and 3. The tabled include one example of use for every analysis element and game, as well as screenshots. The order in which each video game uses these techniques is not relevant so it is not considered in the study.

This comparative analysis corroborates the idea that the principles of organic tutorial design obtained in the present study are applicable to a great variety of video games. Organic tutorials make the players feel capable to learn from their mistakes, consider the options and overcome the challenge, instead of being treated with condescension. The direct help of the developer is not needed: he or she learns in the best possible way, by playing the game.

Table 2. Review of the ten elements for *Super Mario Bros.* and *Dark Souls* (I)

Element	*Super Mario Bros.*	*Dark Souls*
1. Guidance and direct navigation	The path to the left is blocked, only movement to the right is allowed	The whole area is full of corridors, the movement is always forward.
2. Guidance and indirect navigation	The interrogation blocks blink to draw attention: the player unconsciously moves towards them.	The souls are whitish and blurring to draw attention: the player unconsciously moves towards them.
3. Teach through contextual practice	After learning to throw fireballs, the player must used them to kill two consecutive Goombas.	After learning to block with the shield, block the arrows from an enemy.
4. Antepiece, Setpiece and Conveyance	First, practice the jump with no risk of death by fall; then make another jump, now with risk of death.	First practice the combat techniques with unarmed enemies; then fight against an enemy with a sword.
5. Teaching through failing	The first Goomba forces the player to learn the basic jumping ability.	The first boss is impossible to defeat without equipment; it forces the player to escape and to become armed before the fight.

Table 3. Review of the ten elements for *Super Mario Bros.* and *Dark Souls* (II)

Element	Super Mario Bros.	Dark Souls
6. Teaching through accident	When jumping over the red mushroom, the top block is touched, and Mario turns into Super Mario.	When falling from the balcony on the boss, the normal attack turns into a powerful fall attack.
7. Safe areas	The game starts in an area with no enemies, with space to test the controls.	The game starts in a cell with no enemies, with little but sufficient space to test the camera and movement controls.
8. Short iteration cycles	There are two control points: one in the beginning (where it is most likely to die), and another in the middle of the level.	There are three save points: one in the beginning, one in front of the boss and one at the last third of the level.
9. The flow	The first enemies, the Goombas, are the weakest. They are first defeated one by one and then in pairs.	The first enemies, the ones with the sword, are the weakest. They are first defeated one by one and then in pairs.
10. Reward the observant player	The goal flag, which gives extra points, can be seen at the end of the level.	When opening the big door, the boss can be seen on the roof, avoiding the ambush.

4   Design Guide for Organic Tutorials

Organic tutorials, if well designed, are the best choice for teaching players in skill-based video games. Their greatest advantage, their effectiveness as a tool to teach the player, is also their greatest weakness: an improperly designed organic tutorial will leave the player disoriented, without having correctly learned the mechanics of the game. The high implementation difficulty, the risk of an improper design and the limited information available on organic tutorials, make it necessary to propose a document that gathers, condenses, explains and exemplifies the entire process and common techniques for designing this particular type of tutorials.

After analysing the organic tutorials of the sample using the knowledge acquired during the study of the theoretical framework, it is possible to identify three fundamental objectives of a well-designed organic tutorial:

- Be a subliminal guidance for the player
- Address the indirect teaching of the player
- Do not frustrate the player

Each of these objectives is carried out using various techniques of level design and gameplay. A relationship between the fundamental objectives of the organic tutorials and the associated design techniques can be established:

- Get a subliminal guidance for the player, by:
  - Direct guidance
  - Indirect guidance
- Get the indirect teaching of the player, by:
  - Contextual practice
  - The use of antepieces and setpieces
  - The use of failure
  - The use of accidental events
- Do not frustrate the player, by:
  - The use of safe areas
  - Short iteration cycles
  - Maintain the flow of the game
  - The use of the reward for being observant

Once established this relationship, a brief guide can be proposed, made of a list of principles or patterns, aimed at developers interested in designing good organic tutorials (see Table 4). A tutorial meeting most points of the guide would be of organic type, but whether it is a good or a bad ultimately depends on the designer. This guide is not infallible; it is only a tool for the developer to clearly understand the fundamentals and needs of the organic tutorials. It is the designer who decides how to design and structure his own tutorial level to meet the three basic objectives of organic design. Designing around these principles, in an intelligent way and with numerous iterations for testing the results, you can create a quality organic tutorial.

Table 4. Design principles for organic design

	Techniques	Description	Examples
Subliminal guidance	Direct guidance	The tutorial must be linear, to prevent disorientation, but not so obvious that the player realizes that there is a single route	Corridors, rooms with single entrance and exit but with small side rooms, turns, several floors, backtracking, closed doors, blocking enemies, no return points
	Indirect guidance	In wide areas or with several possible paths, the use of various stimuli to attract the attention of the player allows to place and direct him towards the desired area	Focal points, composition, views, landmarks, illumination, color contrast, movement, detail, audio, silhouettes, shape language, tactical zones, guide lines ...
Indirect teaching	Contextual practice	After learning a new skill, the player must put it into practice immediately to memorize it. How and when to use it is up to the player	An obstacle near the place where the new skill was learned, which can only be overcome by using it
	Antepiece and setpiece	During the game the player must practice simple challenges, antepieces, to be able to overcome later, on his own, more complex challenges, setpieces	An obstacle that does not penalize the player when he fails, followed by a similar one in which the error does penalize
	Failure	It is common for the player to fail in a tutorial in which there are no direct explanations. Make sure that the player learns something new from each mistake to make progress	An obstacle in which the player fails in a first attempt, so that he learns to put it into practice in the following attempts
	Accidental events	Make the player perform an action that triggers the accidental discovery of a new playable mechanic. These accidents do not penalize	An enemy near a destructible element of the stage. By attacking the enemy and failing, the element is destroyed

(continued)

Table 4. (*continued*)

	Techniques	Description	Examples
Avoid frustration	Safe areas	The tutorial is the first contact of the player with the video game, so it is necessary to use safe areas in which he can put into practice what he have learned	The beginning of the game must be in a safe area, without enemies, so that the player can freely test the basic controls of the movement and the camera
	Short iterations	Learning through failure requires trial-error. To prevent the player from getting frustrated, these repeat cycles should be short	In the tutorial, the control and save points must be close to each other and to the biggest challenges, such as the fight with bosses
	Flow	The difficulty of the tutorial should initially be minimal, to compensate for the player's low level of skill. It should increase gradually to adjust to the increasing ability	The tutorial should present the most basic and easy enemies and obstacles. As the player progresses, the difficulty can be increased with several simultaneous enemies
	Reward for the observant	Since the level itself guides and teaches the player, it should encourage attention to the scenario	Give clues about traps to players who, instead of running, are attentive to the scene. Place upgrade objects to reward the exploration

5 Conclusions and Further Work

In their origins, video games did not need to explain the controls or the mechanics to the player due to their simplicity: the novice players were able to learn in few minutes how to advance in the game. As technical and playability complexity increased, the need of instruction manuals to explain controls and mechanics arose. These manuals, in their printed form, were a viable option during the 80's and 90's because, despite being more complex, it was still possible to condense all the learning about a video game in a short document. The problem appeared when video games progressed so that a printed manual was not an economically viable option since dozens of pages were required. Moreover, the immediacy that characterizes the digital world, made players not want to read long manuals to start playing. Therefore, an option that began to arise was the use of tutorials integrated in the beginning of the video game. One of the most interesting types of tutorial from this point of view is the organic or indirect tutorial, which teaches the player without the need for text, but by means of an adequate level design, that is, they indirectly teach the player while he plays the tutorial level. These tutorials become key aspects to the success of the video game. After high investment in the development of a video game, designers cannot afford the game to be abandoned by players that are not able to learn how to play it.

In the first place a selection of the games with organic tutorials has been made. They make up the sample for this research work. Eight video games have been analysed as representatives of a broad set of generations, genres and technologies. After analysing the organic tutorials of the sample, three fundamental objectives of a well-designed organic tutorial have been identified: subliminal guidance for the player, indirect teaching and not to frustrate the player. Each one of these objectives are carried out using various techniques of level design and gameplay, and a list of ten techniques are established: direct guidance, indirect guidance, contextual practice, the use of antepieces and setpieces, failure management, the use of accidental events, safe areas, short iteration cycles, flow channel and the use of the reward for being observant. The relationship between the fundamental objectives of the organic tutorials and the associated design techniques has allowed us to write a brief guide. It is made of a list of principles or patterns to implement organic tutorial, aimed at developers interested in designing a good organic tutorial for their video game.

In addition to help video game designers, this guide can be easily transferable to the design of interactive educational materials. This is an advantage if you consider that video games are an excellent learning tool, by complying with all the laws of classical learning in an environment where failure is not seriously penalized. The design of organic tutorials in the world of education opens a door to natural and fluid learning, what we can call subliminal learning. It is not applicable to all types of learning, just as organic tutorials are not used in all types of video games. They are especially suitable in instruction for skills development. They will even be more useful if they are part of a gamified learning proposal. Therefore, this guide can also be used to help teachers to design gamified learning proposals.

References

1. Bevan, W.: Subliminal stimulation: a pervasive problem for psychology. Psychol. Bull. **61**(2), 89–99 (1964)
2. Bycer, J.: Game Wisdom - Theories on Game Design (2017). http://game-wisdom.com/
3. Cobo Romaní, J.C., Moravec, J.W.: Aprendizaje invisible: hacia una nueva ecología de la educación. Publicacions i Edicions de la Universitat de Barcelona, Barcelona (2011)
4. Csikszentmihalyi, M.: Flow: The Psychology of Optimal Experience, 1st edn. Harper & Row, New York (1990)
5. Dijksterhuis, A., Aarts, H., Smith, P.K.: The power of the subliminal: on subliminal persuasion and other potential applications. In: The New Unconscious, pp. 77–106. Oxford University Press, New York (2007)

6. Gallego, F.J., Llorens, F.: Àqué nos enseña pacman? lecciones aprendidas desarrollando videojuegos educativos. In: Actas I Congreso Internacional sobre Aprendizaje, Innovación y Competitividad (CINAIC) (2011)
7. Gallego, F.J., Satorre, R., Llorens, F.: Computer games tell, show involve.. and teach. In: Actas VIII Simposio Internacional de Informática Educativa (SIIE) (2006)
8. Gallego, F.J., Villagrá, C., Satorre, R., Compañ, P., Molina, R., Llorens, F.: Panorámica: serious games, gamification y mucho más. ReVisión (Revista de Investigación en Docencia Universitaria de la Informática) 7(2), 13–23 (2014)
9. Granic, I., Lobel, A., Engels, R.C.M.E.: The benefits of playing video games. Am. Psychol. 69(1), 66–78 (2014)
10. Hamari, J., Shernoff, D.J., Rowe, E., Coller, B., Asbell-Clarke, J., Edwards, T.: Challenging games help students learn: an empirical study on engagement, flow and immersion in game-based learning. Comput. Hum. Behav. 54, 170–179 (2016)
11. Huizinga, J.J.: Homo Ludens: A Study of the Play-element in Culture. Routledge & K. Paul, London (1938)
12. Illanas, A., Gallego, F.J., Satorre, R., Llorens, F.: Conceptual mini-games for learning. In: International Technology, Education and Development Conference (INTED) (2008)
13. Koster, R.: A Theory of Fun for Game Design. Paraglyph Press, Scottsdale (2005)
14. Llorens-Largo, F., Gallego-Durán, F., Villagrá-Arnedo, C., Compañ Rosique, P., Satorre-Cuerda, R., Molina-Carmona, R.: Gamification of the learning process: lessons learned. IEEE Revista Iberoamericana de Tecnologias del Aprendizaje 11(4), 227–234 (2016)
15. McGonigal, J.: Reality is Broken: Why Games Make Us Better and How They Can Change the World. Penguin Group, New York (2011)
16. Minović, M., García-Peñalvo, F.J., Kearney, N.A.: Gamification ecosystems in engineering education. Int. J. Eng. Educ. (IJEE) 32(1B), 308–309 (2016)
17. Prensky, M.: Digital Game-based Learning. New York, Mcgraw Hill (2004)
18. Prensky, M.: "Don't Bother me Mom, I'm Learning!": How Computer and Video Games are Preparing Your Kids for Twenty-first Century Success and How You Can Help! 1st edn. Paragon House, St. Paul (2006)
19. Quesada-Mora, V.: Proyecto Mundo 1–1. Estudio sobre el aprendizaje subliminal de mecánicas a través del diseño de niveles en los videojuegos. Trabajo Fin de Grado, Ingeniería Multimedia, Universidad de Alicante (2016)
20. Reingold, E.M., Merikle, P.M.: Using direct and indirect measures to study perception without awareness. Percept. Psychophysics 44(6), 563–575 (1988)
21. Rodríguez Andrés, R.: Publicidad subliminal en campañas electorales: entre el mito y la realidad. Pensar la Publicidad. Revista Internacional de Investigaciones Publicitarias 9(0), June 2016
22. Seitz, A., Lefebvre, C., Watanabe, T., Jolicoeur, P.: Requirement for high-level processing in subliminal learning. Curr. Biol. 15(22), R901–R936 (2005)
23. Seitz, A.R., Watanabe, T.: Psychophysics: is subliminal learning really passive? Nature 422(6927), 36–36 (2003)
24. Turkle, S.: Alone Together: Why We Expect More From Technology and Less From Each Other, 1st edn. Basic Books, New York (2011)
25. Vygotskij, L.S., Cole, M.: Mind in Society: The Development of Higher Psychological Processes. Harvard University Press, Cambridge (1981). Nachdr. edn
26. Walker, P.: Depicting visual motion in still images: forward leaning and a left to right bias for lateral movement. Perception 44(2), 111–128 (2015)
27. Wright, F.L.: An Organic Architecture: The Architecture of Democracy. The Sir George Watson Lectures of the Sulgrave Manor Board for 1939. Lund Humphries (1939)

Author Index

Printed in the United States
By Bookmasters